AF478098

Meister des Impressionismus

Masters of Impressionism

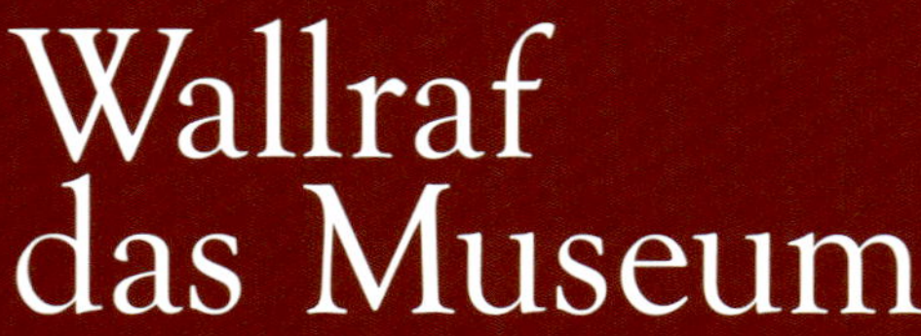
Wallraf
das Museum
WALLRAF-RICHARTZ-MUSEUM & FONDATION CORBOUD

Meister des Impressionismus

Eine Malereigeschichte von 1874 bis 1926

Masters of Impressionism

A History of Painting from 1874 to 1926

Die Kölner Sammlung The Cologne Collection

Wallraf-Richartz-Museum & Fondation Corboud

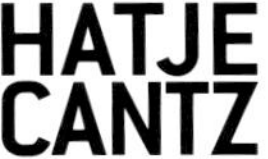

CONTENTS

INHALT

FOREWORD

FRENCH IMPRESSIONISM had not always had a strong lobby in Germany. Modern art, in this case art from the declared "arch enemy," was only gradually accepted by the authorities and those in rule. As late as in 1904, the Reichstag debated Germany's participation at the World's Fair in Saint Louis and the question of which works of art were to represent the country. The liberals and the social democrats even felt obliged to explain the art of Edouard Manet, a painter who had already been dead for twenty-one years, to their fellow assemblymen. In 1911, the Kunsthalle Bremen unleashed a scandal when it purchased a painting by Vincent van Gogh, who had died twenty years prior to that, and the futile attempts by the director of the Nationalgalerie Berlin, Hugo von Tschudi, to communicate Impressionism to Emperor William II are legendary.

Cities such as Hamburg, Bremen, Stettin, Berlin, Dresden, Weimar, Mannheim, Frankfurt am Main, and Munich nevertheless succeeded in assembling a large number of remarkable works. Even in Impressionism's country of origin, France, only few museums have substantial numbers of works done in this style. Impressionism was frowned on in Paris for a long time, and we would have hardly been able to admire paintings there today by artists from Manet to Monet had the painter Gustave Caillebotte not collected works by his comrades-in-arms and bequeathed them to the state—who accepted a mere half of Caillebotte's bequest! Only in America were Impressionist paintings collected on a broad front. There, private individuals brought them in large numbers from Europe across the Atlantic, more because of their bold attitudes than because of their full purses. Today, we look with envy at the museums from Baltimore to Kansas City, institutions that profited from donations by local citizens. This accomplishment cannot be repeated.

VORWORT

DER FRANZÖSISCHE IMPRESSIONISMUS hatte in Deutschland nicht immer eine starke Lobby. Moderne Kunst und noch dazu vom erklärten »Erzfeind« musste mühsam gegen die Behörden und Regierende durchgesetzt werden. Noch 1904 debattierte der Reichstag über die deutsche Beteiligung an der Weltausstellung in Saint Louis und über die Frage, welche Kunst das Land vertreten solle. Dabei sahen sich die Liberalen und Sozialdemokraten noch genötigt, ihren Kollegen Abgeordneten die Kunst von Edouard Manet zu erklären, ein Maler, der zu diesem Zeitpunkt schon 21 Jahre tot war. 1911 entfesselte die Kunsthalle Bremen ungewollt einen Skandal, als sie ein Gemälde des damals auch schon gut zwanzig Jahre verstorbenen Vincent van Gogh erwarb, und die vergeblichen Versuche des Leiters der Nationalgalerie Berlin, Hugo von Tschudi, Kaiser Wilhelm II. den Impressionismus nahezubringen, sind legendär.

Gleichwohl gelang es in Städten wie Hamburg, Bremen, Stettin, Berlin, Dresden, Weimar, Mannheim, Frankfurt am Main und München eine ganze Anzahl beachtlicher Werke zusammenzubringen. Selbst im Ursprungsland des Impressionismus, Frankreich, haben nur wenige Museen wichtige Bestände dieser Richtung. In Paris war der neue Stil lange verpönt, und die Bilder von Manet bis Monet wären dort heute kaum zu bewundern, hätte nicht der Maler Gustave Caillebotte die Werke seiner Mitstreiter gesammelt und dem Staat vermacht. Der hatte von Caillebottes Nachlass nur die Hälfte akzeptiert! Einzig die Amerikaner sammelten auf breiter Front. Dort waren es Privatleute, die eher aufgrund ihrer mutigen Einstellung als aufgrund einer wohlgefüllten Börse Impressionisten in großer Zahl aus Europa über den Atlantik brachten. Jetzt schauen wir mit Neid auf die Museen von Baltimore bis Kansas City, da sie von den Stiftungen ihrer Bürger profitierten. Diese Leistung ist heute nicht wiederholbar.

Not only did the German museums struggle with the great paragons from France, German painters did as well. They could not resist their influence; however, neither could they allow it to be said that they had given up their originality. The great three—Max Liebermann, Lovis Corinth, and Max Slevogt—chose a separate path, either adhering to shades of gray or developing new, informal stylistic elements. In contrast, Paul Baum and Christian Rohlfs were more receptive to experiments with color and brushstroke coming from the other side of the Rhine. Their Dutch and Belgian associates were more open, with Vincent van Gogh at the lead. In Paris, he applied himself to French Impressionism and Neo-Impressionism in rapid motion, later becoming seminal himself in Provence.

Thanks to the French, the epoch between the first Impressionist exhibition in 1874 and Monet's death in 1926 was the height of painting. The names Sisley, Pissarro, Degas, and Renoir ring in our ears and in the tills of the auctioneers. However, we need to go beyond thinking about only the established artists. Even the core group comprises several men and women who have achieved little fame up to now. Was Gustave Caillebotte not added to the canon just over the last fifteen years? And are you familiar, for instance, with Zandomeneghi, Raffaëlli, or De Nittis? They, too, showed their works at the exhibitions of the first Impressionists. It was feminist art historians who first pointed out the artists Berthe Morisot and Mary Cassatt, who now also belong to the circle of stars, not only because of some "quota." Artists such as Martin, Hayet, Lebasque, or Lacombe are also still waiting to be discovered by a broad audience. A sure indication, though, that this discovery is imminent is the art market, where the prices for paintings by these second-generation masters have in the meantime reached levels that not too long ago were reserved for their predecessors.

Nicht nur die deutschen Museen, auch die deutschen Maler rangen mit den großen Vorbildern aus Frankreich. Sie konnten sich ihrem Einfluss nicht entziehen, wollten sich auf der anderen Seite aber auch nicht nachsagen lassen, ihre Eigenständigkeit aufgegeben zu haben. Die großen Drei – Max Liebermann, Lovis Corinth und Max Slevogt – wählten einen Sonderweg, hielten entweder an der grauen Tönung fest oder entwickelten eine neue gestische Formensprache. Paul Baum und Christian Rohlfs zeigten sich hingegen empfänglicher für die Experimente mit Farbe und Pinselstrich von der anderen Seite des Rheins. Offener waren ihre niederländischen und belgischen Kollegen, mit Vincent van Gogh als großem Beispiel. Er verarbeitete in Paris im Zeitraffer den französischen Impressionismus und Neoimpressionismus, um dann in der Provence selbst stilbildend zu wirken.

Die Epoche von der ersten Impressionisten-Ausstellung 1874 bis zum Tod Monets 1926 war dank der Franzosen eine Blütezeit der Malerei. Die Namen Sisley, Pissarro, Degas, Renoir klingen heute in allen Ohren und in den Kassen der Auktionshäuser. Dabei sollten wir nicht nur an die etablierten Künstler denken. Selbst die Kerngruppe umfasst einige Männer und Frauen, die bislang noch wenig Bekanntheit errungen haben. Ist nicht sogar Gustave Caillebotte erst in den vergangenen fünfzehn Jahren zum Kanon hinzugefügt worden? Und kennen Sie etwa Zandomeneghi, Raffaëlli und De Nittis? Auch das waren Maler, die in den Ausstellungen der ersten Impressionisten mit ihren Bildern vertreten waren. Die feministische Kunstgeschichte hat erstmals auf die Künstlerinnen Berthe Morisot und Mary Cassatt hingewiesen, die inzwischen auch zum Kreis der Stars gehören und zwar nicht nur aufgrund irgendeiner »Quote«. Auch Künstler wie Martin, Hayet, Lebasque oder Lacombe warten noch auf ihre Entdeckung durch das breite Publikum. Ein sicheres Anzeichen, dass diese Entdeckung aber bevorsteht, ist der Kunstmarkt, auf dem

There is not another place in Germany (or far beyond it) where the depth and breadth of the history of this style of painting can be better told than at the Wallraf-Richartz-Museum in Cologne. This institution, steeped in tradition, is indebted to the Fondation Corboud for enriching its collection, thus enabling us to display the entire panorama of Impressionism. With precursors, masters, successors, as well as separate German and Dutch paths, the museum can fall back on a store of a good 270 paintings! This treasure has been assembled together in the present volume.
The cooperation between the museum and the donator moves within the bounds of good civic tradition. It was visionary collectors who helped modern art establish itself. They also either founded museums or provided them with content. Modern art and civic commitment have always gone hand in hand, and our museums and our cultural life on the whole would not only be much worse off without them, but would presumably scarcely exist.
Gérard J. and Marisol Corboud count among the ranks of the great donators. Their vision, which they developed with the long-standing director of the Wallraf-Richartz-Museum, Rainer Budde, was to tell the story of Impressionist and Neo-Impressionist painting. They can take pride in saying that they have brought this vision to fruition. Unfortunately, the lack of museum space does not yet allow us to present it in its entirety. The purpose of this book is therefore twofold: the publication of the works comprising this magnificent treasure is intended to delight the reader and the viewer and at the same time add substance to our wish to also be able to present the originals in all their diversity and plurality.
This volume would not have come about without the tireless assistance of the curators at the Wallraf-Richartz-Museum, who attend in particular to nineteenth-century art and

Gemälde dieser Meister der zweiten Generation inzwischen Preise erreichen, die vor gar nicht allzu langer Zeit ihren Vorgängern vorbehalten waren.
Es gibt keinen Ort in Deutschland (und weit darüber hinaus), der die Geschichte dieser Malerei in Breite und Tiefe so gut erzählen kann wie das Wallraf-Richartz-Museum in Köln. Der Fondation Corboud verdankt das traditionsreiche Haus jene Bereicherung, die es in die Lage versetzt, das ganze Panorama des Impressionismus auszubreiten. Mit Vorläufern, Hauptmeistern, Nachfolgern sowie deutschen und niederländischen Sonderwegen kann das Museum auf einen Fundus von gut zweihundertsiebzig Gemälden zurückgreifen! Dieser Schatz ist in diesem Band vereinigt.
Die Zusammenarbeit zwischen Museum und Stifter bewegt sich in einer guten bürgerlichen Tradition. Es waren die visionären Sammler, die der jeweils modernen Kunst halfen, sich zu etablieren. Sie gründeten vielfach auch die Museen beziehungsweise versorgten sie mit Inhalt. Moderne Kunst und bürgerliches Engagement gingen immer miteinander einher, und unsere Museen und unser Kulturleben im Ganzen wären ohne sie nicht nur ärmer, sondern würden wahrscheinlich kaum existieren.
Gérard J. und Marisol Corboud sind dabei in die Reihe der ganz großen Stifter einzuordnen. Es war ihre Vision, die sie mit dem langjährigen Direktor des Wallraf-Richartz-Museums, Rainer Budde, erarbeiteten, die Geschichte der impressionistischen und neoimpressionistischen Malerei zu erzählen. Sie können mit Stolz sagen, diese Vision auch verwirklicht zu haben. Allein der Raummangel des Museums erlaubt es noch nicht, sie vollkommen zur Wirkung kommen zu lassen. Daher ist der Zweck dieses Buches zweierlei: Die Veröffentlichung des reichen Schatzes in seiner Gänze soll die Leser und Betrachter erfreuen und gleichzeitig dem Wunsch Nachdruck verleihen, die Originale auch in ihrer Vielfalt präsentieren zu können.

the Fondation Corboud collection and have published so much on both: Götz Czymmek and Barbara Schaefer. The latter was also responsible for the organization of this book. We would like to thank Eva-Maria Klother for her interesting contribution to the catalogue as well as Hatje Cantz for initiating this project and for their customary professional support. First and foremost, however, we would all like to express our gratitude to Gérard J. and Marisol Corboud, whose collecting enthusiasm allowed this publication to come about and who have filled the museum with their treasures.

Andreas Blühm
Cologne, March 2008

Diese Publikation wäre nicht zustande gekommen ohne die tätige Mithilfe der Kuratoren des Wallraf-Richartz-Museums, die sich um die Kunst des 19. Jahrhunderts und die Sammlung der Fondation Corboud im Besonderen kümmern und darüber schon viel publiziert haben: Götz Czymmek und Barbara Schaefer. Letzterer oblag auch die Organisation dieses Buches. Wir danken Eva-Maria Klother für ihren interessanten Katalogbeitrag und dem Hatje Cantz Verlag für die Initiative zu diesem Projekt und seine gewohnt professionelle Betreuung.
Zuvorderst gilt unser gemeinsamer Dank aber dem Stifterpaar, Gérard J. und Marisol Corboud, deren Sammeleifer und Großzügigkeit dieses Buch entstehen ließen und die das Museum mit ihren Schätzen gefüllt haben.

Andreas Blühm
Köln, im März 2008

Eva-Maria Klother

"WHAT FREEDOM. WHAT LIGHTNESS ..."

"WHAT A STRENUOUS DAY IT WAS, the day I ventured into the first exhibition on the Boulevard des Capucines in the company of landscape painter Josephe Vincent, a student of Bertin and the recipient of medals and awards from various governments. Incautious man that he was, he had gone there quite unsuspecting. He thought he would find good and bad painting—perhaps more bad than good—as one would anywhere, but not such violations of artistic manners, such crimes against the great masters and against form. Yes, form and the masters! We need them no longer, my poor friend! We've changed all that! . . . Ah, that painting over there! What is it supposed to represent? Take a look in the catalogue. 'Impression of a Sunrise.' 'Impression'—That's clear to me. What freedom. What lightness of hand!"[1]

This account by art critic Louis Leroy appeared in the satirical journal *Le Charivari* under the title "L'Exposition des impressionnistes" on April 25, 1874. With biting irony, Leroy recalled his conversations with the landscape painter Josephe Vincent during their tour of the exhibition. The two visitors exchanged scornful comments on the unusual motifs and the unconventional application of paint.

The painting that eventually gave Leroy's article its title and earned an entire group of artists the designation as Impressionists was Claude Monet's *Impression, Soleil levant* (ill. 1). The young artist had painted it in his birthplace of Le Havre. It shows a view of the harbor from a window in his apartment. Cranes, ships' masts and sails, and spewing smokestacks are vaguely discernable behind a veil of finely graduated blues. The deep-orange sun rises over the silhouette of the harbor. In paler tones, it sets the sky aglow and is reflected in a blurred pattern on the water, on which the stencil-like forms of boats are visible. Everything in the picture flickers and remains indistinct. The motif is merely a pretense for the atmosphere Monet has captured in the painting.

»WELCHE FREIHEIT. WELCHE LEICHTIGKEIT ...«

»OH, ES WAR EIN ANSTRENGENDER TAG, als ich mich in Gesellschaft des Landschaftsmalers Josephe Vincent, eines Schülers von Bertin und Empfängers von Medaillen und Auszeichnungen unterschiedlicher Regierungen, in die erste Ausstellung am Boulevard des Capucines wagte. Der Unvorsichtige war, ohne an Böses zu denken, dorthin gegangen. Er dachte, wie überall gute und schlechte – eher schlechte als gute – Malerei zu finden, aber nicht solches Vergehen gegen die künstlerischen Manieren, gegen die großen Meister und die Form. Ja, Form und Meister! Die brauchen wir jetzt nicht mehr, mein armer Freund! Das haben wir alles geändert! [...] Ah, jenes Bild dort! Was soll es darstellen? Sieh im Katalog nach. ›Impression eines Sonnenaufgangs‹. ›Impression‹ – das ist mir klar. Welche Freiheit. Welche Leichtigkeit in der Faktur!«[1]

Dieser Bericht des Kunstkritikers Louis Leroy war am 25. April 1874 in der satirischen Zeitschrift *Le Charivari* unter dem Titel »L'Exposition des impressionnistes« zu lesen. Mit bissiger Ironie gibt Leroy die Gespräche wieder, die er beim Gang durch die Ausstellung mit dem Landschaftsmaler Josephe Vincent geführt hatte. Spöttisch kommentieren die beiden Betrachter die ungewöhnlichen Bildmotive und den eigentümlichen Farbauftrag.

Das Bild schließlich, das dem Artikel Leroys die Überschrift und einer ganzen Gruppe von Künstlern die Bezeichnung als Impressionisten einbringen sollte, war Claude Monets *Impression, Soleil levant* (Abb. 1). Der junge Maler hatte es in seinem Geburtsort Le Havre gemalt. Es zeigt den Blick aus dem Fenster seiner Wohnung auf den Hafen. Die Ladebäume, Schiffstakelagen und rauchenden Schornsteine verschwimmen hinter fein abgestuften Blautönen. Tieforange hängt die aufgehende Sonne über der Silhouette des Hafens. Abgemildert leuchtet sie am Himmel und spiegelt sich verschwommen auf dem Wasser, auf dem Boote schablonenhaft hervortreten. Alles Dargestellte flimmert, bleibt unklar. So ist das Motiv nur ein Vorwand für die Atmosphäre, die Monet im Bild festhielt.

The venue at which these Impressionist paintings were exhibited was no less out of the ordinary than the works themselves. Photographer Gaspar-Félix Tournachon, better know as Nadar, had made his studio spaces on the second floor of the building on Boulevard des Capucines 35 available for the show. Nadar maintained several studios in Paris. The one on Boulevard des Capucines served as a portrait studio. It was frequented by the crème-de-la-crème of the Paris *bohème,* and Nadar took portraits of an entire generation of artists of all persuasions using the still young medium of photography.[2] Thus the venue alone guaranteed the young painters not only an attentive reception by gay Paris society but also scathing commentaries from art critics representing an emerging school of criticism. But did the exhibition really offer these artists any assurance of success?

Named for its venue, the Grand Salon Carré in the Louvre, the official Salon, which took place on a regular basis under government supervision, was still the most important exhibition in Paris. Works were selected for presentation by a jury comprised of ministerial officials and renowned artists, most of whom were also professors at the state art academy in Paris and who made the ultimate decisions on the admission of submitted paintings. The jury evaluated works in accordance with the standards of an academic concept of art and a distinct genre hierarchy in which history painting generally took precedence over the landscape and still life. Moreover, they regularly had several thousand paintings to evaluate. Jury members seldom had the time to undertake a thorough examination of the submitted works. In most cases, they made their decisions on the quality of a given work and thus on its admission to the exhibition on the basis of a cursory glance.

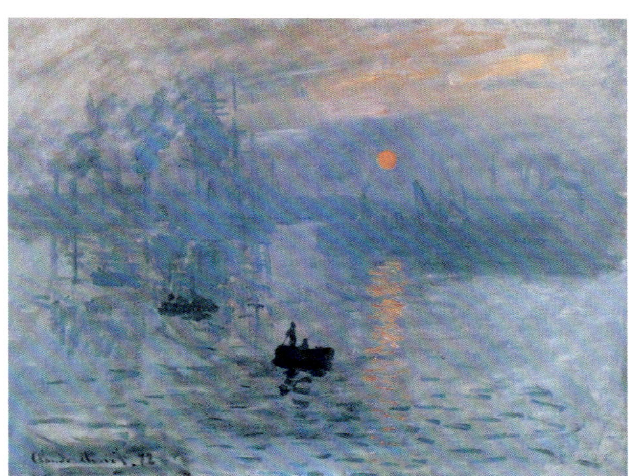

1
Claude Monet
Impression eines Sonnenaufgangs, 1872
Impression: Sunrise
Museé Marmottan, Paris

Nicht weniger ungewöhnlich als die impressionistischen Bilder war der Ort ihrer Präsentation. Der Fotograf Gaspar-Félix Tournachon, besser bekannt unter dem Namen Nadar, hatte seine Atelierräume im ersten Stock des Hauses Boulevard des Capucines Nr. 35 zur Verfügung gestellt. Nadar unterhielt verschiedene Ateliers in Paris. Jenes am Boulevard des Capucines diente ihm als Porträtstudio. Hier tummelte sich alles, was zu jener Zeit in der Pariser Boheme Rang und Namen hatte, und Nadar hielt eine ganze Generation von Künstlern aller Sparten in dem noch jungen Medium der Fotografie fest.[2] So garantierten schon allein die Räumlichkeiten den jungen Malern die Aufmerksamkeit der lebenslustigen Pariser Gesellschaft und die bissigen Kommentare der in dieser Form ebenfalls noch jungen Kunstkritik. Doch war die Ausstellung auch ein Garant für den wirtschaftlichen Erfolg der Maler?

Nach wie vor war die wichtigste Ausstellung in Paris der regelmäßig stattfindende offizielle Salon, so benannt nach den Räumlichkeiten des Grand salon carré im Louvre. Die Ausstellung fand unter staatlicher Regie statt. Es wurde eine Jury eingesetzt, die aus Ministerialbeamten bestand und aus renommierten Künstlern, die meistens auch Professoren an der staatlichen Kunstakademie in Paris waren, und die über die Aufnahme der eingereichten Arbeiten entschied. Sie begutachtete die von den Künstlern eingesandten Werke und legte die akademische Kunstauffassung als Maßstab an. Hierzu zählte die Unterscheidung nach Gattungen, wobei der Historienmalerei allgemein der Vorzug vor der Landschaft und dem Stillleben gegeben wurde. Hinzu kam, dass die Jury einige Tausend Exponate begutachten musste. Zu einem ausführlichen Studium der eingesandten Arbeiten waren die Jurymitglieder in der Regel gar nicht in der Lage. Für die Entscheidung über die Qualität und damit über die Zulassung der Arbeit blieb der Jury nur ein denkbar kurzer Blick.

The public had two to three months to view the works on exhibit. The walls were covered up to the ceiling with several rows of paintings. A spot at eye level was more than a painter could reasonably hope for. Yet for an artist intent upon establishing a reputation beyond the borders of France and finding a good market for his paintings, participation at the Salon was an absolute must.[3]

In no way did Monet's *Impression. Soleil levant* meet the expectations of the jury, who most likely classified it as landscape painting, a genre that had progressed considerably by that time. As a veduta or as heroic or idyllic painting, the eighteenth-century landscape justified its existence entirely on the basis of historical reference. Sketches made in a natural setting served only as studies for paintings executed later in a studio. This changed in the first half of the nineteenth century, when landscape painters became less interested in narration supported by landscape scenes. They had begun to focus their attention on the landscape itself.

In 1830, Camille Corot discovered the one-road village of Barbizon on the fringes of the Forest of Fontainebleau south of Paris as a setting for his painting. The impenetrable forest, in which the Kings of France had once hunted, offered numerous motifs for plein-air painters. Charles-François Daubigny, Jean François Millet, and many other artists followed Corot's example. They leveraged the realistic view of the landscape. Now, any landscape scene could be considered worth depicting.

As an art critic, Charles Baudelaire expressed appreciation for the landscape paintings of Corot and the Barbizon School. "Let us imagine a beautiful spot in nature, where everything flourishes in complete freedom. ... The trees are green, the meadows are green, the moss green; green winds among the branches of the trees; the still unripe stalks are green; green is the basic color of nature, as green is easily wed with all other colors."[4] As if it

Das interessierte Publikum hatte zwei bis drei Monate Zeit, die ausgestellten Werke zu betrachten. Die Wände waren bis unter die Decke in mehreren Reihen mit Bildern behängt. Ein Hängeplatz in Augenhöhe war da mehr als ein Glücksfall. Die Teilnahme am Salon war jedoch für einen Künstler, der über die Grenzen Frankreichs bekannt werden und einen guten Markt für seine Arbeiten finden wollte, unabdingbar.[3]

Monets Bild *Impression, Soleil levant* entsprach in keiner Weise den Vorstellungen der Jury, für die es wohl am ehesten zur Bildgattung der Landschaftsmalerei gehört haben dürfte. Dabei hatte die Landschaftsmalerei bis dahin bereits eine beachtliche Entwicklung vollzogen: Die Landschaft des 18. Jahrhunderts war in ihrer Daseinsberechtigung gänzlich an eine Historie gebunden, ob als Vedute, als heroische oder idyllische Malerei. Eine Skizze direkt vor dem Motiv in der freien Natur diente hierbei nur als Vorbereitung des später im Atelier auszuführenden Gemäldes. Dies änderte sich im frühen 19. Jahrhundert. Die Landschaftsmaler interessierten sich weniger dafür, eine Erzählung mithilfe der Landschaft zu verdeutlichen. Ihre Aufmerksamkeit galt nun der Landschaft selbst.

1830 entdeckte Camille Corot das südlich von Paris gelegene Straßendorf Barbizon am Rande des Waldes von Fontainebleau für seine Malerei. Der undurchdringliche Wald, in dem einst die Könige von Frankreich ihre Treibjagden abgehalten hatten, bot für das Malen im Freien zahlreiche Motive. Charles-François Daubigny, Jean François Millet und viele andere Künstler folgten Corots Vorbild. Sie verhalfen der realistischen Sicht auf die Landschaft zum Durchbruch. Nun konnte jeder beliebige Landschaftsausschnitt bildwürdig werden.

In seiner Tätigkeit als Kunstkritiker sympathisierte Charles Baudelaire mit der Landschaftsmalerei Corots und der Schule von Barbizon: »Denken wir uns eine schöne Stelle in der Natur, wo alles in voller Freiheit grünt. […] Die Bäume sind grün, die Wiesen sind

were the most natural thing in the world, Baudelaire associated the color impressions evoked in nature with the characteristics of material objects, trees, or meadows. And the painters of the Barbizon School actually felt obliged to render local colors as they appeared (ill. 2). That would change with the Impressionists.

Claude Monet had already experienced the rejection of his paintings by the jury of the Salon Officiel on several occasions. As an alternative, the painter exhibited in the art section of the Exposition Maritime Internationale in Le Havre and in the display window of the shop run by art and paint dealer Latouche in Paris. Monet was able to present only a few paintings there, however, and they attracted public attention largely by chance. An independently organized group exhibition appeared to offer the only solution to this problem. With that in mind, Claude Monet and Camille Pissarro, who had become friends during their years of study at the Académie Suisse, and Alfred Sisley consulted on the idea of founding an artists' association. More artists came on board: Johan Barthold Jongkind, Berthe Morisot, Paul Cézanne, Edgar Degas, and others whose names are hardly known today. In December 1873, they formed the Société Anonyme Coopérative des Artistes, which opened its first exhibition at Nadar's studio three-and-a-half months later. The 165 oil paintings, watercolors, pastels, prints, sculptures, and enamel pieces were indexed in a catalogue. The exhibition was open twelve hours a day for one month and attracted a total of some 3,500 curious visitors.

The artists of the Société Anonyme Coopérative des Artistes did not regard themselves as a group united by a common painting style, much less a group with a common platform. Yet the term Impressionists, initially intended as a pejorative designation by critics, was eventually adopted by the artists themselves and has gone down in history as the name of the school of painting they represented.[5]

grün, das Moos grün, das Grün schlängelt sich in den Baumstämmen, die noch nicht reifen Halme sind grün; das Grün ist der Grundton der Natur, weil das Grün sich leicht mit allen anderen Farben vermählt.«[4] Wie selbstverständlich verbindet Baudelaire die Farbeindrücke in der Natur mit der Eigenschaft der materiellen Gegenstände, einem Baum oder einer Wiese. Und tatsächlich blieb die Lokalfarbe für die Maler der Schule von Barbizon verbindlich (Abb. 2). Mit den Impressionisten sollte sich das ändern.

Claude Monet hatte bereits mehrfach eine Ablehnung seiner Bilder durch die Jury des Salon officiel hinnehmen müssen. Alternativ stellte der Maler in der Kunstabteilung der Exposition maritime internationale in Le Havre oder auch im Schaufenster des Kunst- und Farbenhändlers Latouche in Paris aus. Doch konnte Monet hier nur wenige Bilder präsentieren, und die Aufmerksamkeit des Publikums blieb eher zufällig. Eine selbstständig organisierte Gruppenausstellung sollte Abhilfe schaffen. Zu diesem Zweck berieten Claude Monet und Camille Pissarro, Freunde aus der gemeinsamen Studienzeit an der Académie Suisse, sowie Alfred Sisley über eine Künstlervereinigung. Weitere Künstler schlossen sich an, Johan Barthold Jongkind, Berthe Morisot, Paul Cézanne, Edgar Degas und andere, die heute kaum mehr bekannt sind. Im Dezember 1873 gründeten sie die Société anonyme coopérative des artistes, die dreieinhalb Monate später ihre erste Ausstellung in besagtem Atelier von Nadar eröffnete. Die 165 ausgestellten Gemälde, Aquarelle, Pastelle, Druckgrafiken, Skulpturen und Email-Arbeiten waren in einem Katalog verzeichnet. Einen Monat lang konnte die Ausstellung täglich zwölf Stunden besichtigt werden und lockte insgesamt etwa 3500 Neugierige an. Die Künstler der Société anonyme coopérative des artistes verstanden sich allerdings kei-

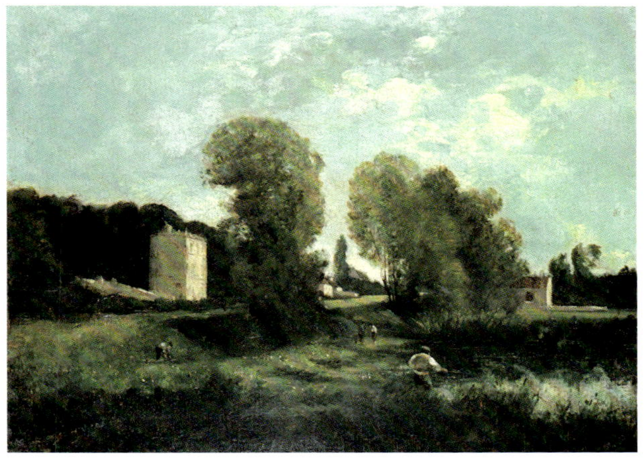

2
Jean-Baptiste-Camille Corot
Bei Avray, ca. 1860/70
Ville d'Avray
Wallraf-Richartz-Museum & Fondation Corboud, Köln Cologne

Louis Napoleon Bonaparte, who had himself crowned Emperor Napoleon III on the basis of a plebiscite in 1852, completely redesigned the city of Paris over the course of the next several decades. What had been a city with a largely medieval character developed into a modern metropolis. Baron Haussmann was commissioned to adapt Paris to the needs of a rapidly growing population and the necessities of industrialization, trade, and transportation. In the process, he was also expected to transform the city into a magnificent capital. The most important and extensive part of his program involved the complete restructuring of the network of streets. The new, broad avenues and boulevards were lined with buildings of uniform height and configuration. Glass-covered shopping arcades and public parks invited people to stroll through the city. The Bois de Boulogne was converted into a recreation and amusement park. The highlight of construction activity for numerous cultural institutions was the new opera house. The railroad linked the city with its suburbs. Huge terminals built of iron and glass, such as the Gare Saint-Lazare, were erected.[6]

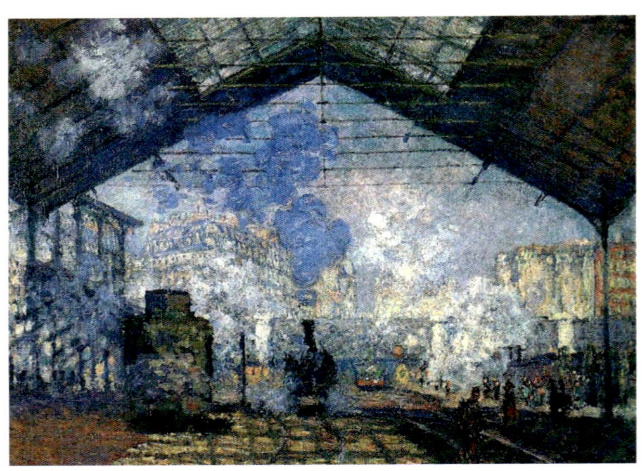

3
Claude Monet
Der Bahnhof Saint-Lazare, 1877
Saint-Lazare Station
Museé d'Orsay, Paris

From that point on, this modern Paris and its suburbs along the Seine became the preferred subjects of the Impressionists. With his Realist approach, Gustave Courbet, who confined himself entirely to the depiction of the visible world, paved the way for the emergence of everyday motifs as subjects worthy of painting.

Claude Monet rented a house with a studio near the Seine in Argenteuil in 1871. There, he had a studio boat built, from which he painted numerous views of the banks of the Seine. Trains ran every hour between Argenteuil and Gare Saint-Lazare in Paris, enabling Monet to work regularly in his Paris studio as well. In 1877, he requested permission to paint in the Saint-Lazare train station. He presented seven views of the station at the

neswegs als eine Gruppe mit einem gemeinsamen Malstil und noch weniger als Gruppe mit einem gemeinsamen Programm. Die zunächst von der Presse abfällig gemeinte Bezeichnung als Impressionisten wurde dann schließlich aber von den Künstlern selbst aufgegriffen und ging als Stilbezeichnung in die Kunstgeschichte ein.[5]

Louis Napoleon Bonaparte, der sich 1852 durch Volksabstimmung als Napoleon III. zum Kaiser der Franzosen erheben ließ, gestaltete Paris in den kommenden Jahrzehnten vollständig um. Aus der noch mittelalterlich geprägten Stadt wurde eine moderne Metropole. Baron Haussmann erhielt den Auftrag, Paris den Bedürfnissen einer rasch wachsenden Bevölkerung, den Notwendigkeiten der Industrialisierung, des Handels und des Verkehrs anzupassen. Gleichzeitig sollte er es zu einer prachtvollen Hauptstadt umgestalten. Die wichtigste und umfassendste Maßnahme war die Neuordnung des Pariser Straßensystems. Die neuen, breit angelegten Straßen und Boulevards wurden gesäumt von Gebäuden mit einheitlicher Höhe und Aufbau. Glas gedeckte Einkaufspassagen und öffentliche Parks und Anlagen lockten zum Flanieren. Der Bois de Boulogne wurde zu einem Vergnügungs- und Erholungspark umgewandelt. Höhepunkt der Baumaßnahmen für zahlreiche kulturelle Institutionen war ein neues Opernhaus. Die Eisenbahn verband die Hauptstadt nun mit den Vorstädten, und es entstanden riesige Gleishallen aus Eisen und Glas wie zum Beispiel die Gare Saint-Lazare.[6]

Dieses moderne Paris sowie die an der Seine gelegenen Vorstädte dienten von nun an als bevorzugte Motive der Impressionisten. Dass dabei Themen des Alltags bildwürdig wurden, war bereits durch Gustave Courbet und seinen Realismus, der sich ganz auf die Darstellung des tatsächlich Sichtbaren beschränkte, vorbereitet worden.

1871 mietete Claude Monet in Argenteuil nahe der Seine ein Haus mit Atelier. Hier ließ sich der Maler ein Atelierboot bauen, und es entstanden zahlreiche Ansichten des Seine-

third Impressionist exhibition that same year, and the paintings caused quite a stir.[7] Emile Zola expressed great enthusiasm ("One hears the thunder of arriving trains; one sees billowing clouds of steam that roll under the expansive halls").[8] But the paintings also reaped criticism as well. Monet's large painting of *La Gare Saint-Lazare* of 1877 (ill. 3), which is now at the Musée d'Orsay in Paris, shows a view into the open terminal. A whirlwind of white and blue steam from a locomotive rises to the glass roof of the hall, enveloping trains and people and obscuring the view of a boulevard. The motifs are merely suggested. Much more striking is the impression evoked by the effects of light, as in the lattice of the glass roof that is projected onto the tracks below. The clothes worn by the people standing on the shaded side of the tracks are rendered in the same colors as the tracks themselves. The sunlit façades of the buildings along the boulevard appear in a golden glow, contrasting with the buildings on the opposite side of the street, which assume the bluish-white coloration of the steam from the locomotive. Thus Monet disregarded the local colors of the objects, thereby giving precedence to the atmosphere and the influence of light on what is being depicted over the motifs themselves.

Regardless of whether it is the urban views and Seine landscapes of Monet and Pissarro, the still lifes of Edouard Manet, Renoir's depictions of people in outdoor settings, or the ballet scenes of Edgar Degas, the atmospheric effects, color changes, and blurring of contours achieved by the Impressionists through their handling of light were indispensable to their concept of painting.[9]

We recognize a crucial innovation in the conceptual approaches of leading Impressionist painters to art.[10] Paul Cézanne spoke of the existence of a purely painterly truth of things. "Painting from nature does not, however, mean copying an object; it means realizing color impressions. ... I have nothing in mind when I paint. I see colors that arrange themselves

Ufers. Stündlich verkehrte ein Zug zwischen Argenteuil und dem Bahnhof Saint-Lazare in Paris, sodass Monet auch regelmäßig in seinem Pariser Atelier arbeiten konnte. 1877 bemühte er sich um die Erlaubnis, im Bahnhof Saint-Lazare zu malen. Auf der im gleichen Jahr stattfindenden dritten Impressionisten-Ausstellung konnte er sieben Ansichten des Bahnhofs präsentieren, die großes Aufsehen hervorriefen.[7] Während Emile Zola sich begeisterte (»Man hört das Getöse der einrollenden Züge, man sieht die überquellenden Dampfwolken, die sich unter den weiten Hallen wälzen«),[8] ernteten diese Bilder auch Kritik. Monets großformatiges Gemälde *La Gare Saint-Lazare* von 1877 (Abb. 3), das sich heute im Musée d'Orsay in Paris befindet, zeigt einen Blick in die offene Gleishalle. Ein Wirbel aus weißem und blauem Dampf einer Lokomotive staut sich unter dem Glasdach der Halle und verhüllt Züge, Menschen und den Blick auf einen Boulevard. Die Motive sind nur angedeutet; stärker berührt der Eindruck der Lichteffekte, wie der des Gitternetzes des Glasdaches, der sich hell auf die Gleisanlagen legt. In der Kleidung der auf der verschatteten Seite der Gleise stehenden Menschen finden sich die gleichen Farben wie bei den Gleisen selbst. Die von der Sonne beschienenen Häuser des Boulevards leuchten golden, wogegen die Häuser auf der anderen Straßenseite die blau-weiße Farbigkeit des Dampfes der Lokomotive angenommen haben. So verzichtet Monet also auf die Lokalfarbe der Gegenstände. Damit erhalten die Atmosphäre und der Einfluss des Lichtes auf das Dargestellte den Vorzug vor dem Motiv.

Ganz gleich, ob Stadtbild oder Seine-Landschaft wie bei Monet und Pissarro, ob Stillleben wie bei Edouard Manet oder die Darstellung von Personen in freier Natur wie bei Auguste Renoir oder des Balletts wie bei Edgar Degas, die atmosphärischen Einwirkungen, die Veränderungen der Farbe und das Verschwimmen der Konturen durch das Licht, dies alles war für die Impressionisten unverzichtbarer Bildbestandteil.[9]

as they will. Everything is organized—trees, fields, and houses—by spots of color."[11] Monet had quite naturally associated his color impressions with the central perspective in his painting of the Gare Saint-Lazare. Cézanne, however, abandoned the idea that the eye seeks a fixed vanishing point. In his view, it is the impressions of color that dictate the composition of the painting and offer multiple perspectives to the viewer's eye within the same picture. In Cézanne's *Dans la plaine de Bellevue* (ill. 4), for example, the landscape is composed of individual bands that evoke a certain sense of depth only in the slanted roofs of the houses. Architecture and nature are abstracted into self-enclosed geometric surfaces and forms.

Several years later, another art critic coined the term for a new artistic movement. In 1886, Félix Fénéon visited an exhibition that included Georges Seurat's *Un Dimanche après-midi à la Grande Jatte* (ill. 5). In his rave review of the painting, he used the term "Pointillism" to describe the painting style developed by Georges Seurat, which would influence such artists as Paul Signac and Camille Pissarro. Seurat's painting shows the Seine island of Grande Jatte northwest of Paris. The figures in the scene are city-dwellers clad in chic Paris fashions who are amusing themselves during their excursion. Seurat composed the entire painting with strokes of equal size which, when viewed from a certain distance, blend to form fields of color. The painter proceeded on the basis of visual laws in developing his coloration. He was influenced primarily by the theories of the physicist and chemist Michel-Eugène Chevreul on the phenomenon of simultaneous color contrast. According to Chevreul, colors should not be mixed but instead set individually and side by side on the canvas, so that they actually blend only in the viewer's eye.

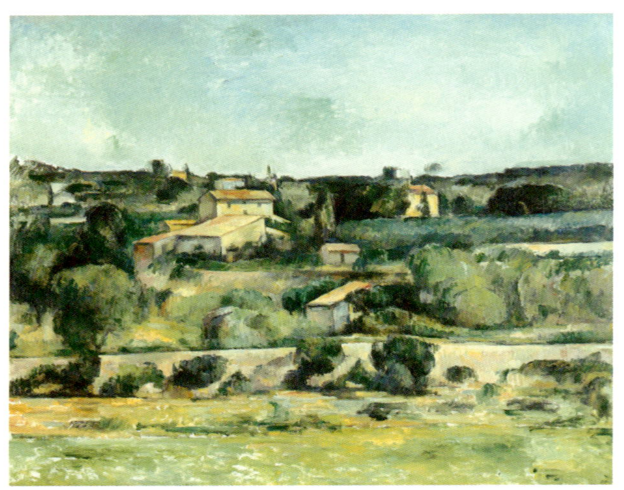

4
Paul Cezanne
Landschaft im Westen von Aix-en-Provence, 1885/88
Landscape in the West of Aix-en-Provence
Wallraf-Richartz-Museum & Fondation Corboud, Köln Cologne

So zeigt sich bei den Malerpersönlichkeiten des Impressionismus eine entscheidende Neuerung der künstlerischen Vorstellungen.[10] Paul Cézanne sprach davon, dass es eine rein malerische Wahrheit der Dinge gäbe. »Nach der Natur malen bedeutet aber nicht, das Objekt kopieren, sondern Farbeindrücke realisieren. [...] Ich denke an nichts, wenn ich male, ich sehe Farben, sie ordnen sich, wie sie wollen, alles organisiert sich, die Bäume, Felder, Häuser, durch Farbflecken.«[11] Monet hatte in seinem Bild vom Bahnhof Saint-Lazare die Farbeindrücke wie selbstverständlich mit der Zentralperspektive verbunden. Cézanne hingegen trennte sich von der Vorstellung, dass das Auge einen festen Fluchtpunkt sucht. Bei ihm sind es Farbeindrücke, die die Bildkomposition vorgeben und dem Auge des Betrachters mehrere Perspektiven im Bild anbieten. In Cézannes *Dans la plaine de Bellevue* (Abb. 4) beispielsweise setzt sich die Landschaft aus einzelnen Bildstreifen zusammen, die nur in den Dachschrägen der Häuser eine gewisse Tiefenwirkung aufweisen. Architektur und Natur abstrahieren sich zu geschlossenen geometrischen Flächen und Formen.

Einige Jahre später sollte es wiederum ein Kunstkritiker sein, der die Bezeichnung für eine neue Stilrichtung prägte. 1886 besuchte Félix Fénéon eine Ausstellung, in der Georges Seurats Gemälde *Un Dimanche après-midi à la Grande Jatte* (Abb. 5) zu sehen war. In seiner begeisterten Besprechung dieses Bildes prägte er den Begriff »Pointillismus«, mit dem in der Folge der Malstil bezeichnet wurde, den Georges Seurat entwickelt hatte und damit unter anderen Paul Signac und Camille Pissarro beeinflusste. Seurats Bild zeigt die nordwestlich von Paris in der Seine gelegene Insel Grande Jatte. Es sind städtische Ausflügler, modisch gekleidet im Pariser Schick, die hier ihren Vergnügungen nachgehen. Seurat setzte das ganze Bild aus gleich großen Strichen zusammen, die sich, mit einigem Abstand betrachtet, zu Farbfeldern vermischen. In seiner Farbgebung ging

Thus, for example, a gray field on a black background appears lighter than it does on a white background. Yet not only the degree of lightness but also the intensity of a given color is influenced by its adjacent one. Yellow looks more orange next to a clear blue and tends toward green next to a dark blue. Seurat used this method of breaking down colors also to achieve harmony. "Art is harmony. And harmony is the unity of contrasts and the unity of like phenomena, in tone, in color, and in line. ... All of these harmonies are distinguishable as those of tranquility, happiness, or sorrow."[12] In this way, colors reveal something about moods and states of mind. Many artists sympathetic to Pointillism developed their own unique approaches to the laws of color posited by Seurat.[13]

The Dutch artist Vincent van Gogh arrived in Paris in 1886. He got to know Emile Bernard, Camille Pissarro, and Georges Seurat, who introduced him to the new currents in painting. Van Gogh went on to experiment with the Impressionist brushwork technique and the Pointillist style while bringing himself up to date with the latest color theories. He consistently strove to achieve a style of his own.

After two years in Paris, van Gogh turned his back on city life and moved to Arles in the South of France. Aside from the tranquility of the rural setting, the artist was attracted to Provence and to nature untainted by civilization, the radiant sunlight, and the colors of the South. It was here that van Gogh developed an entirely autonomous concept of color, which interprets objects on the basis of their coloration. He did not use colors as they appear in nature but instead intensified them to the extreme as a means of expressing emotional intensity. In 1888, van Gogh painted *Le Café de nuit, Place Lamartine, Arles* (ill. 6). He wrote the following remarks on the painting in a letter to his brother Théo: "I tried to express the horrible suffering of these people with red and green.—It is a color, not literally true from the standpoint of Realism, the deceiver of the eye, but a suggestive

der Maler nach optischen Gesetzen vor. Dabei beeinflussten ihn vor allem auch die Farbtheorien des Physikers und Chemikers Michel-Eugène Chevreul zum Simultankontrast: Gemäß diesen Theorien sollten Farben nicht gemischt, sondern einzeln und nebeneinander auf die Leinwand gesetzt werden, sodass sie sich erst im Auge des Betrachters vermischen. So wirkt eine graue Fläche vor einem schwarzen Hintergrund optisch heller als vor einem weißen. Aber nicht nur der Helligkeitswert, sondern auch die Intensität einer Farbe steigert sich in Bezug auf ihre benachbarte Farbe. So wirkt Gelb neben einem klaren Blau eher wie Orange und neben einem dunklen Blau grünlich. Mit dieser Farbzerlegung strebte Seurat auch Harmonie an. »Kunst ist Harmonie. Harmonie wiederum ist Einheit von Kontrasten und Einheit von Ähnlichem, im Ton, in der Farbe, in der Linie. […] Alle diese Harmonien scheiden sich in solche der Ruhe, der Heiterkeit und der Trauer.«[12] Die Farben geben somit Auskunft über Stimmung und Befindlichkeit. Zahlreiche Künstler, die mit dem Pointillismus sympathisierten, fanden dabei einen ganz individuellen Weg im Umgang mit den von Seurat aufgestellten Farbgesetzen.[13]

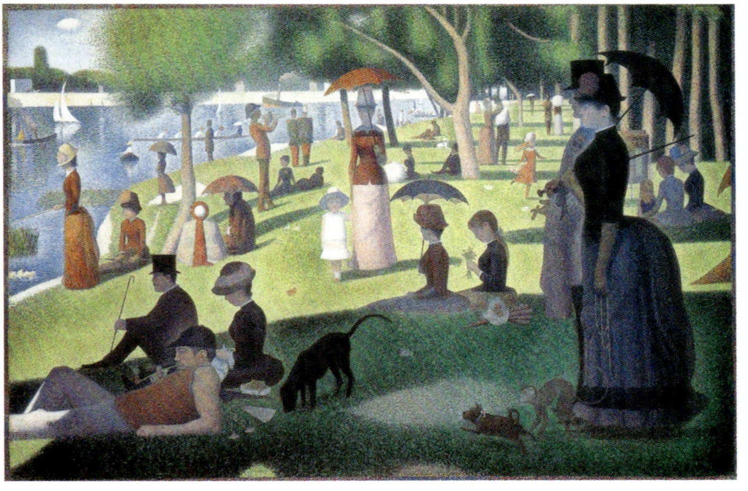

5
Georges Seurat
Ein Sonntagnachmittag auf der Insel La Grande Jatte, 1884–86
A Sunday Afternoon on the Island of Grande Jatte
The Art Institute of Chicago

1886 traf der Niederländer Vincent van Gogh in Paris ein. Er knüpfte Kontakte zu Emile Bernard, Camille Pissarro und Georges Seurat, die ihm die neuen Strömungen der Malerei vermittelten. Van Gogh experimentierte daraufhin mit dem impressionistischen Pinselstrich und der Malweise des Pointillismus und brachte seine Kenntnisse im Bereich der Farbenlehre auf den neuesten Stand. Stets bemühte er sich dabei um einen eigenen Stil.

color that expresses the movement of glowing emotion."[14] Using these "suggestive" colors, as he called them, and a specific brushstroke technique, van Gogh also painted other typical motifs of Provence: the local people, cypresses, and olive groves. The painter found his own distinct style in this southern landscape.[15]

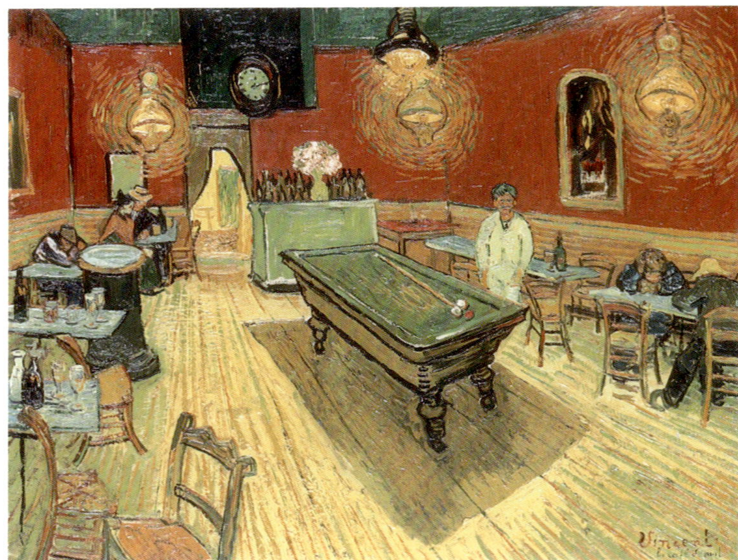

6
Vincent van Gogh
Das Nachtcafé an der Place Lamartine in Arles, 1888
The Night Café in the Place Lamartine in Arles
Yale University Art Gallery, New Haven, CT

The art of the Impressionists had in the meantime become socially acceptable, and the artists of the avant-garde who succeeded them were able to count on the support of art critics, art patrons, and art dealers. Paris was still the crucial proving ground for an artist's success.

Vincent van Gogh was not the only artist to abandon the city as motif and setting for his artistic work. Paul Gauguin traveled to Brittany in 1886 and settled in the rural town of Pont-Aven. The artist felt that life in Brittany offered symbolic proof that the virtues of piety, simplicity, and community still existed in the country. Gauguin idealized these virtues in his iconic depictions of Breton women. The women in his *Vision after the Sermon* of 1888 (ill. 7) are recognizable primarily by their headwear. Dark lines frame the women's faces, bonnets, and bodies. In this work, Gauguin developed a style of painting that was inspired by medieval religious art. His vivid contours resemble the metal wires used in the *cloisonné* enamel technique or the lead rods used to join the separate colored segments in stained-glass art. Color and space bear witness to a bold antinaturalism. It is a visionary approach to color that is not empirical but instead expresses a spiritual character.[16]

Nach zwei Jahren kehrte van Gogh dem Stadtleben den Rücken und zog ins südfranzösische Arles. Neben der ländlichen Ruhe suchte der Künstler in der Provence die von der Zivilisation unbelastete Natur, das strahlende Sonnenlicht und die Farben des Südens. Hier gelangte van Gogh zu einer ganz eigenständigen Farbauffassung, die den Gegenstand mithilfe der Farbgebung interpretiert. Er setzte die Farben nicht so ein, wie sie in der Natur erscheinen, sondern übersteigerte sie, um eine emotionale Intensität widerzuspiegeln. 1888 malte van Gogh *Le Café de nuit, Place Lamartine, Arles* (Abb. 6). Zu diesem Bild schrieb er seinem Bruder Théo: »Ich versuchte mit dem Rot und dem Grün die schreckliche Leidenschaft der Menschen auszudrücken. – Es ist eine Farbe, nicht wörtlich wahr vom Standpunkt des Realismus, der Augentäuscher, aber eine suggestive Farbe, welche eine Bewegung des glühenden Gefühls ausdrückt.«[14] Mit diesen, wie er sie nannte, »suggestiven« Farben und einem spezifischen Pinselstrich malte van Gogh auch andere charakteristische Motive der Provence: die einheimische Bevölkerung, Zypressen und Olivenhaine. Der Maler hatte hier im Süden seinen individuellen Stil gefunden.[15]

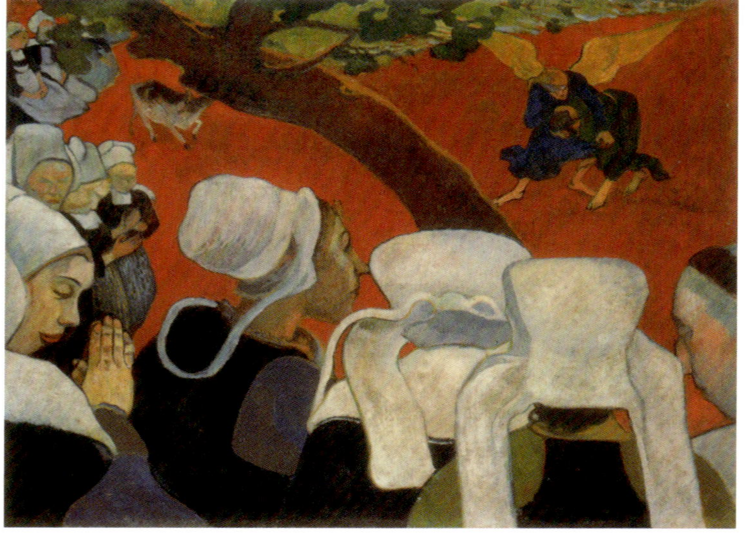

7
Paul Gauguin
Vision nach der Predigt oder
Der Kampf Jakobs mit dem Engel, 1888
Vision after the Sermon
National Gallery of Scotland, Edinburgh

Die Kunst der Impressionisten war mittlerweile salonfähig geworden, und die Künstler der nachfolgenden Avantgarde konnten auf die Förderung durch die Kunstkritik, die Kunstmäzene und den Kunsthandel zählen. Noch immer war Paris der entscheidende Ort für den Erfolg eines Künstlers.

Dabei war Vincent van Gogh nicht der einzige Künstler, der der Stadt als Motiv und als Ort seiner künstlerischen Tätigkeit den Rücken kehrte. 1886 reiste beispielsweise Paul

Gauguin, Emile Bernard, and Paul Sérusier attracted a number of followers some of which founded the artists' group known as the Nabis (Prophets) under the leadership of Maurice Denis in 1888. Denis, who regarded painting as a kind of religious calling, used color as a means of expressing mental states. Incorporated within a decorative, abstract form, it became a symbol of a subjective state of mind.

The decisive changes in conceptual approaches to art introduced by the Impressionists paved the way for the various modern-art movements of the twentieth century. Pointillism, Cloisonnism, Symbolism, Cubism, and Expressionism all trace their routes to Impressionism.

Gauguin in die Bretagne und ließ sich in dem ländlichen Ort Pont-Aven nieder. Der Künstler empfand das bretonische Leben als ein Sinnbild dafür, dass die Tugenden der Frömmigkeit und Schlichtheit und der Gemeinschaft auf dem Lande noch existierten. Diese Tugenden idealisierte Gauguin in der ikonenhaften Darstellung der bretonischen Frauen. In der *Vision nach der Predigt* von 1888 (Abb. 7) sind die Frauen vorwiegend an ihren Kopfbedeckungen zu erkennen. Dunkle Linien umfassen die Gesichter, Hauben und Körper der Frauen. Gauguin entwickelte hier einen Malstil, der von der religiösen Kunst des Mittelalters inspiriert war. So vollziehen die klaren Konturen die bei der Email-Zellenschmelz-Technik (cloisonné) verwendeten Metallstege oder die in der Glasmalerei zur Verbindung der farbigen Einzelstücke eingesetzten Bleiruten nach. Farbe und Raum zeugen von einem kühnen Antinaturalismus. Es ist eine visionäre Farbgebung, die nicht empirisch ist, sondern einen spirituellen Charakter veranschaulicht.[16]

Gemeinsam mit Emile Bernard und Paul Sérusier versammelte Gauguin eine Schar von Anhängern um sich, aus der 1888 unter der Führung von Maurice Denis die Künstlergruppe der Nabis (Propheten) hervorging. Denis, der die Malerei als Art religiöse Berufung empfand, diente die Farbe als Ausdruck des Seelenzustands. In eine dekorative, abstrakte Form eingebunden, wurde sie zum Symbol subjektiver Befindlichkeit.

Die entscheidenden Veränderungen des künstlerischen Denkens der Impressionisten waren Voraussetzung für die verschiedenen Richtungen der modernen Kunst des 20. Jahrhunderts: Pointillismus, Cloisonismus, Symbolismus, Kubismus und Expressionismus fanden hier ihren Anfang.

1 Louis Leroy, "L'Exposition des impressionnistes," in *Le Charivari*, April 25, 1874, cited in and translated from John Rewald, *Die Geschichte des Impressionismus* (Cologne, 1979), p. 191.

2 Unda Hörner, *Madame Man Ray: Fotografinnen der Avantgarde in Paris* (Berlin, 2002), pp. 144f.

3 Götz Czymmek, *Bildhefte zur Sammlung*, vol. 12: *Französische Malerei des 19. Jahrhunderts I (mit Ausnahme der Bilder der Fondation Corboud)*, ed. Wallraf-Richartz-Museum—Fondation Corboud (Cologne, 2005), pp. 10–12.

4 Charles Baudelaire, "Salon (1846)," cited in and translated from Werner Busch, ed., *Landschaftsmalerei* (Berlin, 1997), p. 295.

5 Czymmek 2005 (see note 3), pp. 38f.

6 Jürgen Paul, "Großstadt und Lebensstil: London und Paris im 19. Jahrhundert," in *Moderne Kunst: Das Funkkolleg zum Verständnis der Gegenwartskunst*, vol. 1, ed. Monika Wagner (Hamburg, 1992), pp. 50–74.

7 Dorothee Hansen, "Monet und Camille—Biographie einer Beziehung," in *Monet und Camille: Frauenporträts im Impressionismus*, eds. Dorothee Hansen and Wulf Herzogenrath, exh. cat. Kunsthalle Bremen (Bremen, 2005/06), pp. 31–34.

8 "Impressionismus: Monet, Renoir, Pissarro, Sisley, vor 1880," in Caroline Mathieu, *Musée d'Orsay: Führer* (Paris, 1987), p. 122.

9 Czymmek 2005 (see note 3), p. 40.

10 Walter Hess, *Dokumente zum Verständnis der modernen Malerei* (Hamburg, 1993), p. 13.

11 Joachim Gasquet, "Cézanne: Gespräche (Paris 1921)," in Hess 1993 (see note 10), pp. 21, 25.

12 "Seurat, von seinem Biographen niedergeschriebenes Diktat," cited in and translated from Jules Christophe, "Seurat (Paris 1890)," in Hess 1993 (see note 10), p. 31.

13 Barbara Schaefer, *Bildhefte zur Sammlung*, vol. 13: *Französische Malerei des 19. Jahrhunderts II: Die Impressionisten und ihre Nachfolger—Die Bilder der Fondation Corboud: Mit einem Beitrag von Götz Czymmek*, ed. Wallraf-Richartz-Museum & Fondation Corboud (Cologne, 2006).

14 Vincent van Gogh, "Briefe an seinen Bruder," in Hess 1993 (see note 10), p. 38.

15 Cornelia Homburg, "Vincent van Goghs Avantgardestrategien," in *Vincent van Gogh und die Maler des Petit Boulevard*, ed. id., exh. cat. Saint Louis Art Museum; Städelsches Kunstinstitut und Städtische Galerie, Frankfurt am Main (Ostfildern-Ruit, 2001), pp. 23–58.

16 Elizabeth C. Childs, "Auf der Suche nach dem Atelier des Südens: Van Gogh, Gauguin und die Identität des Avantgardekünstlers," in Homburg 2001 (see note 15), pp. 115–118.

1 Louis Leroy, »L'Exposition des impressionnistes«, in: *Le Charivari*, 25.4.1874, zit. nach: John Rewald, *Die Geschichte des Impressionismus*, Köln 1979, S. 191.

2 Unda Hörner, *Madame Man Ray. Fotografinnen der Avantgarde in Paris*, Berlin 2002, S. 144 f.

3 Götz Czymmek, *Französische Malerei des 19. Jahrhunderts I – mit Ausnahme der Bilder der Fondation Corboud (Wallraf-Richartz-Museum – Fondation Corboud, Köln. Bildhefte zur Sammlung*, Bd. 12), Köln 2005, S. 10–12.

4 Charles Baudelaire, »Salon (1846)«, in: Werner Busch (Hrsg.), *Landschaftsmalerei*, Berlin 1997, S. 295.

5 Czymmek 2005 (wie Anm. 3), S. 38 f.

6 Jürgen Paul, »Großstadt und Lebensstil. London und Paris im 19. Jahrhundert«, in: Monika Wagner (Hrsg.), *Moderne Kunst. Das Funkkolleg zum Verständnis der Gegenwartskunst*, Bd. 1, Hamburg 1992, S. 50–74.

7 Dorothee Hansen, »Monet und Camille – Biographie einer Beziehung«, in: Dorothee Hansen und Wulf Herzogenrath (Hrsg.), *Monet und Camille. Frauenporträts im Impressionismus*, Ausst.-Kat. Kunsthalle Bremen, 2005/06, S. 31–34.

8 »Impressionismus. Monet, Renoir, Pissarro, Sisley, vor 1880«, in: Caroline Mathieu, *Musée d'Orsay. Führer*, Paris 1987, S. 122.

9 Czymmek 2005 (wie Anm. 3), S. 40.

10 Walter Hess, *Dokumente zum Verständnis der modernen Malerei*, Hamburg 1993, S. 13.

11 Joachim Gasquet, »Cézanne. Gespräche (Paris 1921)«, in: Hess 1993 (wie Anm. 10), S. 21, 25.

12 »Seurat, von seinem Biographen niedergeschriebenes Diktat«, zit. nach: Jules Christophe, »Seurat (Paris 1890)«, in: Hess 1993 (wie Anm. 10), S. 31.

13 Barbara Schaefer, *Französische Malerei des 19. Jahrhunderts II – Die Impressionisten und ihre Nachfolger – Die Bilder der Fondation Corboud. Mit einem Beitrag von Götz Czymmek (Wallraf-Richartz-Museum & Fondation Corboud, Köln. Bildhefte zur Sammlung*, Bd. 13), Köln 2006.

14 Vincent van Gogh, »Briefe an seinen Bruder«, in: Hess 1993 (wie Anm. 10), S. 38.

15 Cornelia Homburg, »Vincent van Goghs Avantgardestrategien«, in: Cornelia Homburg (Hrsg.), *Vincent van Gogh und die Maler des Petit Boulevard*, Ausst.-Kat. Saint Louis Art Museum; Städelsches Kunstinstitut und Städtische Galerie, Frankfurt a. M., Ostfildern-Ruit 2001, S. 23–58.

16 Elizabeth C. Childs, *Auf der Suche nach dem Atelier des Südens. Van Gogh, Gauguin und die Identität des Avantgardekünstlers*, in: Homburg 2001 (wie Anm. 15), S. 115-118.

PLATES

TAFELTEIL

The Precursors

Die Vorläufer

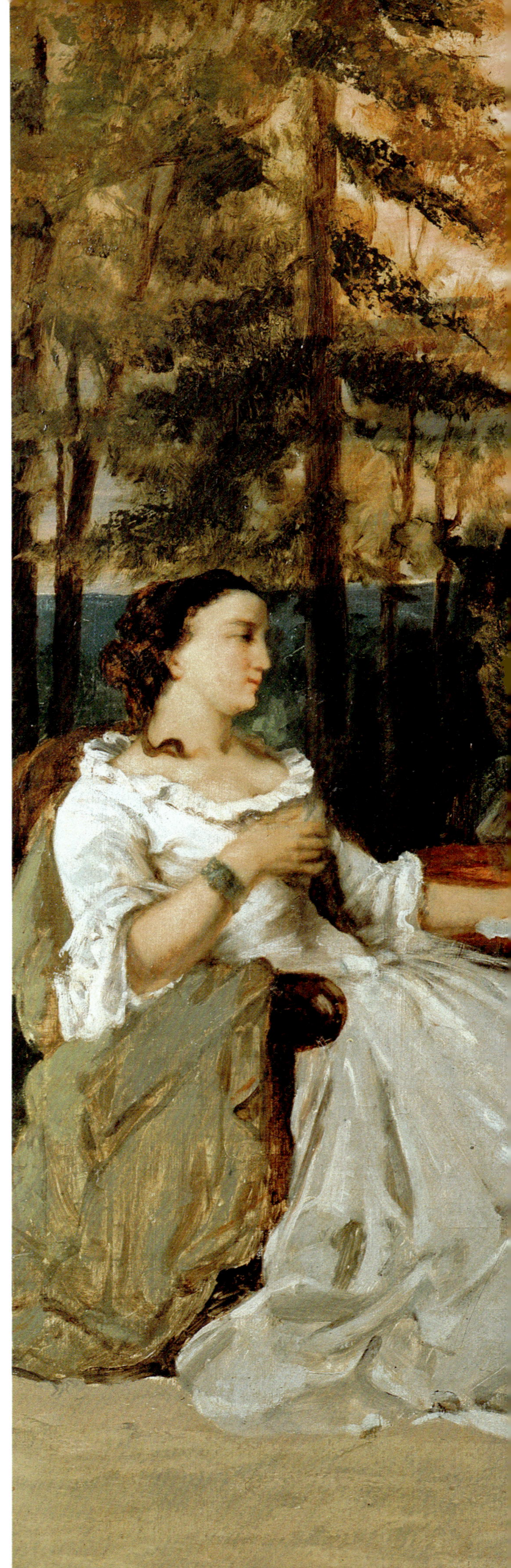

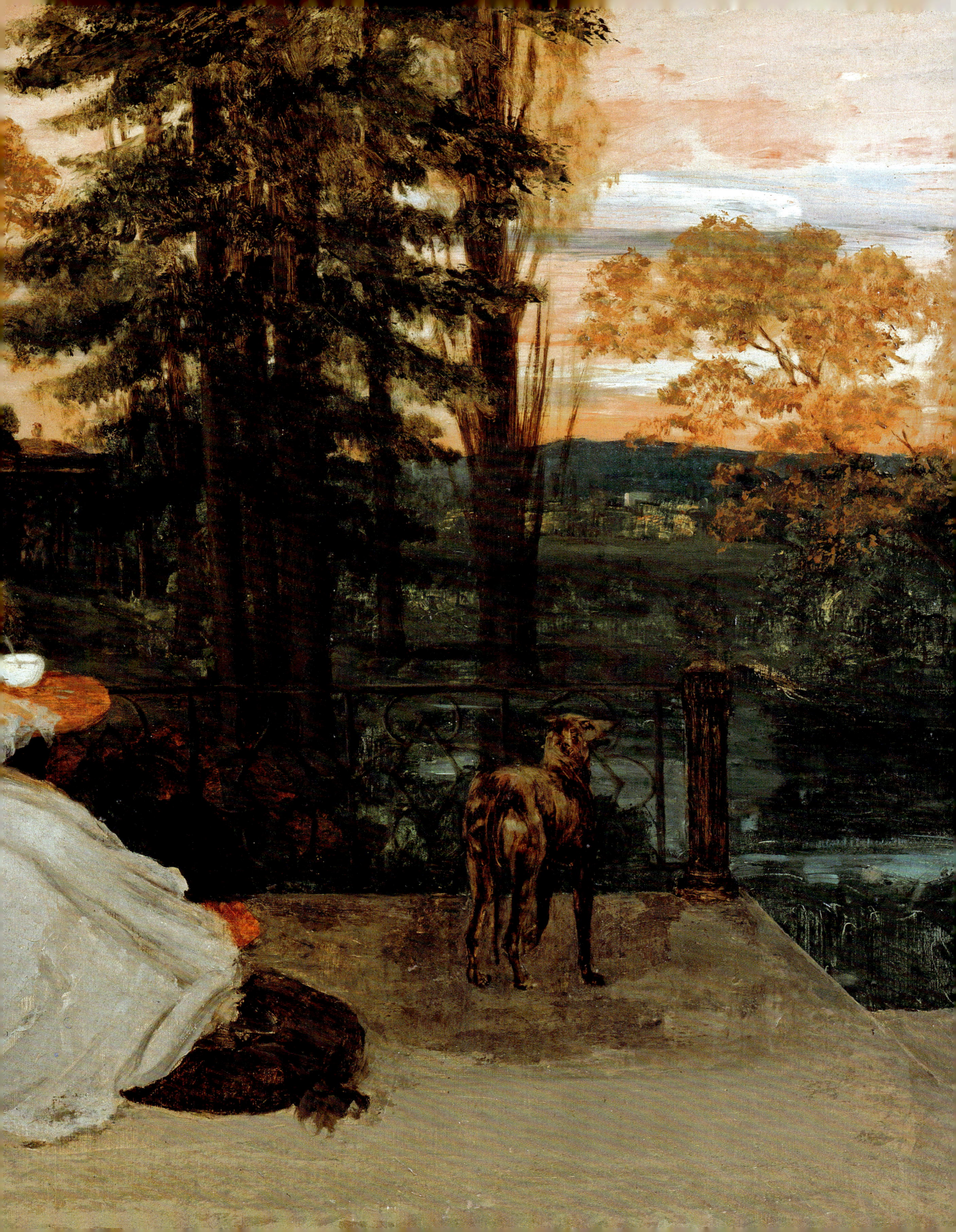

Jean-Baptiste-Camille Corot
Poetry
Die Dichtkunst, ca. 1865/70

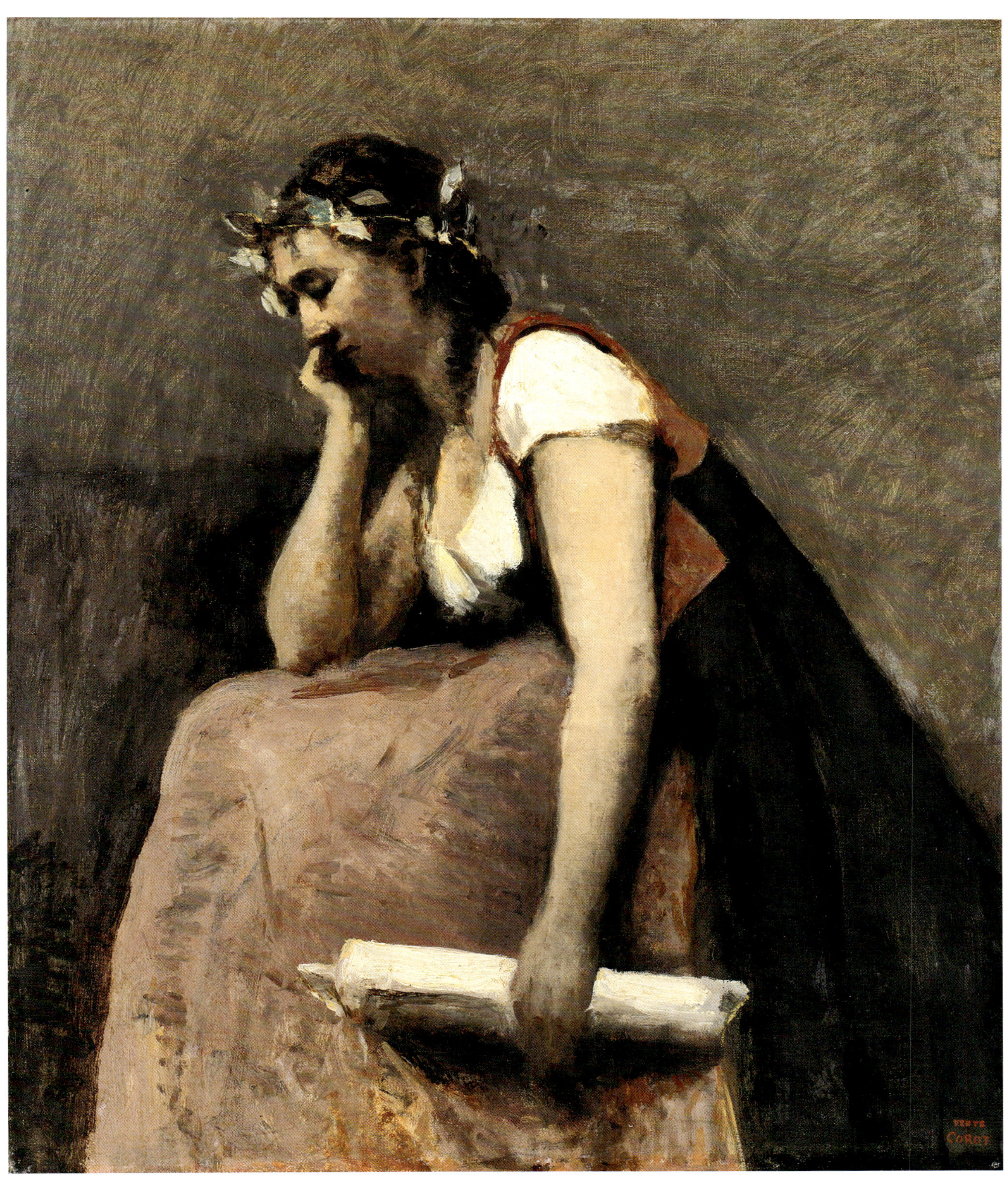
VENTE
COROT

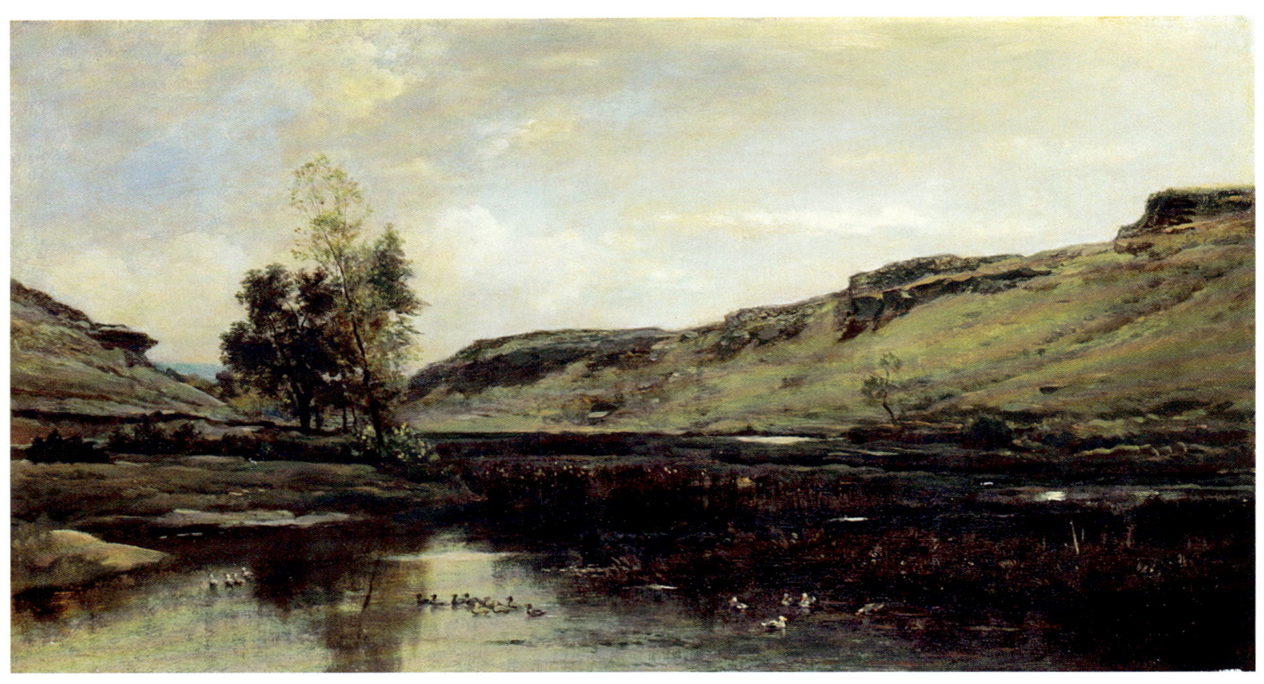

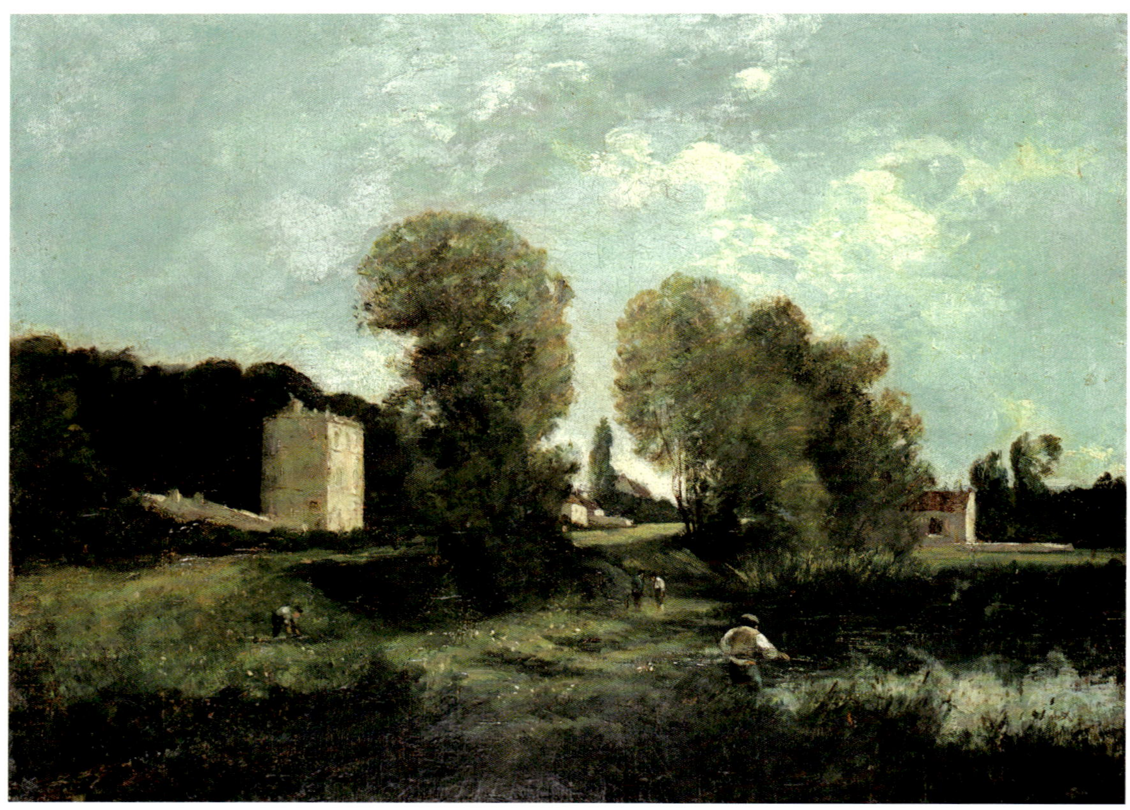

Charles-François Daubigny
Gylieu Pond at Optevoz
Der Weiher von Gylieu bei Optevoz, 1856

Jean-Baptiste-Camille Corot
Ville d'Avray
Bei Avray, ca. 1860/70

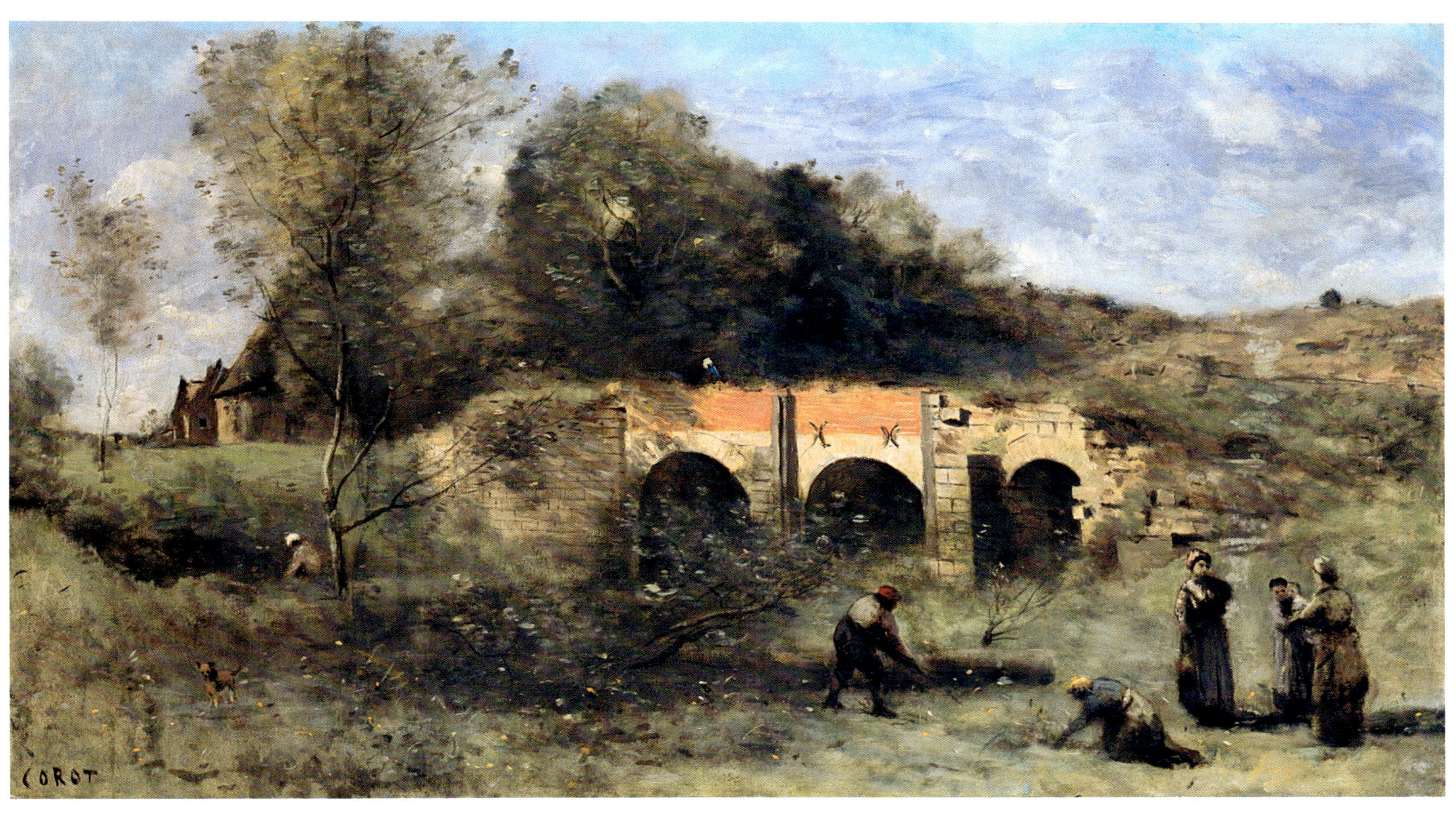

JEAN-BAPTISTE-CAMILLE COROT
The Old Brick Bridge at Arleux-Palluel
Die alte Ziegelsteinbrücke bei Arleux-Palluel, 1871

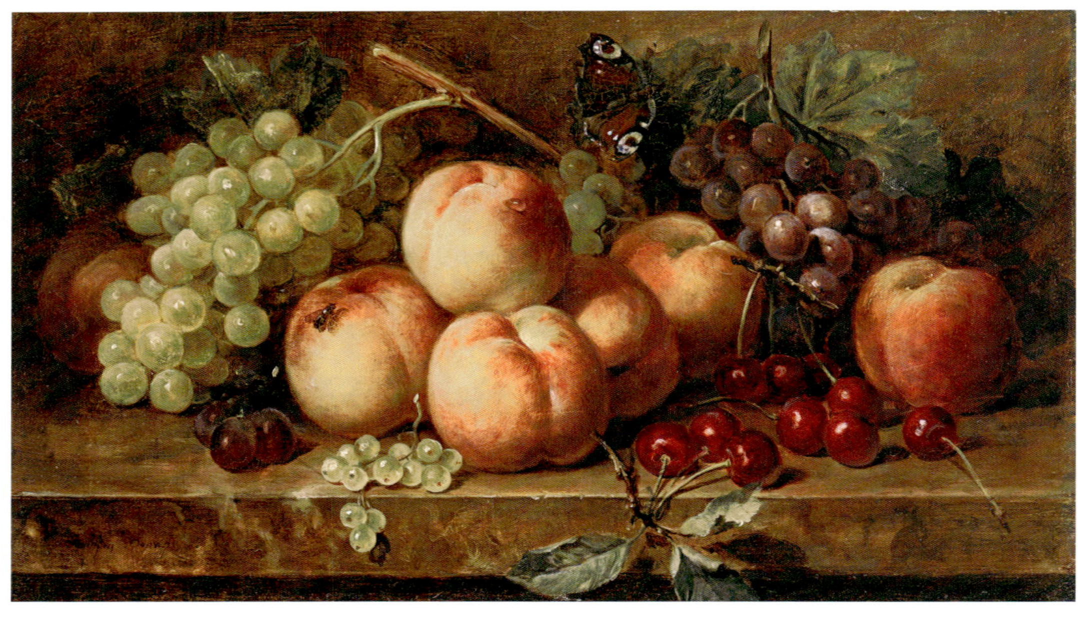

François Bonvin
Still Life with Grapes, Peaches, and Cherries, n.d.
Stillleben mit Weintrauben, Pfirsichen und Kirschen, o. J.

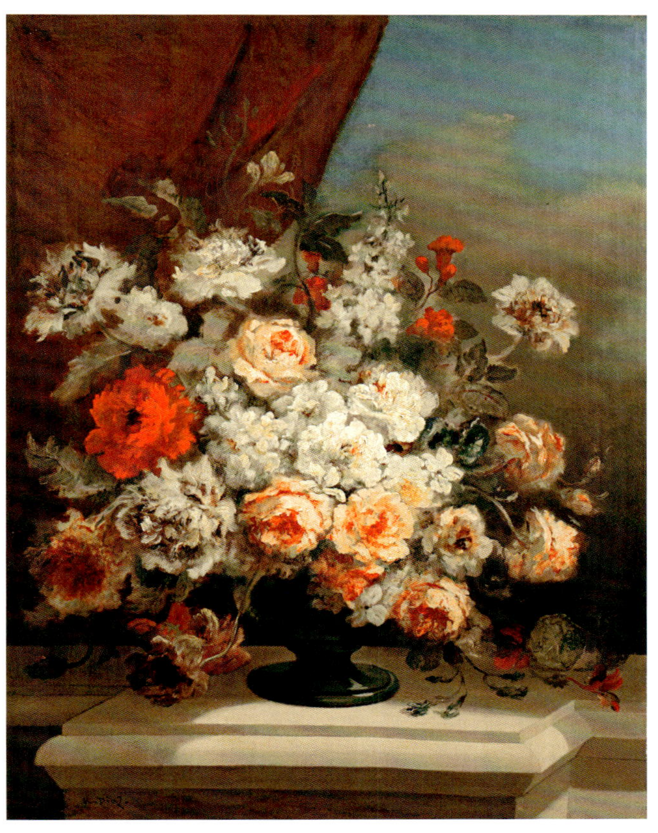

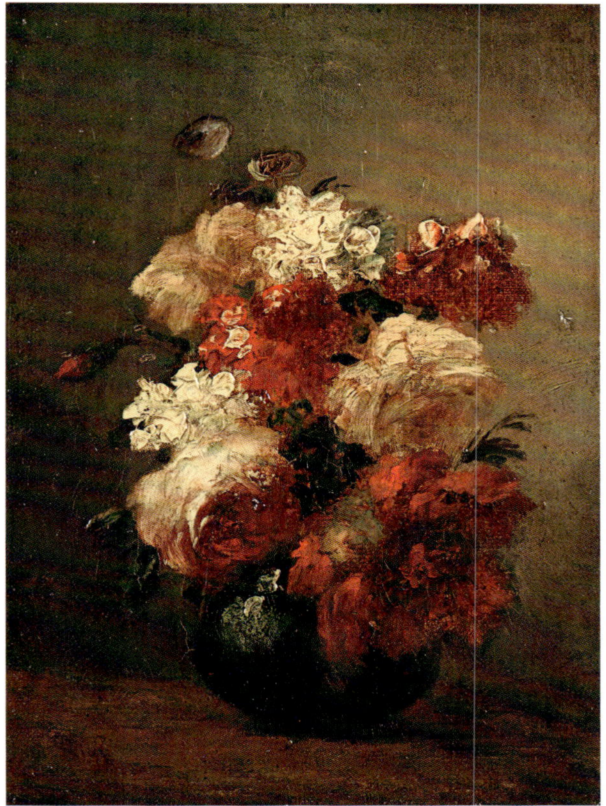

VIRGILIO NARCISSO DIAZ DE LA PENA
Still Life with Flowers, n.d.
Blumenstillleben, o. J.

VIRGILIO NARCISSO DIAZ DE LA PENA
Bouquet of Flowers in a Clay Vase, n.d.
Blumenstrauß in Tonvase, o. J.

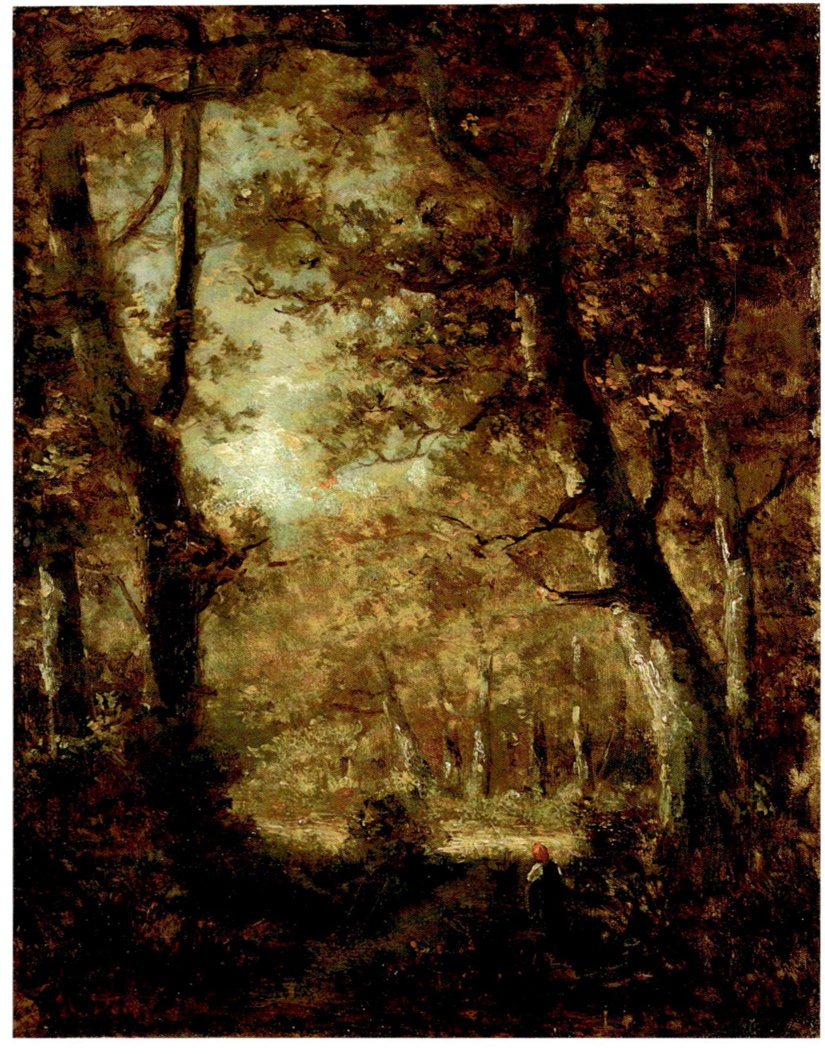

Virgilio Narcisso Diaz de la Pena
Forest Path, n.d.
Waldweg, o. J.

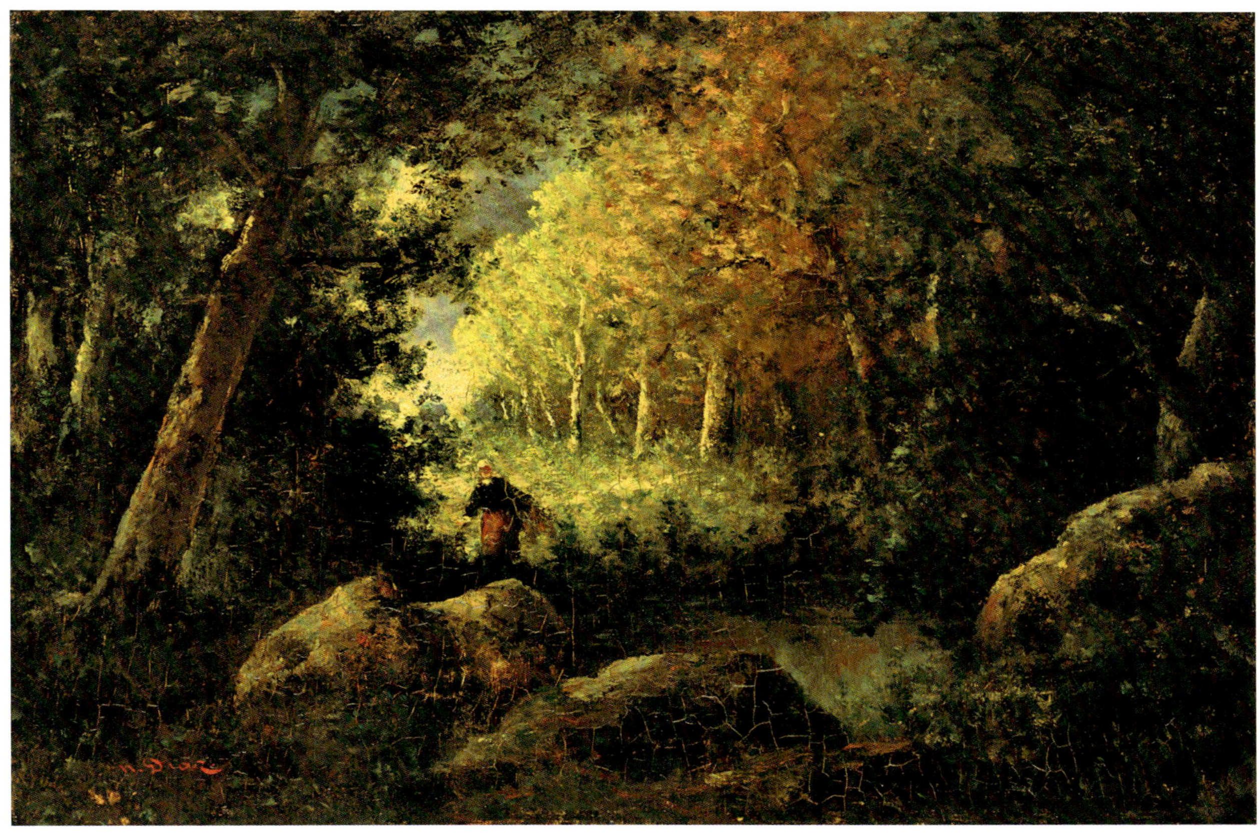

Virgilio Narcisso Diaz de la Pena
Autumn in the Forest of Fontainebleau, n.d.
Herbst im Wald von Fontainebleau, o. J.

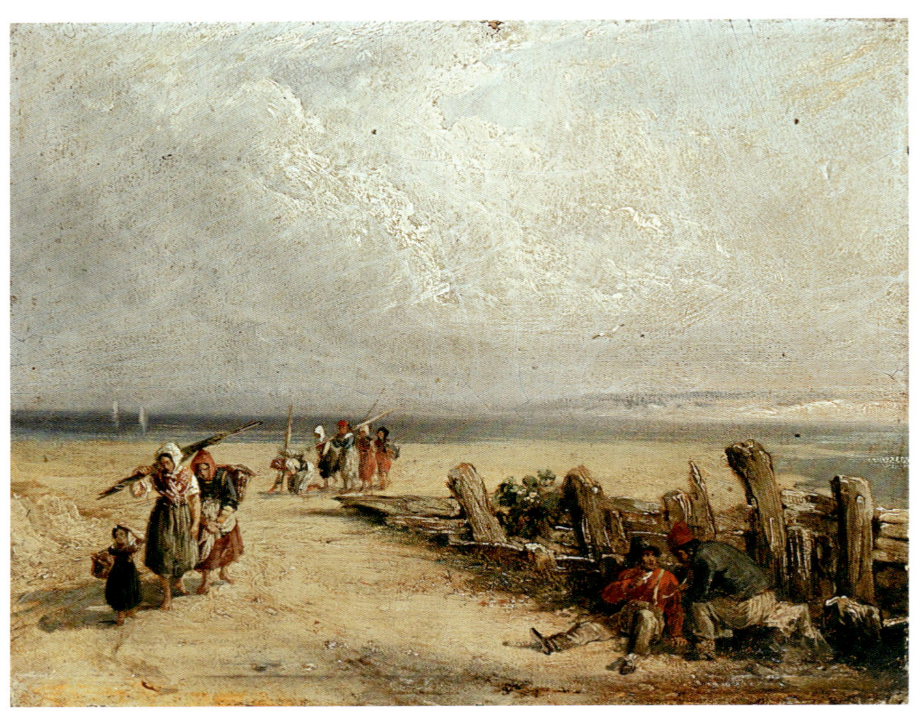

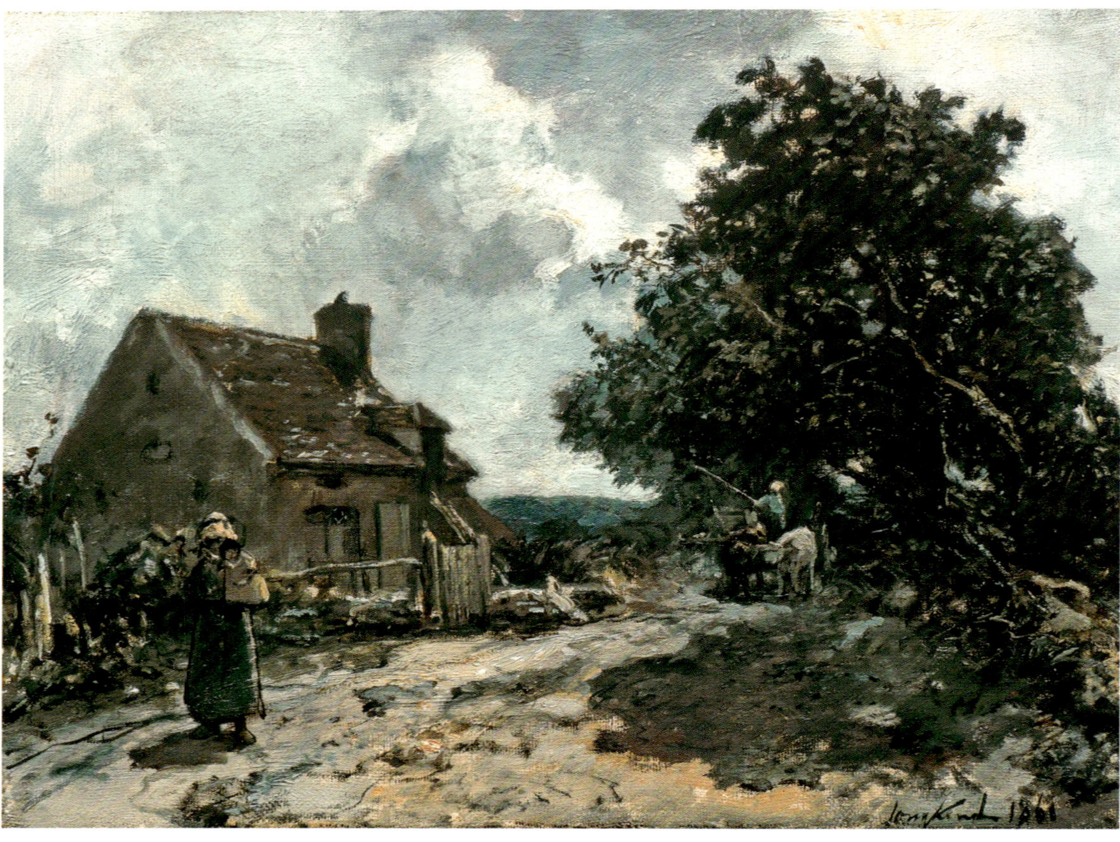

Eugene Isabey
Return from Fishing, n.d.
Rückkehr vom Fischfang, o. J.

Johan Barthold Jongkind
In the Environs of Nevers or *Farm in Saint-Parize-le-Chatel*
In der Umgebung von Nevers oder *Bauernhof in Saint-Parize-le-Chatel*, 1861

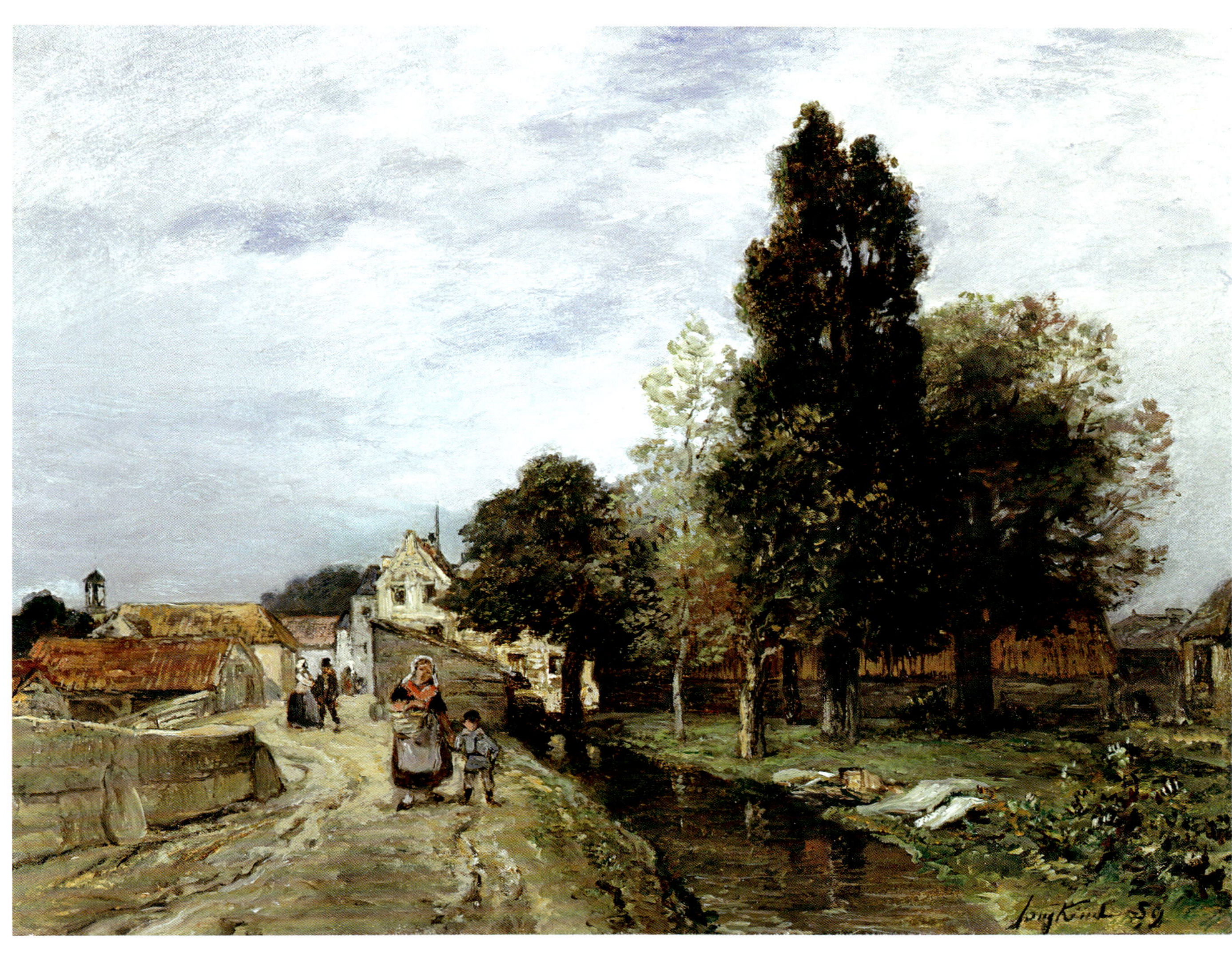

Johan Barthold Jongkind
Landscape in Normandy
Normannische Landschaft, 1859/61

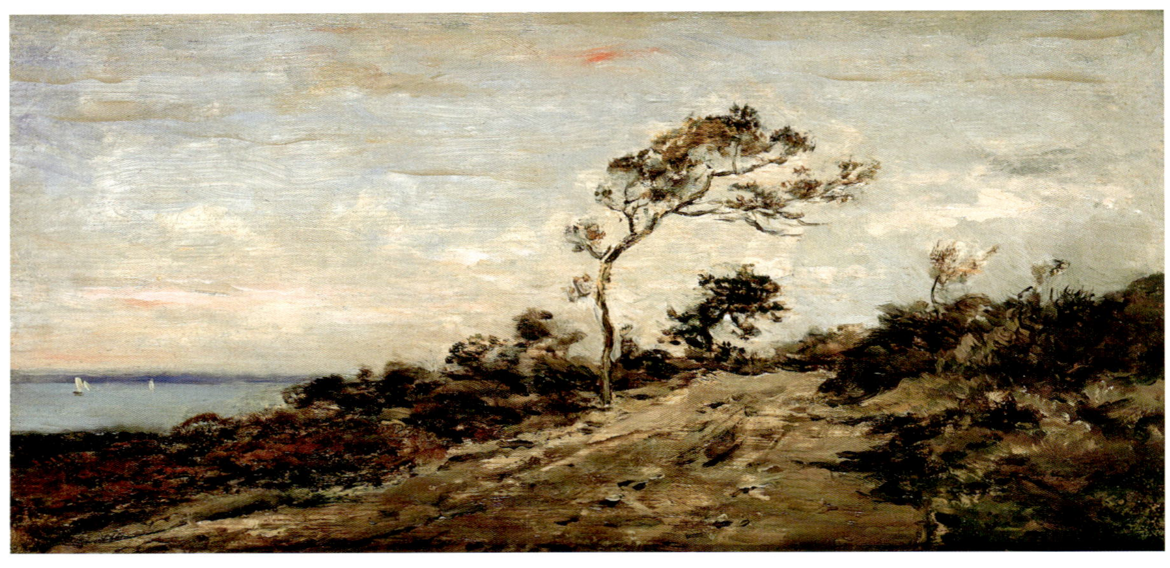

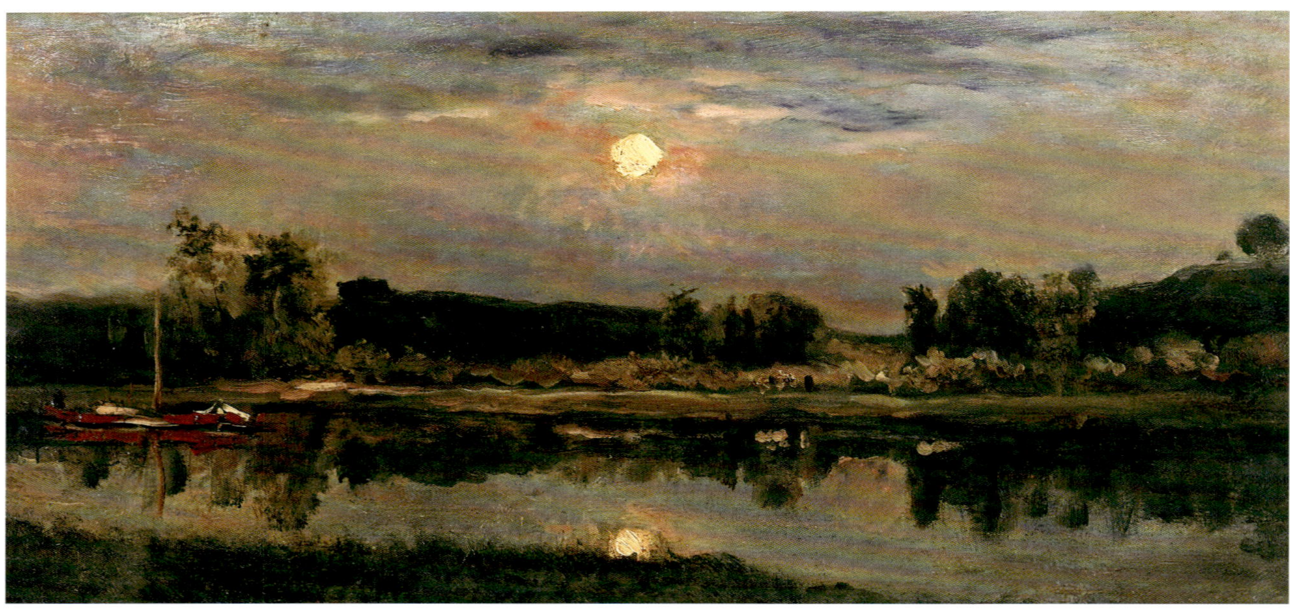

Charles-François Daubigny
Track across the Fields, Villerville
Feldweg, Villerville, ca. 1865

Charles-François Daubigny
Moonlight on the Riverbank or *The Banks of the Oise*
Mondschein am Flussufer oder *Die Ufer der Oise*, ca. 1869

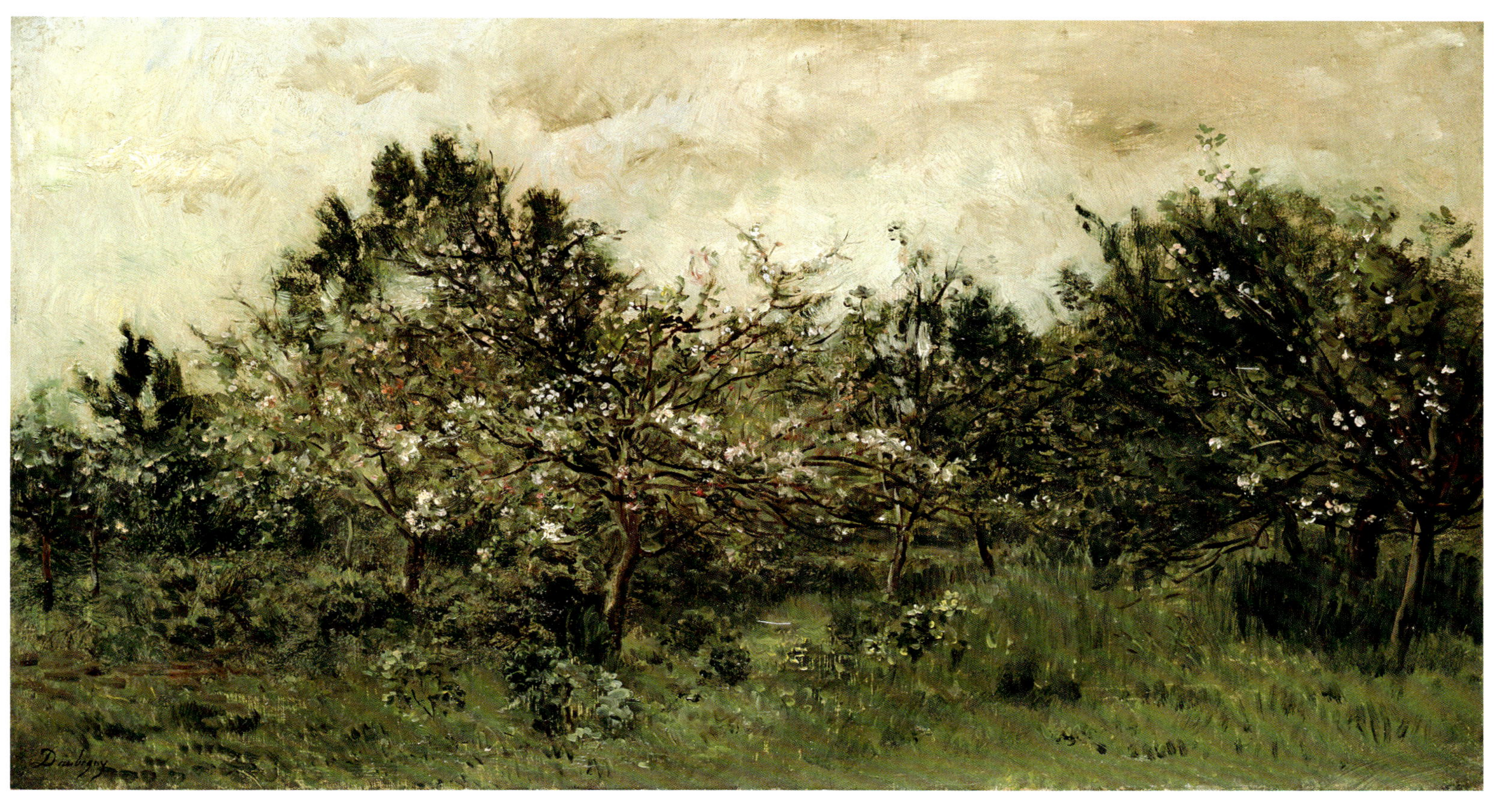

CHARLES-FRANÇOIS DAUBIGNY
Meadow with Blossoming Fruit Trees
Wiese mit blühenden Obstbäumen, ca. 1870

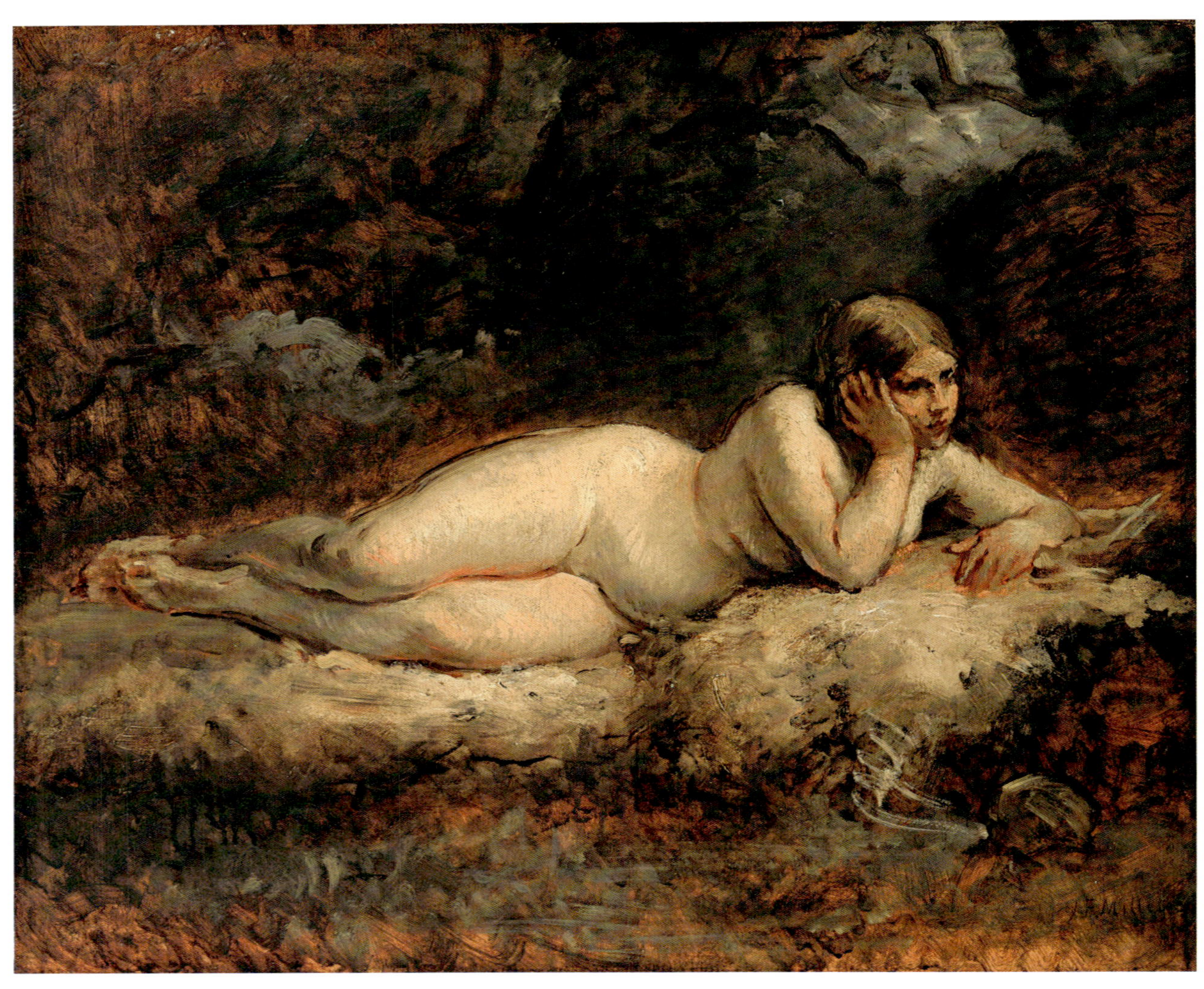

Jean François Millet ?
Reclining Nude, n.d.
Liegender Frauenakt, o. J.

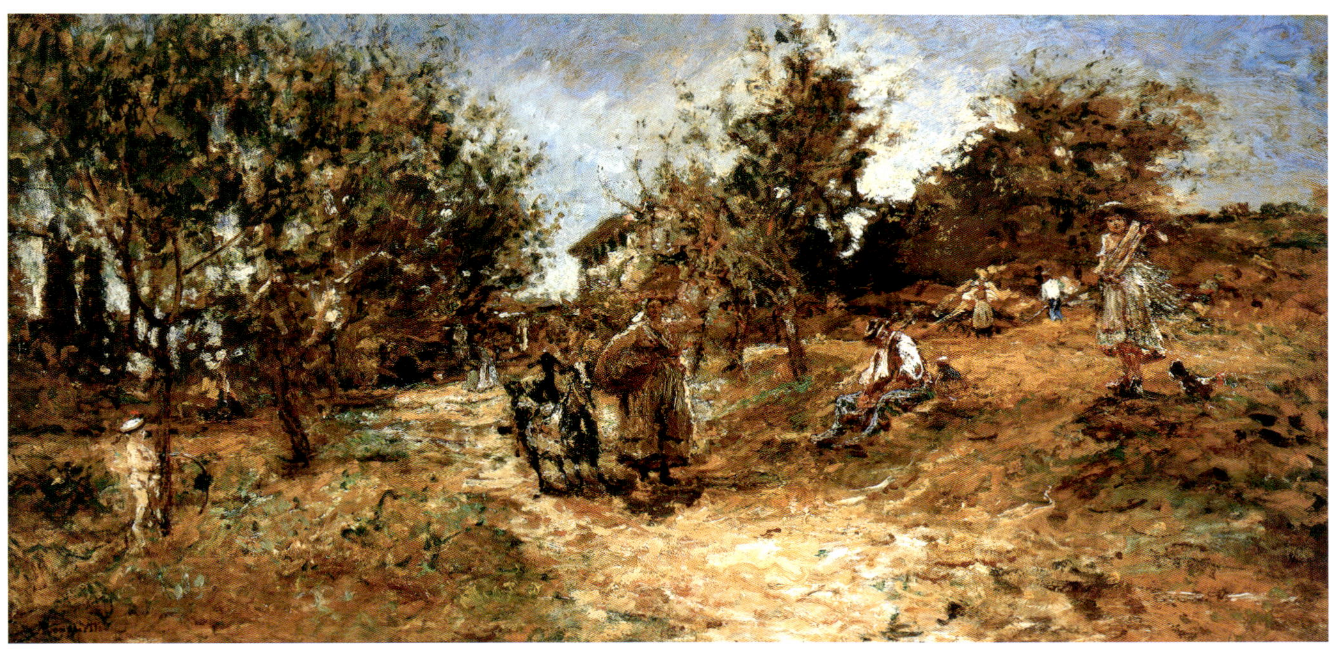

ADOLPHE MONTICELLI
Landscape at Ganagobie
Landschaft bei Ganagobie, 1872

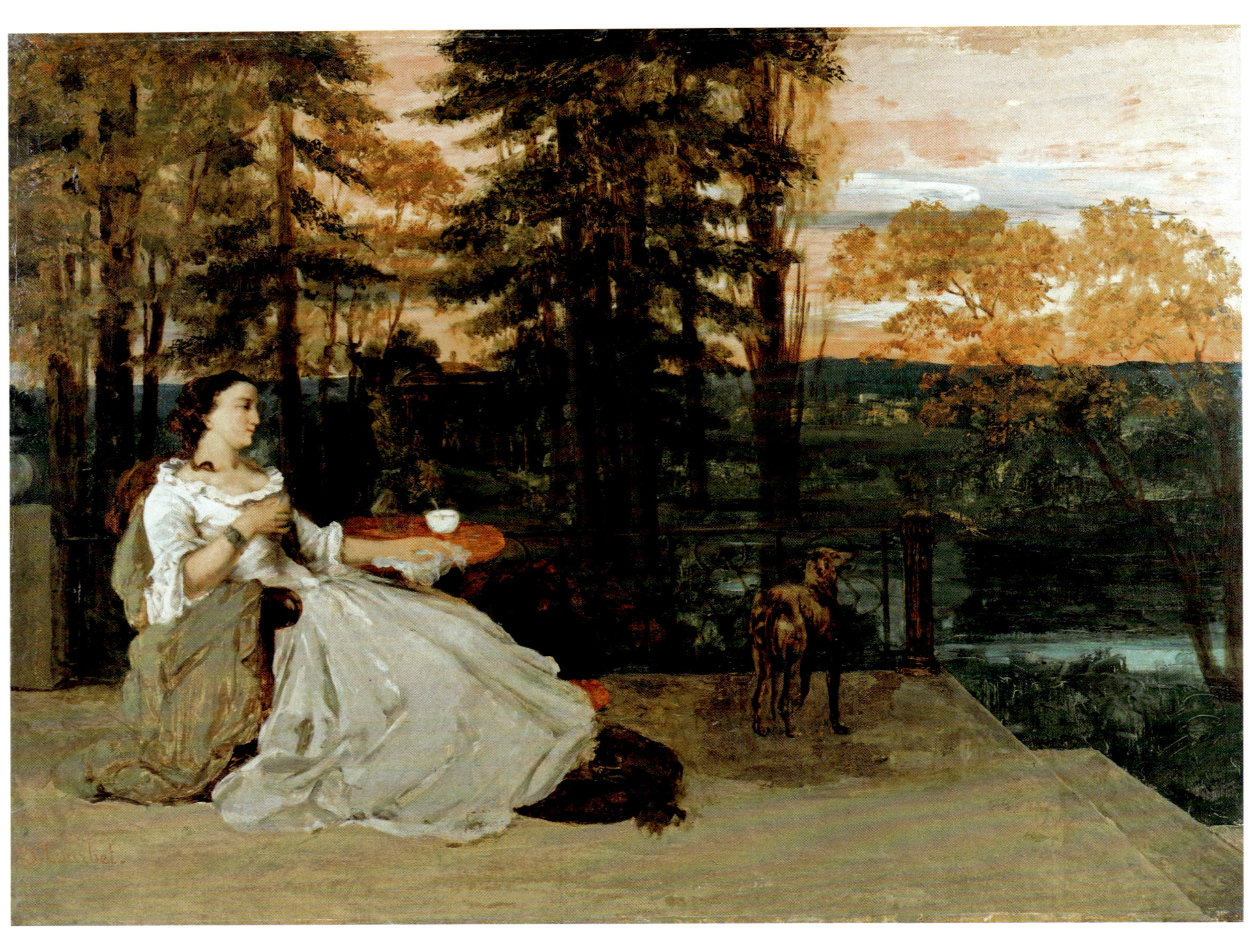

Gustave Courbet
Lady on the Terrace (Lady of Frankfurt)
Dame auf der Terrasse, 1858

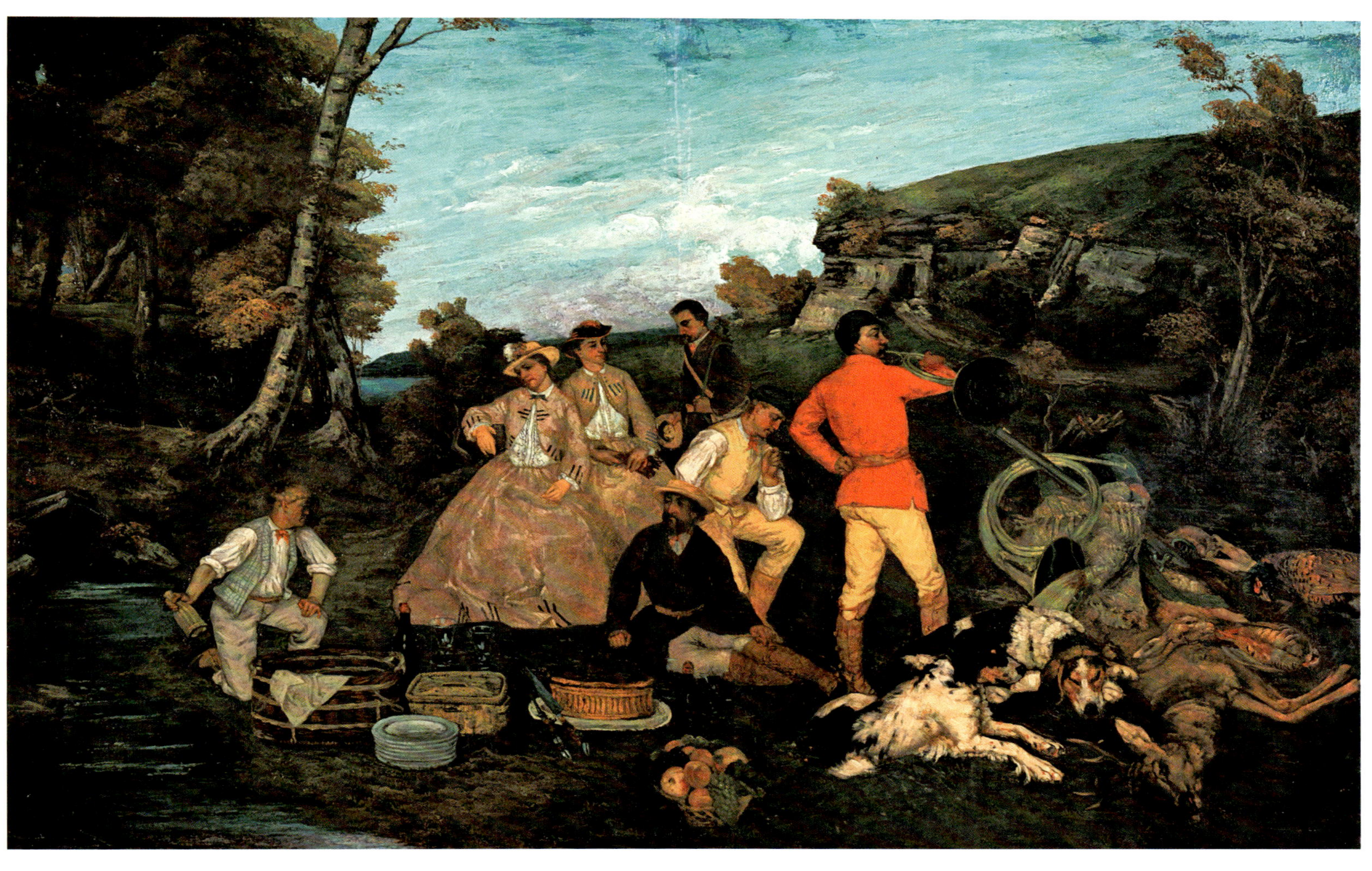

Gustave Courbet
The Hunters' Breakfast
Das Jagdfrühstück, 1858

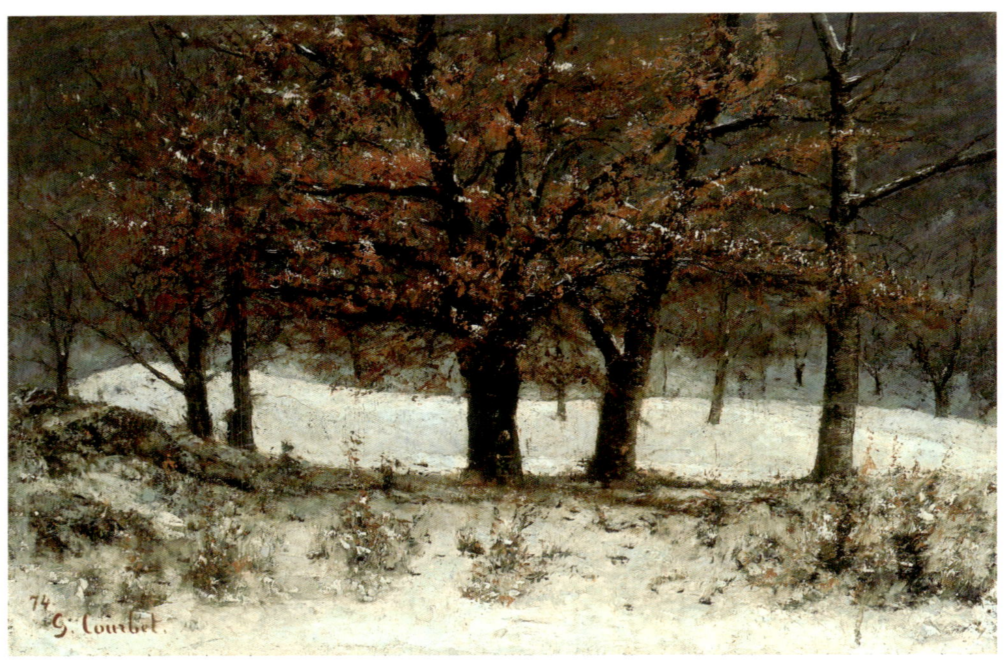

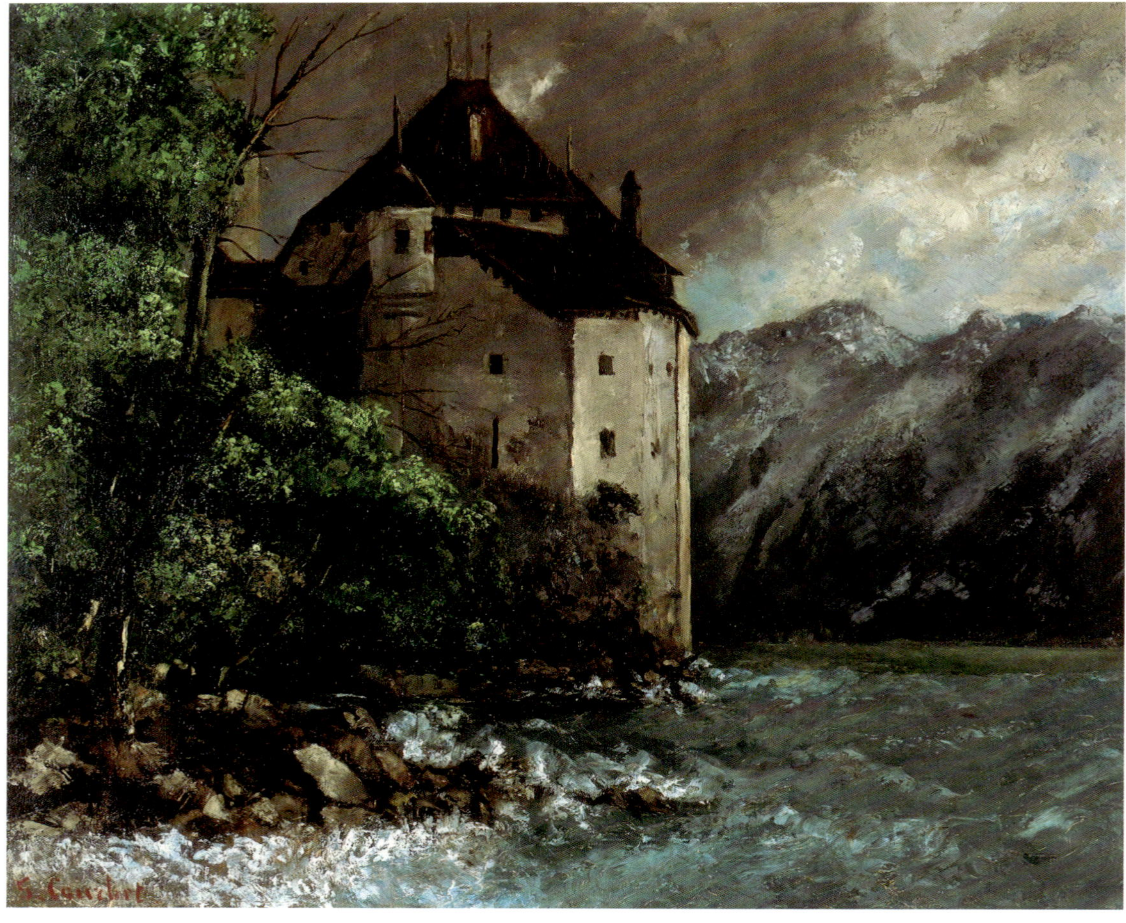

Gustave Courbet
View of the Parc des Crêtes above Clarens
Ansicht des Parc des Crêtes, oberhalb von Clarens, 1874

Gustave Courbet
Château de Chillon, 1873

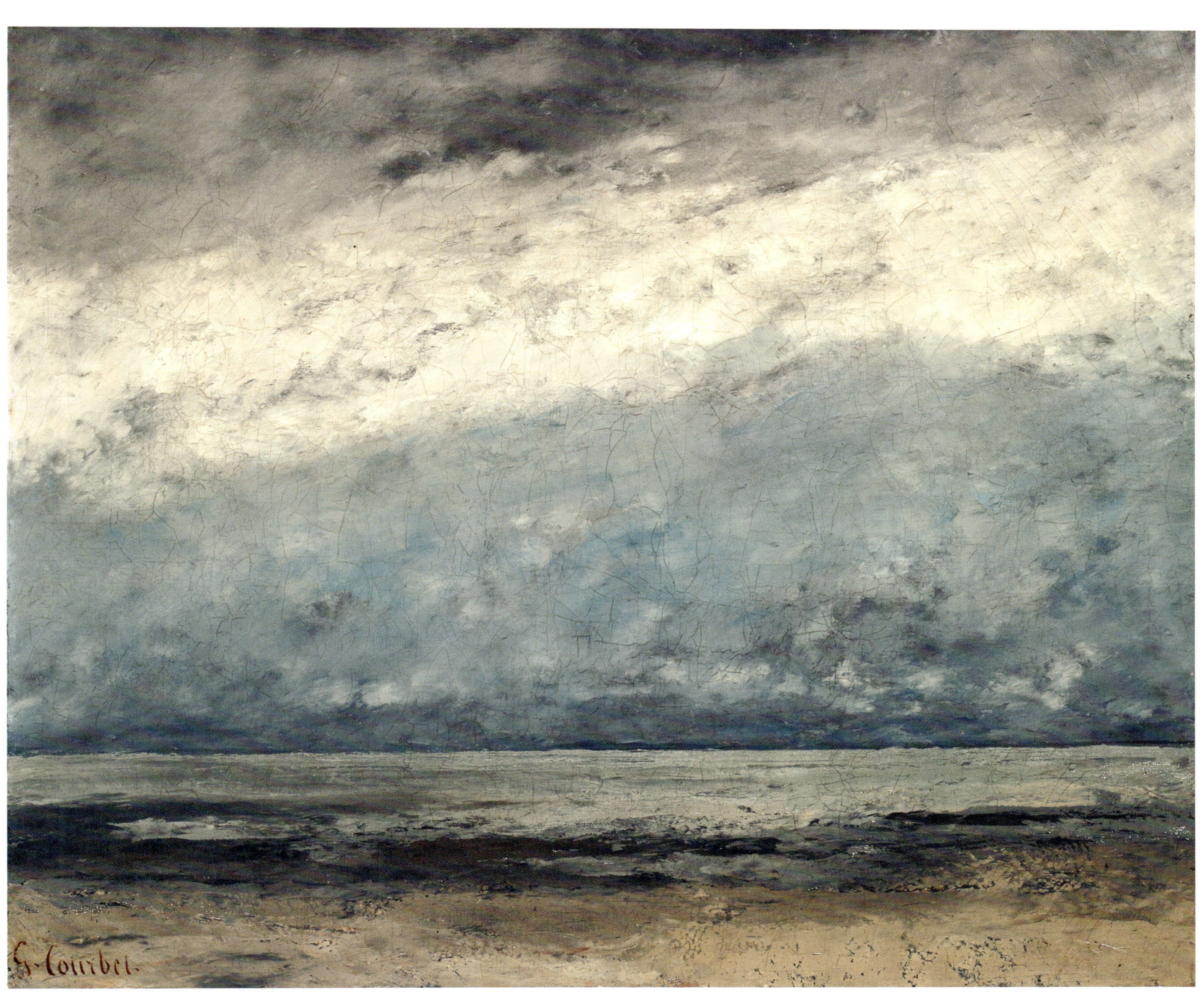

Gustave Courbet
Seascape
Meeresstrand, 1865

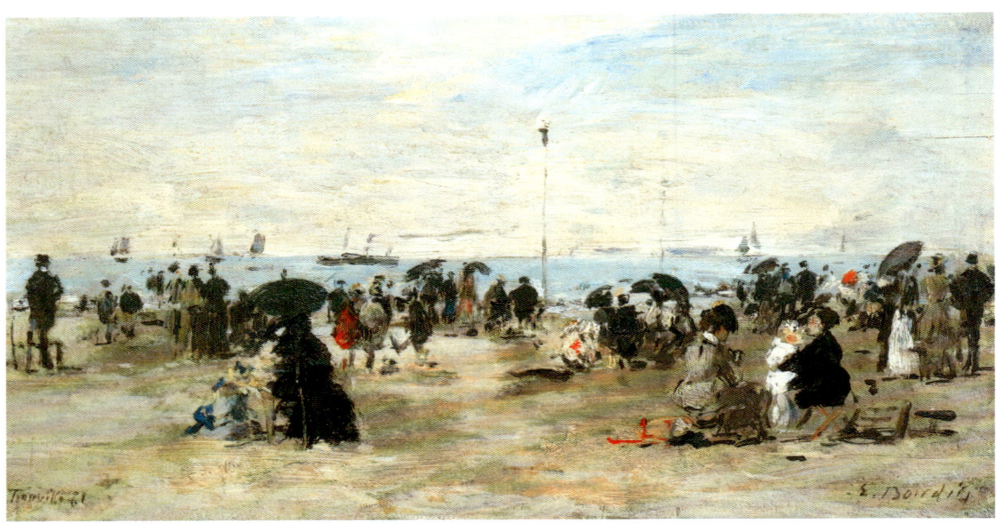

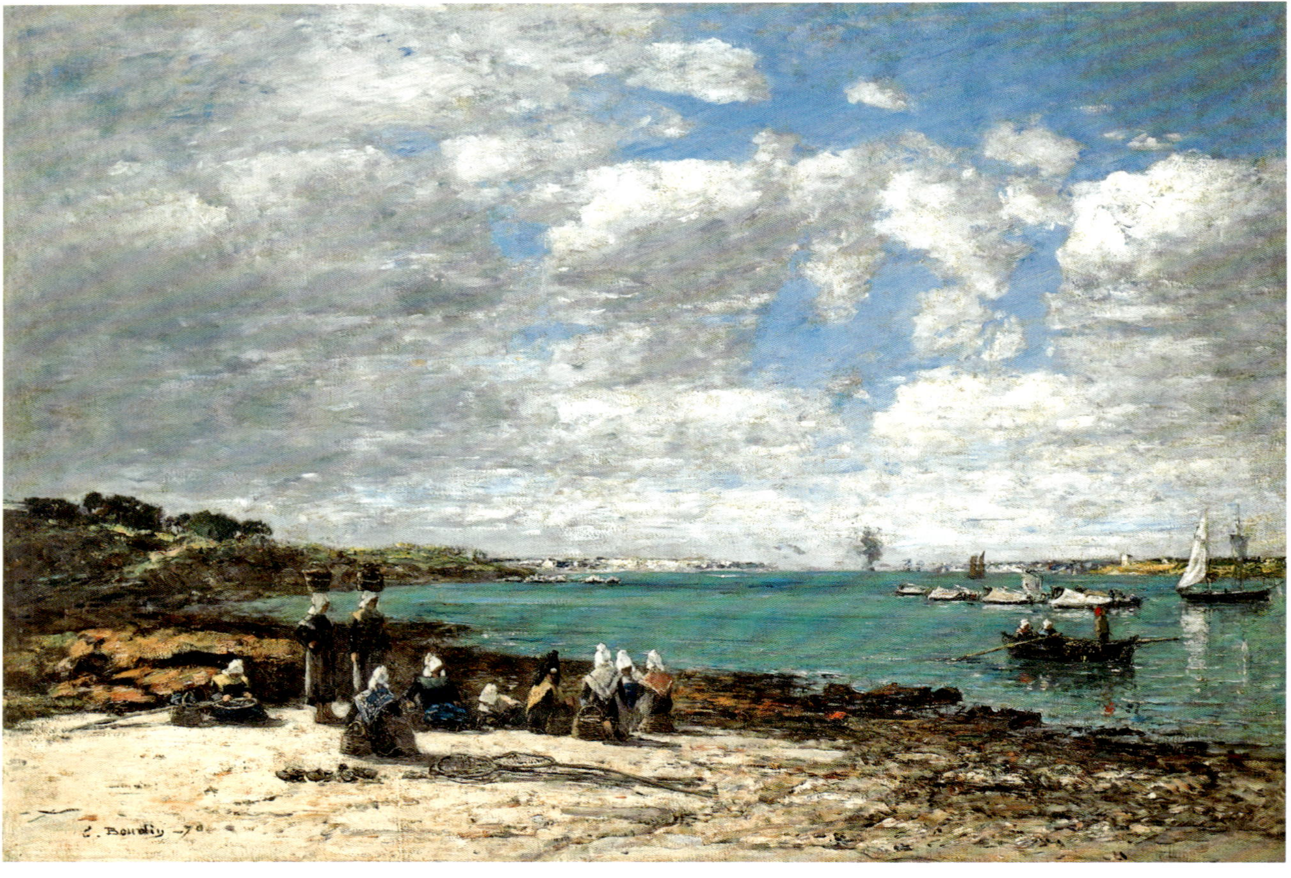

Eugene Boudin
Trouville, Beach Scene
Trouville, Strandszene, 1881

Eugene Boudin
Kerhor, Fisherwomen
Kerhor, Fischerinnen, 1870

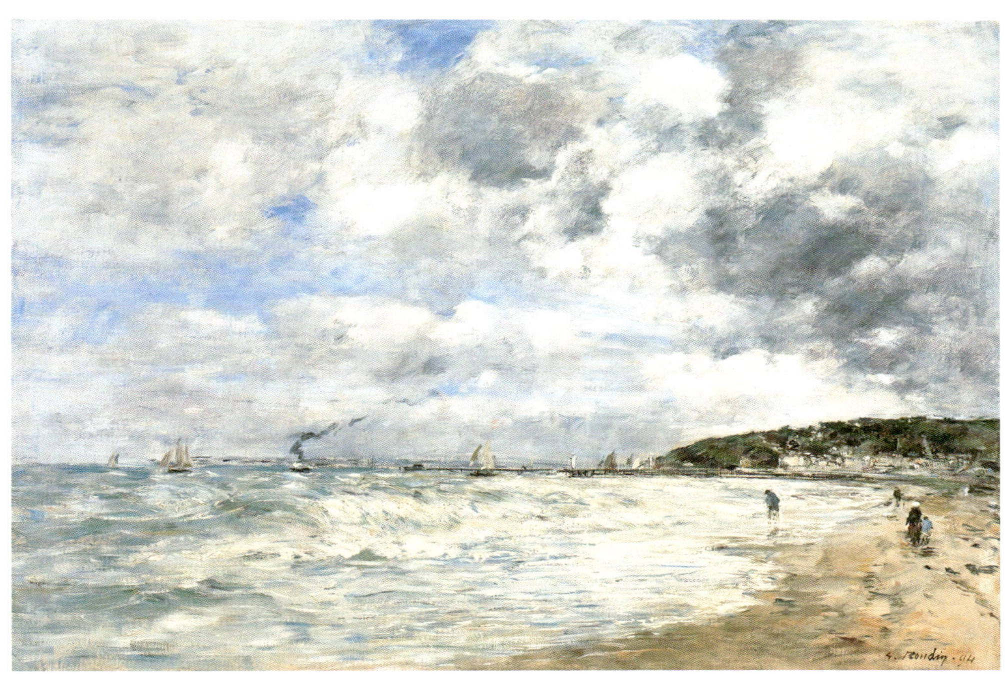

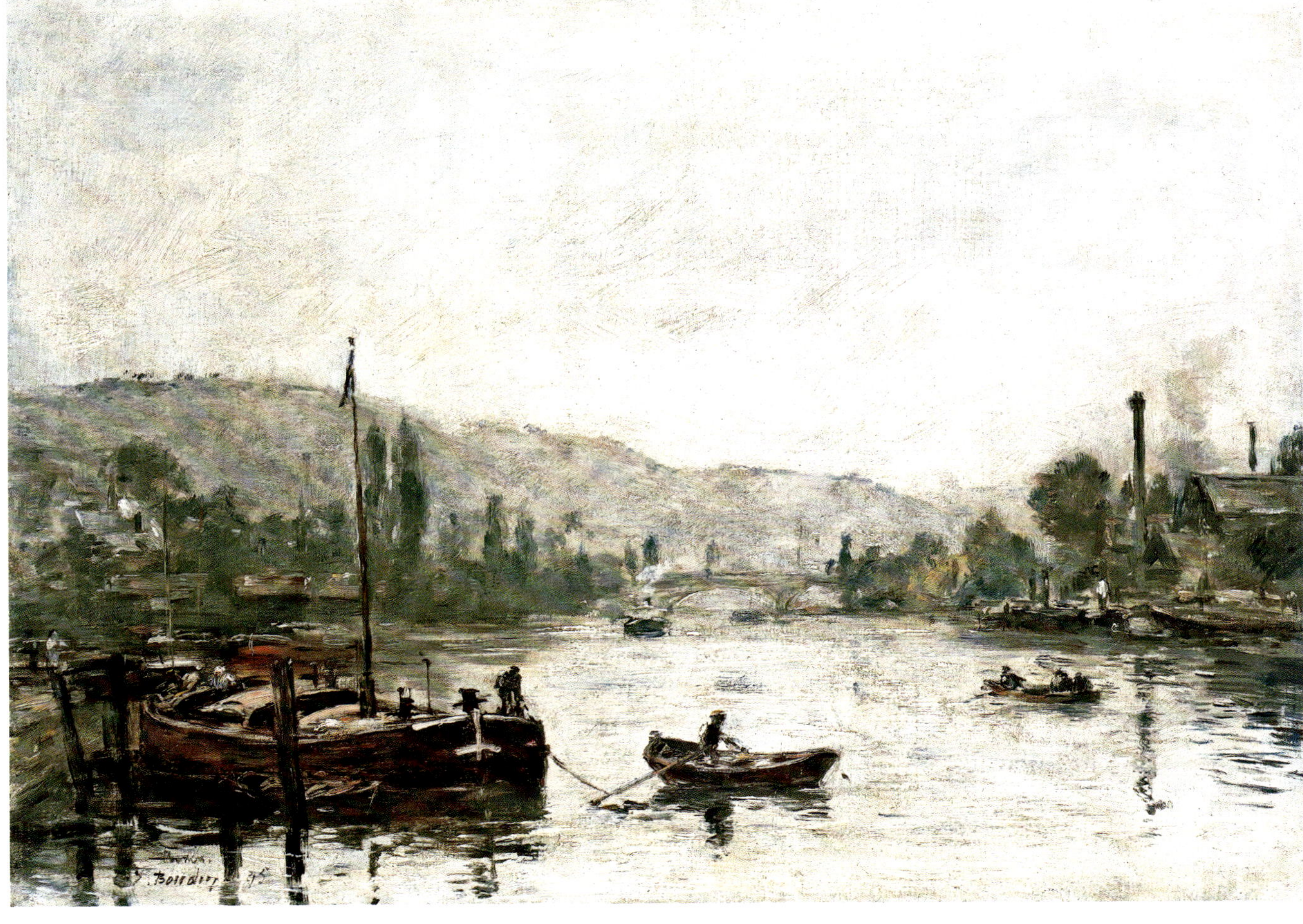

Eugene Boudin
The Coast at Trouville
Die Küste von Trouville, 1894

Eugene Boudin
Rouen – Côte Sainte-Catherine in the Morning Mist
Rouen – Côte Sainte-Catherine im Morgennebel, 1895

The Beginnings

Die Anfänge

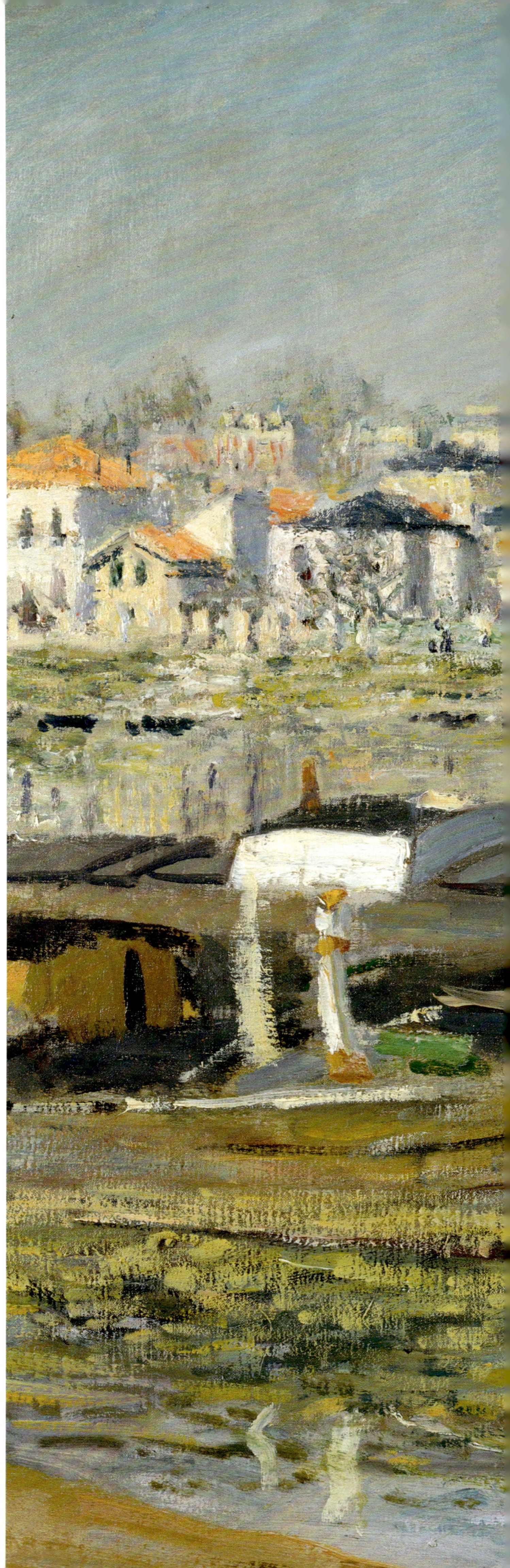

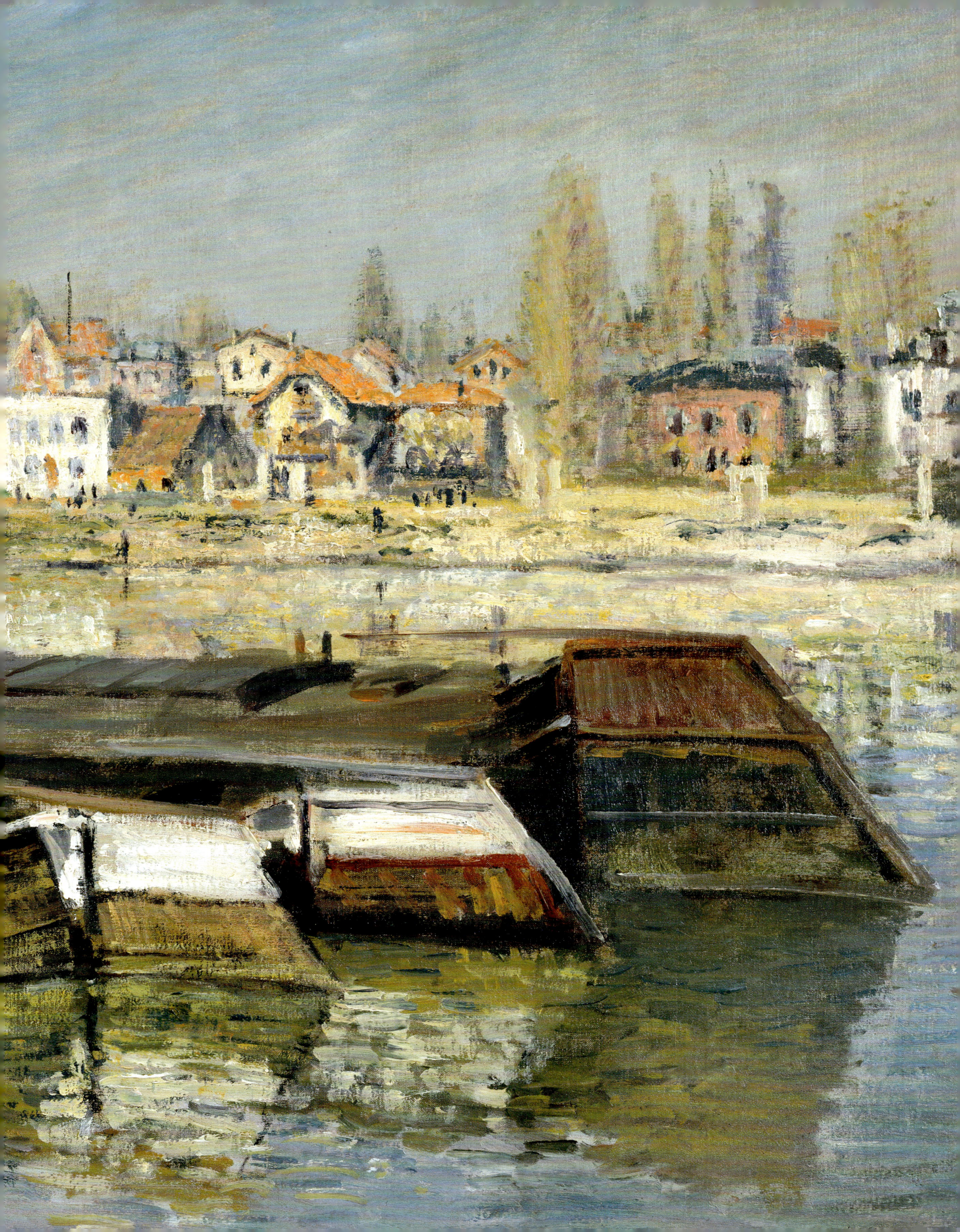

Auguste Renoir
The Fiancés
Ein Paar im Grünen, ca. 1868

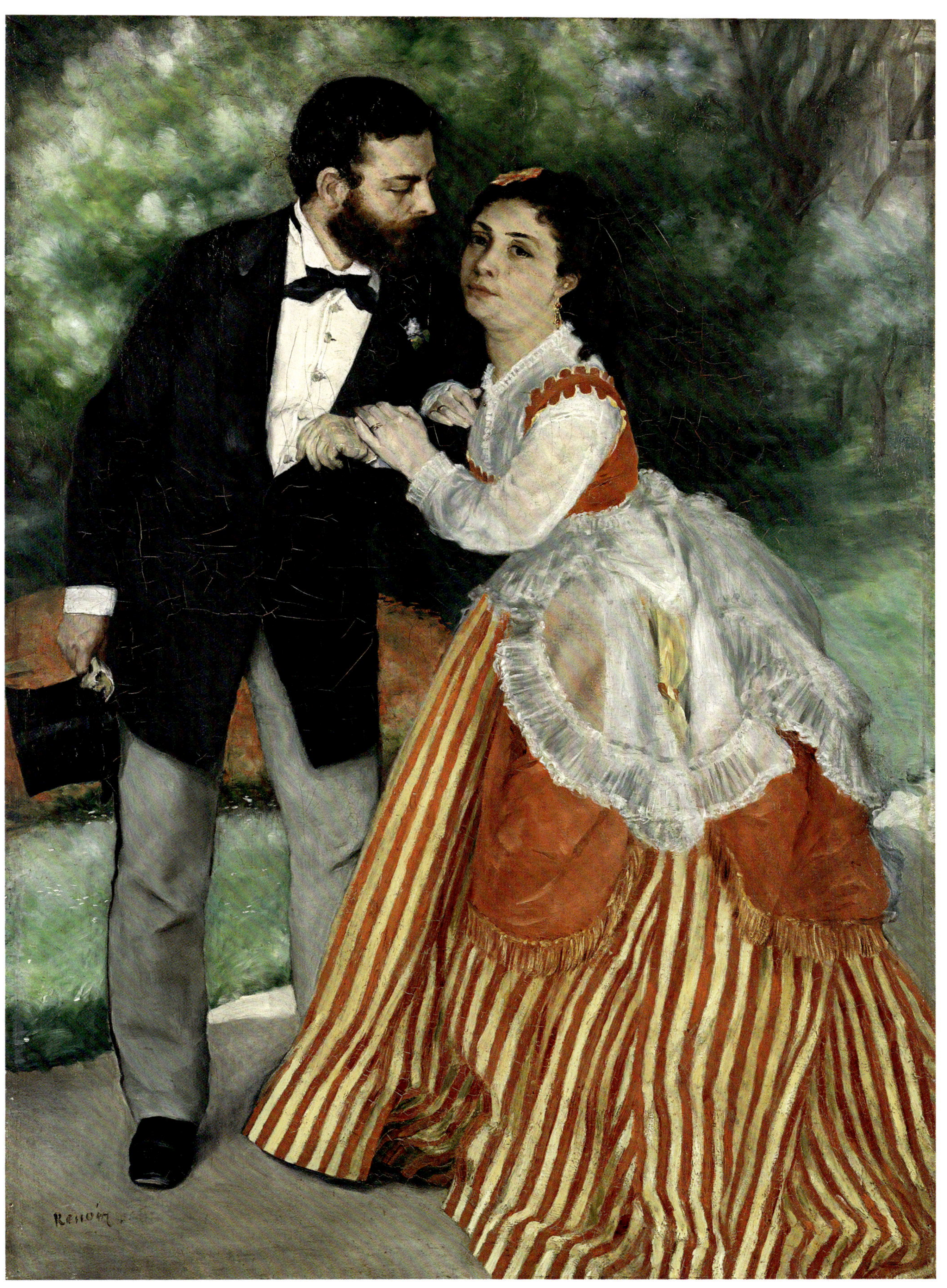

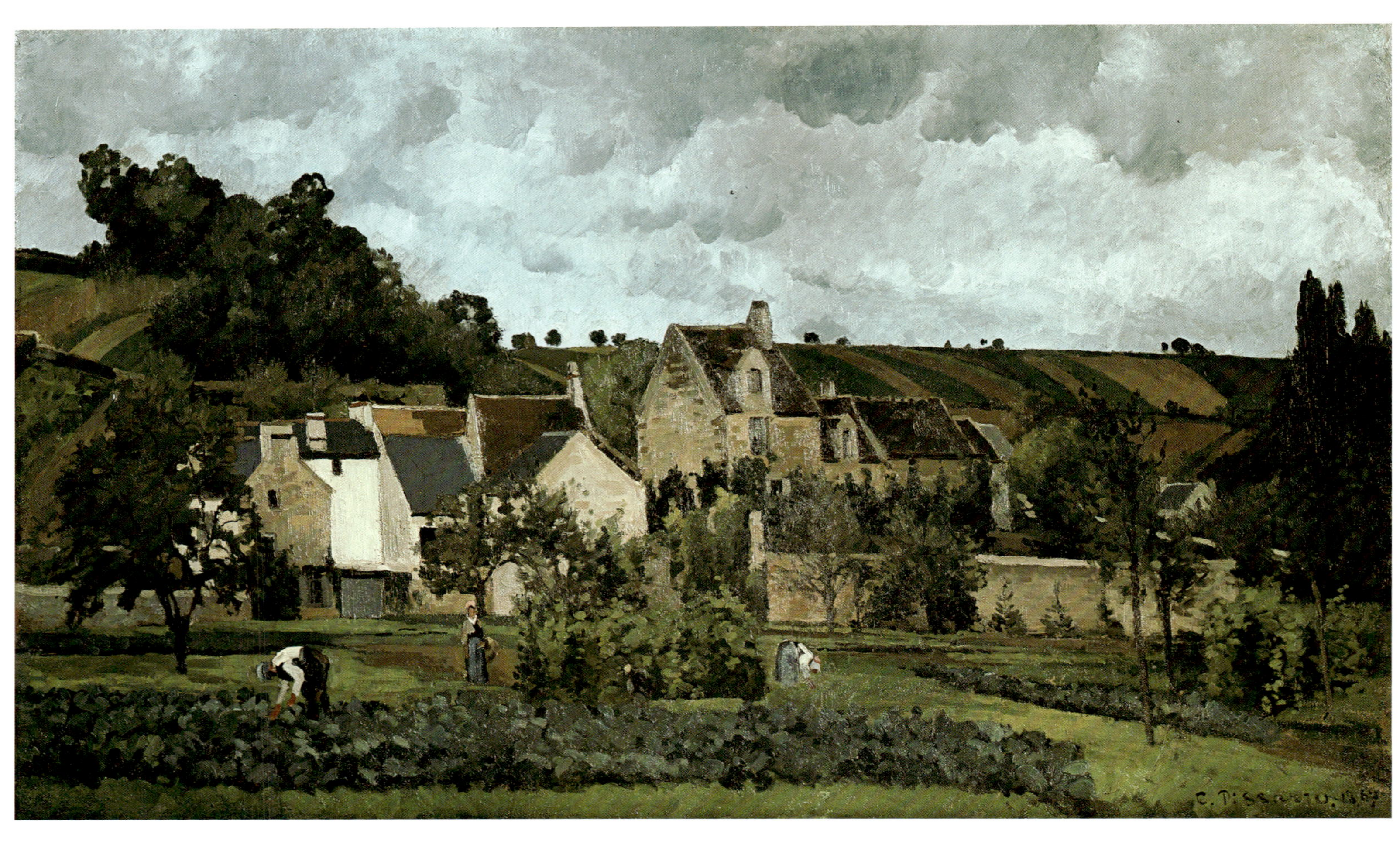

Camille Pissarro
The Hermitage at Pontoise
L'Hermitage bei Pontoise, 1867

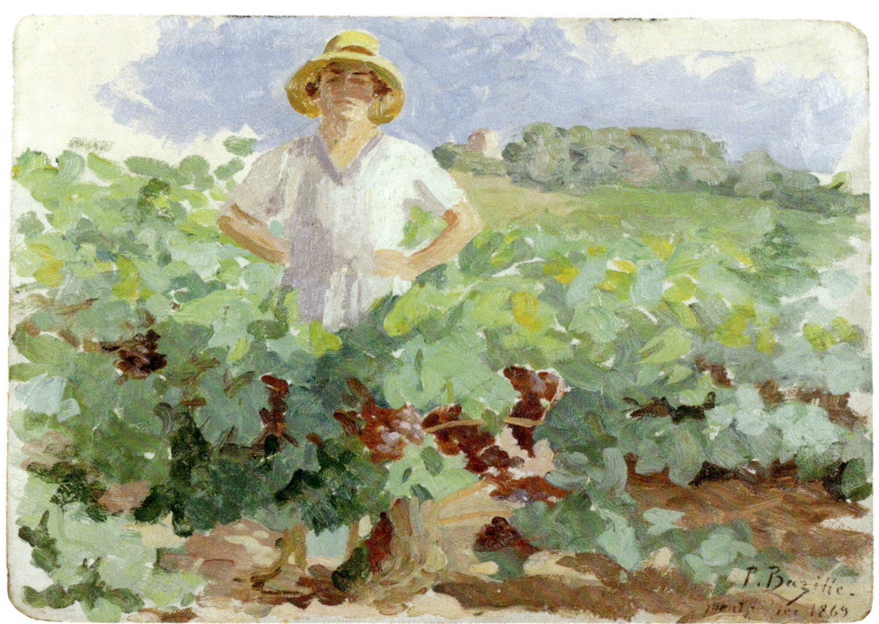

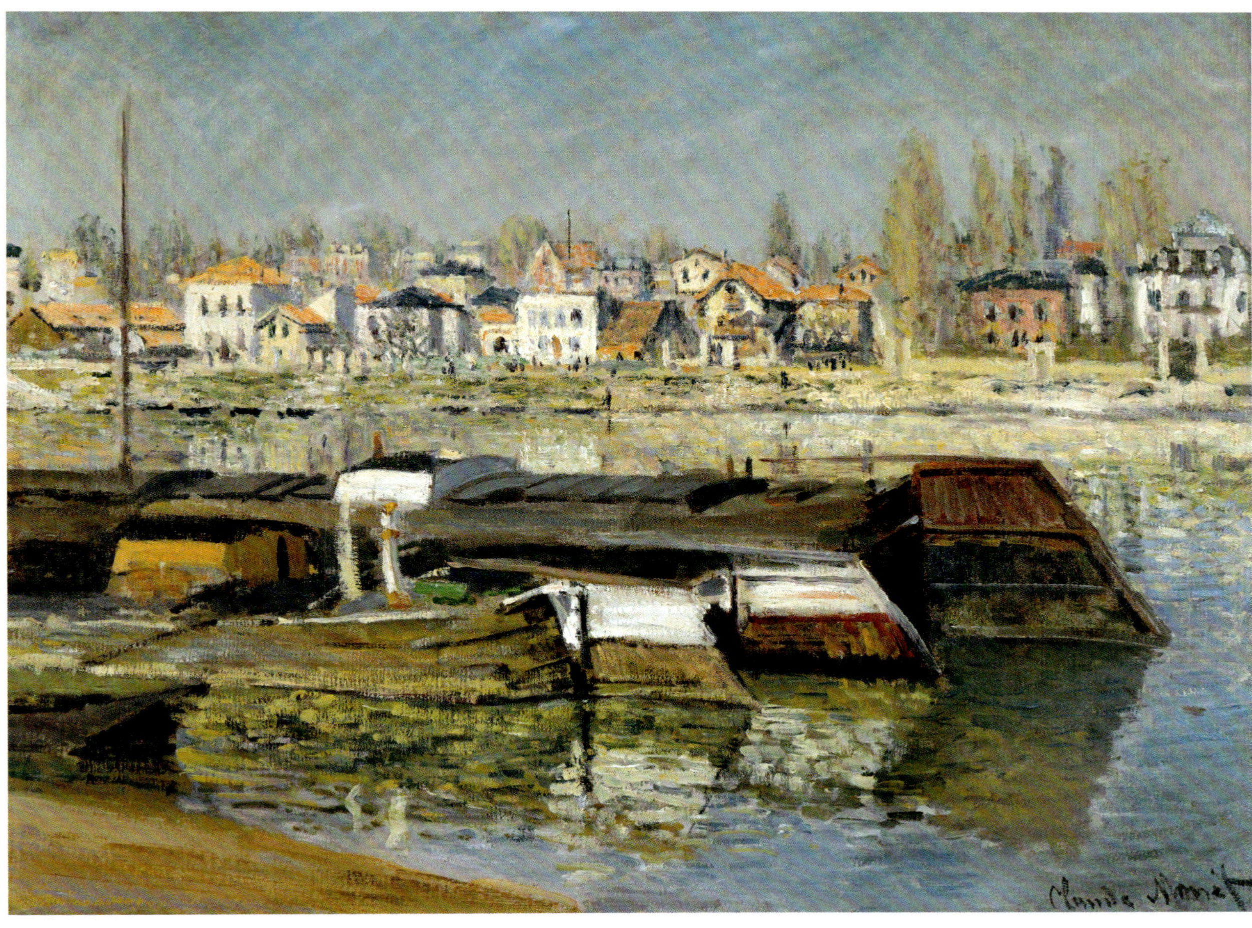

Claude Monet
The Seine at Asnières
Die Seine bei Asnières, 1873

Jean-Frederic Bazille
Young Woman in a Vineyard
Junge Frau zwischen Weinstöcken, 1869

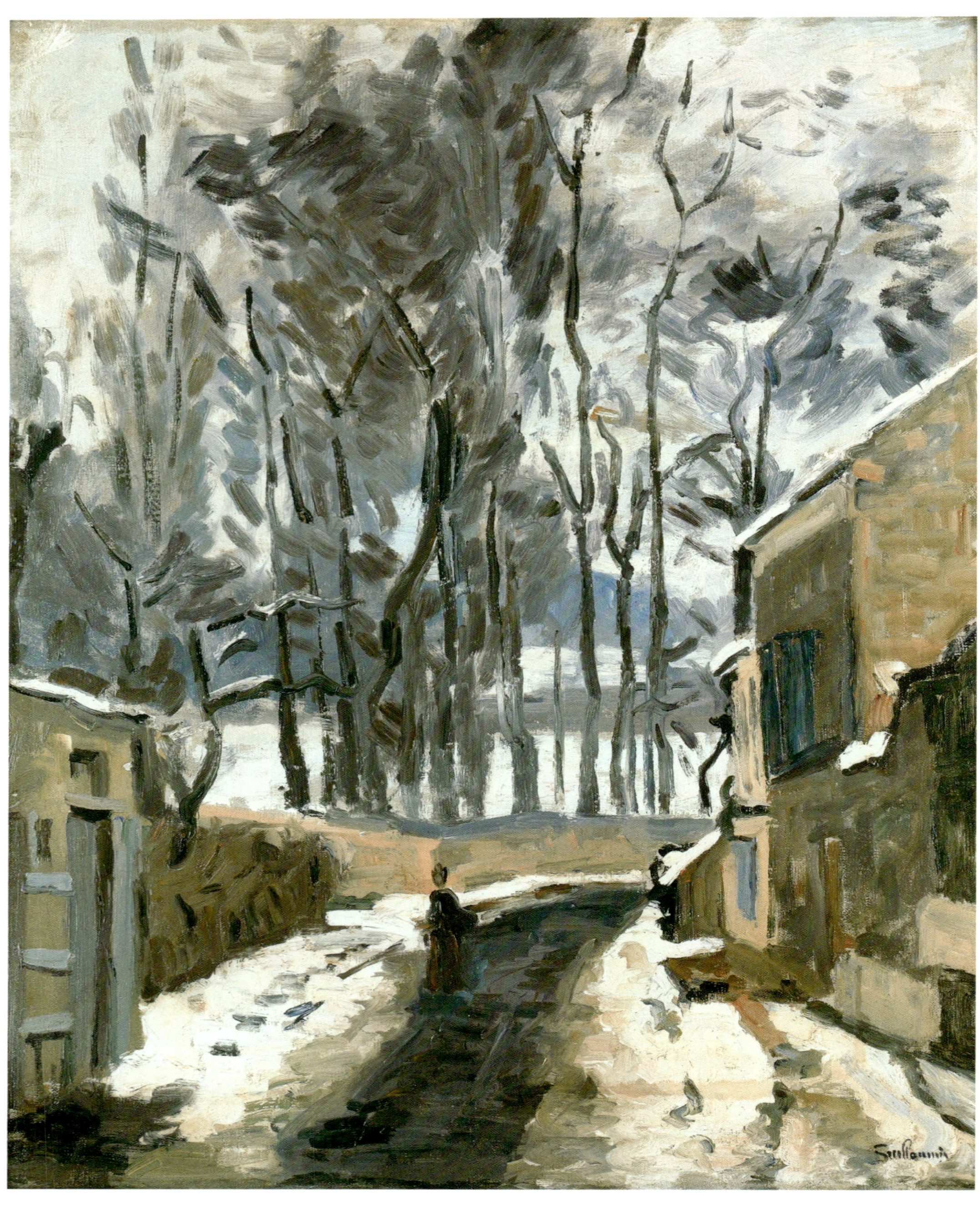

Armand Guillaumin
Landscape, Louveciennes
Landschaft von Louveciennes, ca. 1872

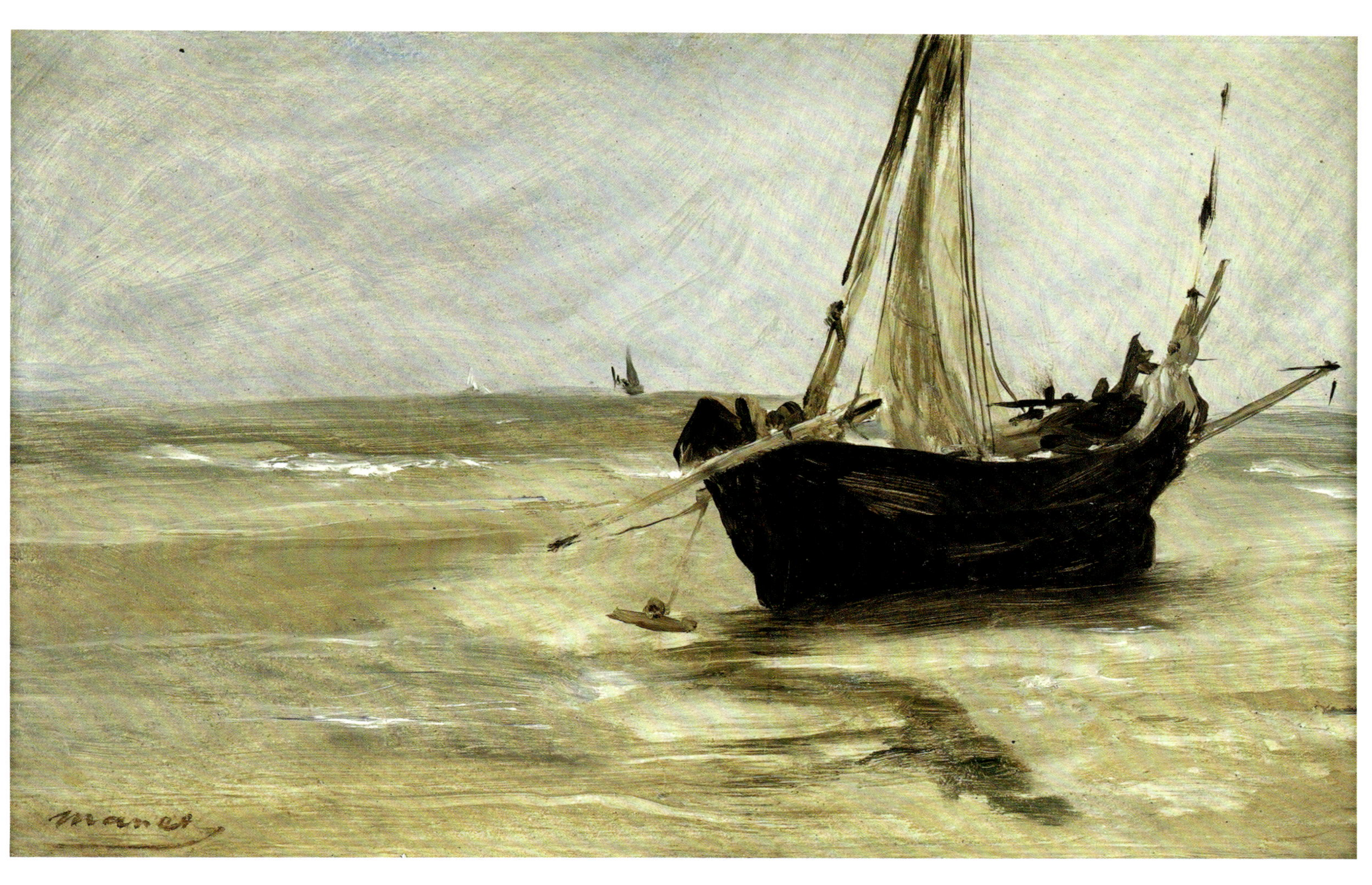

EDOUARD MANET
Fishing Boat on the Beach at Berck
Schwarzes Boot bei Berck, 1873

The Years of the Impressionist Exhibitions 1874–1886
The Classic Period

Die Jahre der Impressionisten-Ausstellungen 1874–1886
Die Klassische Periode

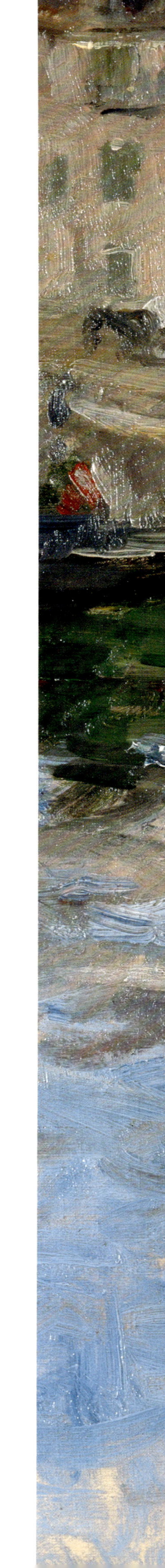

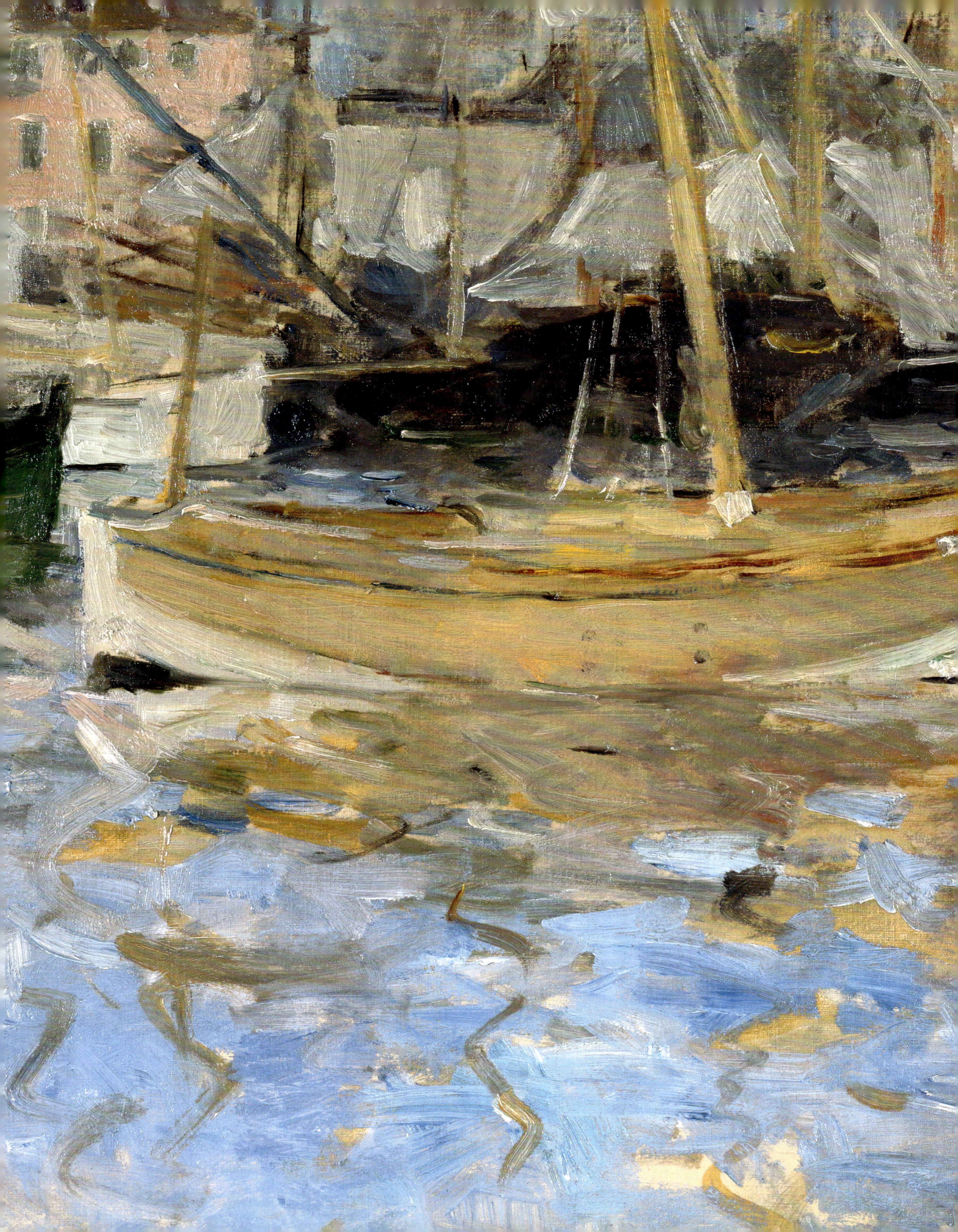

Alfred Sisley
Bridge at Hampton Court
Brücke bei Hampton Court, 1874

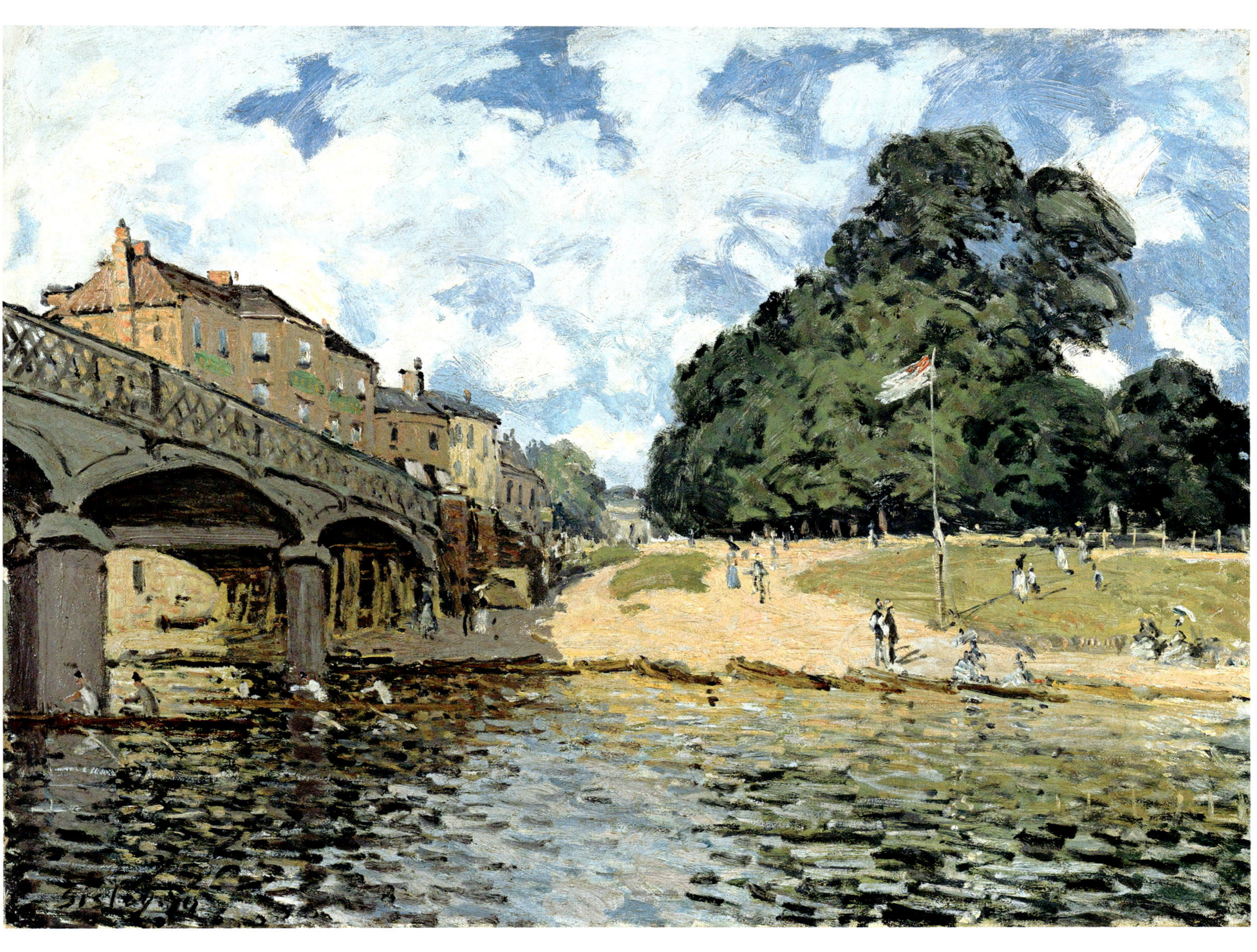

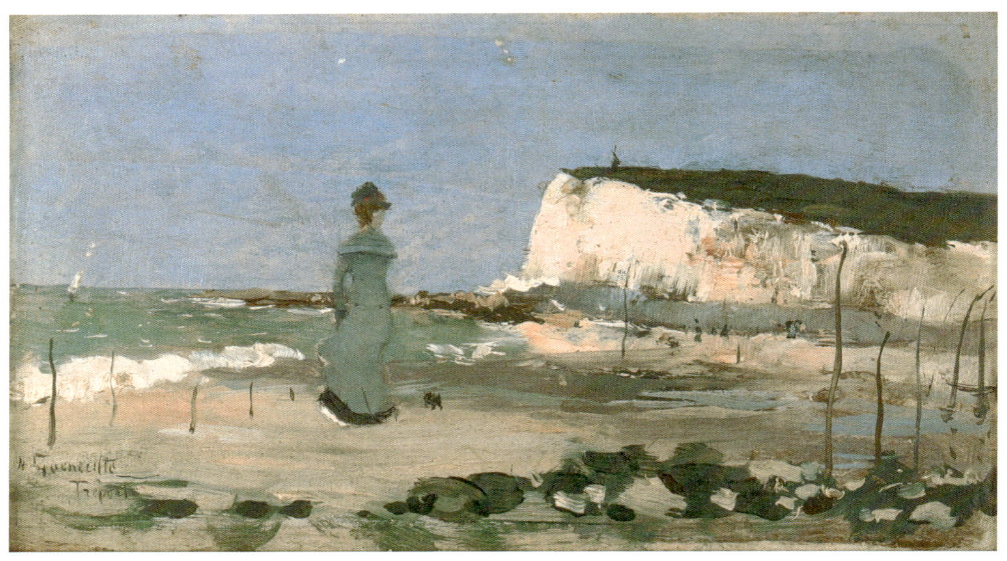

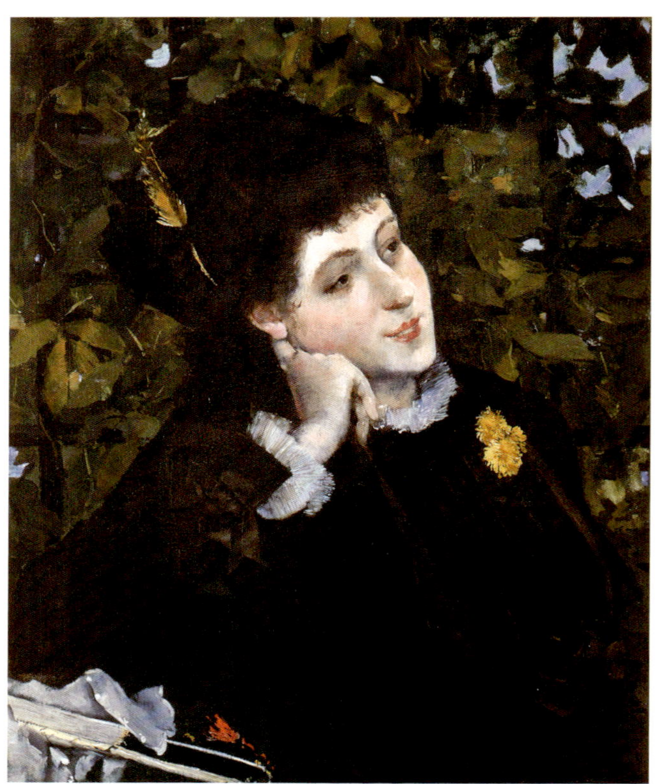

NORBERT GOENEUTTE
Elegant Lady on the Beach, n.d.
Elegante Dame am Strand, o. J.

NORBERT GOENEUTTE
Portrait of a Woman (Berthe Morisot?)
Porträt einer Frau (Berthe Morisot?), ca. 1875

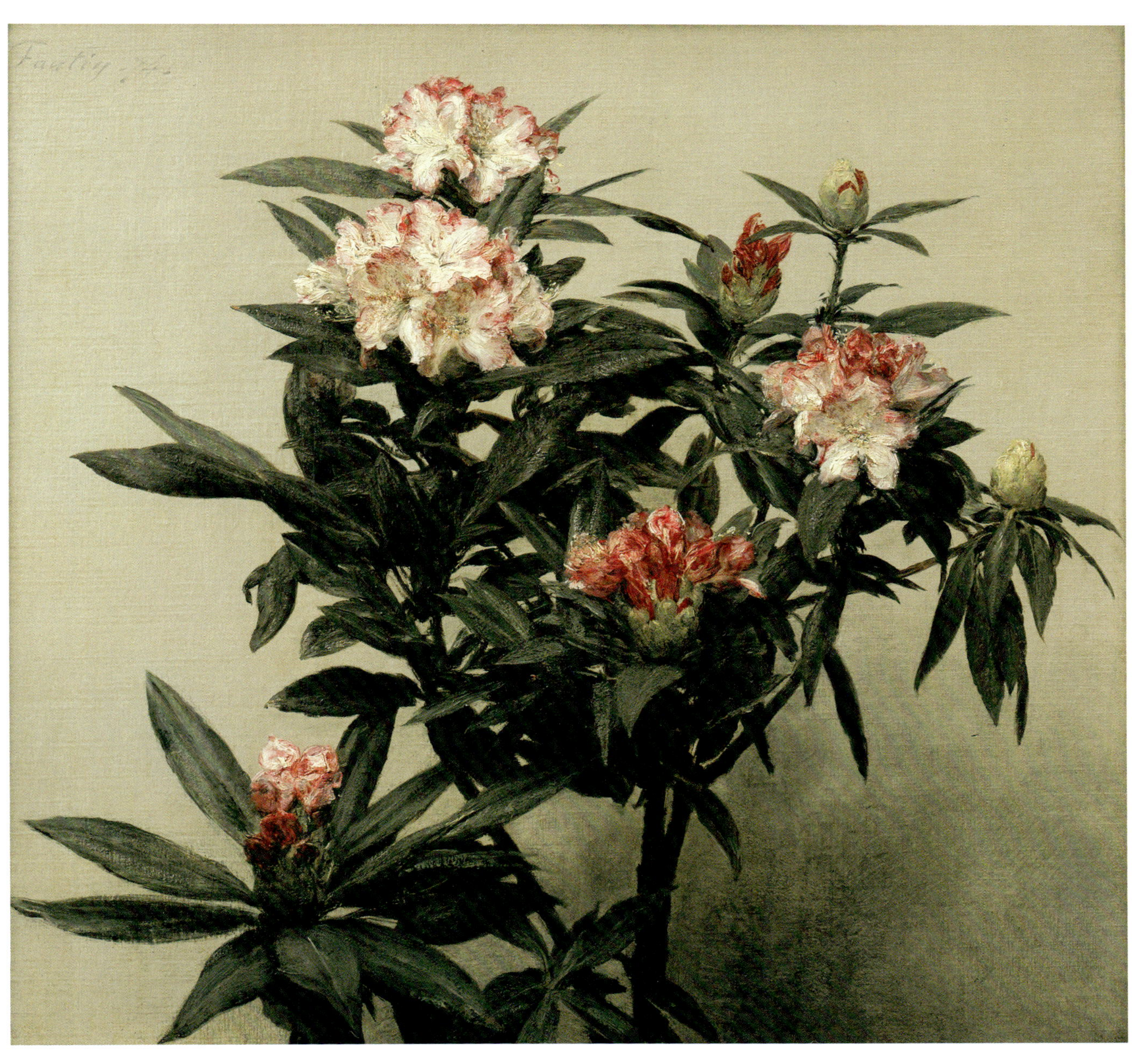

Henri Fantin-Latour
Rhododendron Branch in Bloom
Blühender Rhododendronzweig, 1874

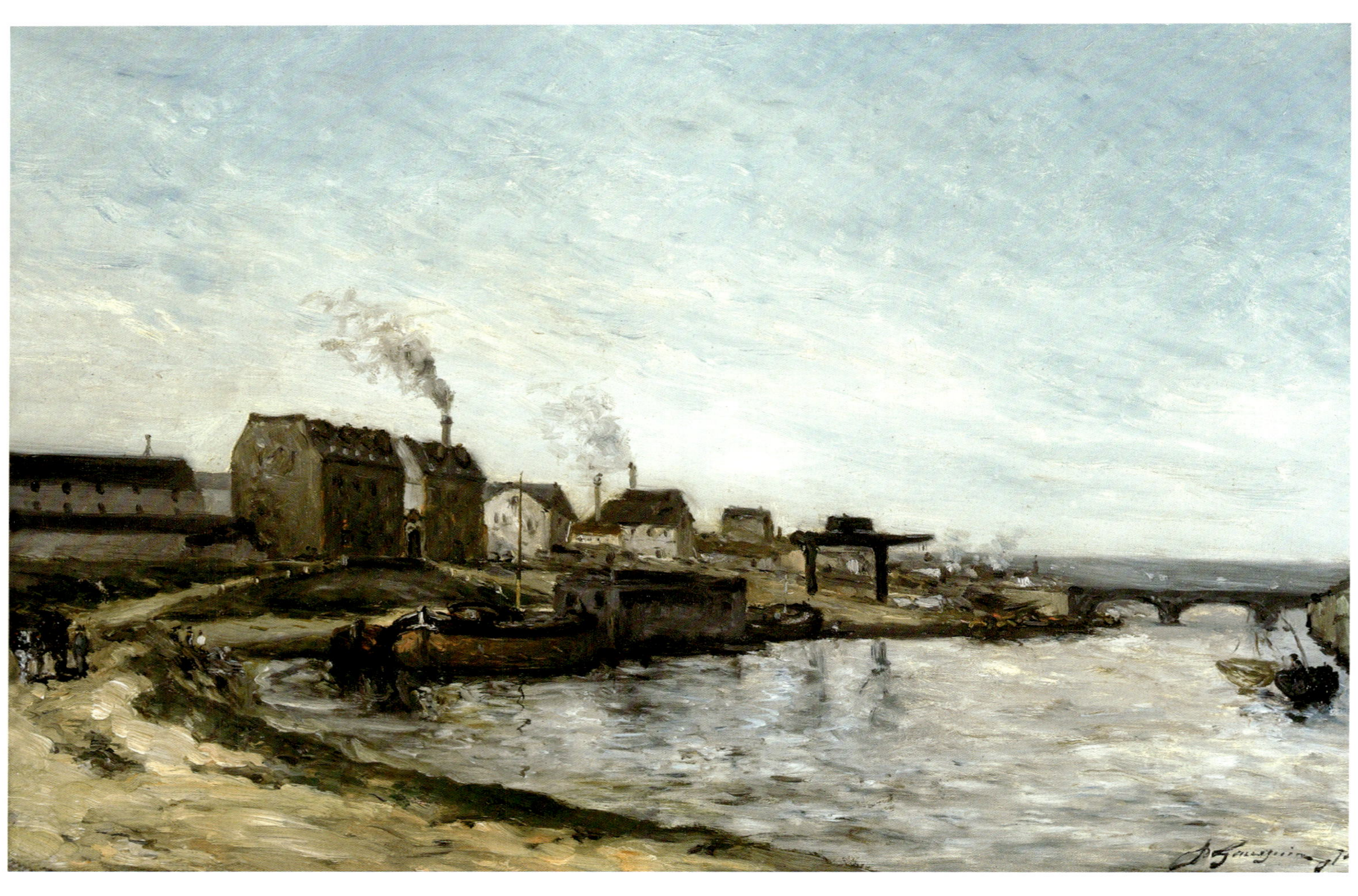

Paul Gauguin
The Seine at the Pont de Grenelle
Die Seine beim Pont de Grenelle, 1875

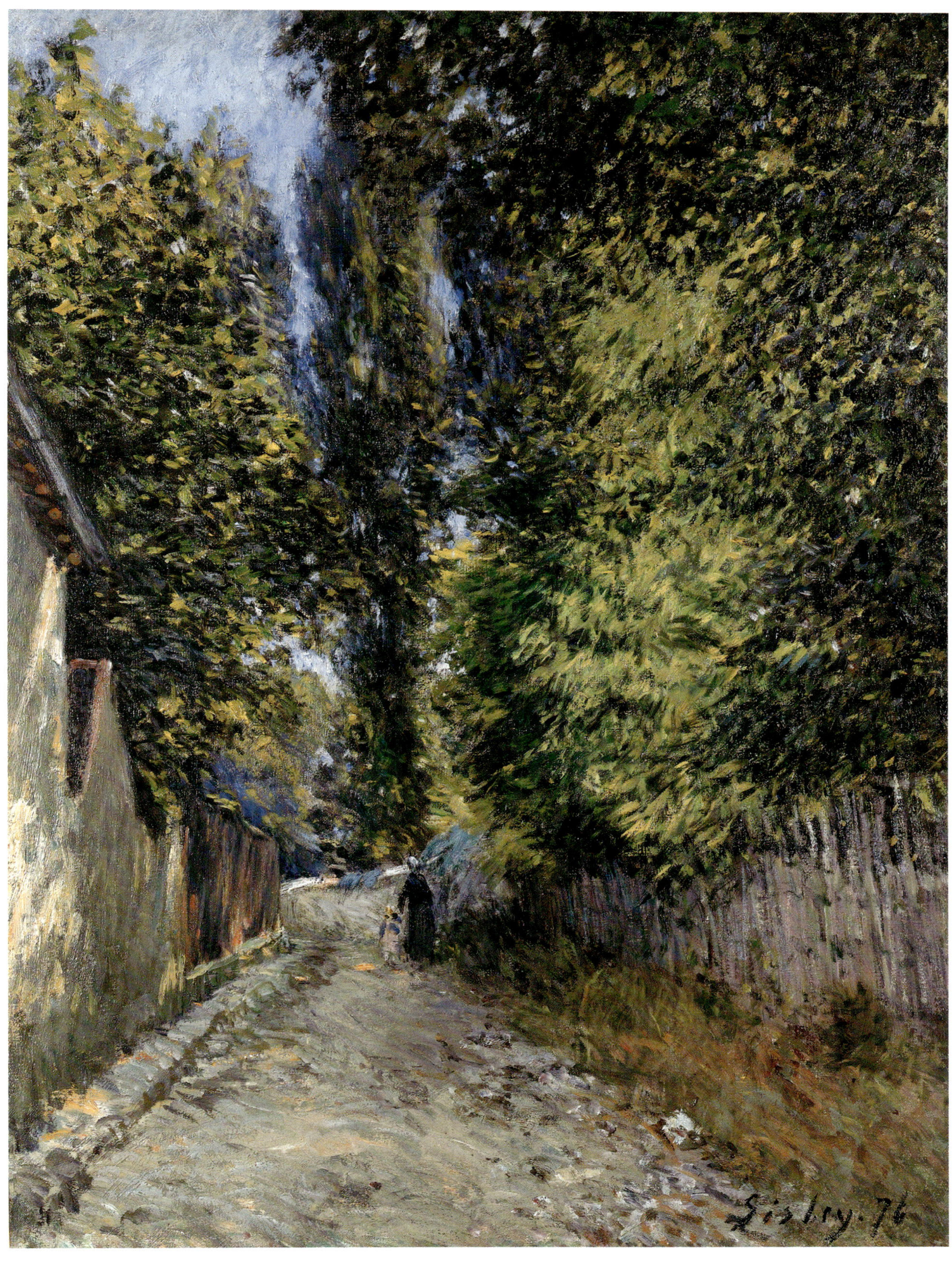

Alfred Sisley
The Environs of Louveciennes
Umgebung von Louveciennes, 1876

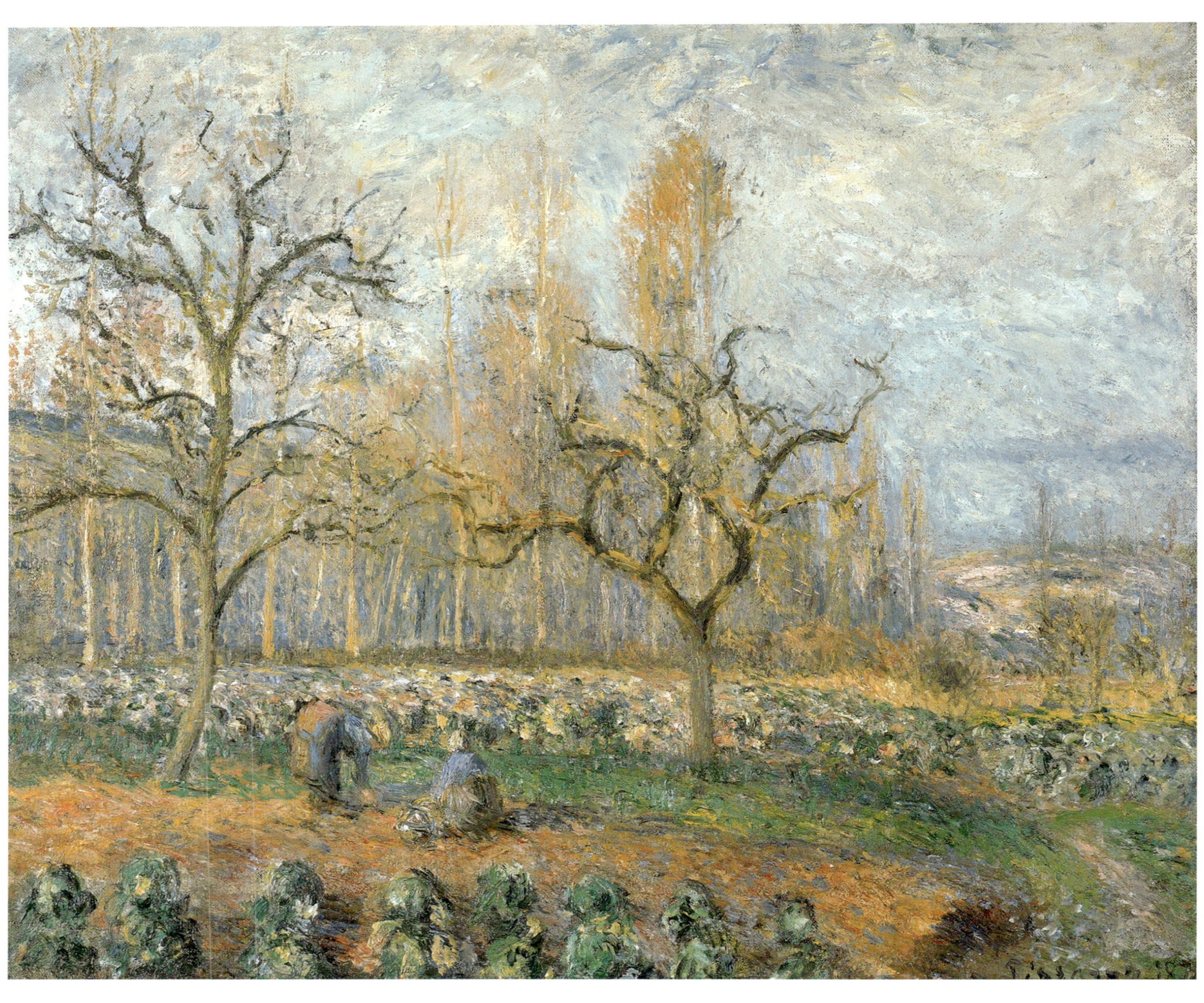

Camille Pissarro
Orchard in Pontoise at Sunset
Obstgarten in Pontoise bei Sonnenuntergang, 1878

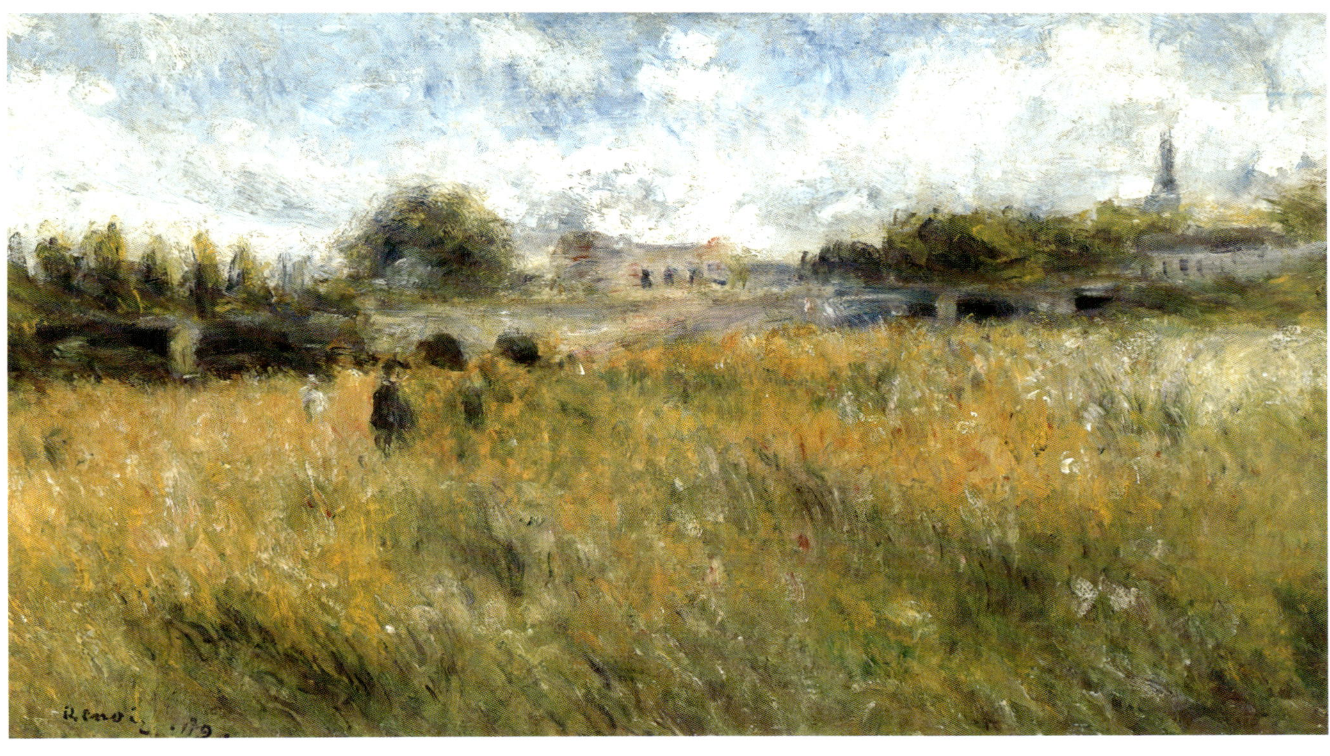

Auguste Renoir
On the Banks of the Seine at Rueil
Die Ufer der Seine bei Rueil, 1879

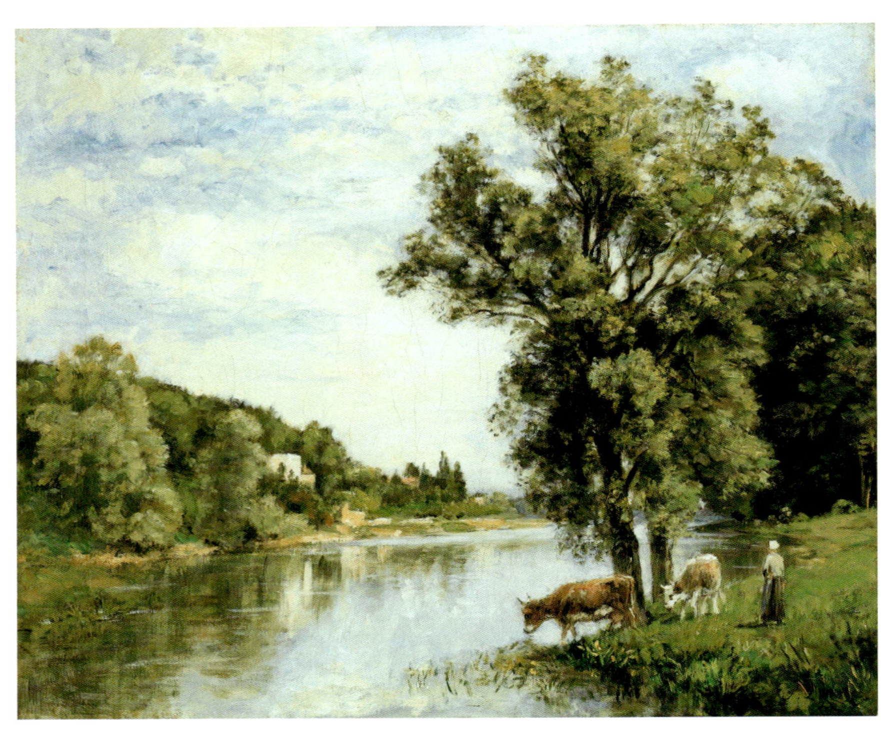

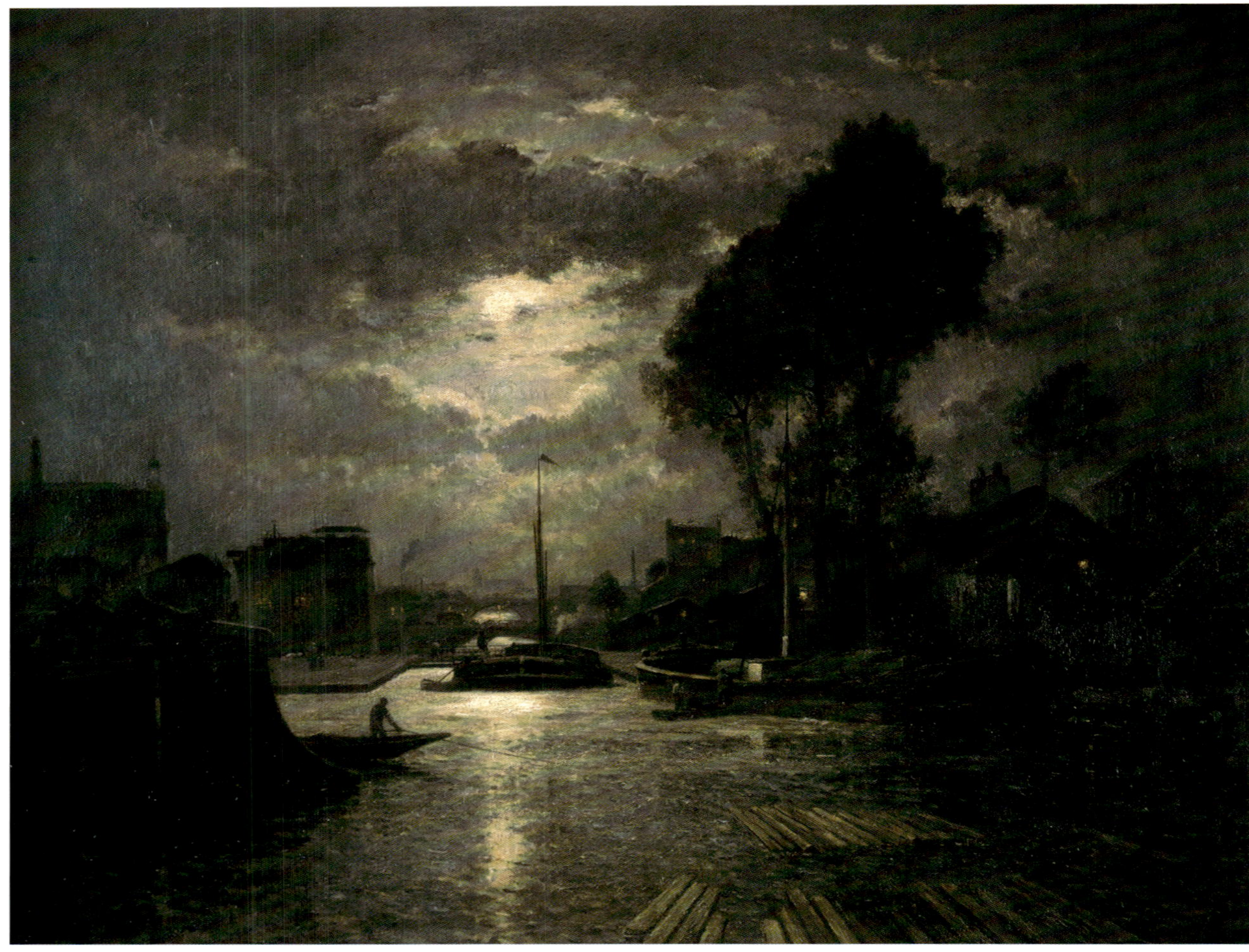

Stanislas Lepine
The Saint-Denis Canal in the Moonlight, Viewed from the Harbor at Metz
Der Kanal Saint-Denis im Mondschein, vom Hafen von Metz aus gesehen, ca. 1876/79

Stanislas Lepine
The Island of Grande Jatte
Die Insel Grande Jatte, ca. 1877/82

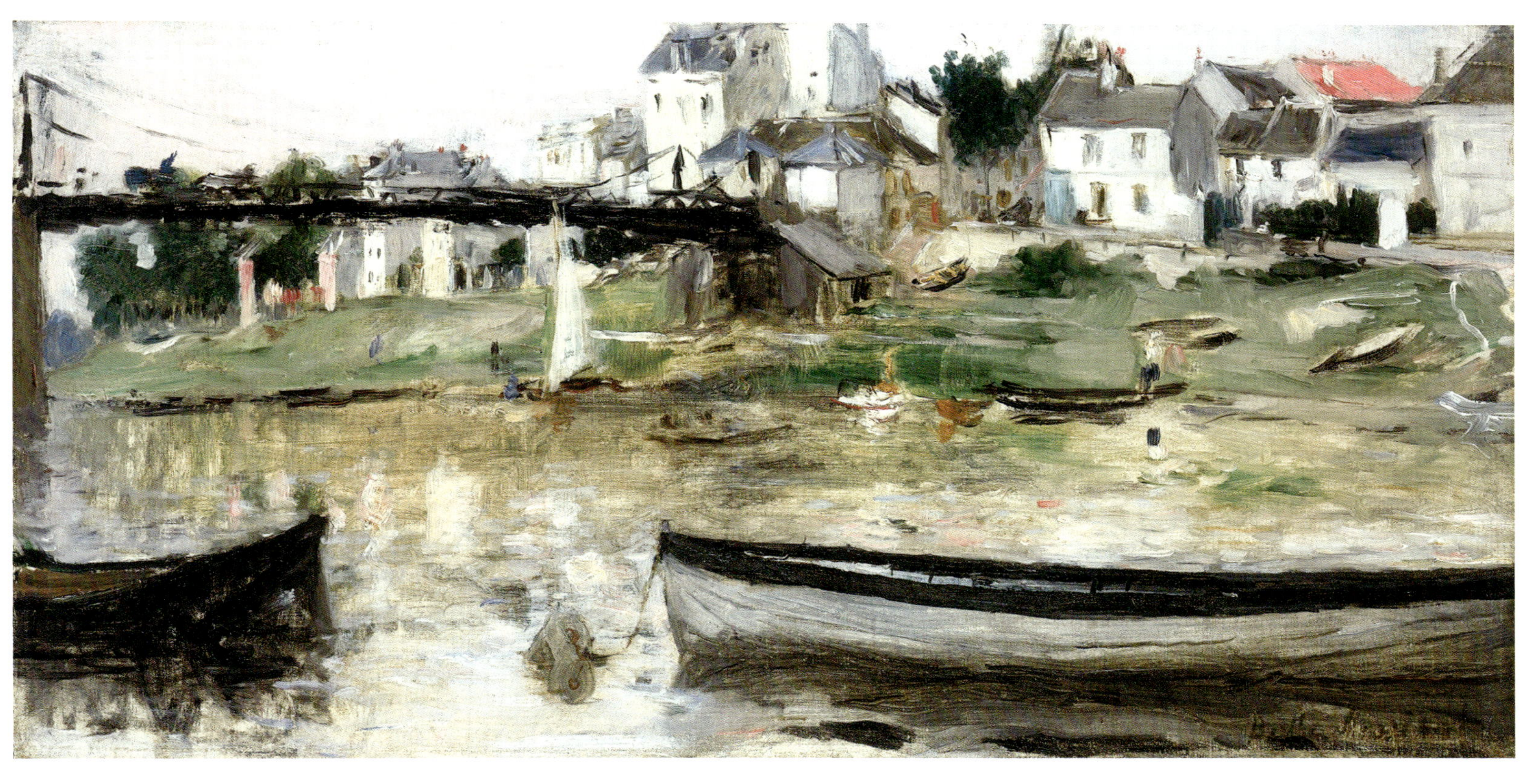

Berthe Morisot
Boats on the Seine
Boote auf der Seine, ca. 1879/80

EDOUARD MANET
A Bunch of Asparagus
Spargel-Stillleben, 1880

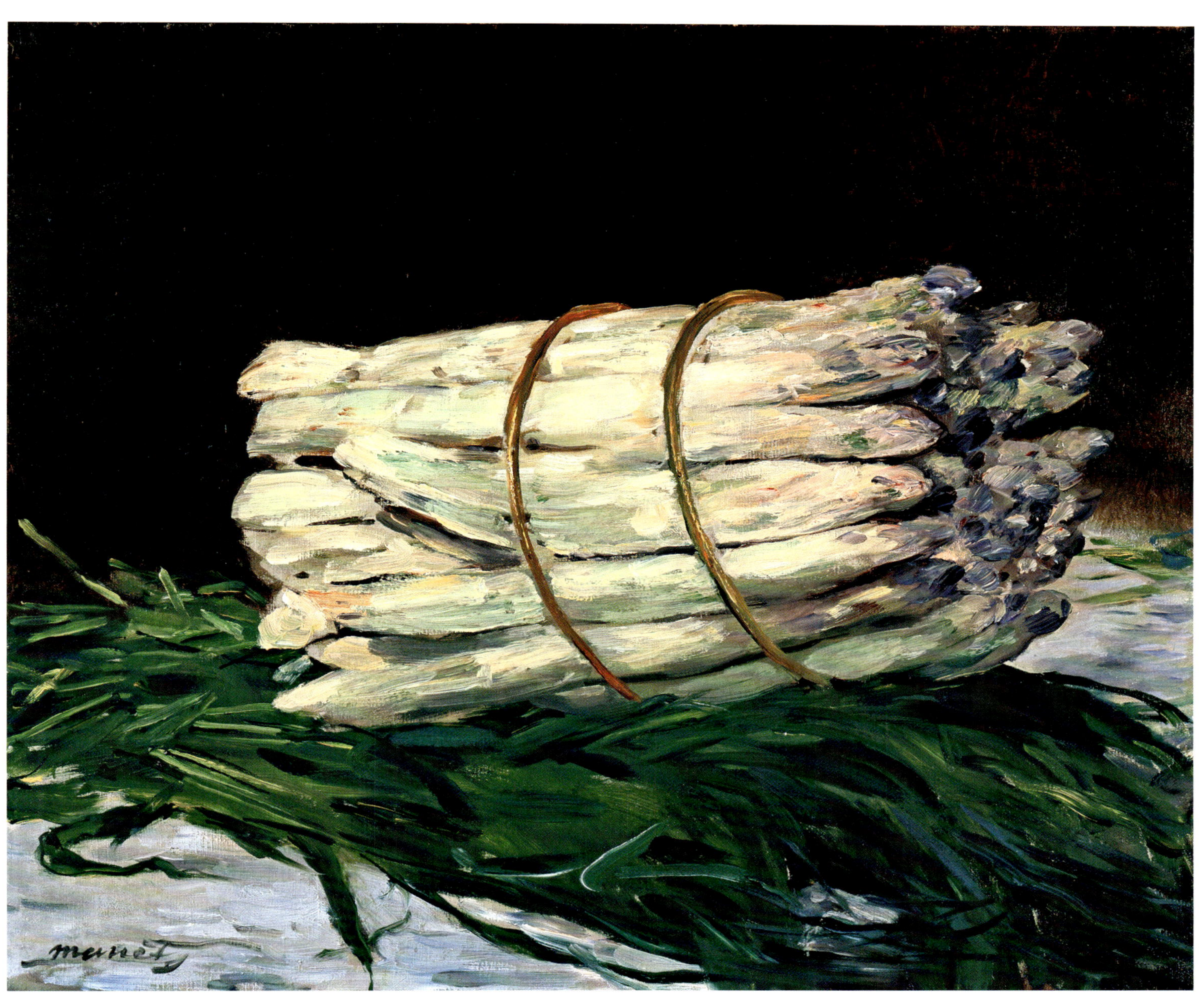
manet

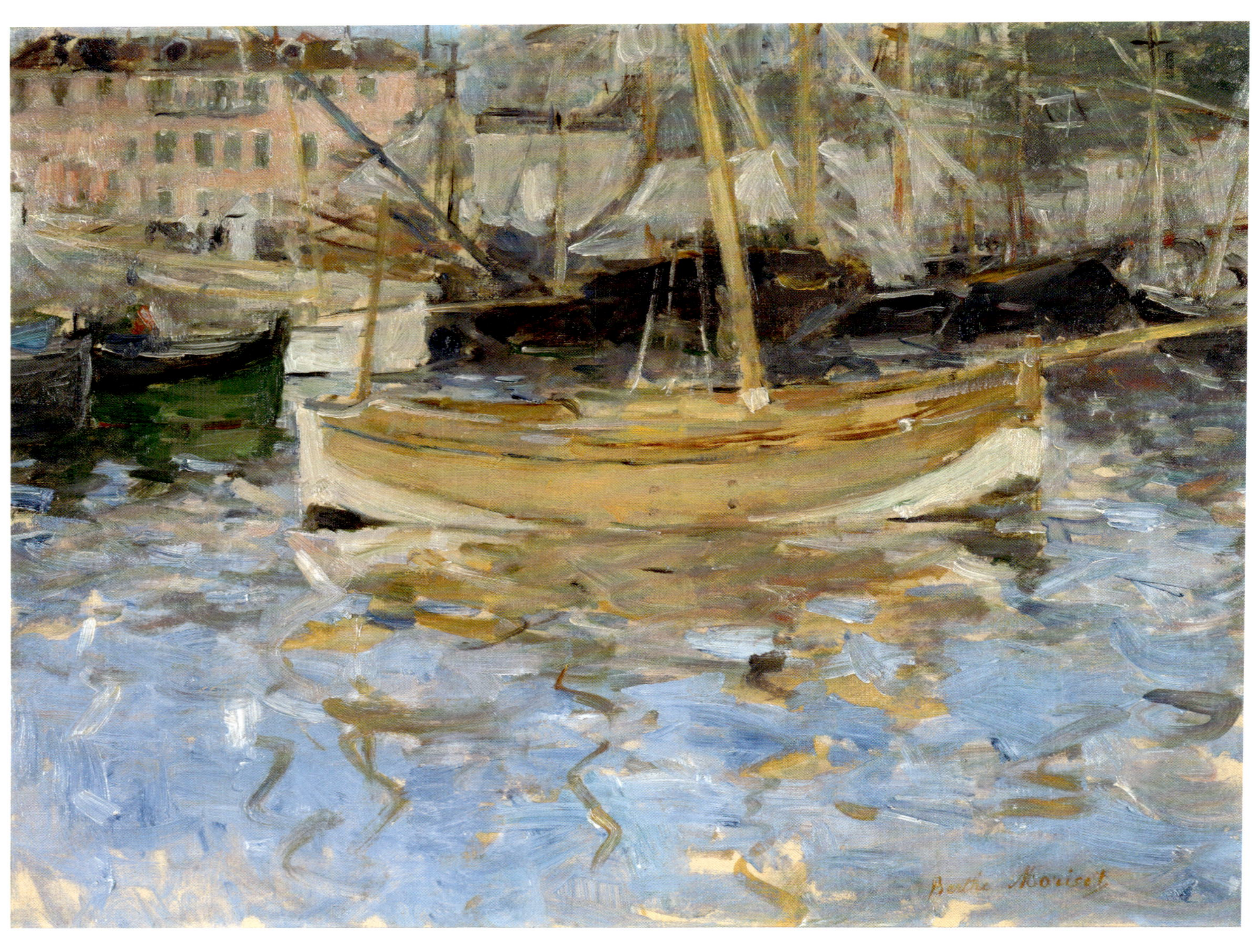

Berthe Morisot
The Harbor of Nice
Der Hafen von Nizza, 1881/82

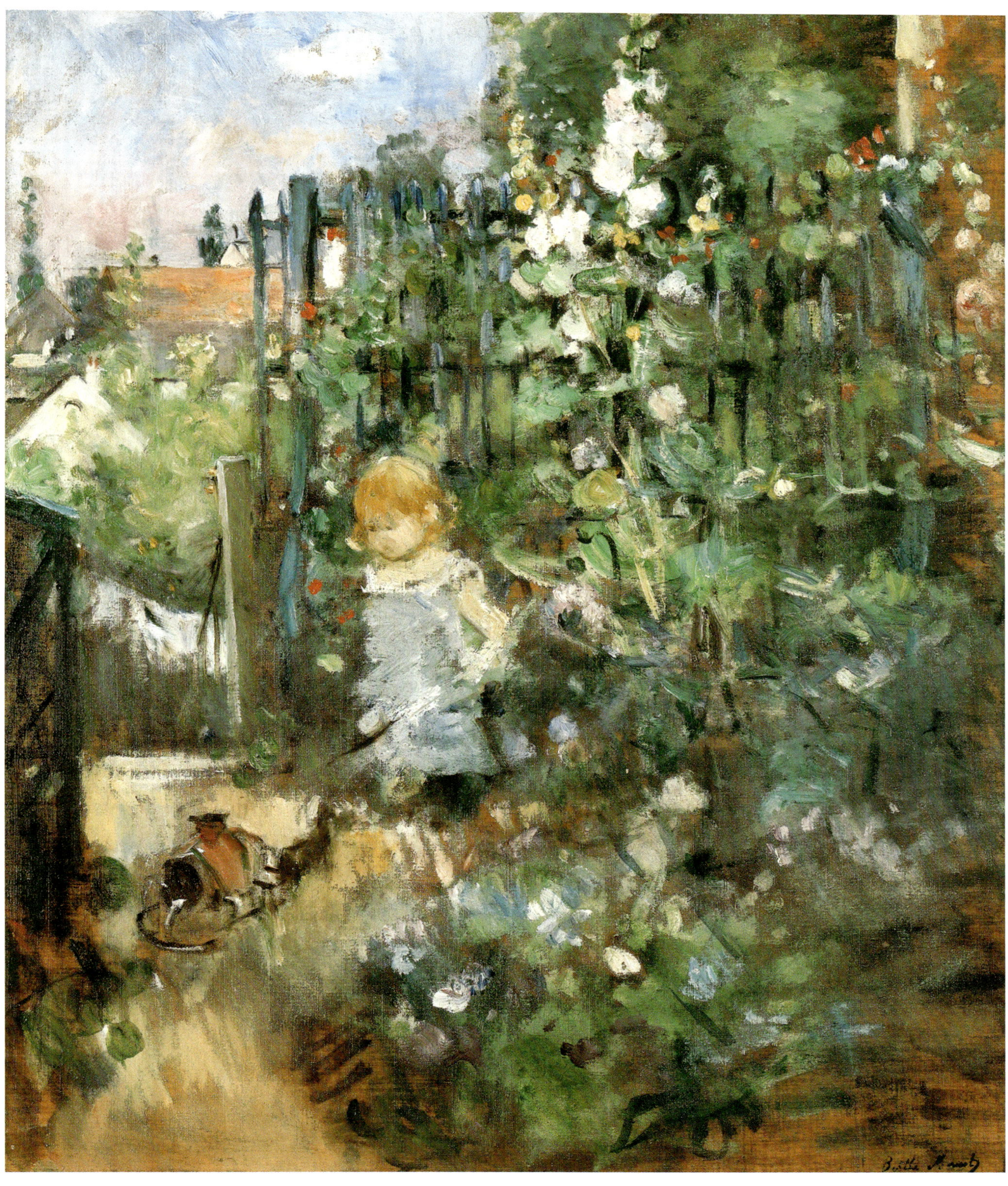

Berthe Morisot
Child in the Hollyhocks
Kind zwischen Stockrosen, 1881

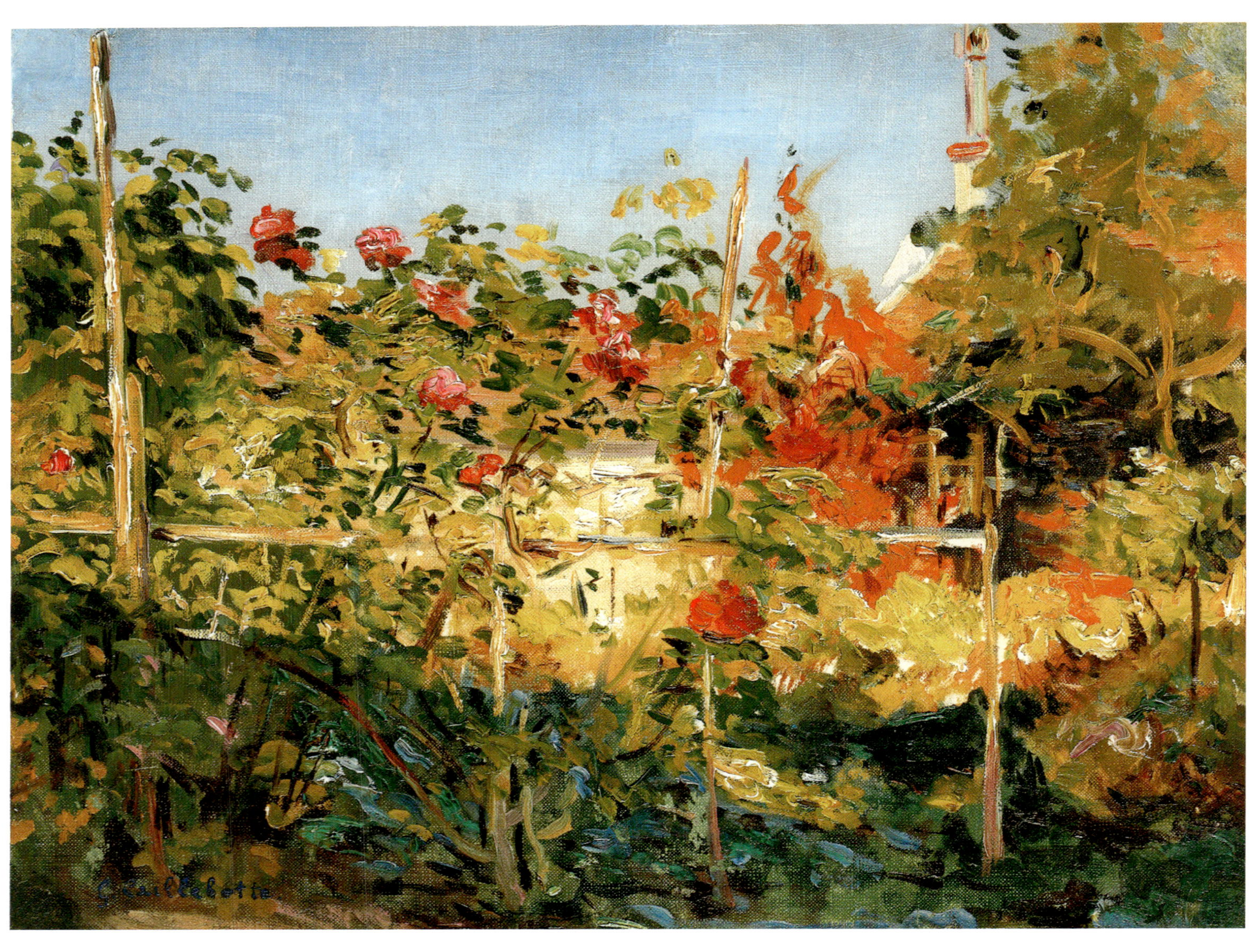

Gustave Caillebotte
Garden in Trouville
Garten in Trouville, ca. 1882

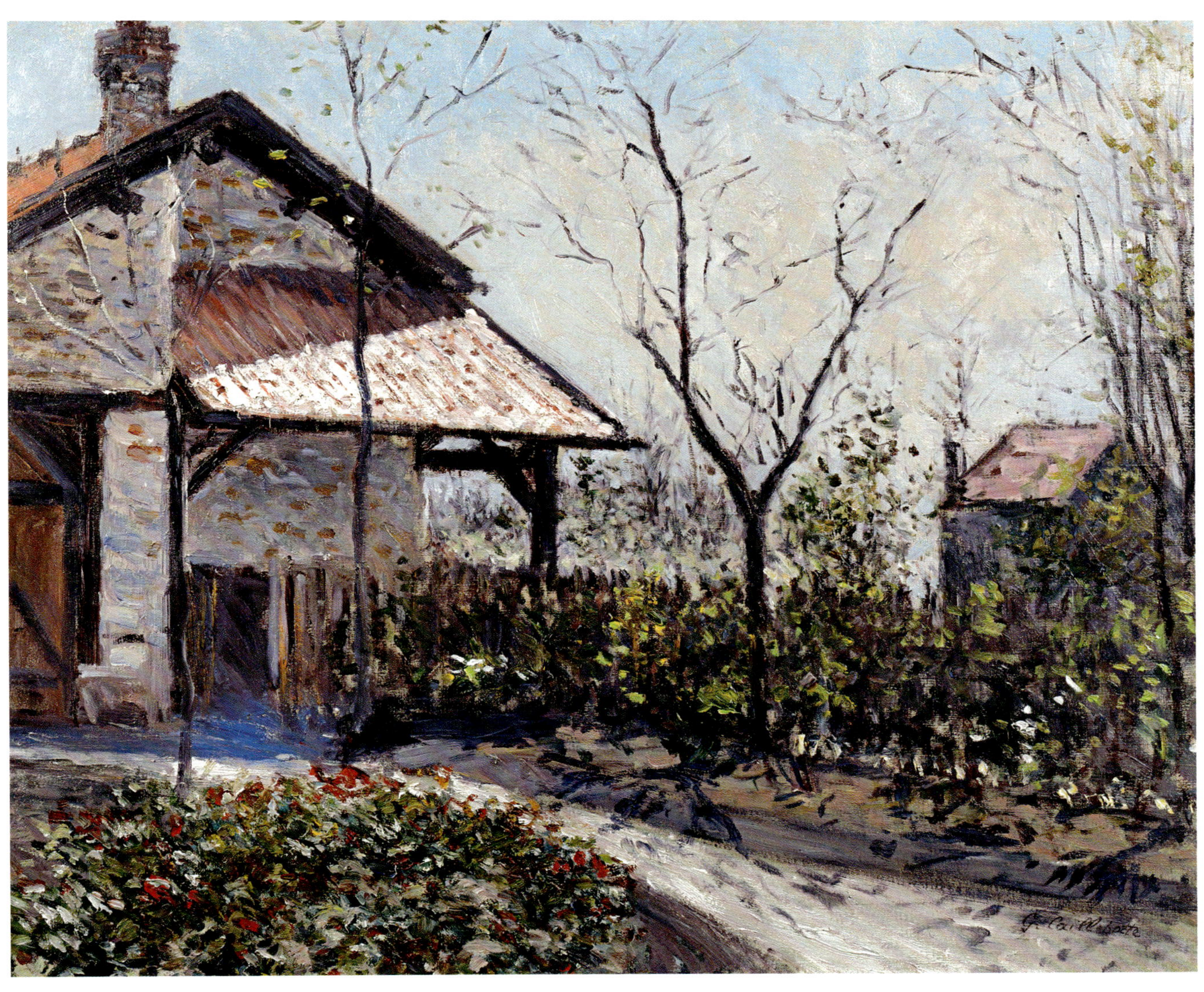

Gustave Caillebotte
Shed in the Garden in Petit-Gennevilliers
Schuppen im Garten von Petit-Gennevilliers, 1882

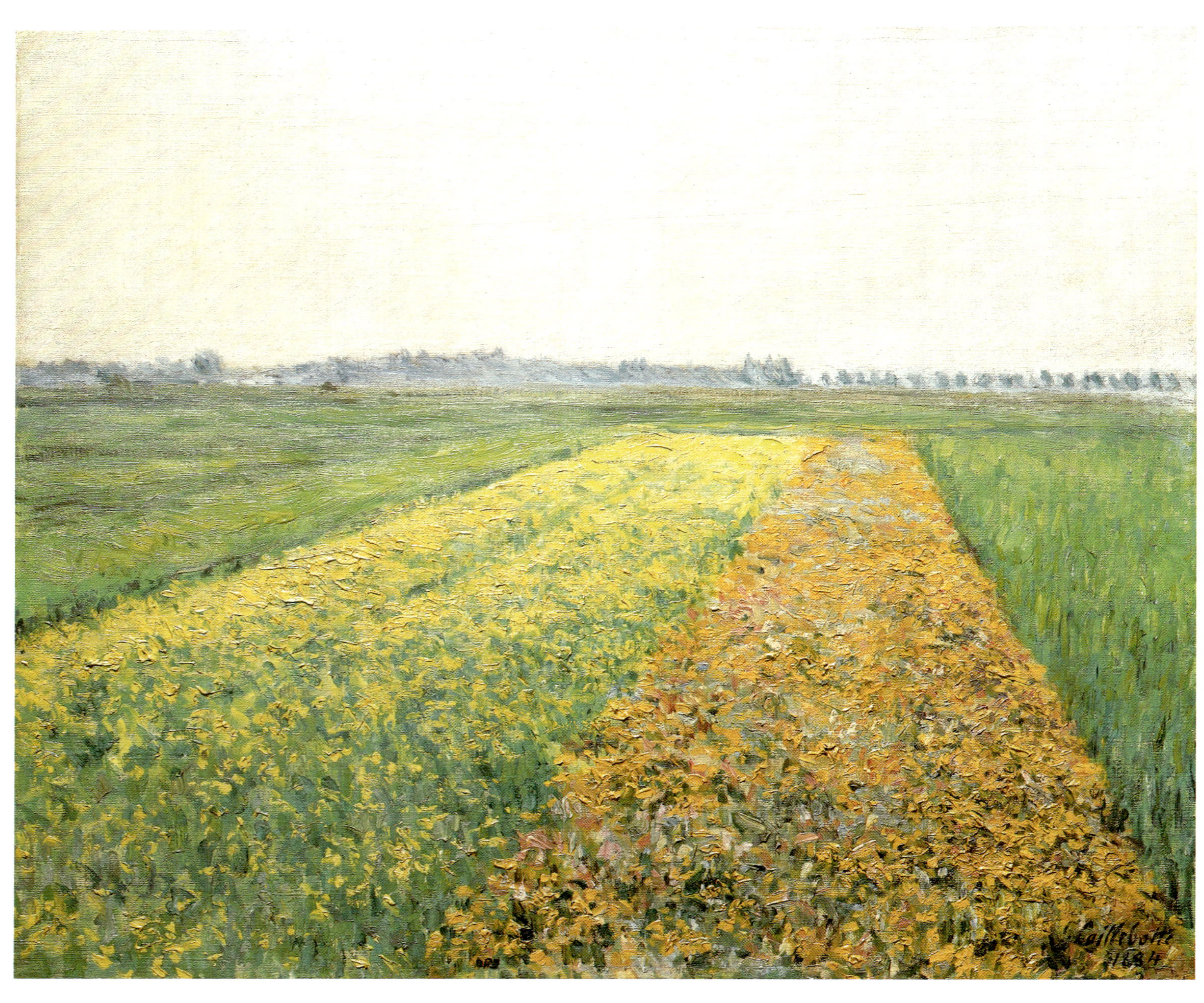

Gustave Caillebotte
The Yellow Fields at Gennevilliers
Die Ebene von Gennevilliers, gelbe Felder, 1884

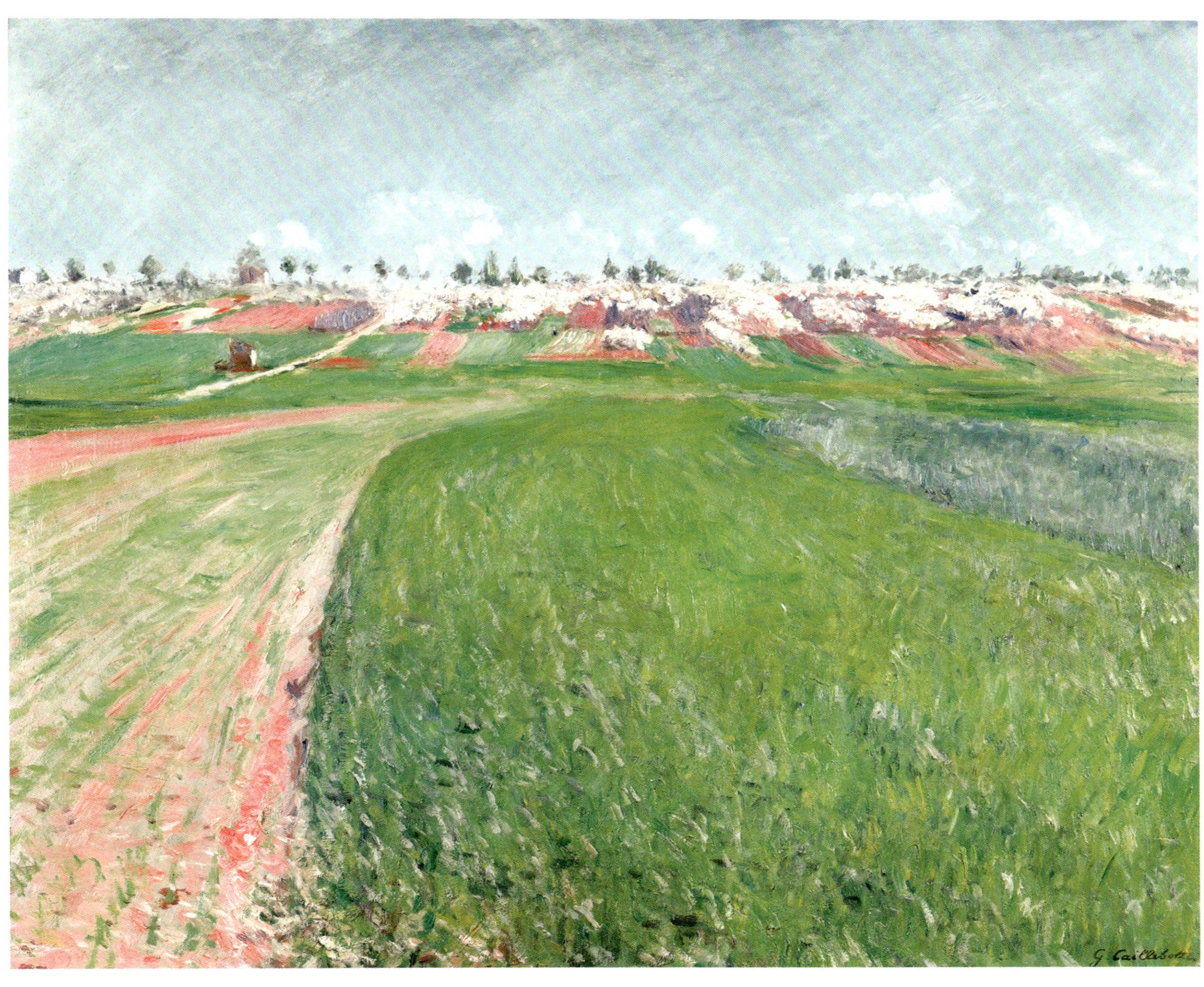

Gustave Caillebotte
Hill at Colombes
Hügel bei Colombes, 1884

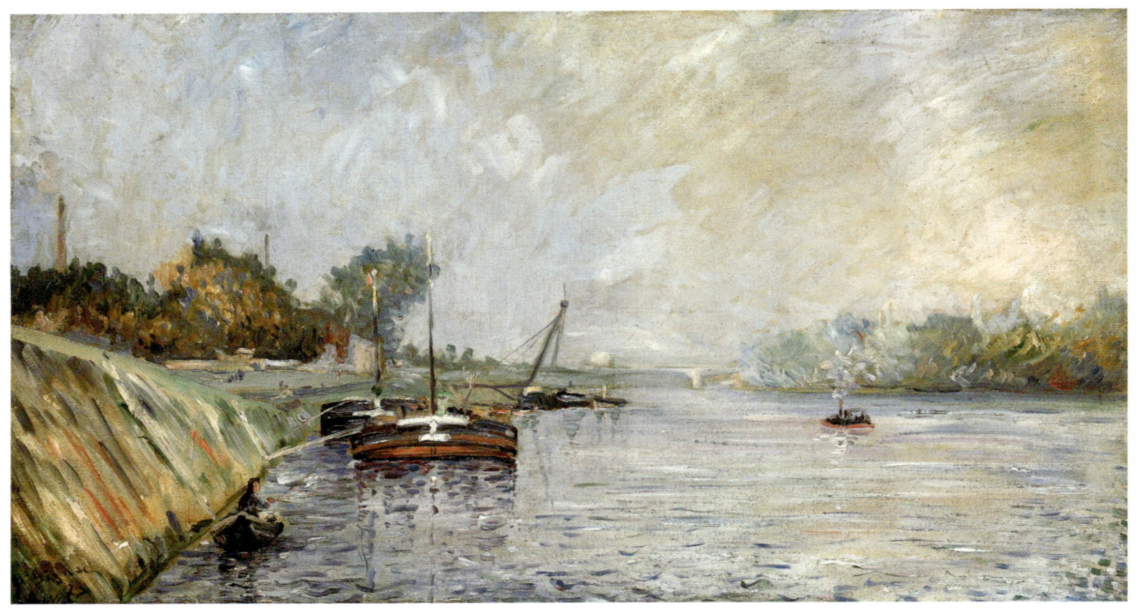

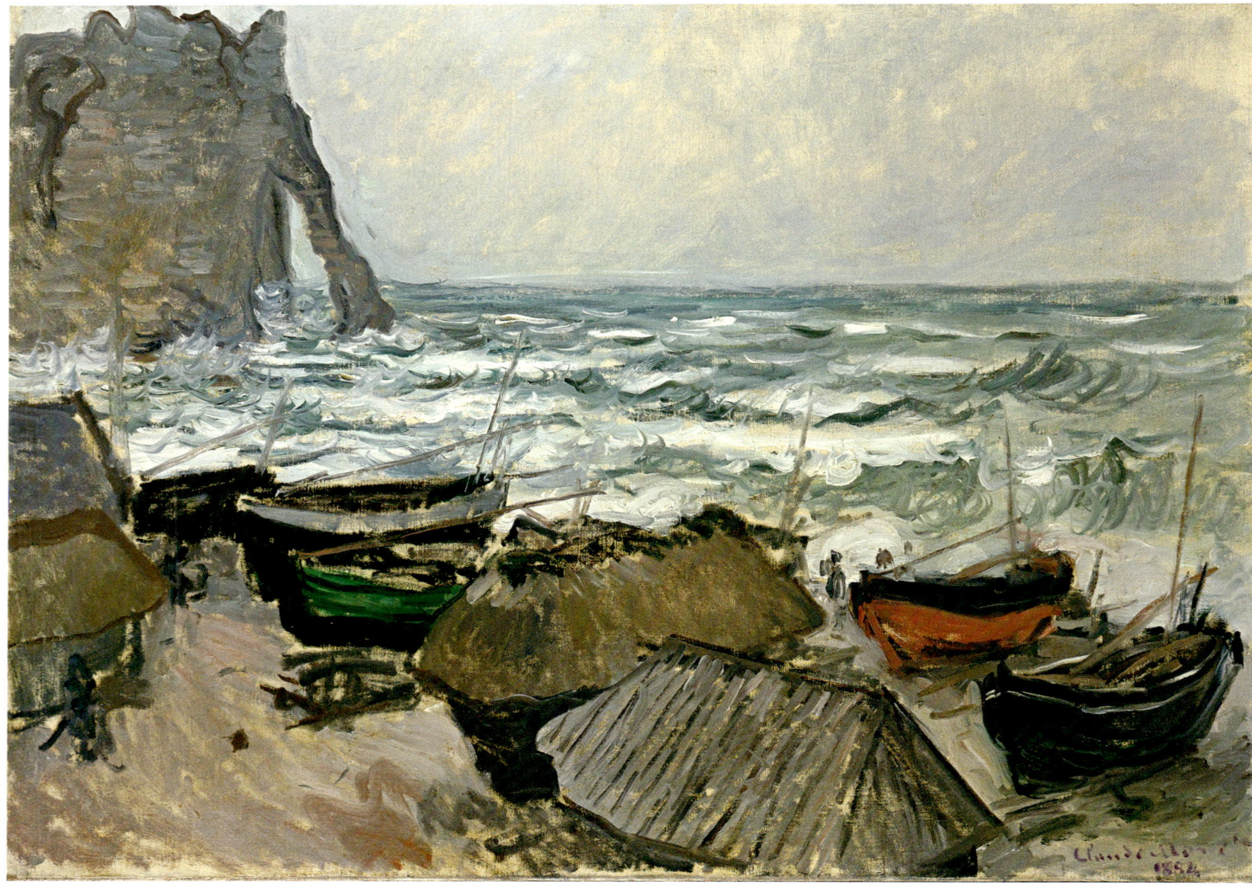

Paul Signac
The Seine at Courbevoie (Riverscape)
Die Seine bei Courbevoie (Flusslandschaft), 1883

Claude Monet
Fishing Boats at the Beach at Etretat
Fischerboote am Strand von Etretat, ca. 1883/84

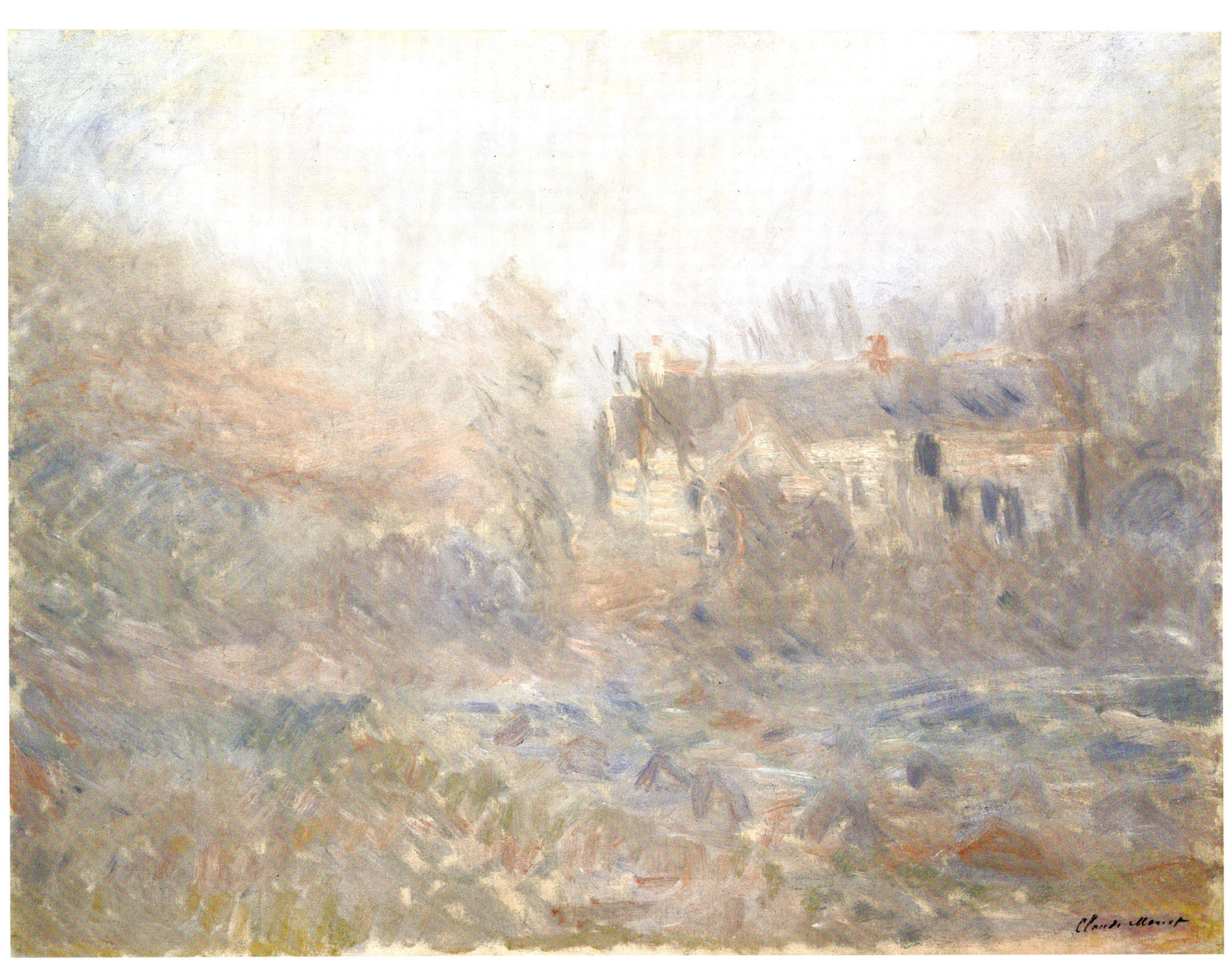

Claude Monet
Houses in Falaise in the Fog
Häuser in Falaise im Nebel, 1885

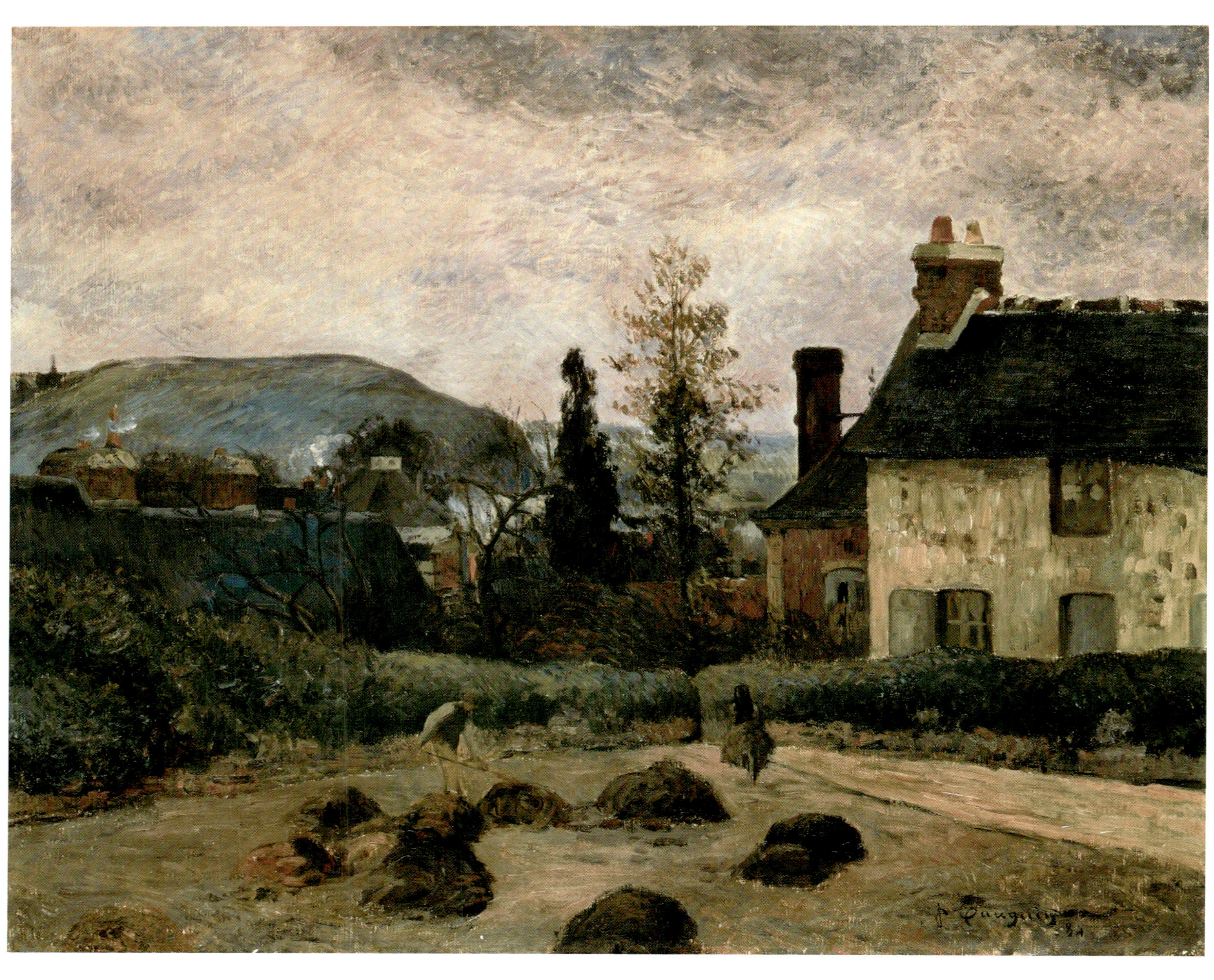

Paul Gauguin
Manuring
Das Ausbringen des Mists, 1884

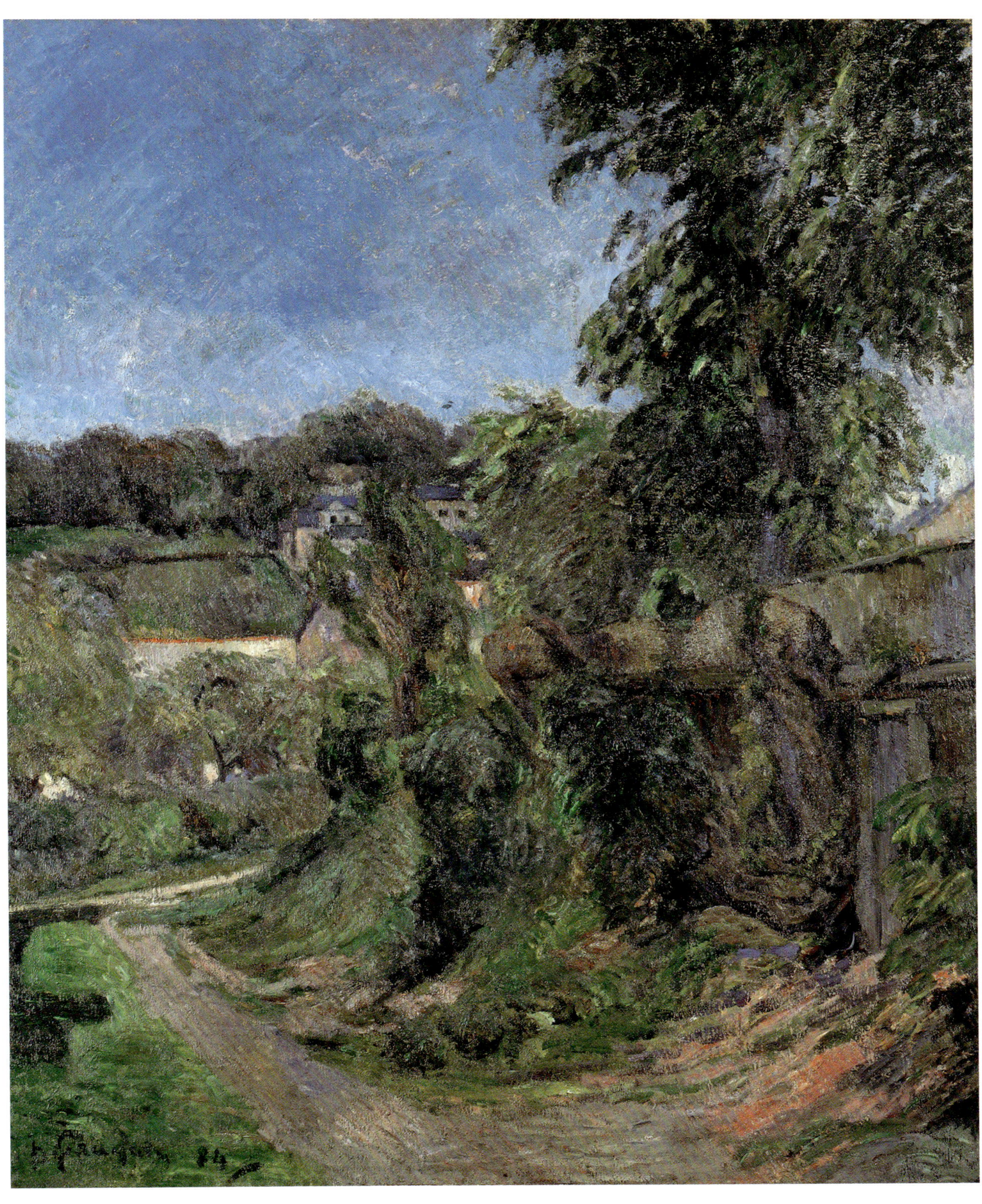

PAUL GAUGUIN
Rouen Landscape
Landschaft bei Rouen, 1884

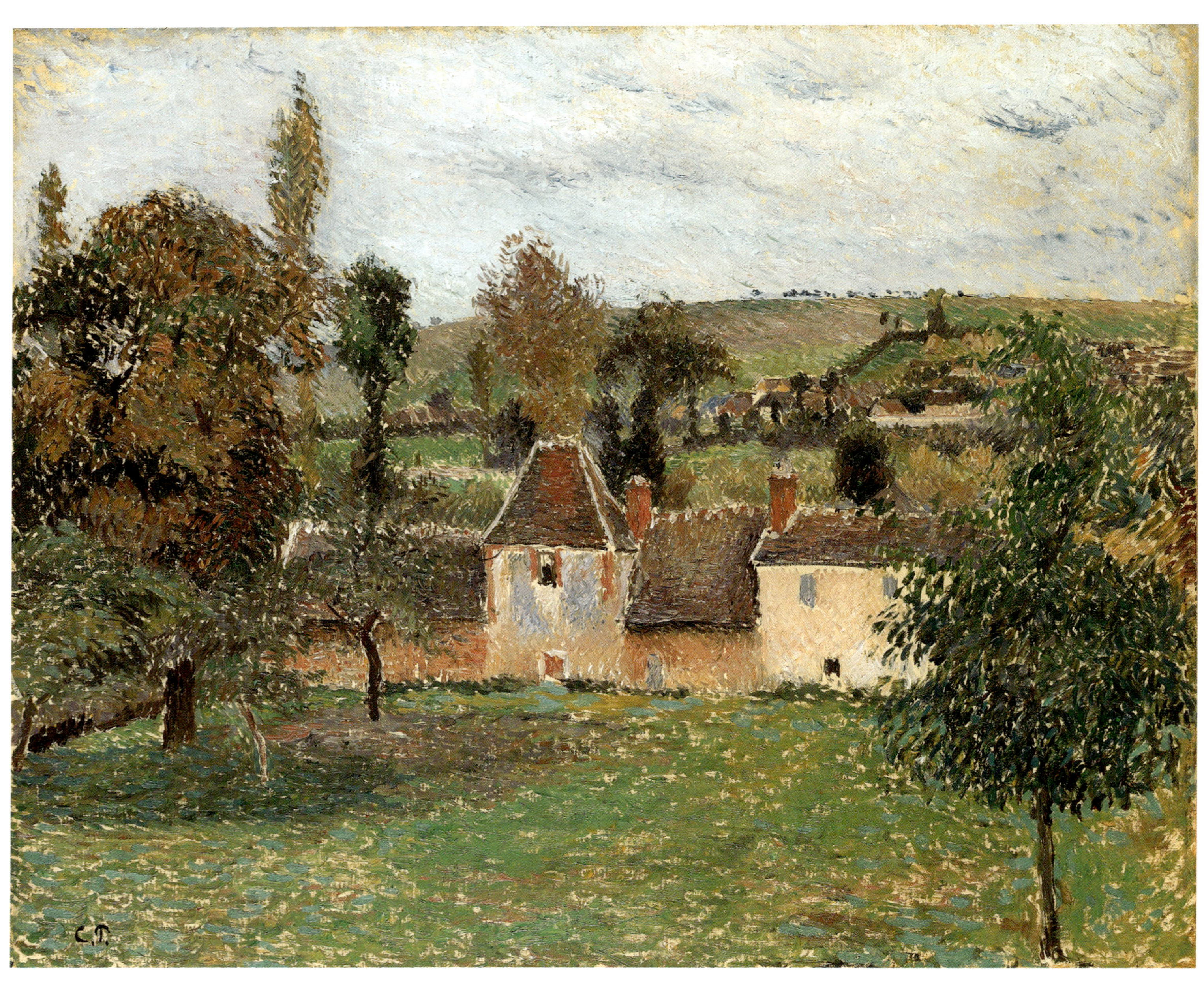

Camille Pissarro
Farm in Bazincourt
Bauernhof in Bazincourt, 1884

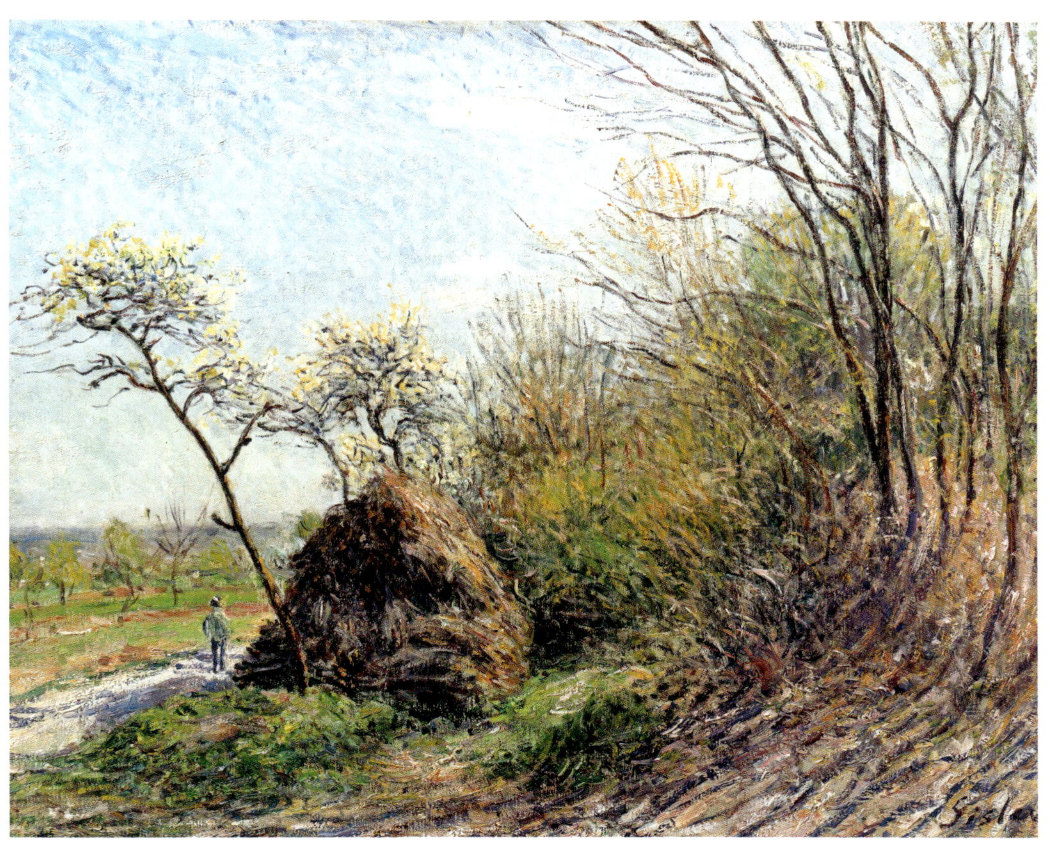

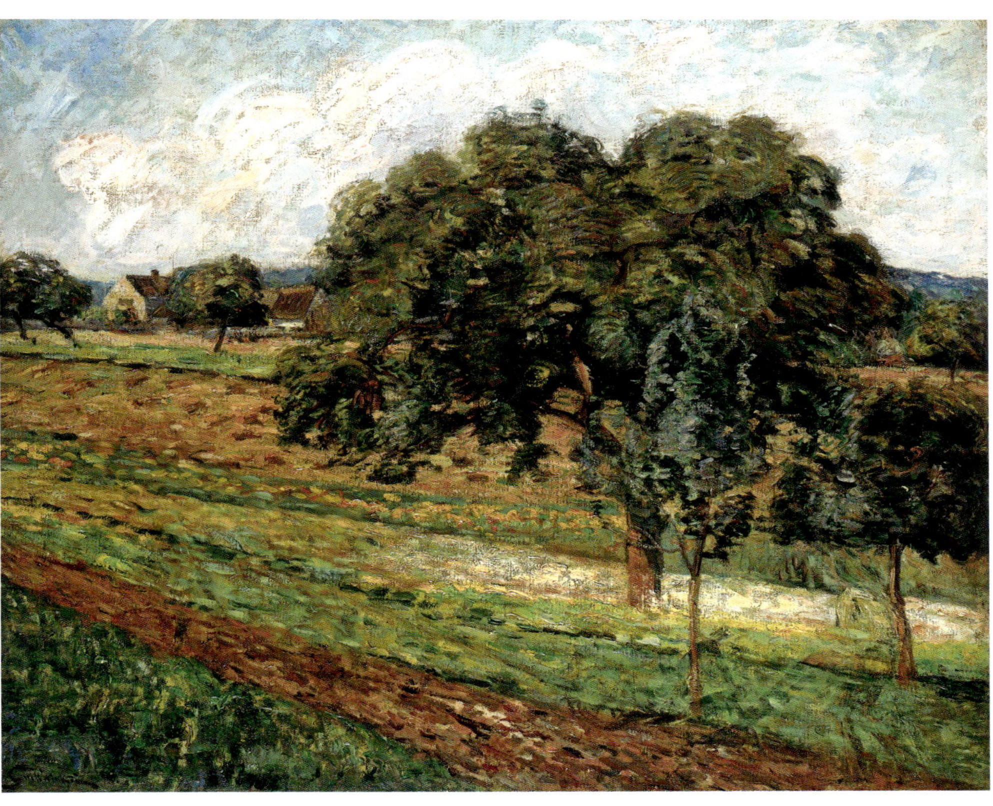

Alfred Sisley
At the Edge of the Forest – Les Sablons
Am Waldrand – Les Sablons, ca. 1884/85

Armand Guillaumin
Trees and Flowers, Landscape at Damiette
Bäume und Blumen, Landschaft bei Damiette, ca. 1885

PAUL CEZANNE
Still Life with Pears
Stillleben mit Birnen, ca. 1885

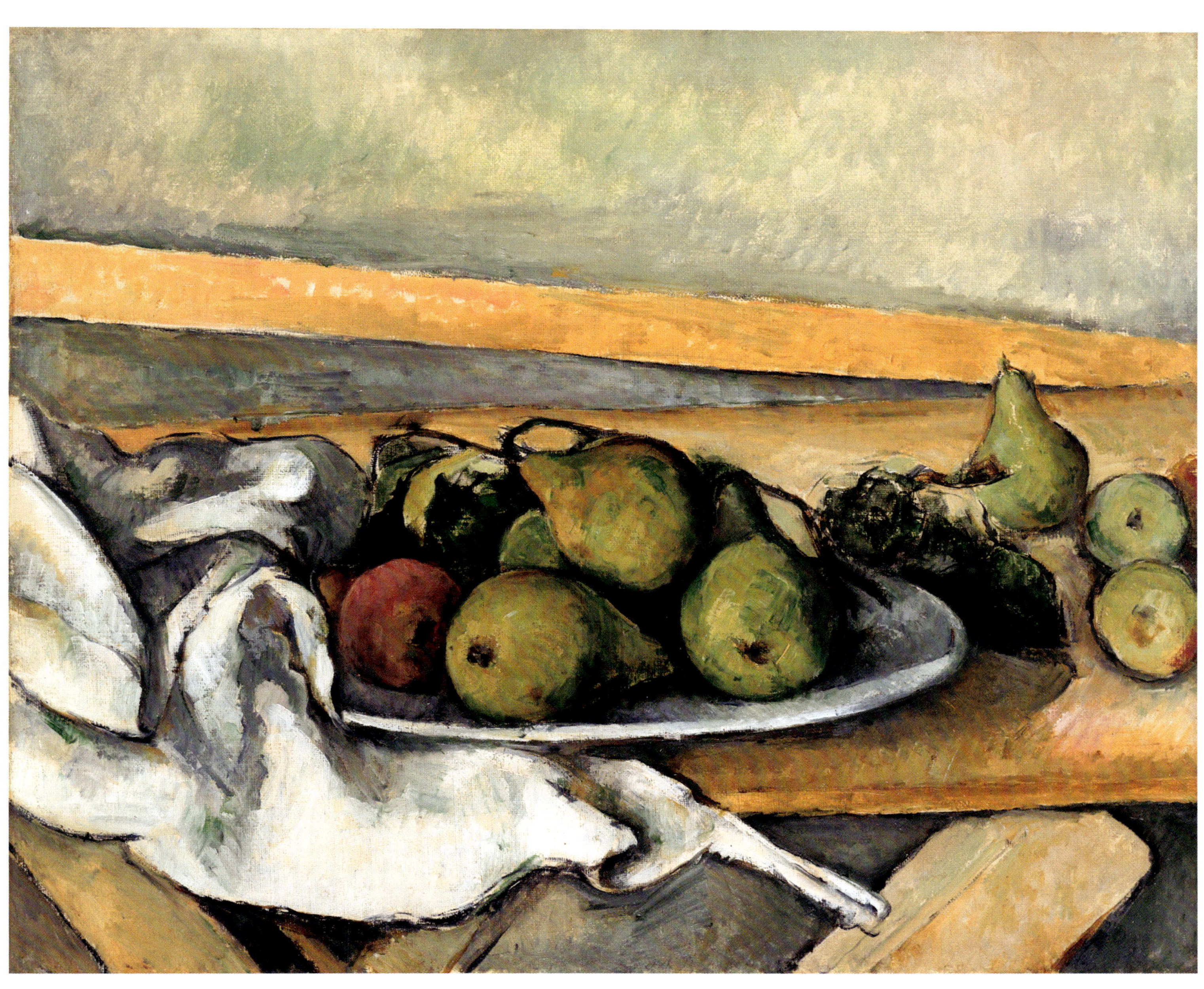

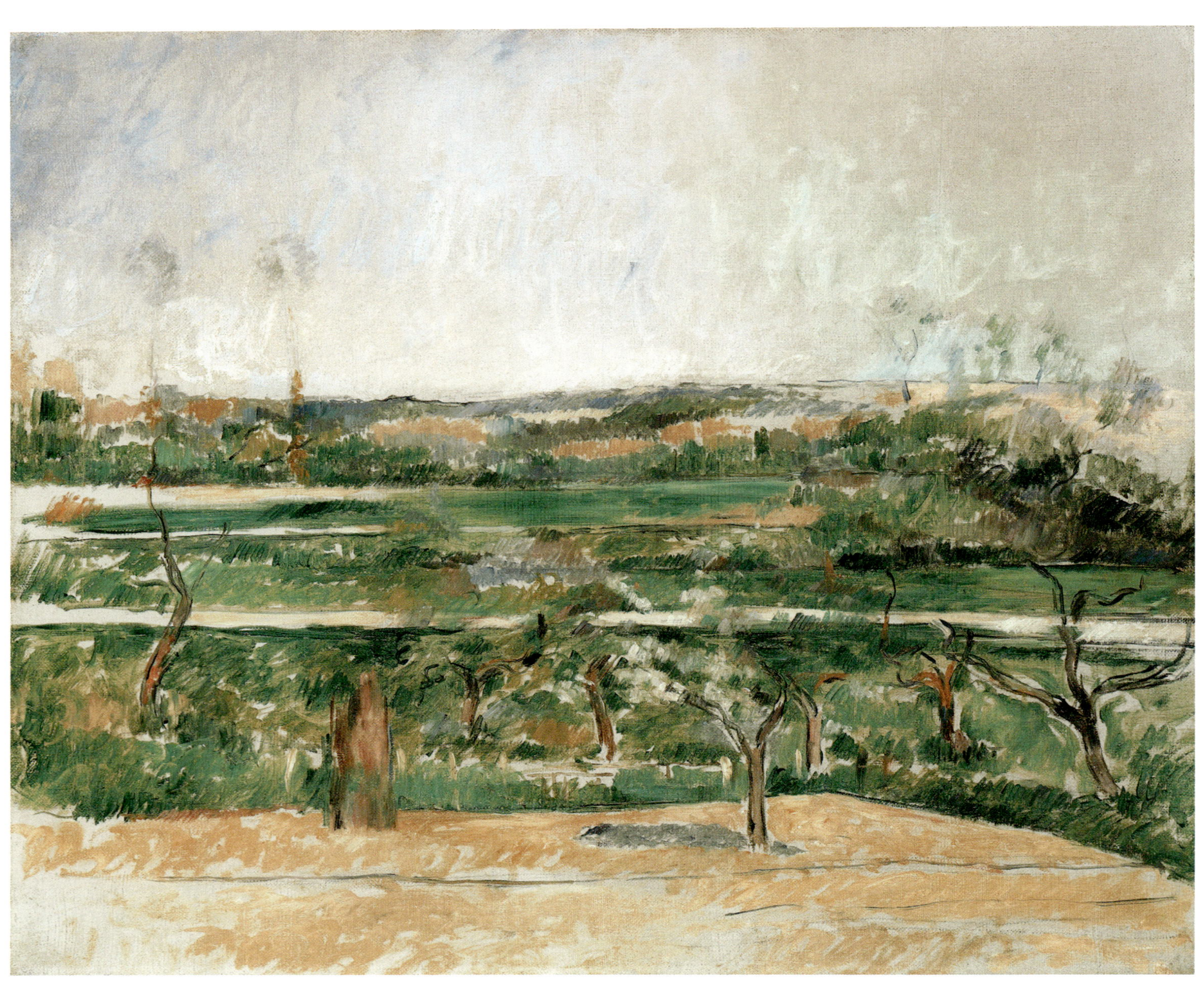

Paul Cezanne
Landscape at Aix-en-Provence
Landschaft bei Aix-en-Provence, ca. 1879

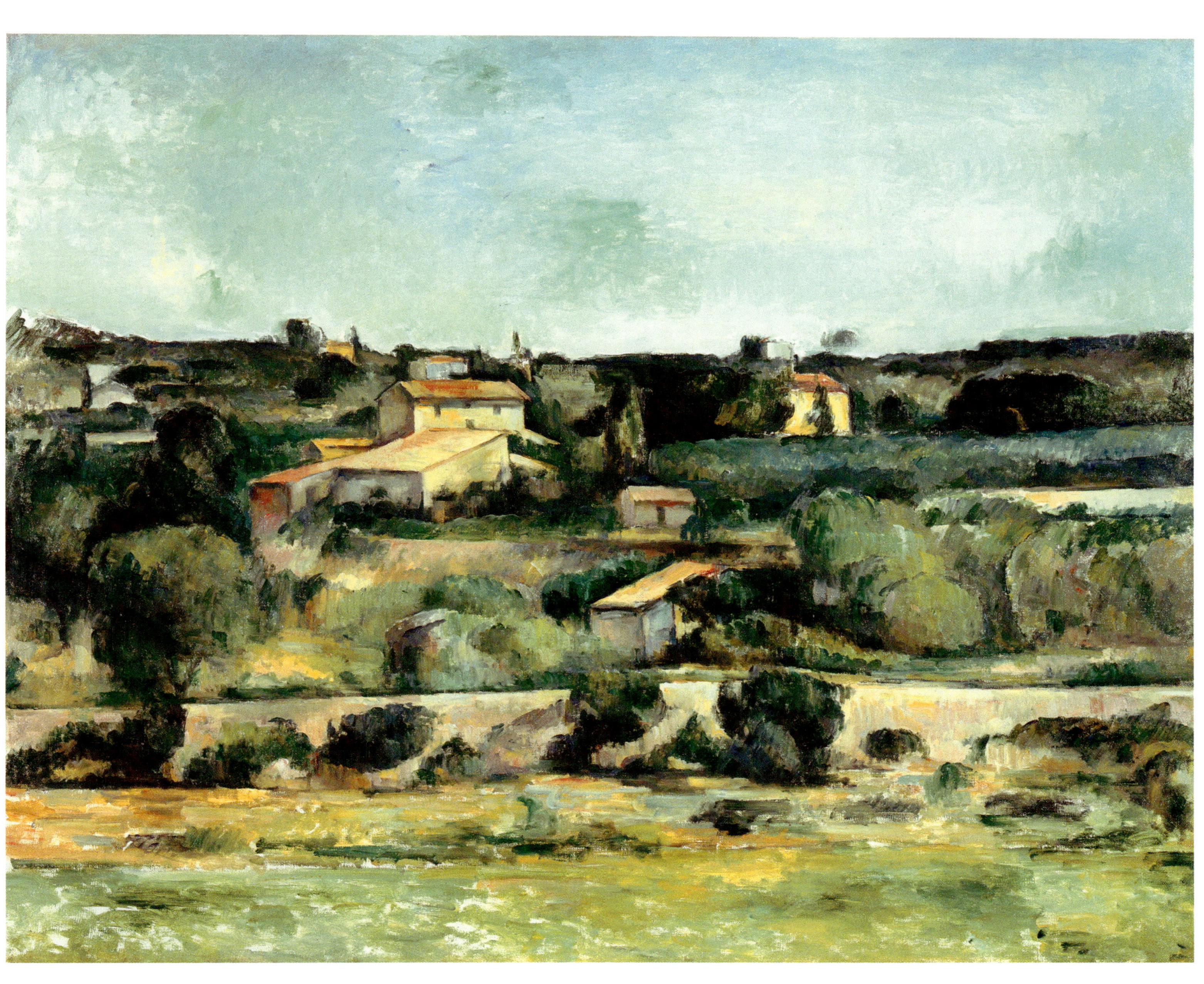

Paul Cezanne
Landscape in the West of Aix-en-Provence
Landschaft im Westen von Aix-en-Provence, 1885/88

The Mature Years

Die Zeit der Reife

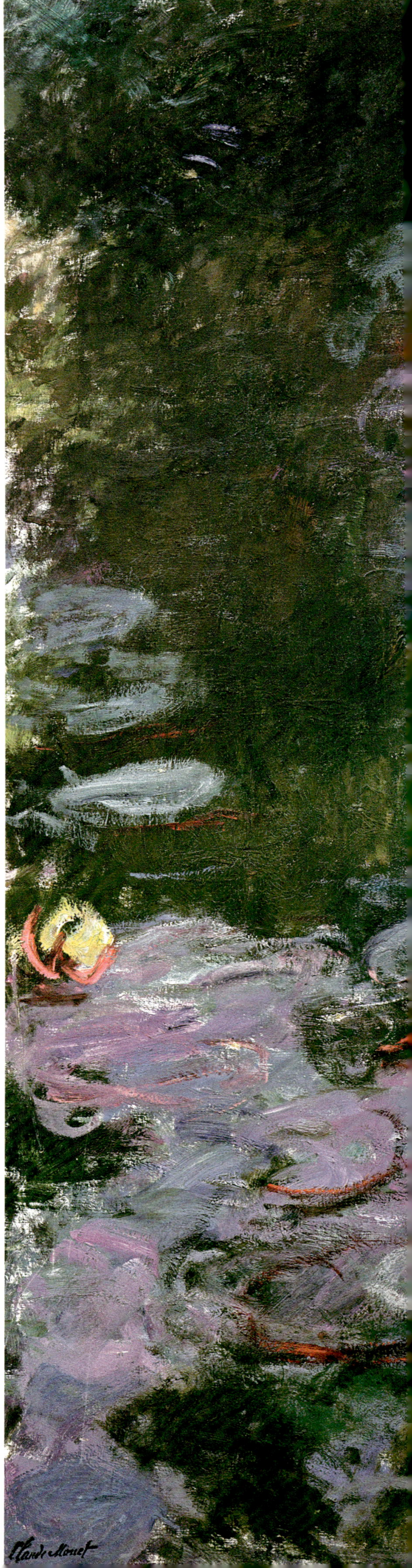

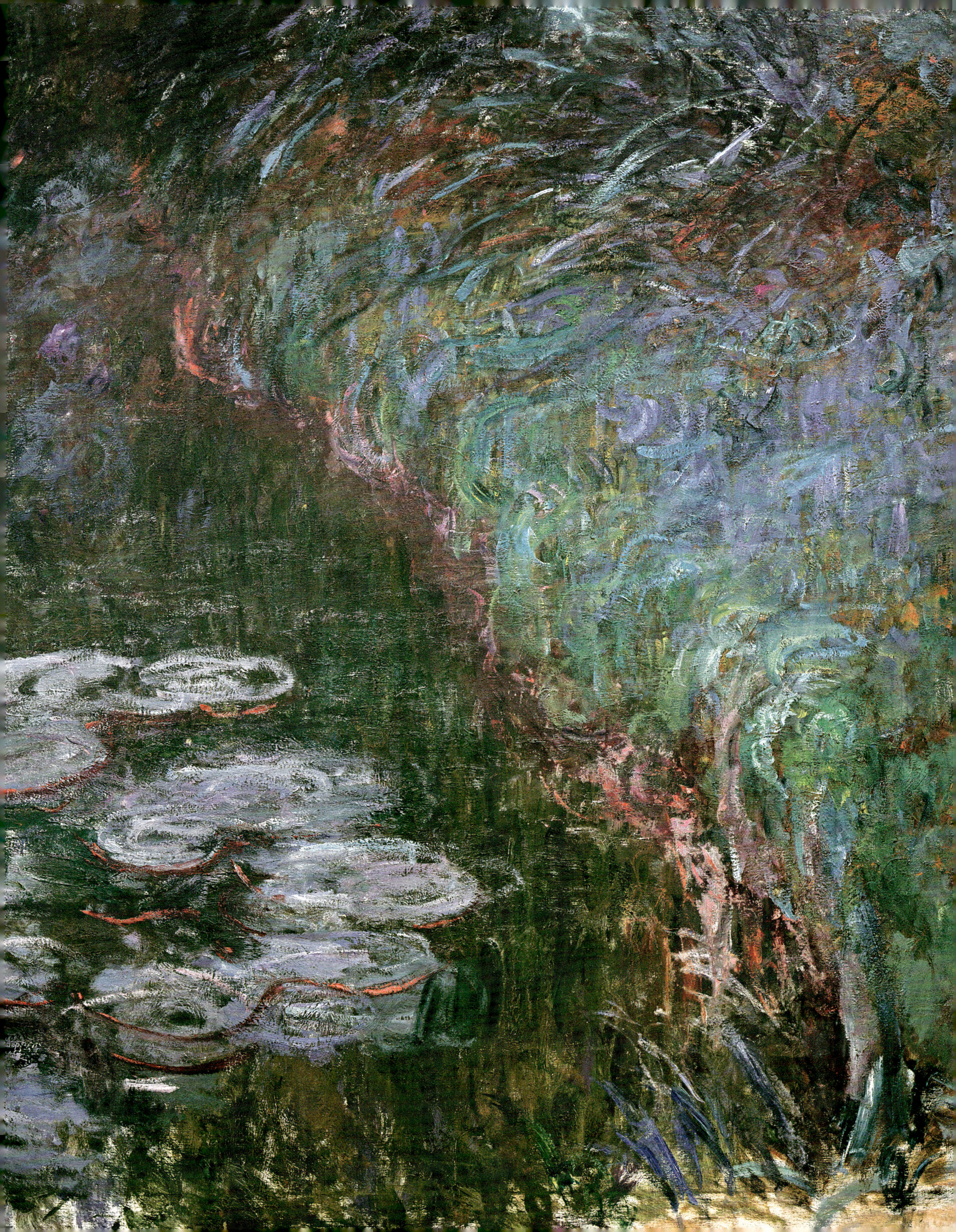

Gustave Caillebotte
Laundry Drying on the Banks of the Seine
Trocknende Wäsche am Ufer der Seine, ca. 1892

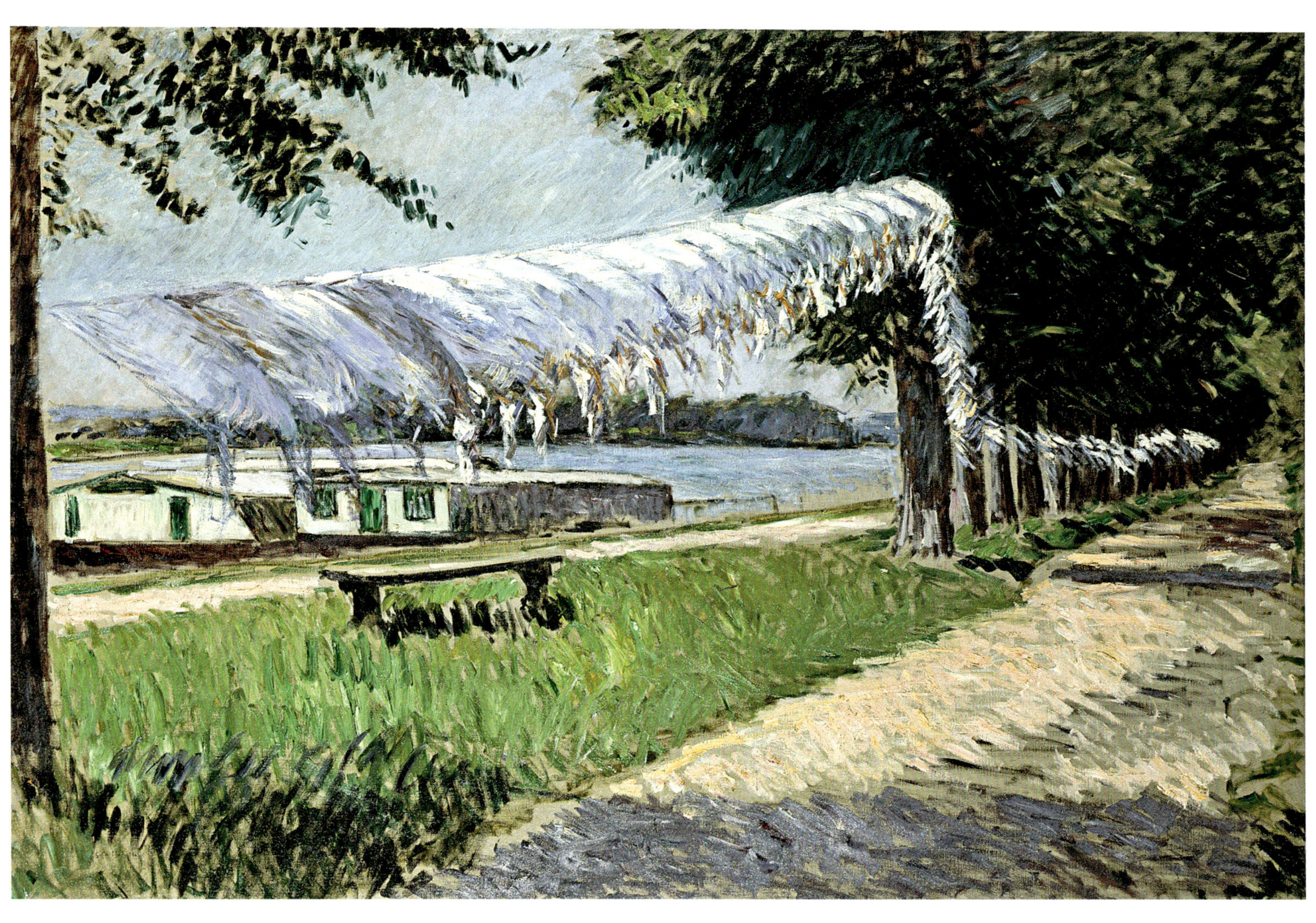

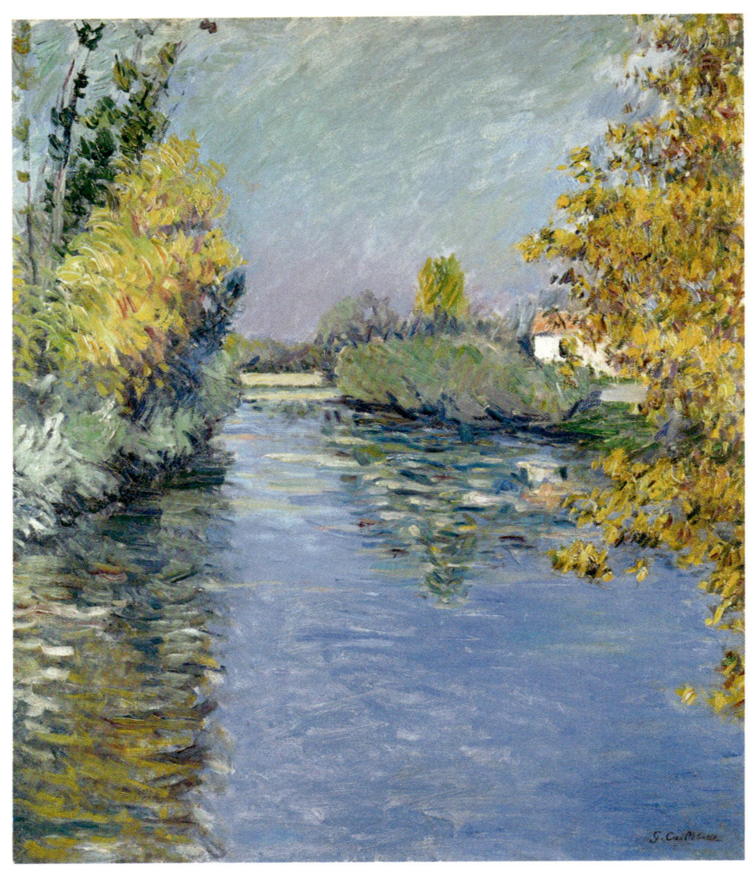

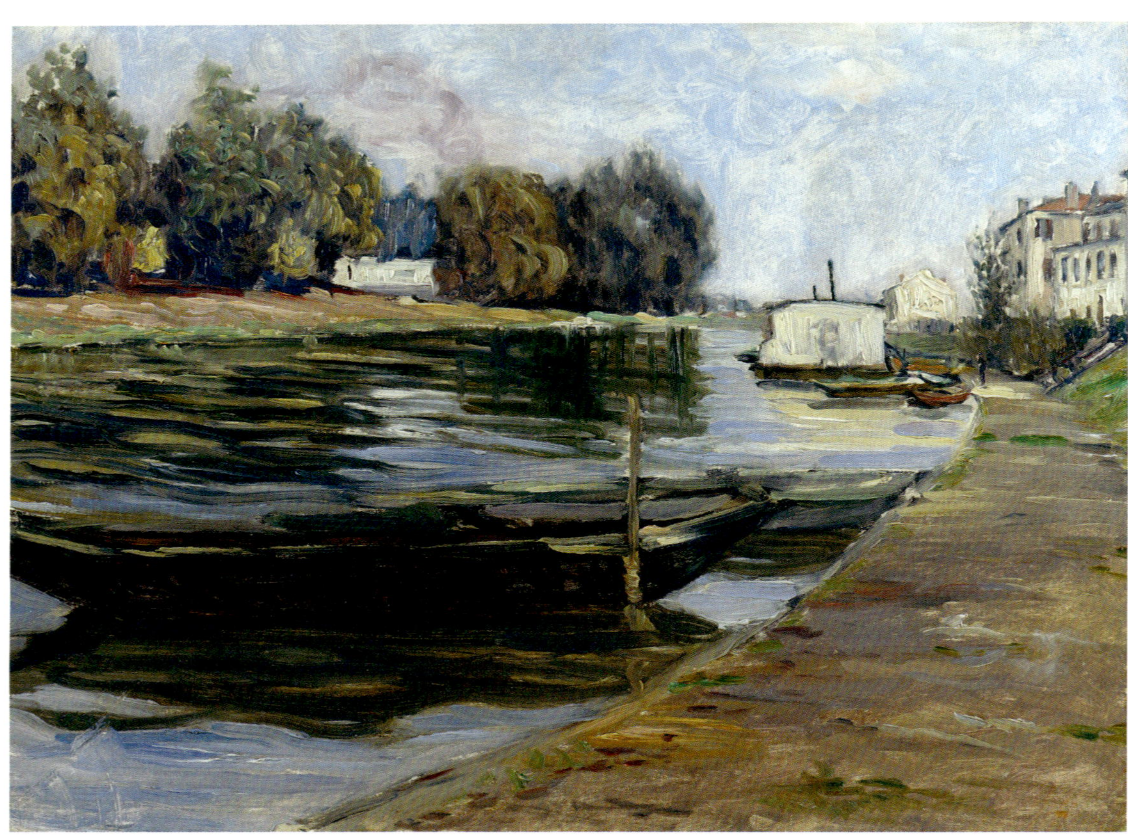

GUSTAVE CAILLEBOTTE
Branch of the Seine in Autumn
Nebenarm der Seine, Herbststimmung, 1890

GUSTAVE CAILLEBOTTE
Banks of the Seine
Ufer der Seine, 1891

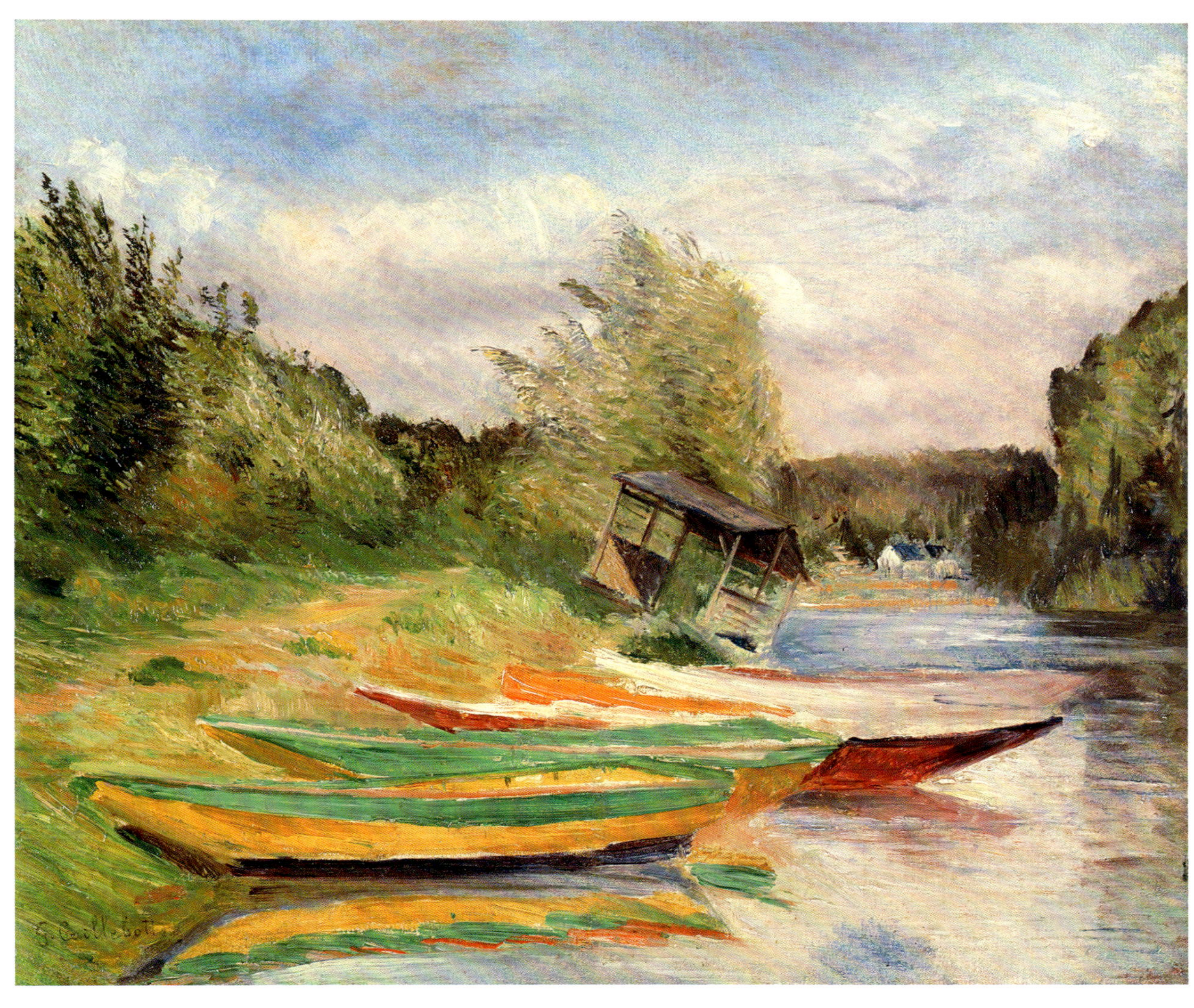

Gustave Caillebotte
Boats and Shed on the Banks of the Seine
Boote und Schuppen am Ufer der Seine, 1891

Gustave Caillebotte
Sailboat on the Seine at Argenteuil
Segelboot auf der Seine bei Argenteuil, 1893

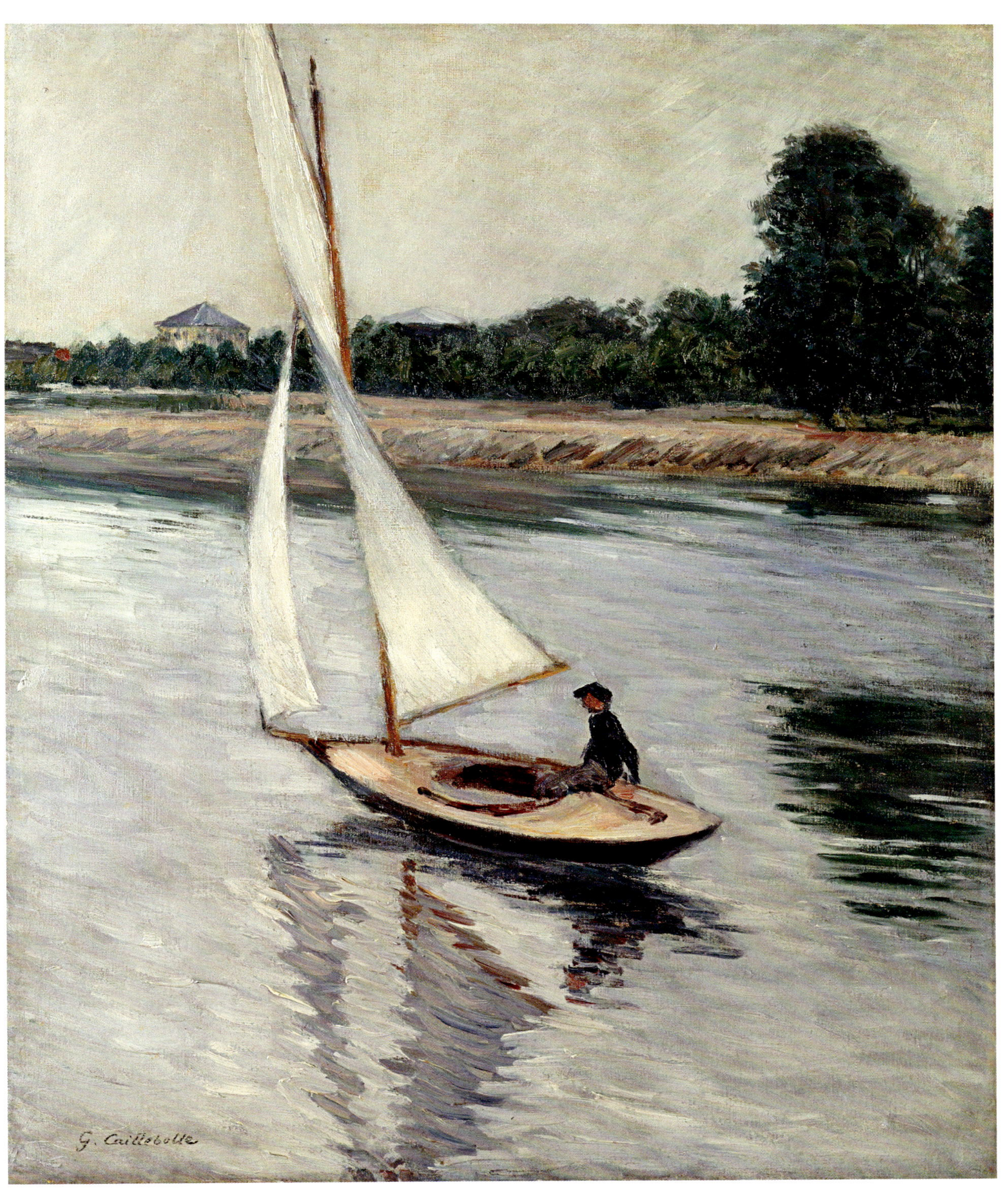
G. Caillebotte

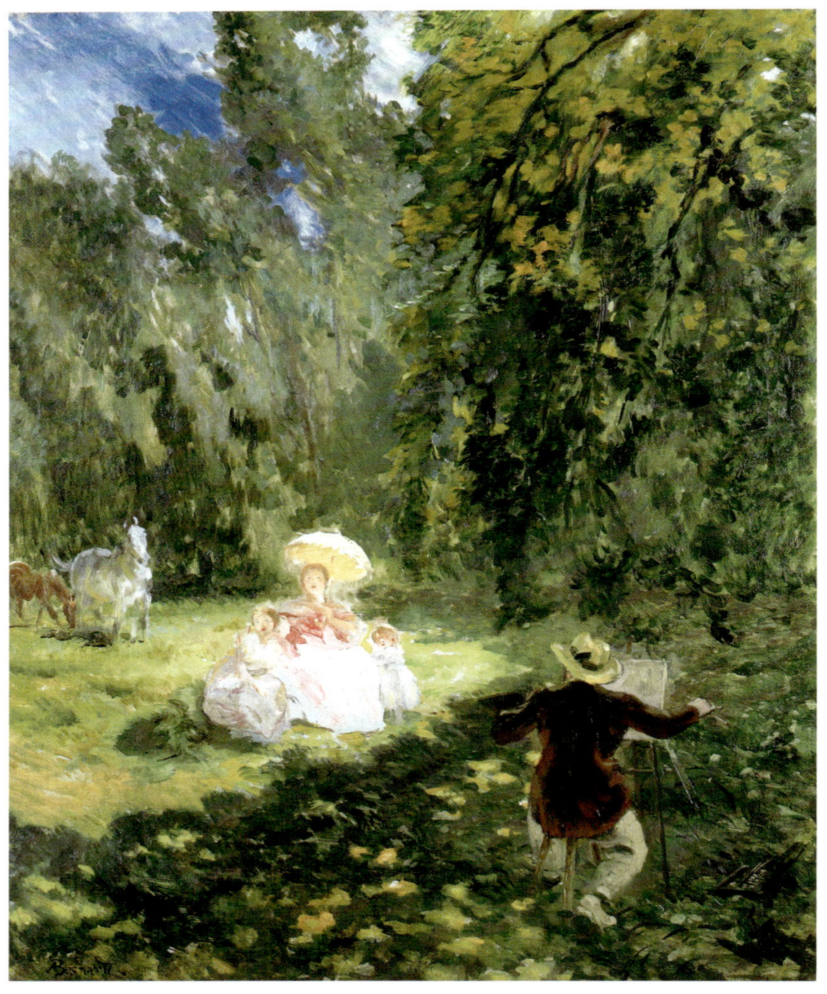

ALBERT BESNARD
A Meadow in the Park in Calais
Eine Wiese im Park von Calais, 1890

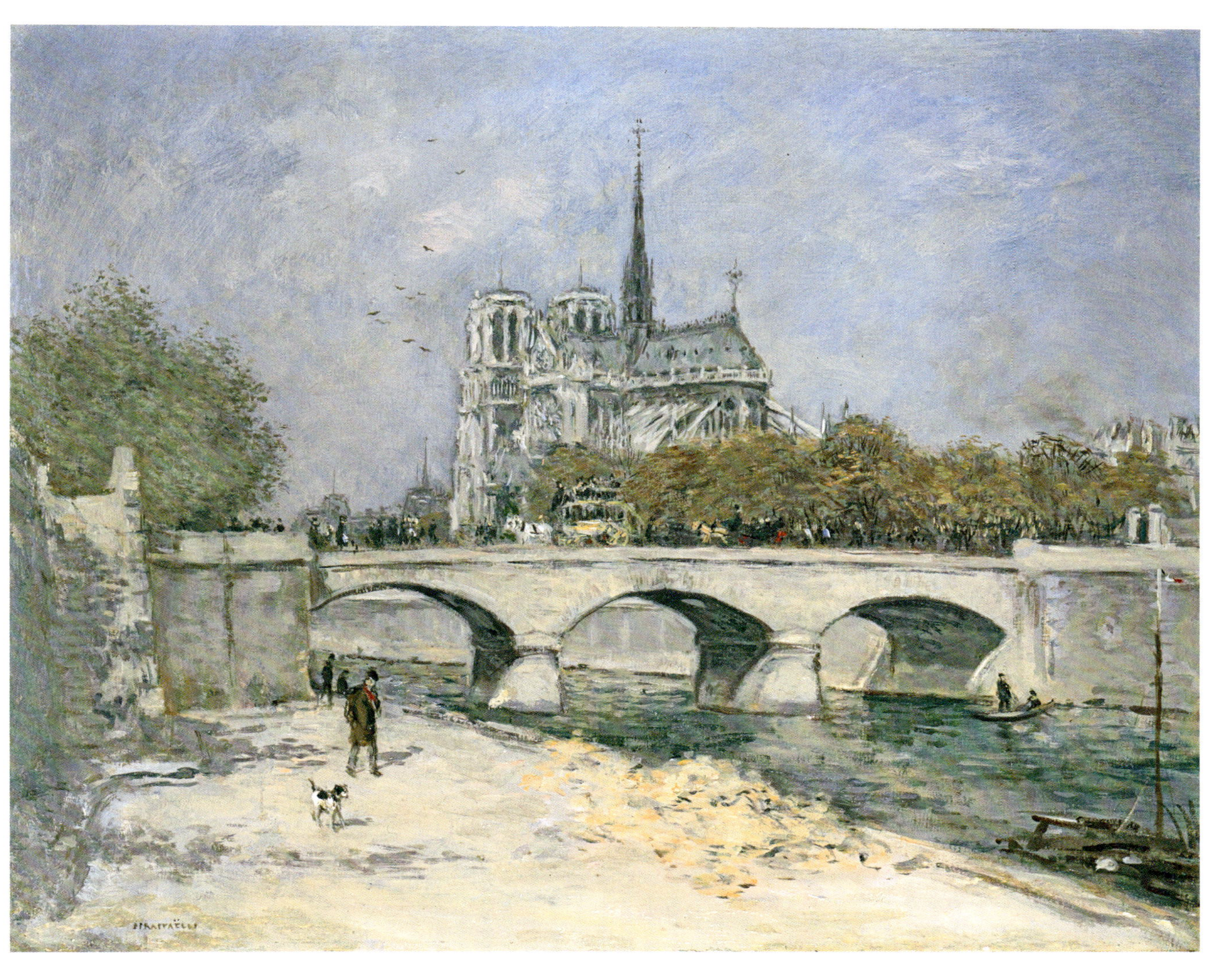

Jean-François Raffaelli
Notre-Dame de Paris
Notre-Dame, Paris, ca. 1890

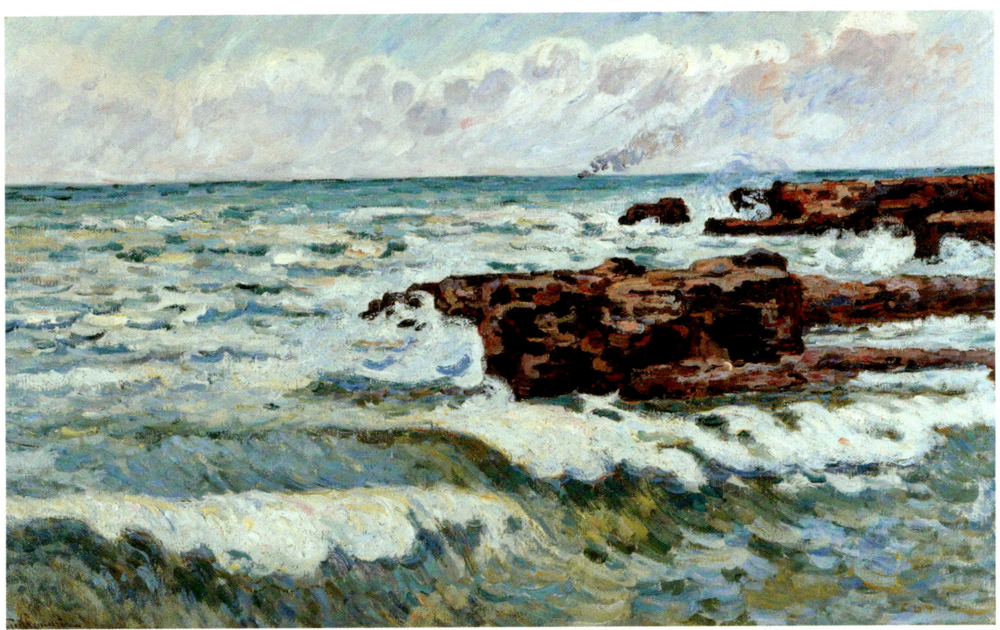

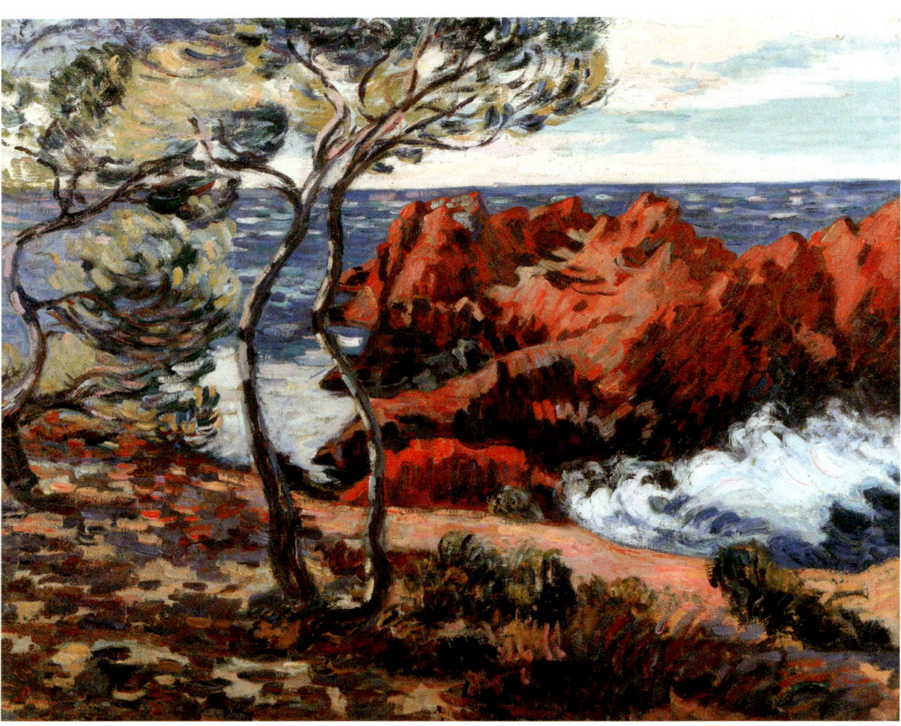

ARMAND GUILLAUMIN
The Sea at Saint-Palais
Meer bei Saint-Palais, 1892

ARMAND GUILLAUMIN
The Ile Besse at Agay, Morning Scene
Die Ile Besse bei Agay, am Morgen, 1901

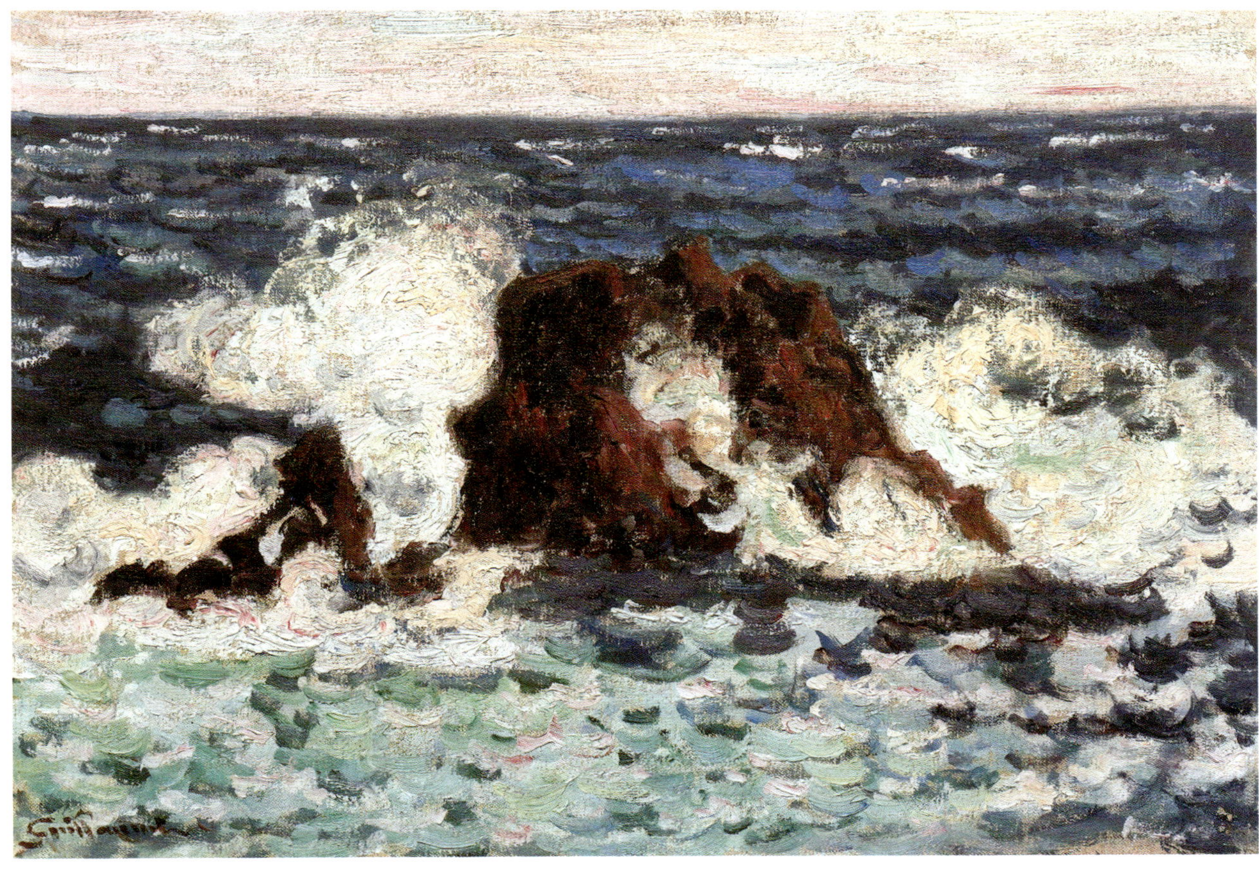

Armand Guillaumin
Rocks at the Spit of La Baumette
Felsklippe an der Landzunge von La Baumette, 1893

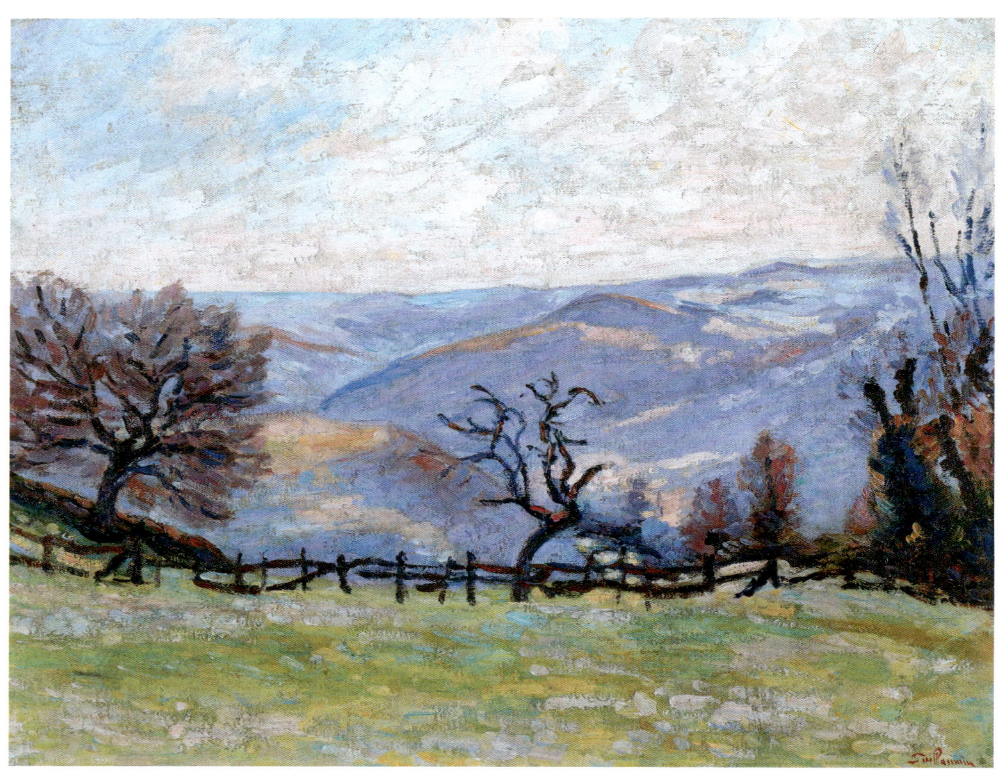

Armand Guillaumin
Mount Bariou, Crozant
Der Berg Bariou, Crozant, 1918

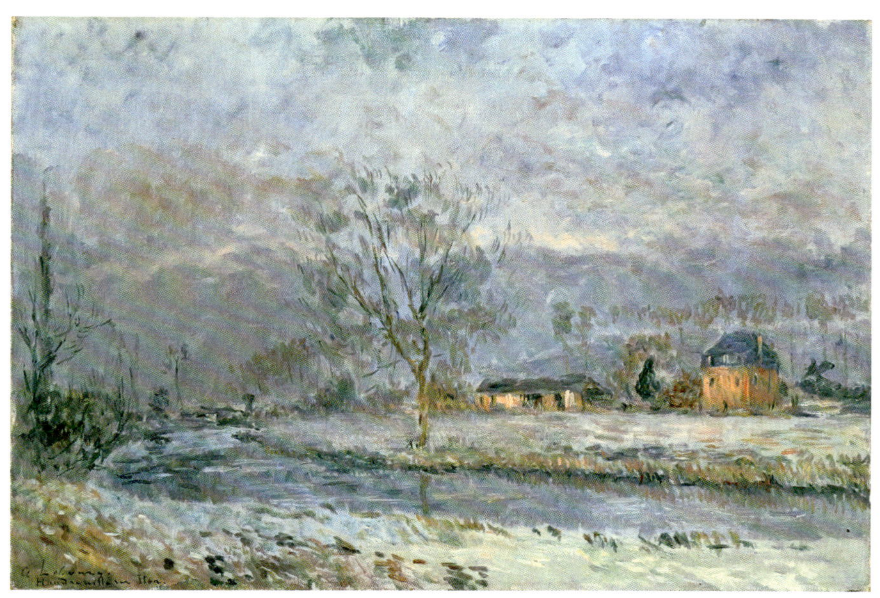

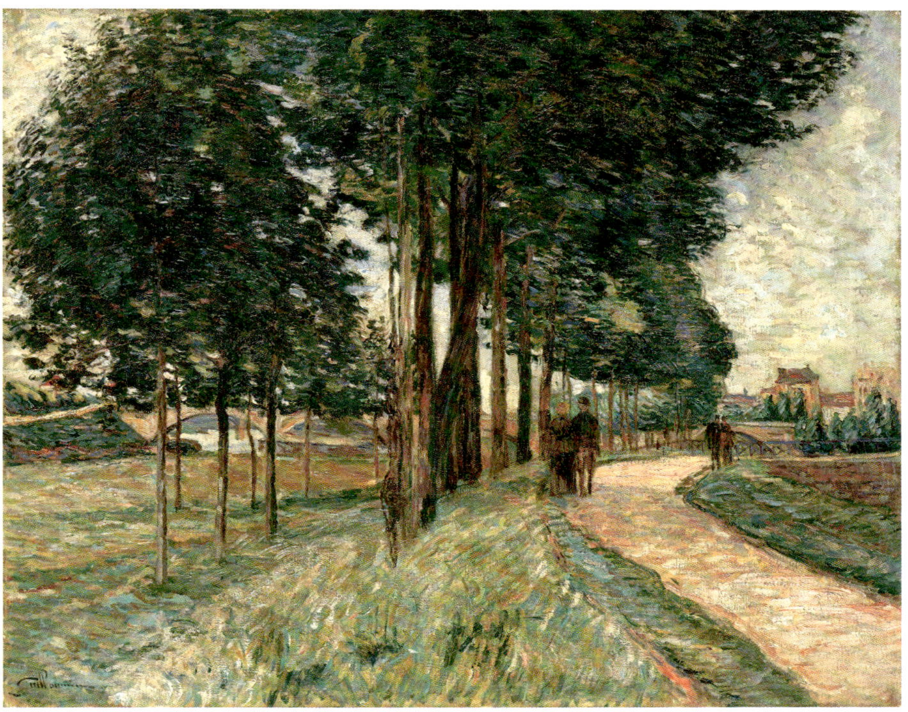

Albert Charles Lebourg
Hondouville-sur-Iton in the Fog
Hondouville-sur-Iton im Nebel, ca. 1890/92

Armand Guillaumin
On the Canal
Am Kanal, ca. 1888/89

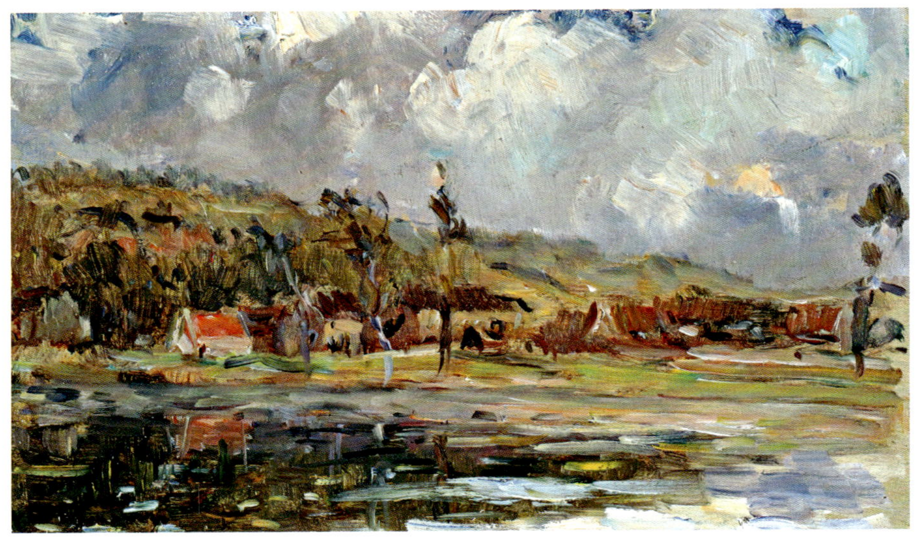

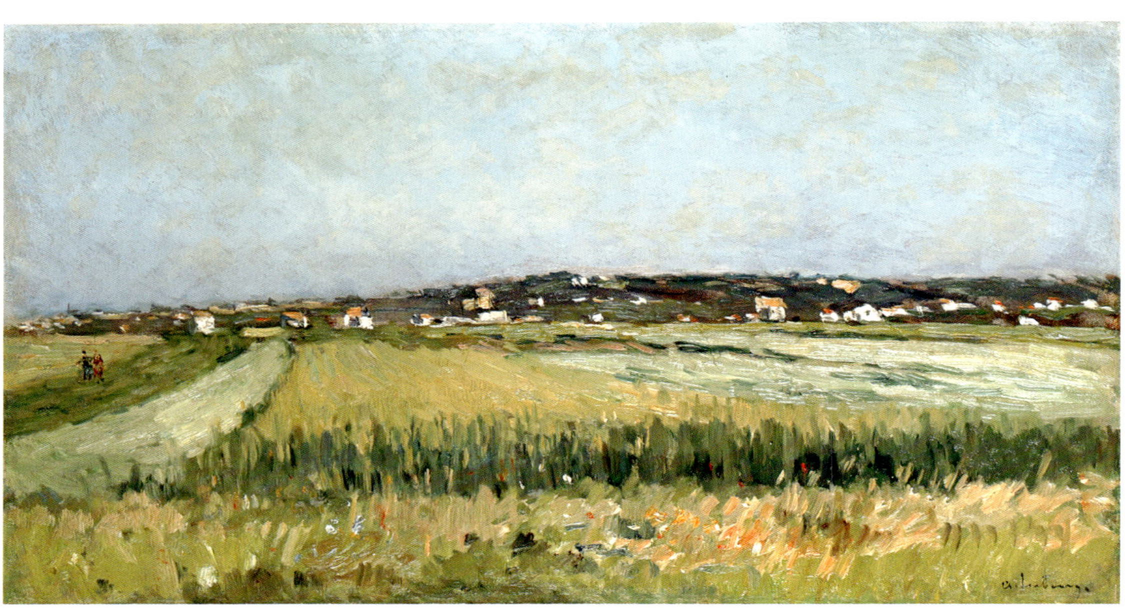

Albert Charles Lebourg
Pond
Weiher, ca. 1900

Albert Charles Lebourg
Environs of Clermont-Ferrand
Umgebung von Clermont-Ferrand, ca. 1900

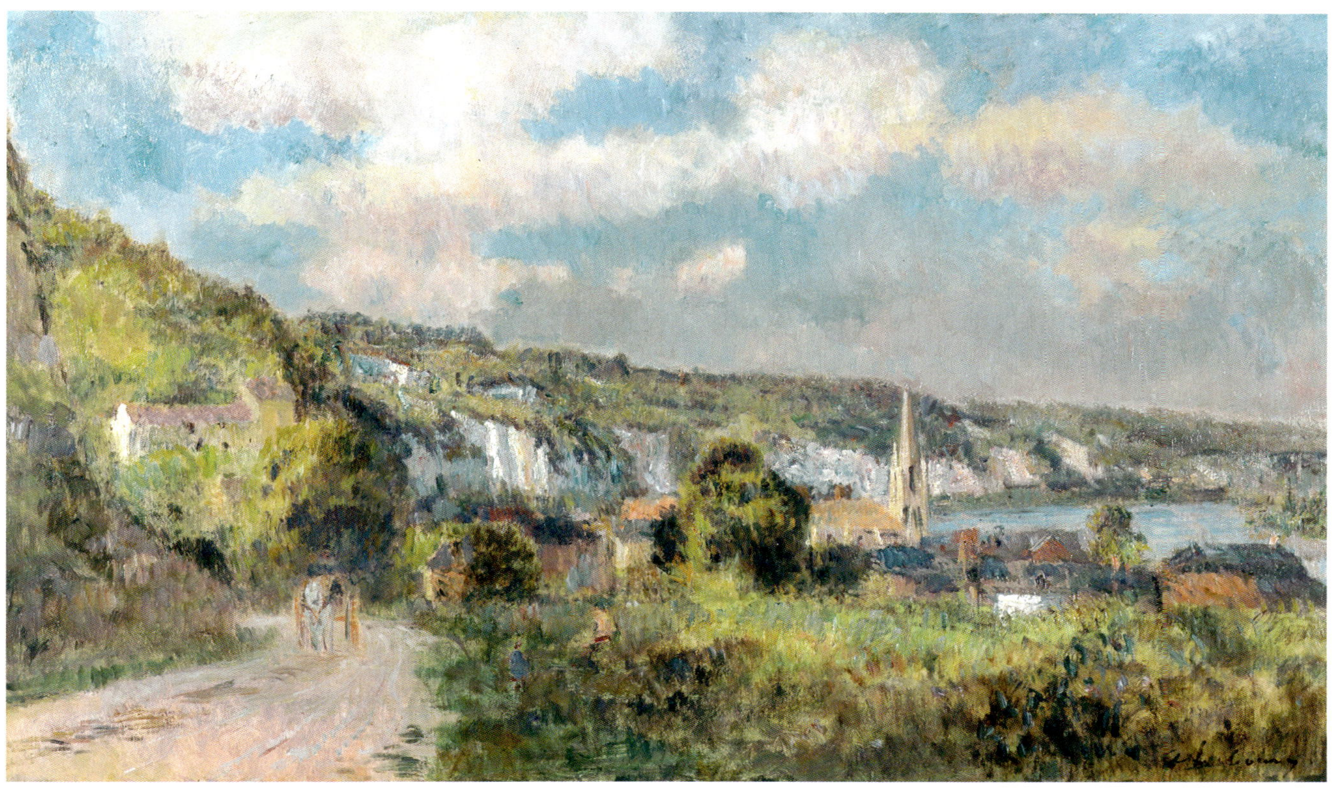

Albert Charles Lebourg
View of Bouille
Ansicht von Bouille, ca. 1900

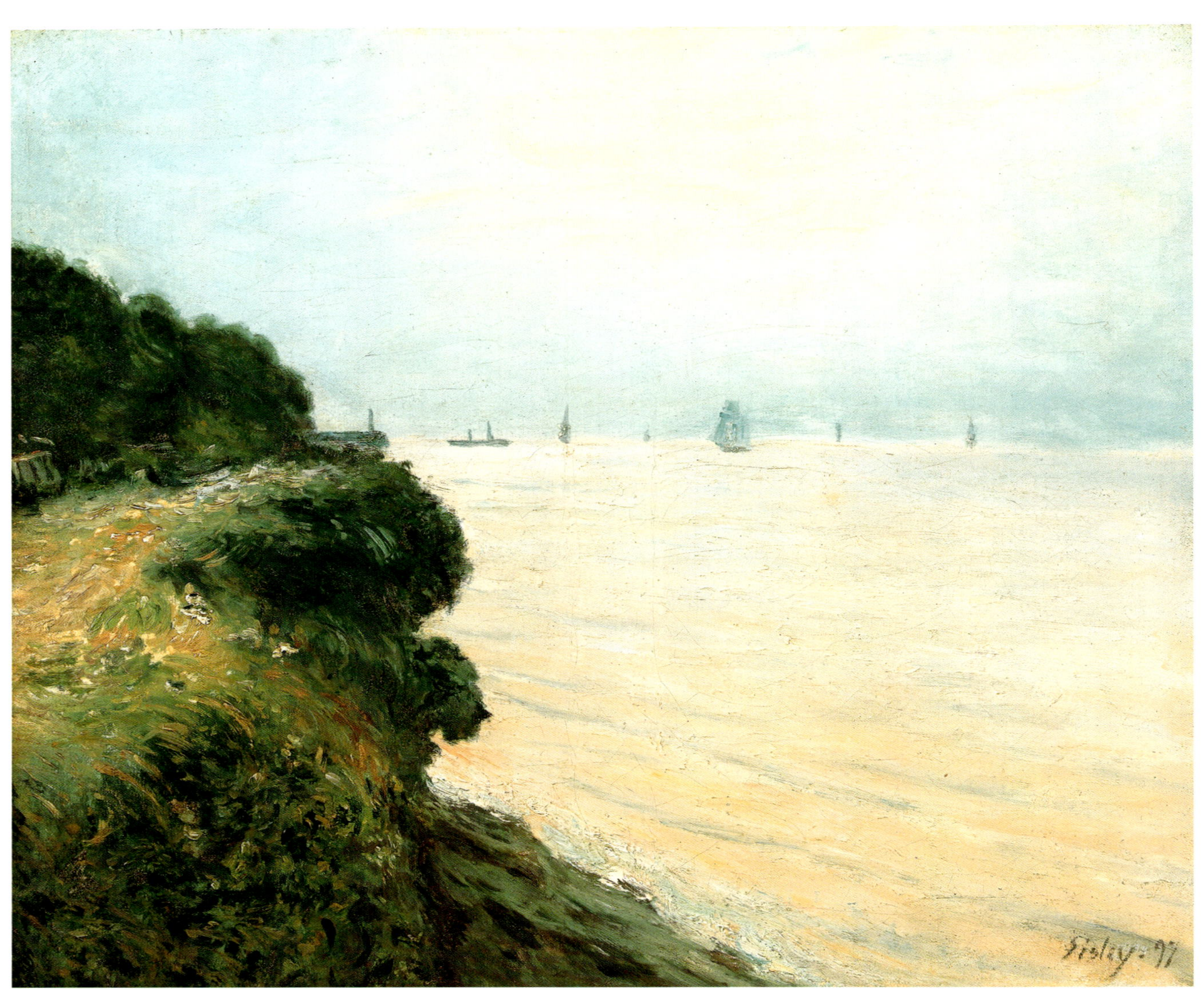

Alfred Sisley
Langland Bay
Die Bucht von Langland, 1897

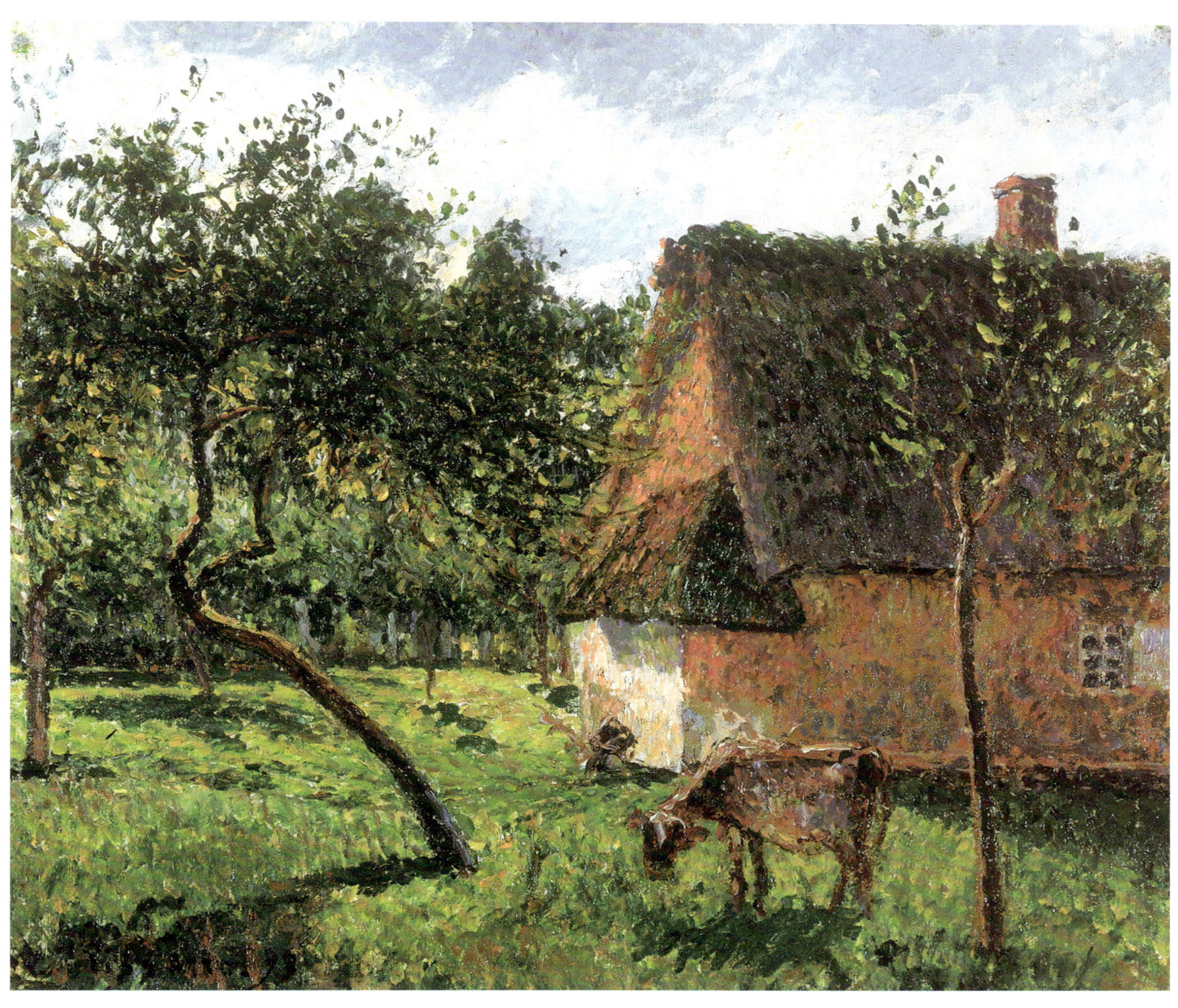

Camille Pissarro
Orchard in Varengeville
Obstgarten in Varengeville, 1899

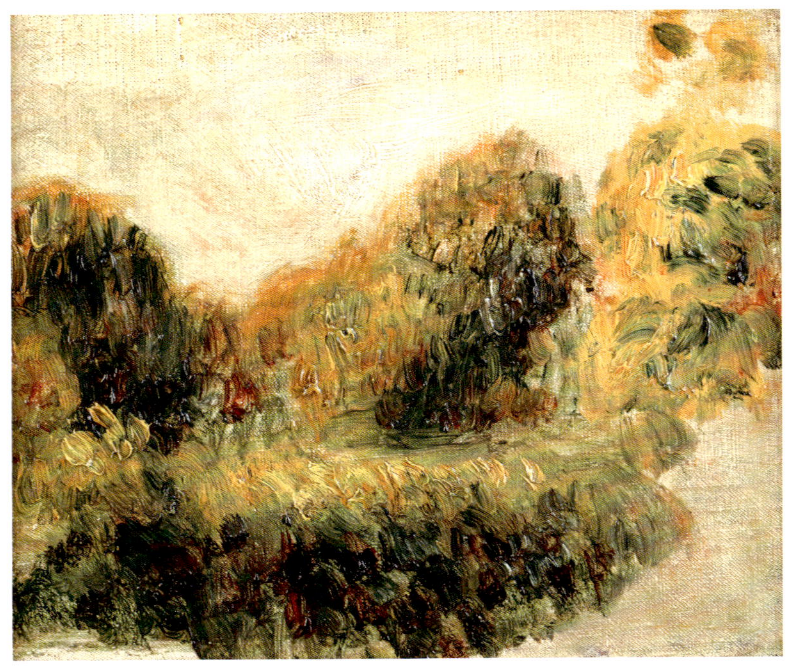

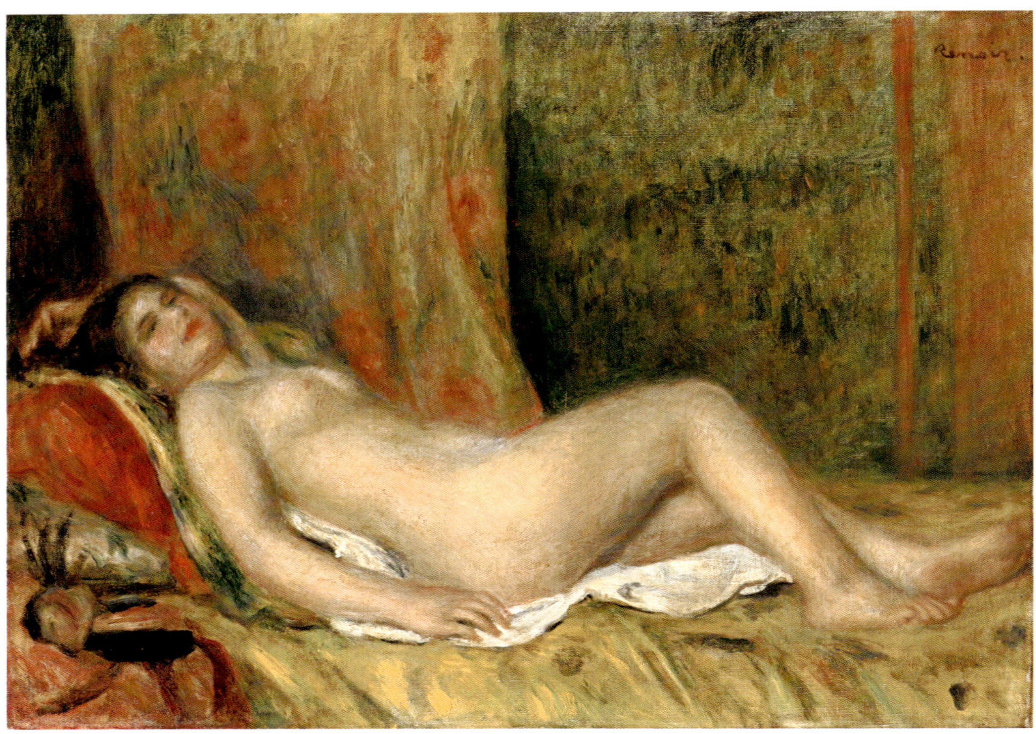

Auguste Renoir
Landscape Study, n.d.
Landschaftsstudie, o. J.

Auguste Renoir
Resting Nude
Ruhender Akt, 1890/95

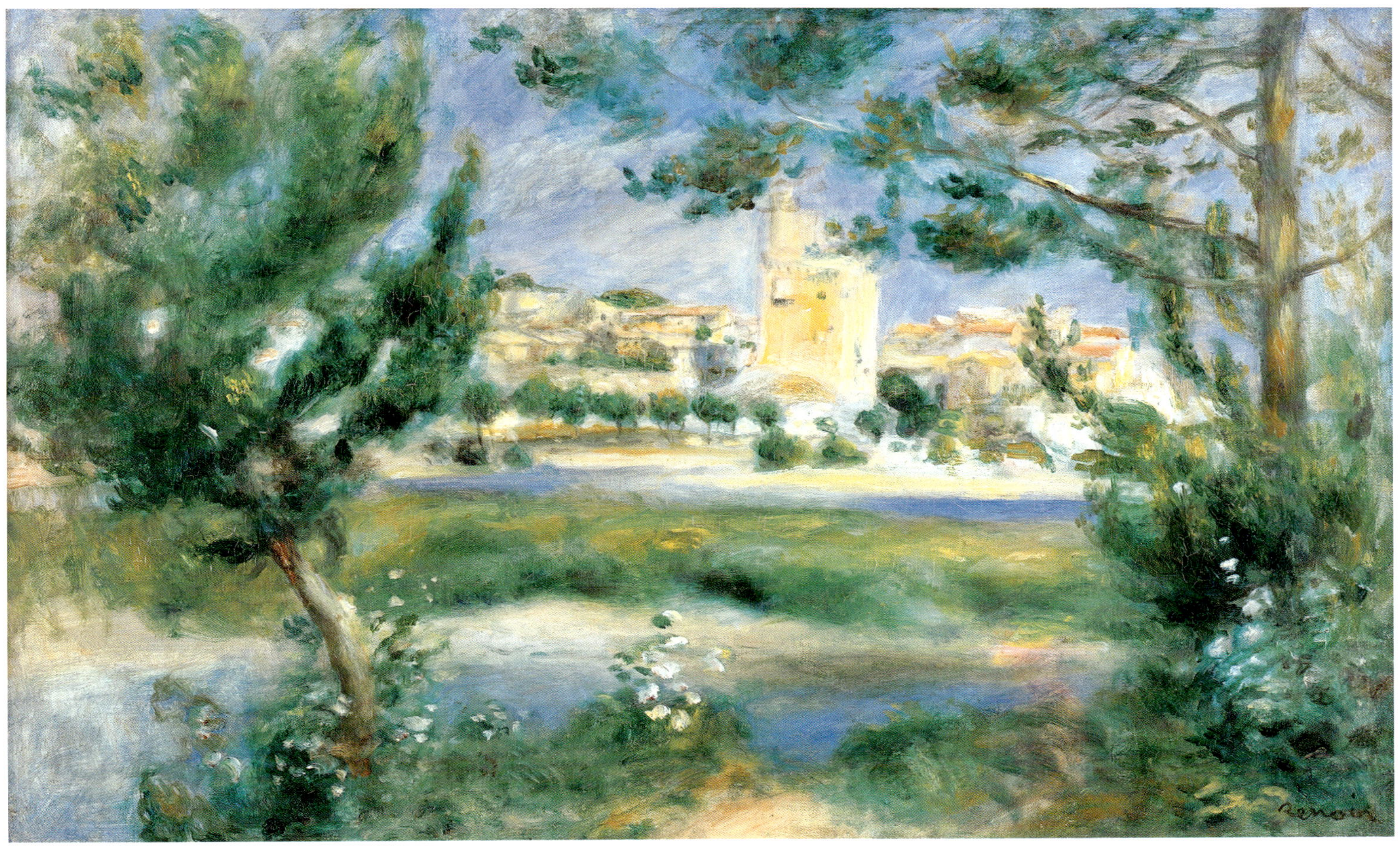

Auguste Renoir
Villeneuve-les-Avignon, 1901

Auguste Renoir
Jean Renoir Sewing
Jean Renoir nähend, 1900

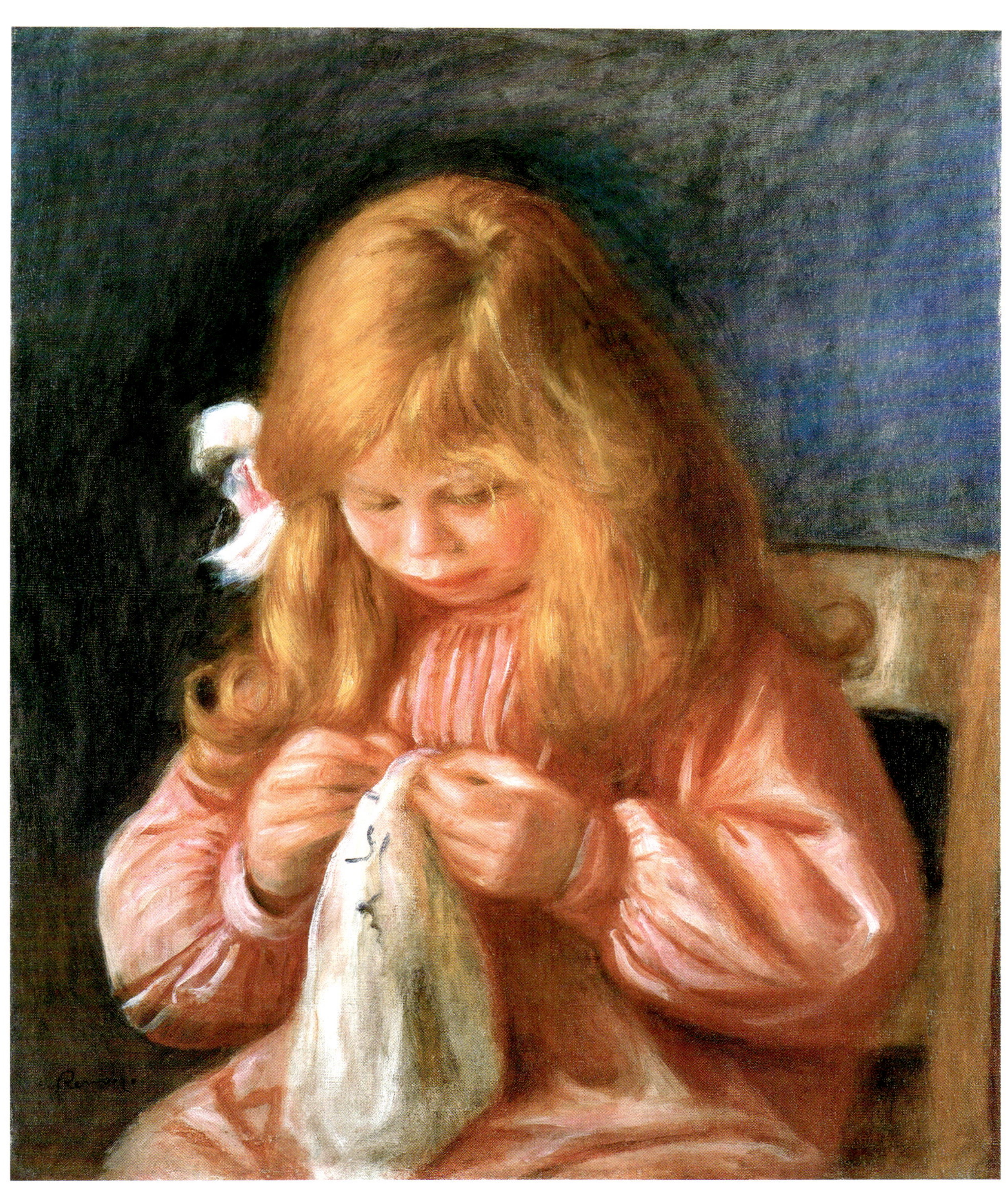

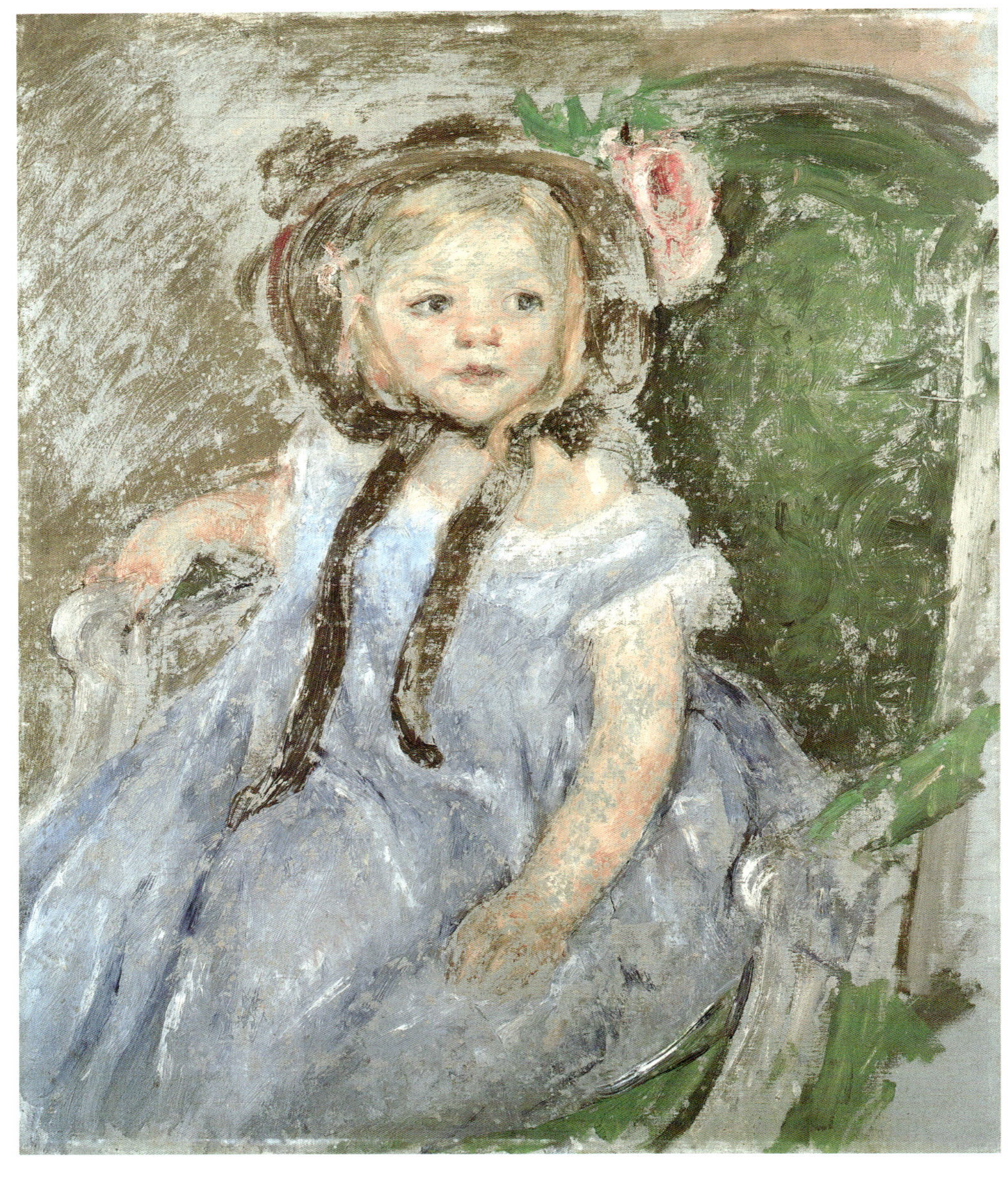

Mary Cassatt
Sara in a Dark Bonnet with Right Hand on Arm of Chair
Sara mit einem dunklen Häubchen, 1901

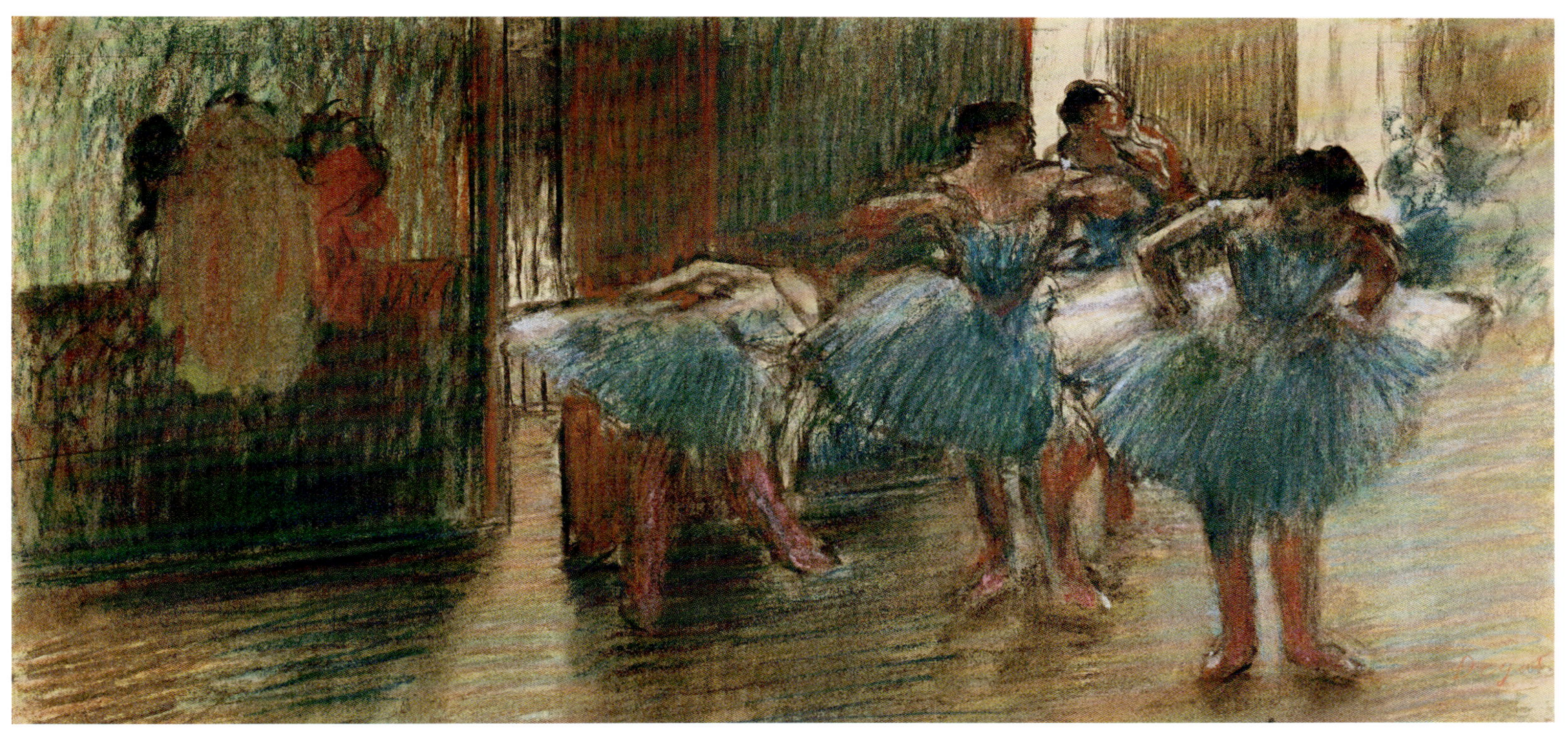

Edgar Degas
Dancers
Tänzerinnen, ca. 1905

Claude Monet
Water Lilies
Seerosen, ca. 1915/17

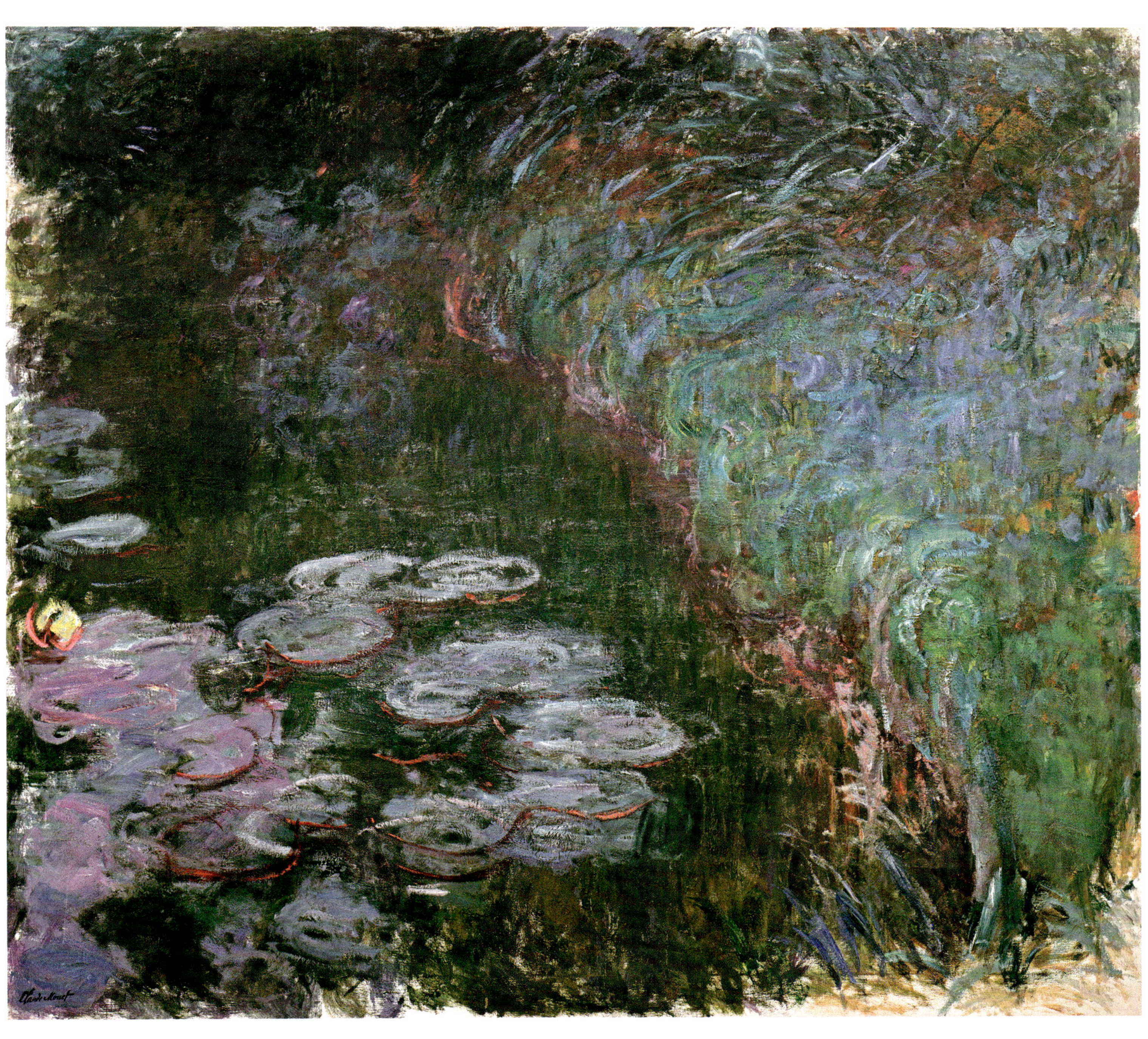

Neo-Impressionism

Der Neoimpressionismus

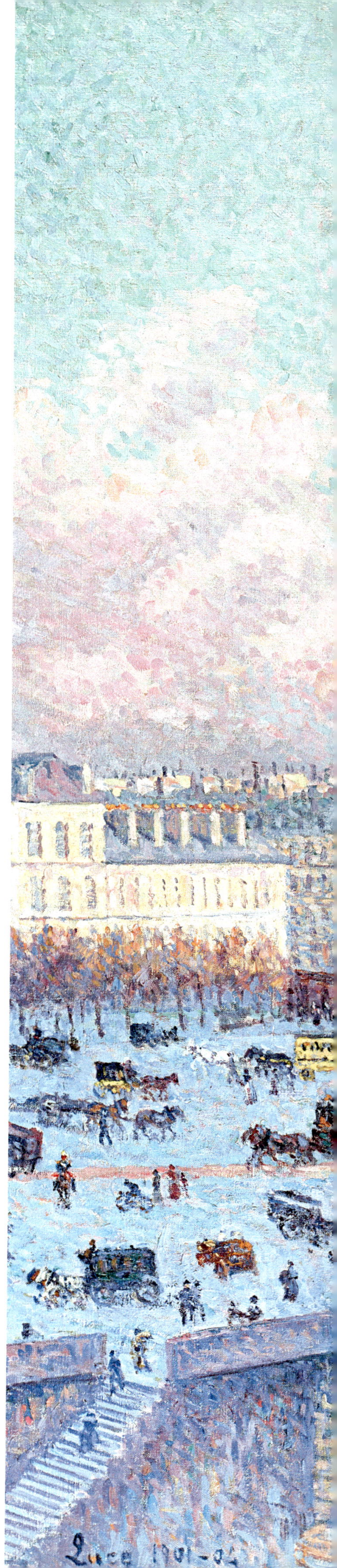

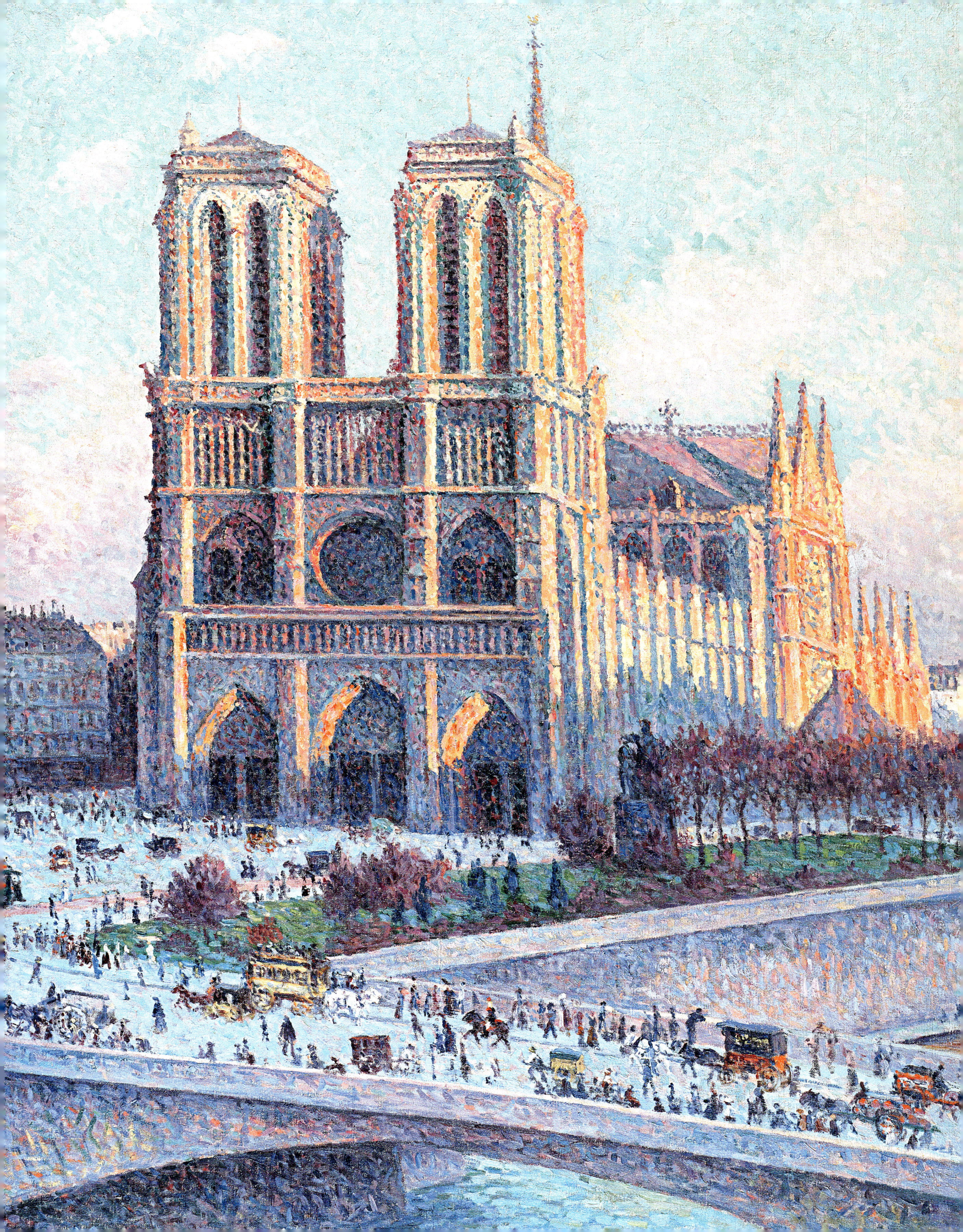

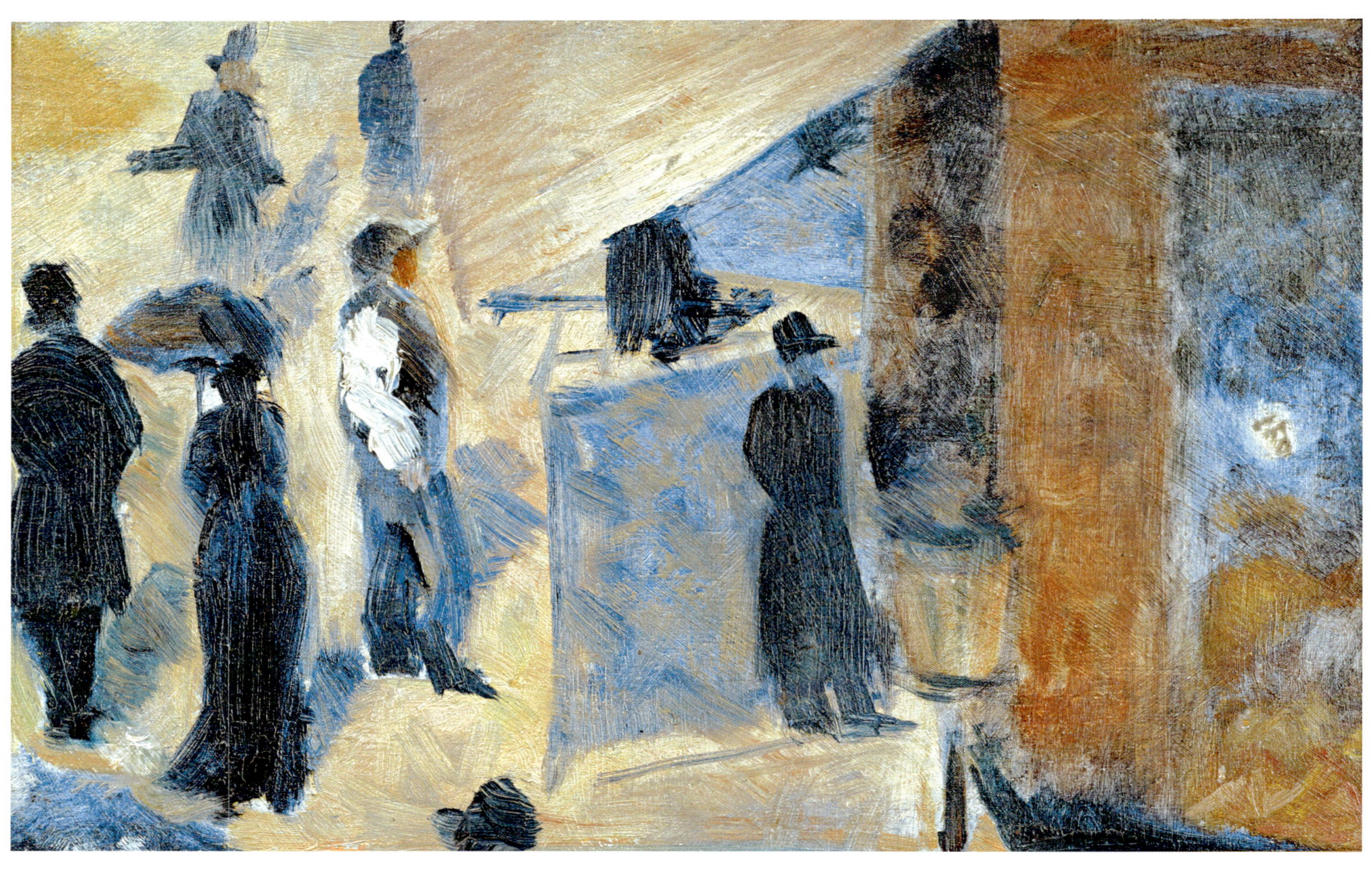

Georges Seurat
Street Scene
Straßenszene, ca. 1883

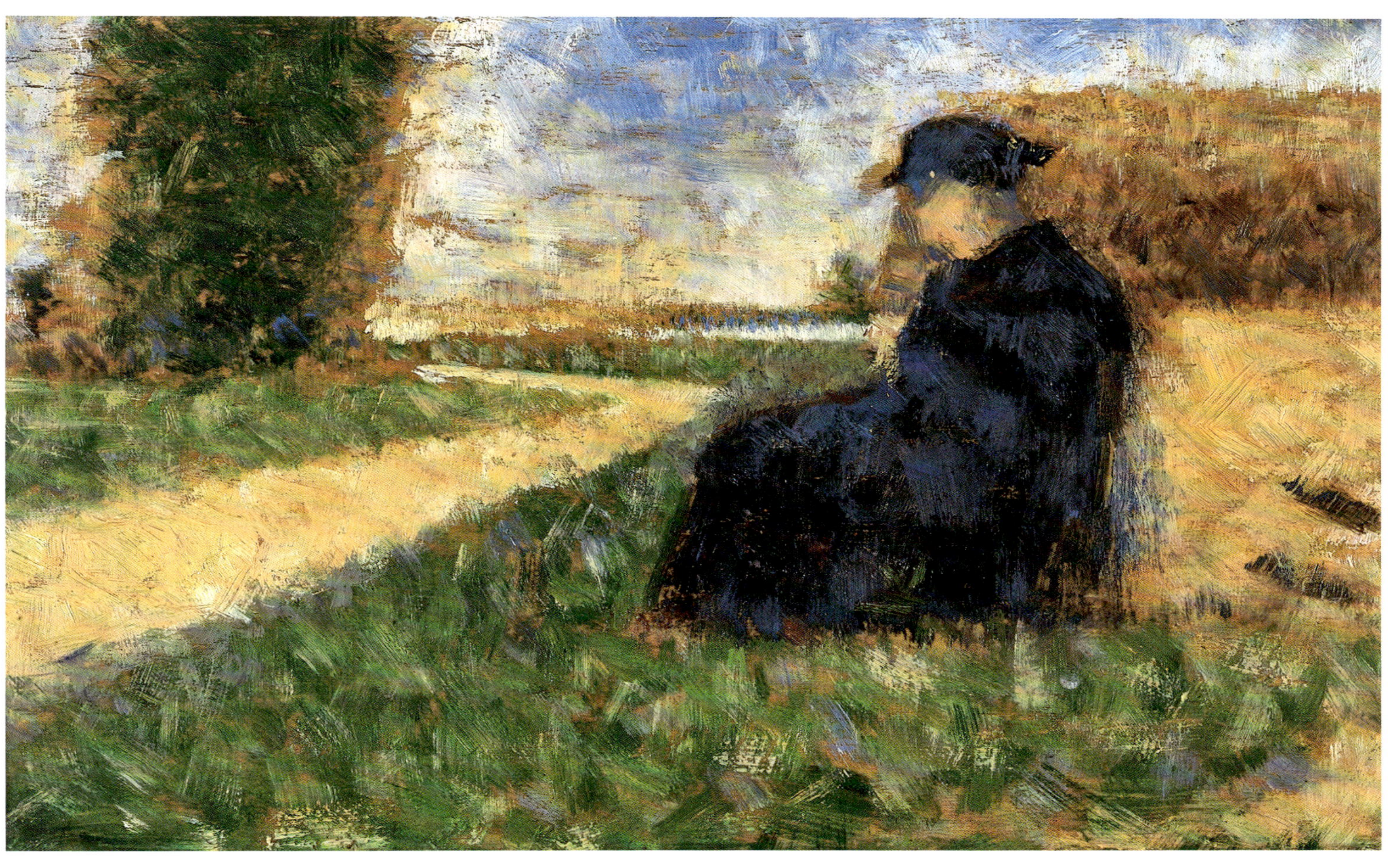

Georges Seurat
Figure in a Landscape at Barbizon
Gestalt in einer Landschaft bei Barbizon, ca. 1882

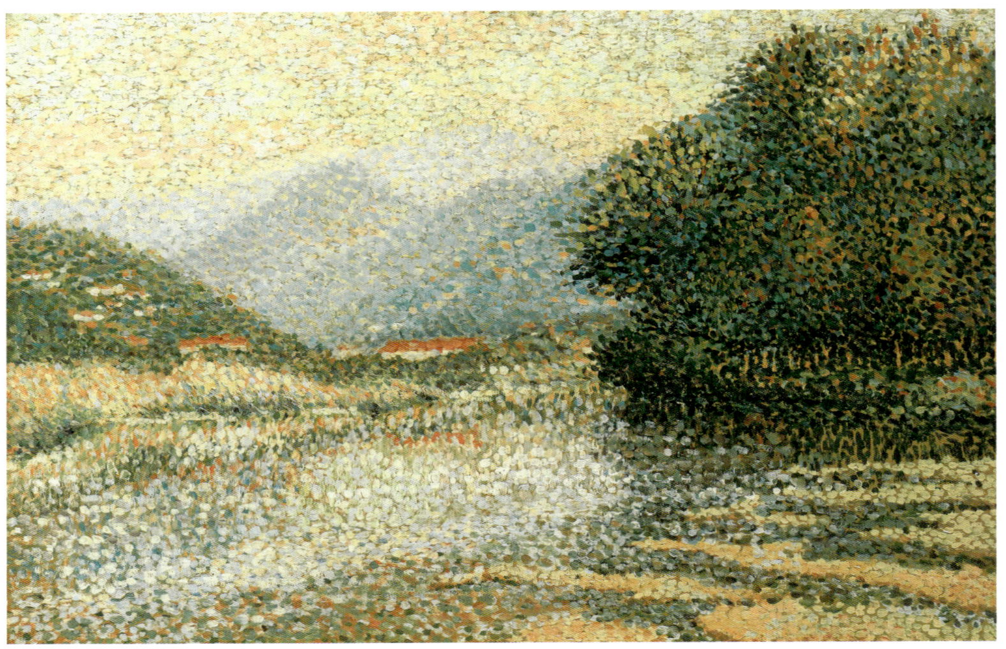

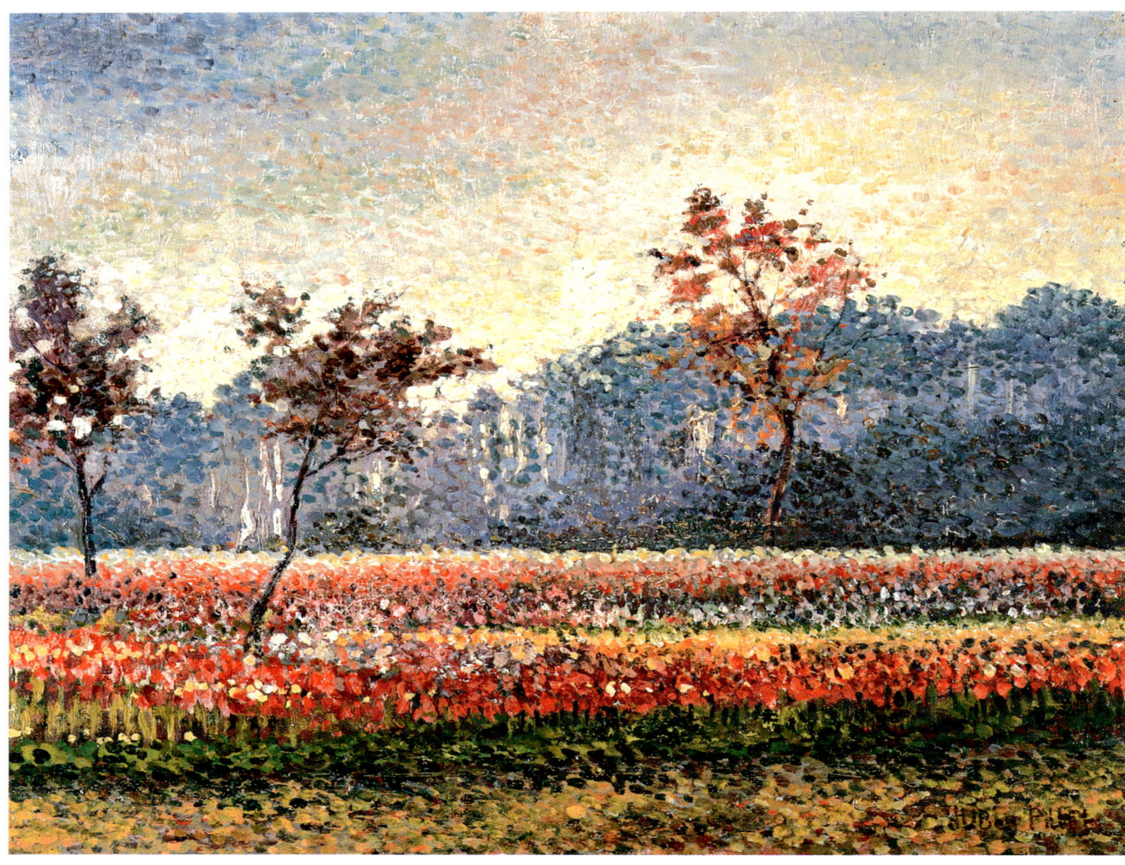

ALBERT DUBOIS-PILLET
Landscape, n.d.
Landschaft, o. J.

ALBERT DUBOIS-PILLET
Fields, Ile-de-France
Felder in der Ile-de-France, ca. 1889/90

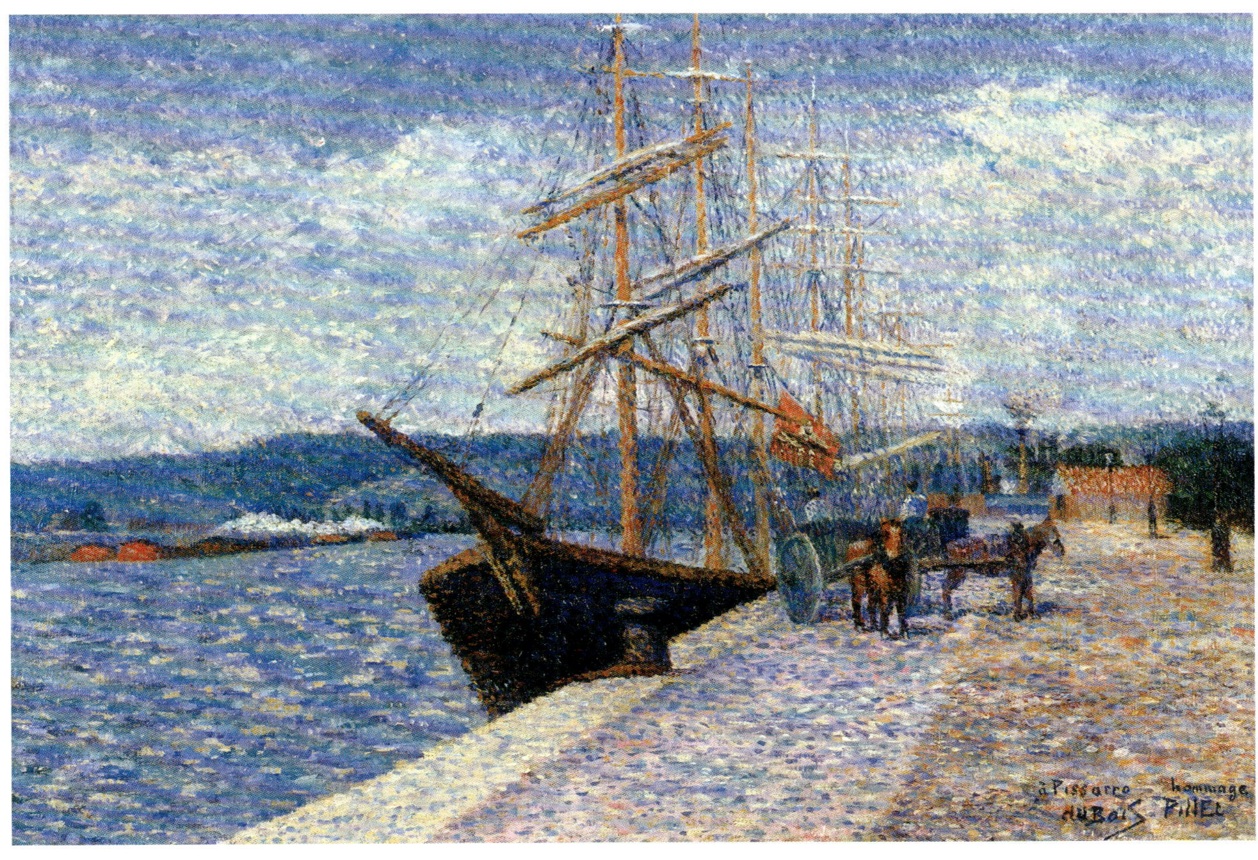

Albert Dubois-Pillet
Quai de Lesseps – Rouen, ca. 1887

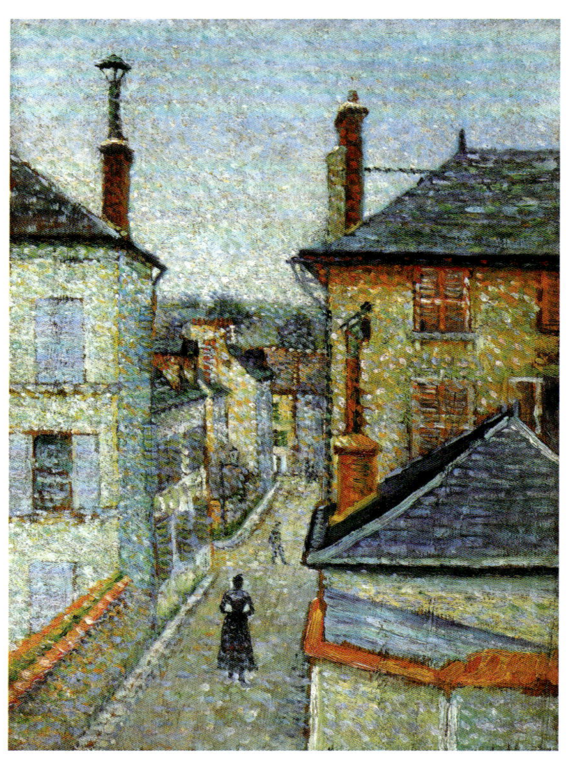

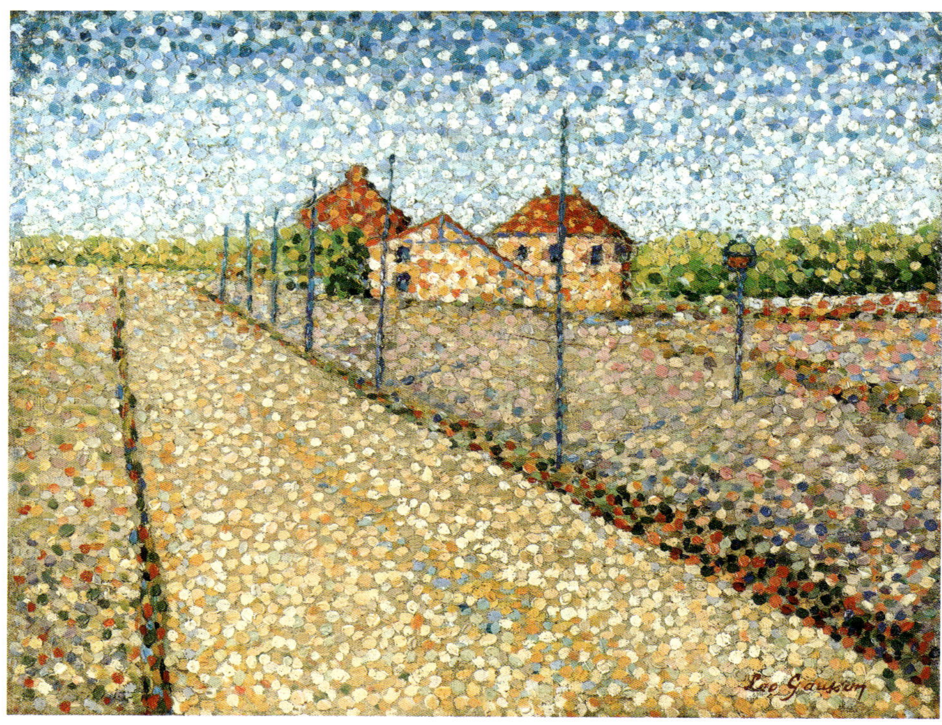

Leo Gausson
The Rue des Etuves in Lagny-sur-Marne (View of Lagny-sur-Marne) or *Woman on the Street*
Die Rue des Etuves in Lagny-sur-Marne (Ansicht von Lagny-sur-Marne) oder *Frau auf der Straße*, ca. 1885

Leo Gausson
Landscape near Lagny
Landschaft in der Umgebung von Lagny, ca. 1887/89

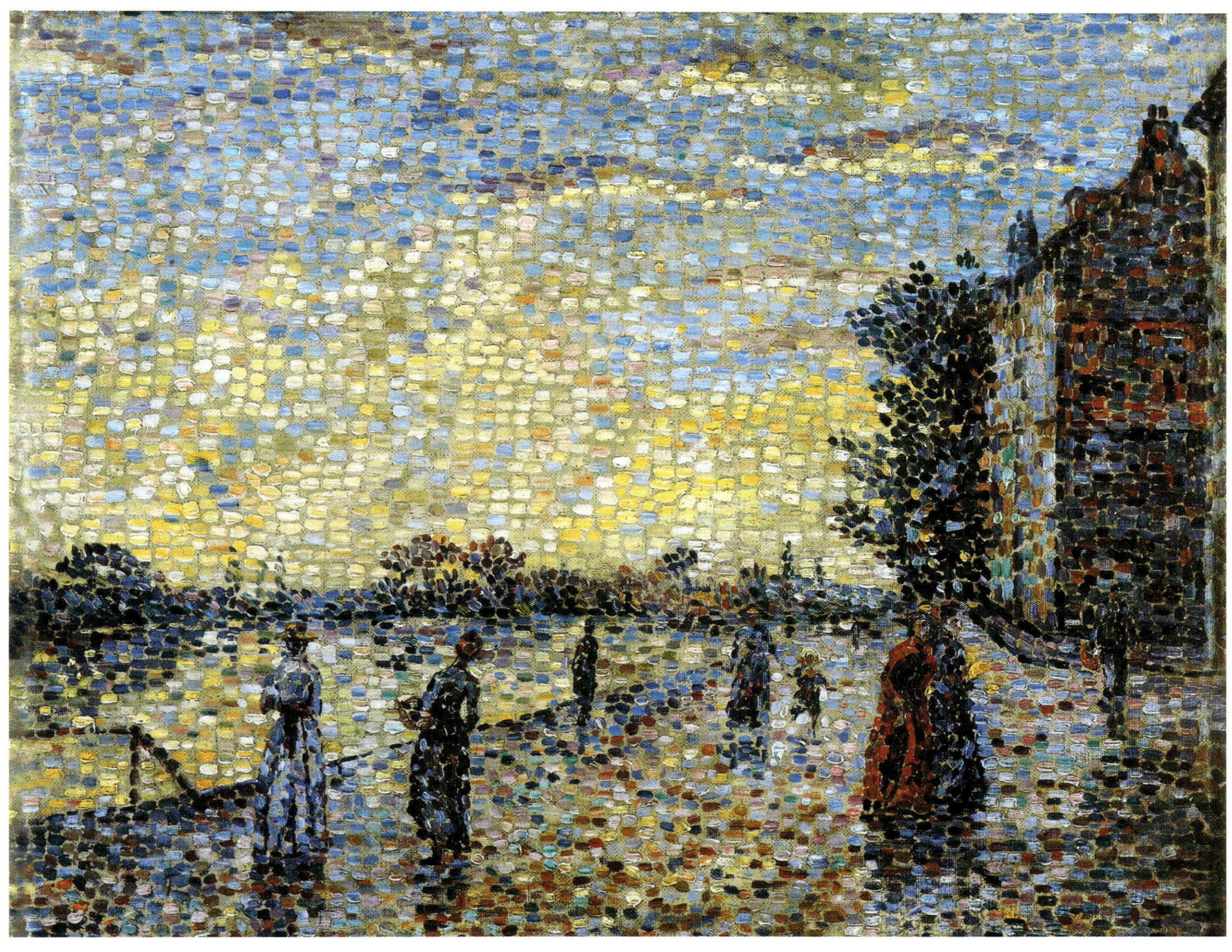

Achille Lauge
Promenade on the Riverside
Promenade am Flussufer, 1888

Alfred William (genannt known as Willy) Finch
Village near the North Sea Coast
Dorf nahe der Nordseeküste, ca. 1889

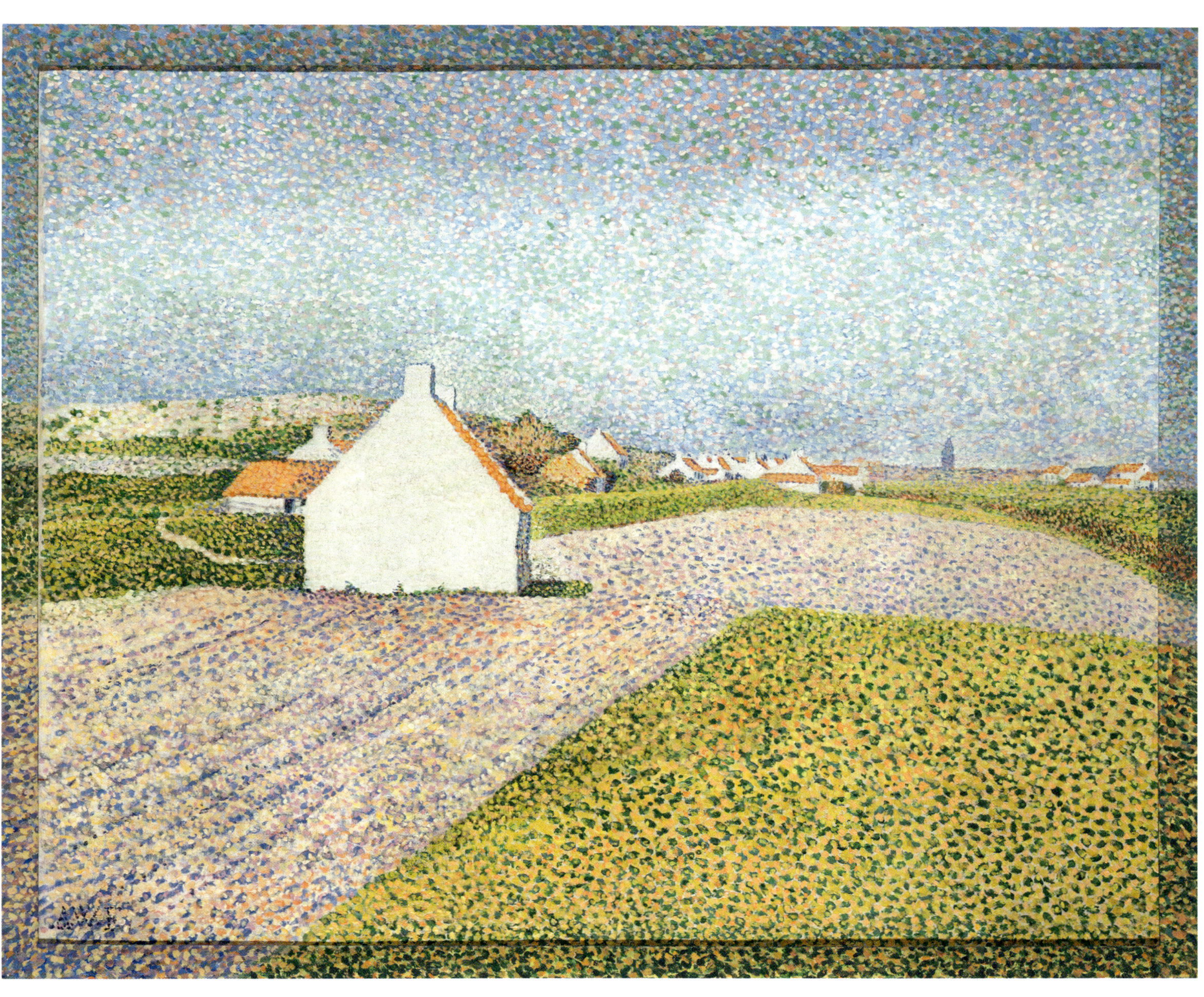

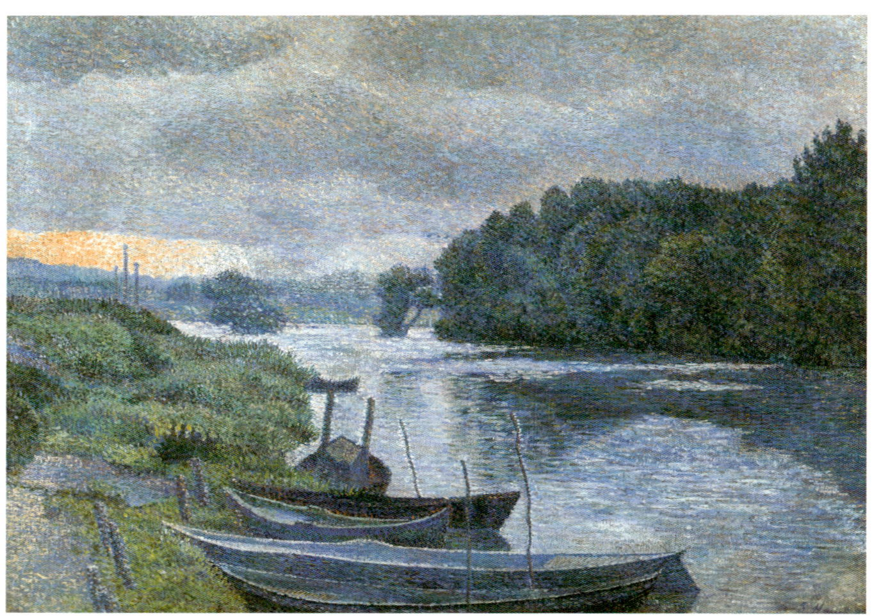

Louis Hayet
Riverside
Am Flussufer, 1888

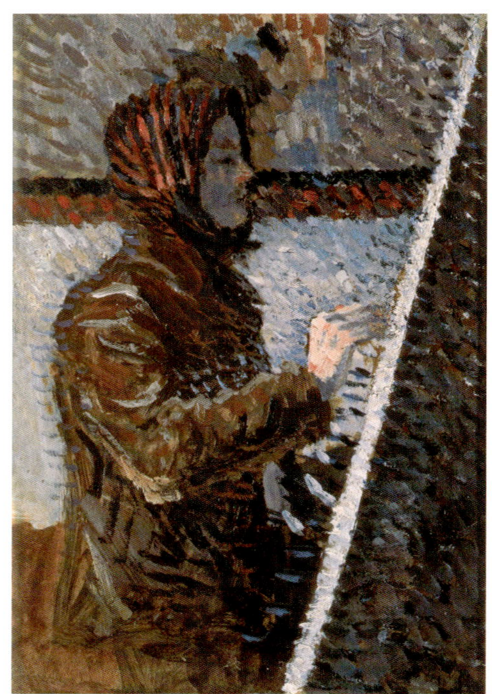

Louis Hayet
Young Woman Drawing at her Easel
Junge Frau beim Zeichnen vor ihrer Staffelei,
ca. 1892/94

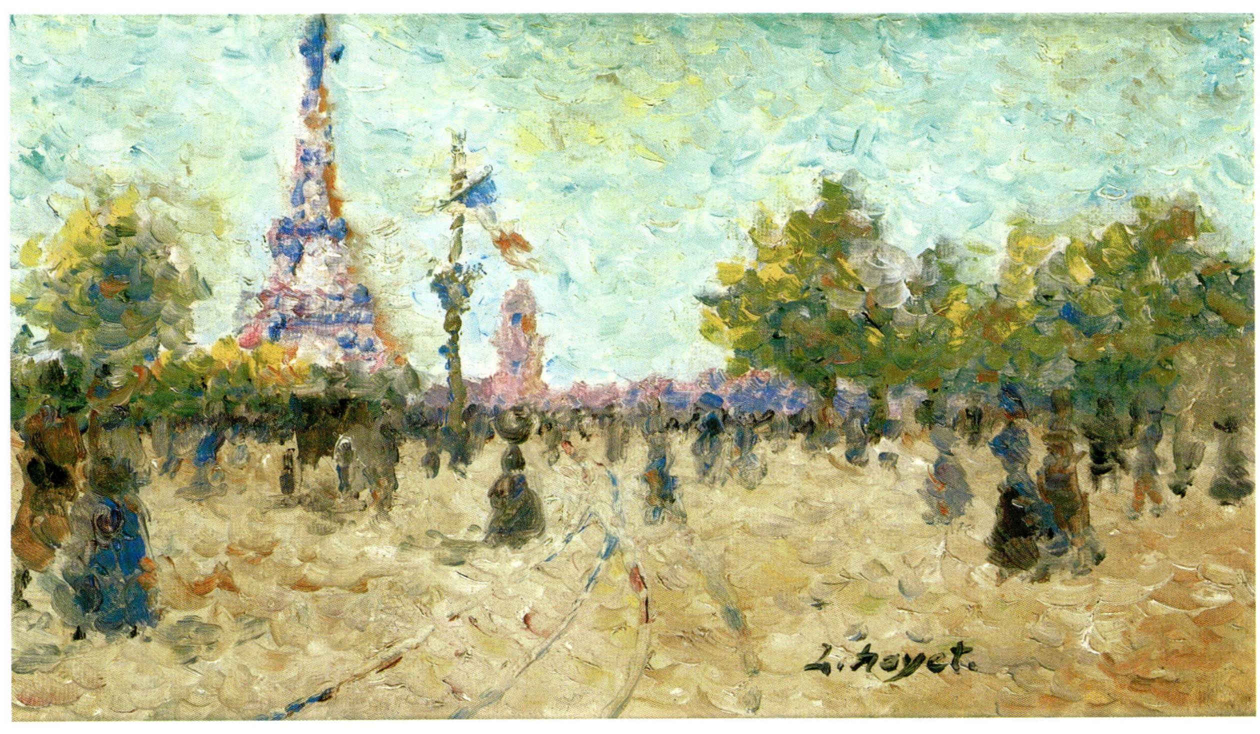

Louis Hayet
Paris, the Eiffel Tower
Paris, der Eiffelturm, ca. 1889/90

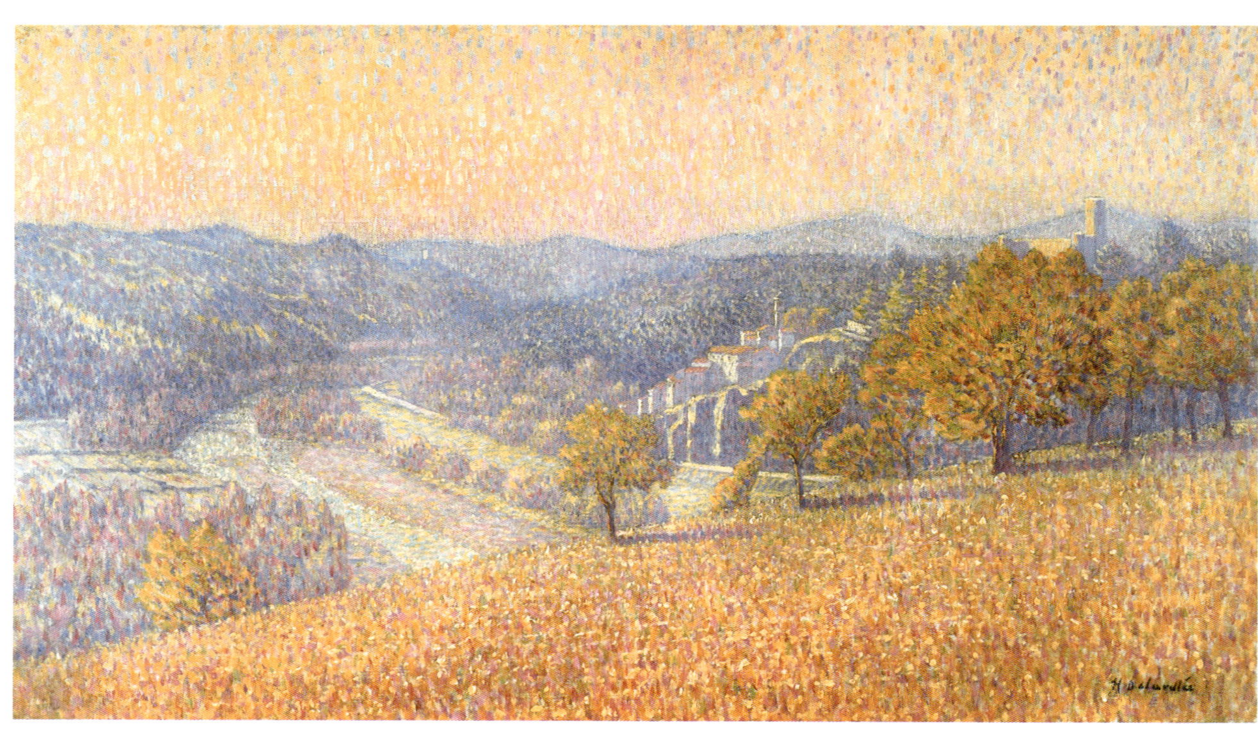

Henri Delavallee
Autumn, Village in the Valley
Herbst, Dorf im Tal, ca. 1887

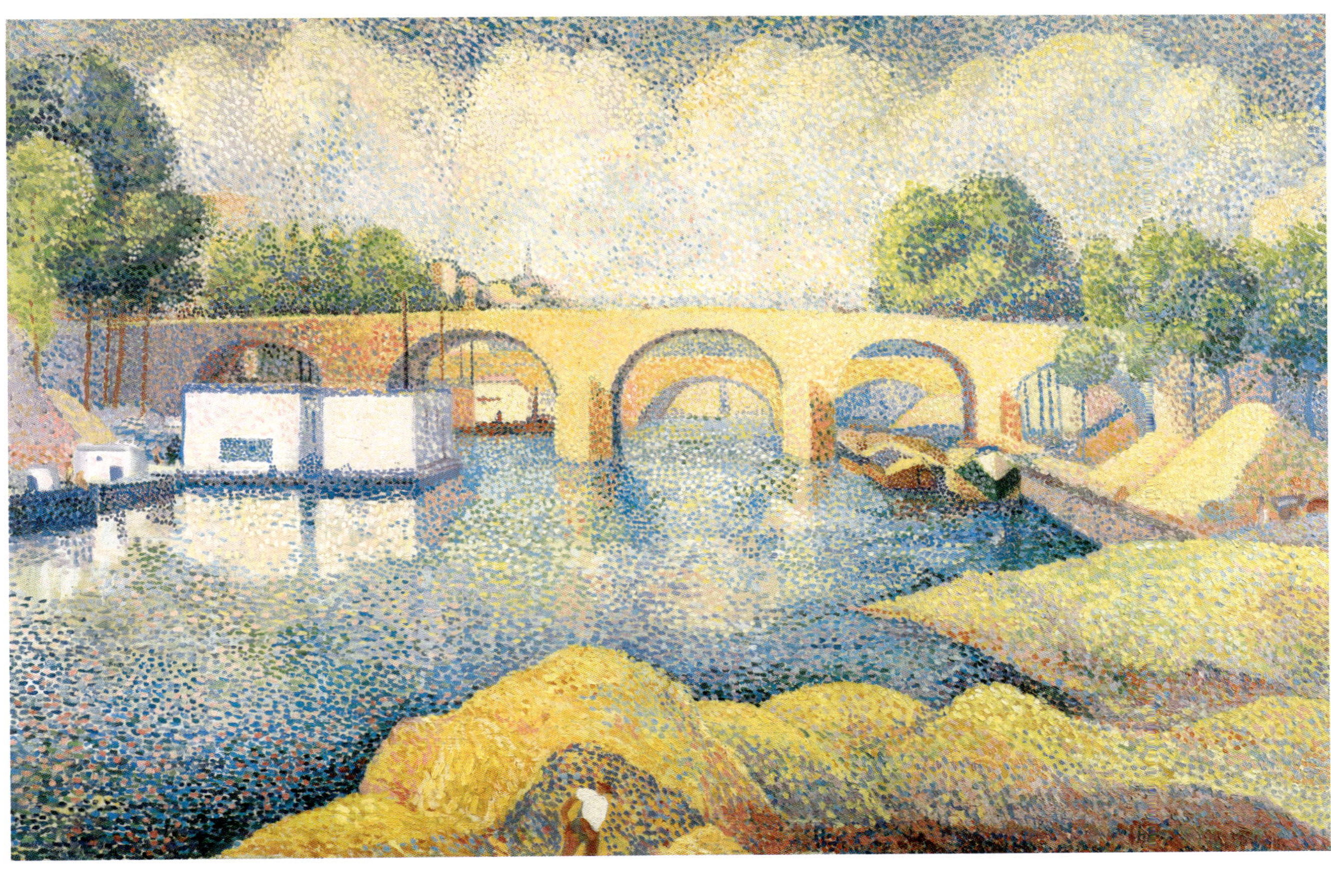

Hippolyte Petitjean
The Bridge
Die Brücke, ca. 1890

Georges Lemmen
On the Dyke – The Beach at Ostend
Auf dem Deich – Der Strand von Ostende, 1890–92

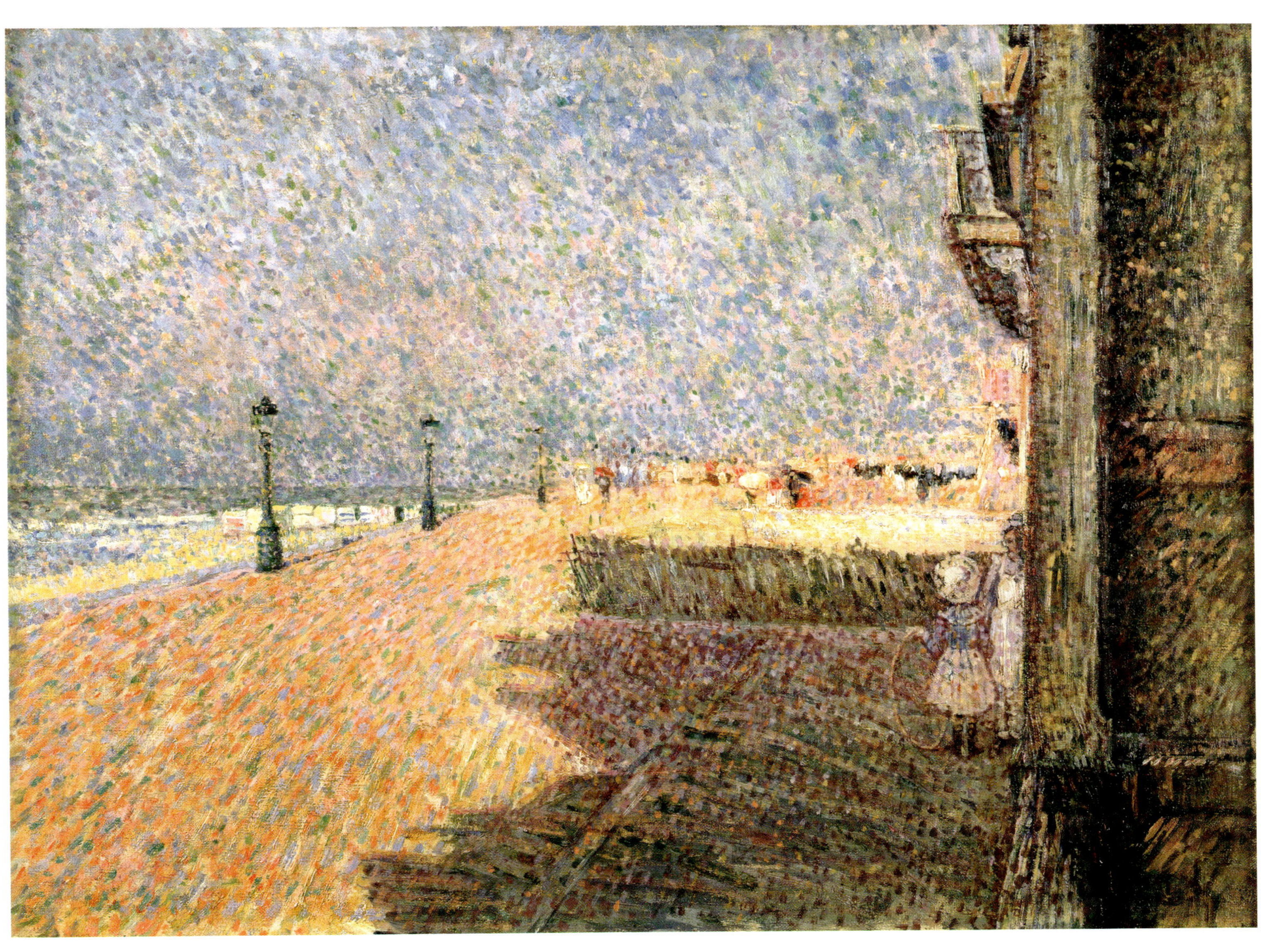

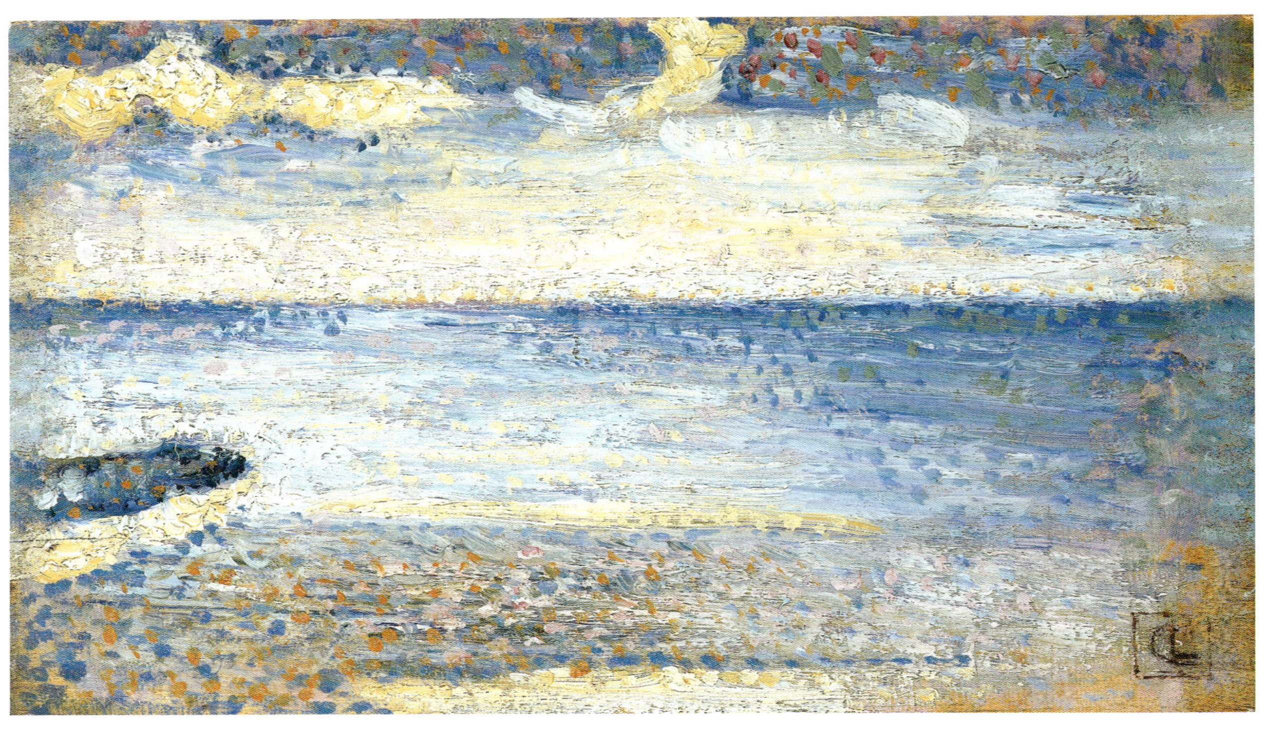

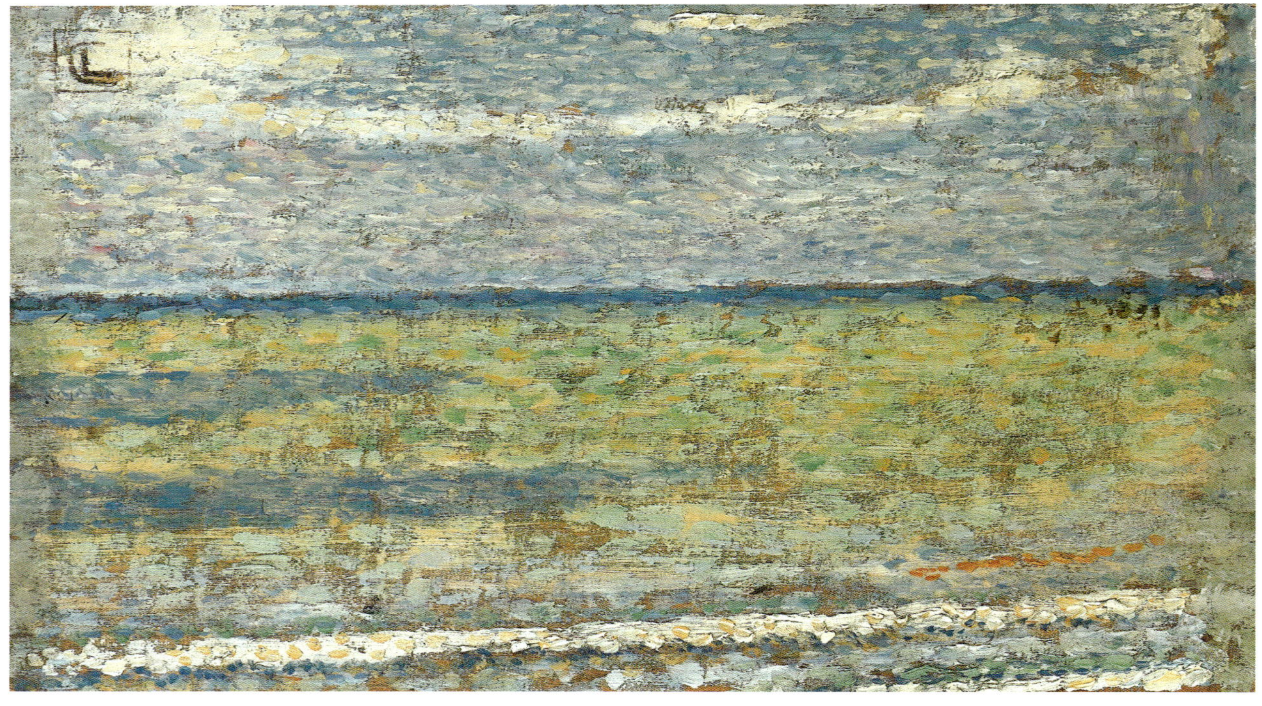

Georges Lemmen
The Coast at Heyst
Die Küste von Heyst, 1891

Georges Lemmen
The Coast at Heyst, Low Tide
Die Küste von Heyst bei fallendem Wasser, 1891

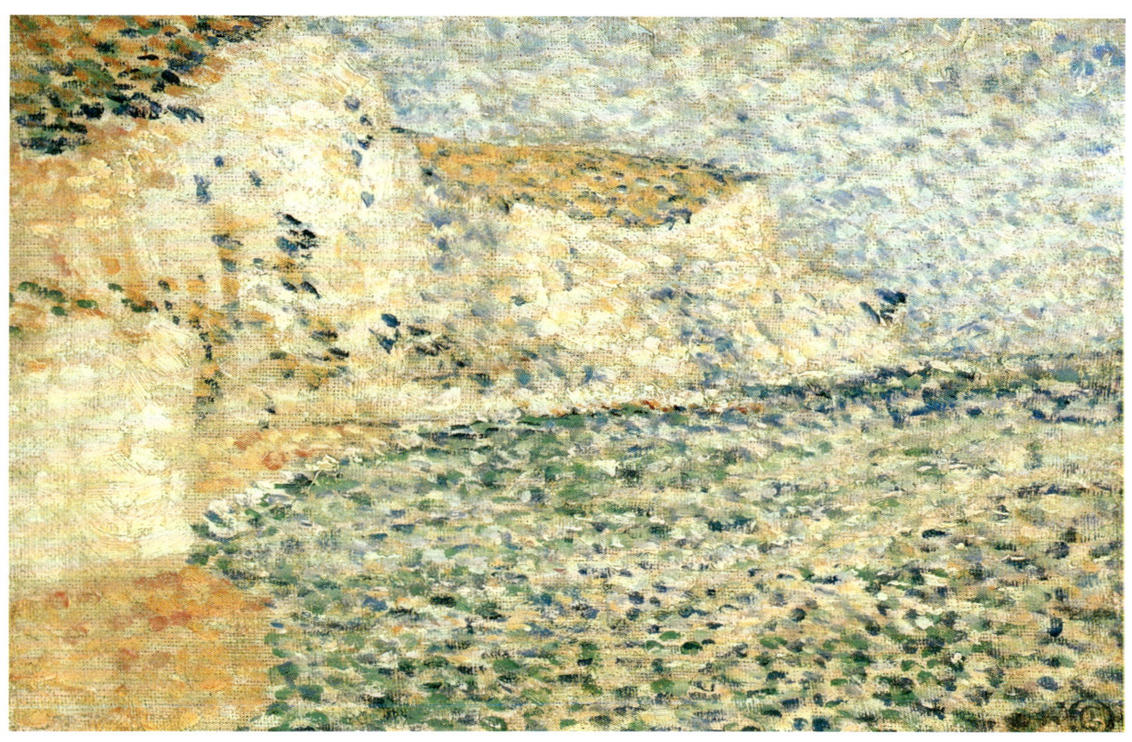

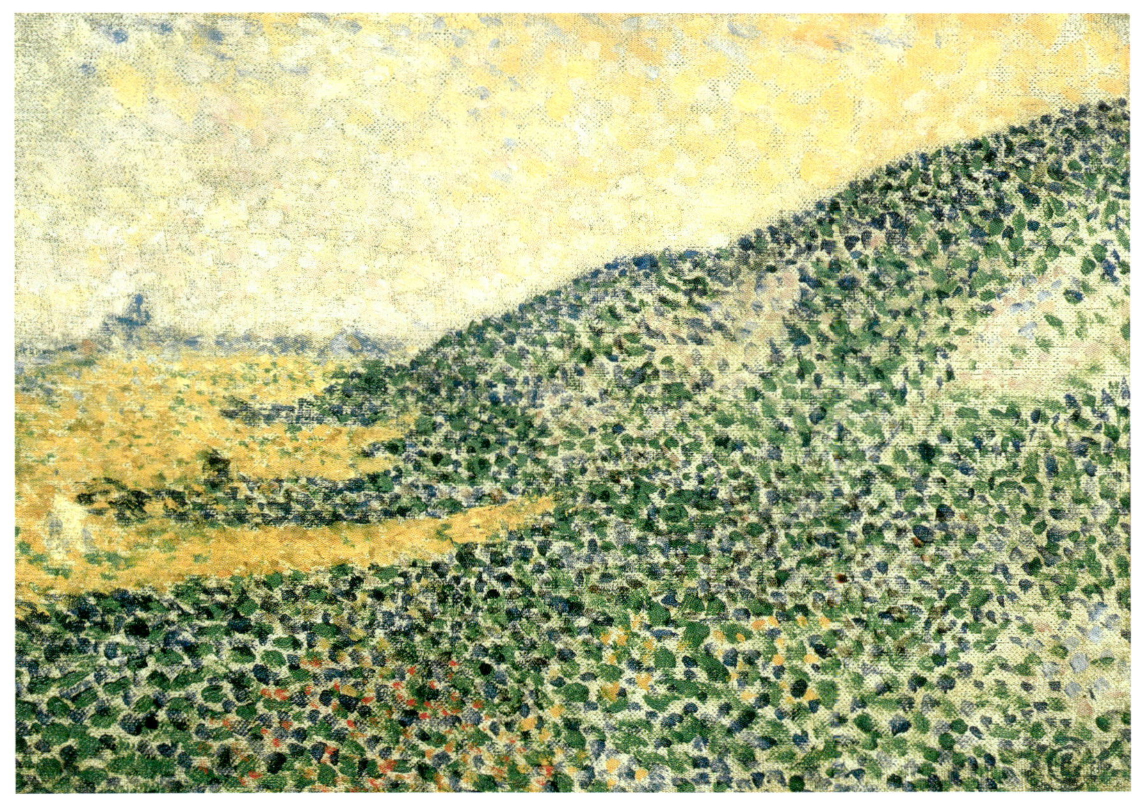

Georges Lemmen
The Cliffs of Dover
Die Klippen von Dover, 1892

Georges Lemmen
View of a Green Coast
Blick auf eine grüne Küste, 1891/92

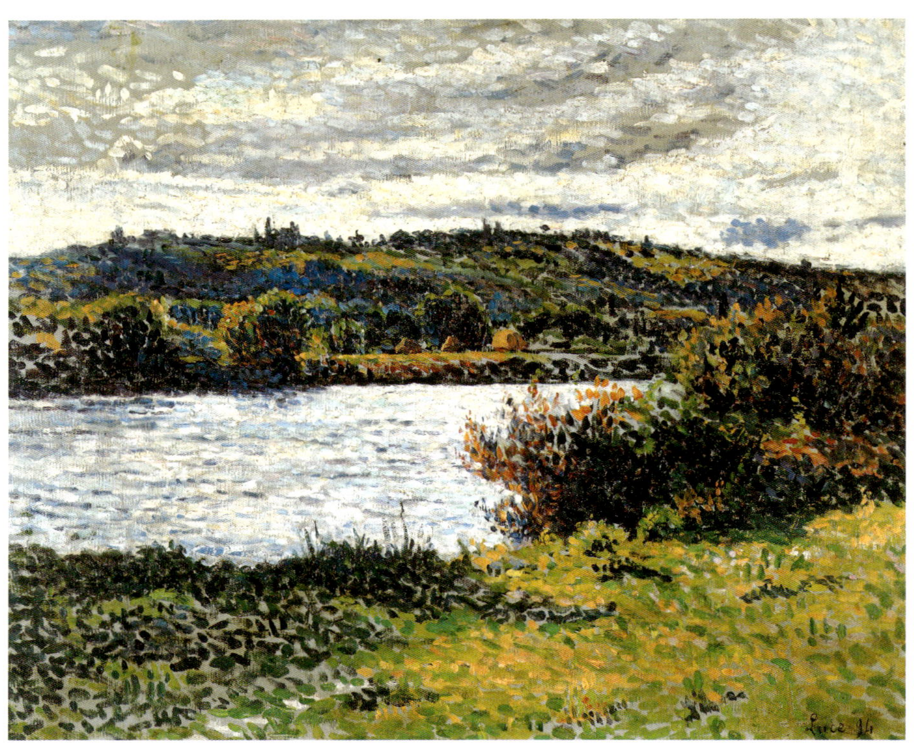

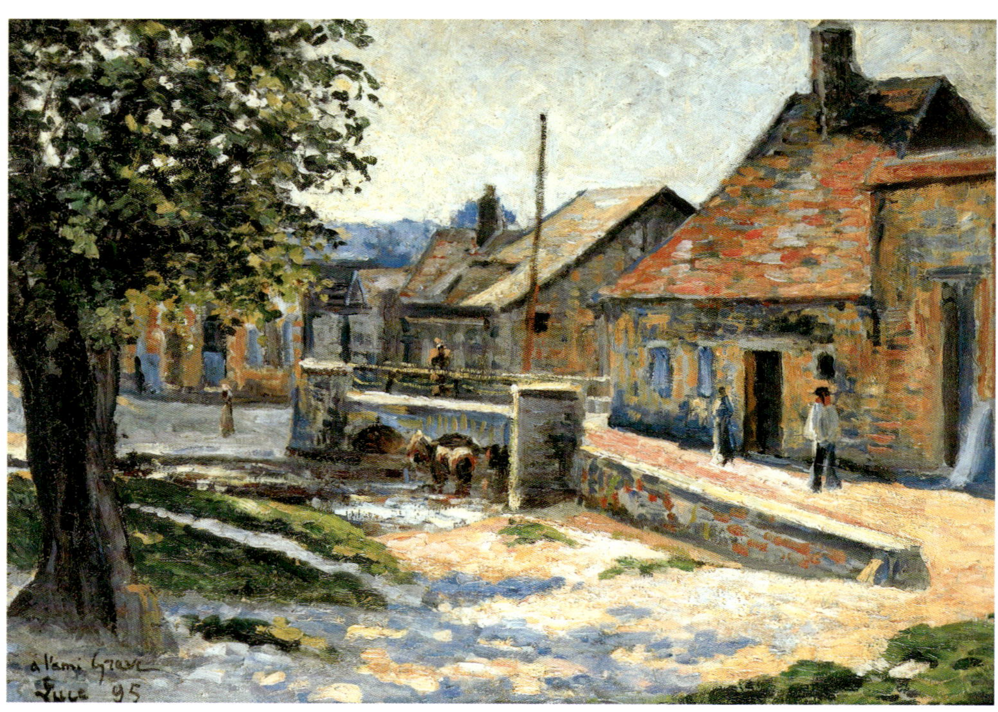

Maximilien Luce
The Seine in the Rain
Regenstimmung über der Seine, 1894

Maximilien Luce
Street Scene in Gisors
Straßenszene in Gisors, 1895

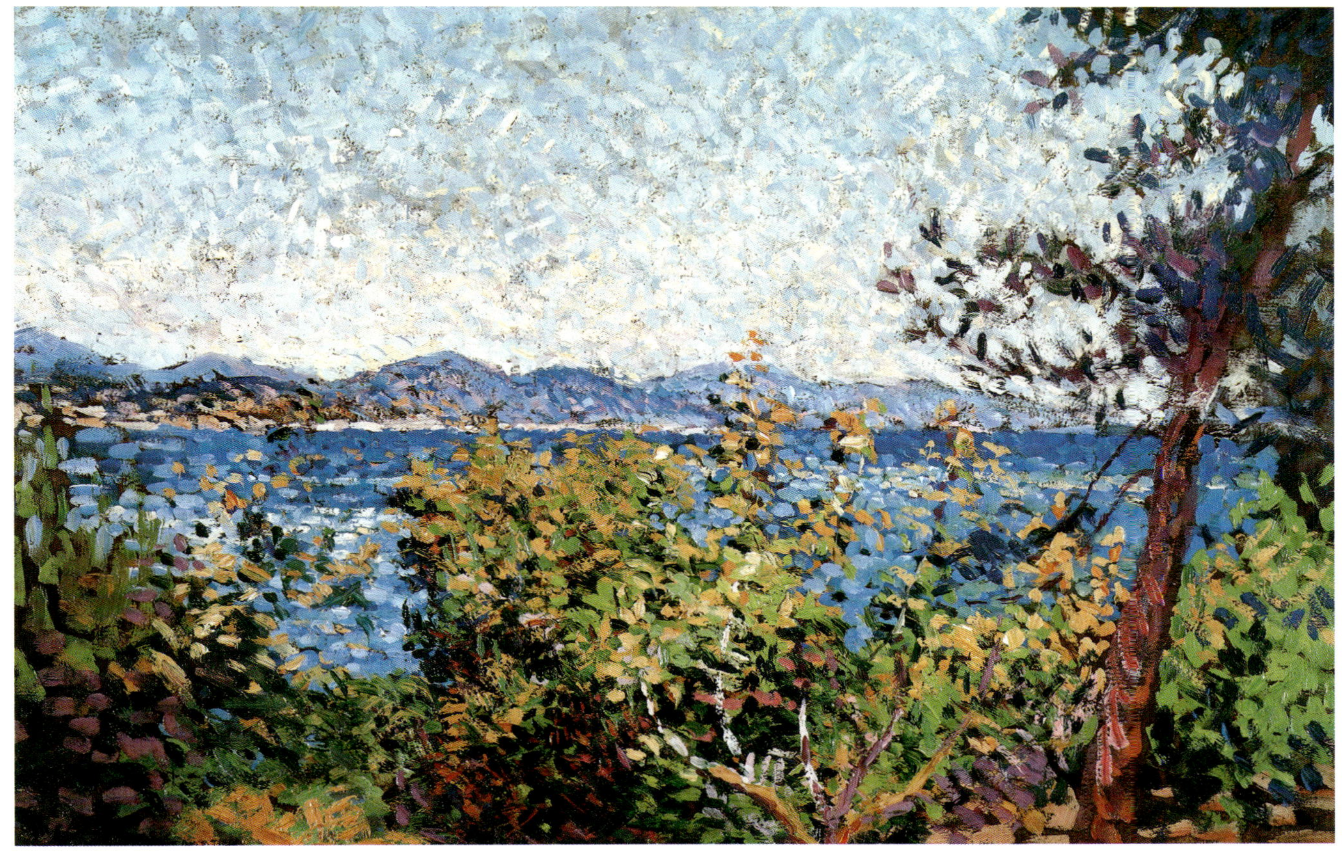

Maximilien Luce
Saint-Tropez, 1892

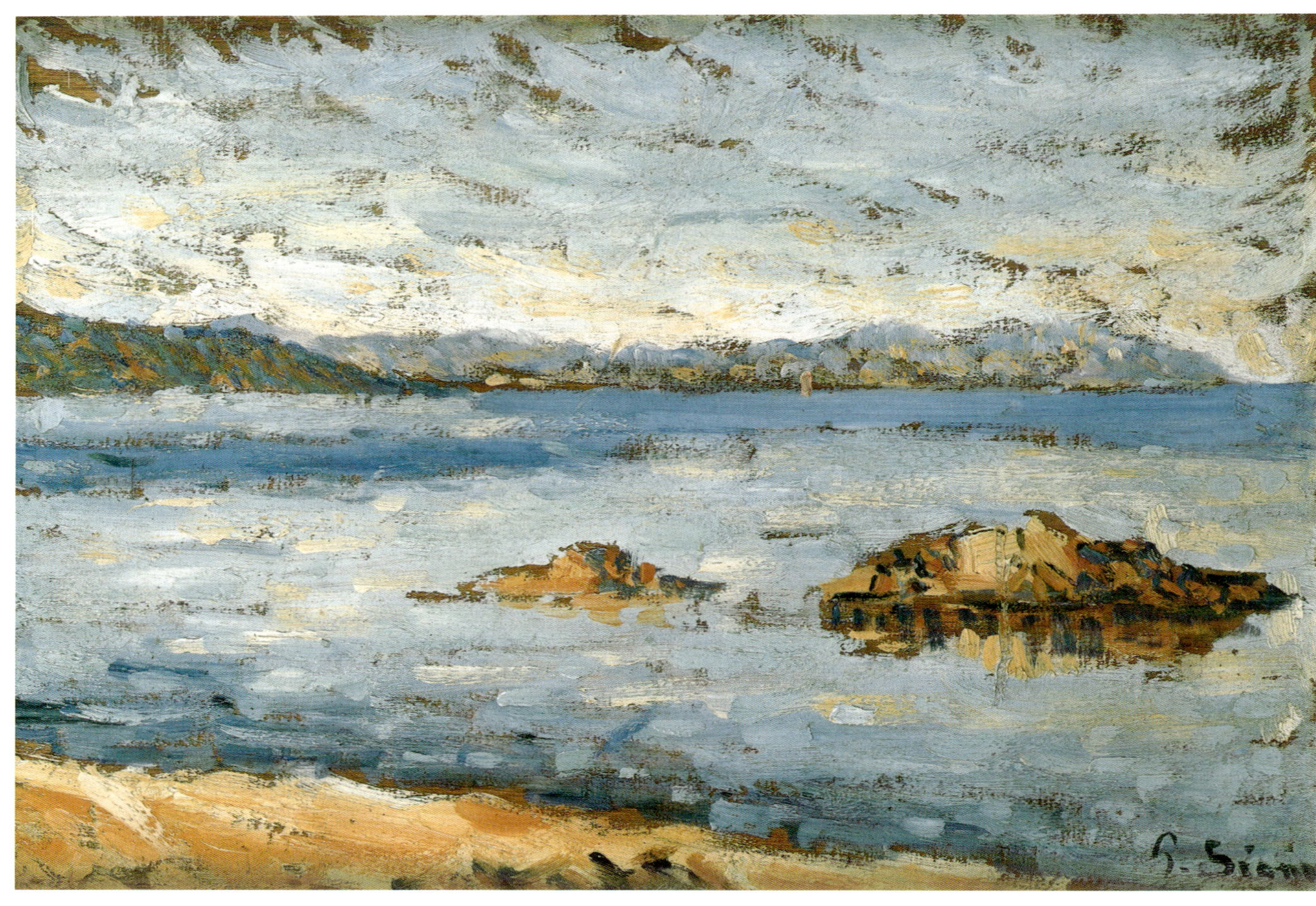

Paul Signac
Saint-Tropez, Calm
Saint-Tropez, Windstille, 1895

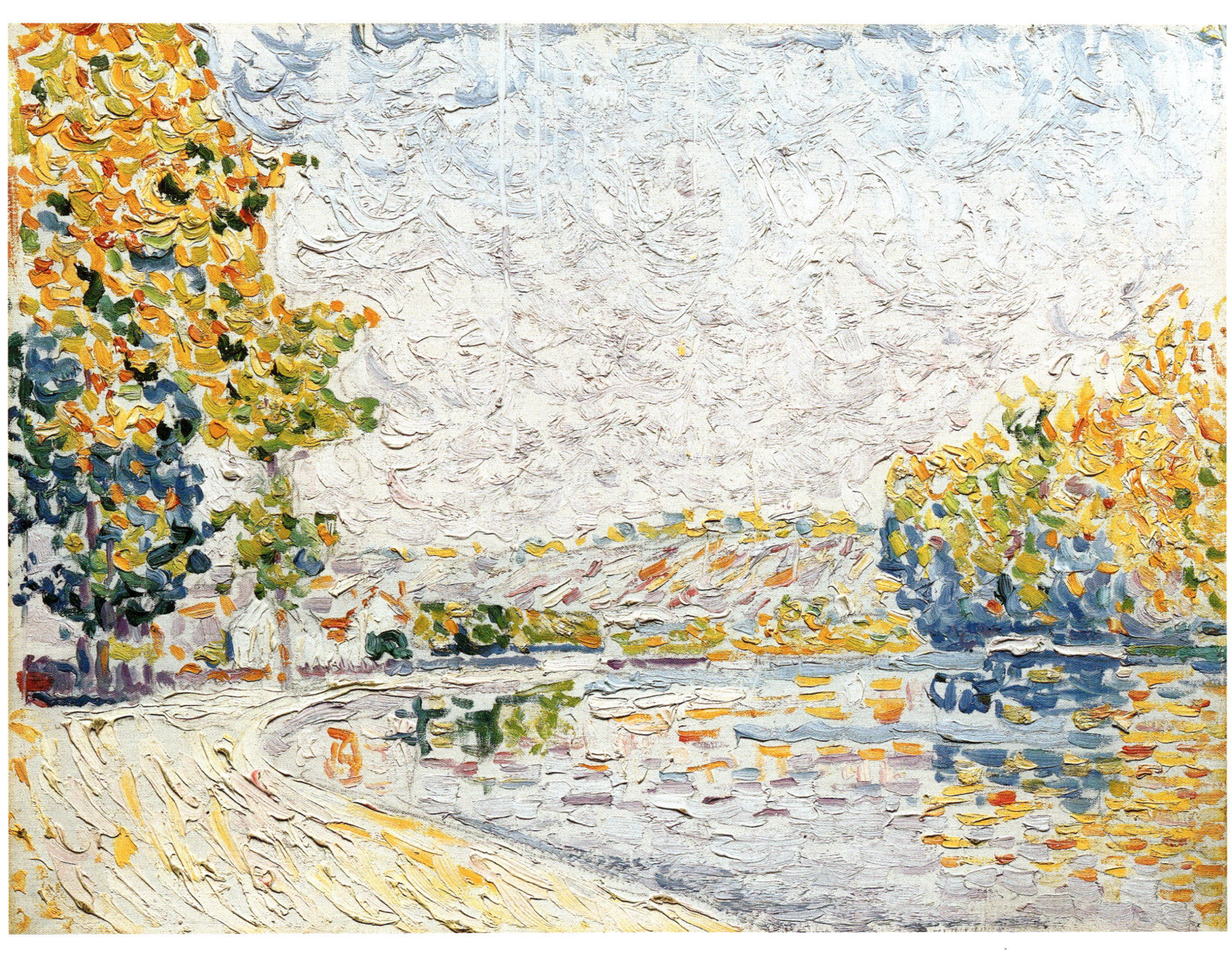

Paul Signac
Samois, Study No. 8 (The Seine at Samois)
Samois, Studie Nr. 8 (Die Seine bei Samois), 1899

Paul Signac
Capo di Noli, 1898

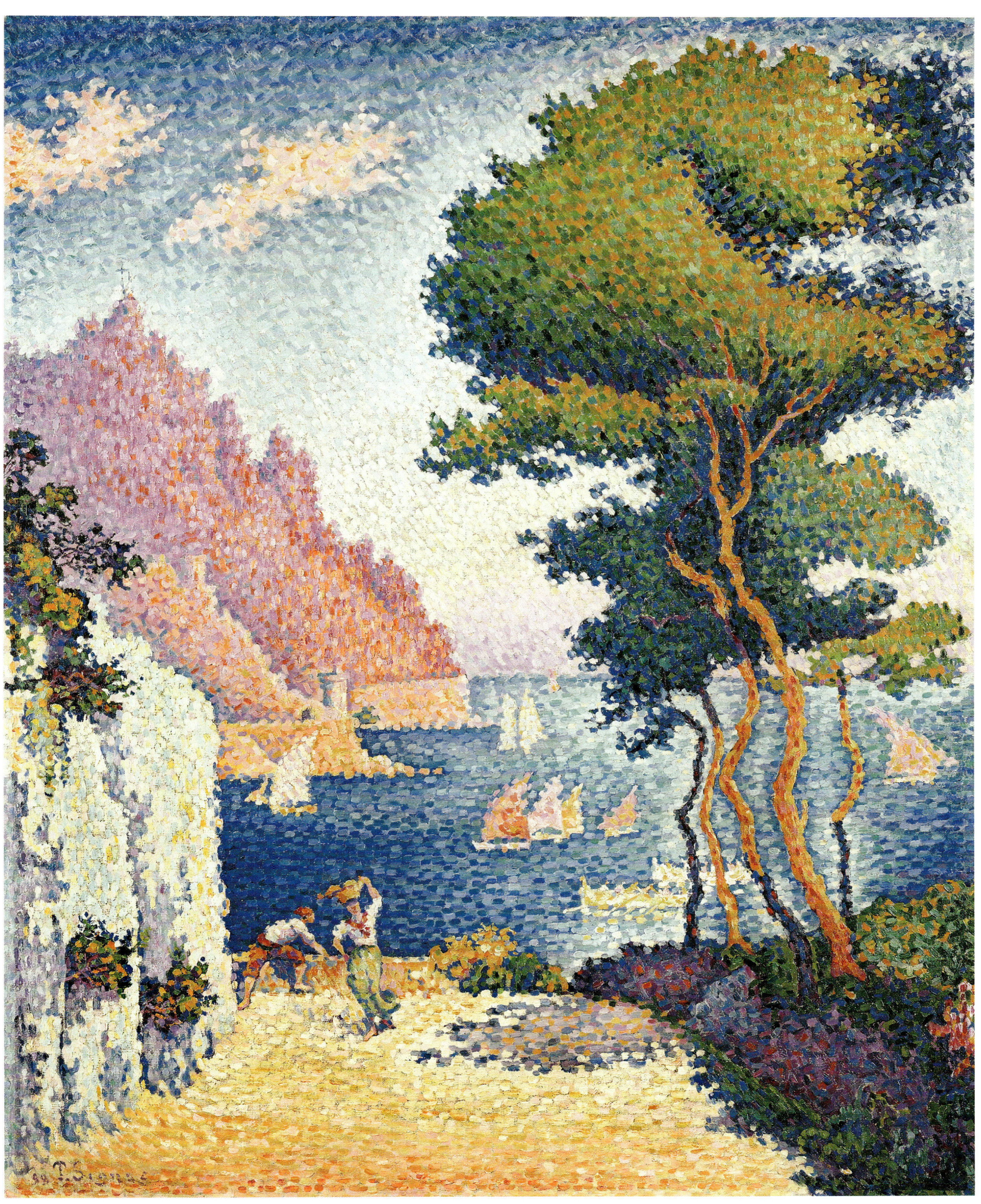

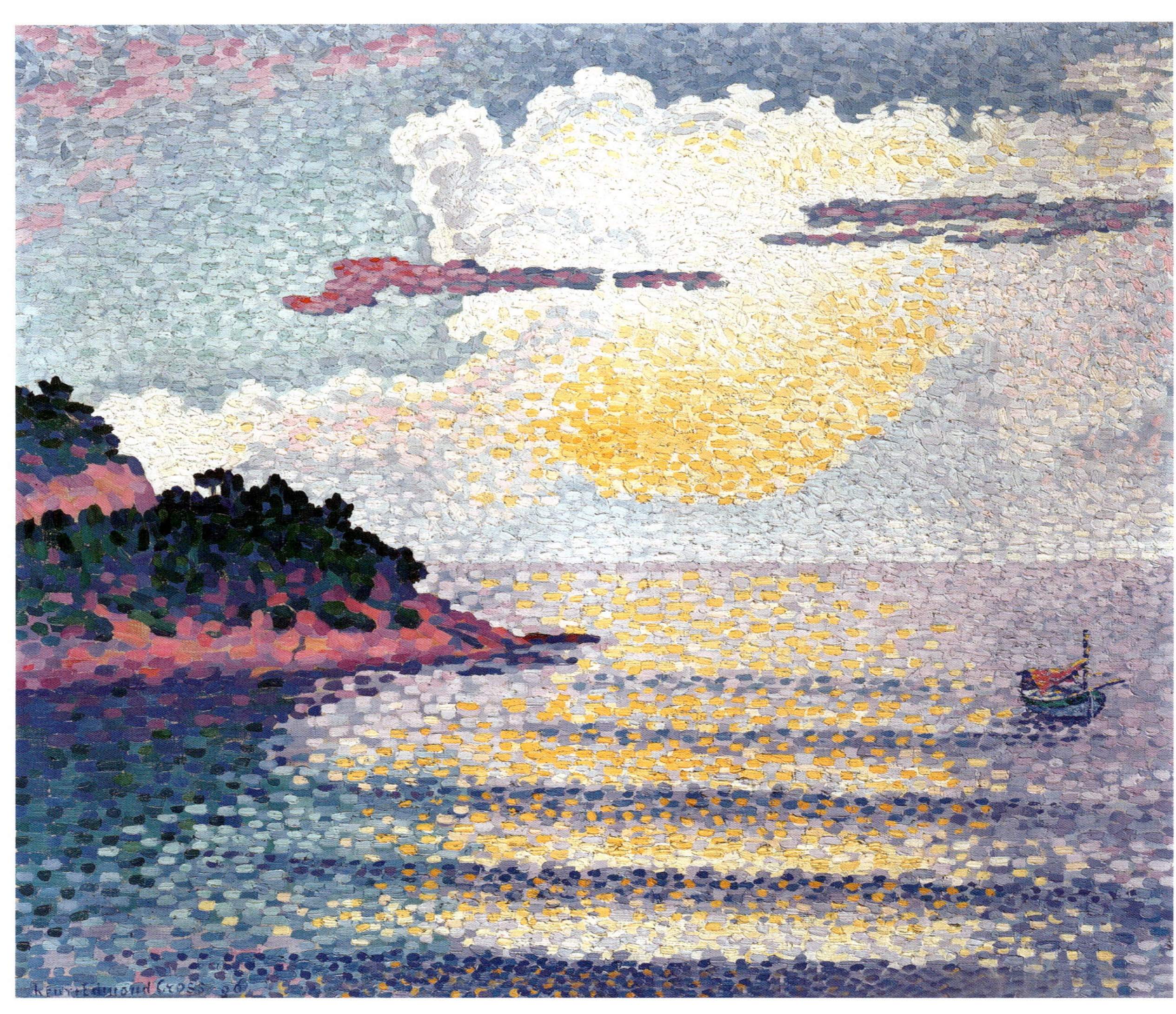

Henri Edmond Cross
Sunset over the Sea
Sonnenuntergang über dem Meer, 1896

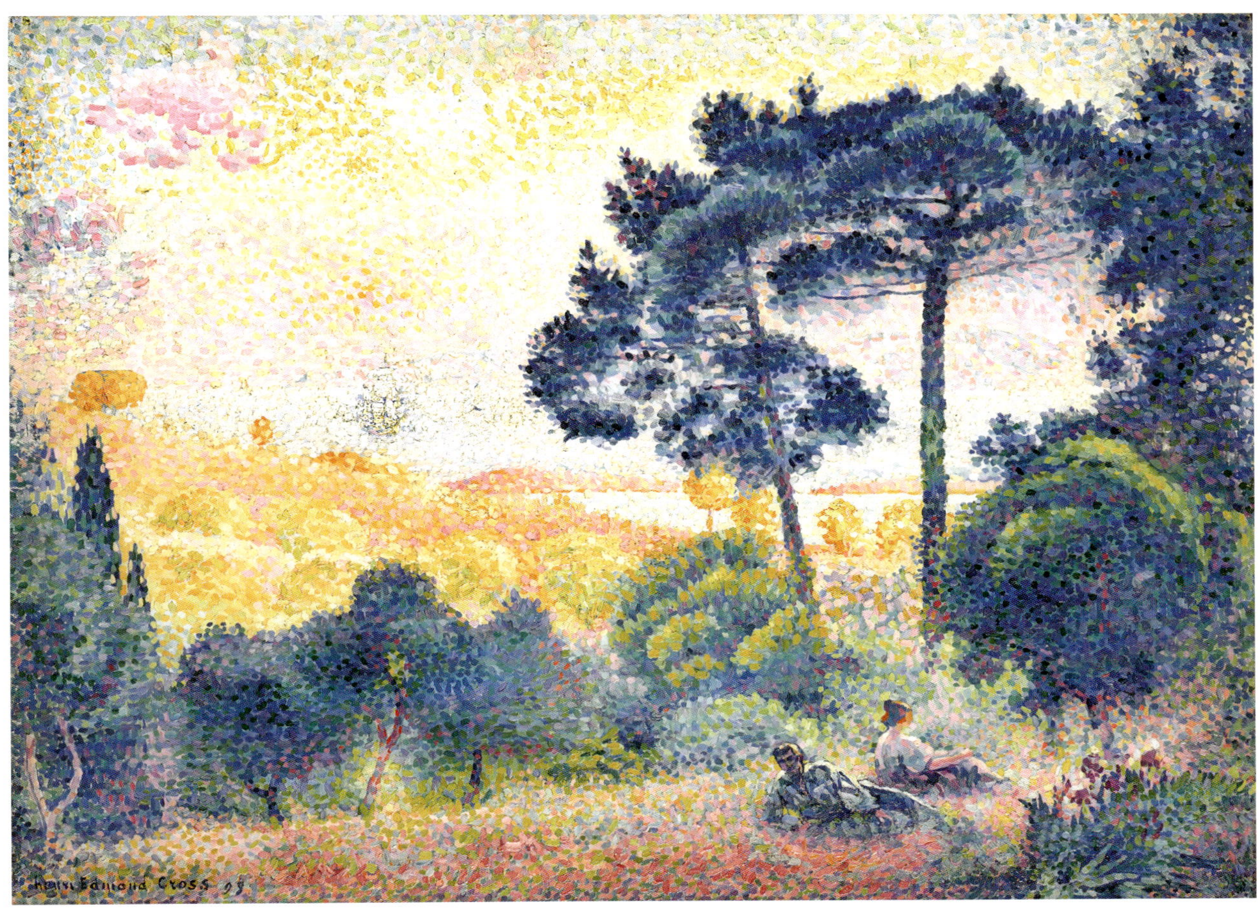

Henri Edmond Cross
Landscape in Provence
Landschaft der Provence, 1898

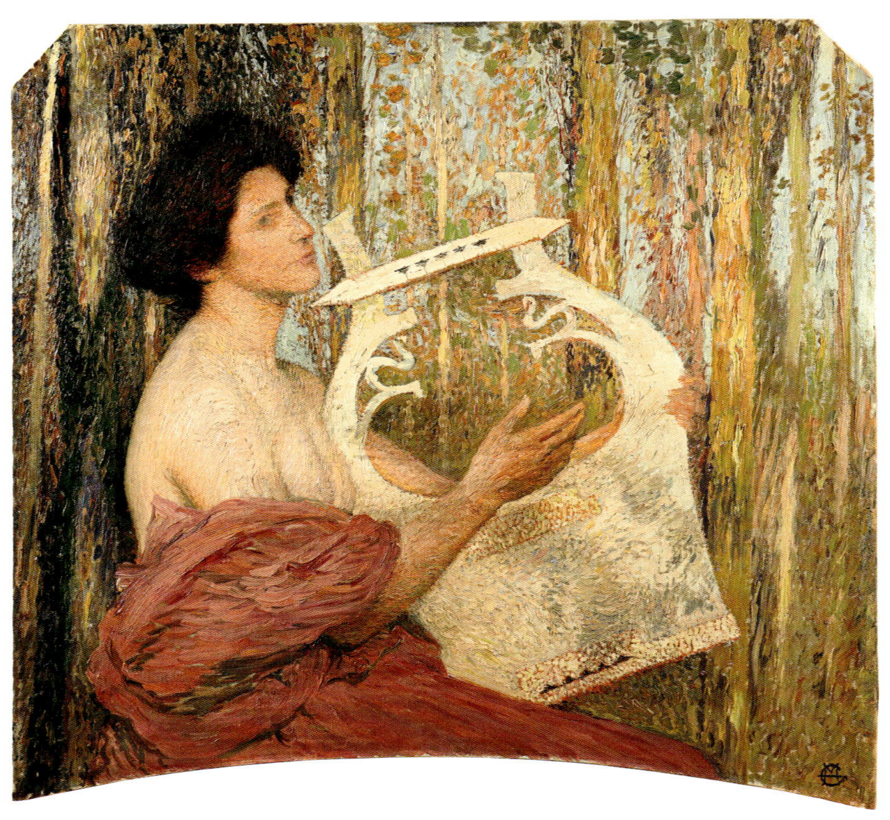

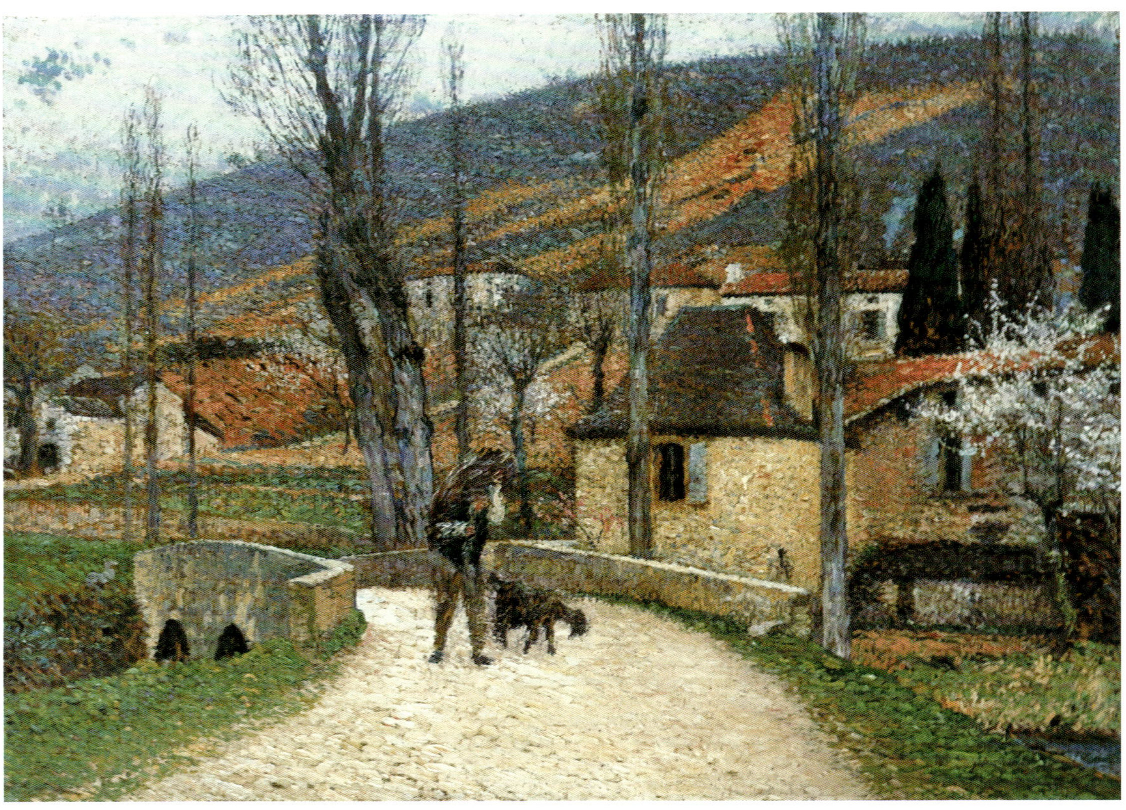

Henri Martin
Muse with Lyre
Muse mit Lyra, ca. 1890

Henri Martin
Peasant Returning to the Village
Ins Dorf heimkehrender Bauer, ca. 1898

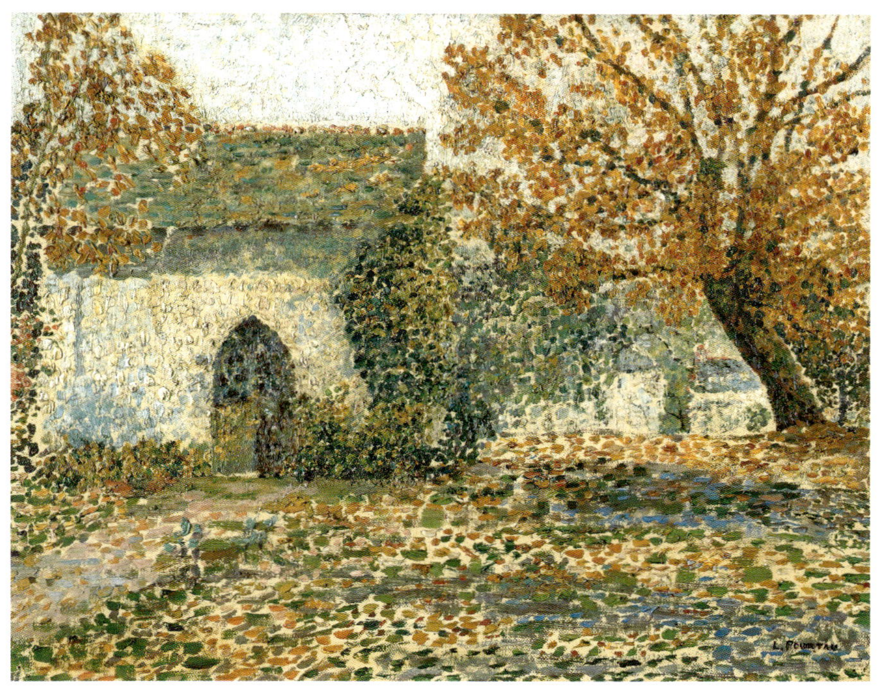

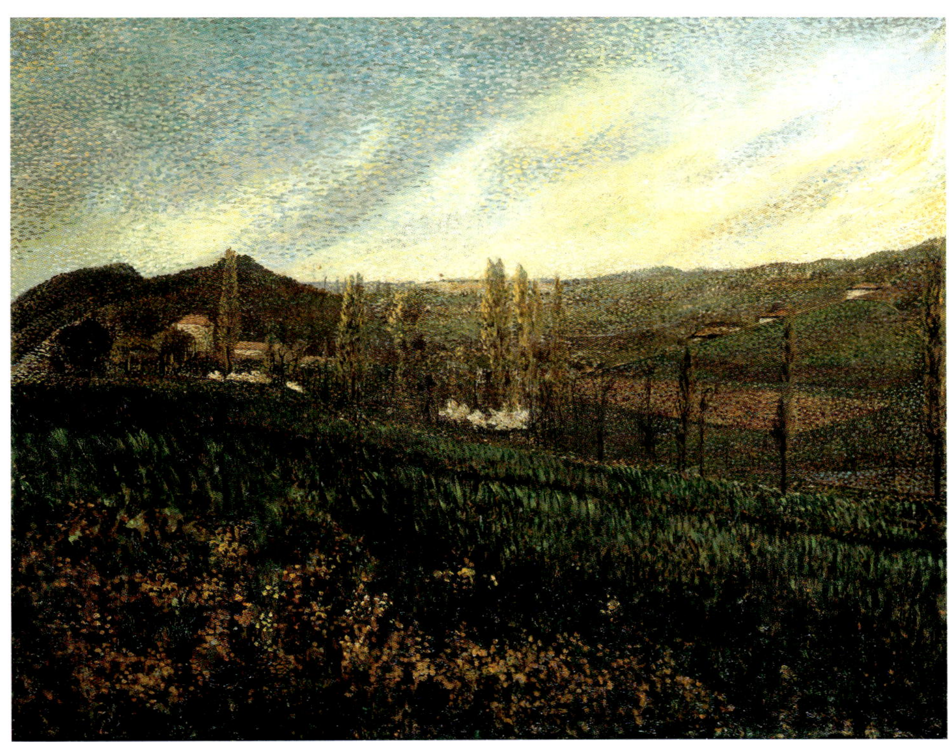

LEON POURTAU
Valley in Spring
Tal im Frühling, 1893

LEON POURTAU
The Chapel of Sainte-Adresse
Die Kapelle von Sainte-Adresse, ca. 1897

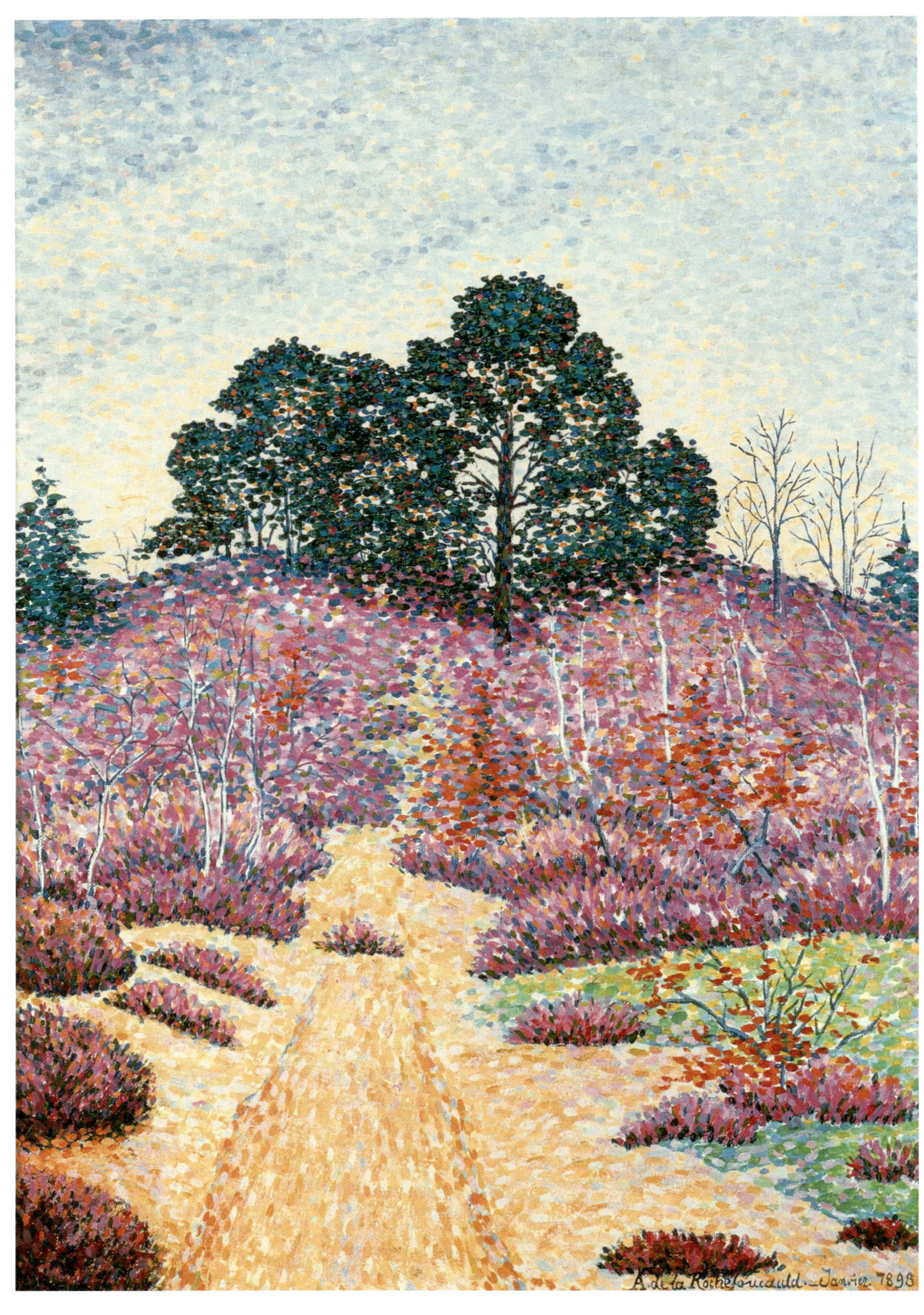

Antoine de la Rochefoucauld
Neo-Impressionist Landscape
Neoimpressionistische Landschaft, 1898

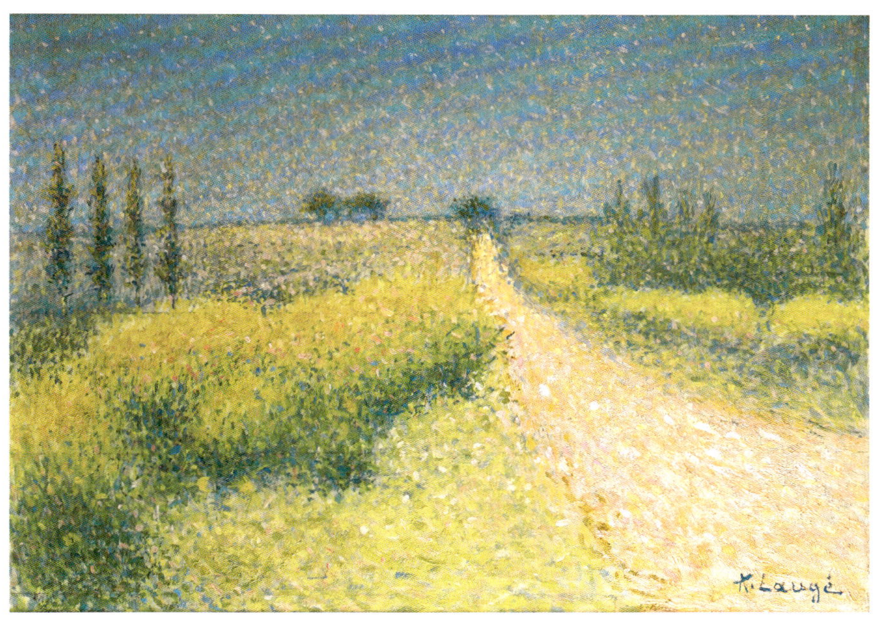

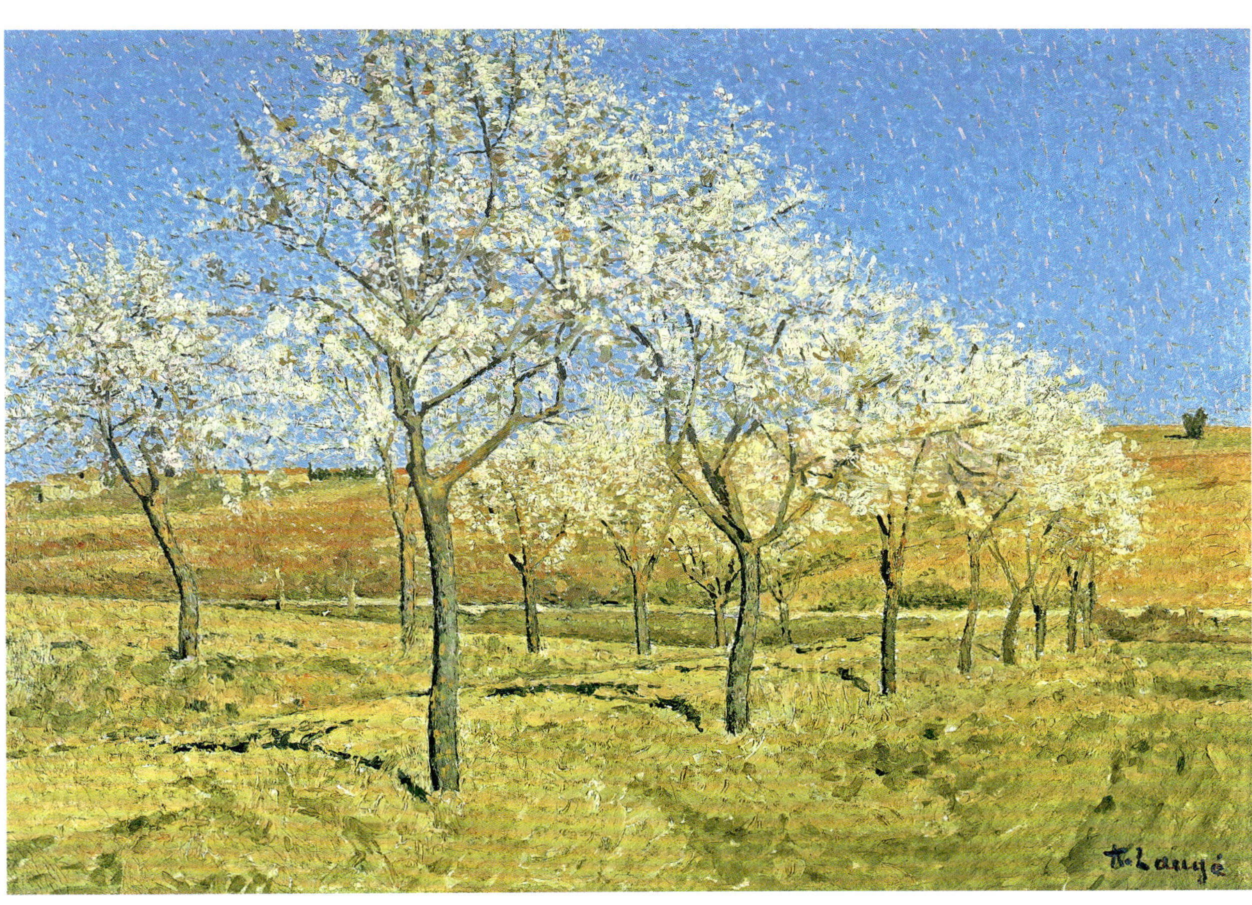

Achille Lauge
Landscape with Trees in Bloom
Landschaft mit blühenden Bäumen, 1898

Achille Lauge
Path with Gorse
Weg mit Ginster, ca. 1900

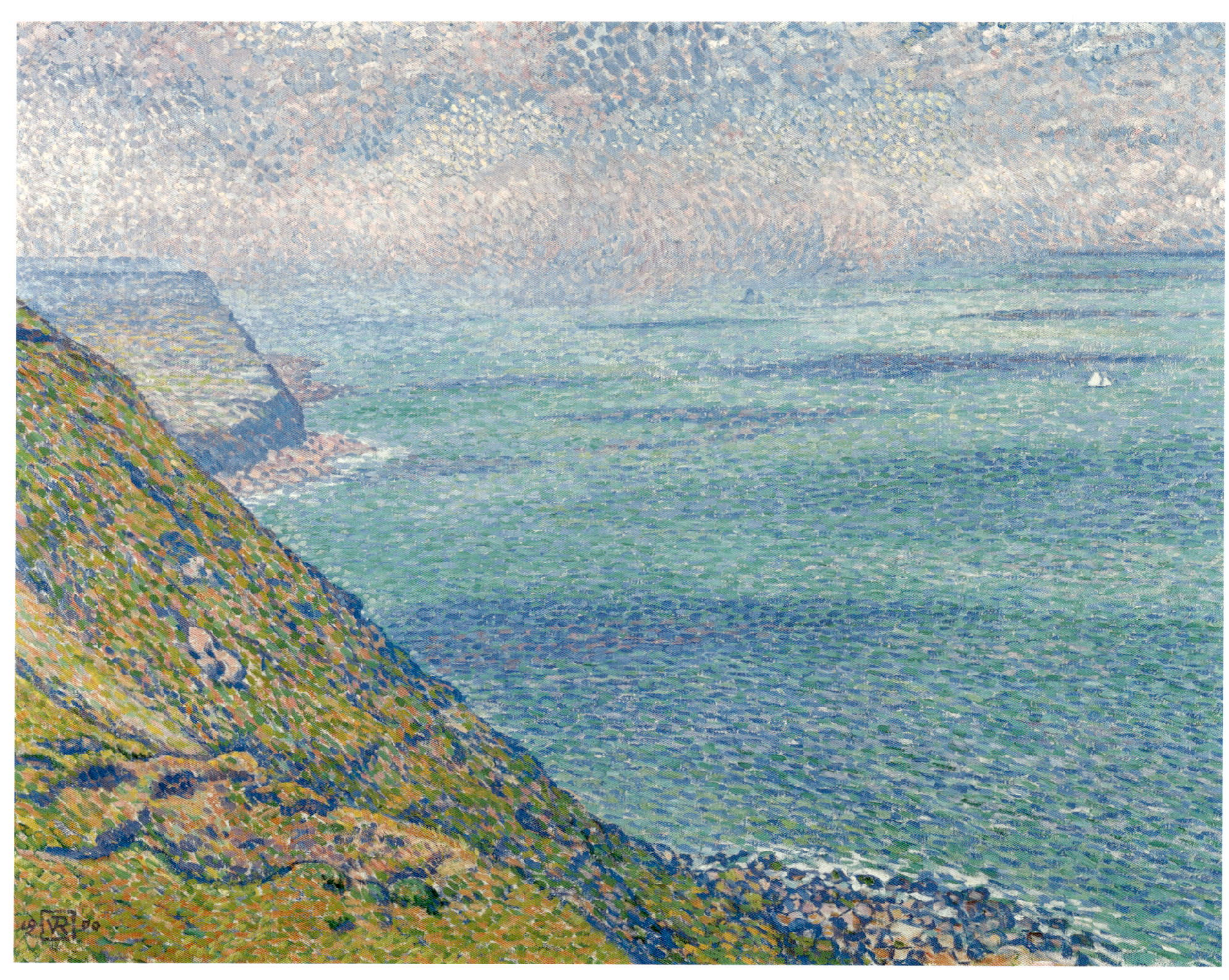

Theo van Rysselberghe
Cape Gris-Nez or *Summer Mist*
Das Kap Gris-Nez oder *Sommernebel*, 1900

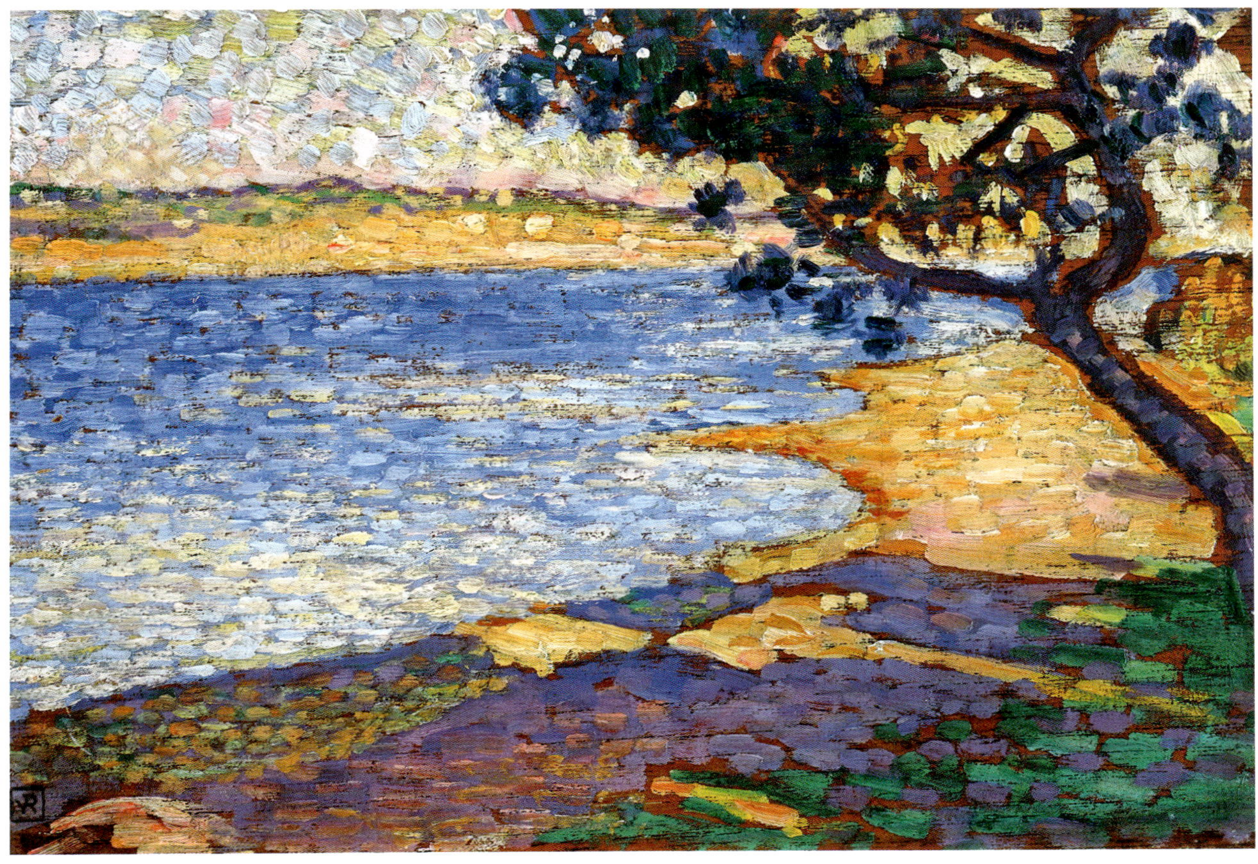

Theo van Rysselberghe
Saint-Tropez, 1895

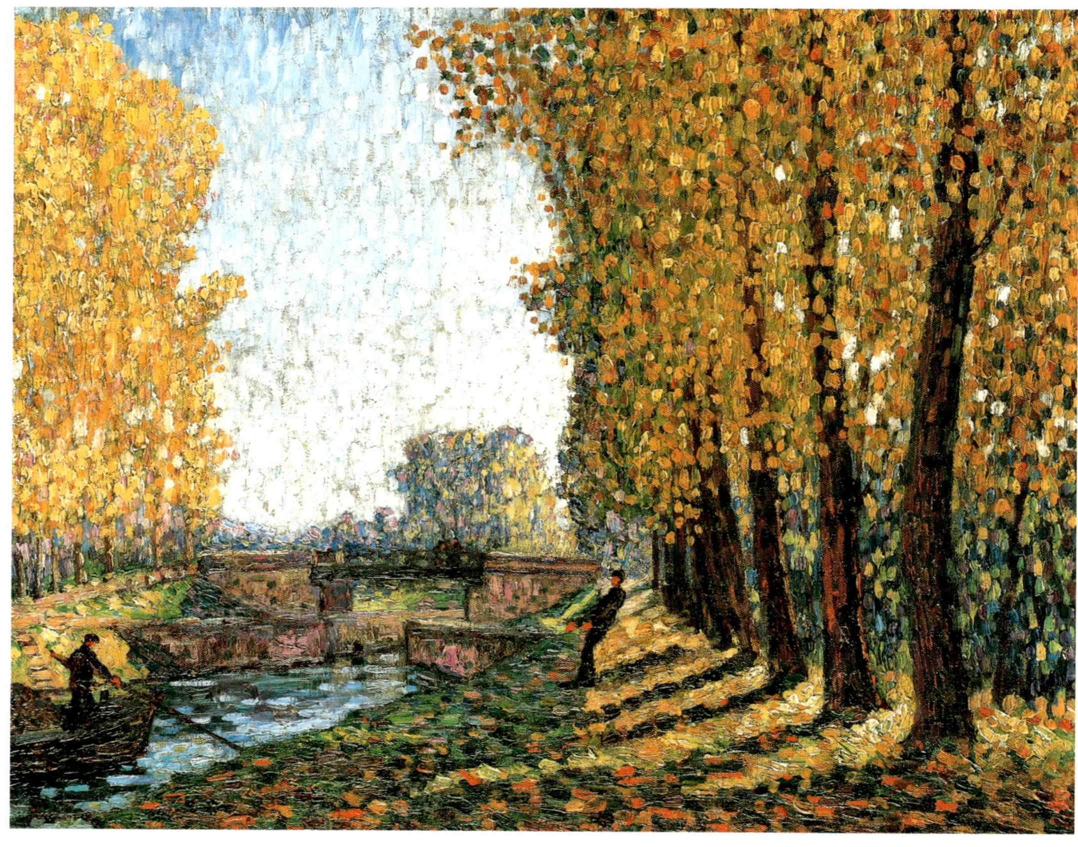

Francis Picabia
Morning Sun in Autumn
Morgensonne im Herbst, ca. 1898

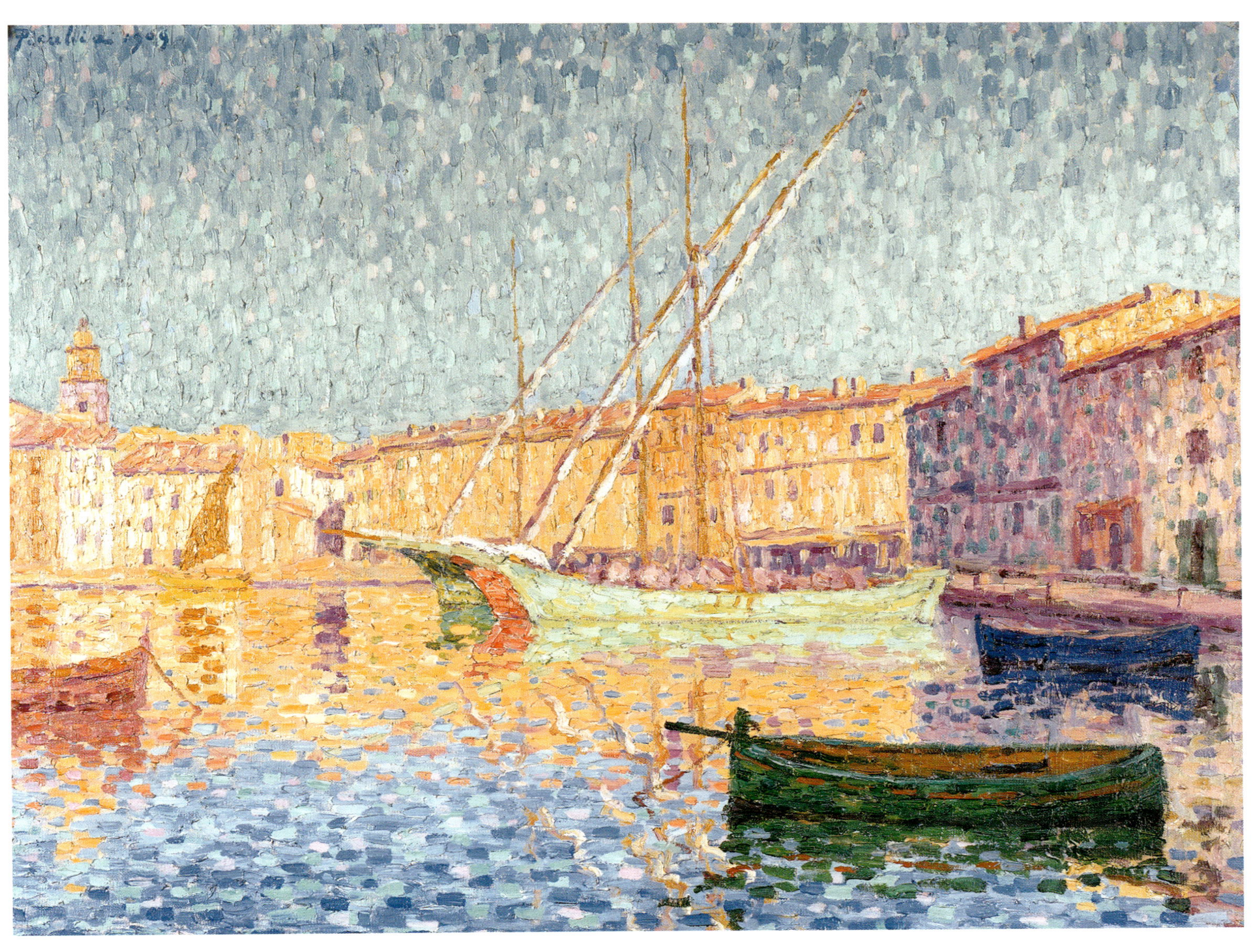

Francis Picabia
The Harbor of Saint-Tropez in the Sunlight
Der Hafen von Saint-Tropez im Sonnenlicht, 1909

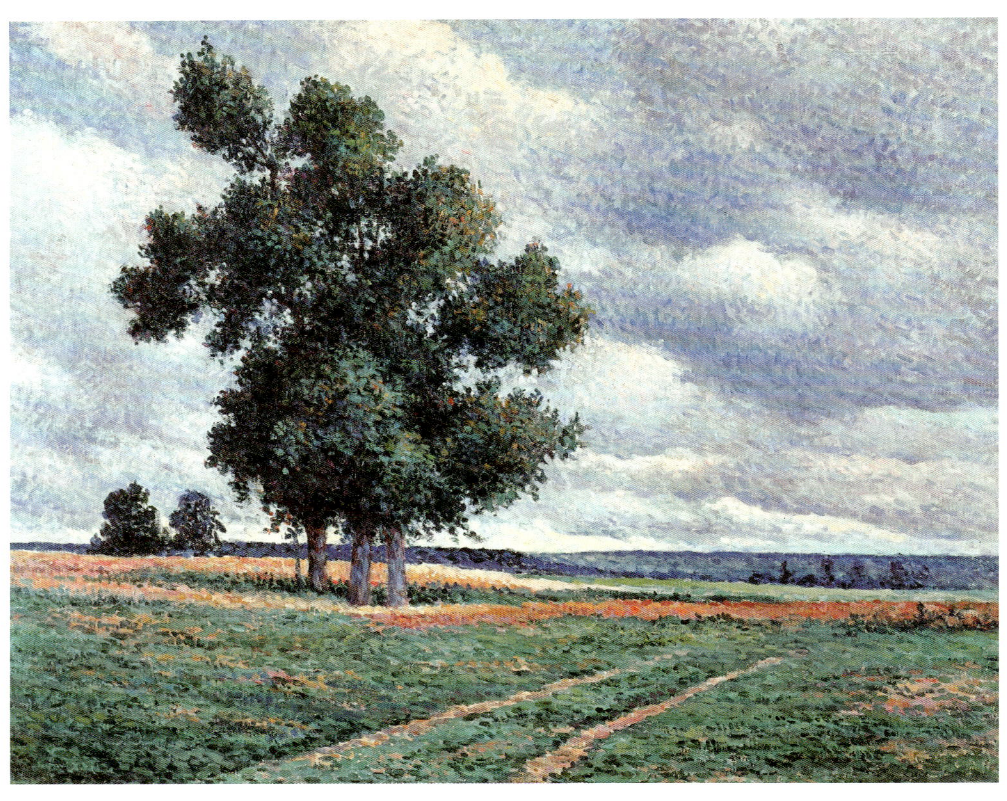

MAXIMILIEN LUCE
The Plain of Les Grésillons, Poissy
Die Ebene von Les Grésillons, Poissy, 1899

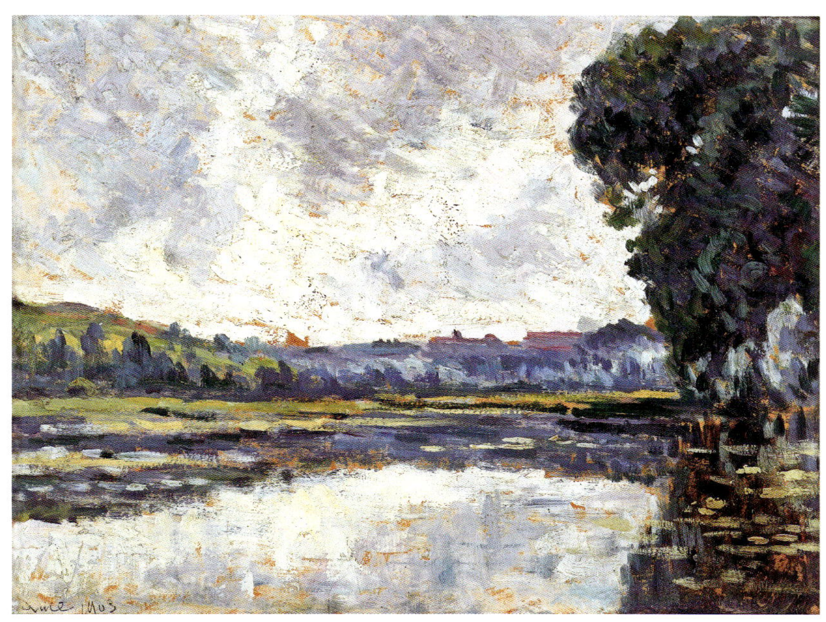

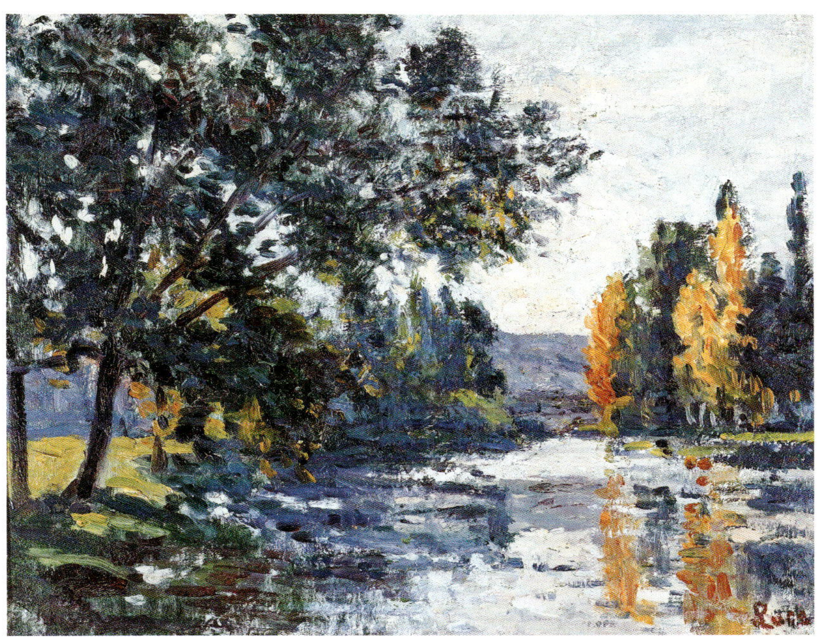

Maximilien Luce
On the Banks of the River
Am Flussufer, 1903

Maximilien Luce
The River Eure near Garennes
Der Fluss Eure bei Garennes, ca. 1901

Maximilien Luce
Notre-Dame, Viewed from the Quai Saint-Michel
Notre-Dame, Ansicht vom Quai Saint-Michel aus, 1901–04

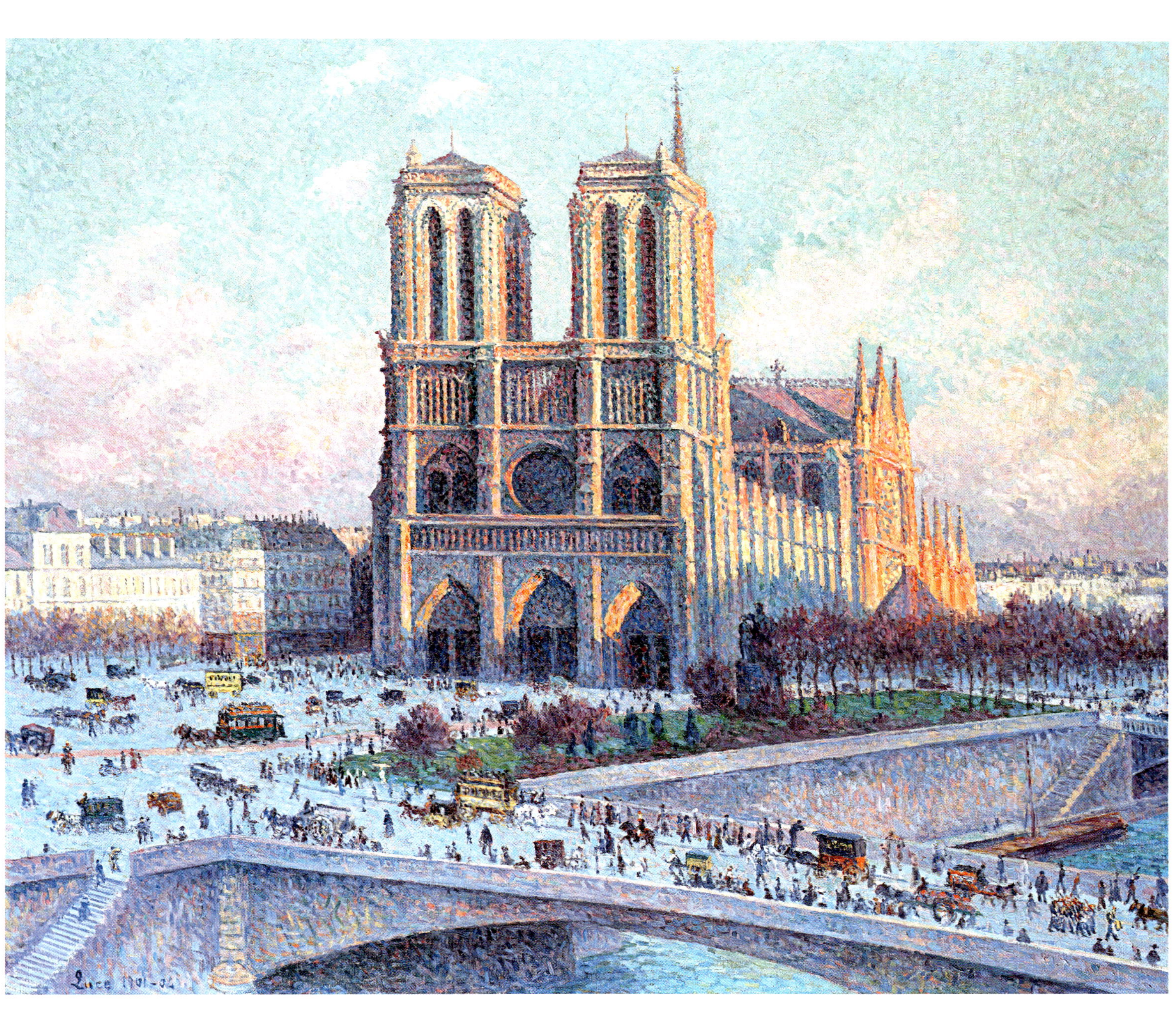

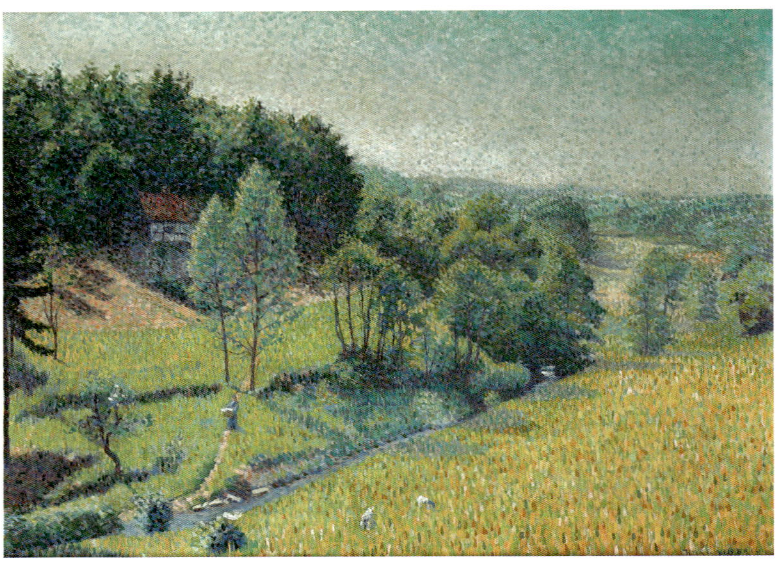

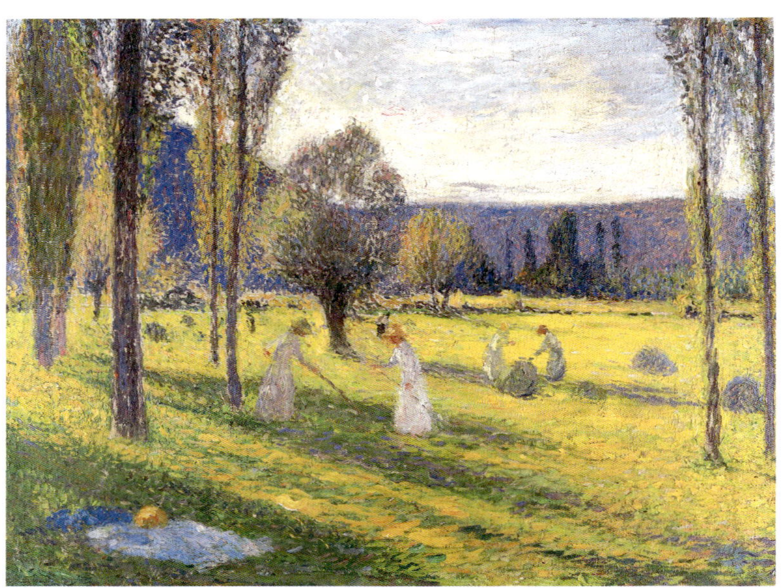

Ferdinand Hart-Nibbrig
Geuldal, Province of Limburg
Geuldal, Provinz Limburg, ca. 1904/05

Henri Martin
La Bastide-du-Vert, ca. 1905

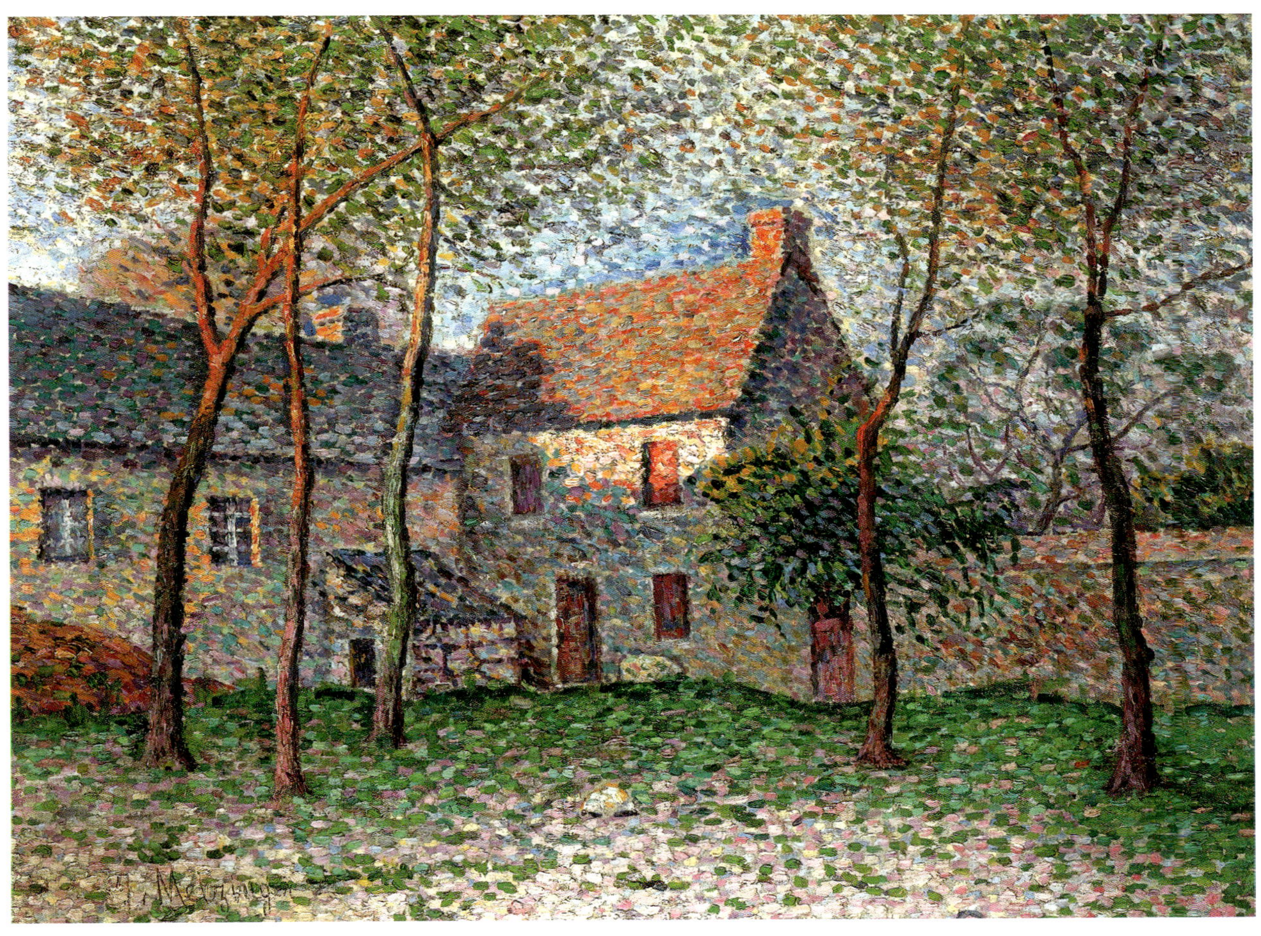

JEAN METZINGER
Farm, before 1906
Bauernhof, vor 1906

Jean Metzinger
Landscape with Tree
Landschaft mit Baum, ca. 1906

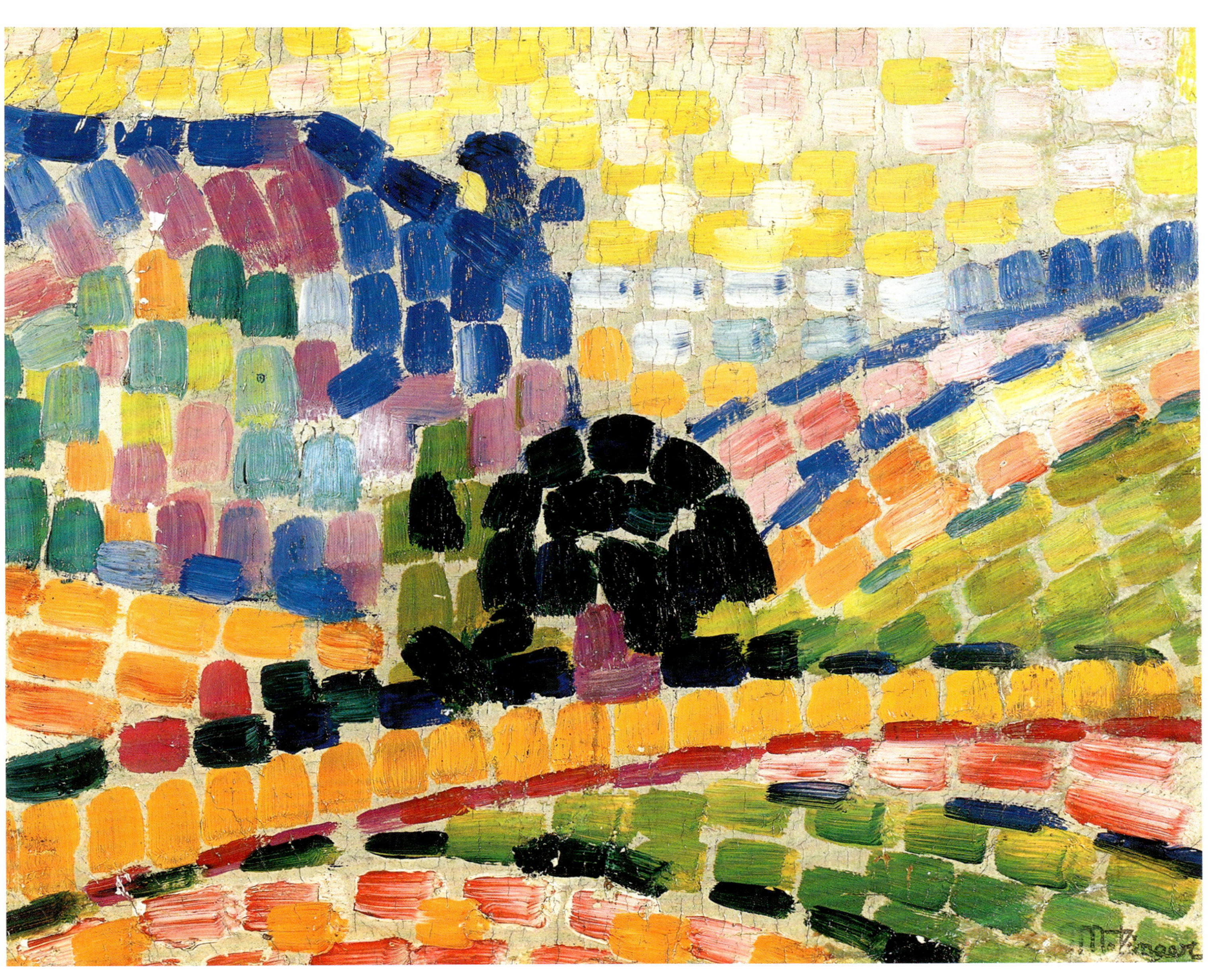

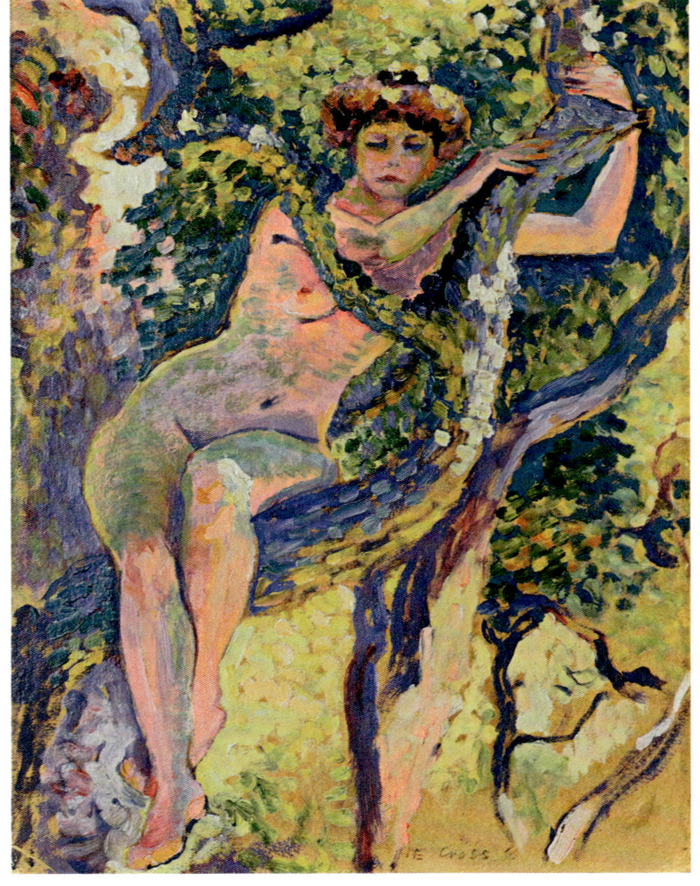

Henri Edmond Cross
Nude in a Tree or *Woman in a Tree*
Akt in einem Baum oder *Frau im Baum*, ca. 1906

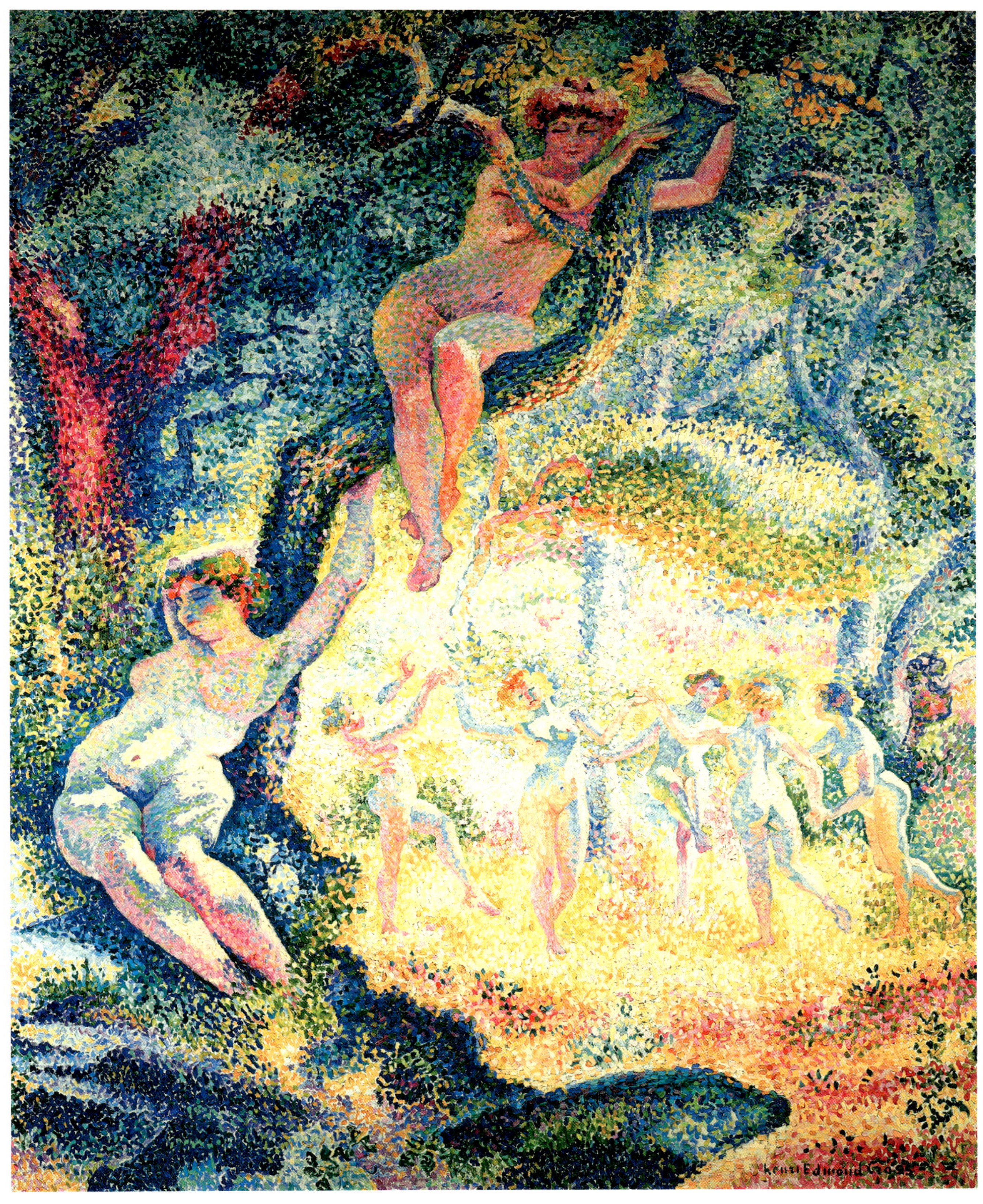

Henri Edmond Cross
The Clearing
Die Lichtung, 1906–07

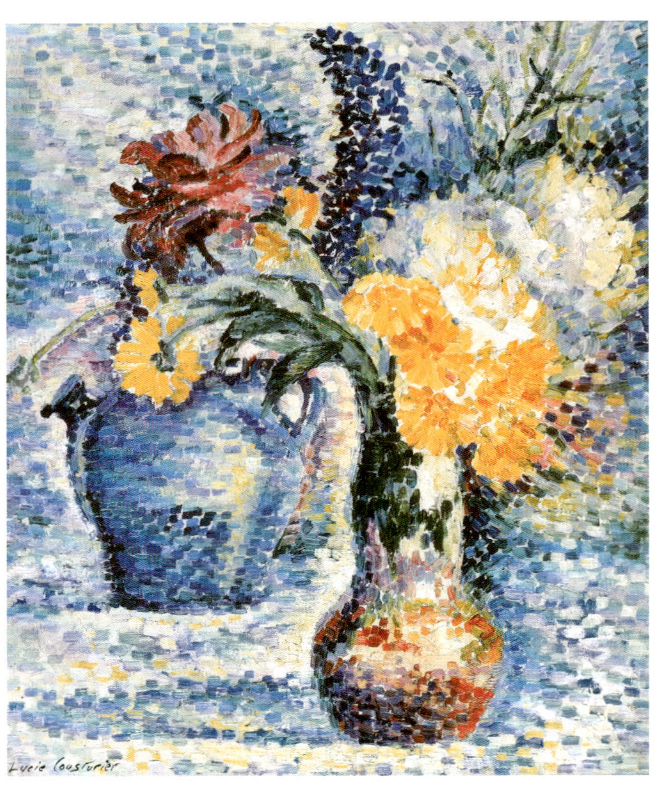

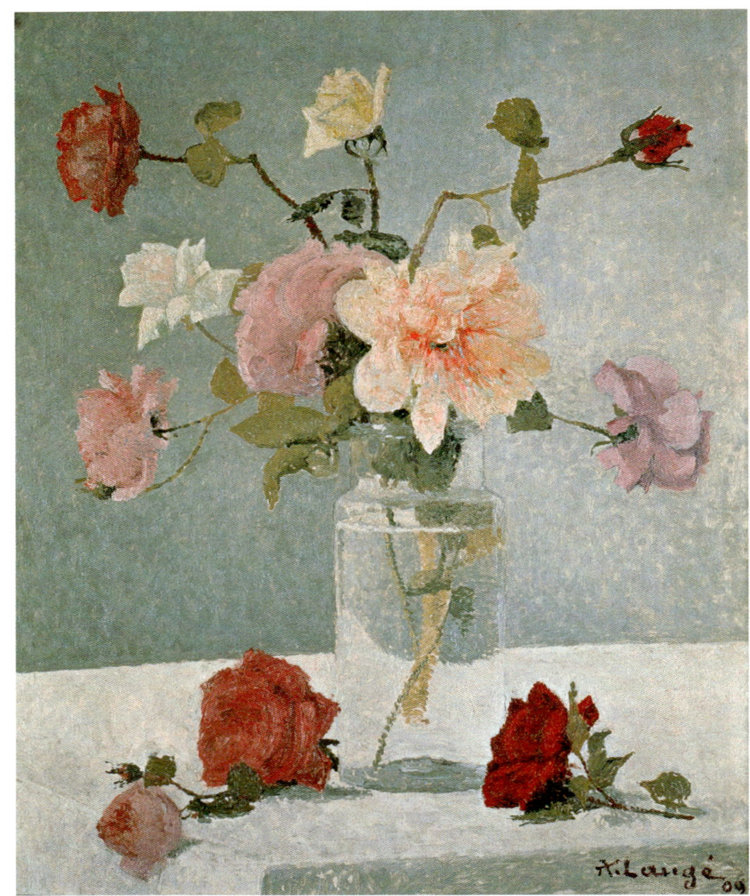

Lucie Cousturier
Bouquet of Flowers
Blumenstrauß, 1910

Achille Lauge
Vase with Roses
Vase mit Rosen, 1909

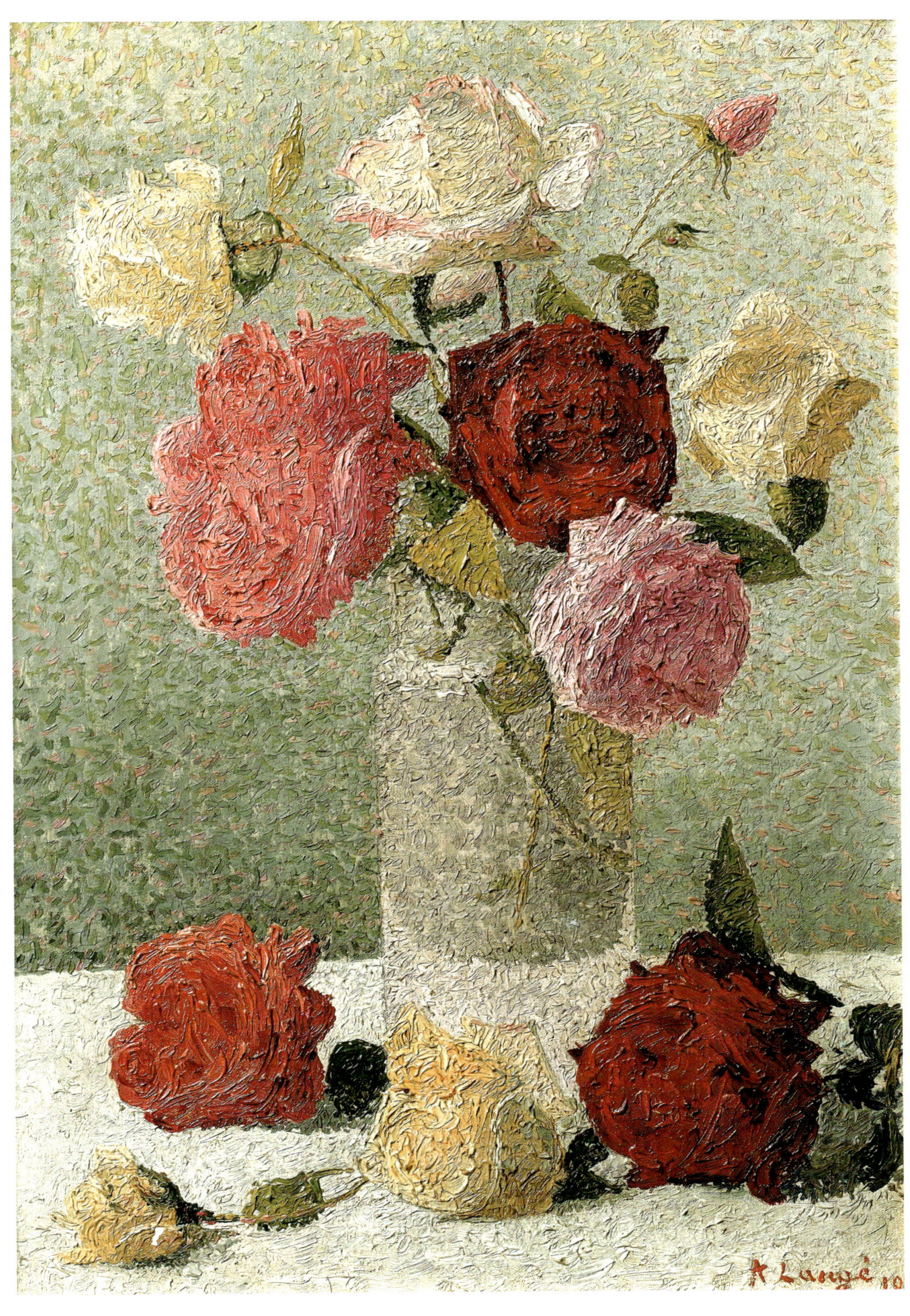

ACHILLE LAUGE
Roses
Rosen, 1910

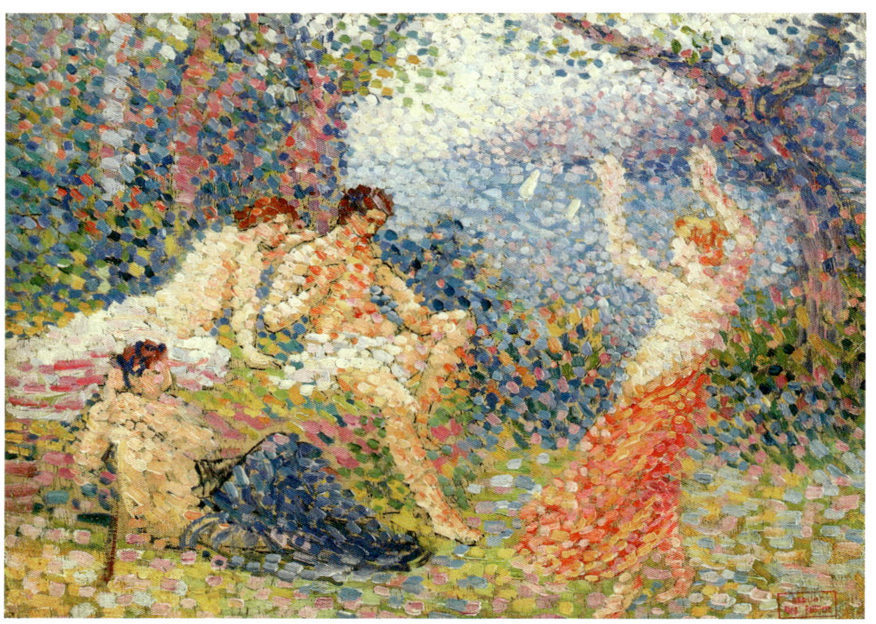

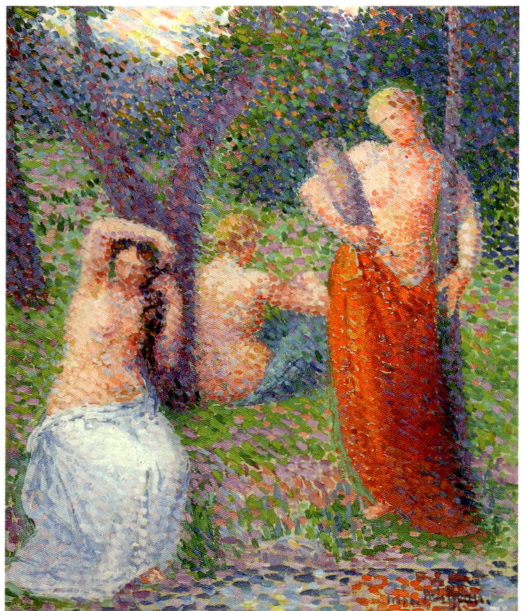

Hippolyte Petitjean
Rural Scene
Ländliche Szene, ca. 1898

Hippolyte Petitjean
The Three Graces
Die drei Grazien, 1917

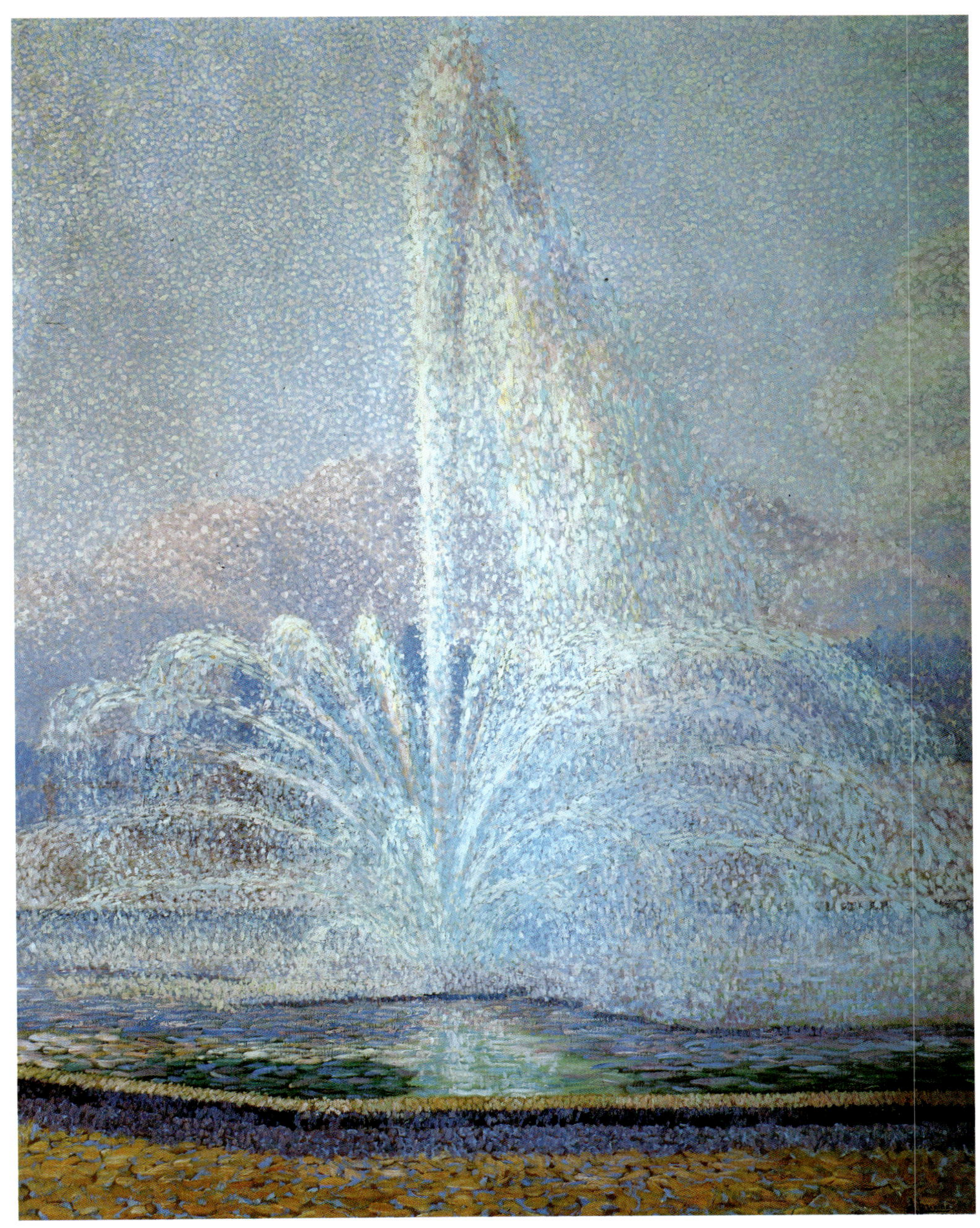

Andre Leveille
Fountain
Springbrunnen, ca. 1903

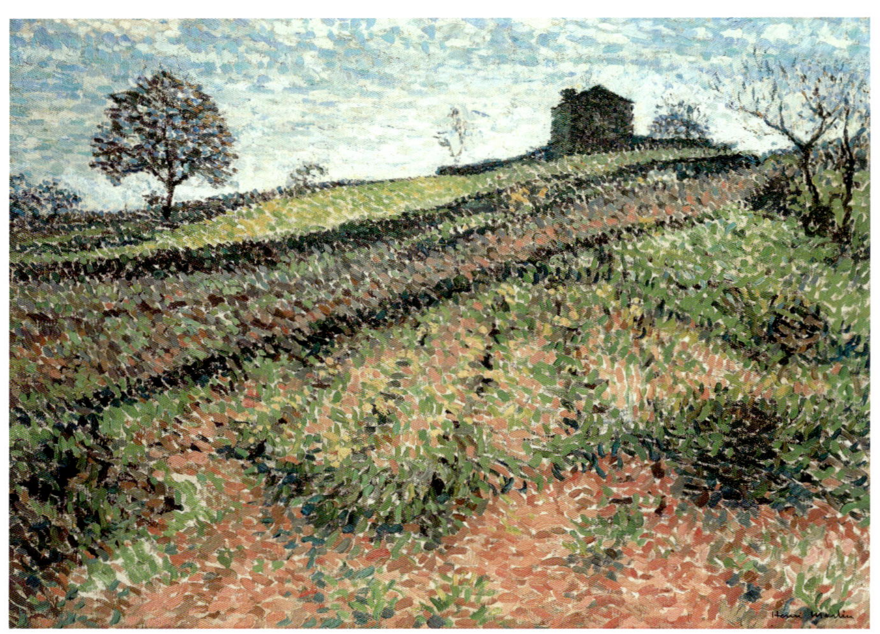

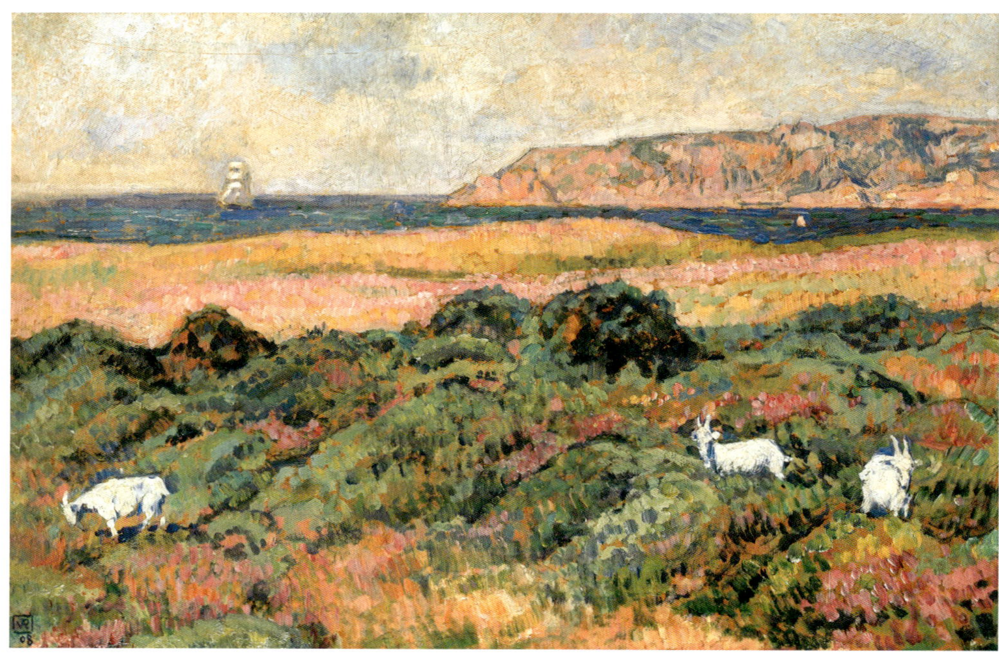

Henri Martin
Landscape – House in the Country
Landschaft – Haus auf dem Lande, ca. 1910

Theo van Rysselberghe
Le Lavandou, Var, 1908

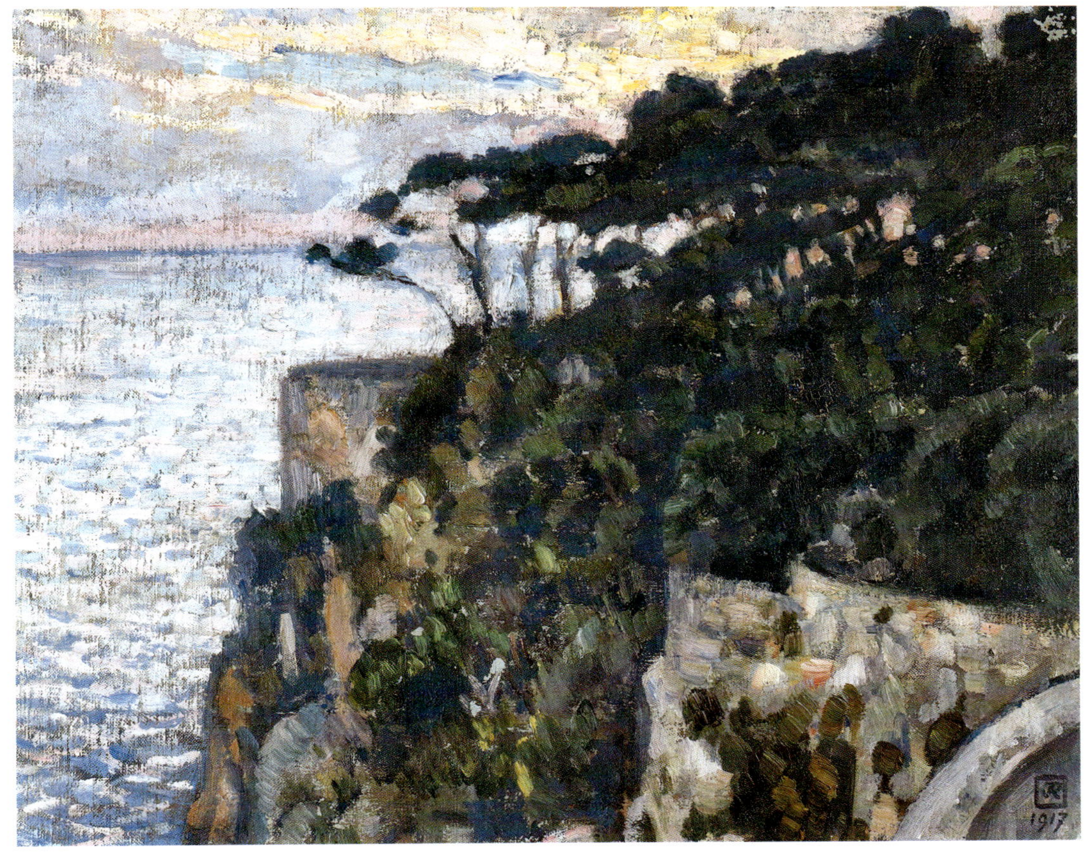

THEO VAN RYSSELBERGHE
Pines in Monaco
Pinien in Monaco, 1917

Paul Signac
The Harbor at Concarneau
Der Hafen von Concarneau, 1933

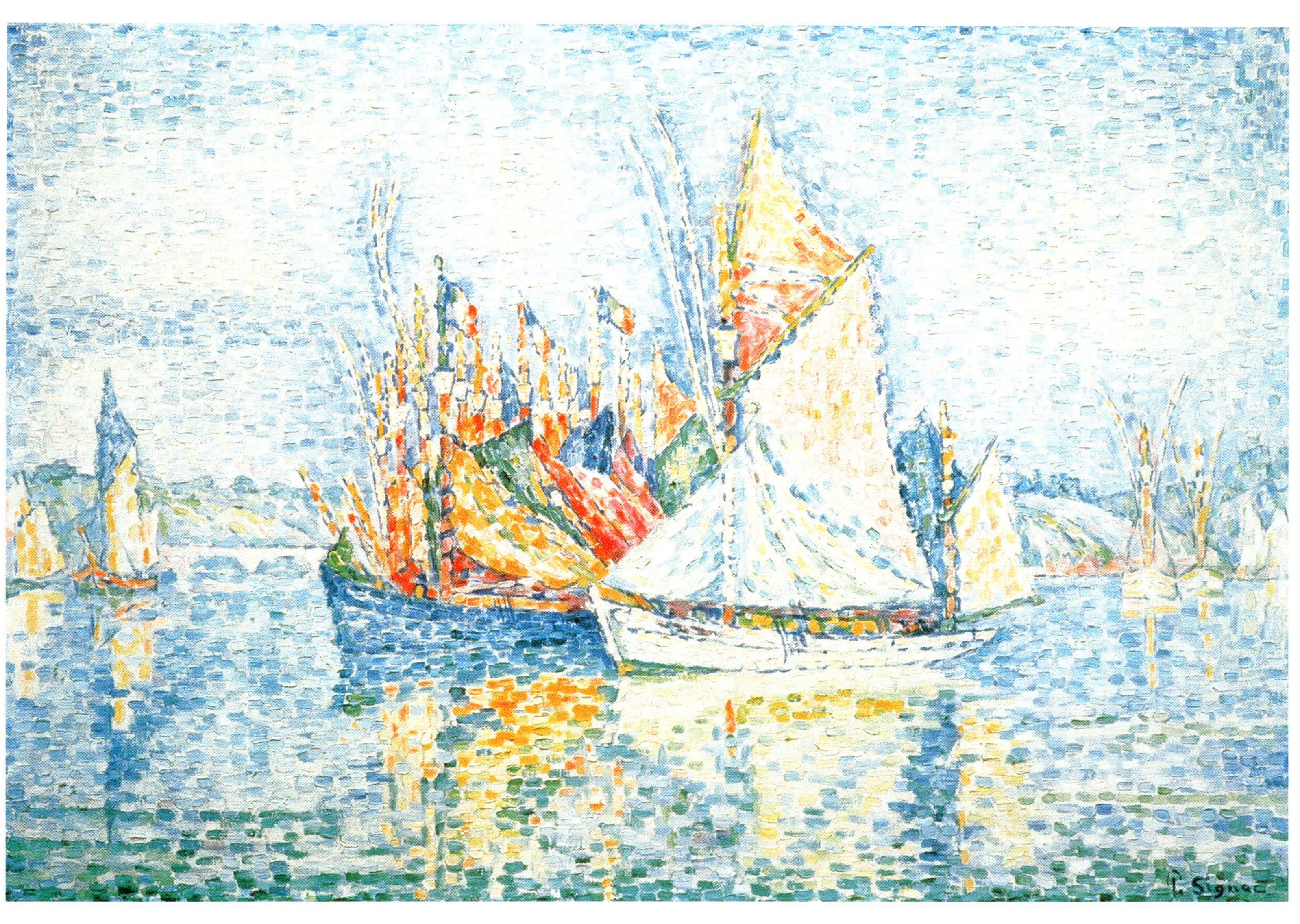
P. Signac

Van Gogh, Gauguin, and the Pont-Aven Group

Van Gogh, Gauguin und der Kreis von Pont-Aven

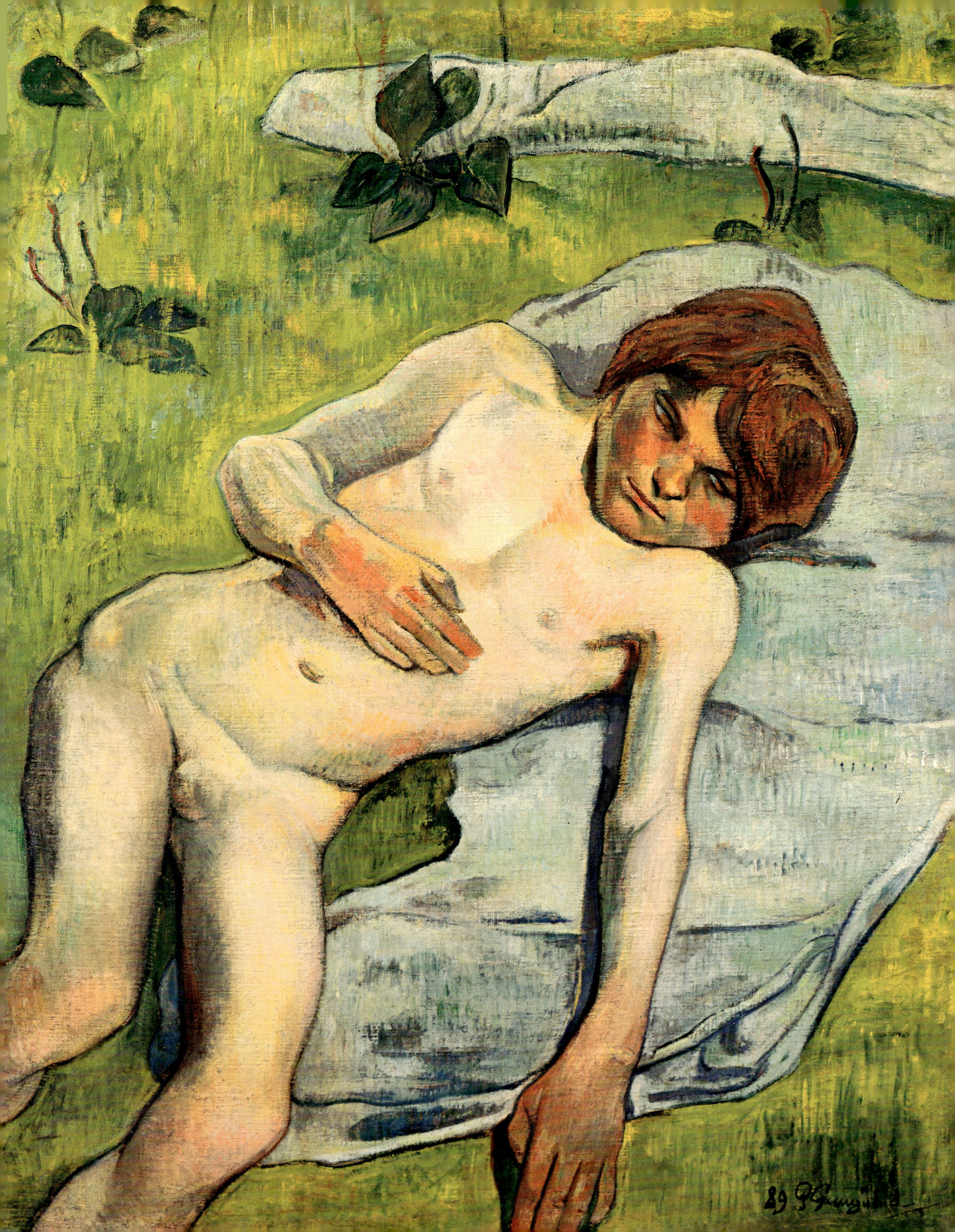

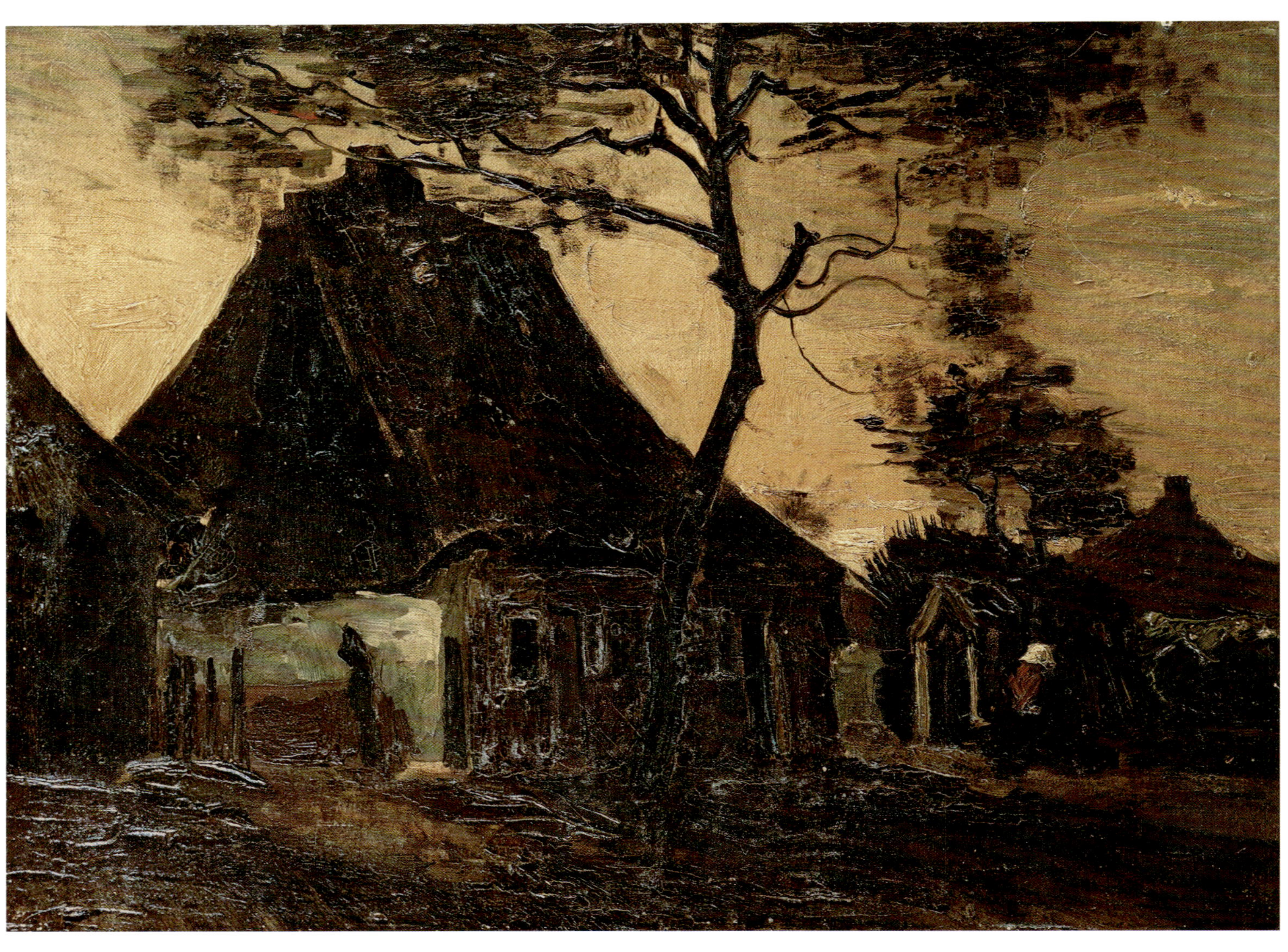

Vincent van Gogh
Farmhouse in Nuenen
Bauernkate in Nuenen, 1885

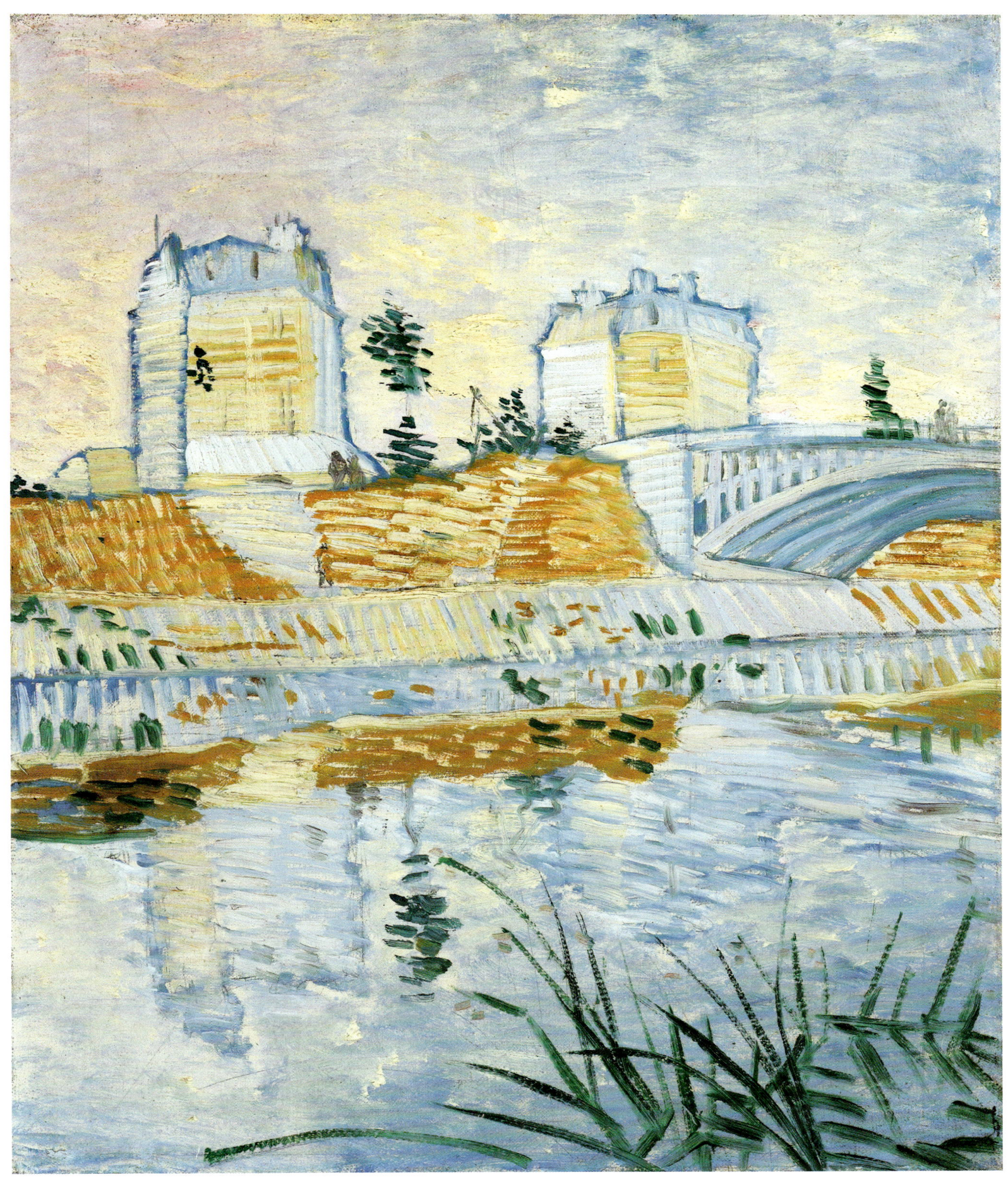

Vincent van Gogh
Bridge at Clichy
Brücke von Clichy, 1887

Vincent van Gogh
The Drawbridge
Die Zugbrücke, 1888

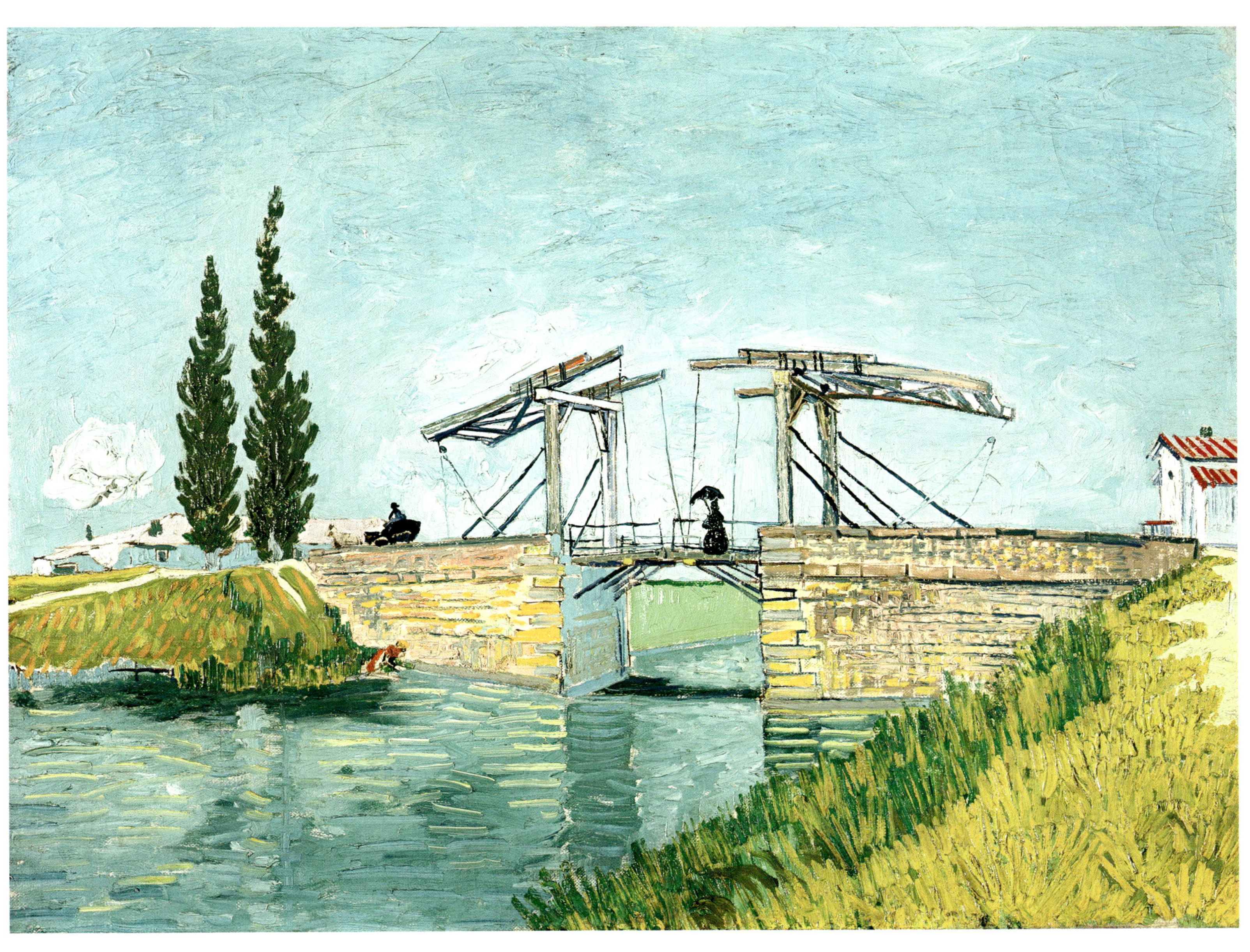

Paul Gauguin
Nude Breton Boy
Ein bretonischer Junge, 1889

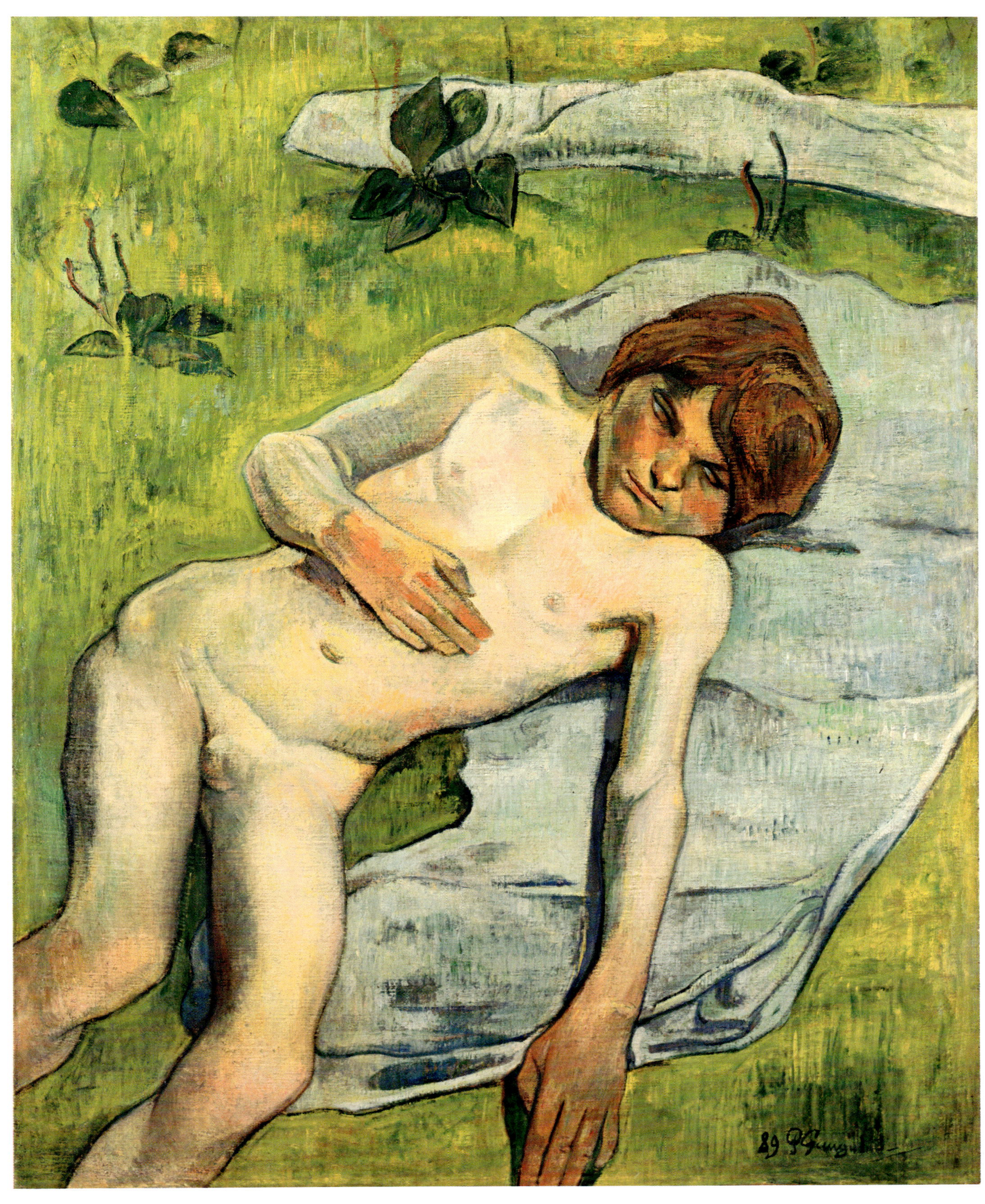

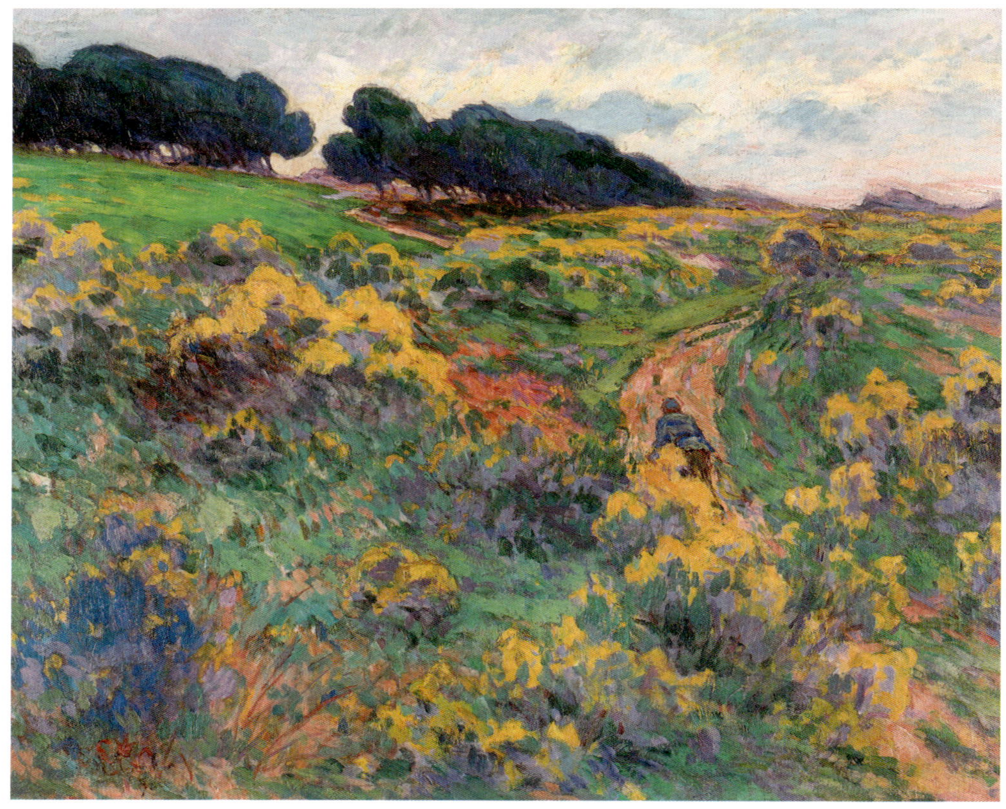

CLAUDE-EMILE SCHUFFENECKER
Figure in a Breton Heathland (Path over a Hill in Bloom or *The Ascending Path)*
Figur in bretonischer Heidelandschaft (Weg über einen blühenden Hügel oder *Der ansteigende Weg)*, 1886

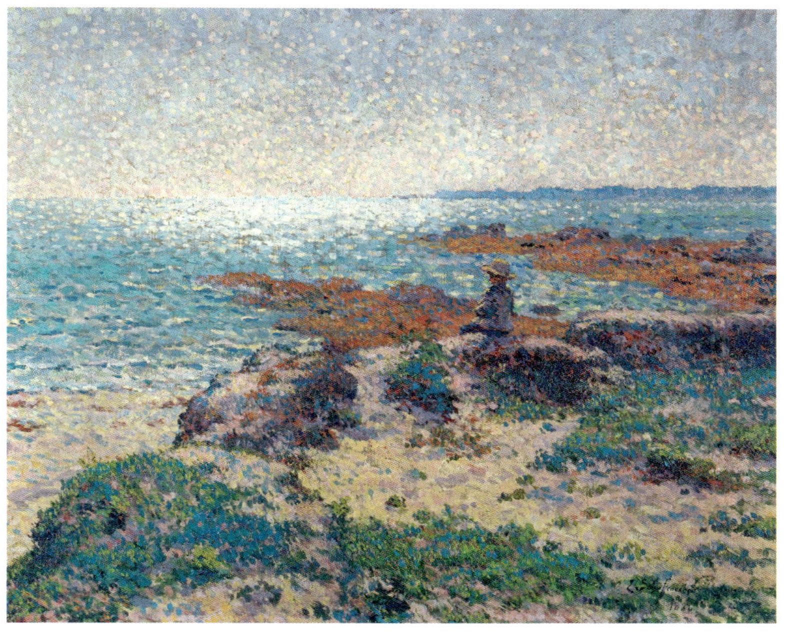

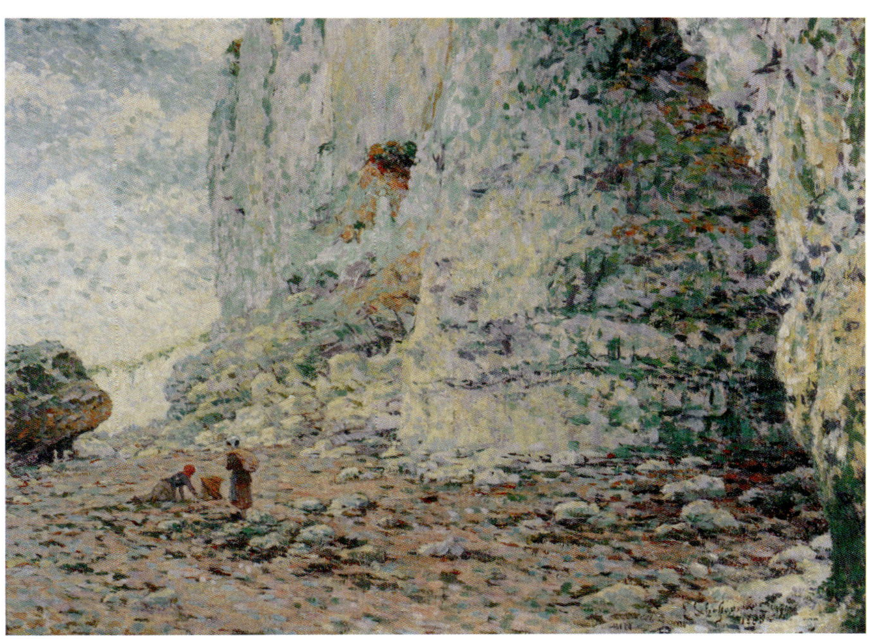

Claude-Emile Schuffenecker
Kelp Gatherers (At the Foot of the Cliffs or *Two Breton Women on the Beach at Low Tide)*
Seetang-Sammlerinnen (Am Fuße der Klippen oder *Zwei bretonische Frauen am Strand bei Ebbe)*, 1888

Claude-Emile Schuffenecker
Child Dreaming on the Seashore at Sunset
Träumendes Kind am Meer, bei Sonnenuntergang, 1884

Claude-Emile Schuffenecker
Notre-Dame de Paris (Notre-Dame in the Snow)
Notre-Dame von Paris (Notre-Dame im Schnee), 1889

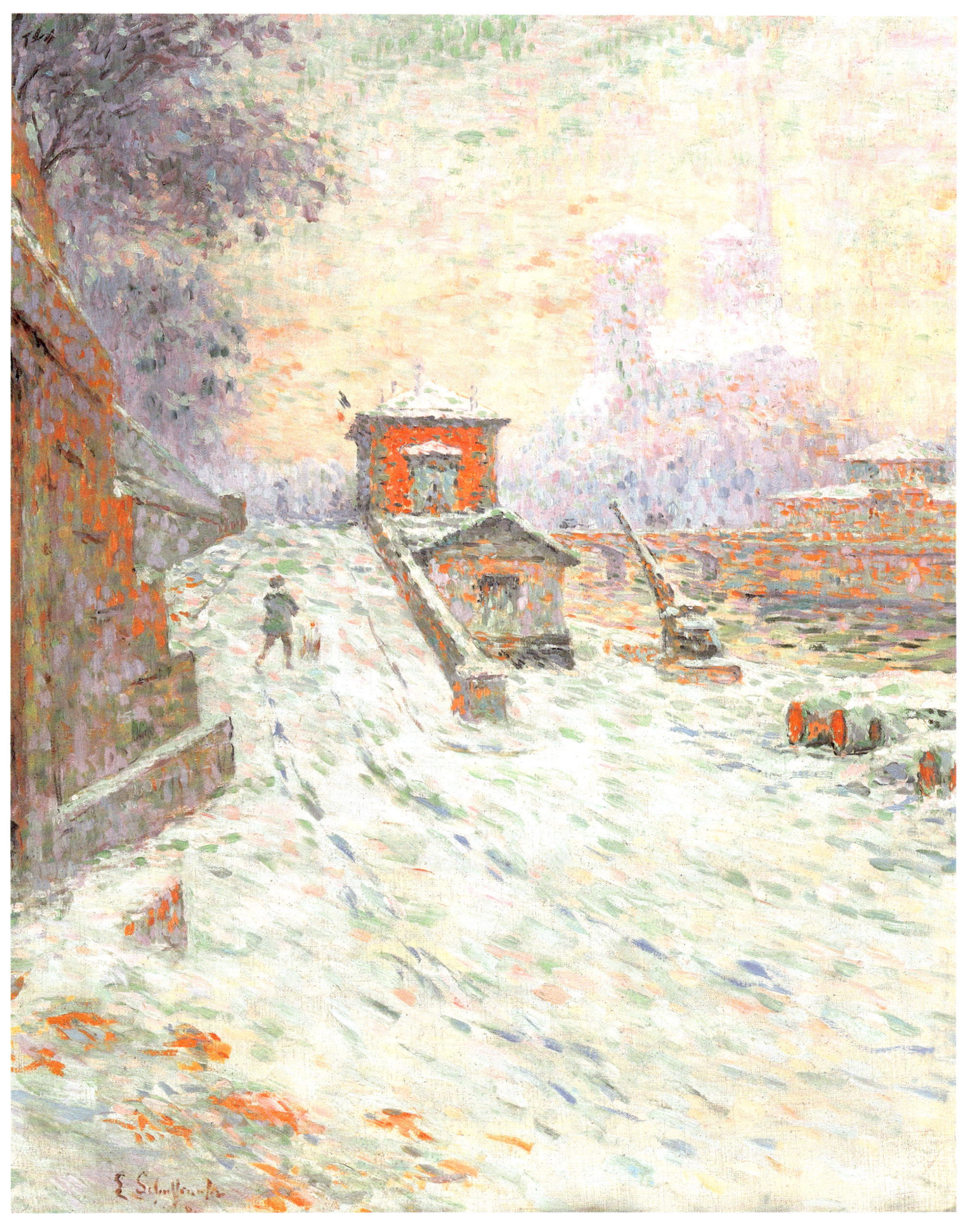

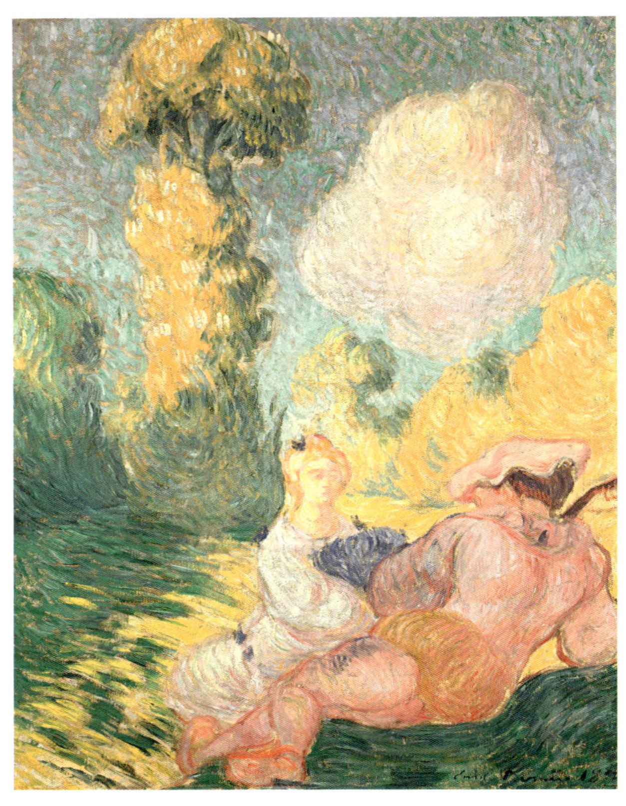

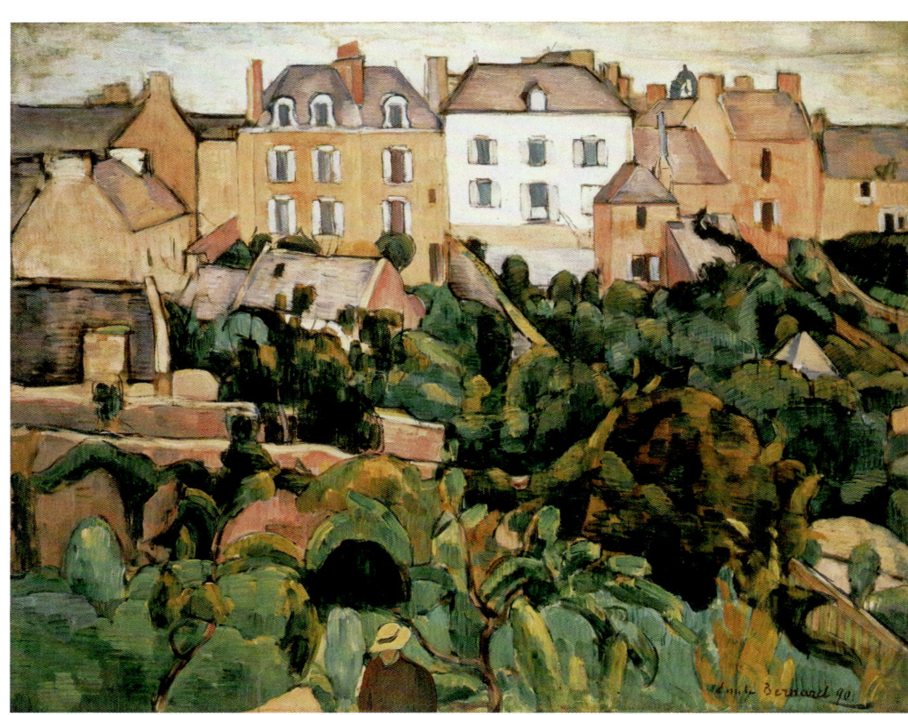

EMILE BERNARD
Houses in Pont-Aven
Häuser in Pont-Aven, 1890

EMILE BERNARD
Lovers
Liebespaar, 1891

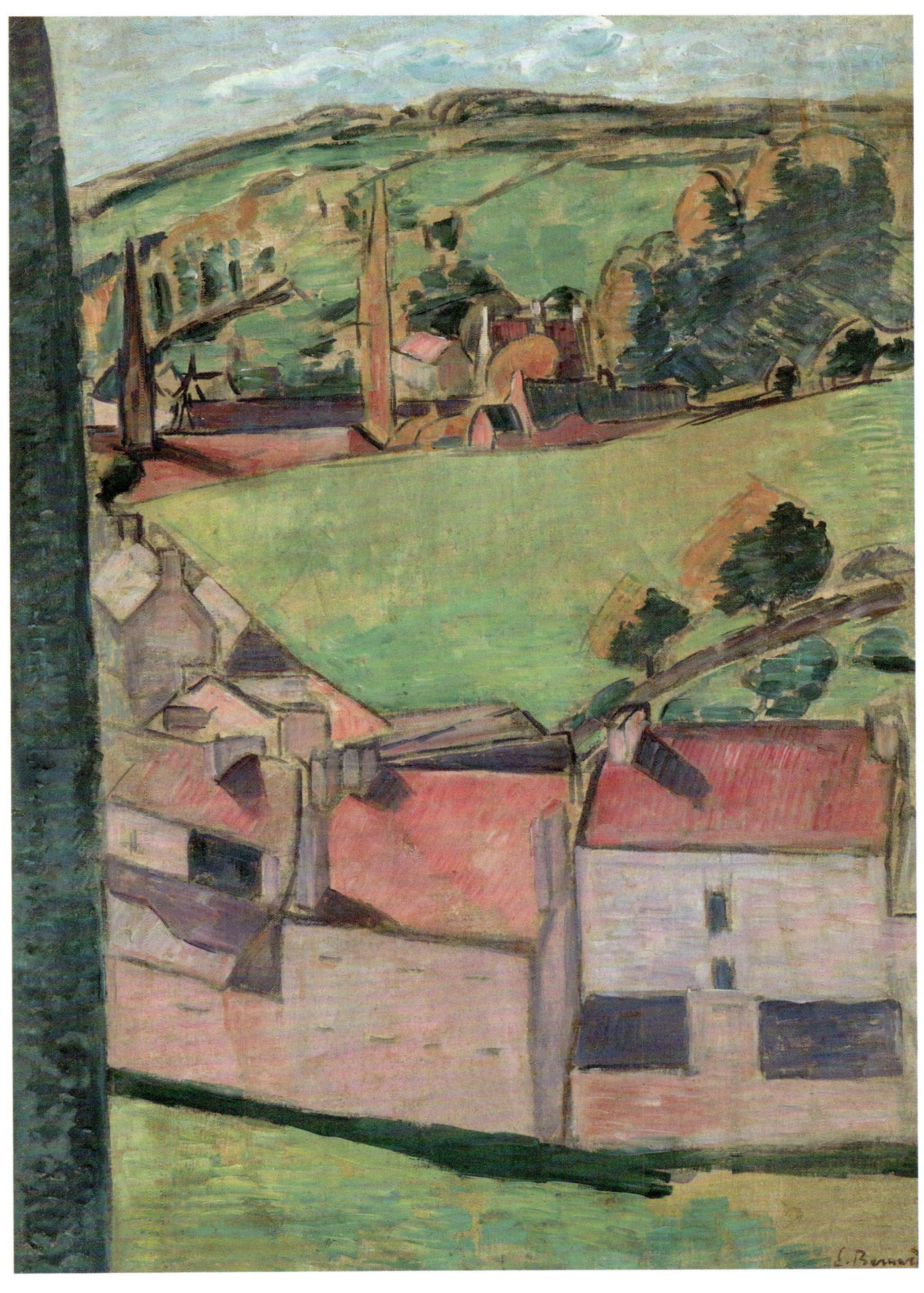

Emile Bernard
View of Pont-Aven (Landscape at Pont-Aven or *View of the Bois d'Amour)*
Ansicht von Pont-Aven (Landschaft von Pont-Aven oder *Ansicht des Bois d'Amour)*, 1888

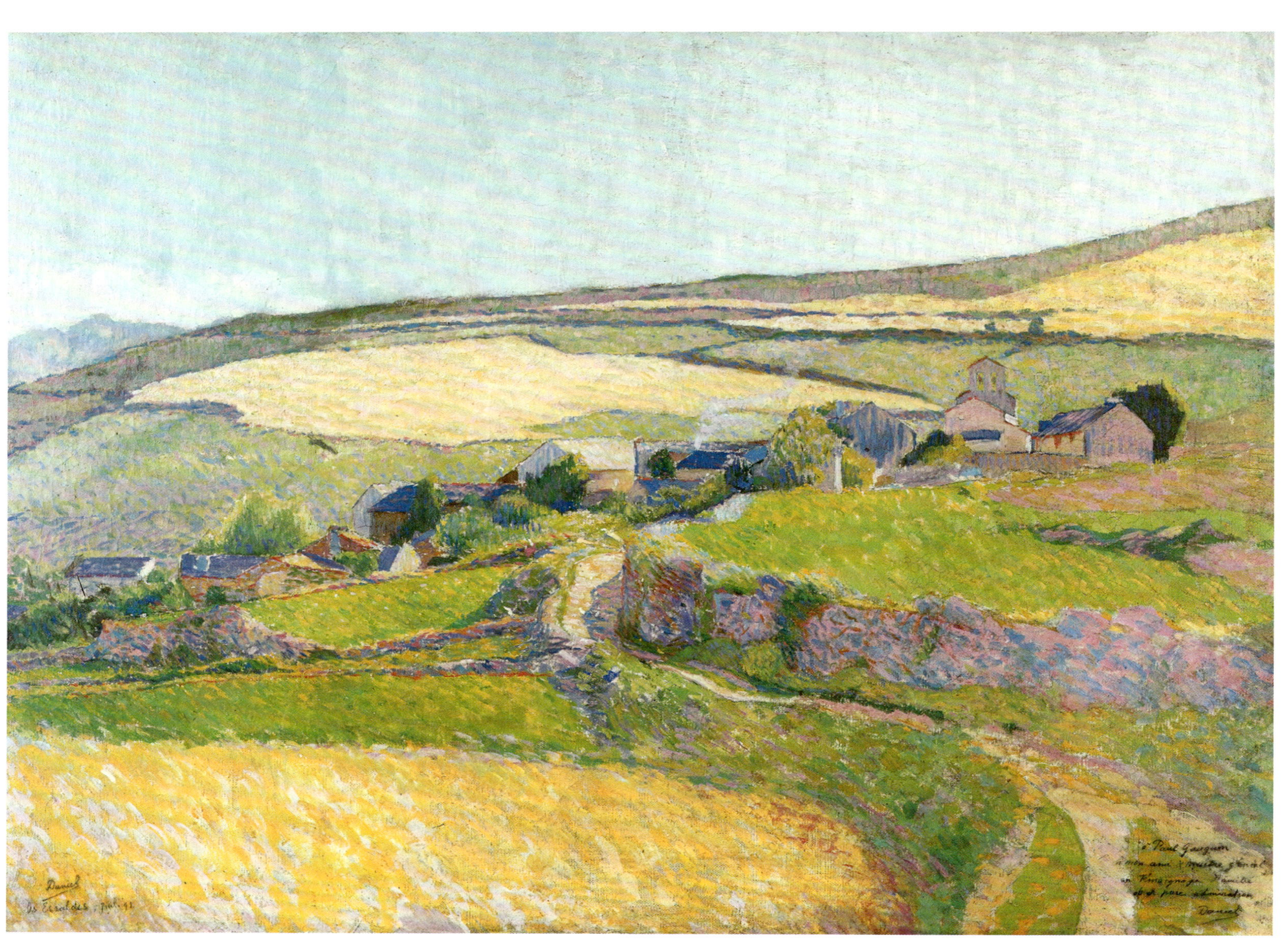

Georges Daniel de Monfreid
Landscape near Banyuls
Landschaft in der Umgebung von Banyuls, 1891

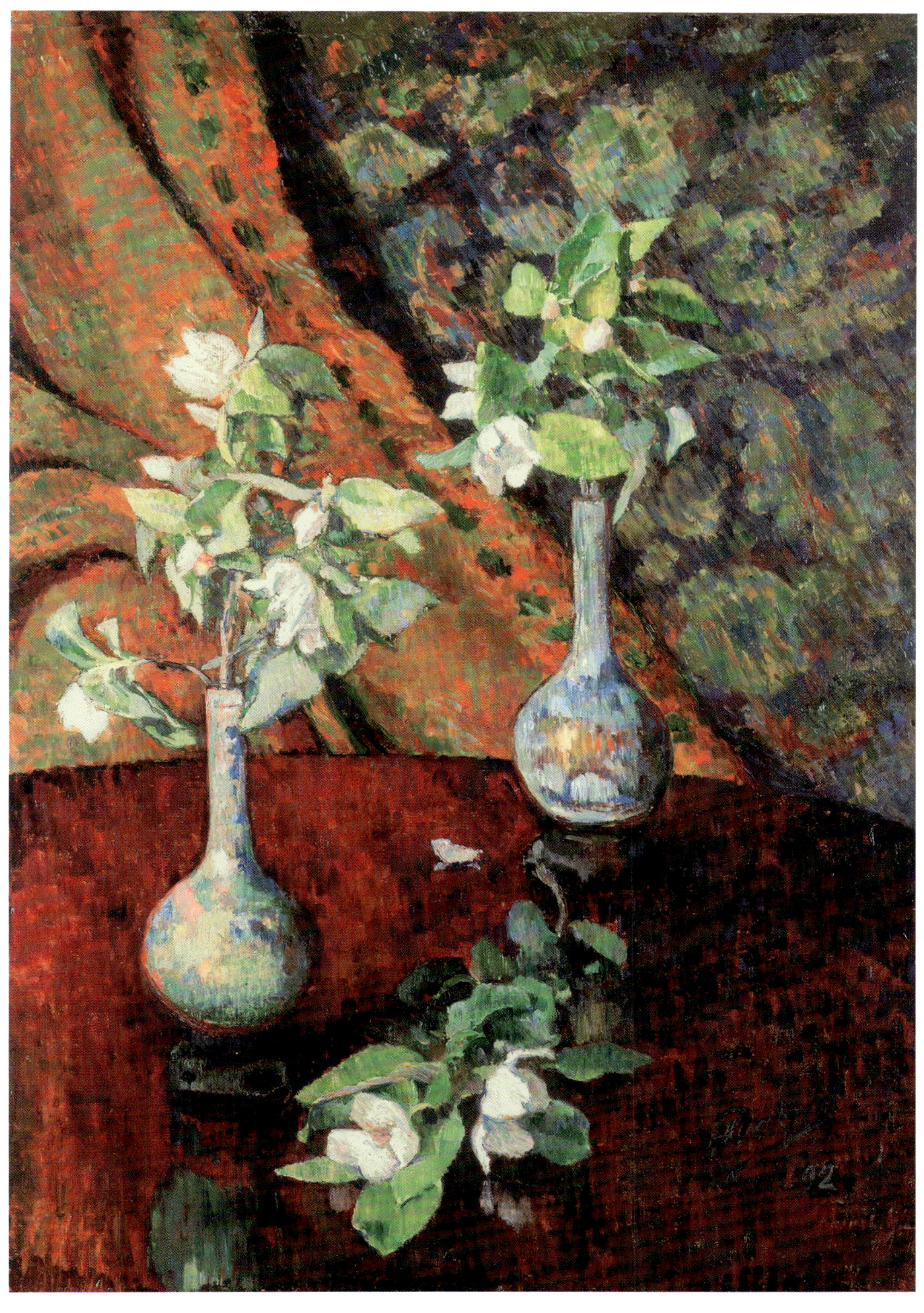

Georges Daniel de Monfreid
Chinese Vases (Flowers)
Chinesische Vasen (Blumen), 1892

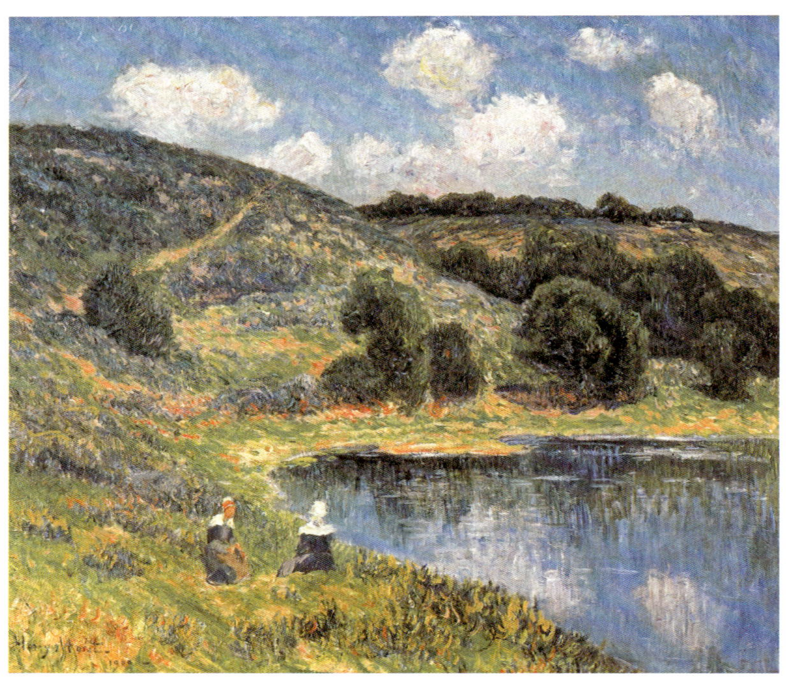

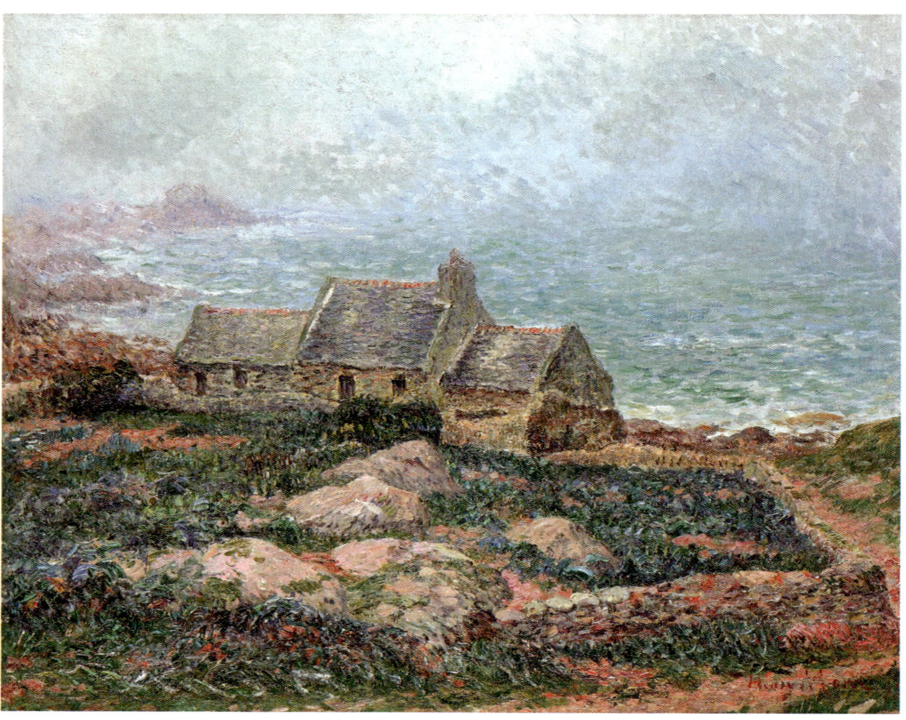

Henry Moret
Heathland in Saint-Guinolé near Pont-Aven
Heidelandschaft von Saint-Guinolé bei Pont-Aven, 1900

Henry Moret
The Customs House, Finistère
Die Zollstation, Finistère, 1899

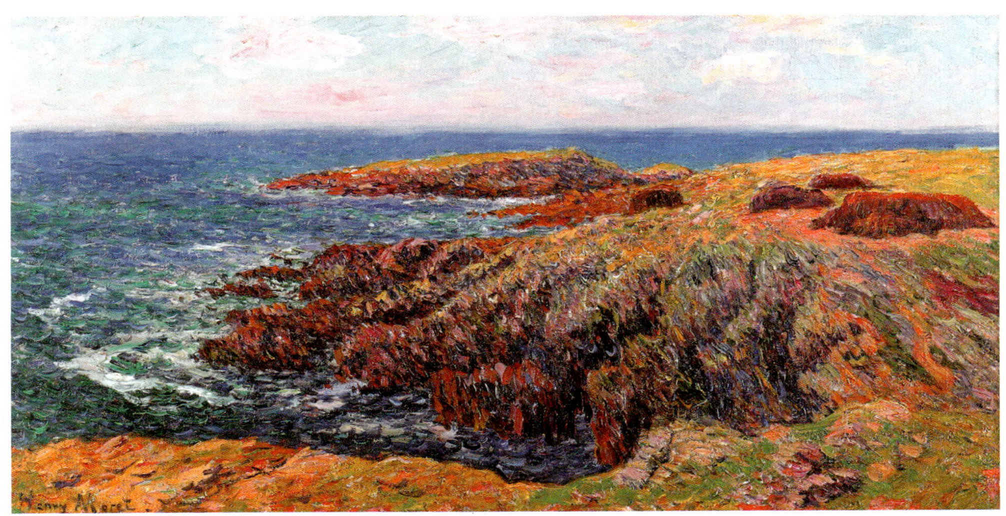

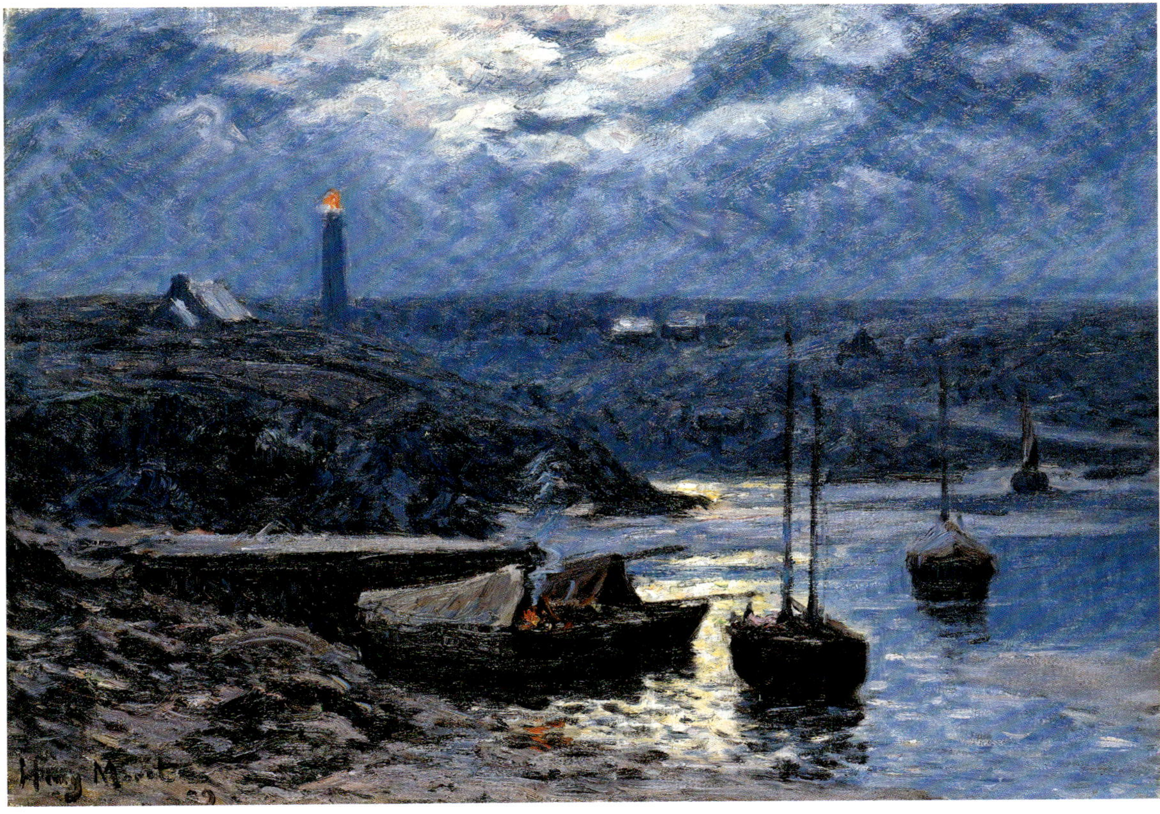

Henry Moret
Douelan at Night
Nacht in Douelan, 1909

Henry Moret
Coast at Belon, Finistère
Küste bei Belon, Finistère, ca. 1900

Paul Serusier
Still Life with Pears
Stillleben mit Birnen, 1923

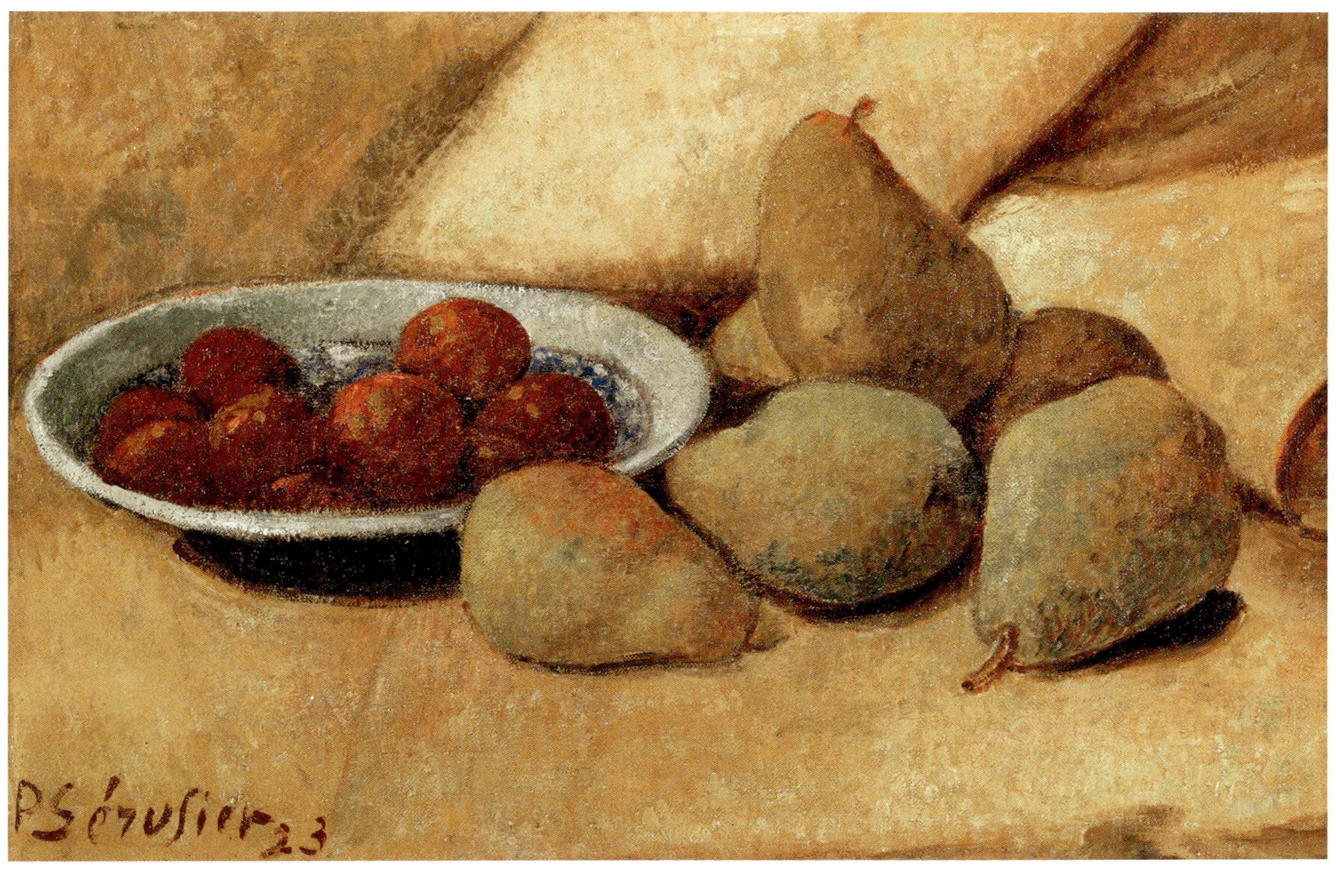
P Sérusier 23

The Moderns

Die Modernen

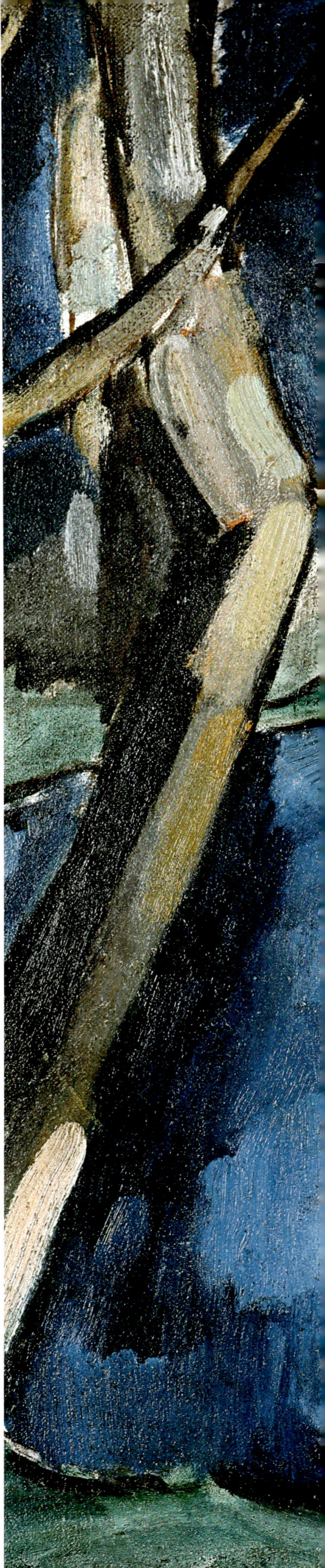

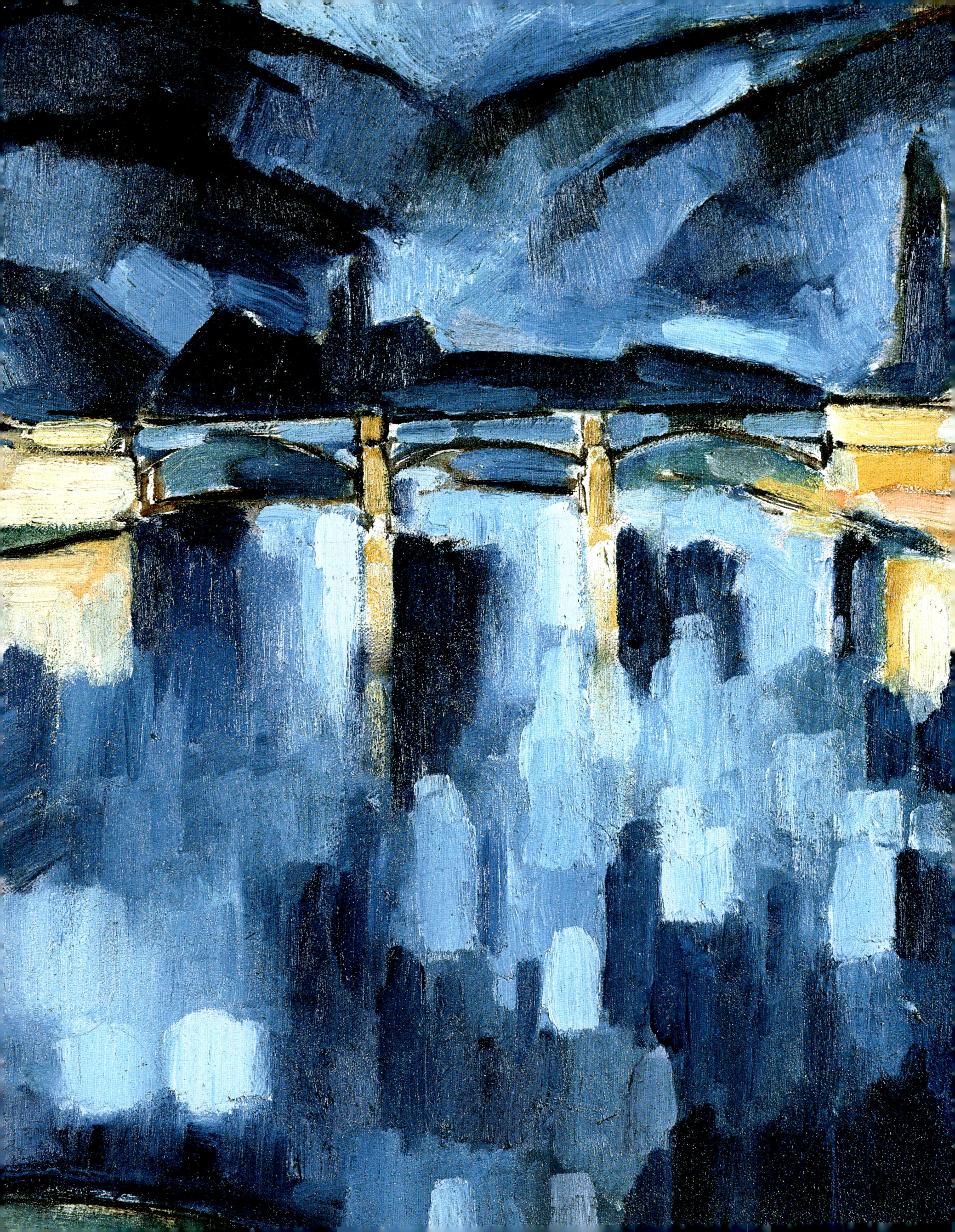

Albert Marquet
Suburb of Paris
Vorort von Paris, 1899

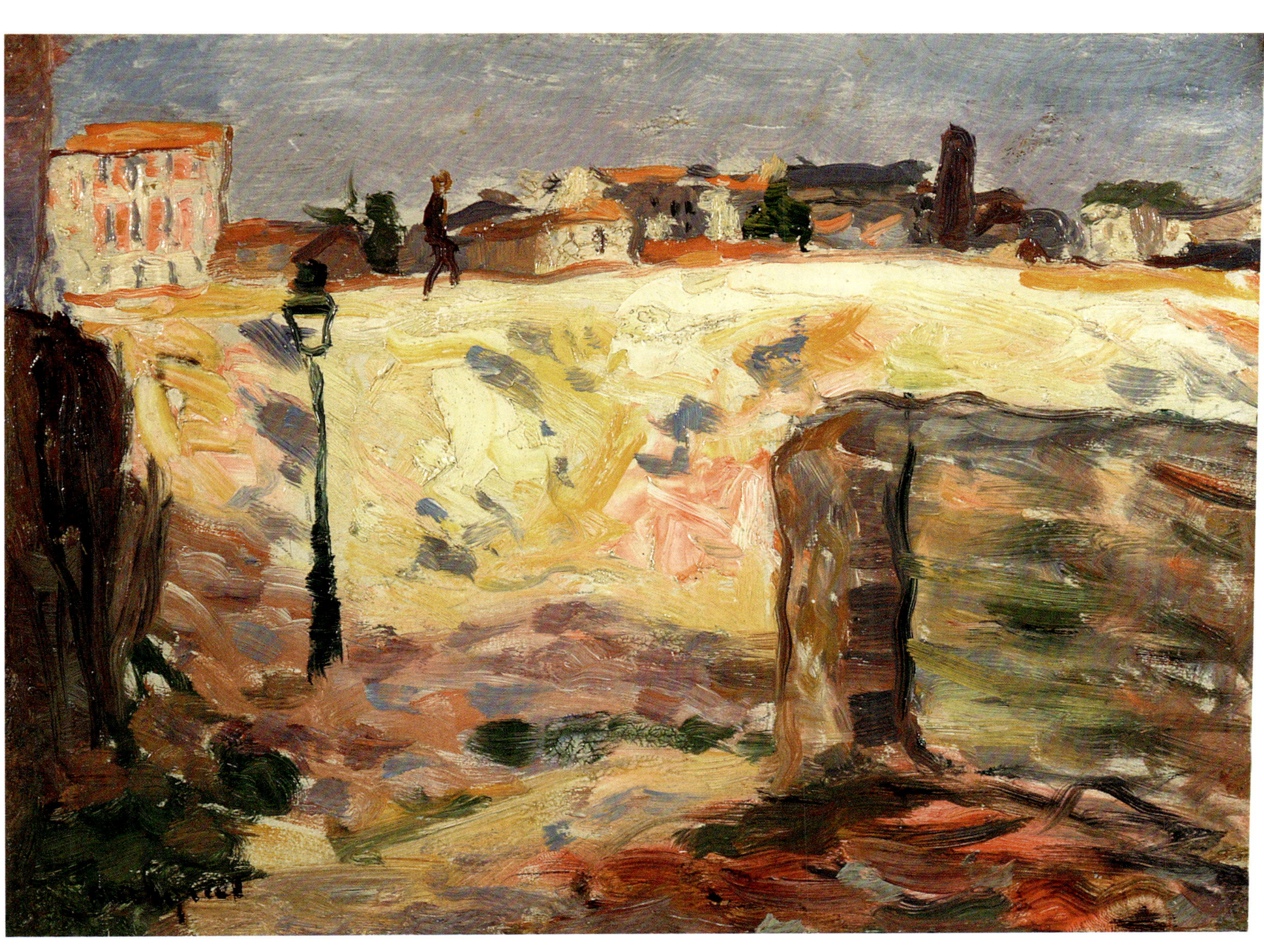

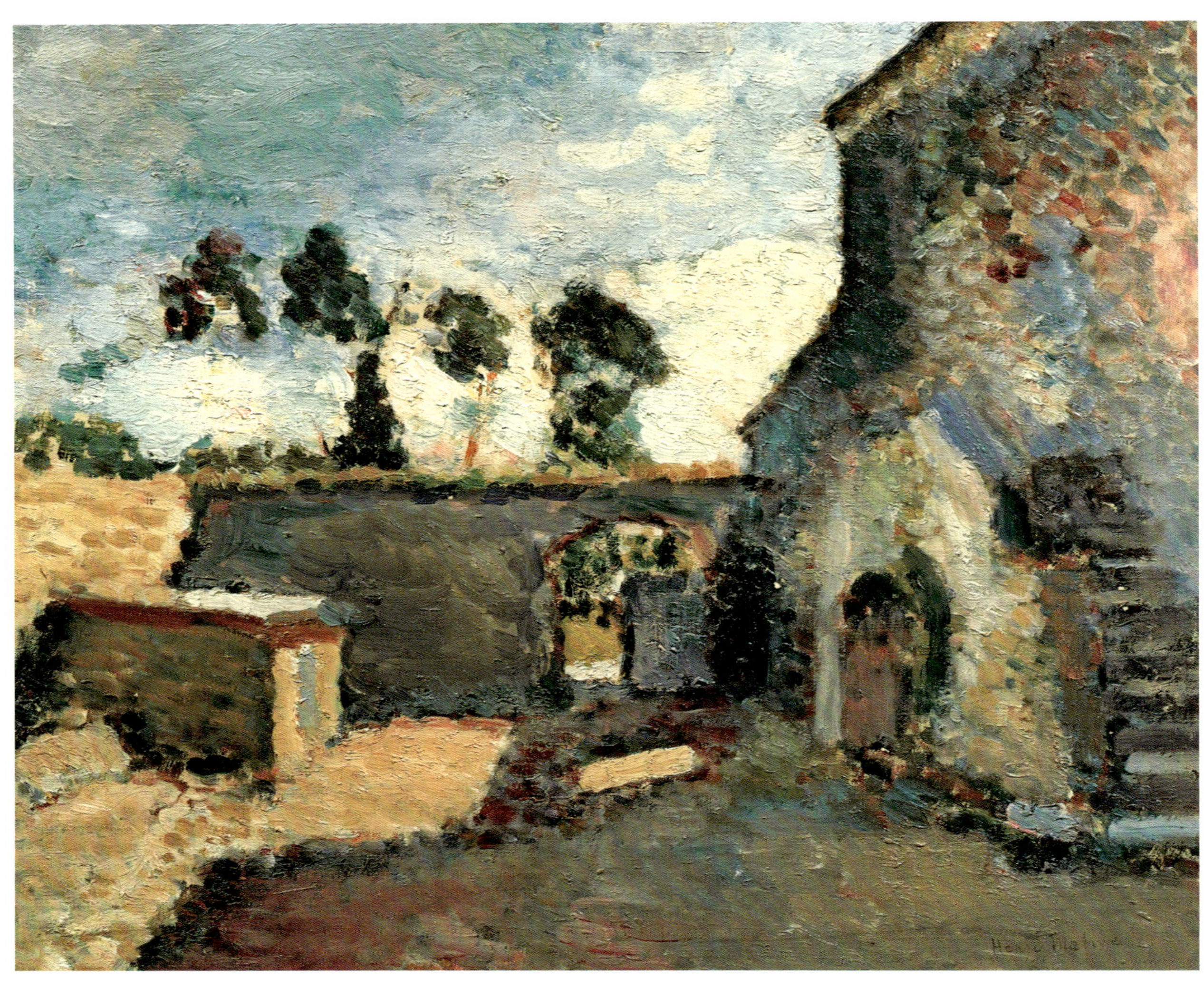

Henri Matisse
Corsica, the Old Mill (Mill Courtyard in Ajaccio I)
Korsika, die alte Mühle (Hof der Mühle in Ajaccio I), 1898

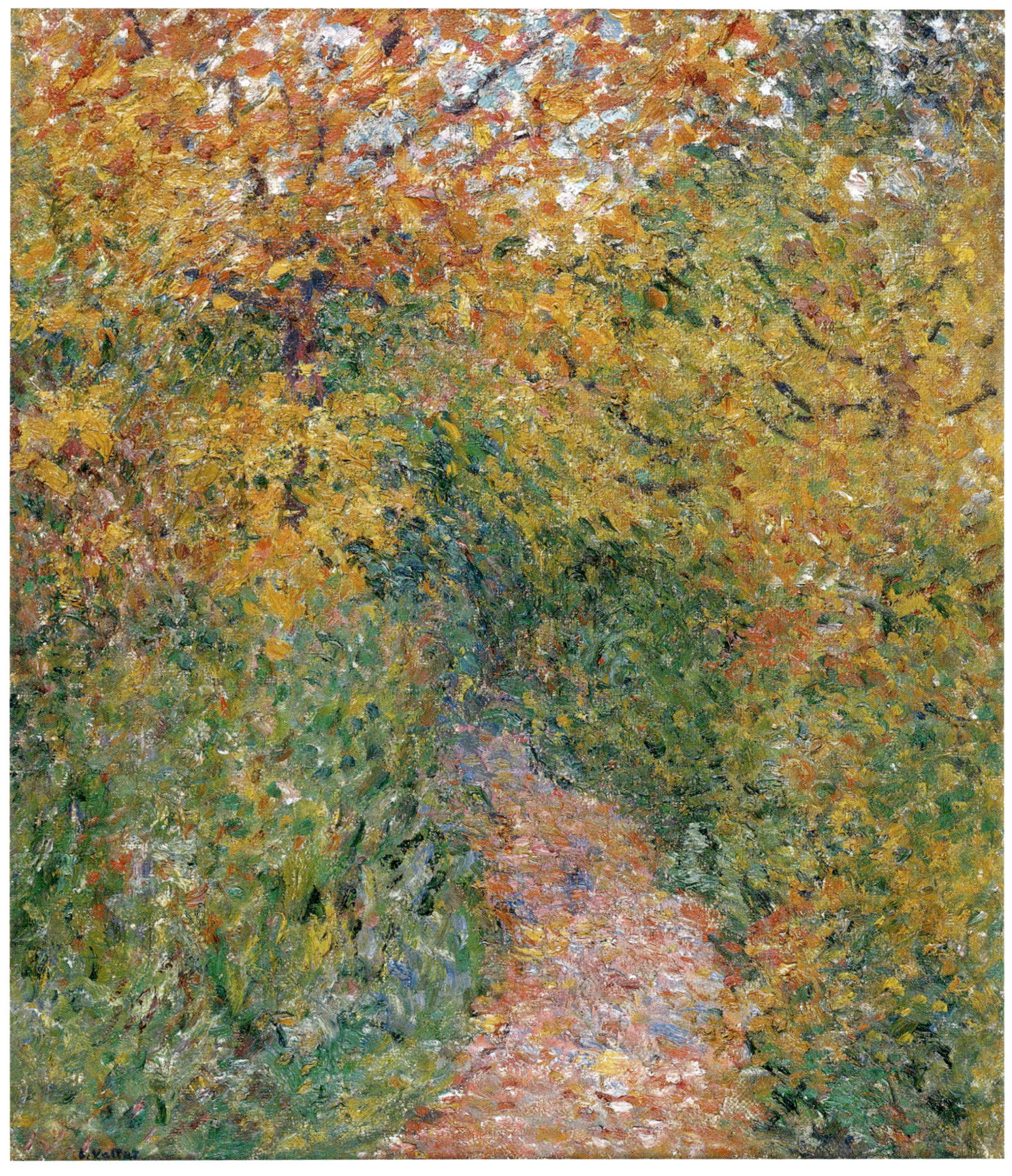

Louis Valtat
Undergrowth
Unterholz, ca. 1898

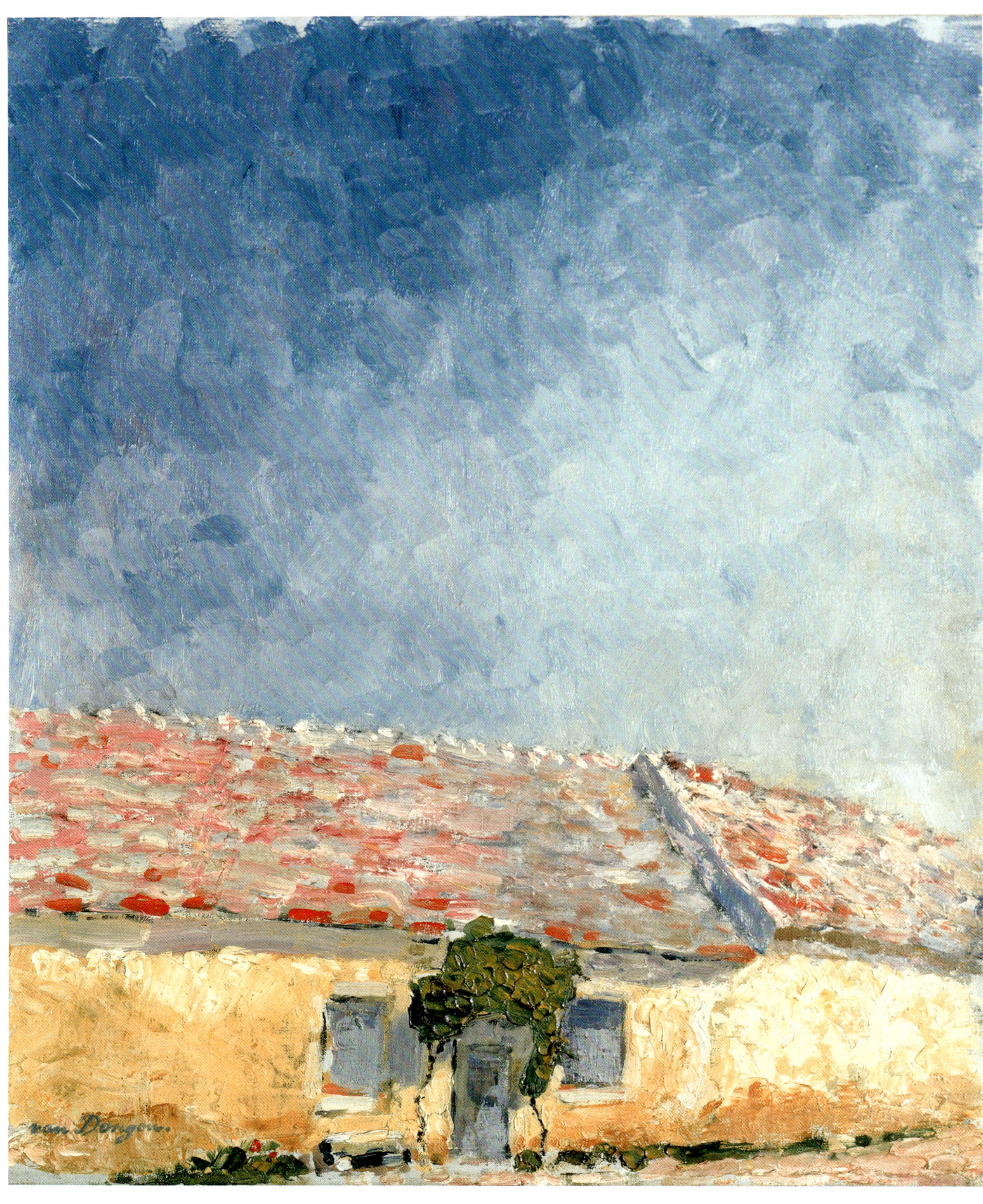

Kees van Dongen
House in Fleury
Haus in Fleury, 1905

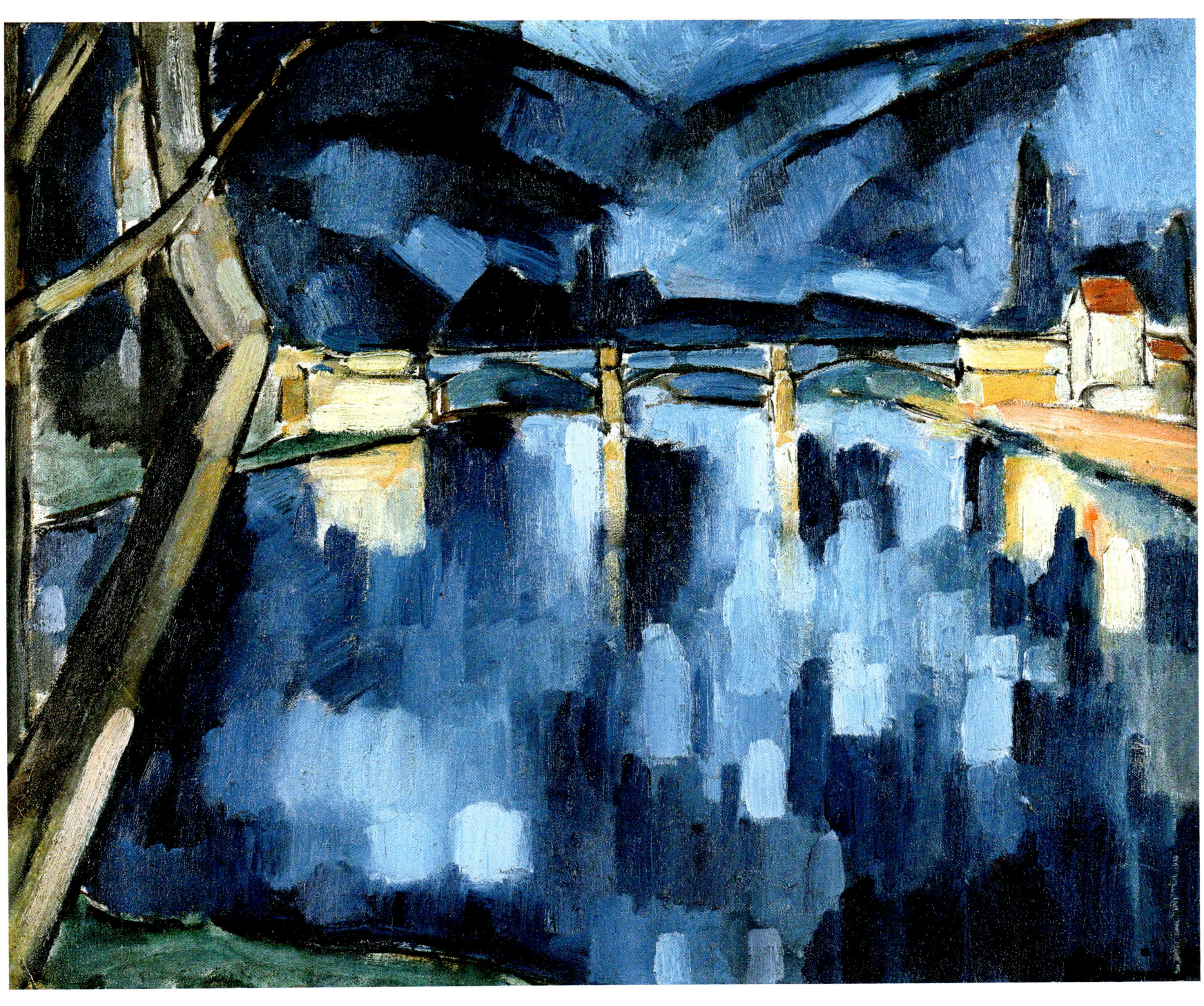

Maurice de Vlaminck
The Bridge at Chatou
Die Brücke von Chatou, 1908

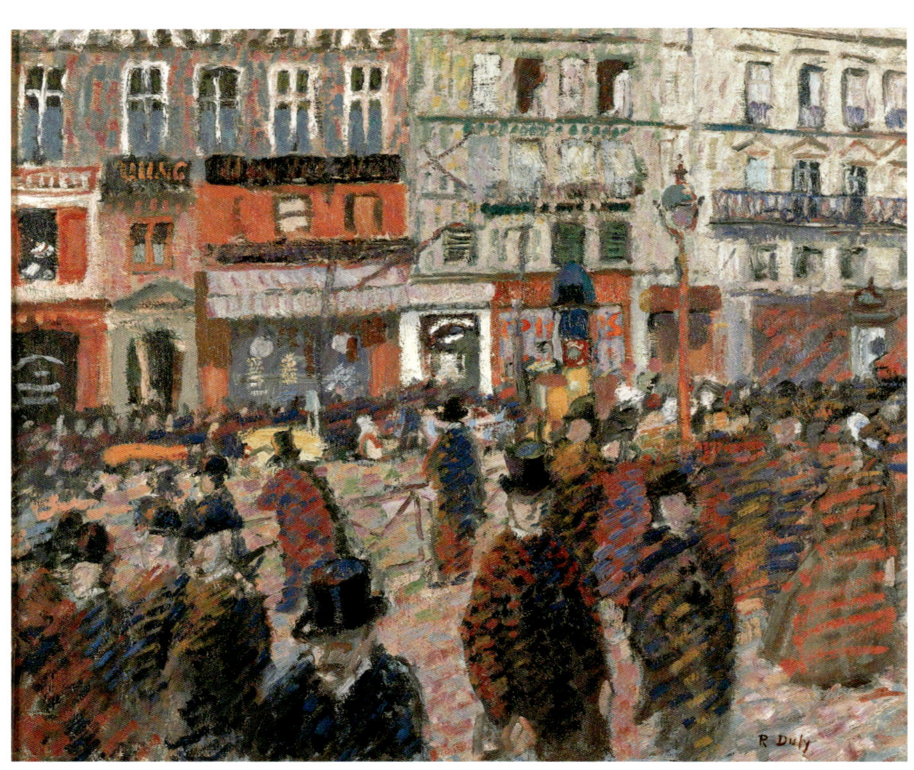

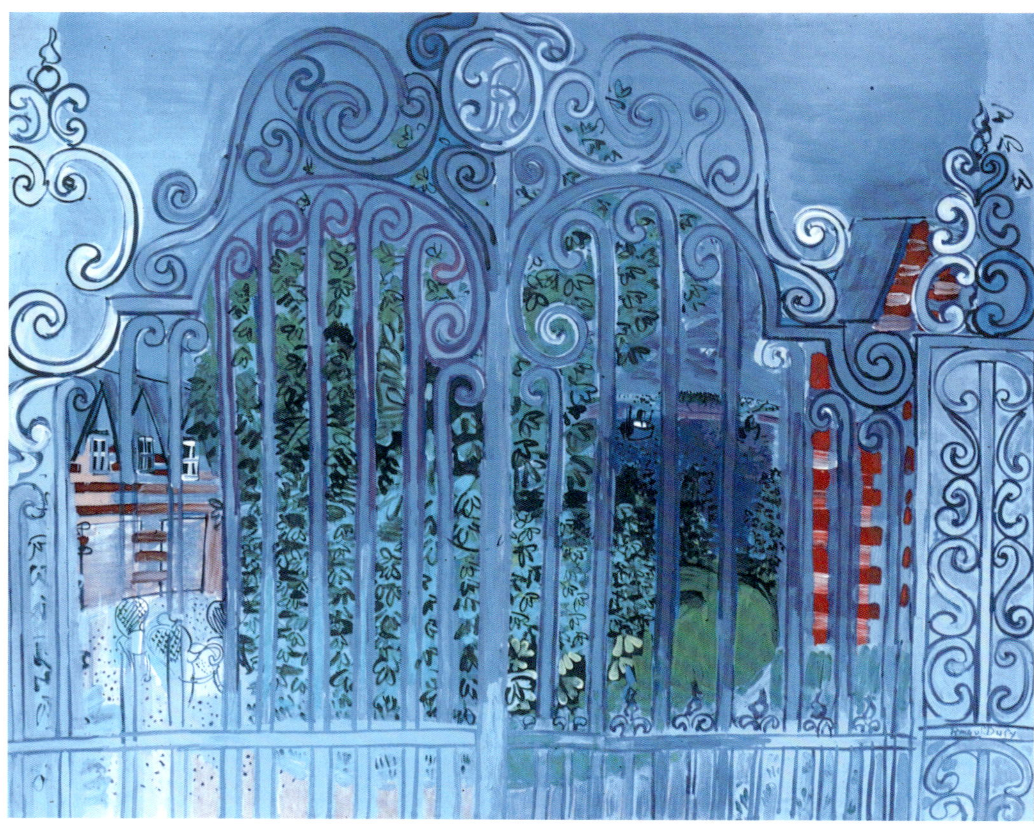

Raoul Dufy
Boulevard Saint-Martin, 1903

Raoul Dufy
Paled Gate
Gittertor, 1930

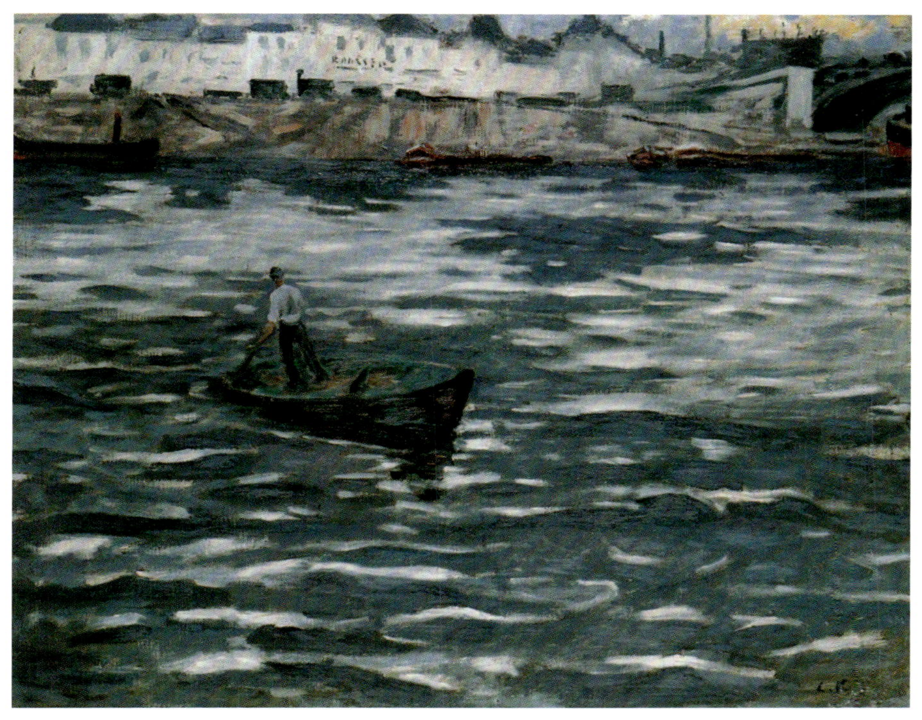

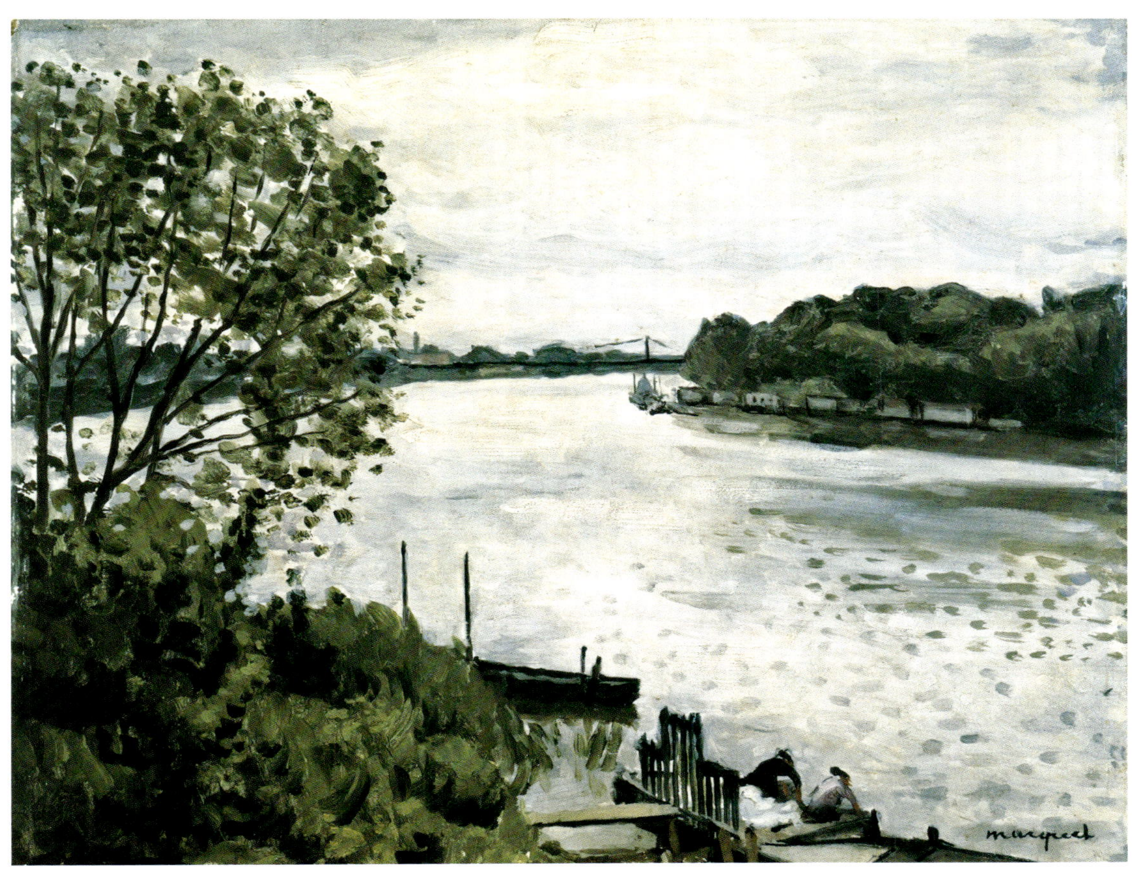

Albert Marquet
Washerwomen, Triel-sur-Seine
Waschfrauen, Triel-sur-Seine, 1931

Louis Valtat
The Ferryman
Der Fährmann, ca. 1905

EDOUARD VUILLARD
Girl at the Linen Cupboard
Mädchen am Wäscheschrank, ca. 1894/95

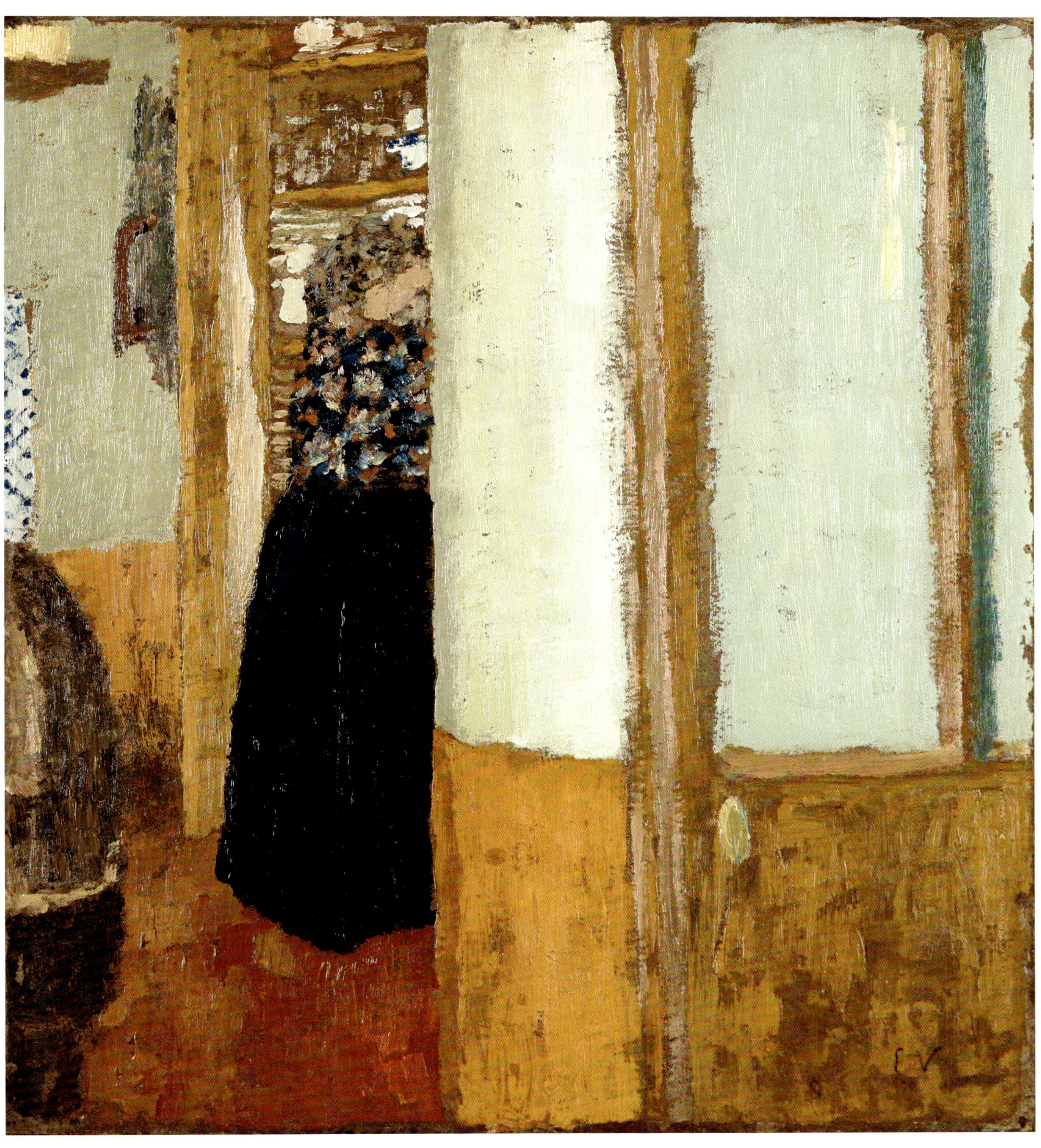

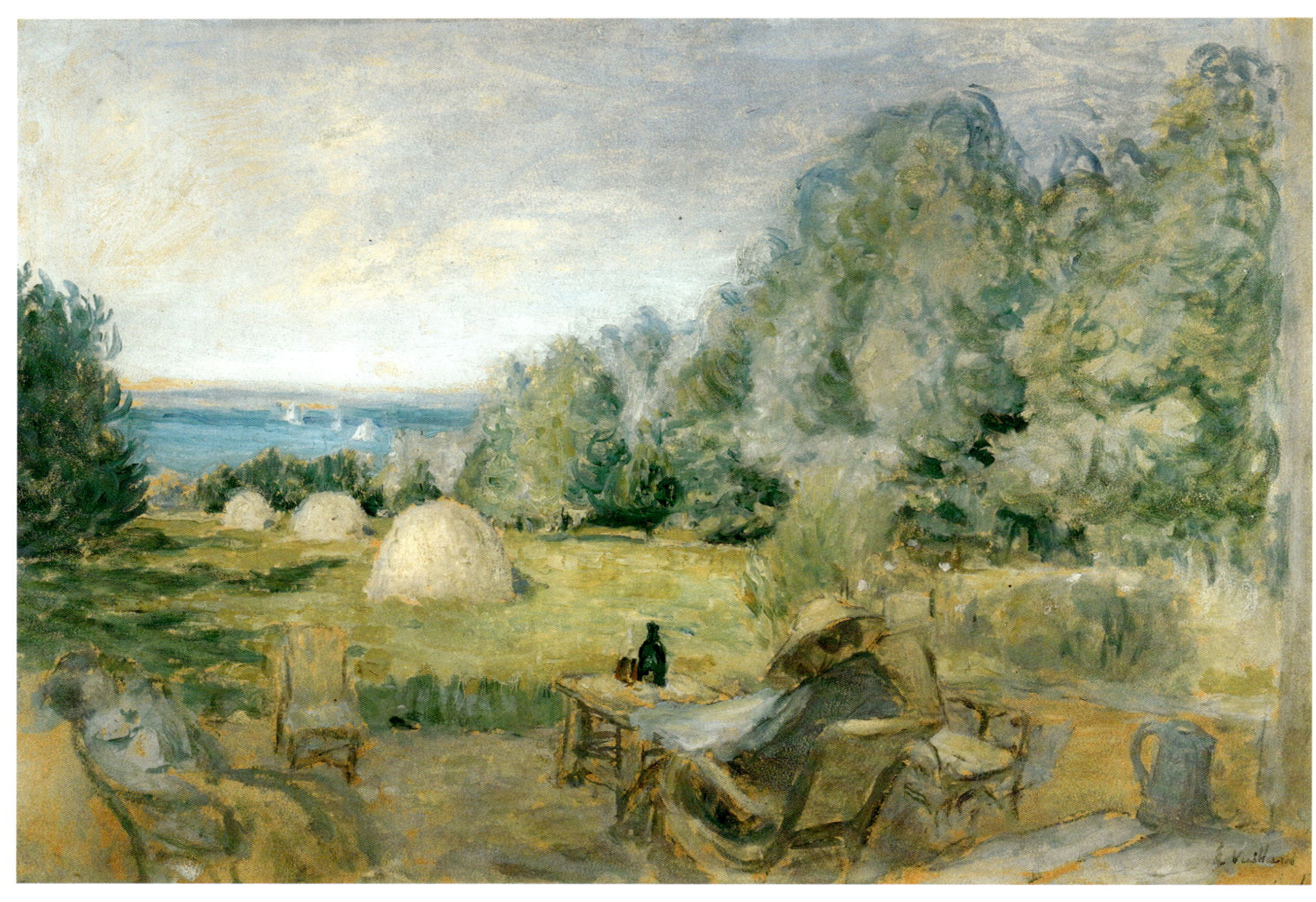

Edouard Vuillard
Haystacks in the "Jardin des Etincelles" in Criqueboeuf
Heuhaufen im »Jardin des Etincelles« in Criqueboeuf, 1902

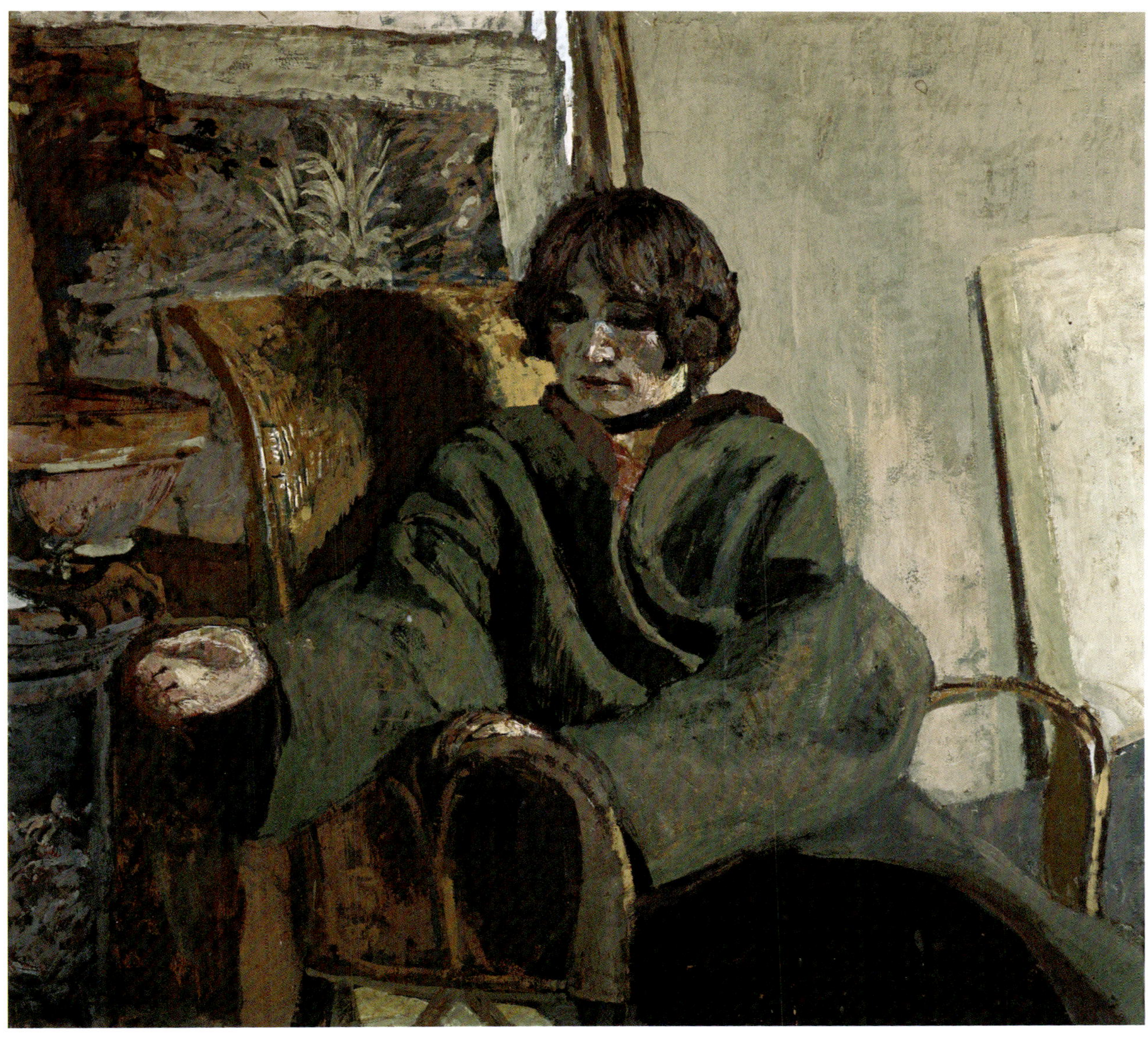

Edouard Vuillard
Portrait of the Actress Lucie Belin (Woman in the Studio)
Bildnis der Schauspielerin Lucie Belin (Frau im Atelier), 1914/15

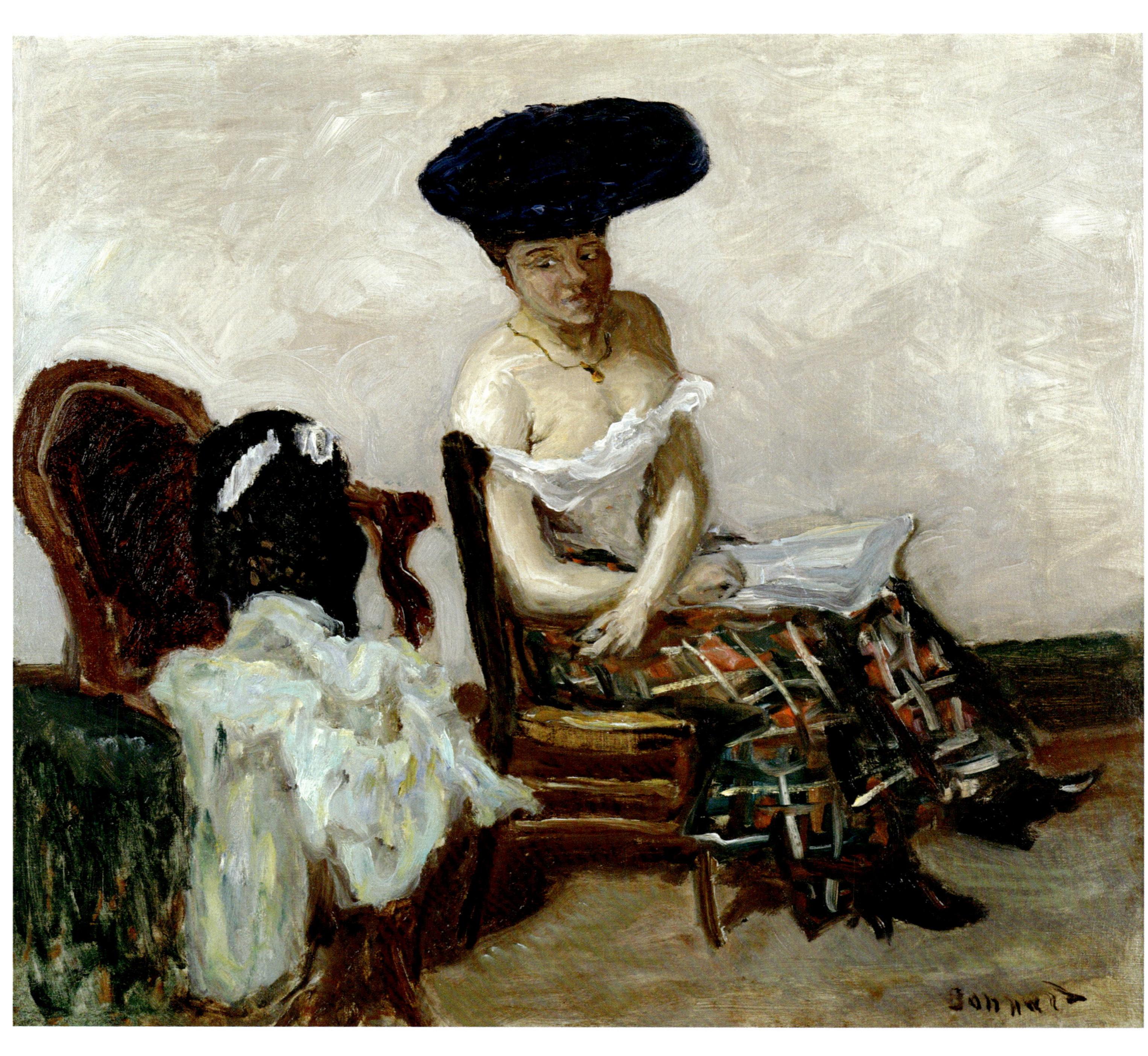

Pierre Bonnard
Model with a Large Hat
Modell mit großem Hut, 1907

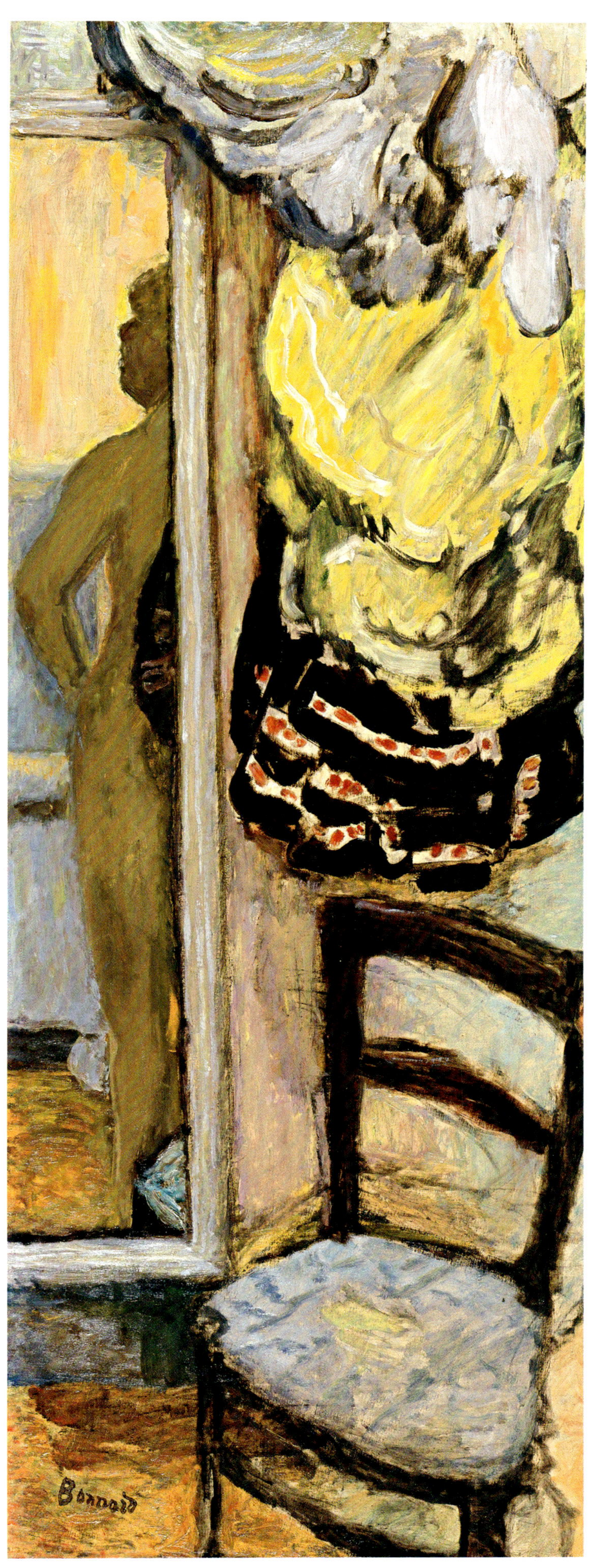

Pierre Bonnard
Female Nude in the Mirror
Frauenakt im Spiegel, 1910

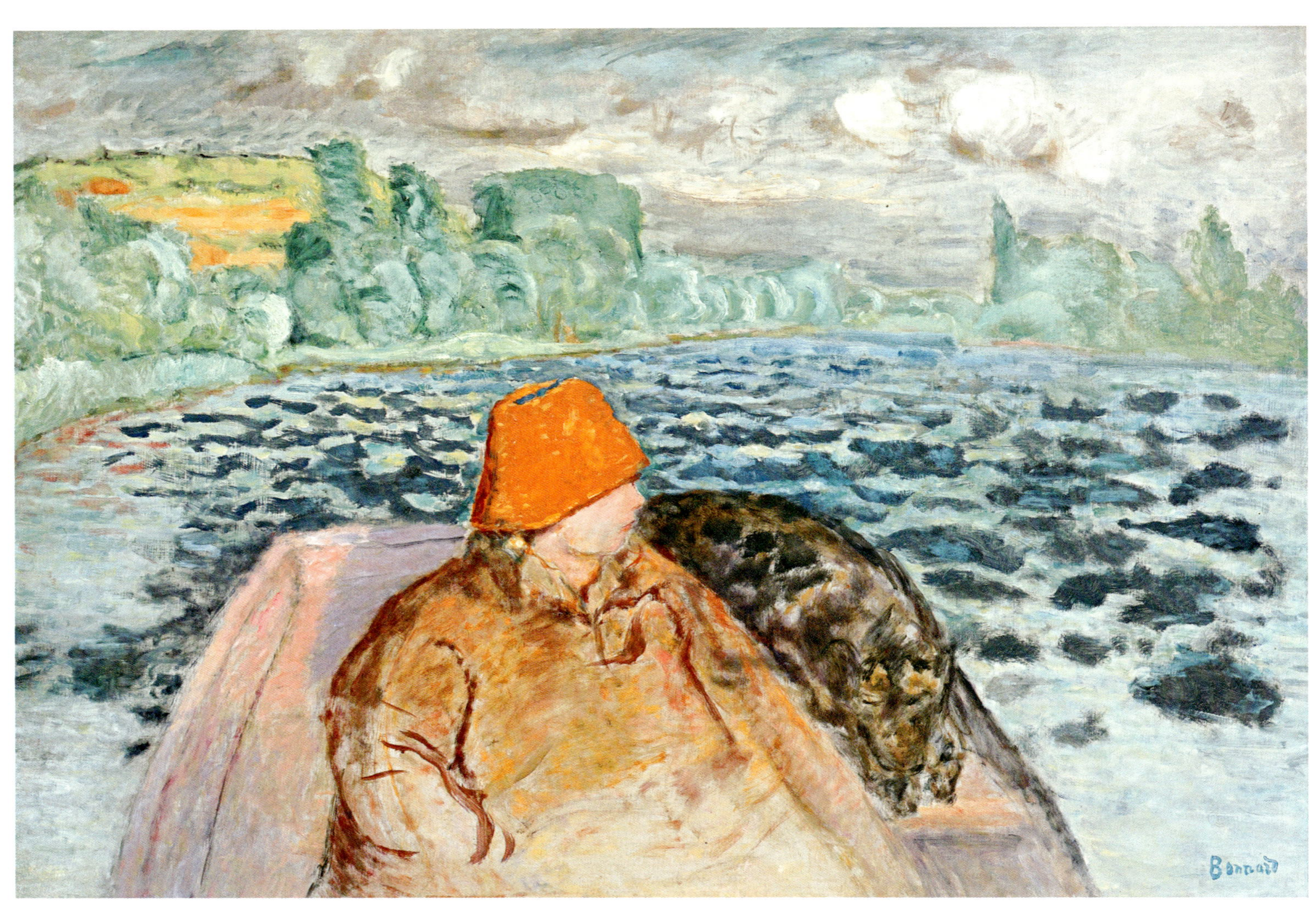

Pierre Bonnard
In a Rowboat (Vernon)
Im Kahn (Bei Vernon), 1912

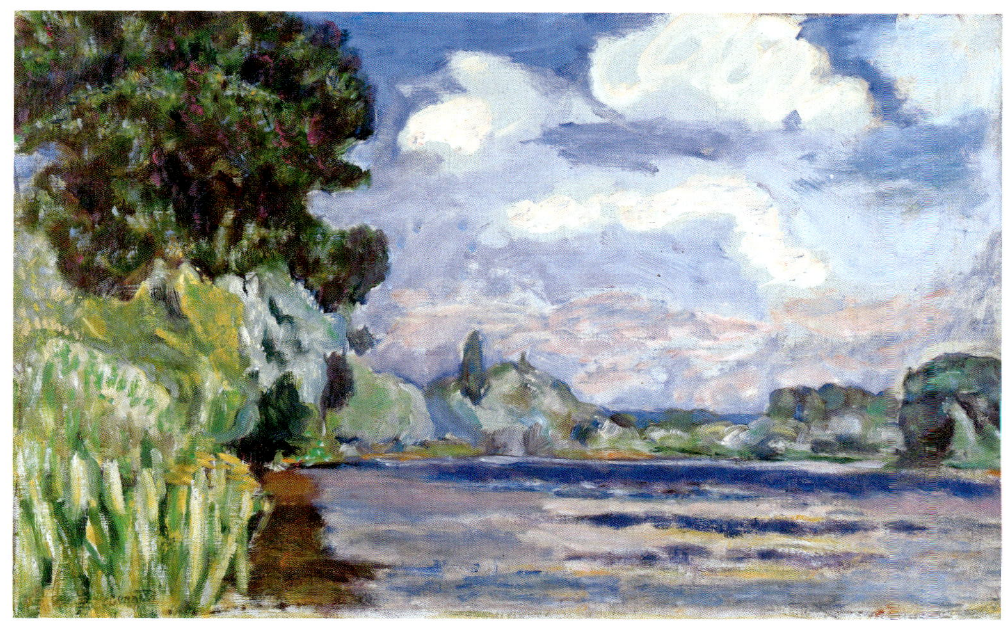

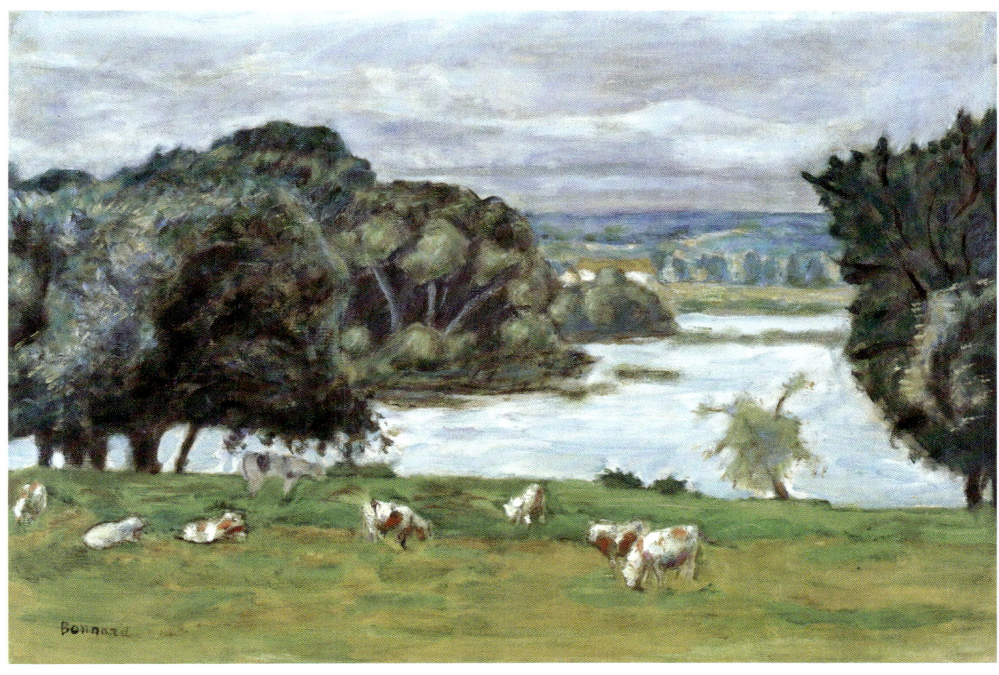

PIERRE BONNARD
Pasture on the Banks of the Seine
Weideland am Ufer der Seine, ca. 1913

PIERRE BONNARD
The Seine at Vernon
Die Seine bei Vernon, ca. 1922

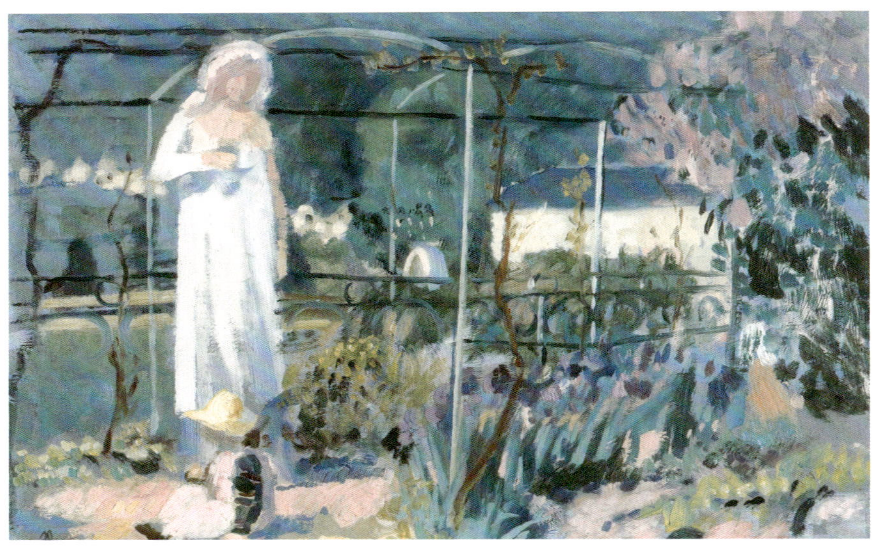

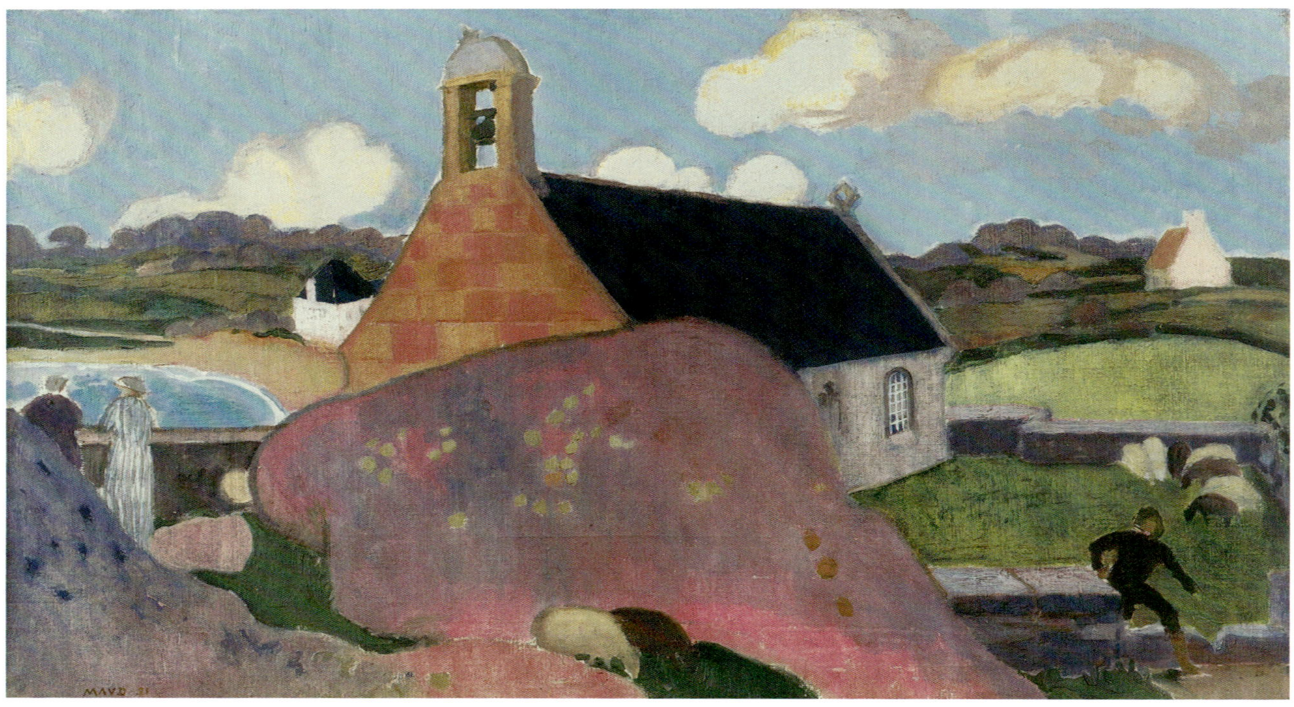

Maurice Denis
Vine Bower in Saint-Germain
Weinlaube in Saint-Germain, ca. 1903/05

Maurice Denis
The Pink Church – Tilloloy
Die roséfarbene Kirche – Tilloloy, 1921

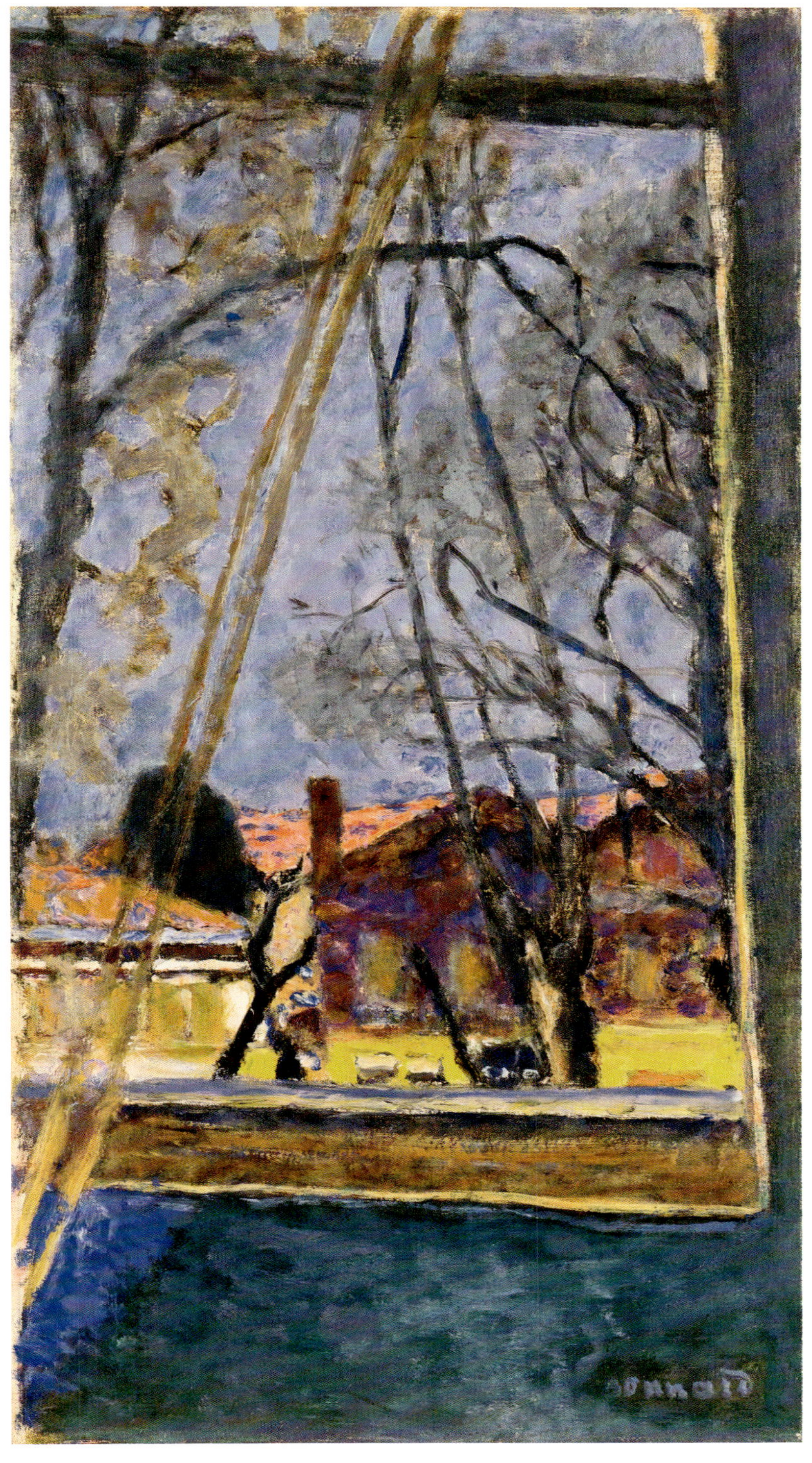

Pierre Bonnard
View of a Landscape through a Window
Blick durch ein Fenster in eine Landschaft, ca. 1918

France
The Younger Generation

Frankreich
Die jüngere Generation

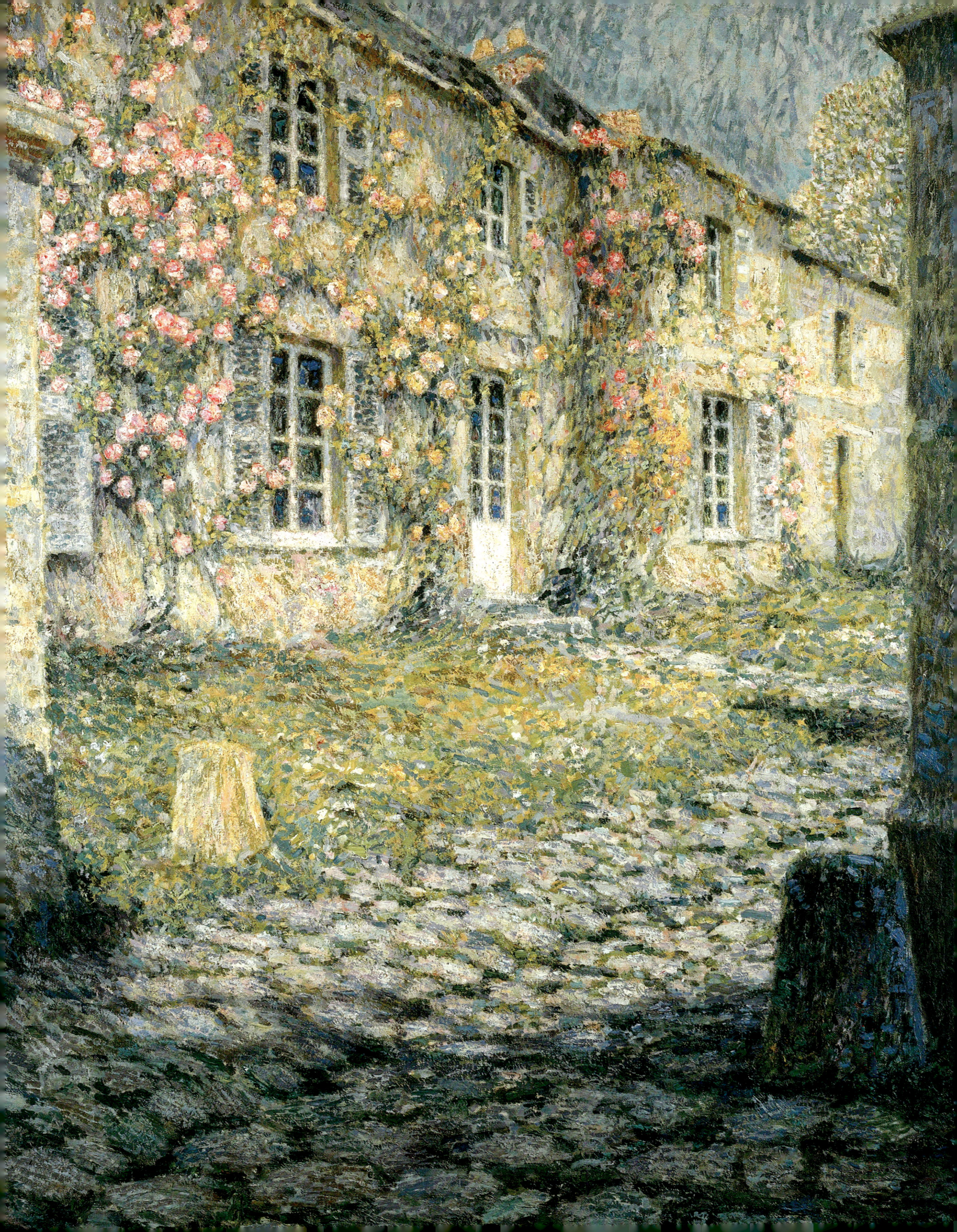

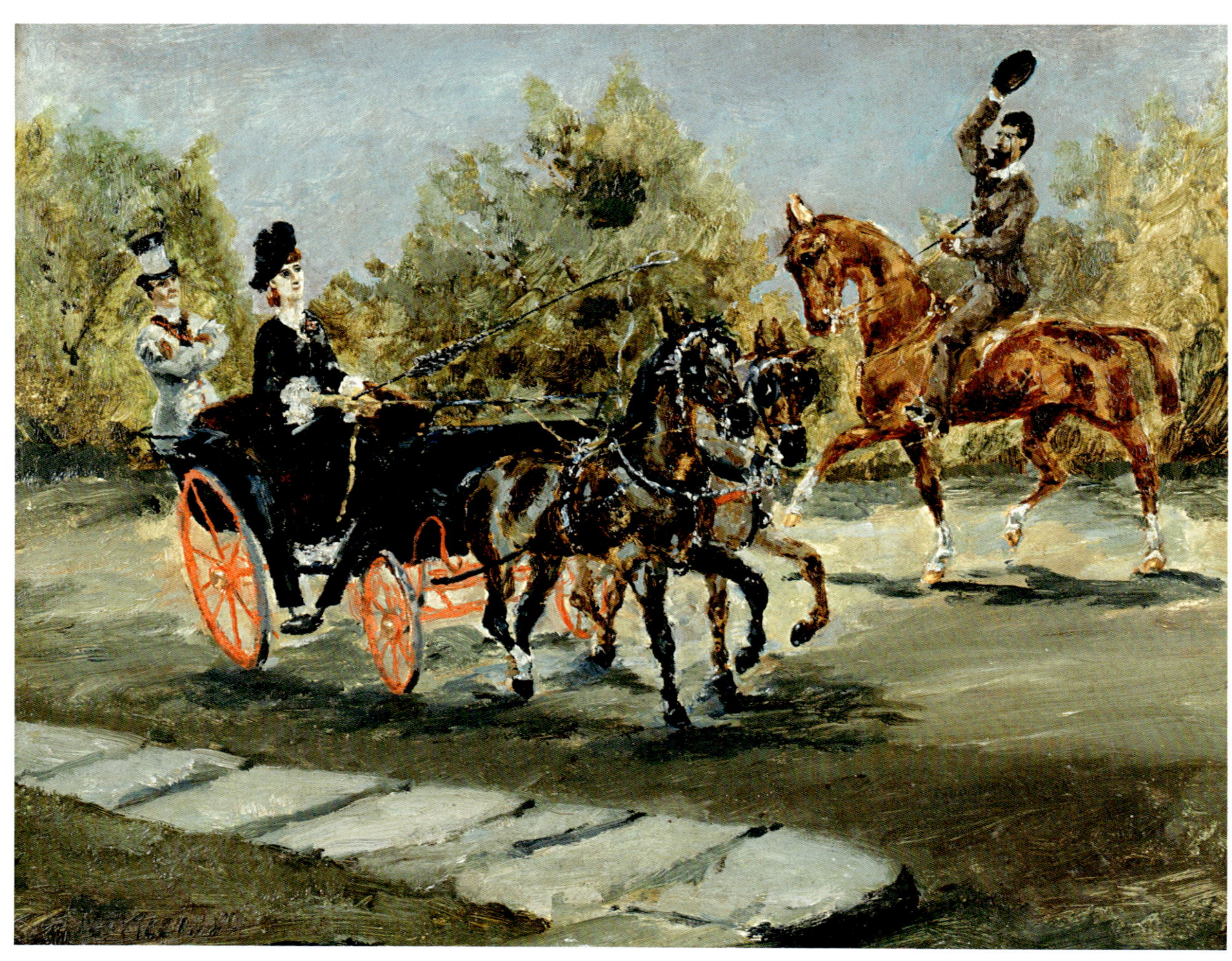

Henri de Toulouse-Lautrec
Nice – On the "Promenade des Anglais"
Nizza – Auf der »Promenade des Anglais«, 1880

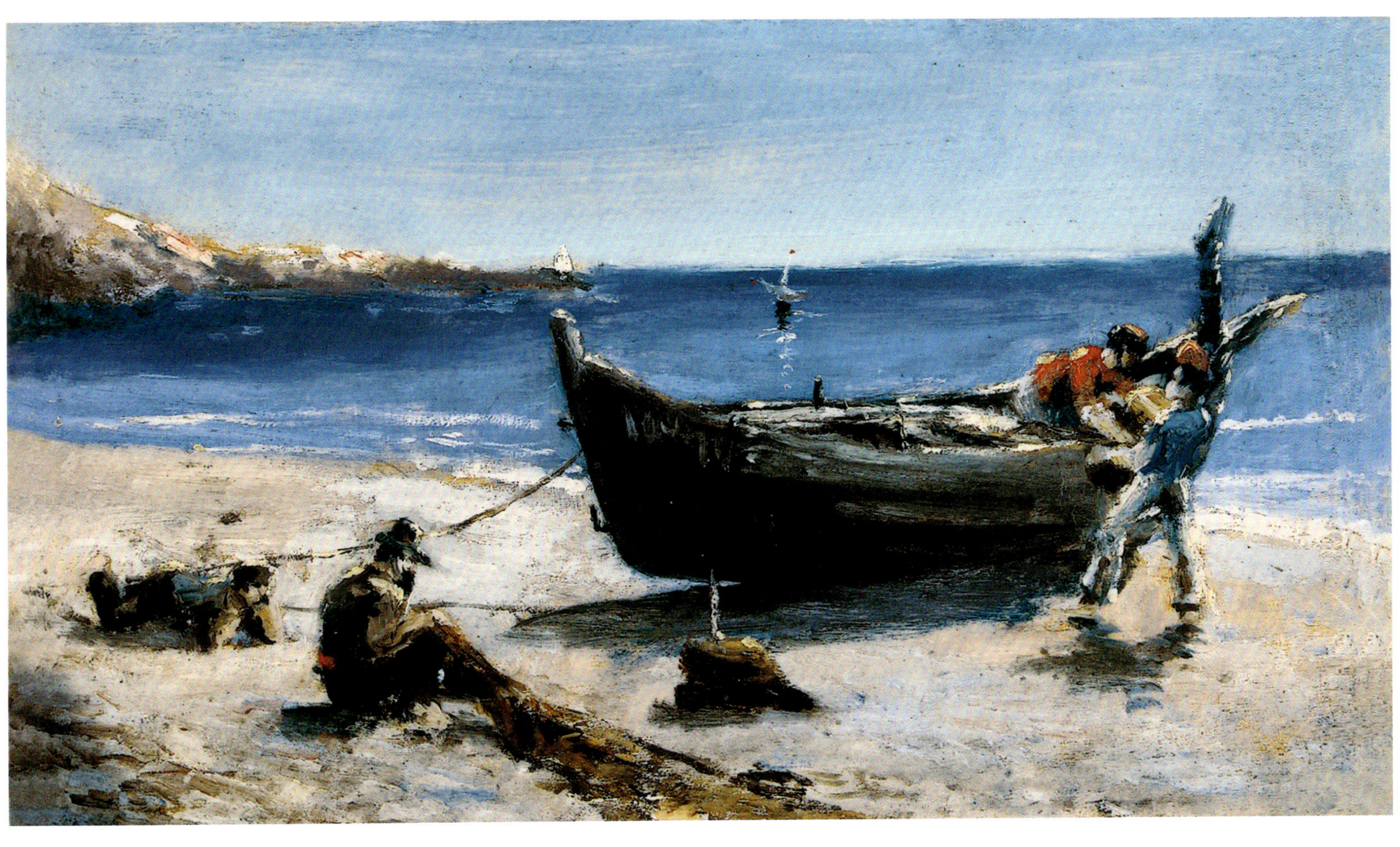

Henri de Toulouse-Lautrec
Fishing Boat
Fischerboot, 1880

Henri Lebasque
The Village of Champigné, Maine-et-Loire
Das Dorf Champigné, Maine-et-Loire, 1893

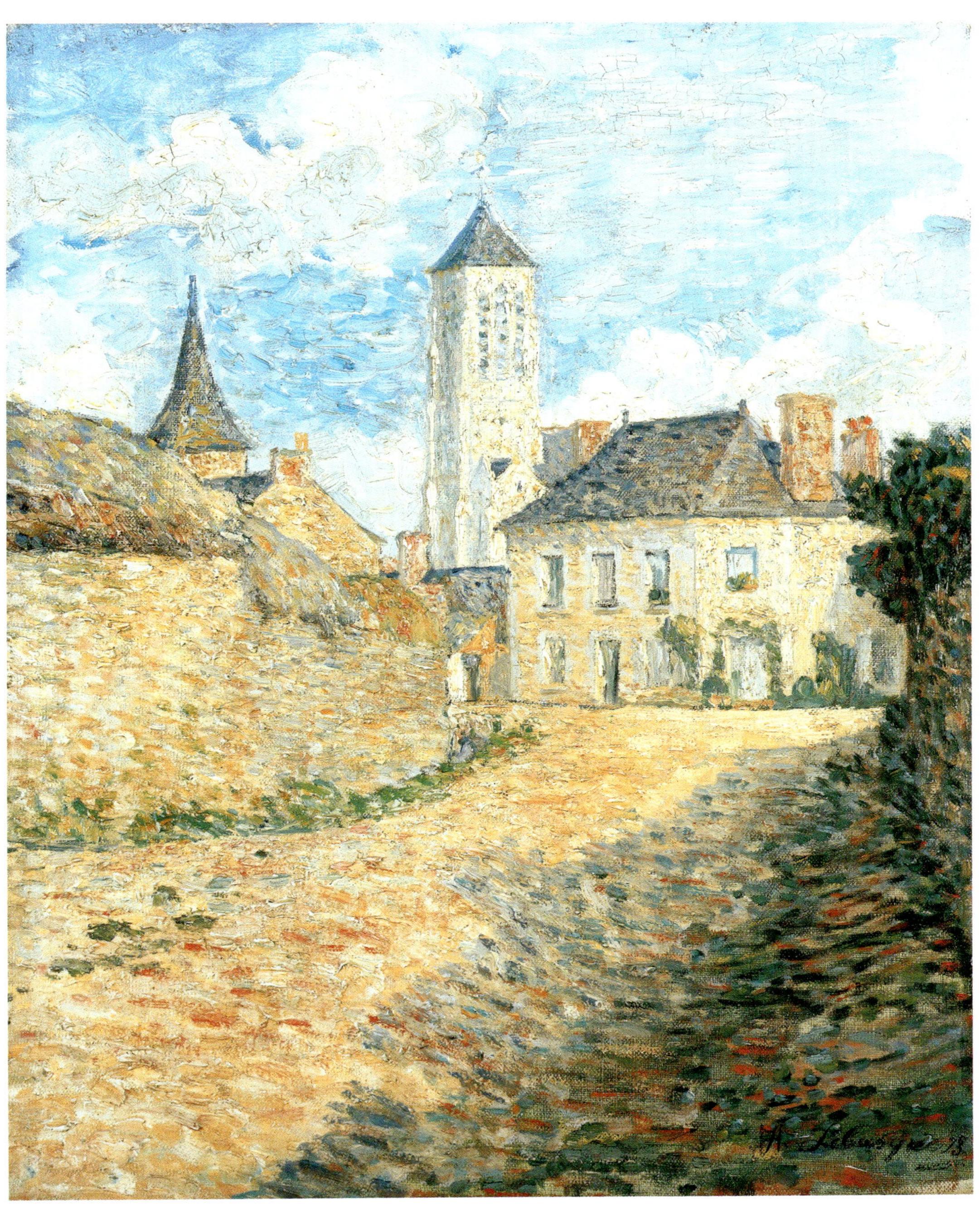

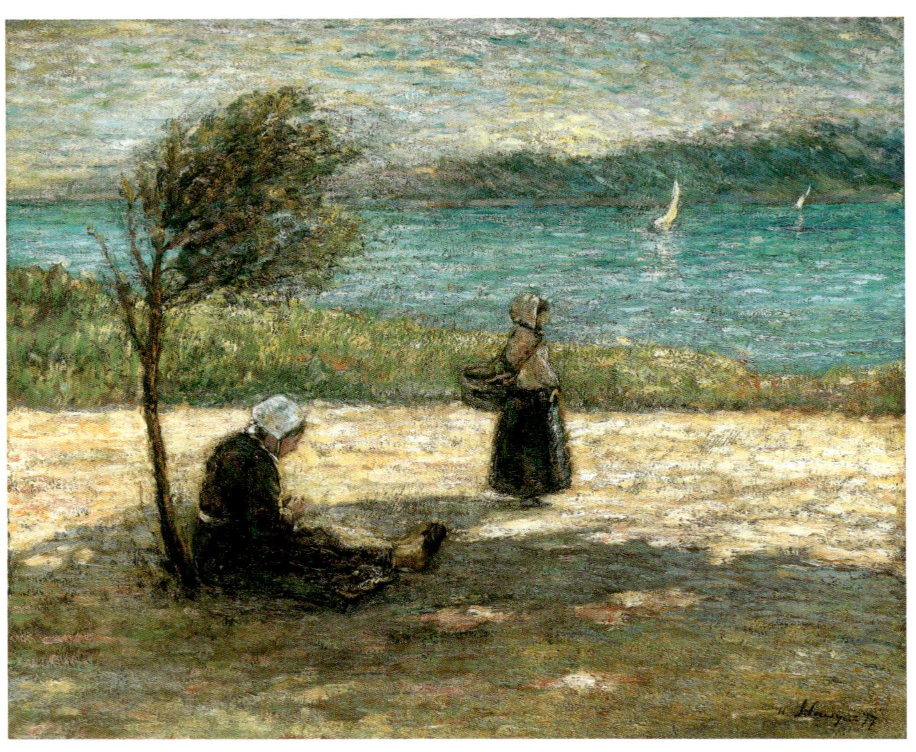

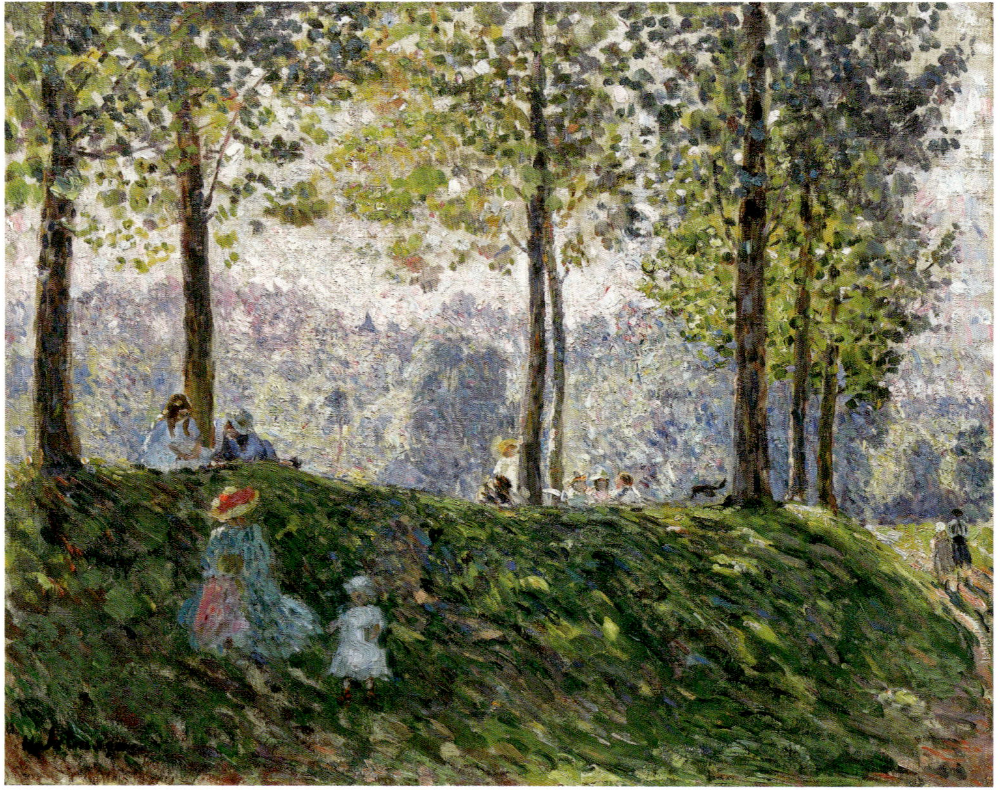

Henri Lebasque
Two Breton Women on the Seashore
Zwei bretonische Frauen am Meer, 1897

Henri Lebasque
An Afternoon in the Park
Ein Nachmittag im Park, ca. 1898

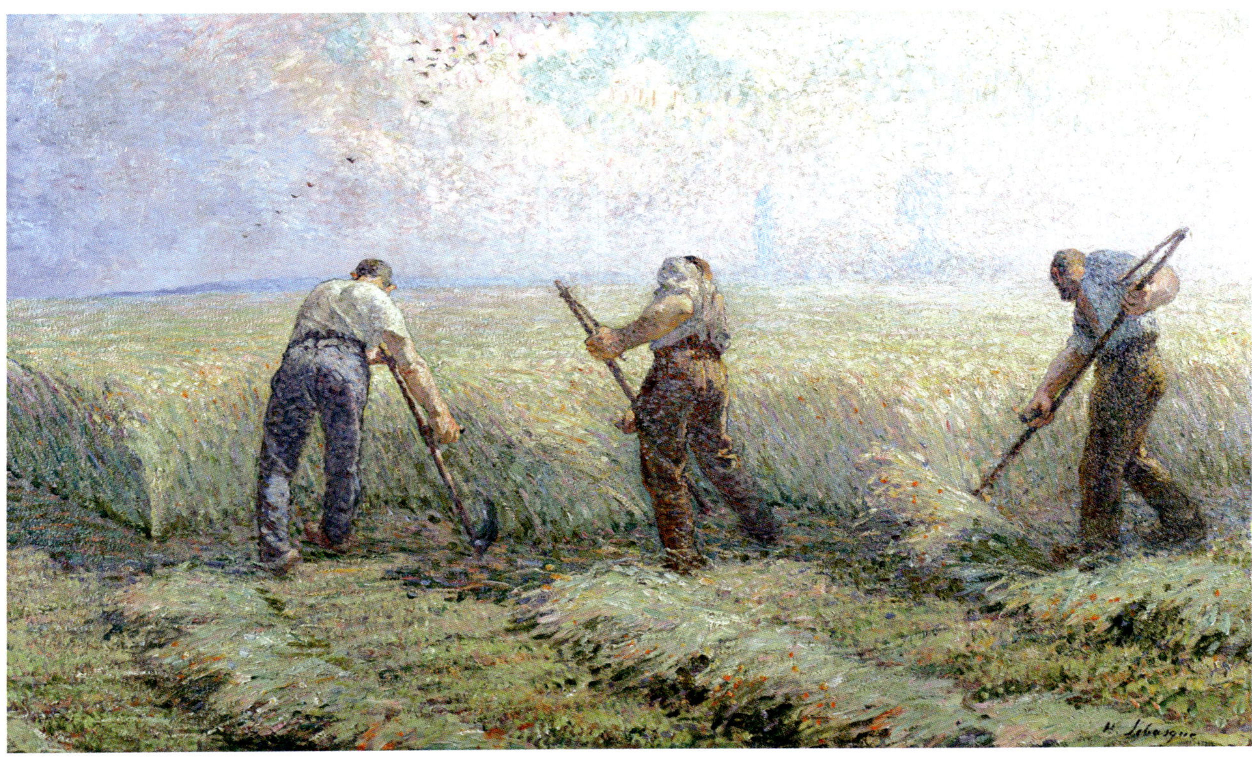

Henri Lebasque
Reapers near Lagny
Schnitter in der Umgebung von Lagny, ca. 1899/1900

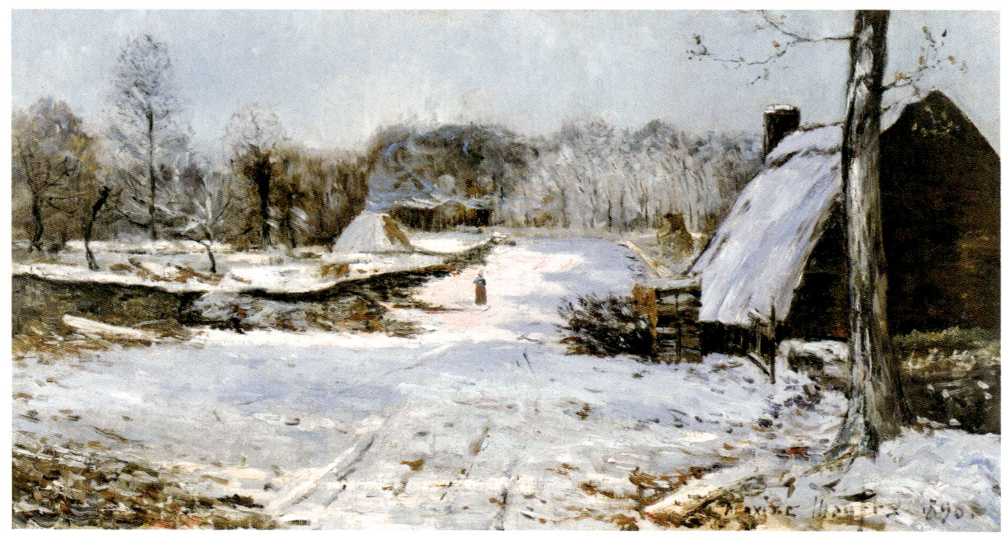

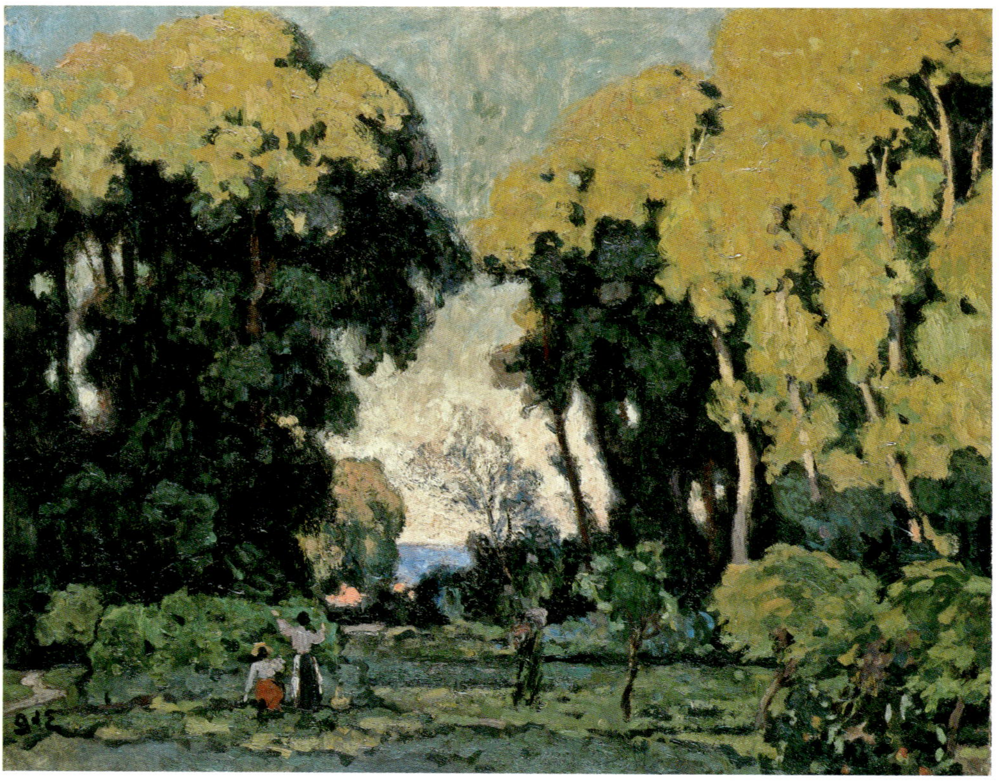

Maxime Maufra
Winter Landscape
Winterlandschaft, 1890

Georges d'Espagnat
Garden in Verneuil
Garten in Verneuil, 1892/95

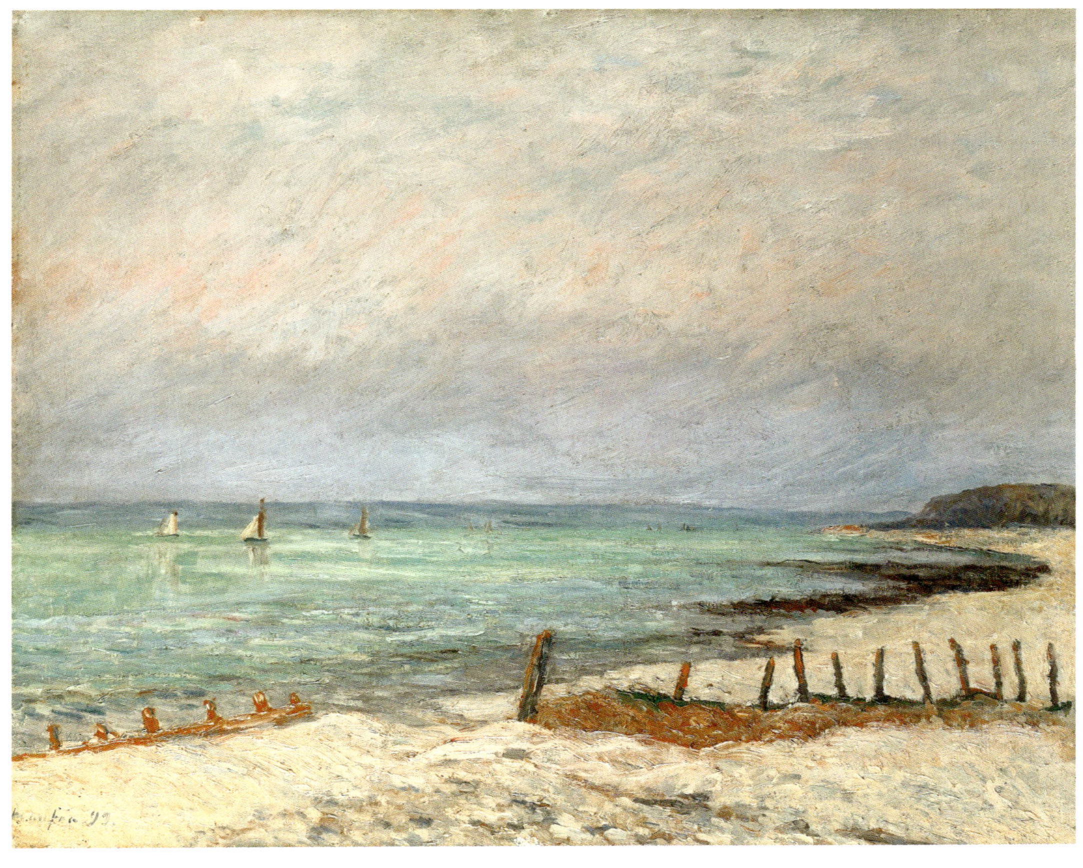

MAXIME MAUFRA
Sailboats in a Bay of the Seine
Segelboote in einer Bucht der Seine, 1899

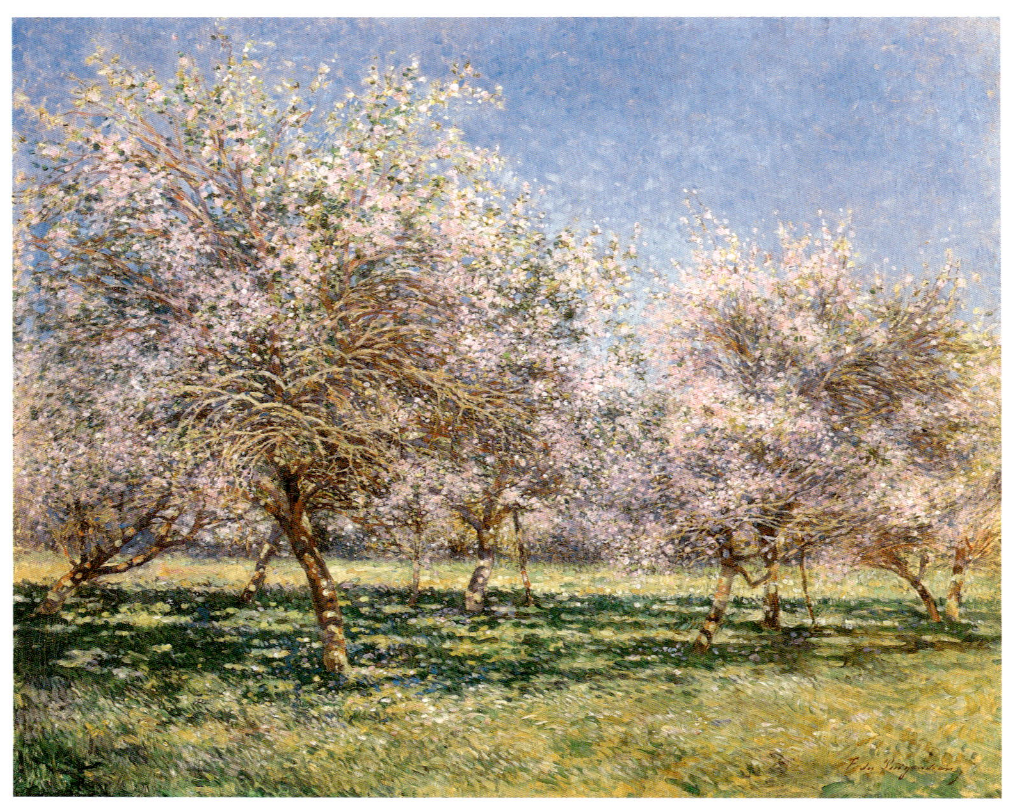

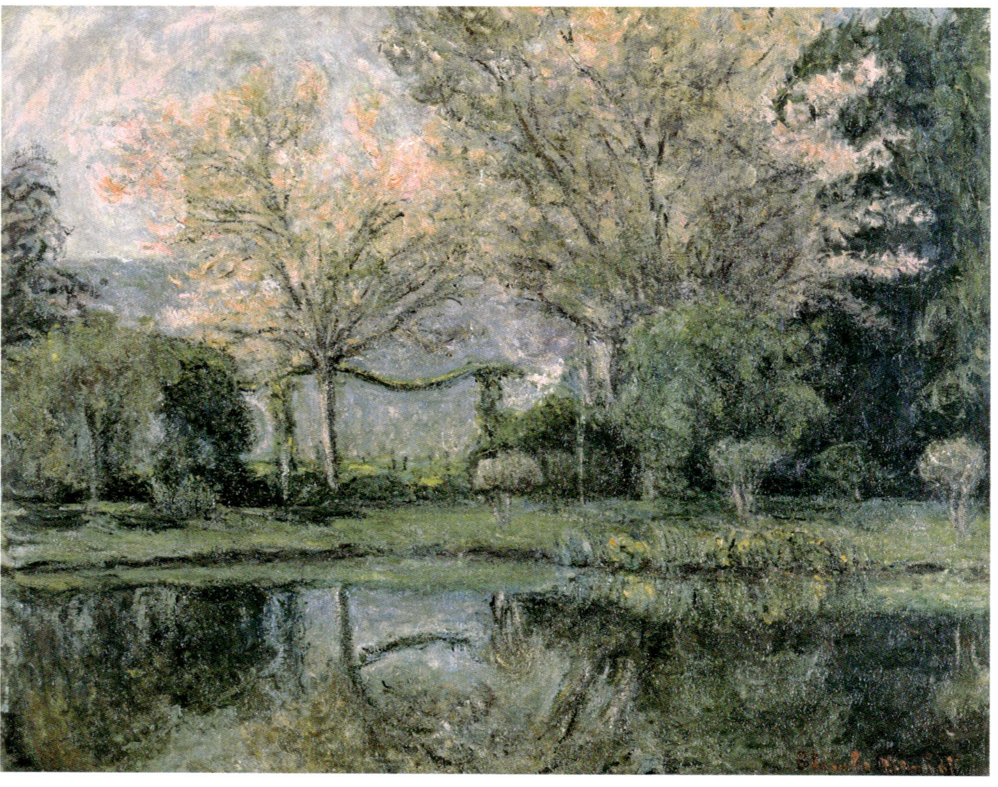

Fernand Loyen du Puigaudeau
Apple Trees in Bloom
Blühende Apfelbäume, ca. 1900

Blanche Hoschede-Monet
Pond in Giverny or *The Garden*, n.d.
Weiher in Giverny oder *Der Garten*, o. J.

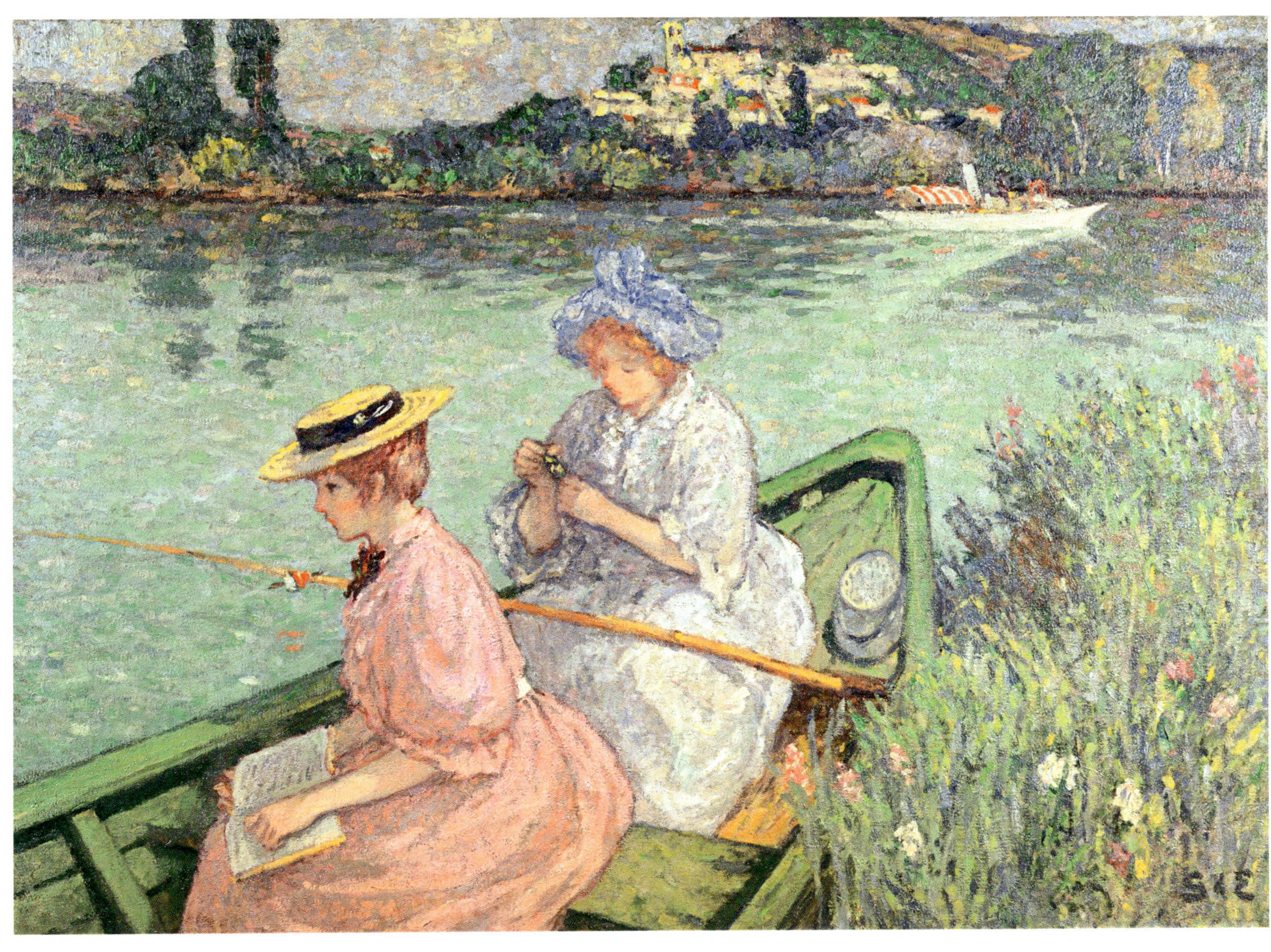

Georges d'Espagnat
The Anglers, n.d.
Die Anglerinnen, o. J.

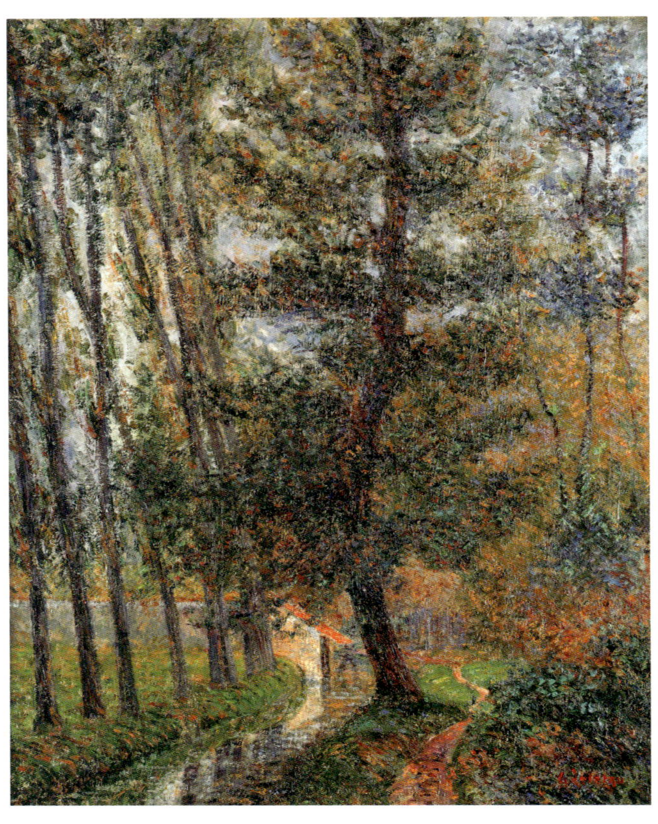

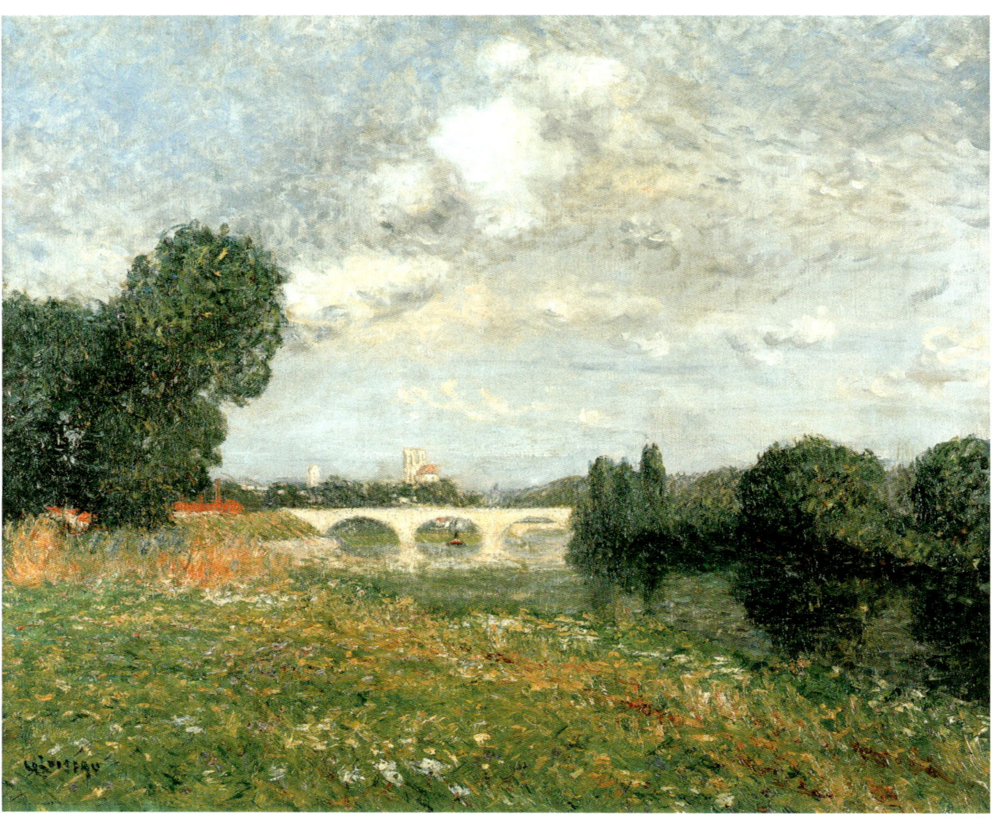

Gustave Loiseau
Banks of the River Sausseron at Nesles
Die Ufer des Flusses Sausseron, bei Nesles, ca. 1897

Gustave Loiseau
Pont Perronet in Mantes
Der Pont Perronet in Mantes, ca. 1898

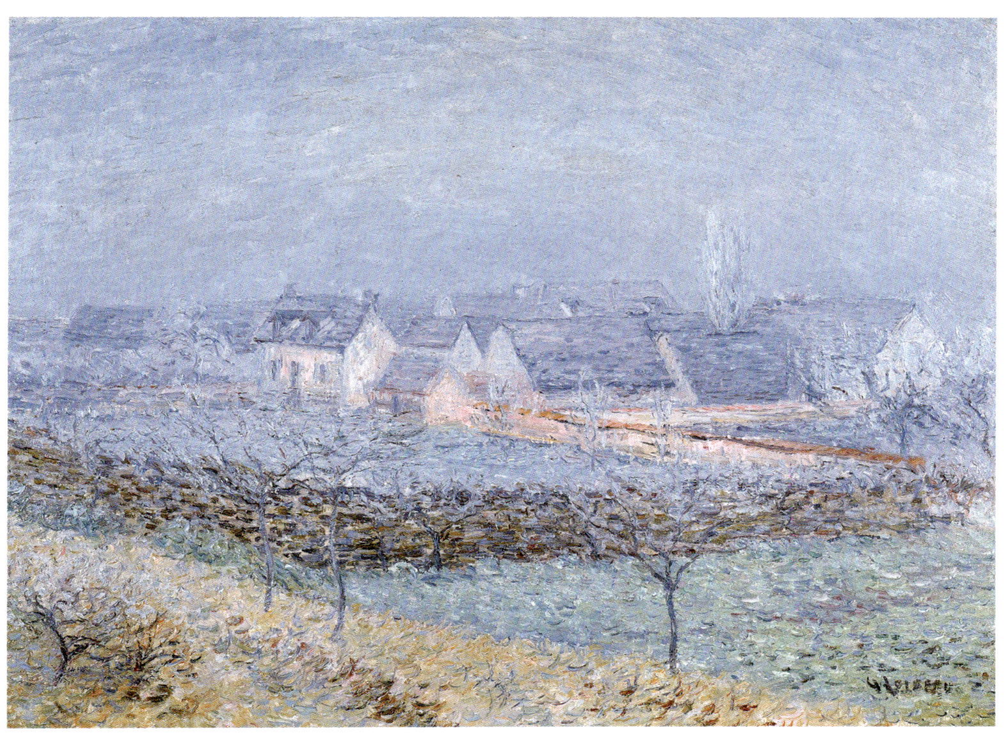

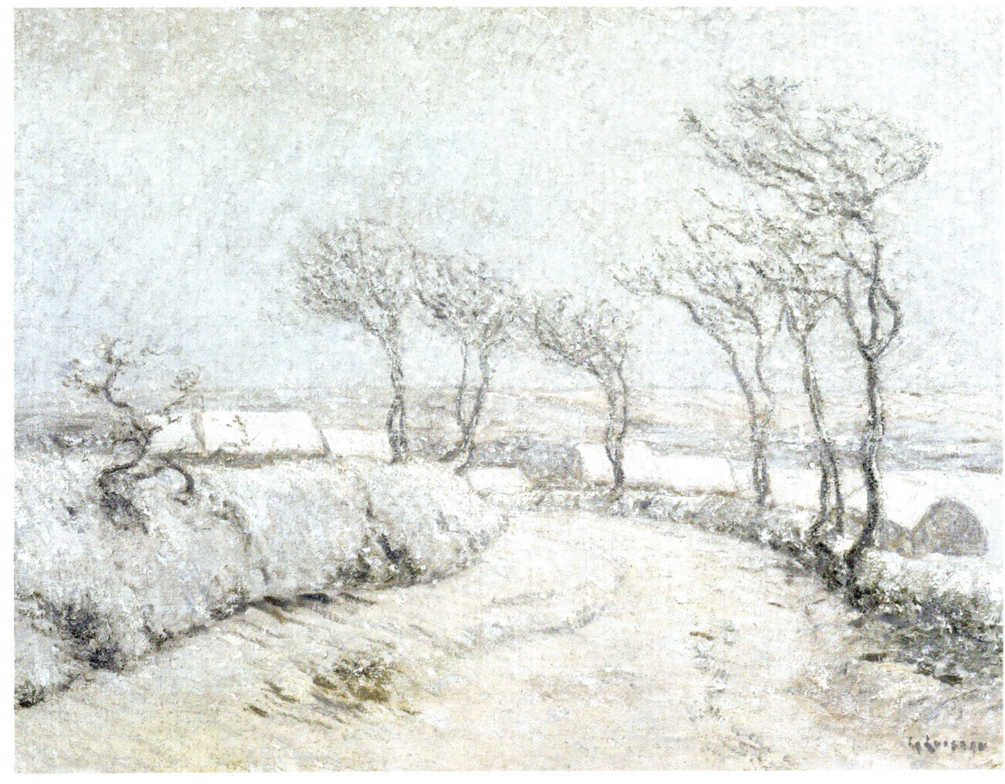

Gustave Loiseau
Village in Spring, the Seine Valley at Les Damps
Dorf im Frühling, das Tal der Seine bei Les Damps, ca. 1898

Gustave Loiseau
Landscape in the Snow, Entrance to a Village in Brittany
Landschaft im Schnee, Dorfeingang in der Bretagne, ca. 1897/1900

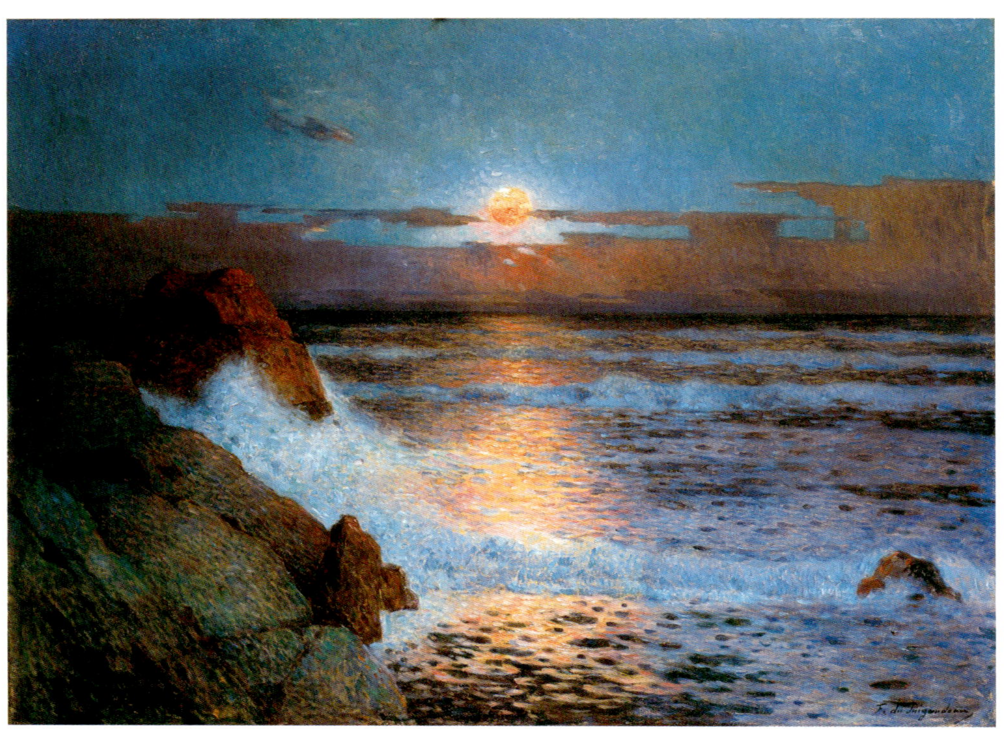

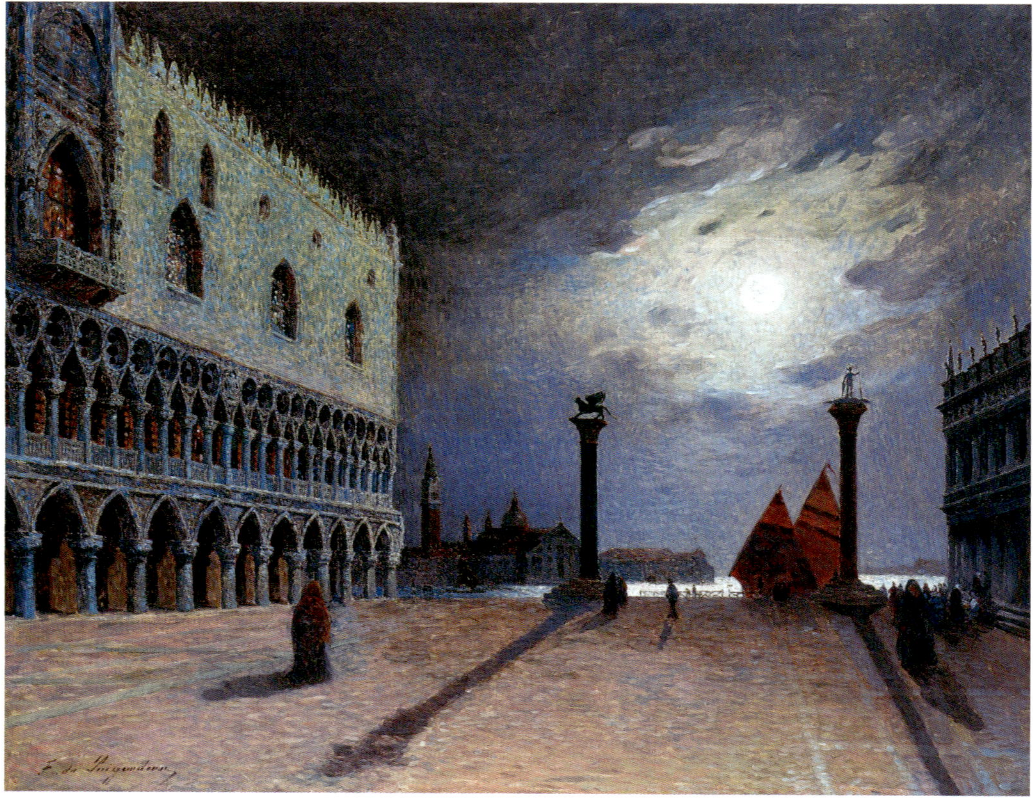

Fernand Loyen du Puigaudeau
Sunset at Croisic, Breton Landscape
Sonnenuntergang bei Croisic, bretonische Landschaft, 1895

Fernand Loyen du Puigaudeau
Piazza San Marco in Venice at Night, n.d.
Der Markusplatz in Venedig bei Nacht, o. J.

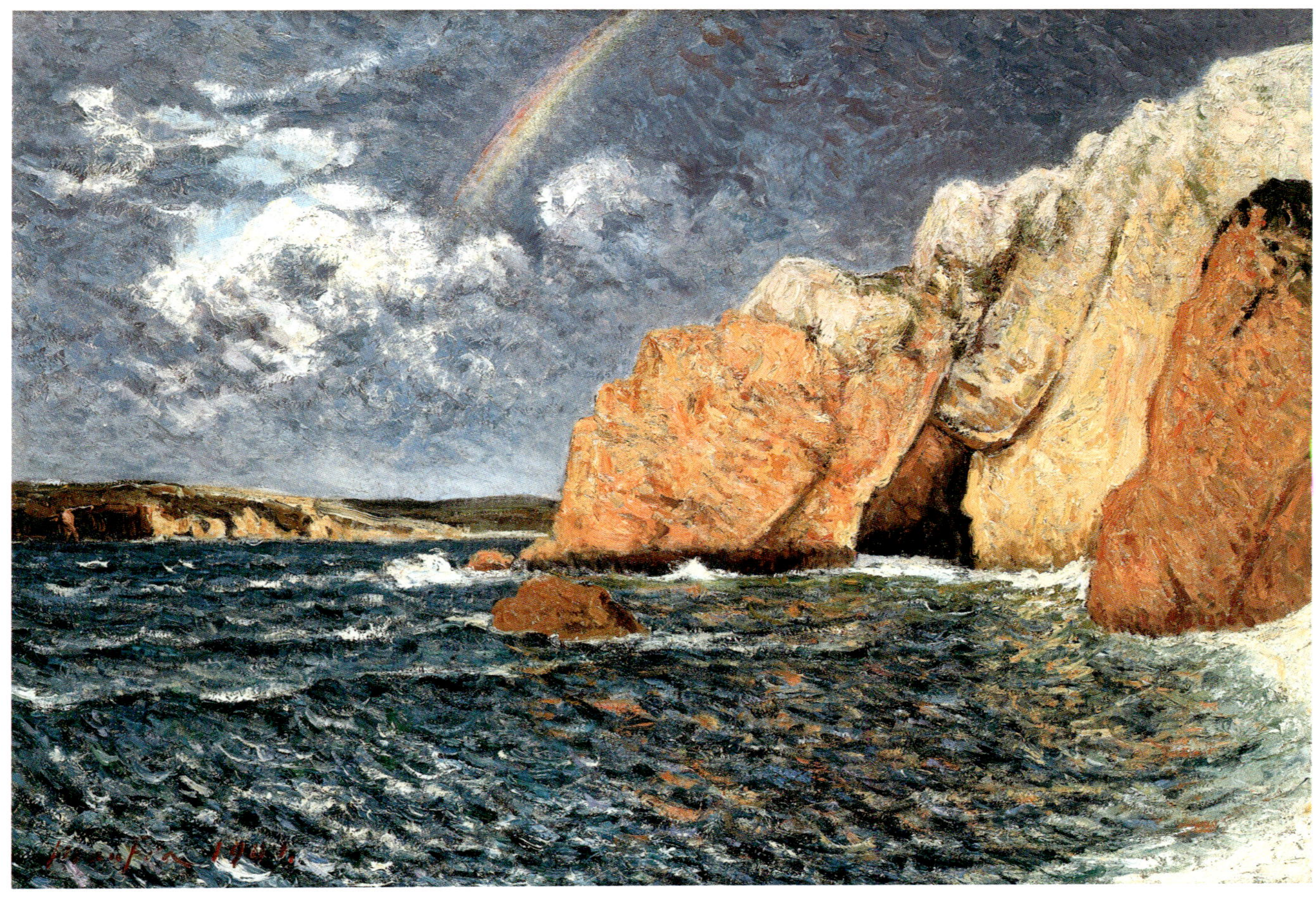

Maxime Maufra
Rainbow
Regenbogen, 1901

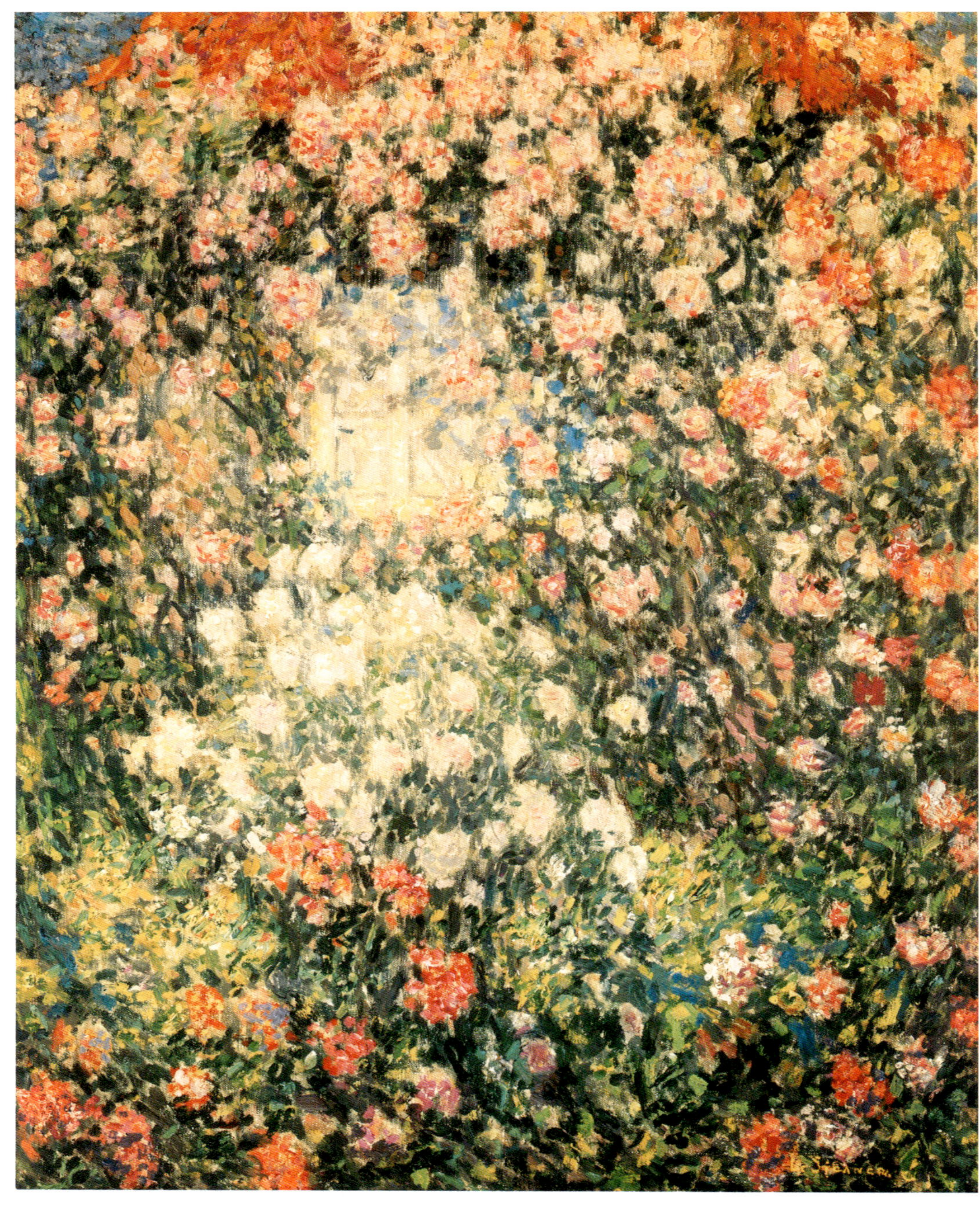

Henri le Sidaner
Pavilion with Roses – Gerberoy, after 1902
Pavillon mit Rosen – Gerberoy, nach 1902

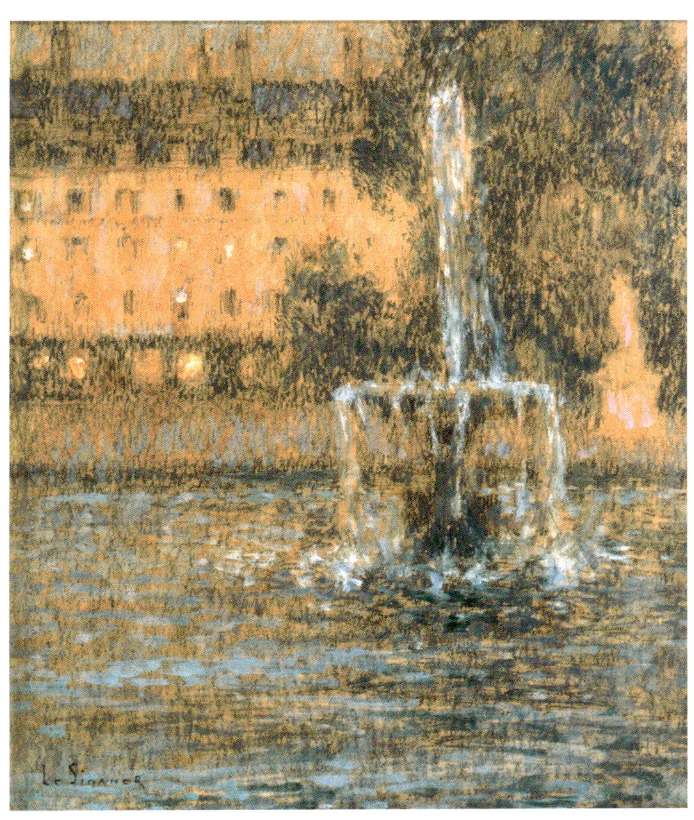

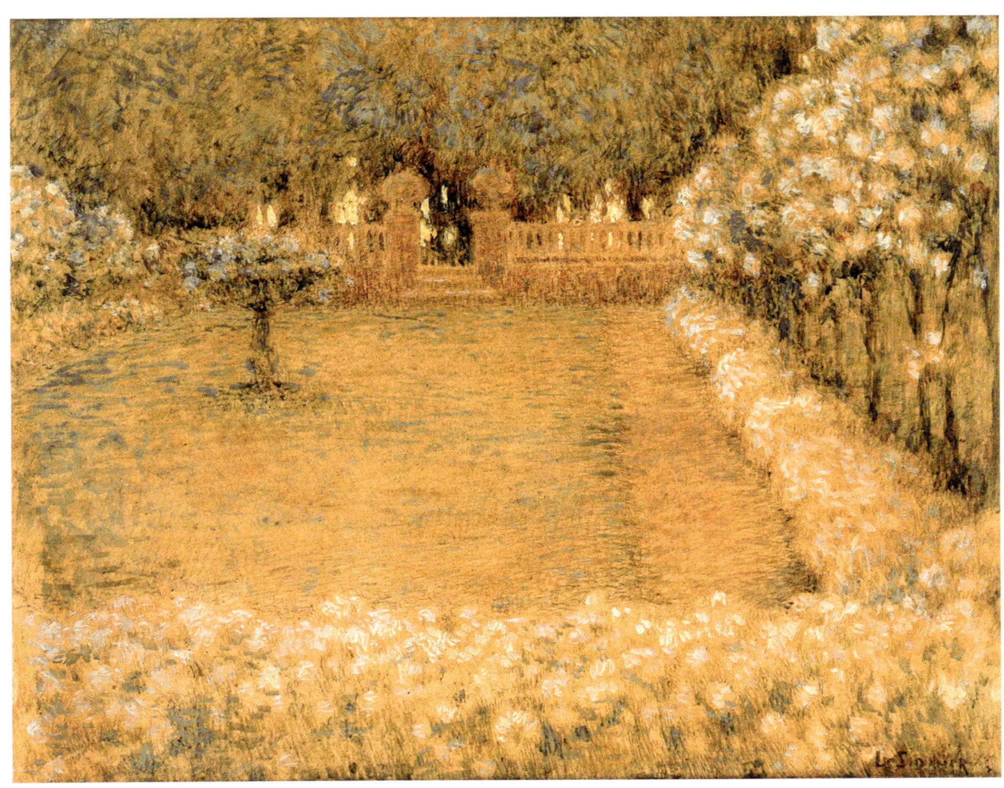

Henri le Sidaner
Fountain in the Tuileries
Brunnen in den Tuilerien, ca. 1900

Henri le Sidaner
The "White Garden" of Gerberoy at Dusk
Der »Weiße Garten« von Gerberoy in der Dämmerung, ca. 1907

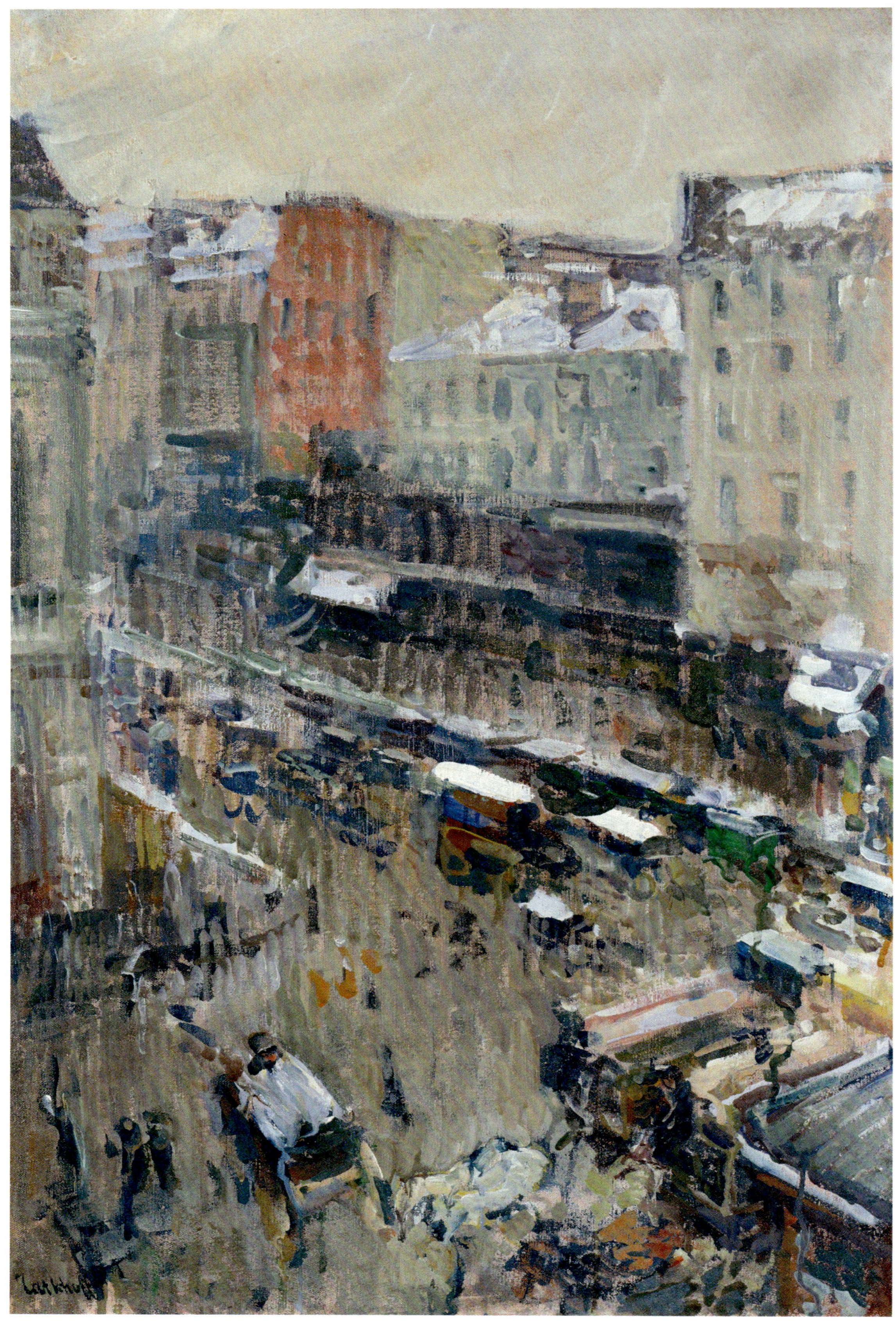

Nicolas Tarkhoff
Boulevard St. Denis, 1901

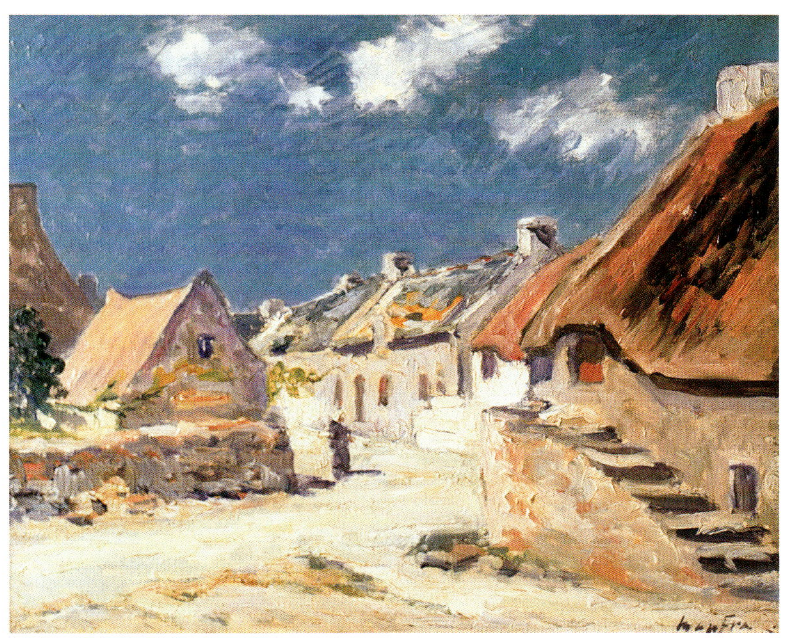

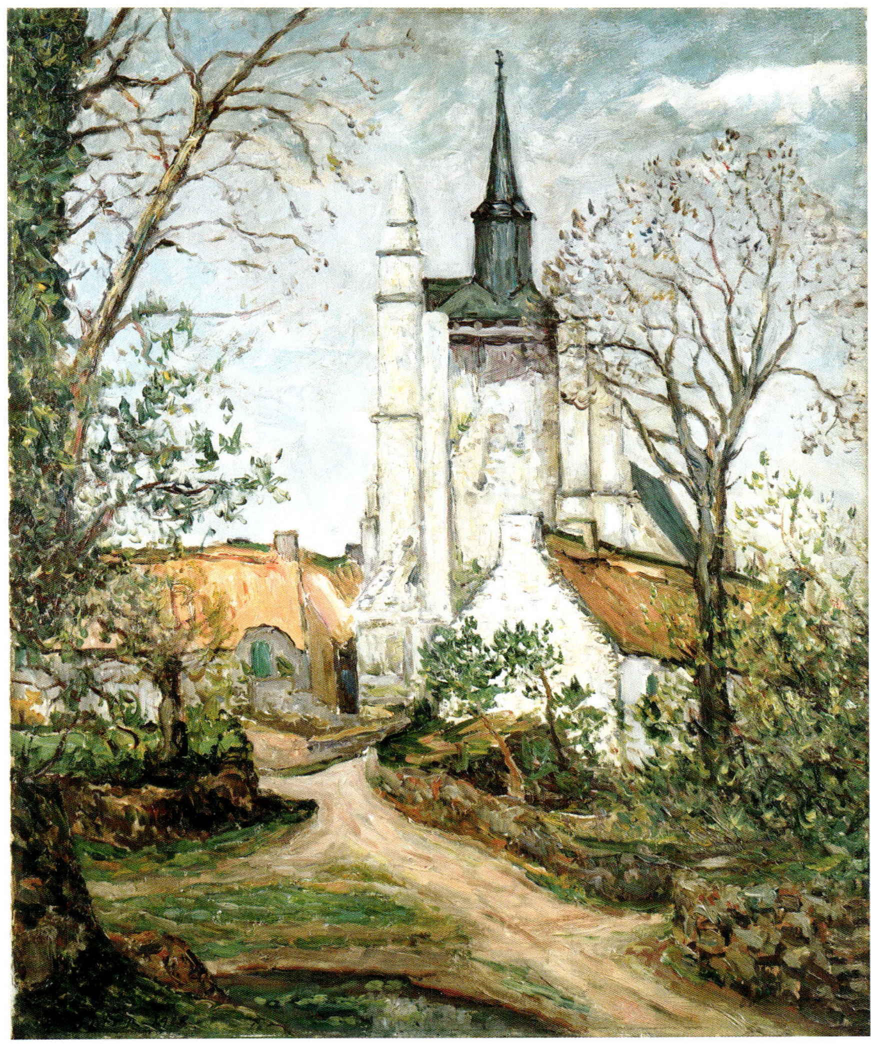

Maxime Maufra
Kerhostin, nach after 1903

Maxime Maufra
The Chapel of Sainte-Avoye, Morbihan
Die Kapelle von Sainte-Avoye, Morbihan, 1908

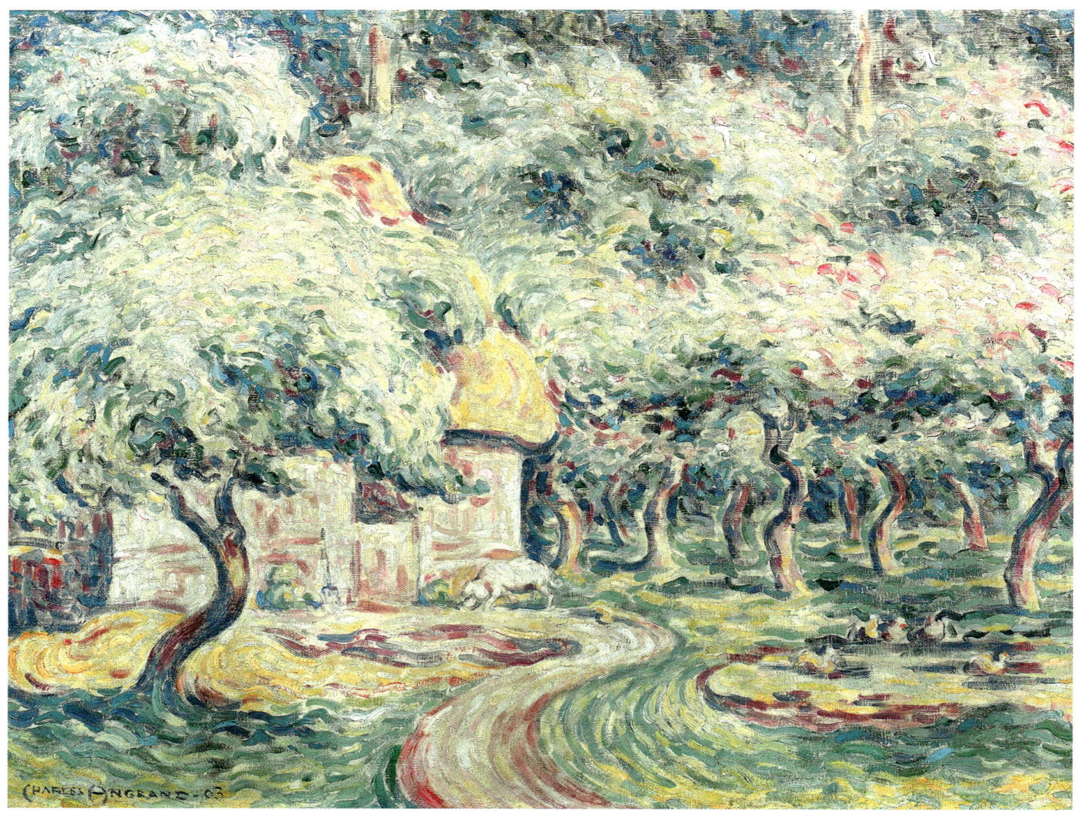

Charles Angrand
House under Olive Trees or *Hut in an Orchard*
Haus unter Ölbäumen oder *Hütte in einem Obstgarten*, 1903

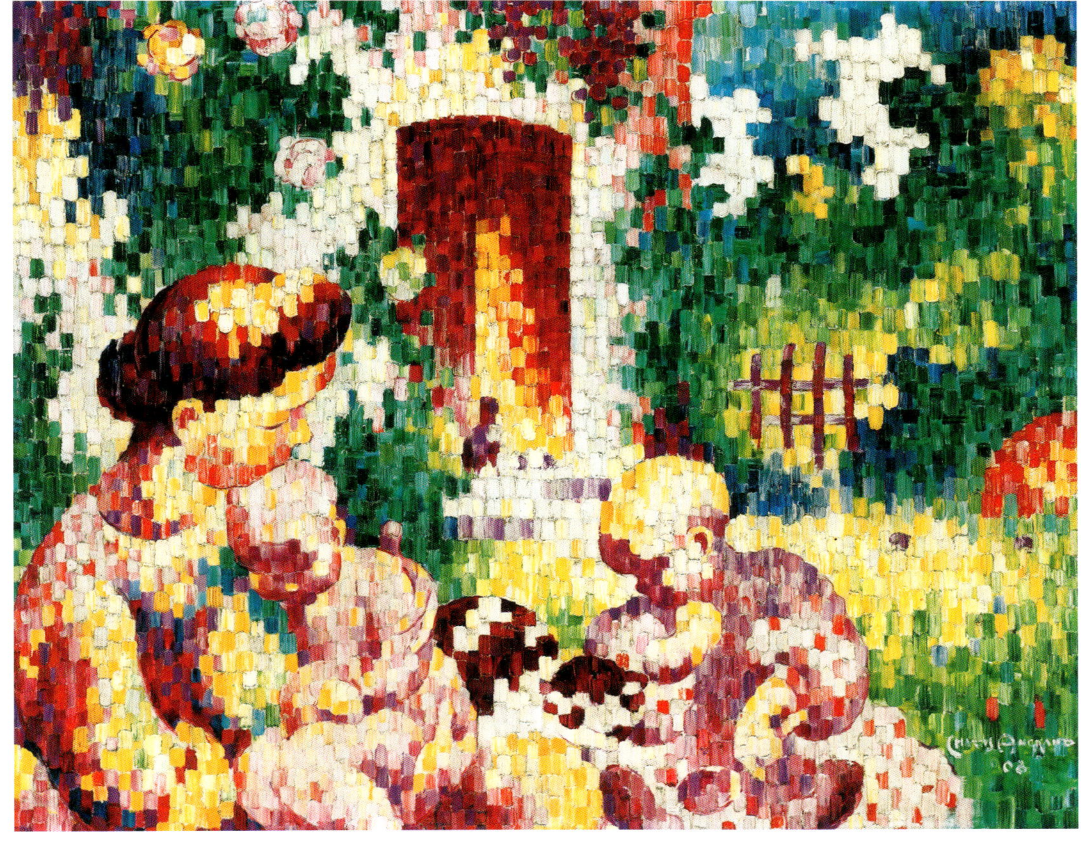

Charles Angrand
On the Threshold or *The Milk Pot*
An der Schwelle oder *Der Milchtopf,* 1908

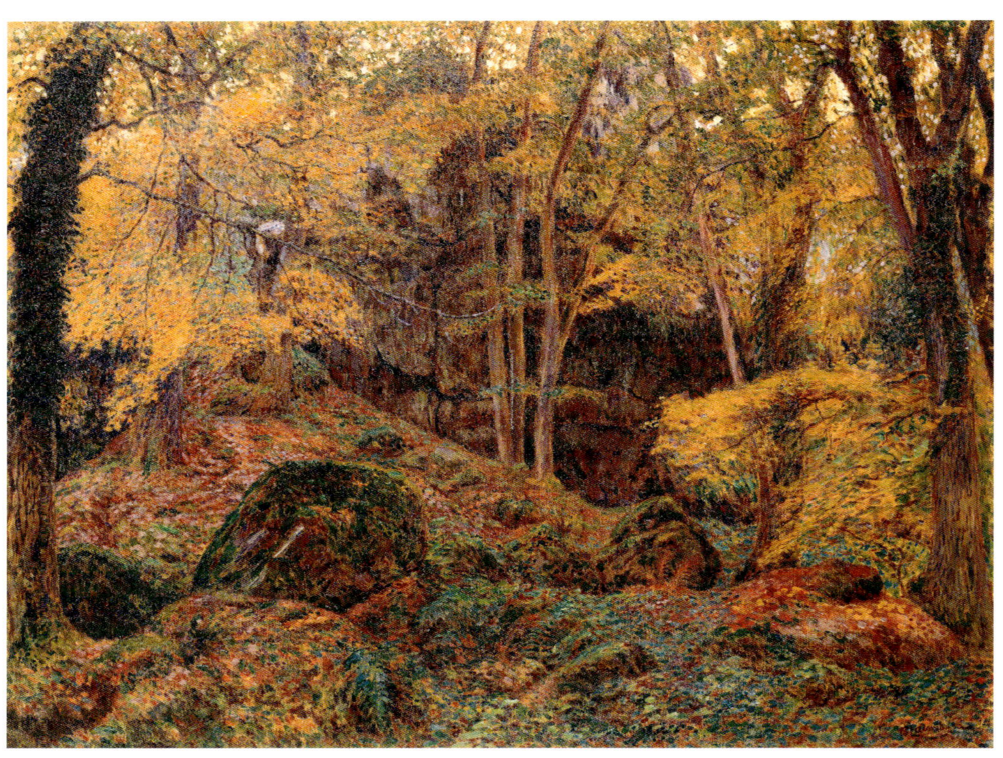

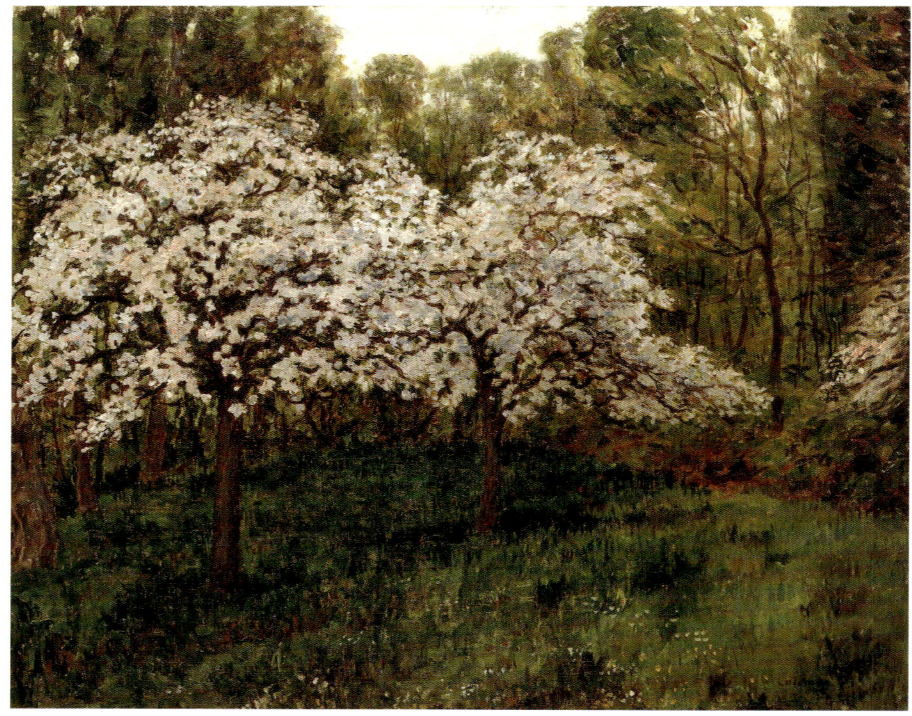

Georges Lacombe
Rocks at Vignage, Forest of Ecouves
Felsen bei Vignage, Wald von Ecouves, ca. 1904/08

Georges Lacombe
Apple Trees in Bloom or *Two Blossoming Apple Trees in a Grove near Vignage*
Blühende Apfelbäume oder *Zwei blühende Bäume in einem Waldstück bei Vignage*, ca. 1910/14

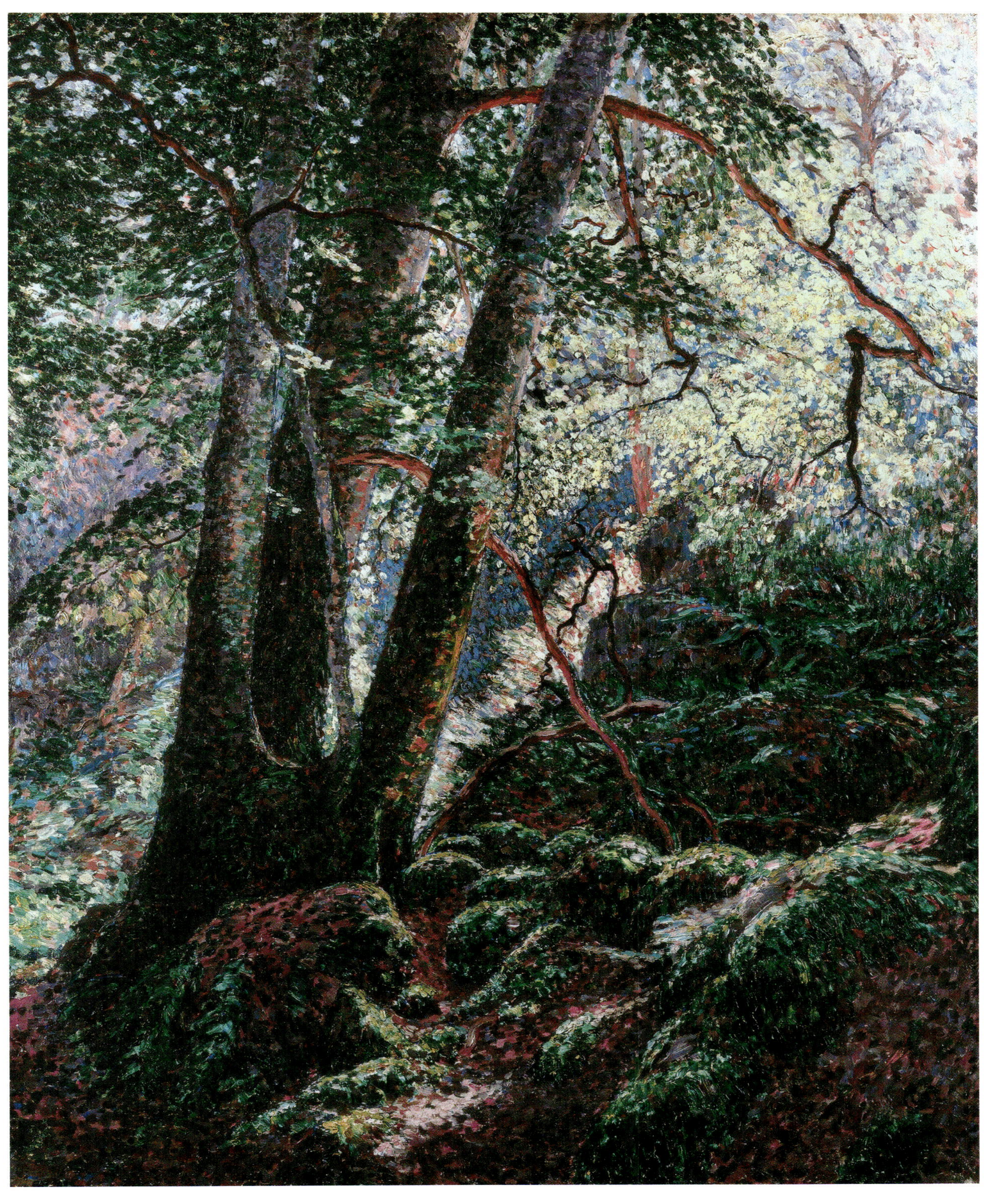

Georges Lacombe
Rocks at Vignage, Forest of Ecouves or *Sunshine on the Beeches*
Felsen bei Vignage, Wald von Ecouves oder *Sonnenlicht auf den Buchen*, ca. 1905/08

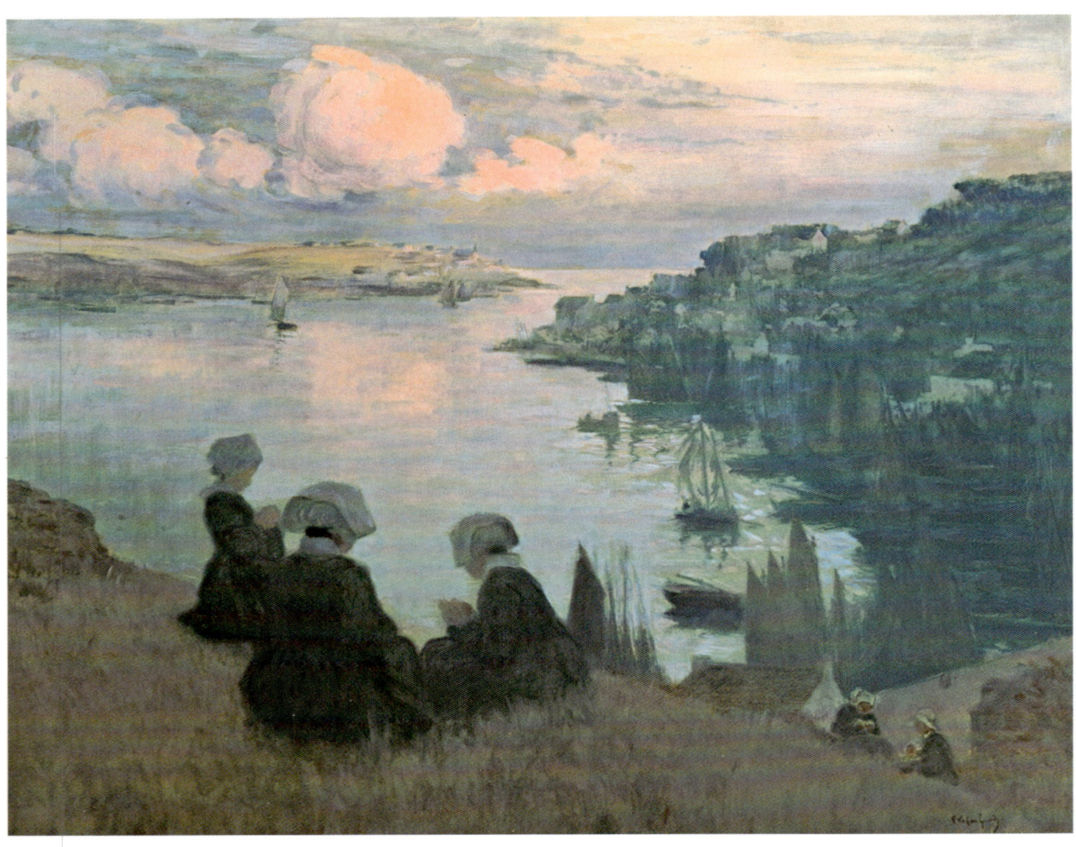

Fernand Marie Eugene le Gout-Gerard
Women Knitting
Strickerinnen, ca. 1906

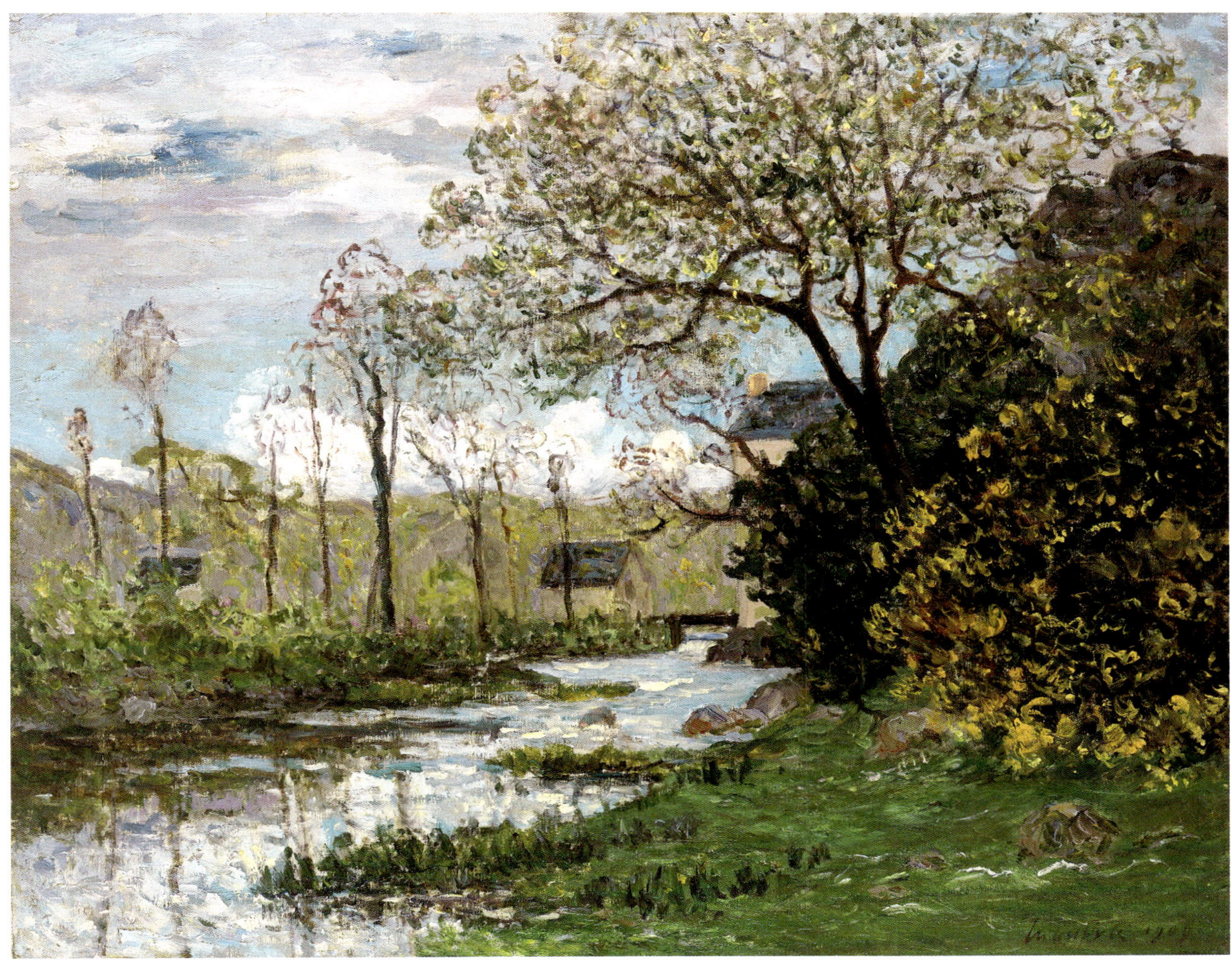

MAXIME MAUFRA
River near Auray
Fluss bei Auray, 1909

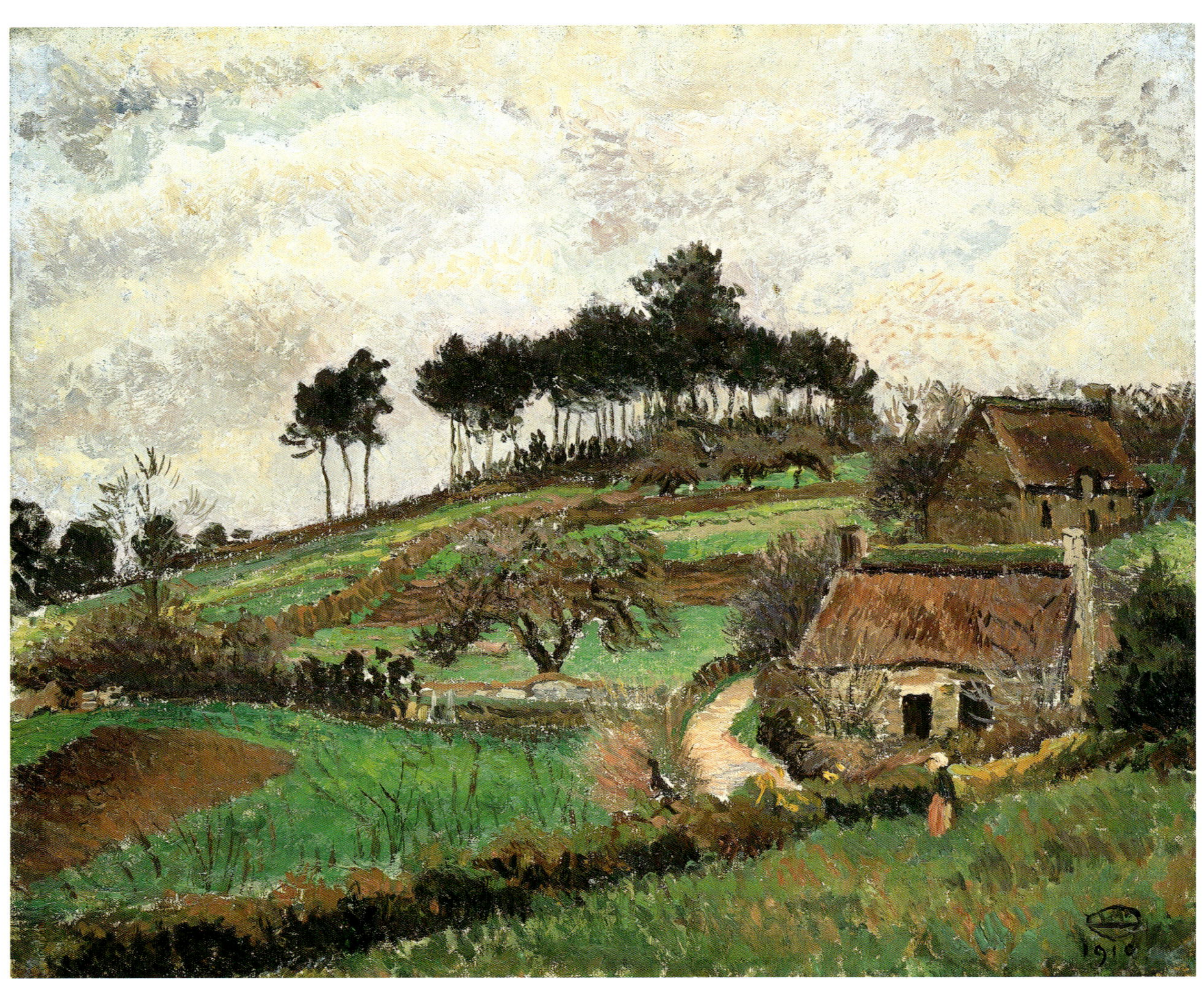

Lucien Pissarro
Brittany Cottages, Riec
Bauernhäuser in der Bretagne, Riec, 1910

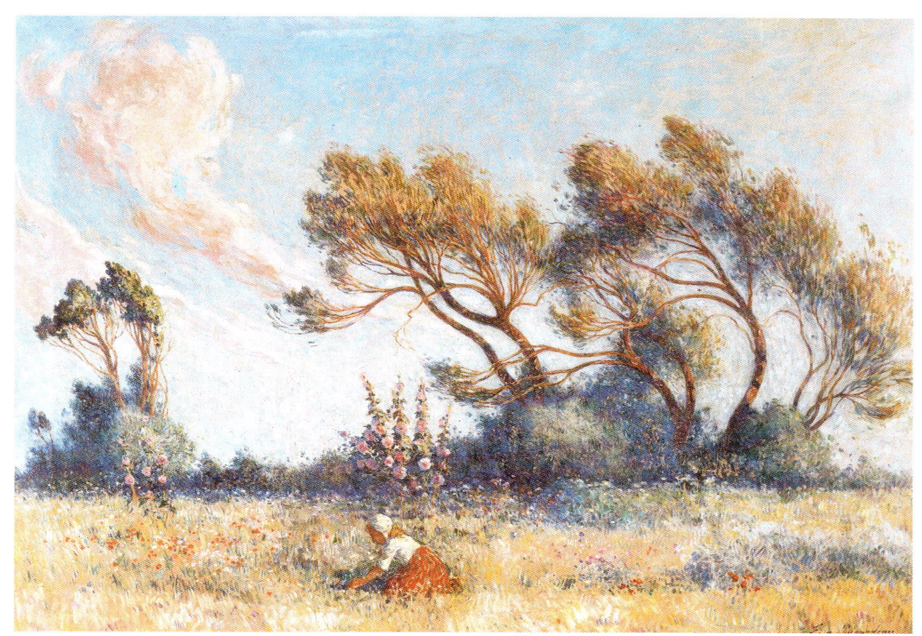

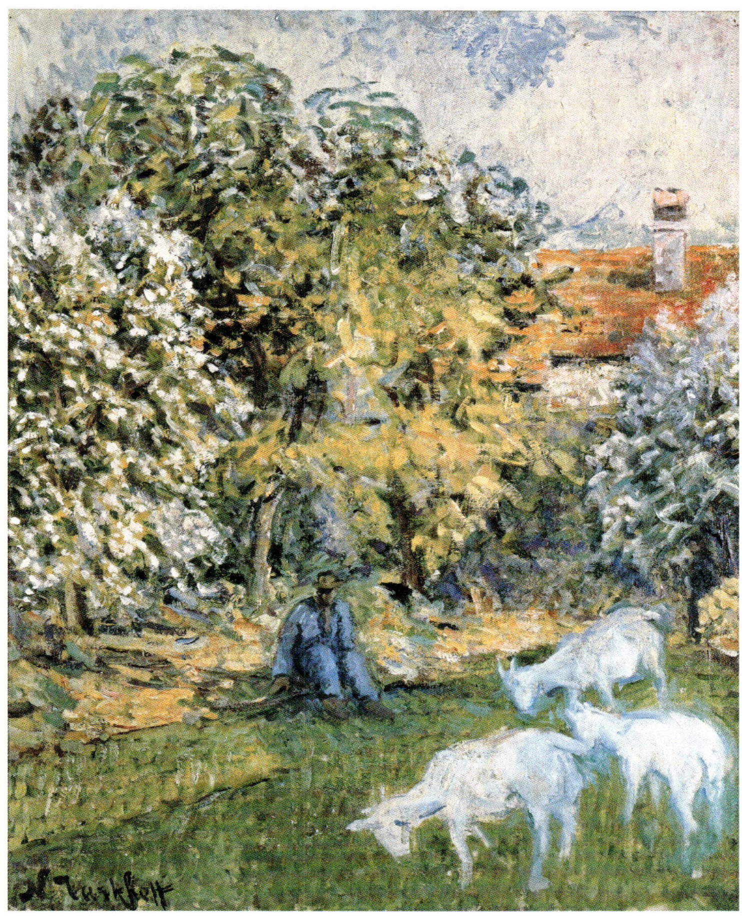

FERNAND LOYEN DU PUIGAUDEAU
Picking Hollyhocks
Beim Pflücken der Stockrosen, ca. 1904

NICOLAS TARKHOFF
A Morning in Spring (The Painter in his Garden)
Ein Morgen im Frühling (Der Maler in seinem Garten), ca. 1911

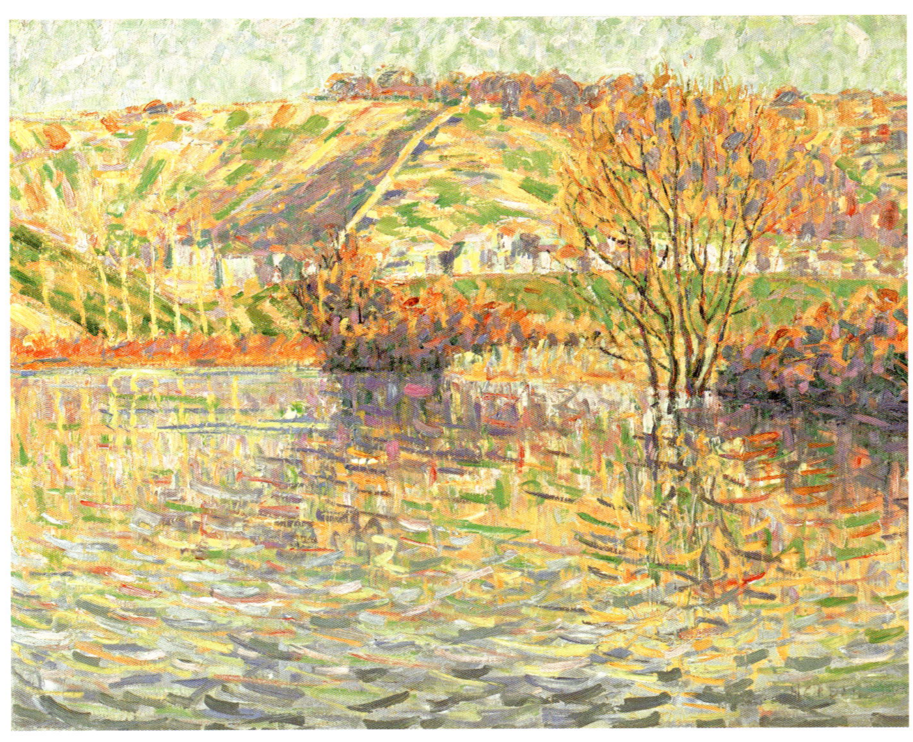

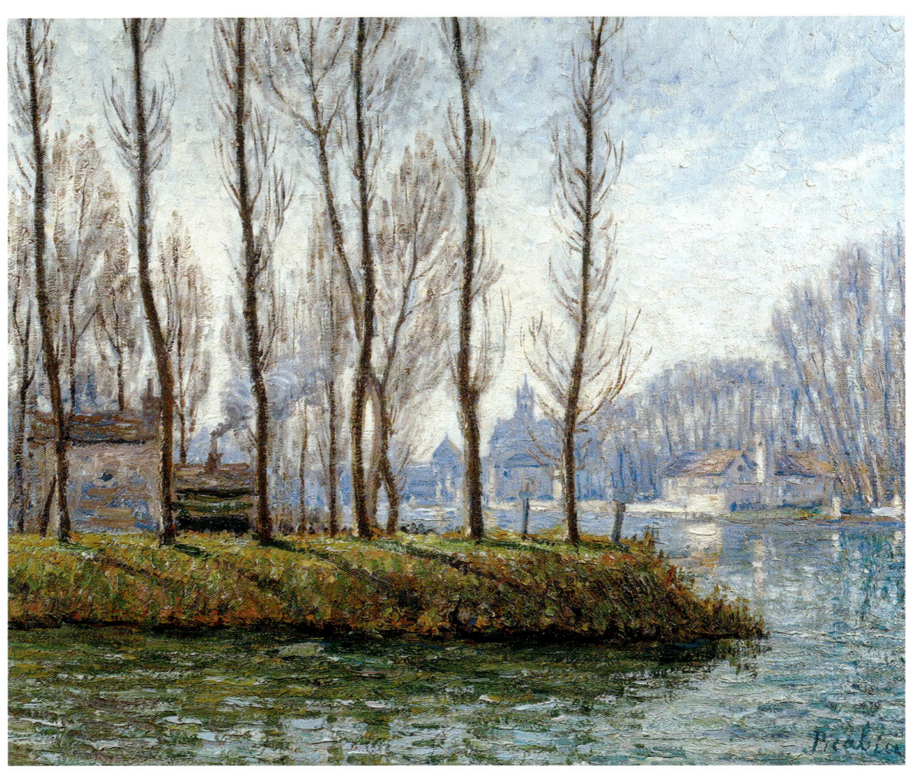

Auguste Herbin
The Hills of Haute-Isle, Val-d'Oise
Die Hügel von Haute-Isle, Val-d'Oise, 1906

Francis Picabia
Moret-sur-Loing in Winter
Moret-sur-Loing im Winter, 1907

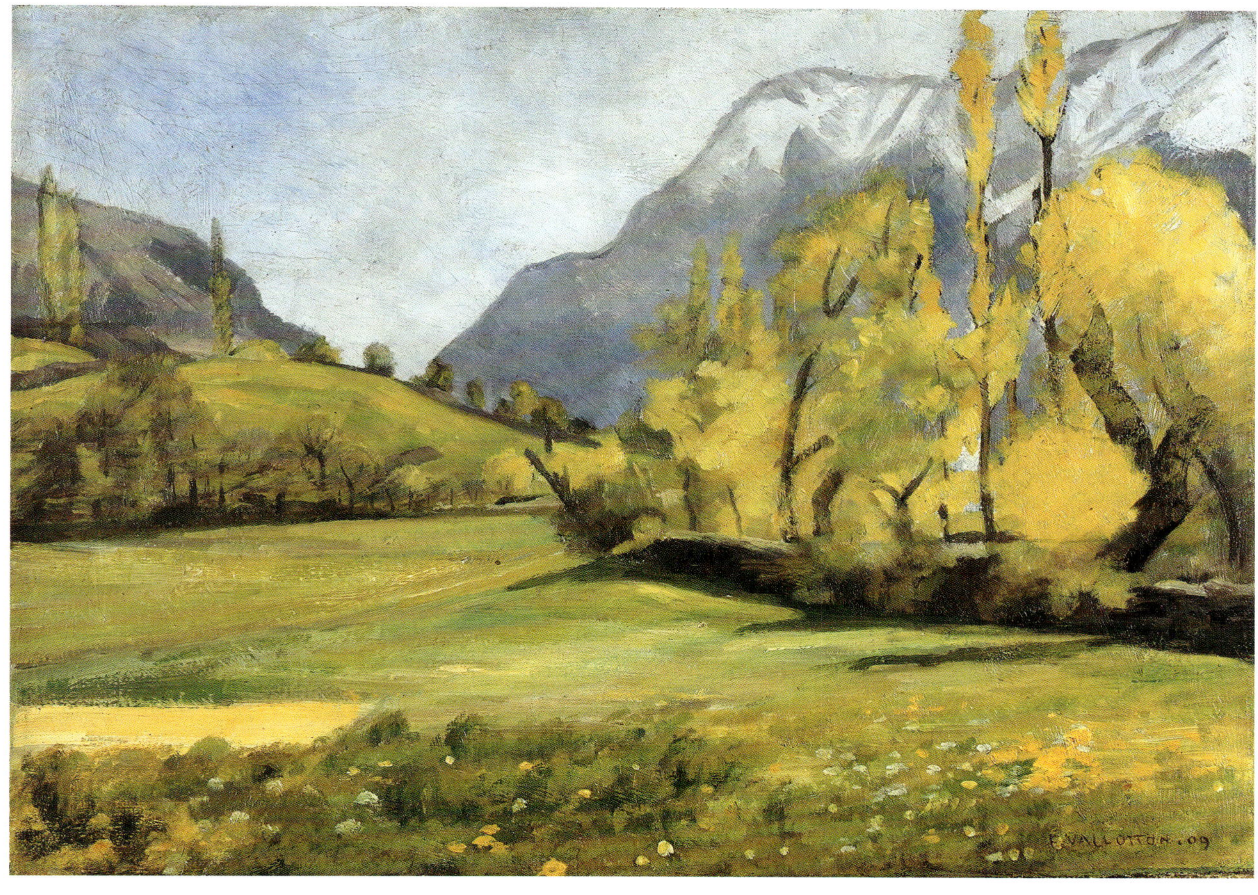

Felix Vallotton
The Environs of Bex, the Valley of St. Maurice
Umgebung von Bex, das Tal von St. Maurice, 1909

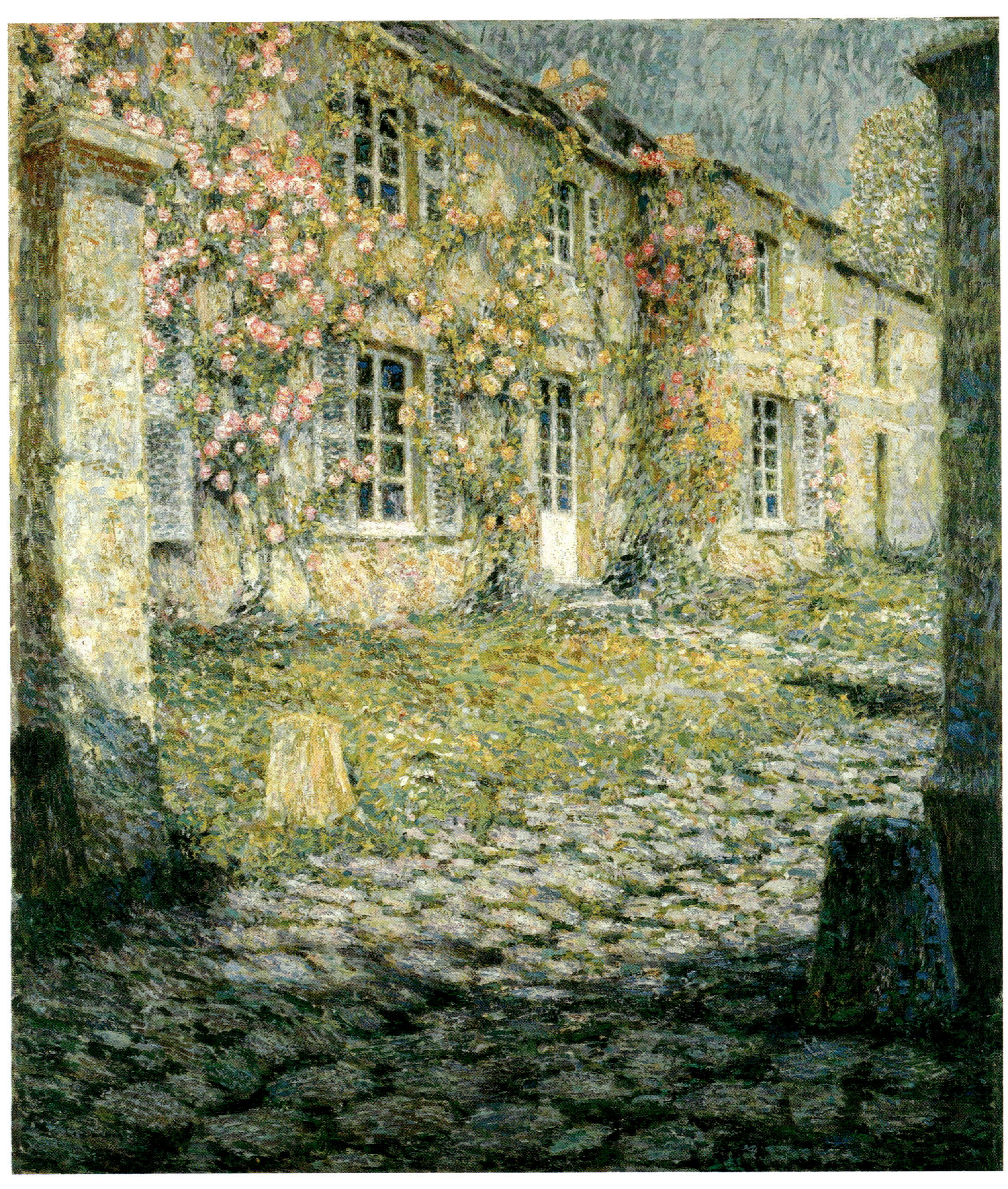

Henri le Sidaner
House with Roses in Versailles
Haus mit Rosen in Versailles, 1918

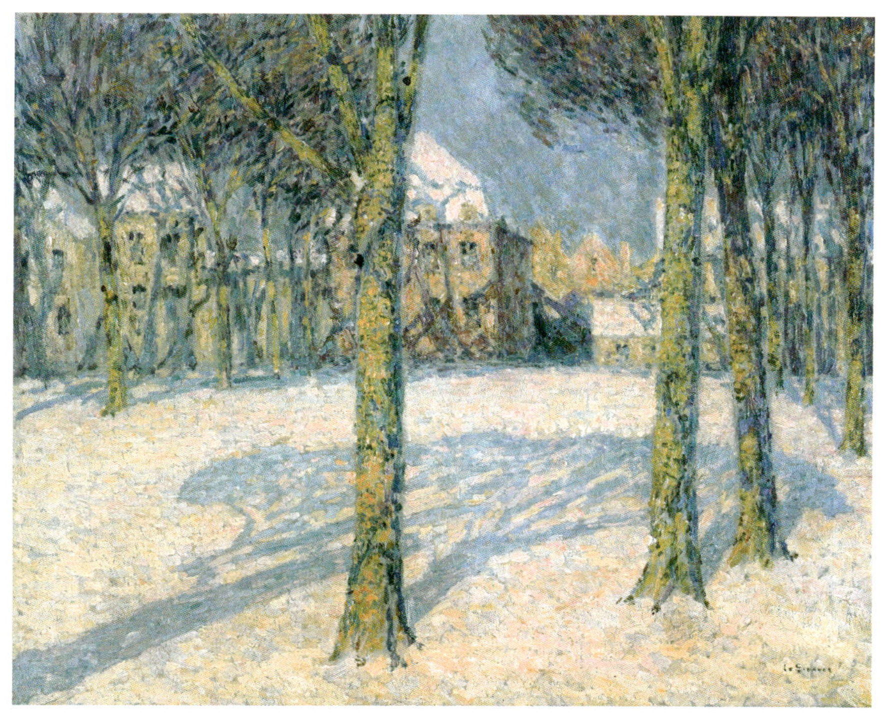

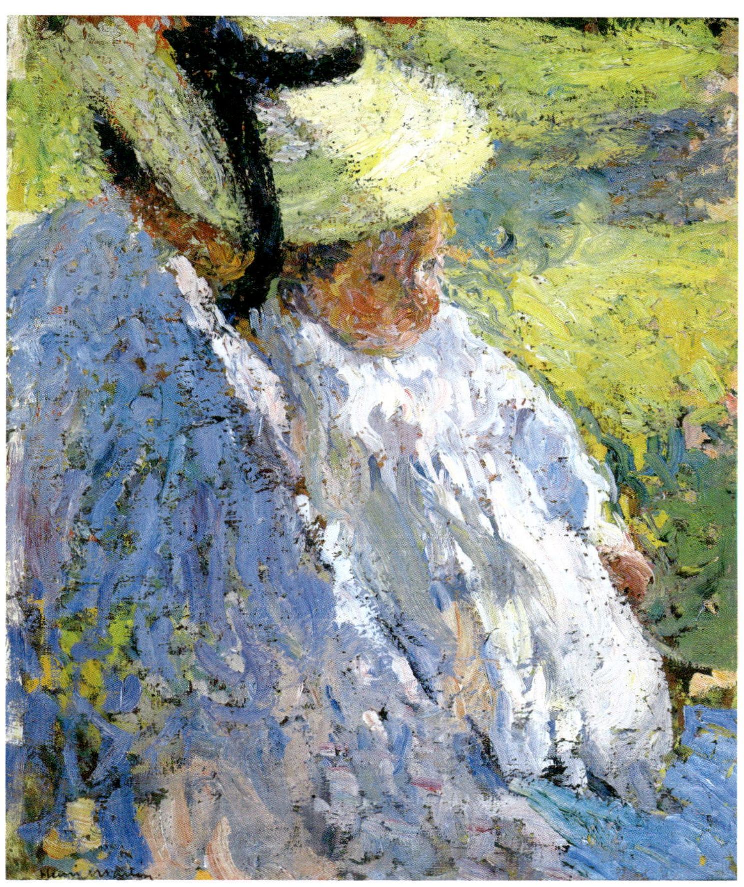

Henri le Sidaner
Small Square in Chartres in the Snow
Verschneiter kleiner Platz in Chartres, 1919

Henri Martin
Child in the Arms of a Woman Wearing a Hat or *Mother and Child*
Kind in den Armen einer Frau mit Hut oder *Mutter und Kind*, ca. 1920

MAURICE UTRILLO
The Circus or *The Festival of Vaugirard*
Der Zirkus oder *Fest von Vaugirard*, 1927

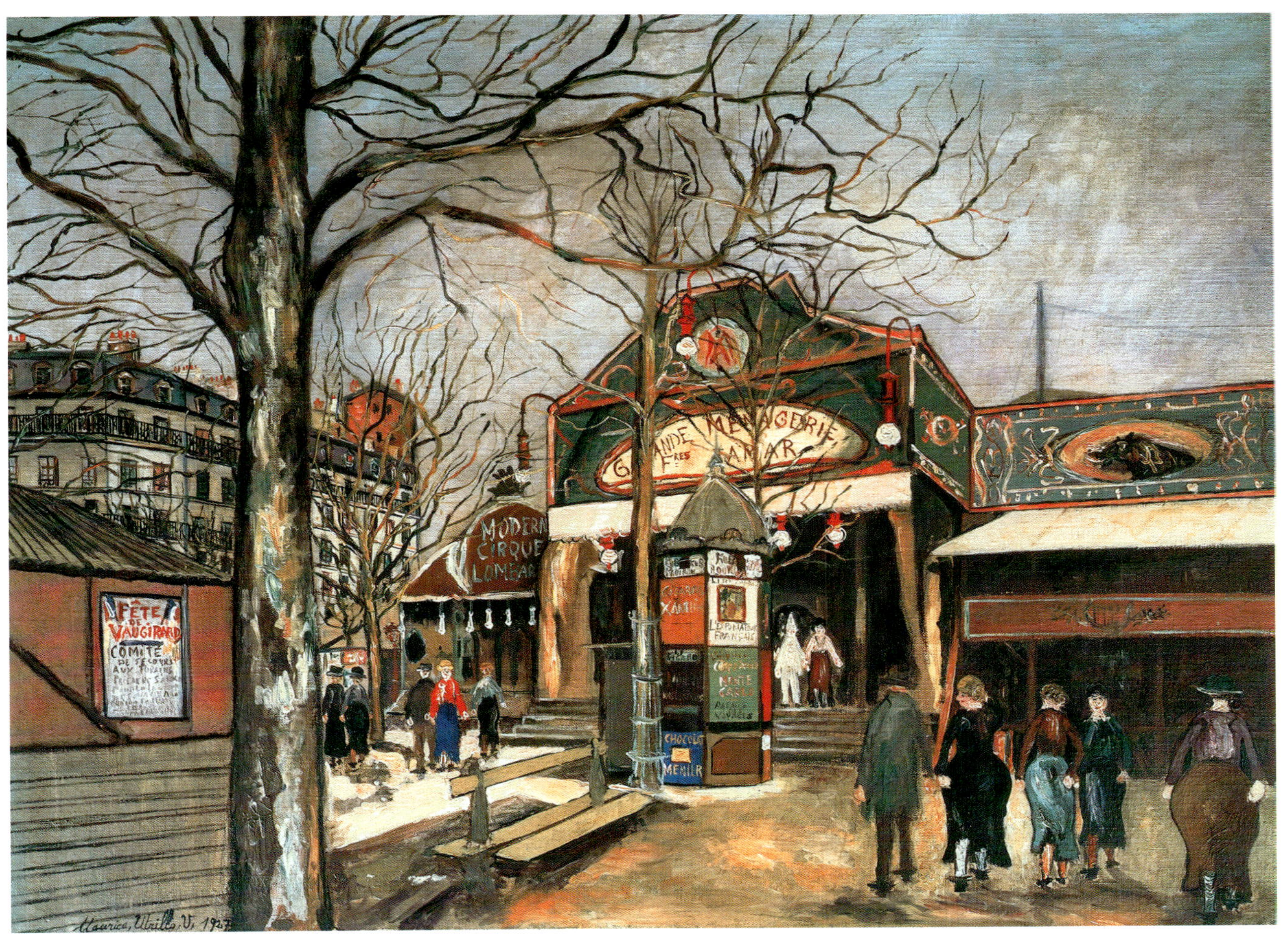
GRANDE MENAGERIE
MODERN
CIRQUE
FÊTE DE VAUGIRARD
COMITE
MENIER

Impressionism and Symbolism
Symbolism in Europe

Impressionismus und Symbolismus
Symbolismus in Europa

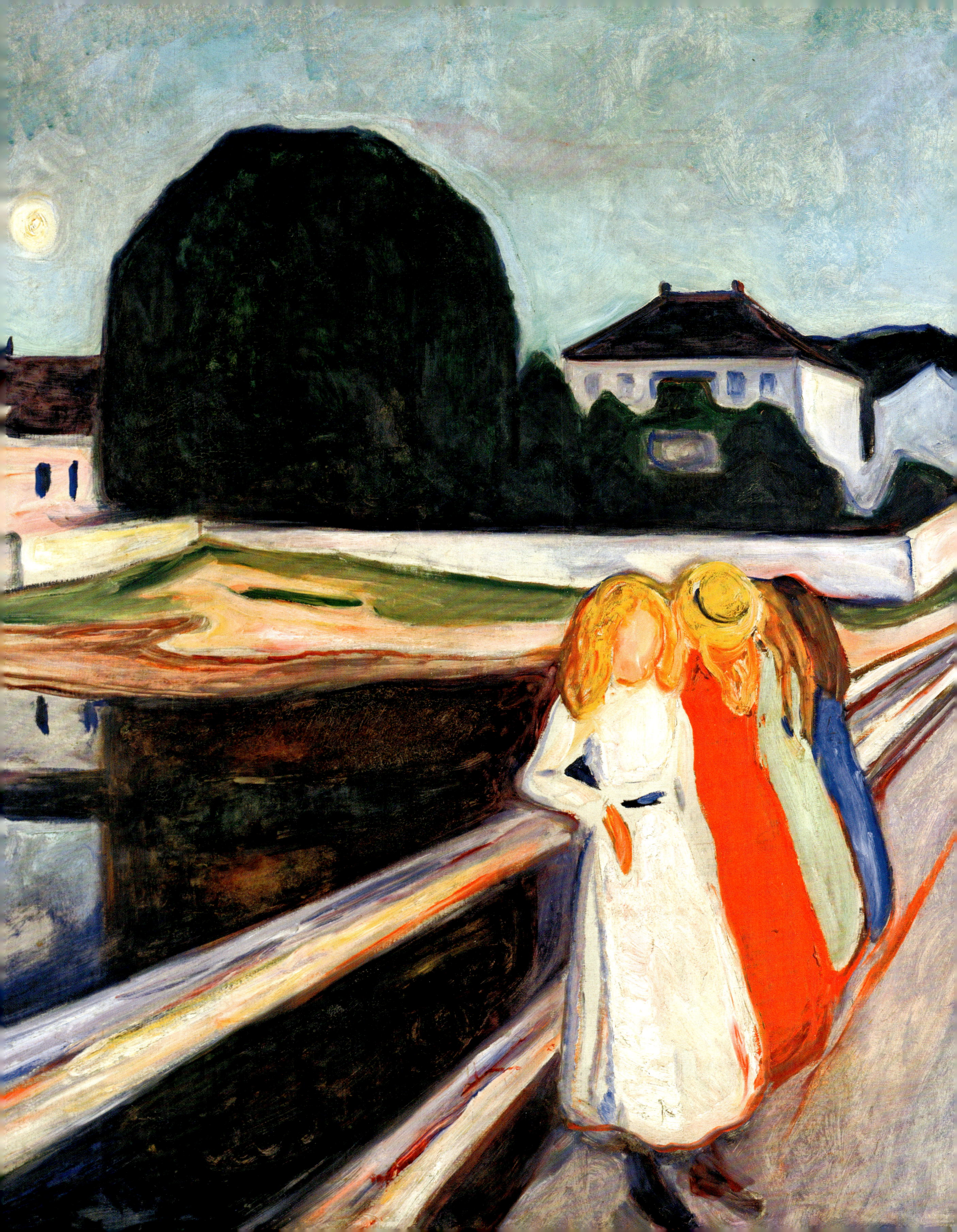

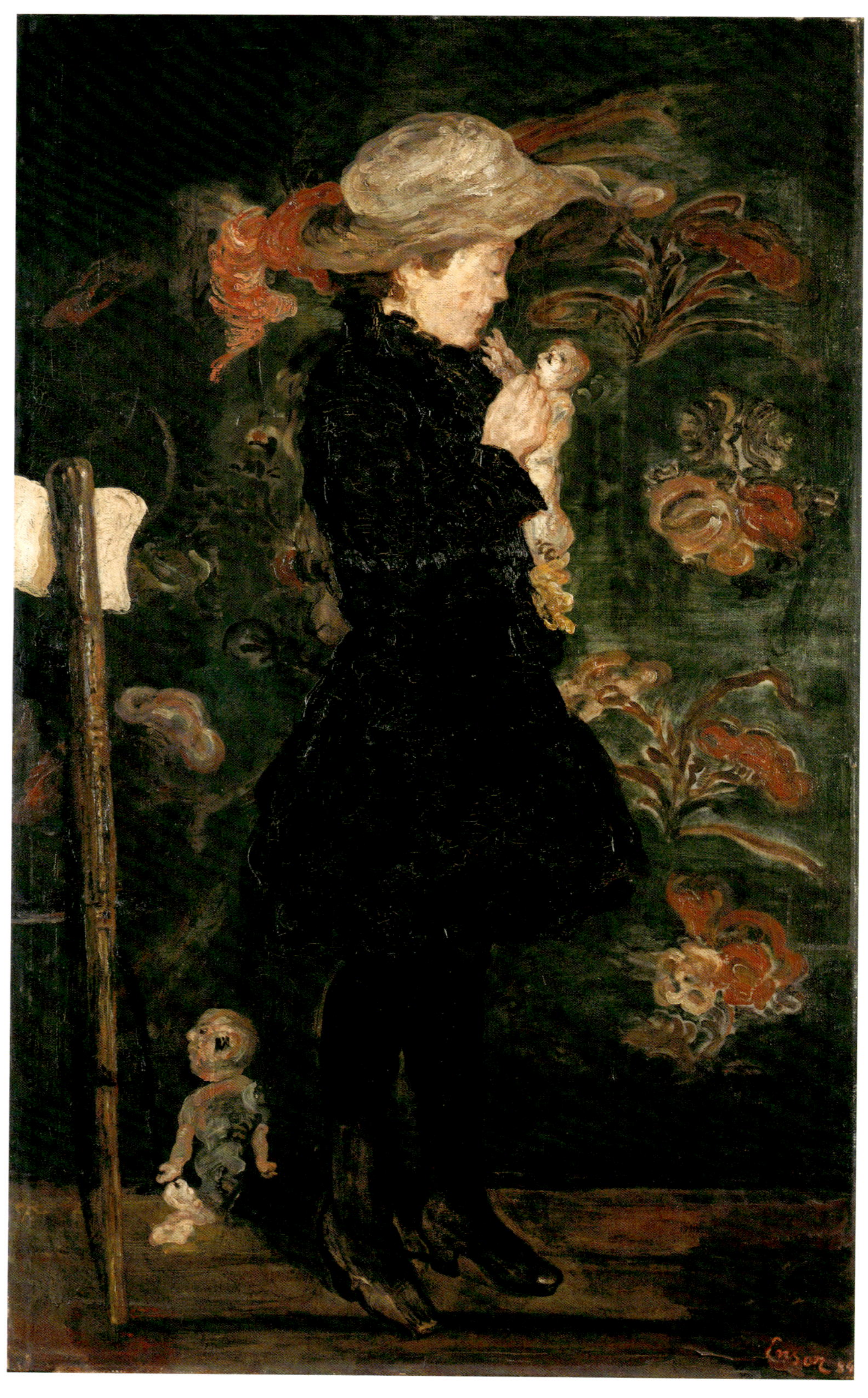

James Ensor
Young Girl with a Doll
Mädchen mit Puppe, 1884

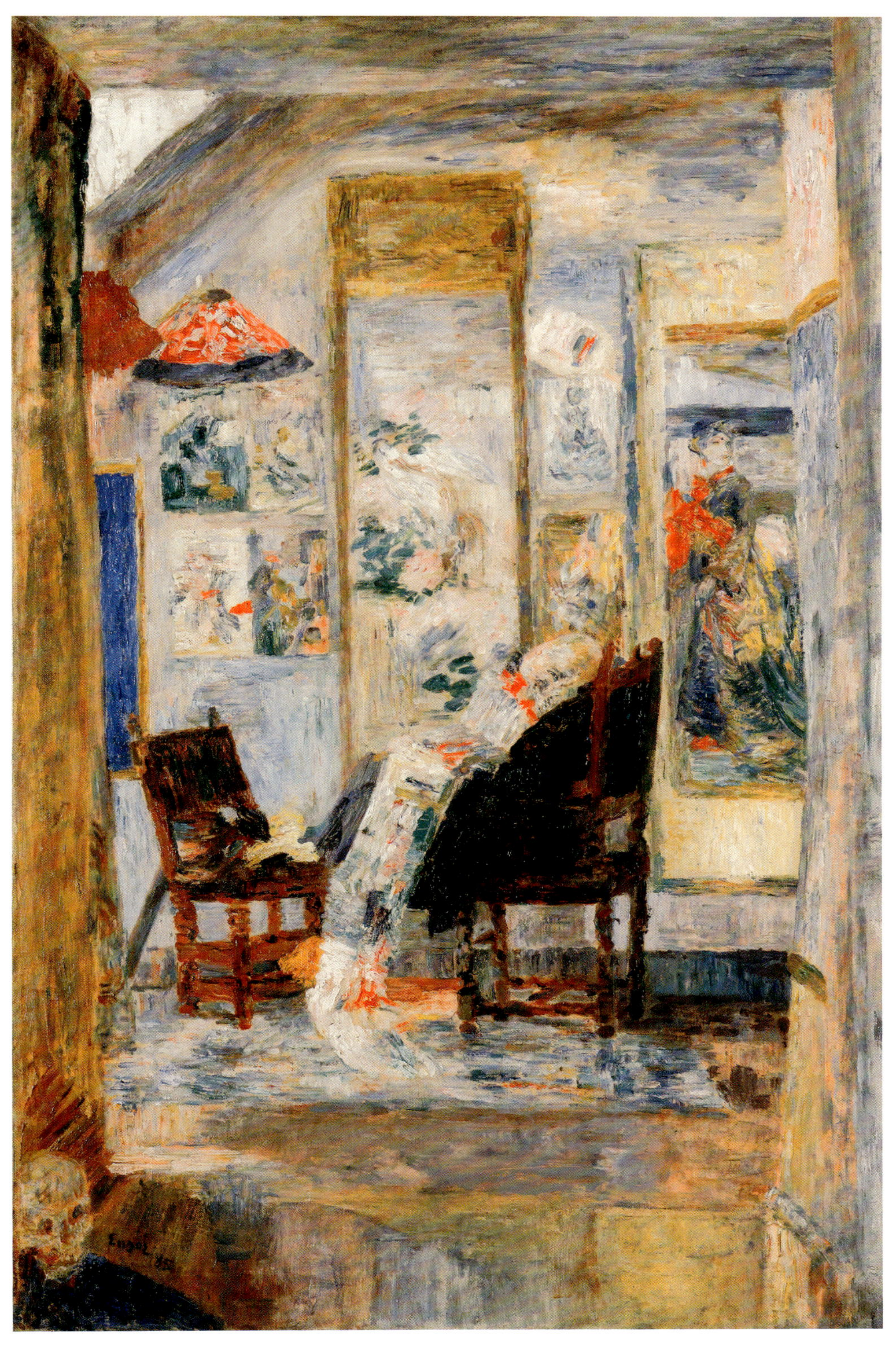

James Ensor
Skeleton Gazing at Chinoiseries
Skelett, Chinoiserien betrachtend, 1885

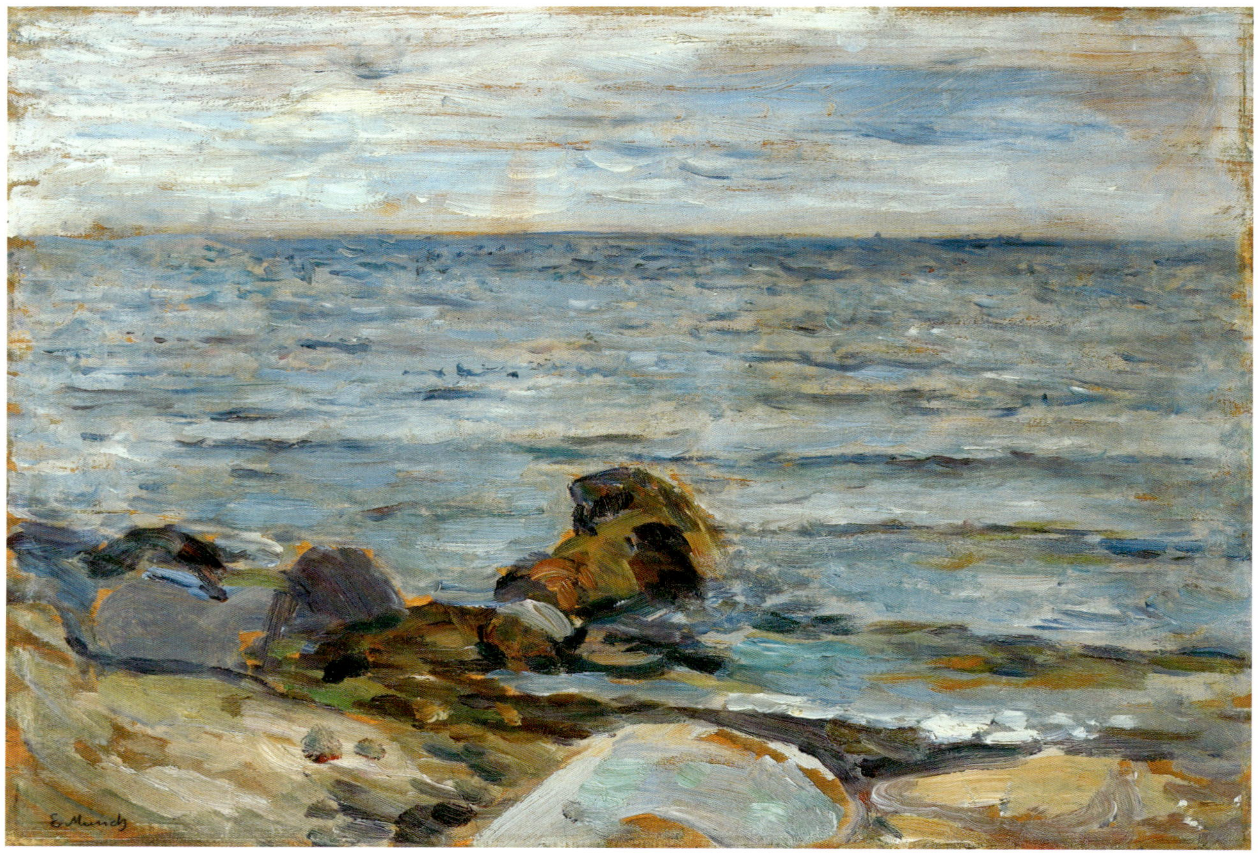

Edvard Munch
Åsgårdstrand, 1888/90

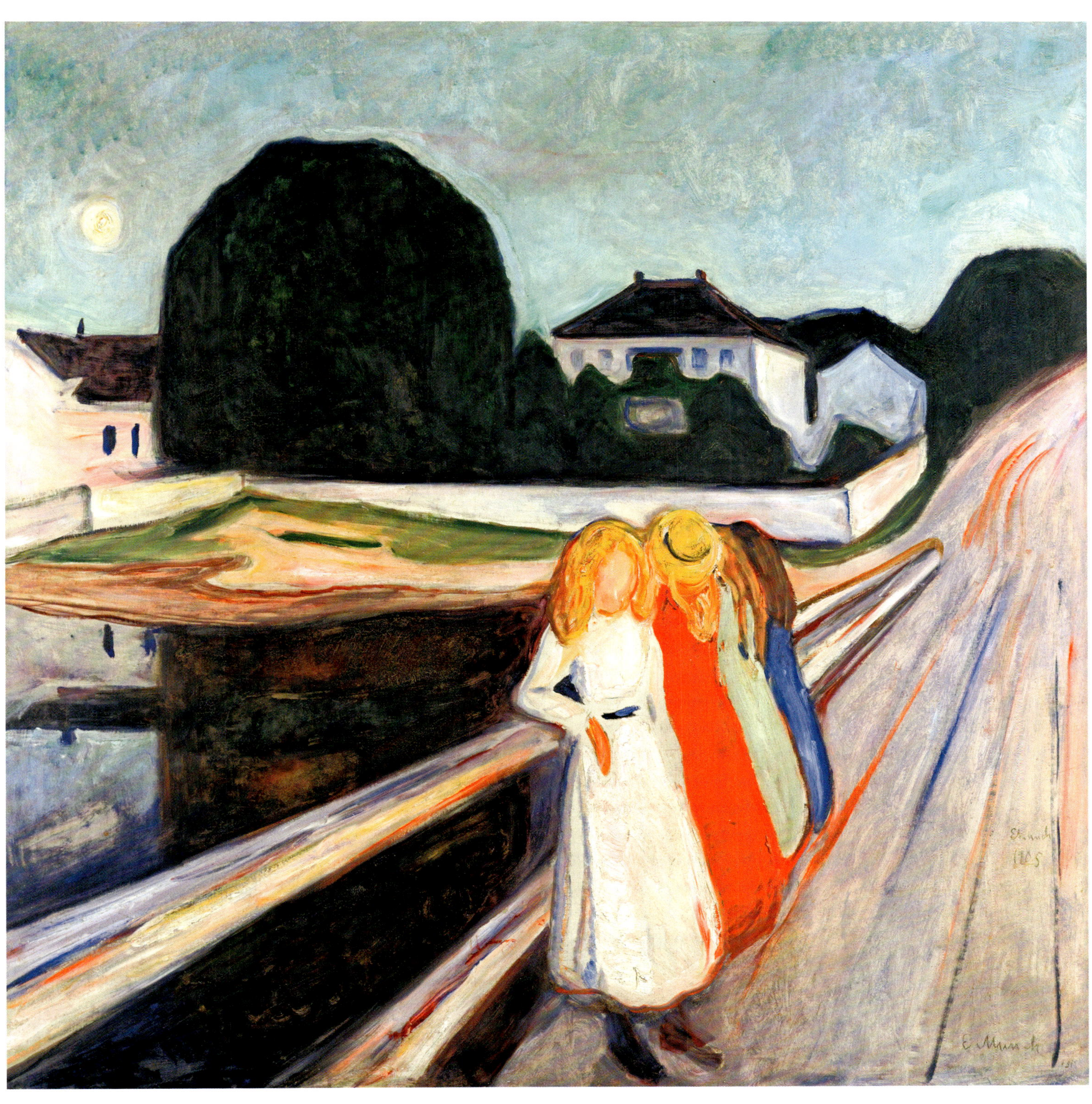

Edvard Munch
Four Girls on the Bridge
Vier Mädchen auf der Brücke, 1905

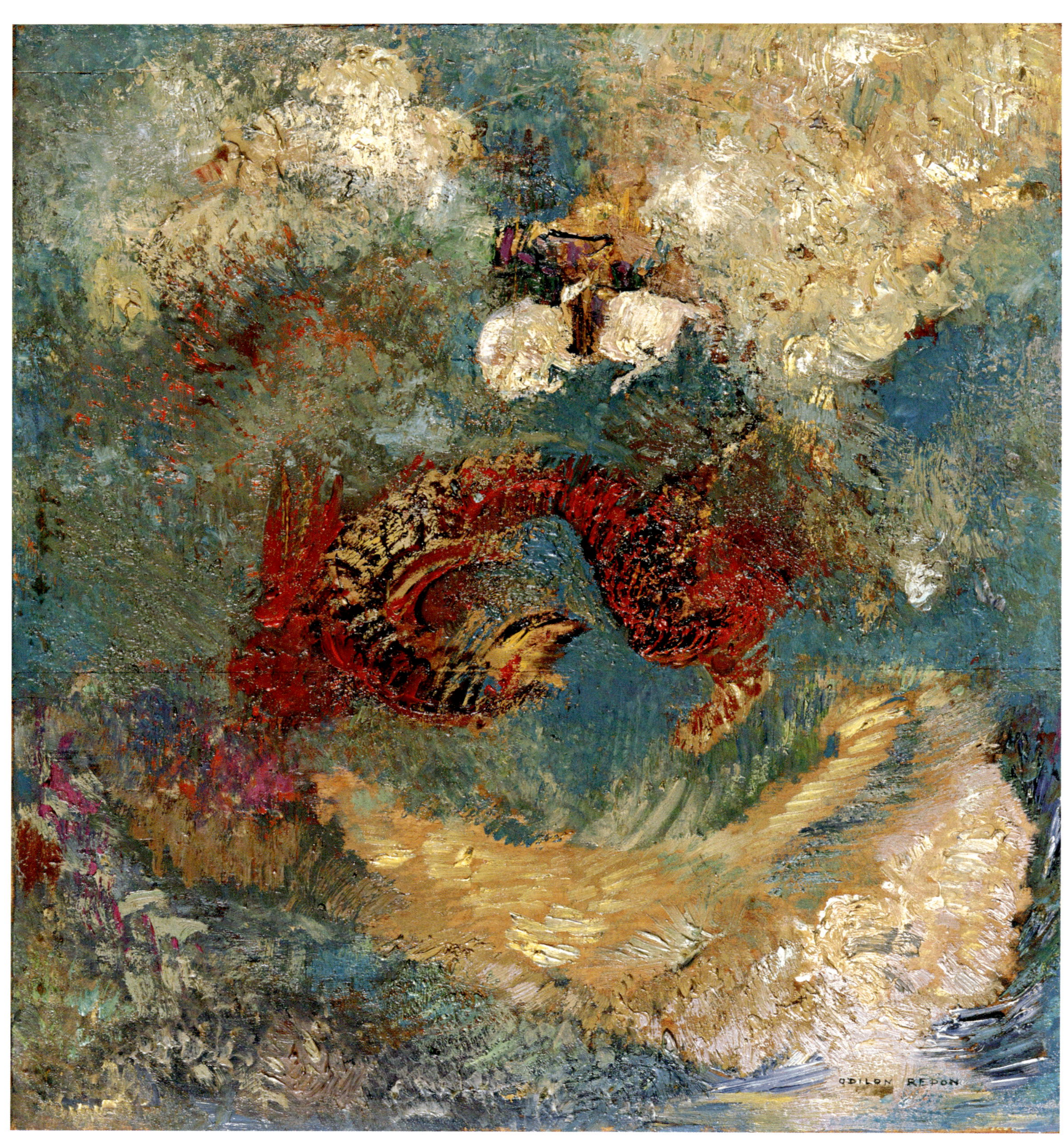

Odilon Redon
Saint George and the Dragon
Der Kampf mit dem Drachen, ca. 1907

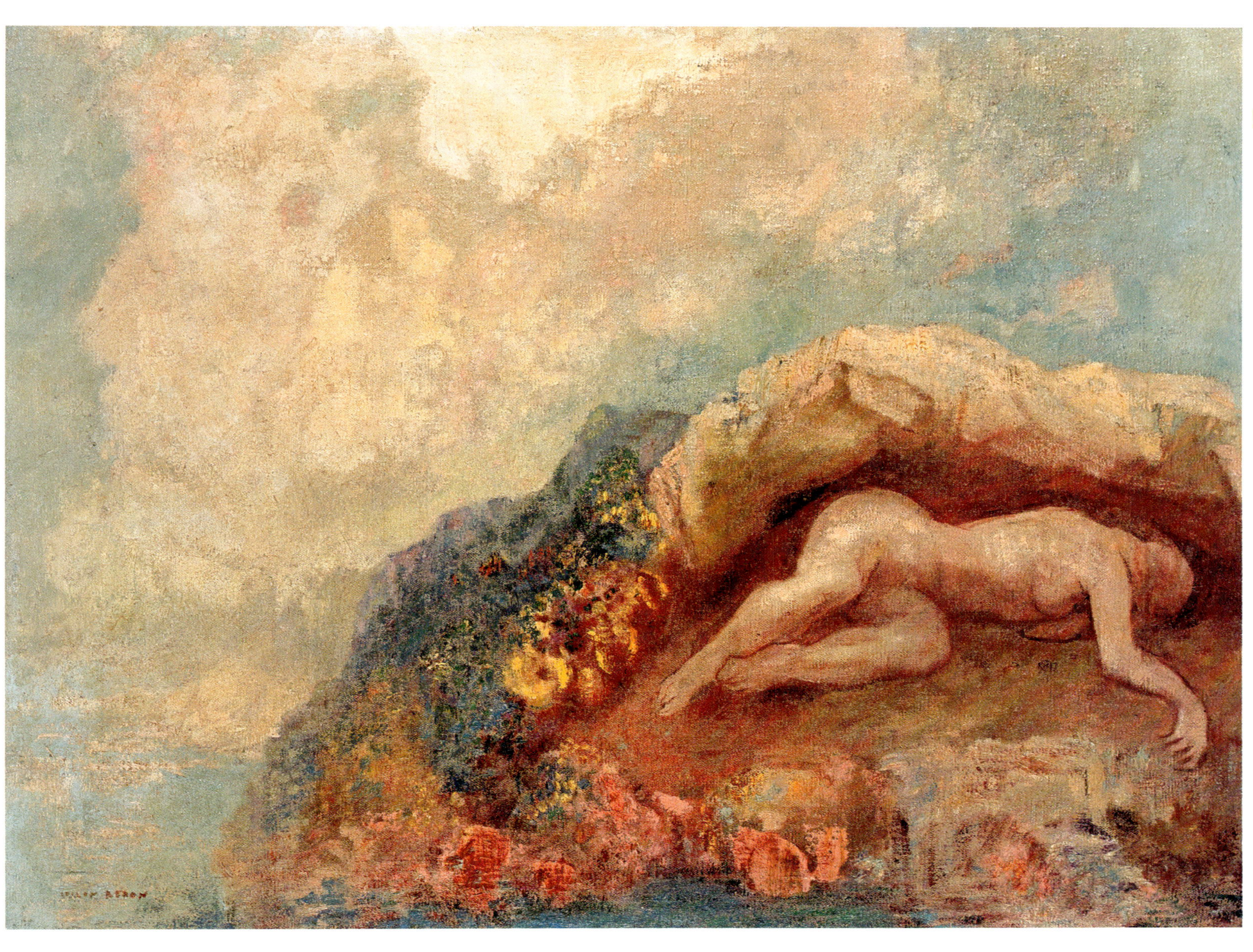

Odilon Redon
The Prisoner
Die Gefangene, 1910

Odilon Redon
Butterflies
Schmetterlinge, 1910

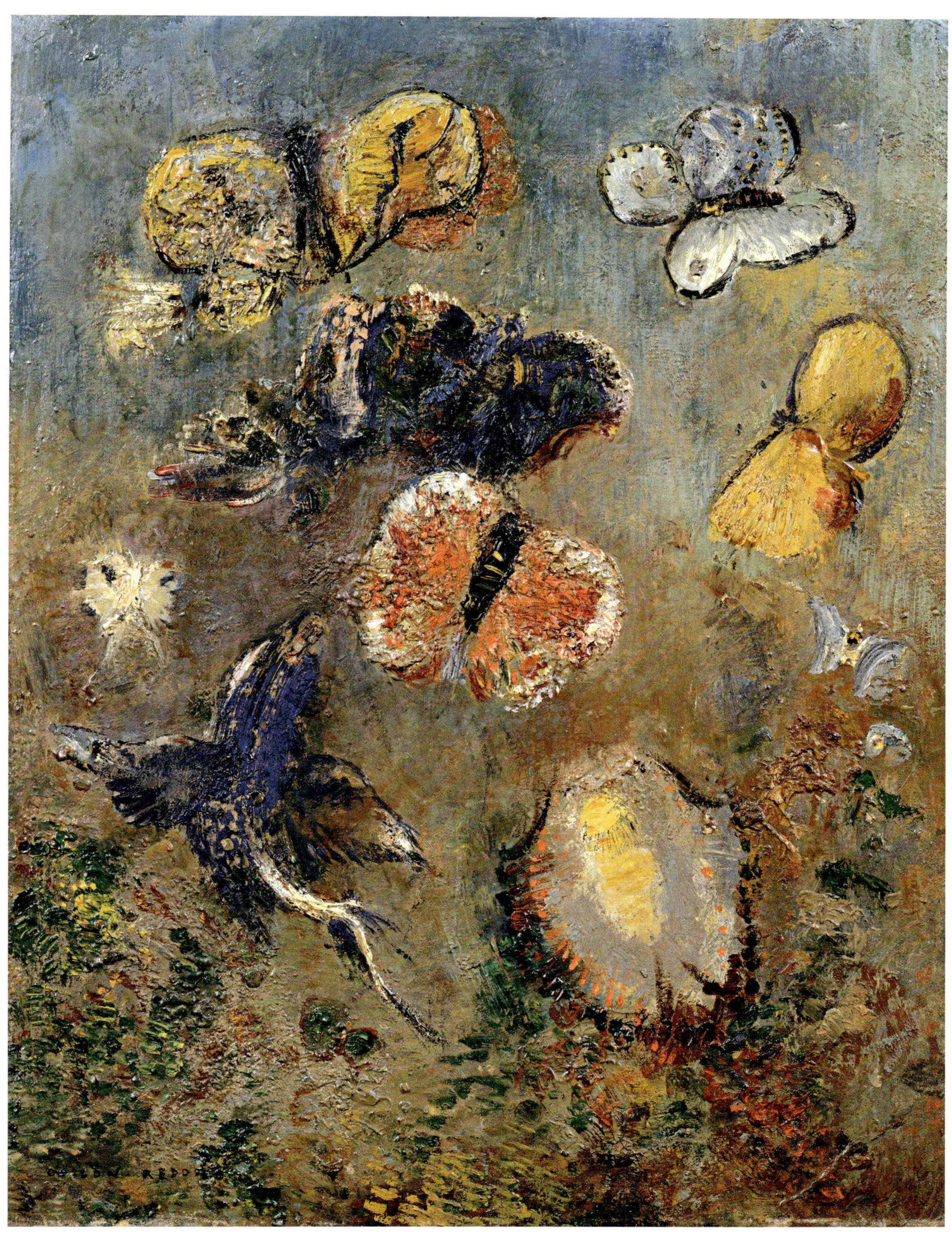

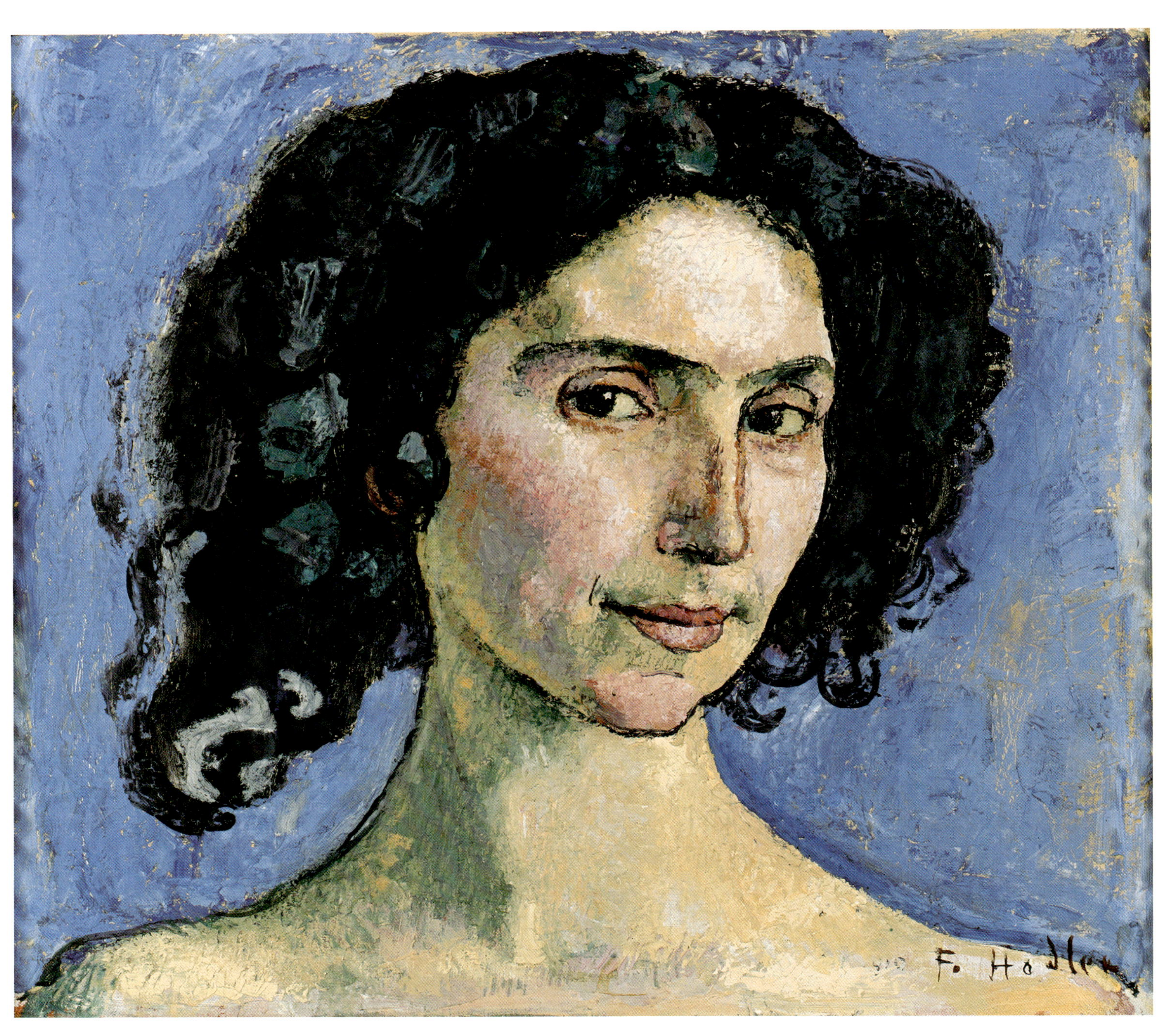

Ferdinand Hodler
Study of the Head of an Italian Woman (Giulia Leonardi)
Kopfstudie einer Italienerin (Giulia Leonardi), 1910

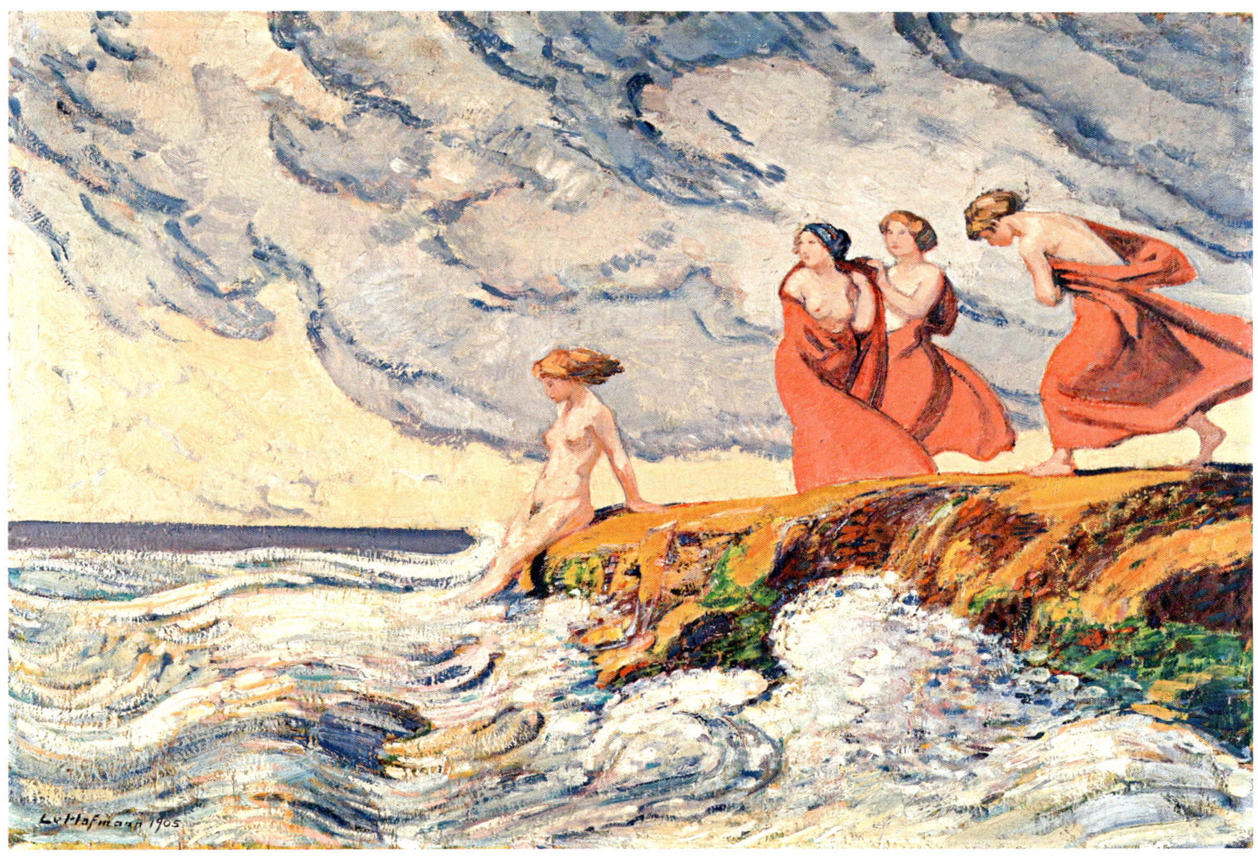

Ludwig von Hofmann
Surf
Brandung, 1905

William Degouve de Nuncques
Snowy Landscape
Schneelandschaft, ca. 1910/20

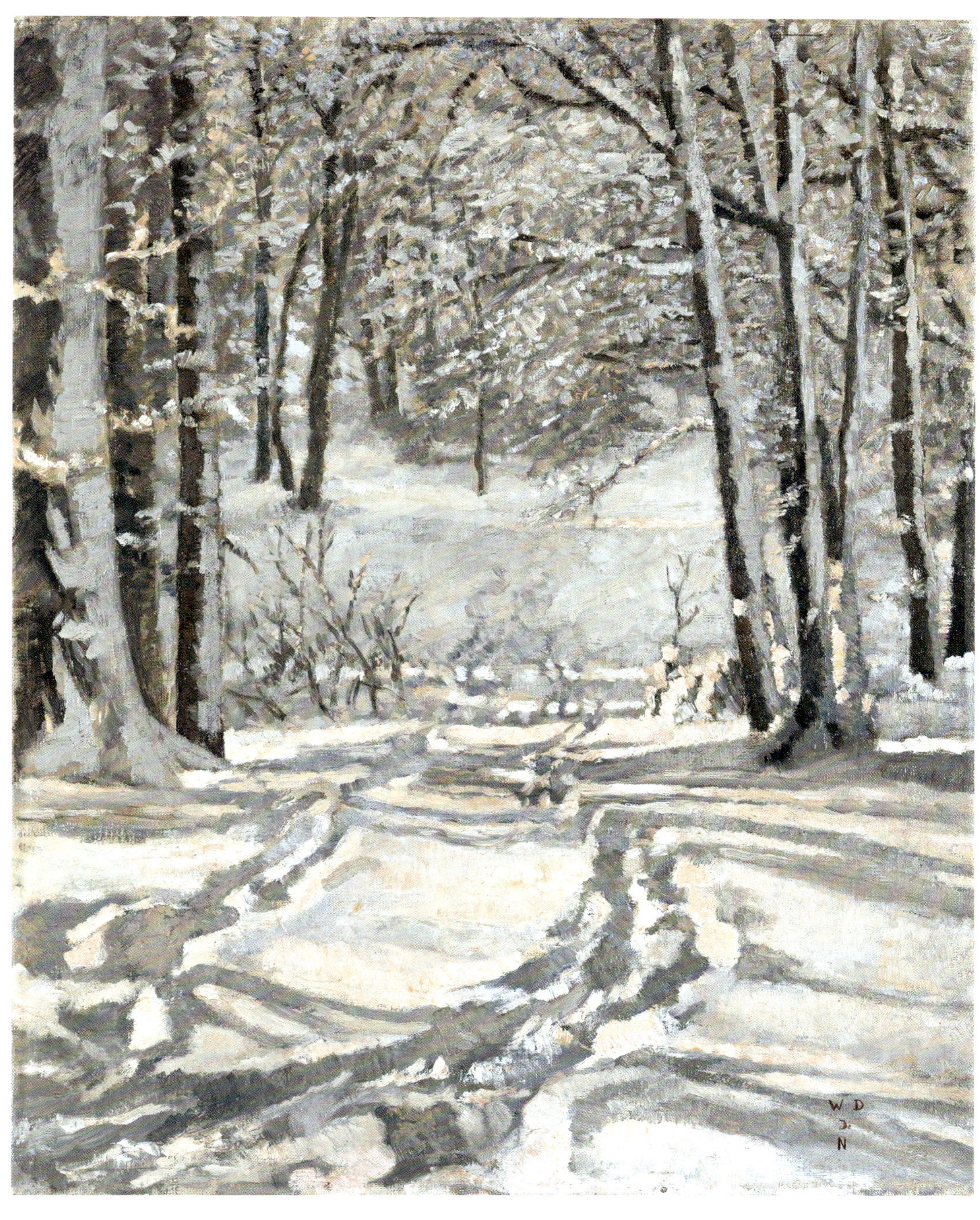

The Germans

Die Deutschen

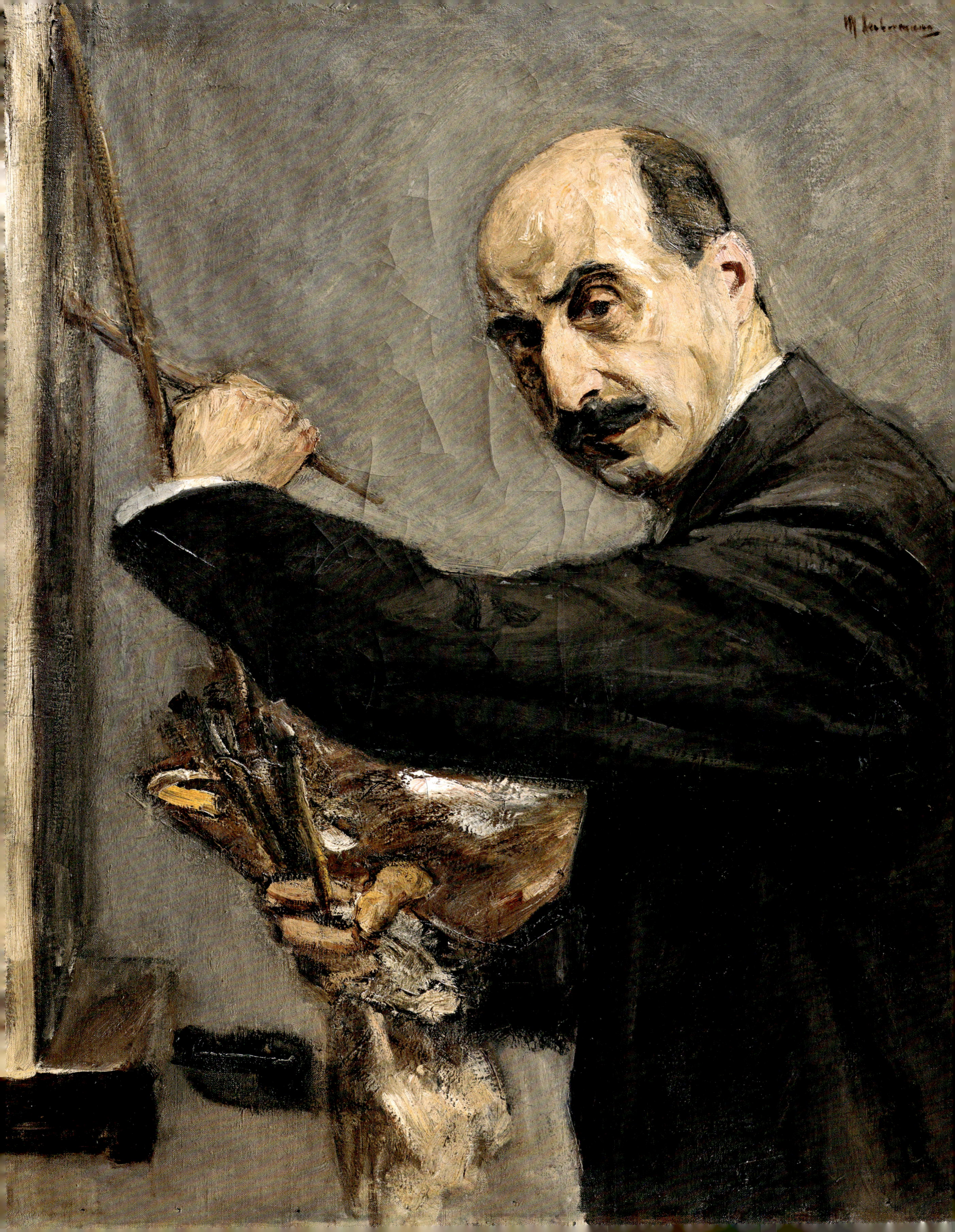

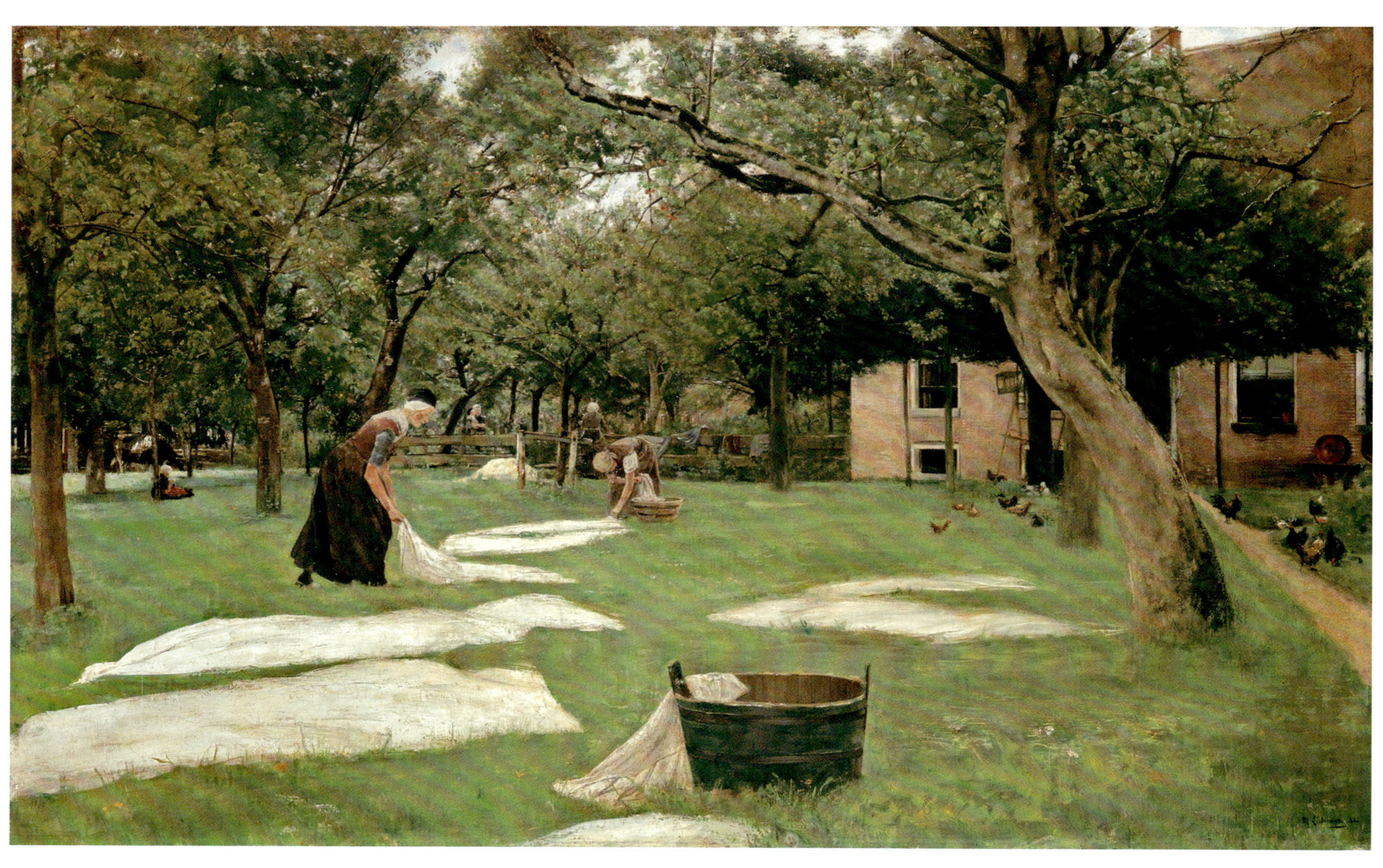

Max Liebermann
The Bleaching Ground
Die Rasenbleiche, 1882

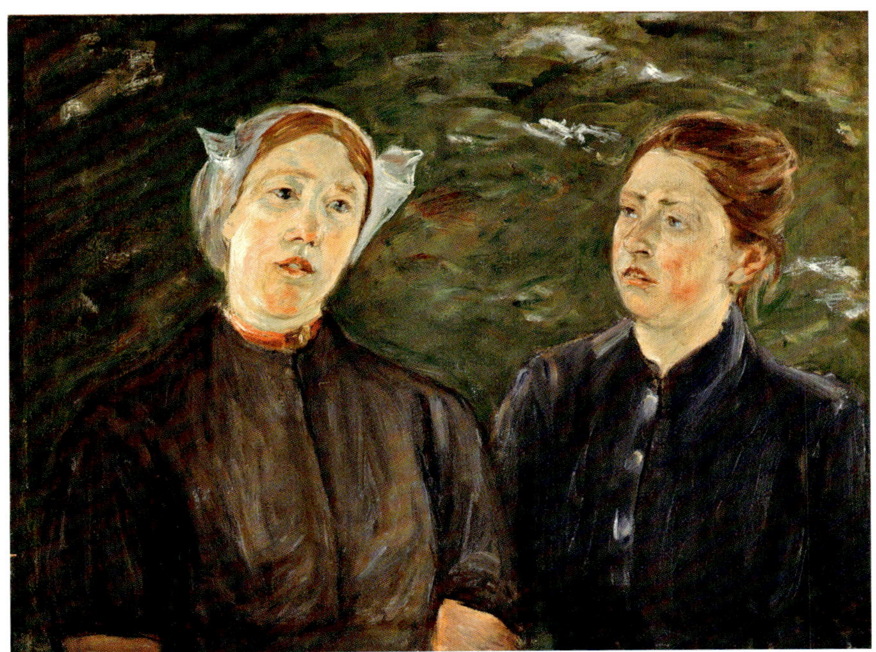

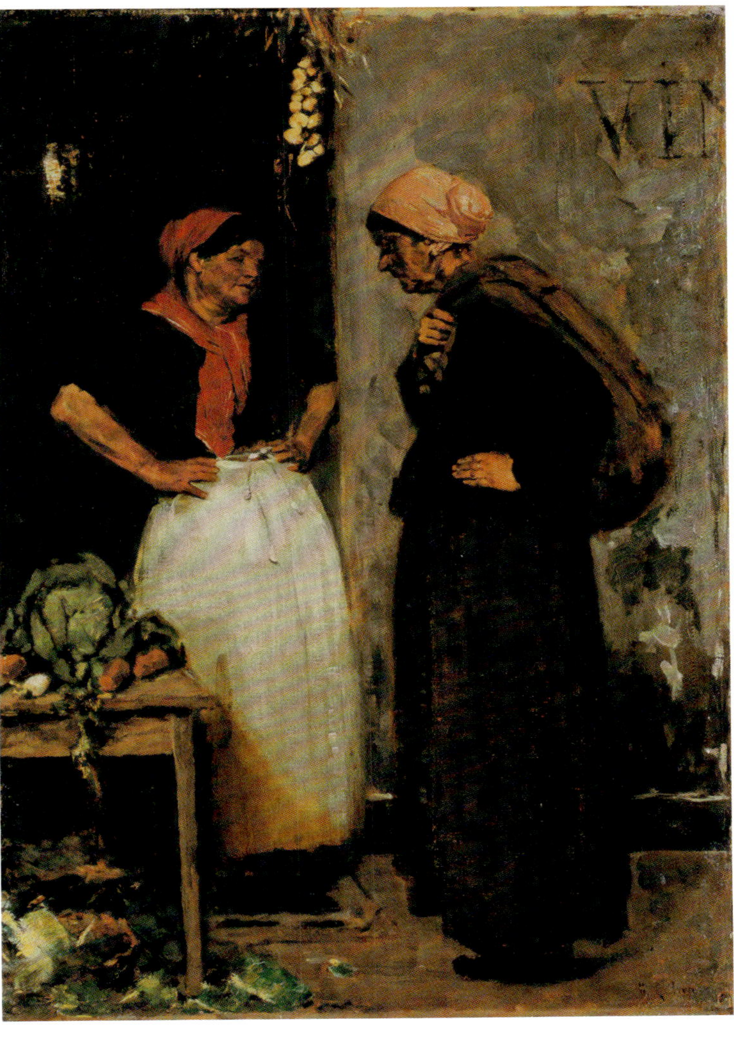

Max Liebermann
Two Dutch Peasant Women
Zwei holländische Bäuerinnen, 1898

Max Liebermann
Market Scene
Marktszene, 1874

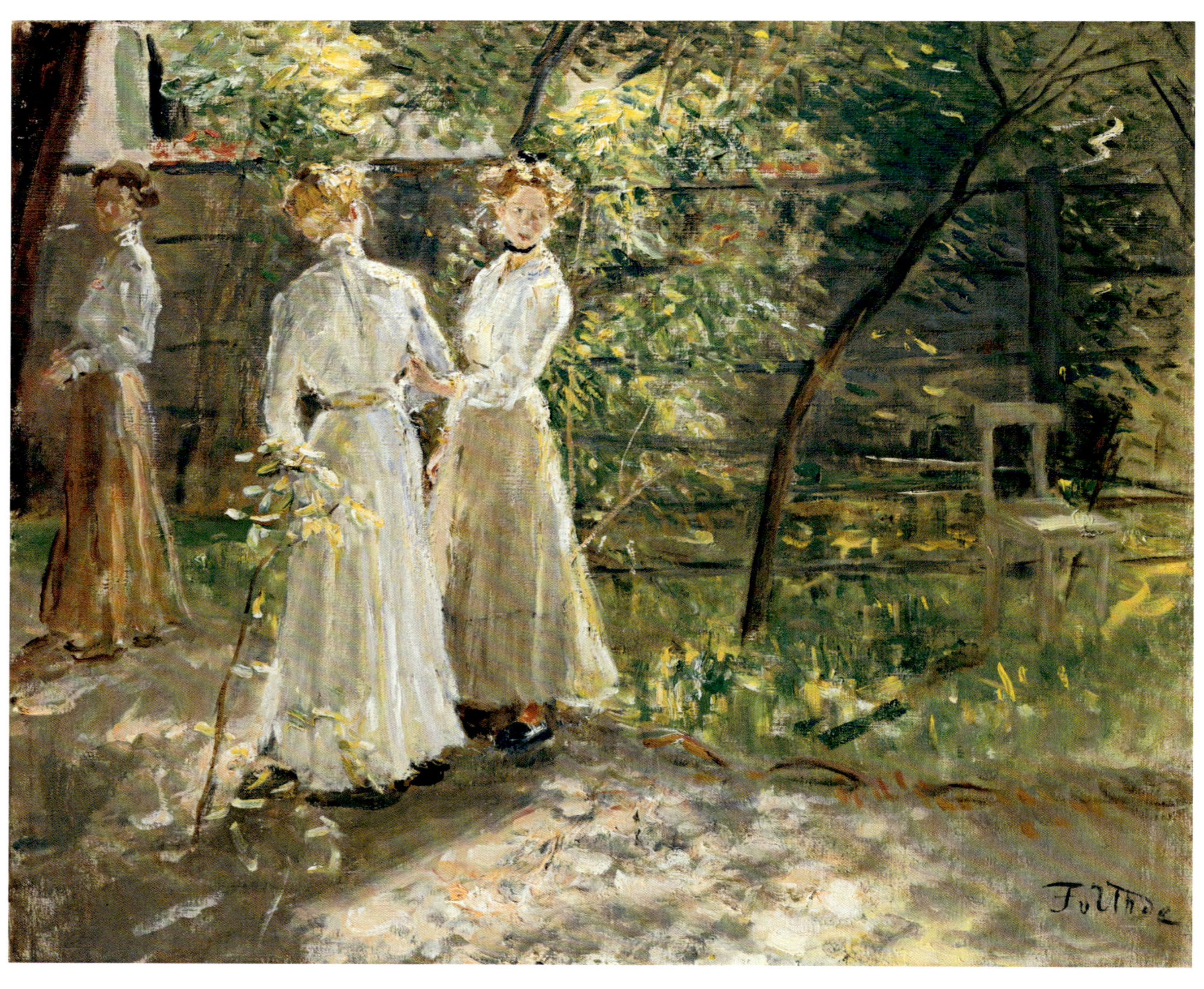

Fritz von Uhde
The Painter's Three Daughters in the Garden
Die drei Töchter des Malers im Garten, ca. 1885

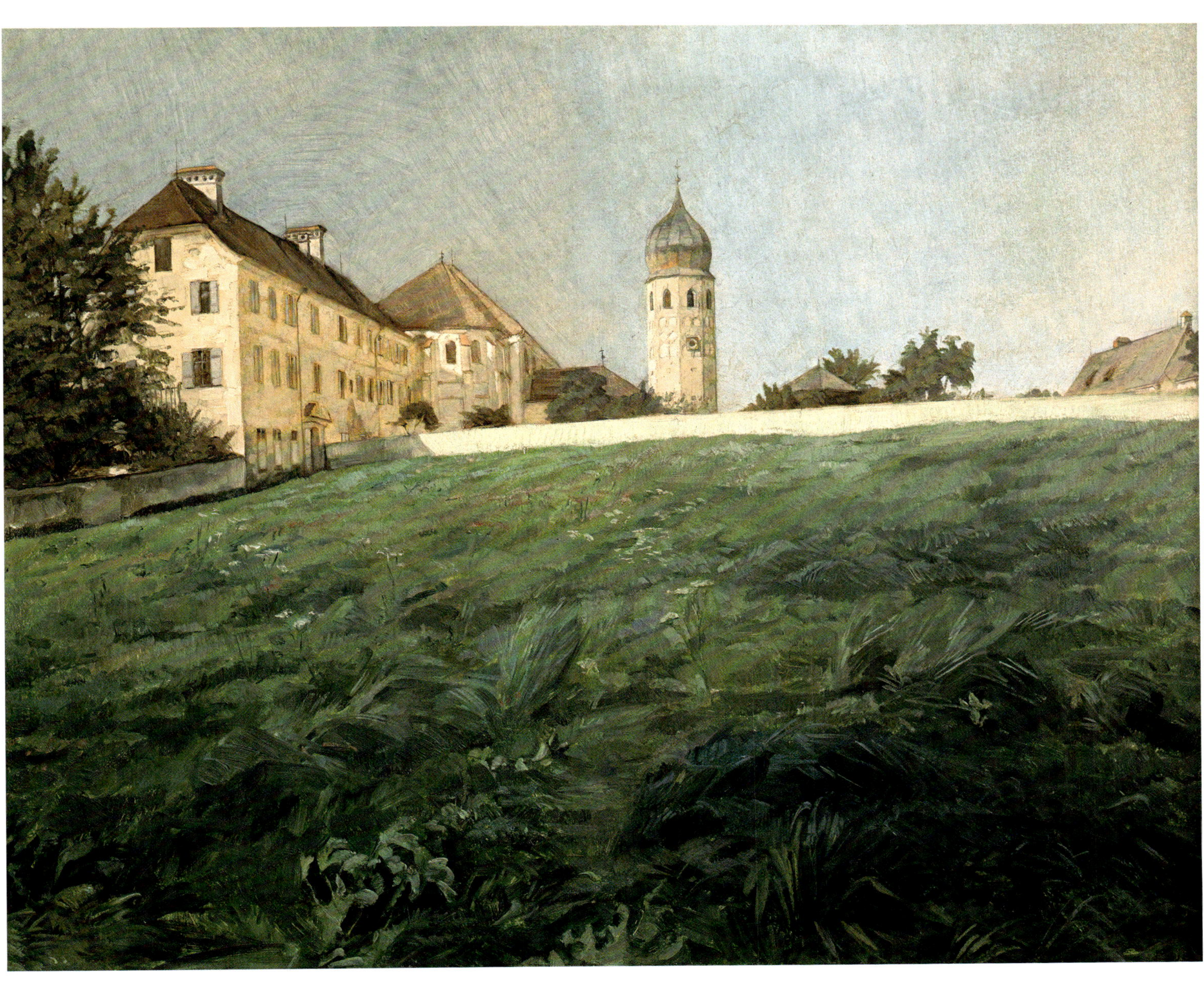

HEINRICH WILHELM TRÜBNER
On Frauenchiemsee
Auf Frauenchiemsee, ca. 1891

Lovis Corinth
Descent from the Cross
Kreuzabnahme, 1895

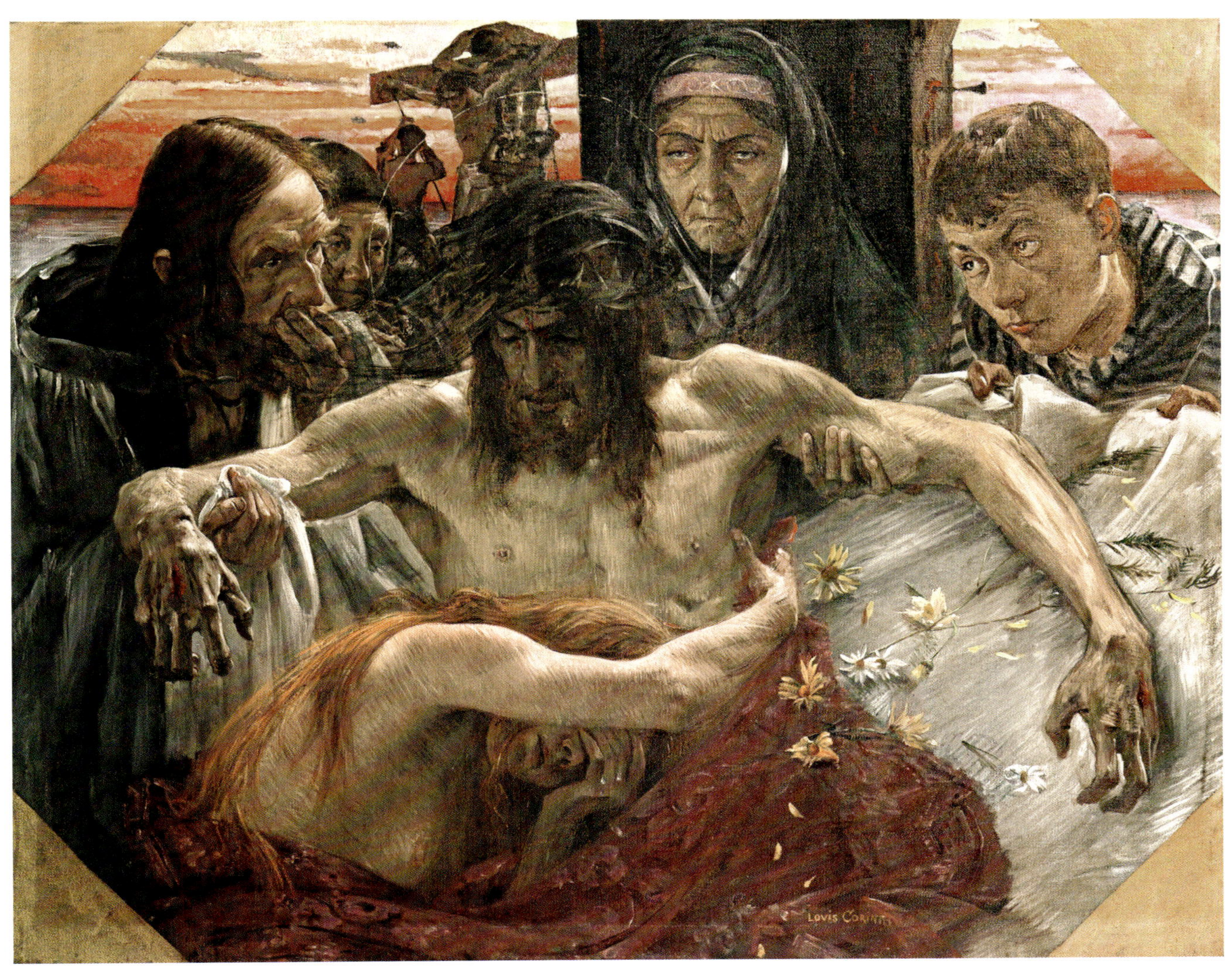
LOVIS CORINTH

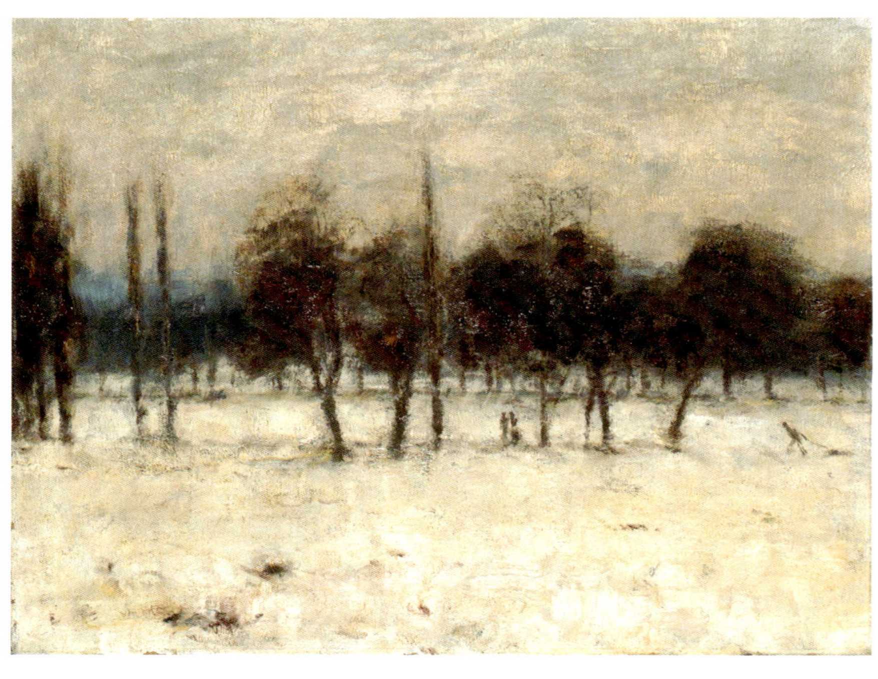

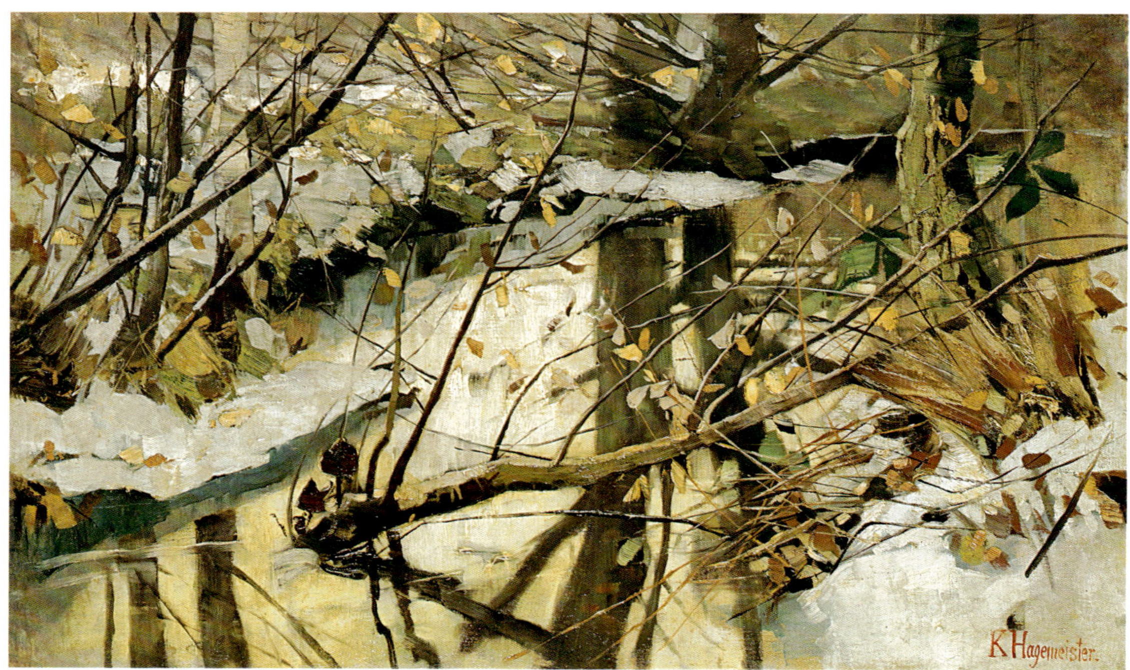

CHRISTIAN ROHLFS
Fruit Trees in the Snow
Obstbäume im Schnee (Am Sandweg vor Weimar-Ehringsdorf), ca. 1898

KARL HAGEMEISTER
Forest Stream in Early Spring
Waldbach im Vorfrühling, ca. 1900

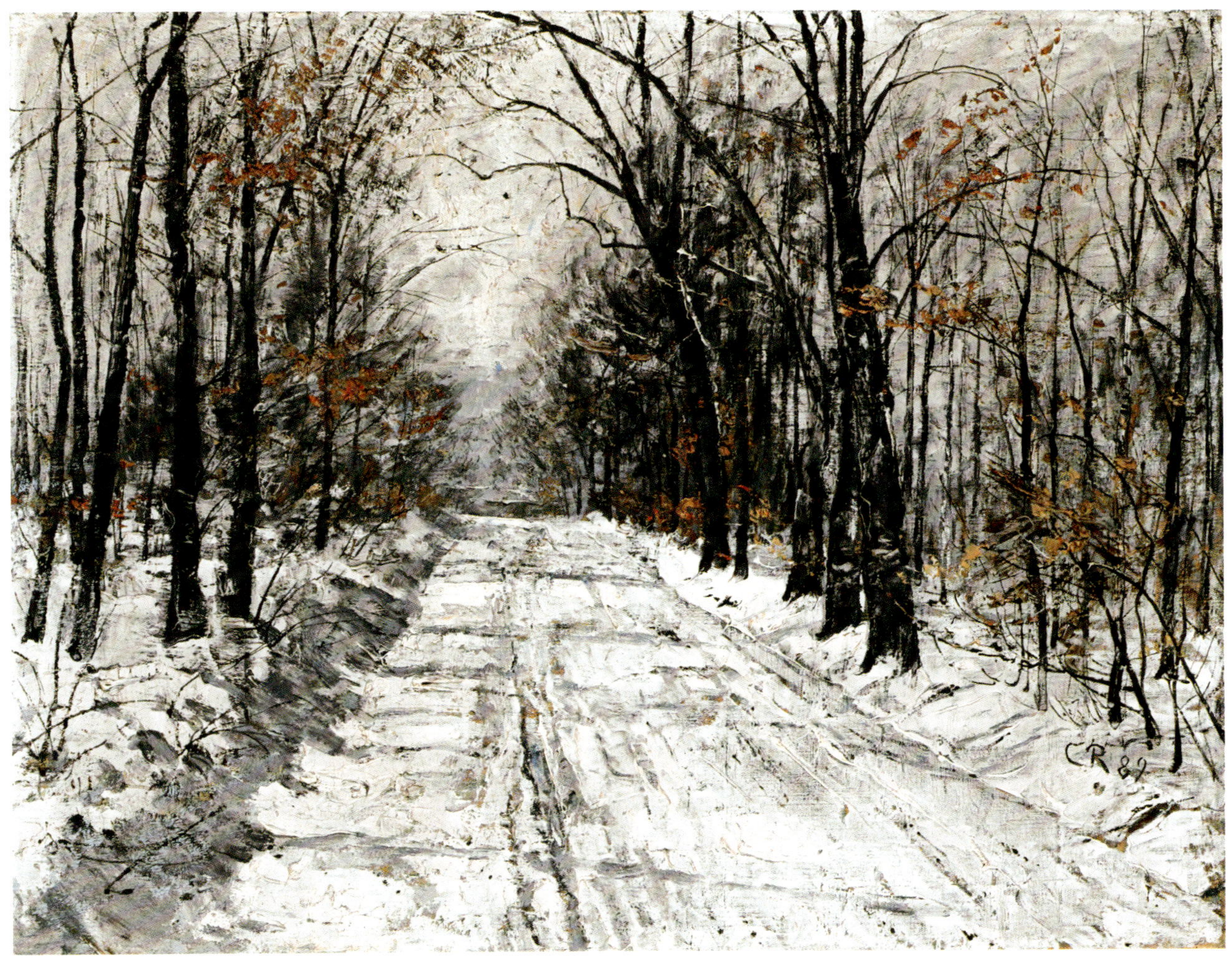

Christian Rohlfs
Forest Path in Winter (Road to Tiefurt in Webicht near Weimar)
Waldweg im Winter (Chaussee nach Tiefurt im Webicht bei Weimar), 1889

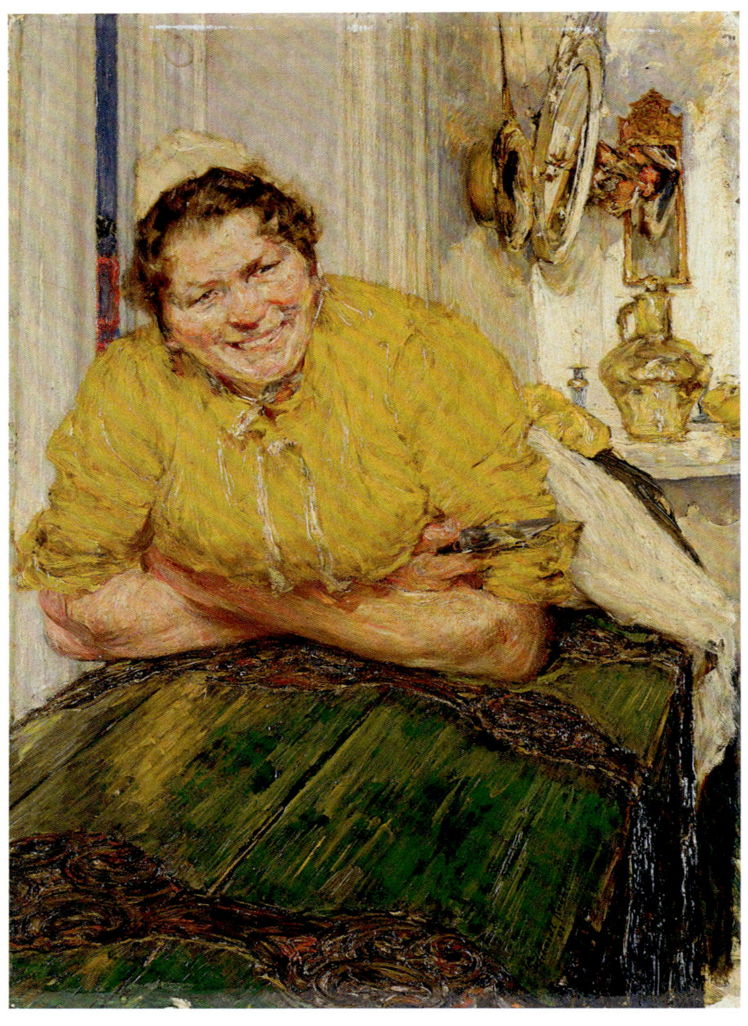

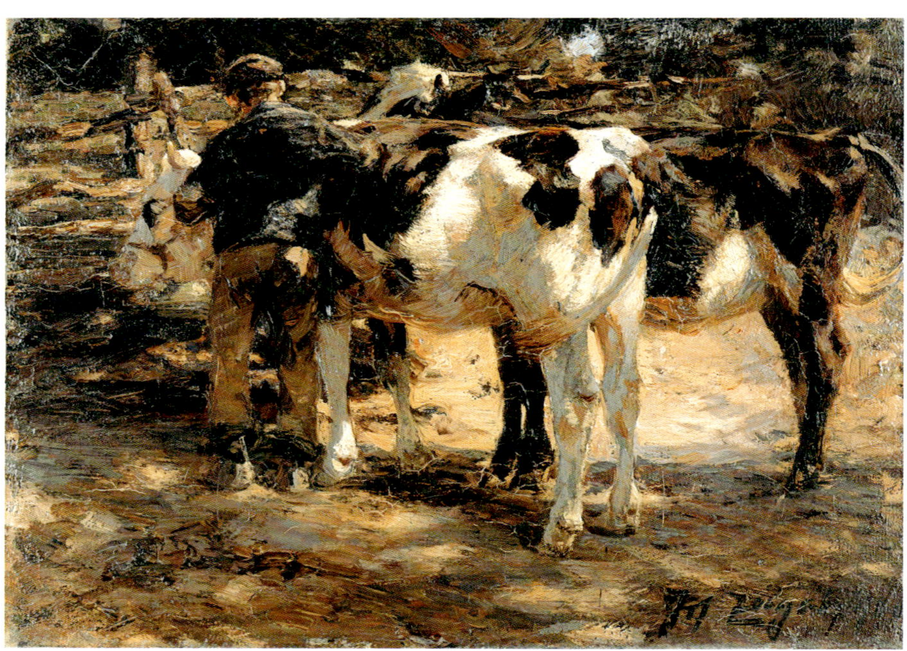

Gotthardt Kuehl
Young Girl Laughing
Lachendes Mädchen, 1903

Heinrich von Zügel
Cattle
Rindvieh, 1900

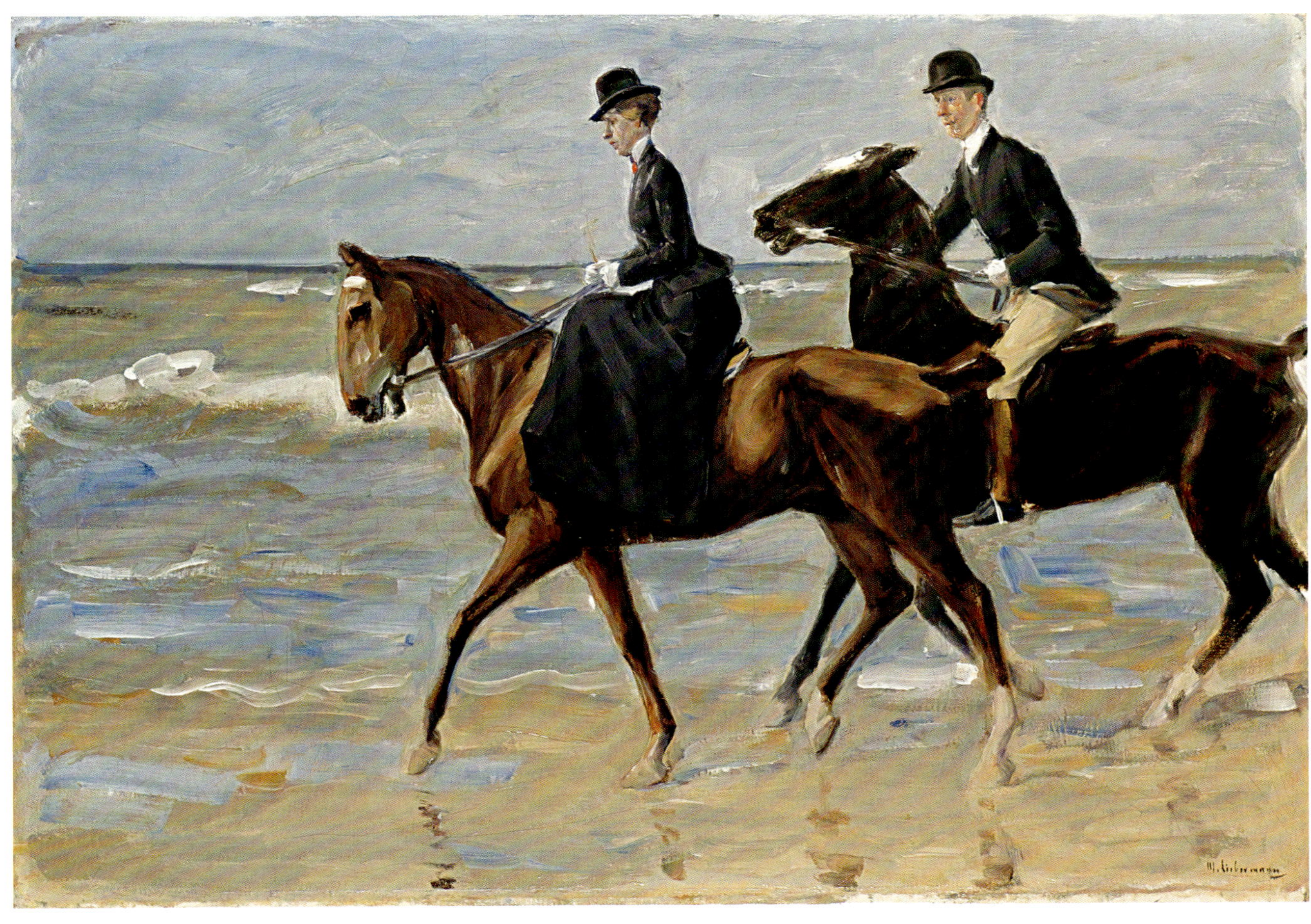

Max Liebermann
Riders on the Beach
Reiter und Reiterin am Strand, 1903

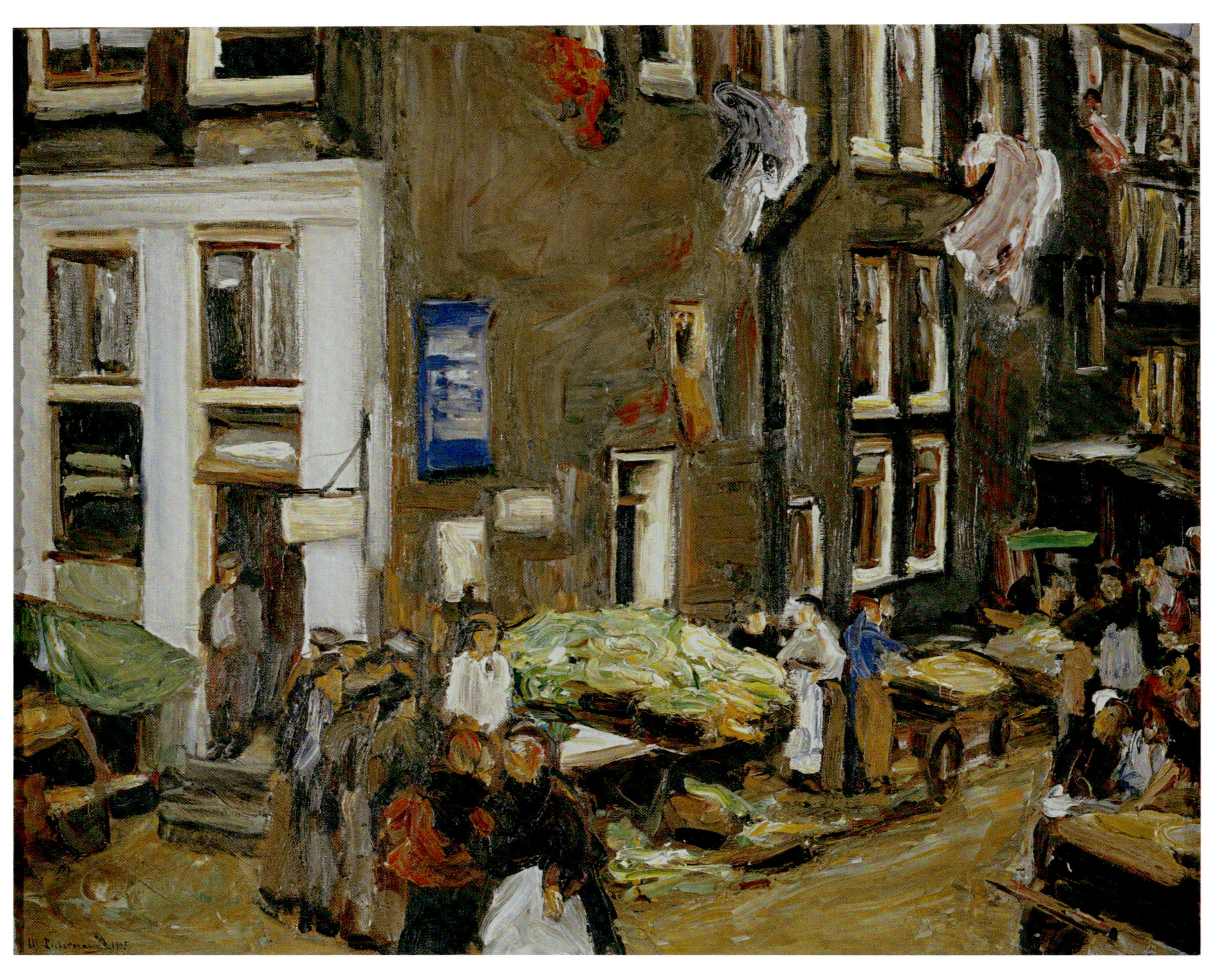

Max Liebermann
Jewish Quarter in Amsterdam
Judengasse in Amsterdam, 1905

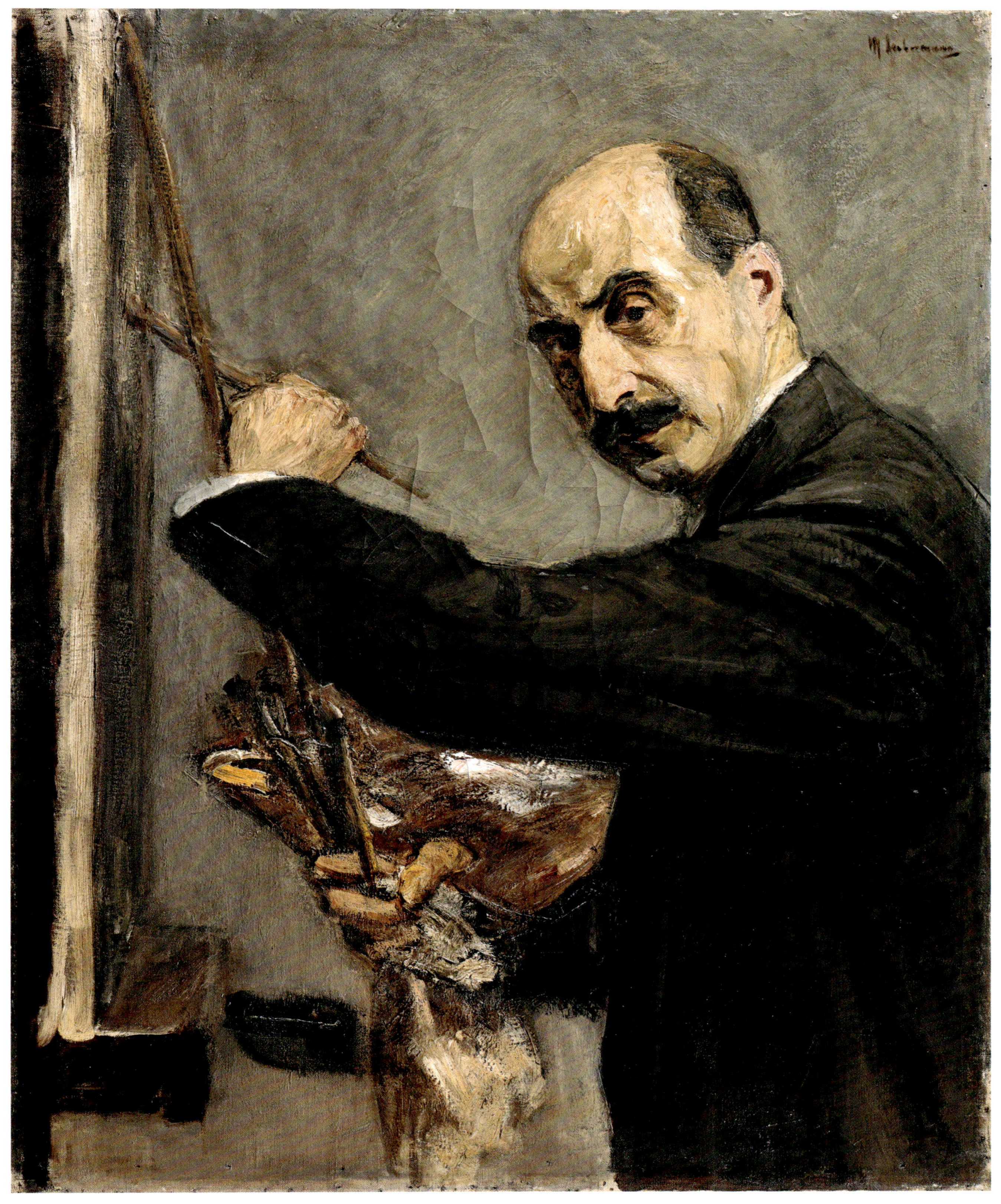

Max Liebermann
Self-Portrait
Selbstbildnis, 1908

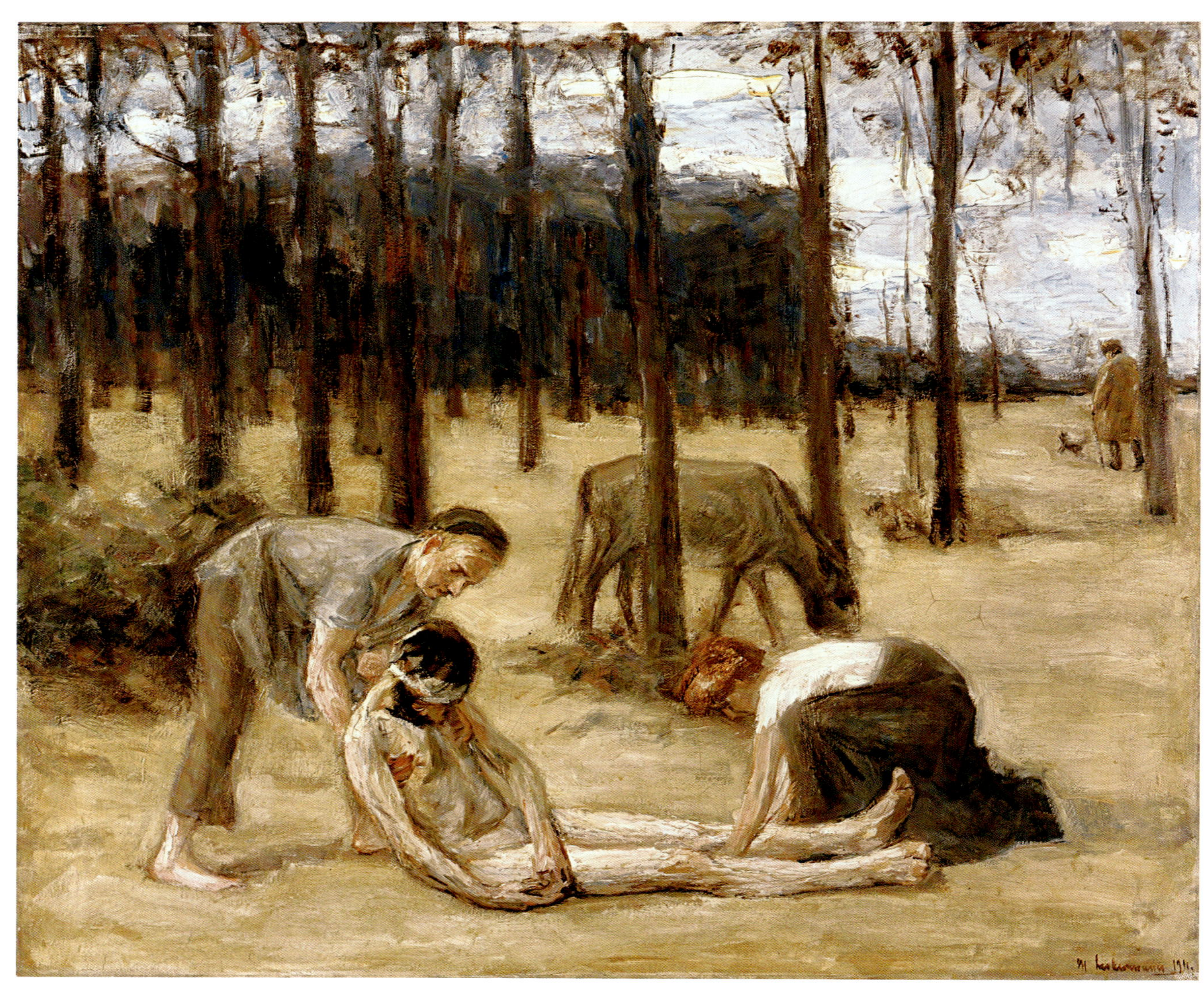

Max Liebermann
The Good Samaritan
Der barmherzige Samariter, 1911

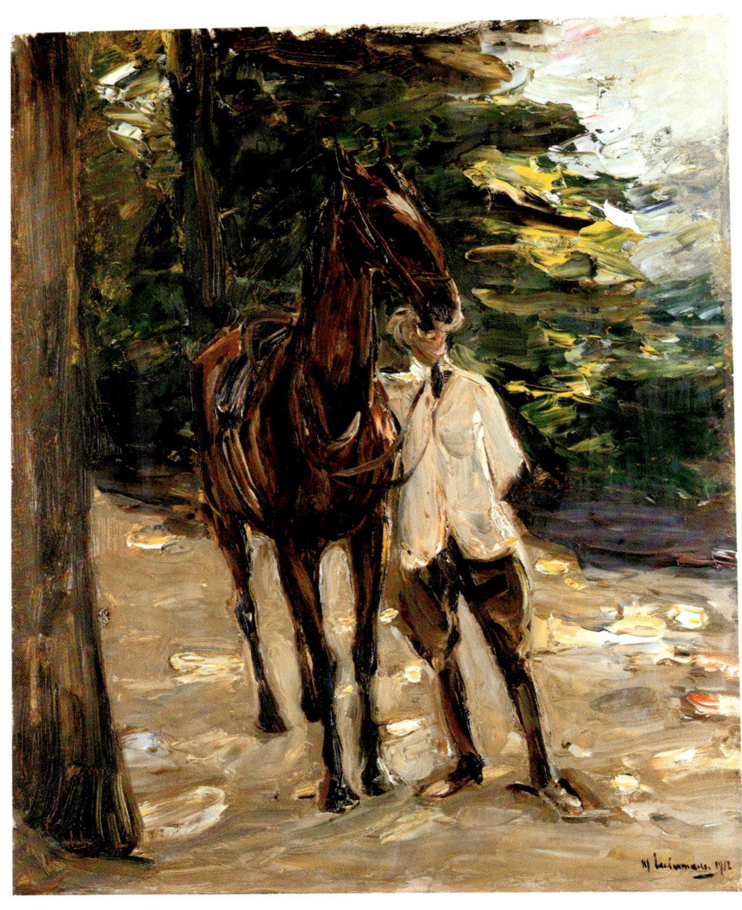

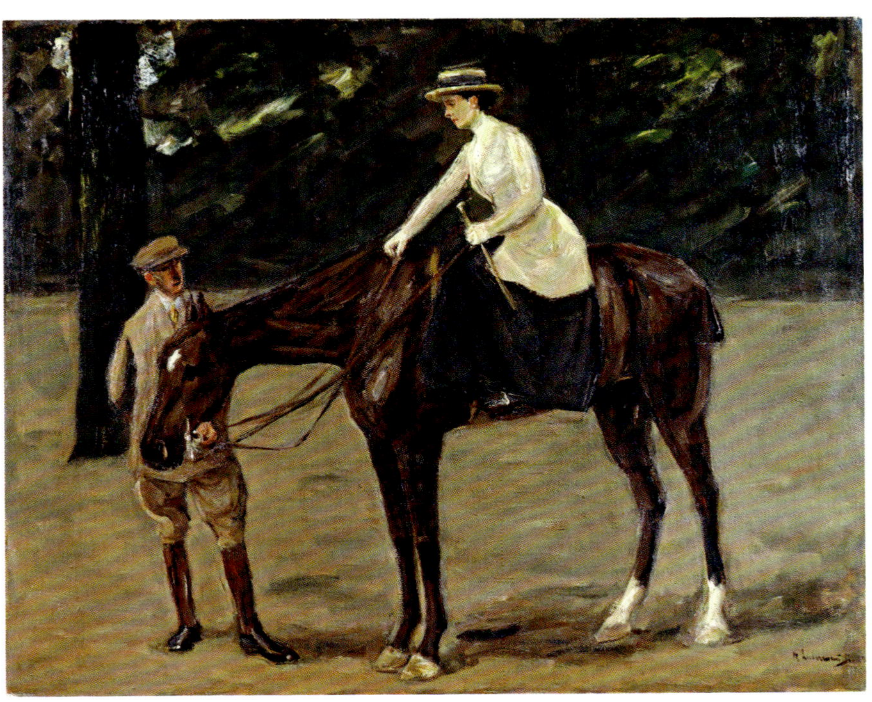

Max Liebermann
Groom with Horse
Reitknecht mit Pferd, 1912

Max Liebermann
Käthe, the Painter's Daughter, on Horseback
Käthe, die Tochter des Malers, zu Pferd, 1913

Lovis Corinth
Self-Portrait in a White Smock
Selbstbildnis im weißen Kittel, 1918

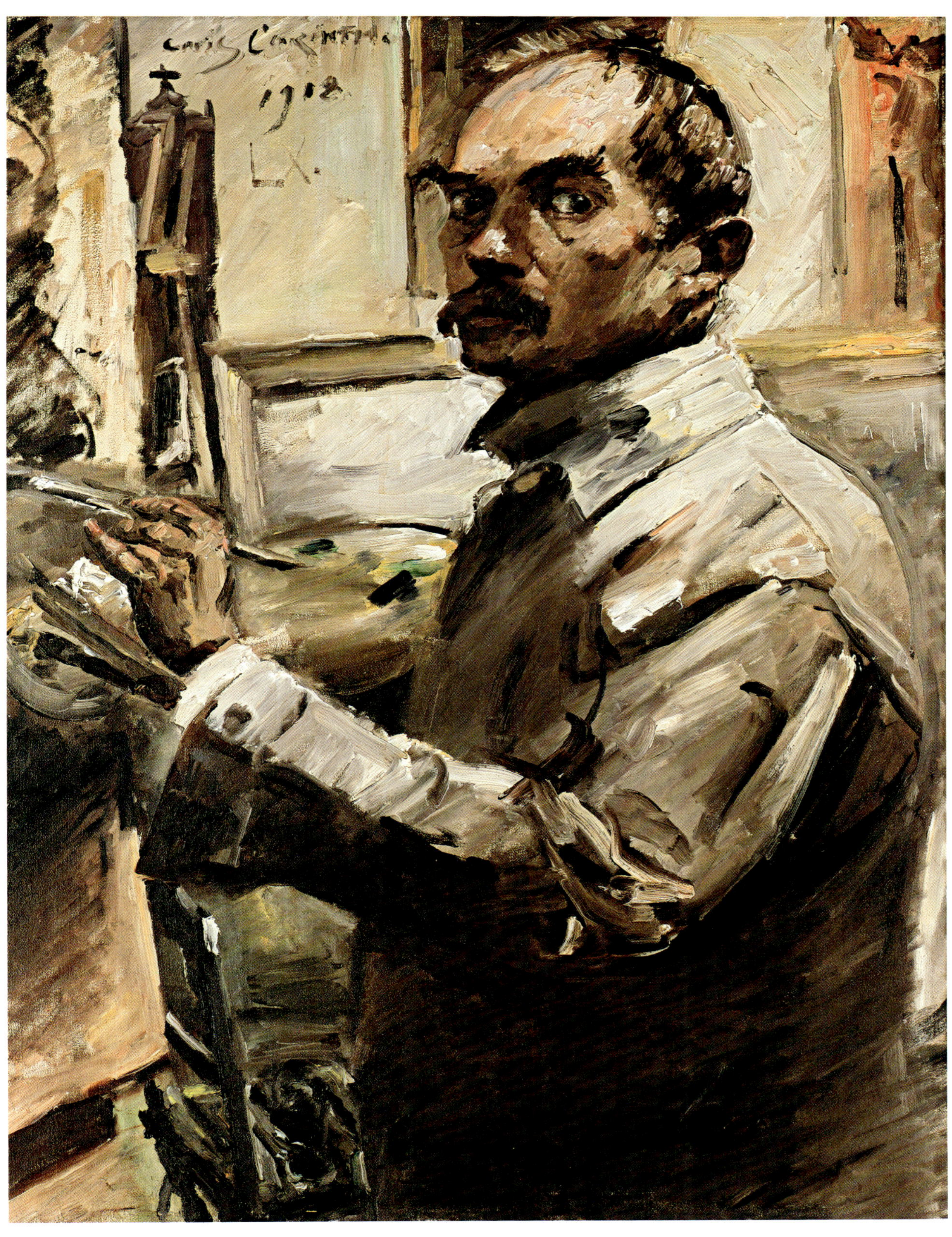

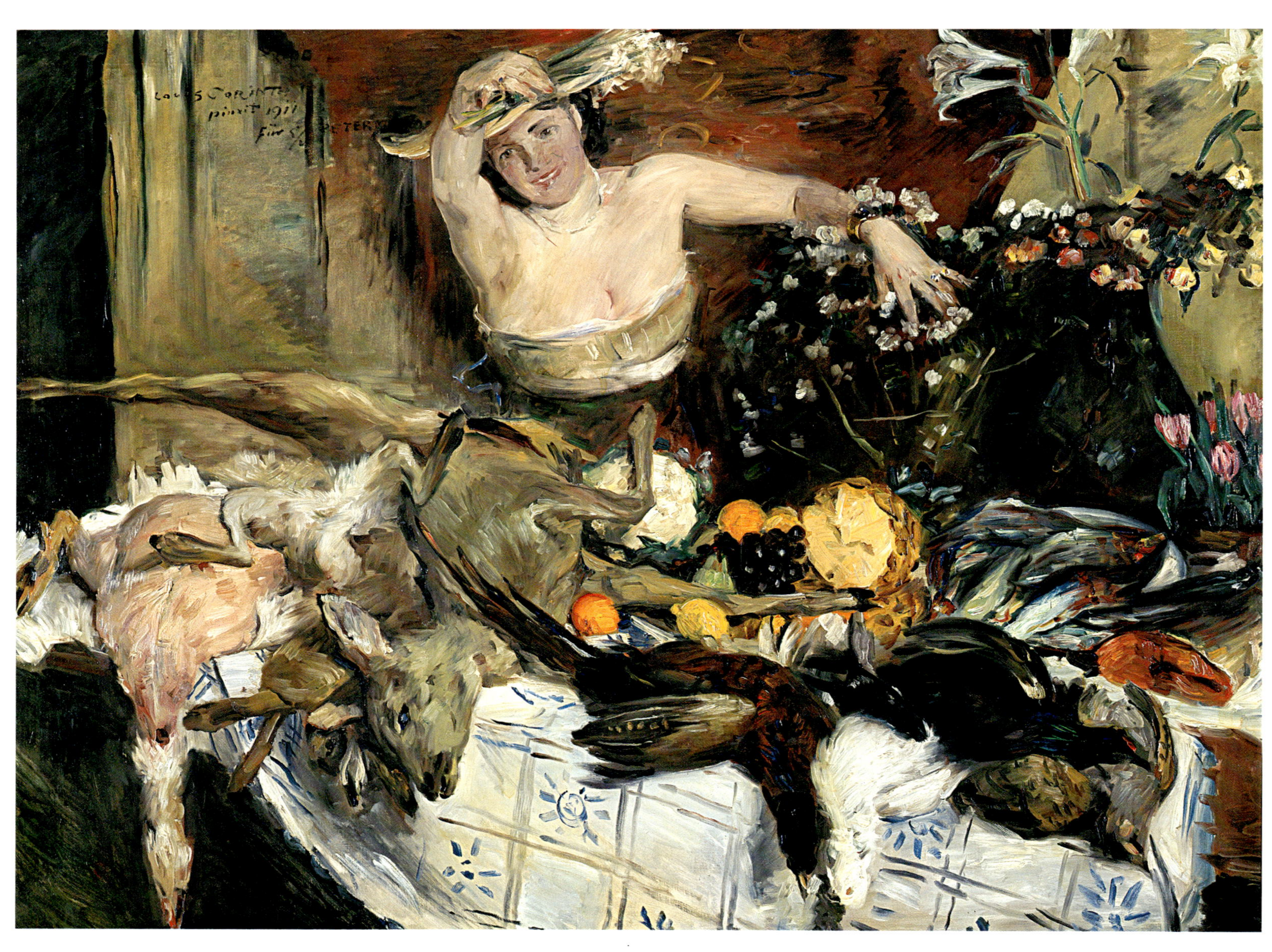

Lovis Corinth
Large Still Life with Figure (Birthday Painting)
Großes Stillleben mit Figur (Geburtstagsbild), 1911

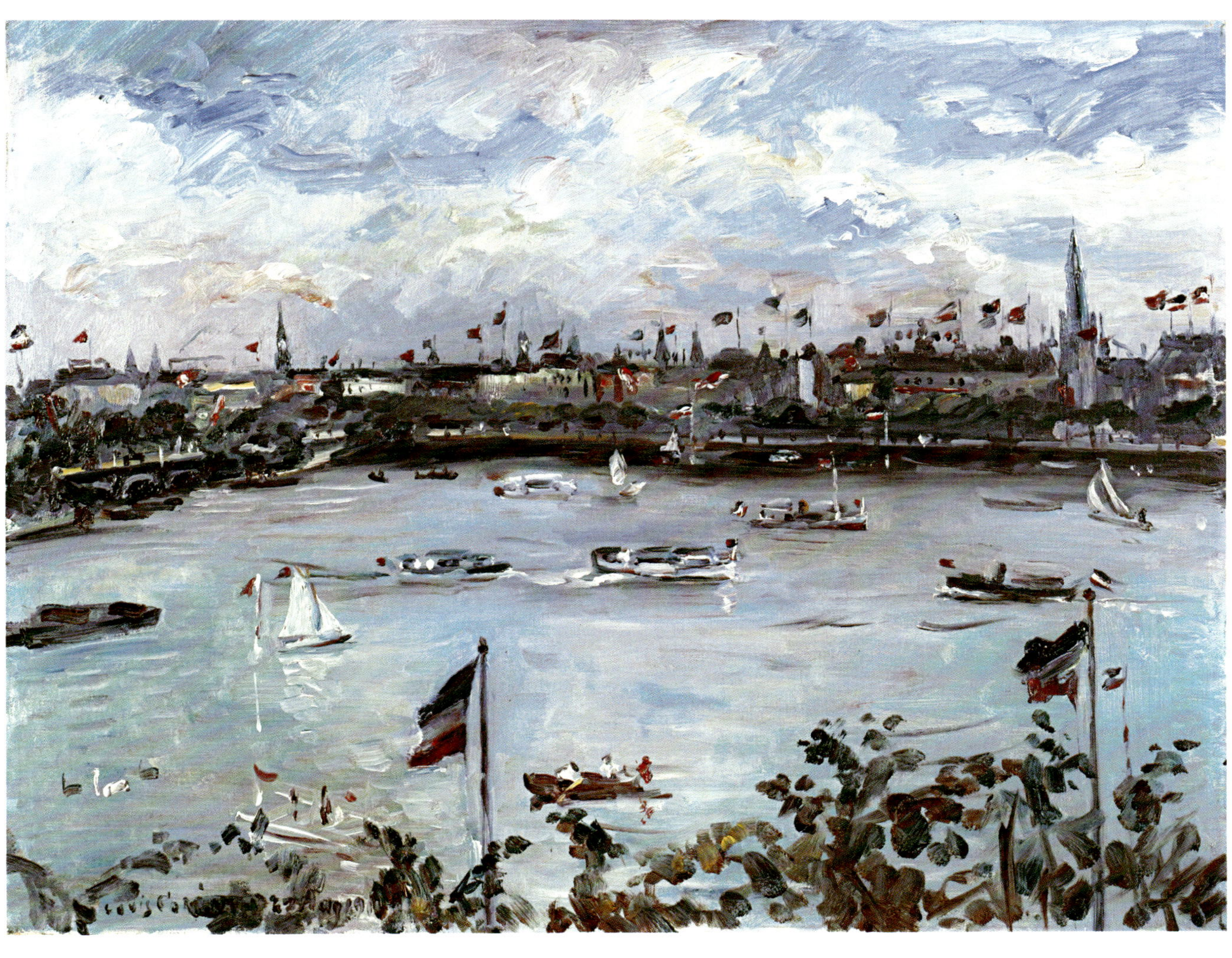

Lovis Corinth
Emperor's Day in Hamburg
Kaisertag in Hamburg, 1911

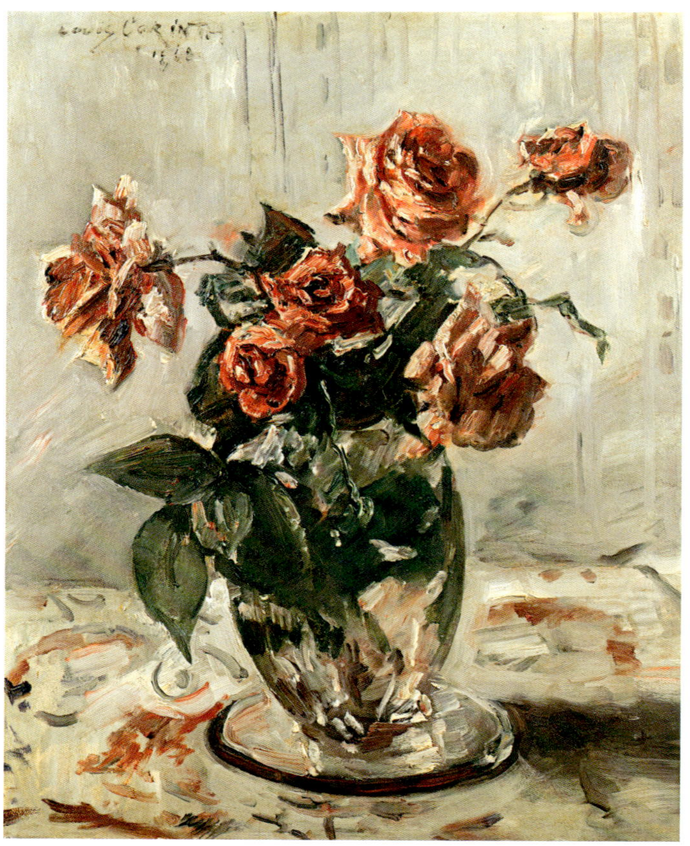

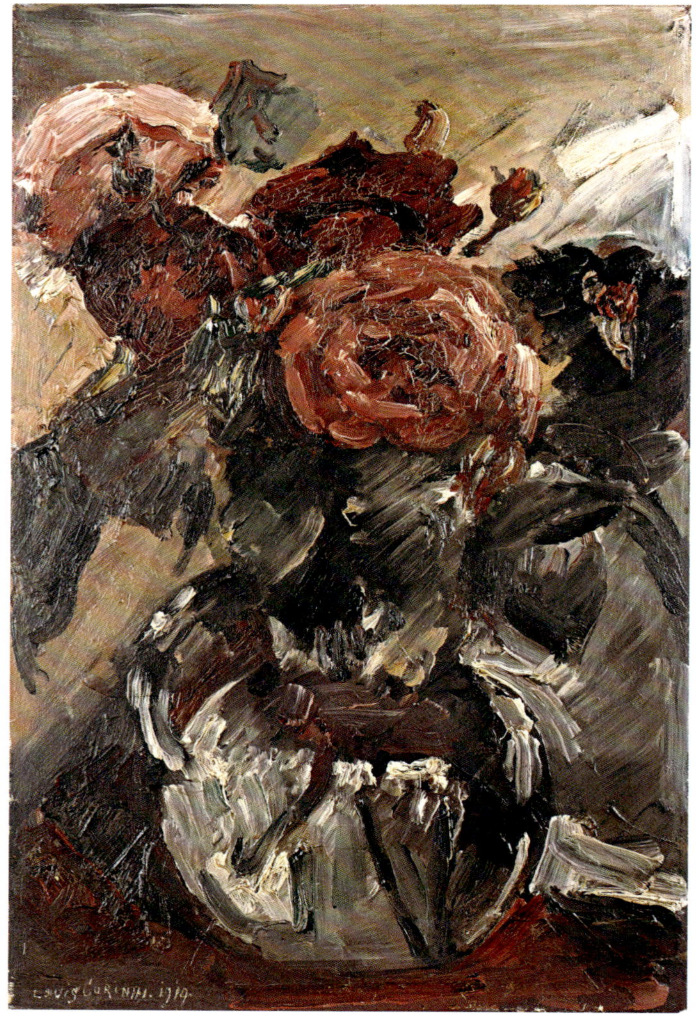

Lovis Corinth
Pink Roses
Rosa Rosen, 1918

Lovis Corinth
Red Roses in a Glass Jug
Rote Rosen in einem Glaskrug, 1919

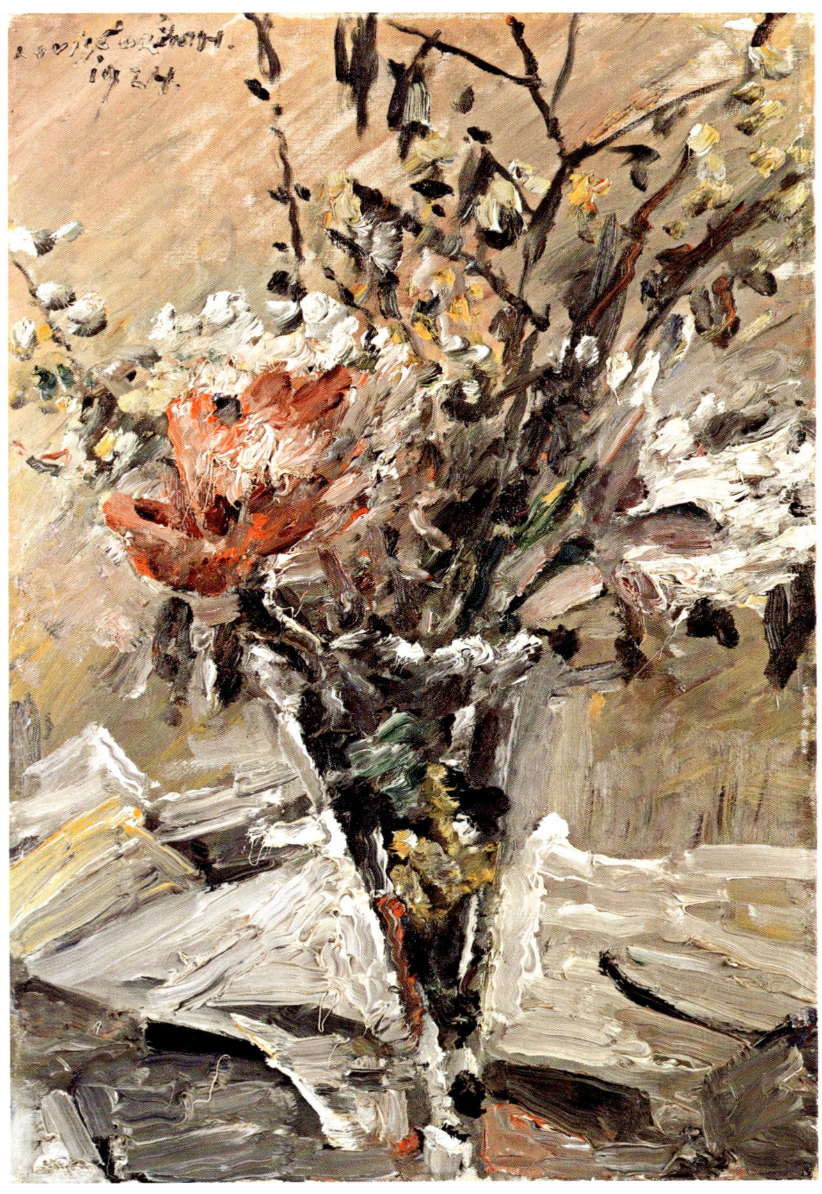

Lovis Corinth
Spring Flowers in a Goblet
Frühlingsblumen im Kelchglas, 1924

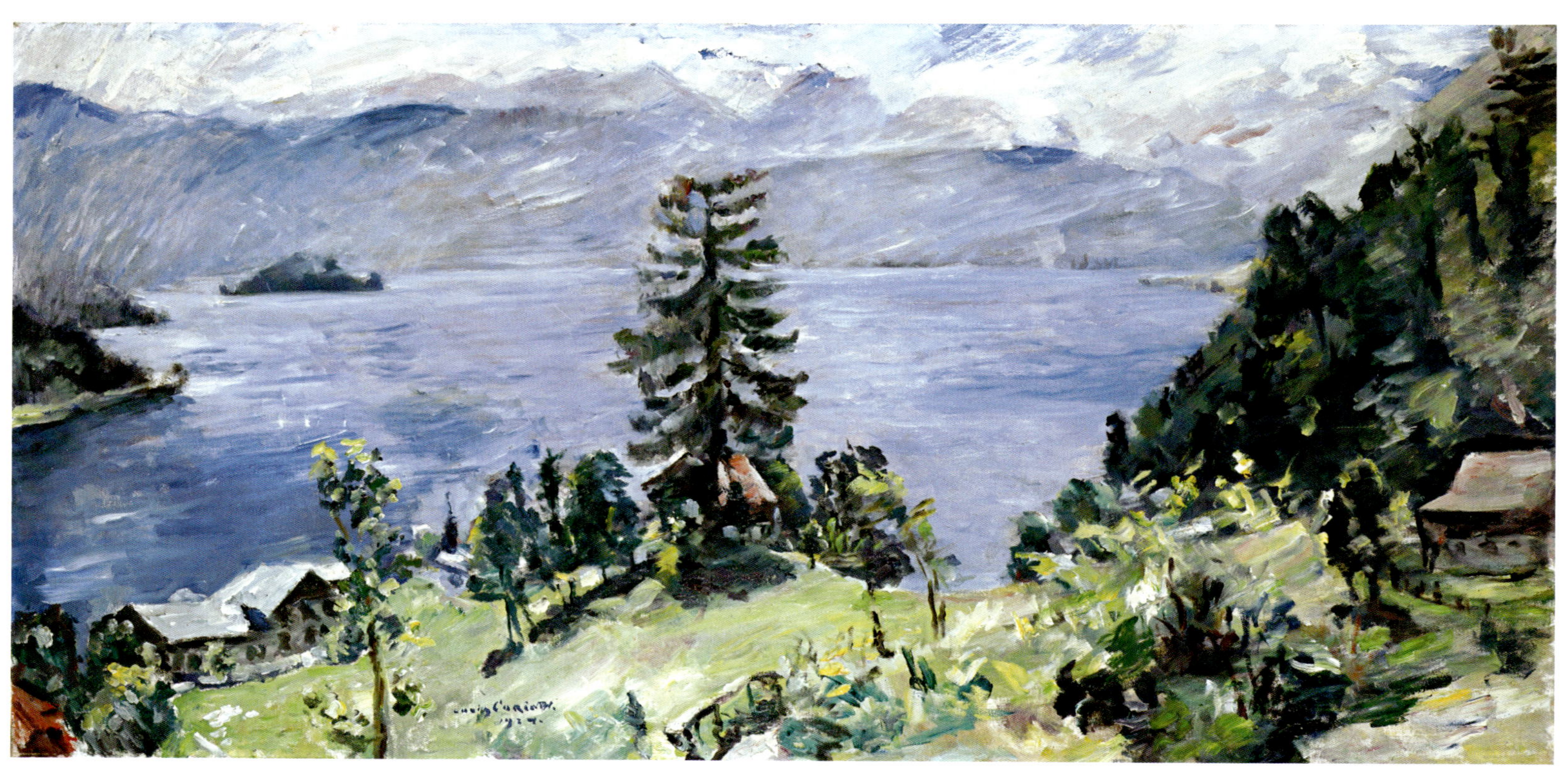

Lovis Corinth
Lake Walchen Panorama
Walchensee-Panorama (Walchensee, Blick von der Kanzel), 1924

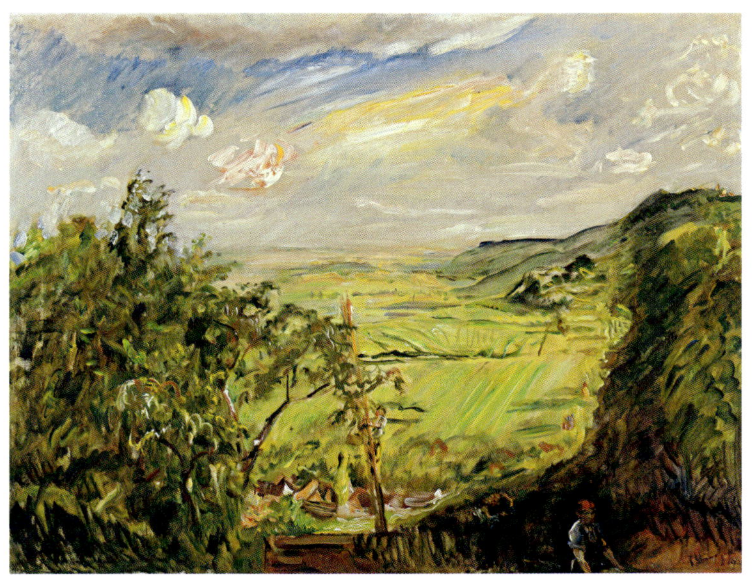

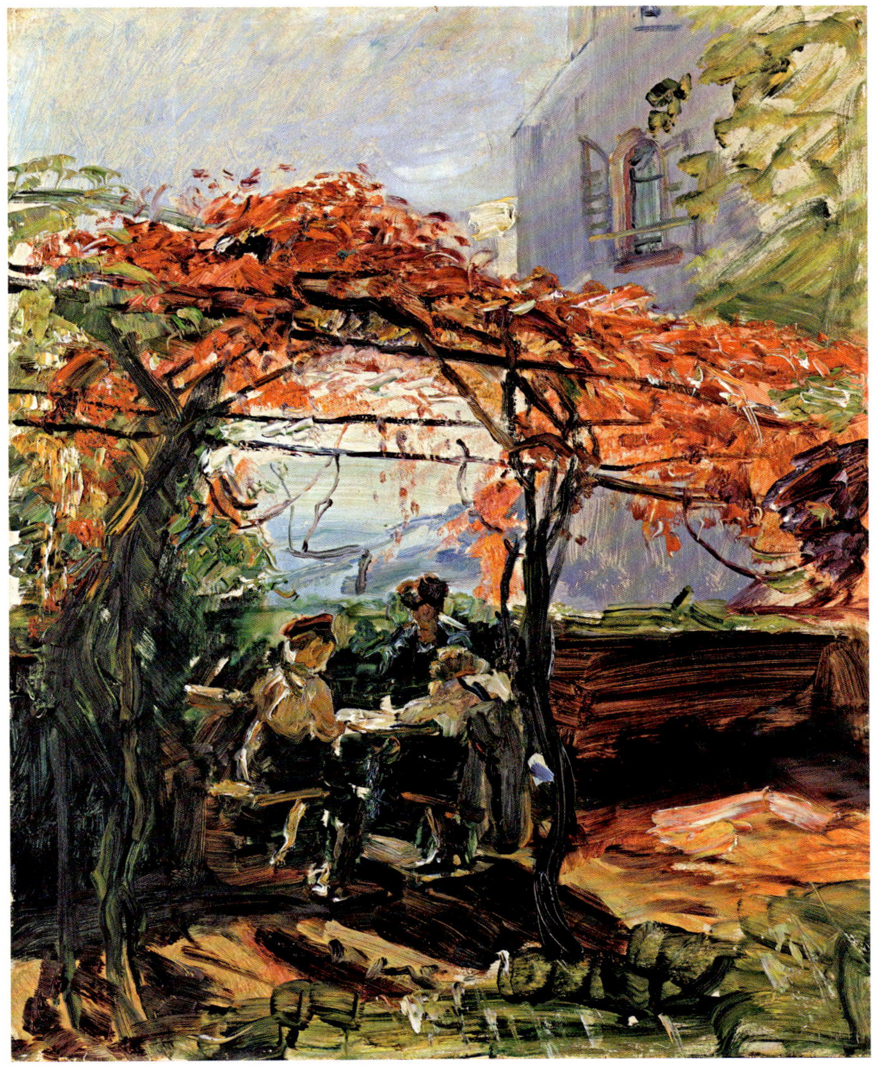

Max Slevogt
Vine Bower in Neukastel
Weinlaube auf Neukastel, 1917

Max Slevogt
Cherry Harvest. View from Neukastel to the South
Kirschenernte, Blick von Neukastel nach Süden, 1926

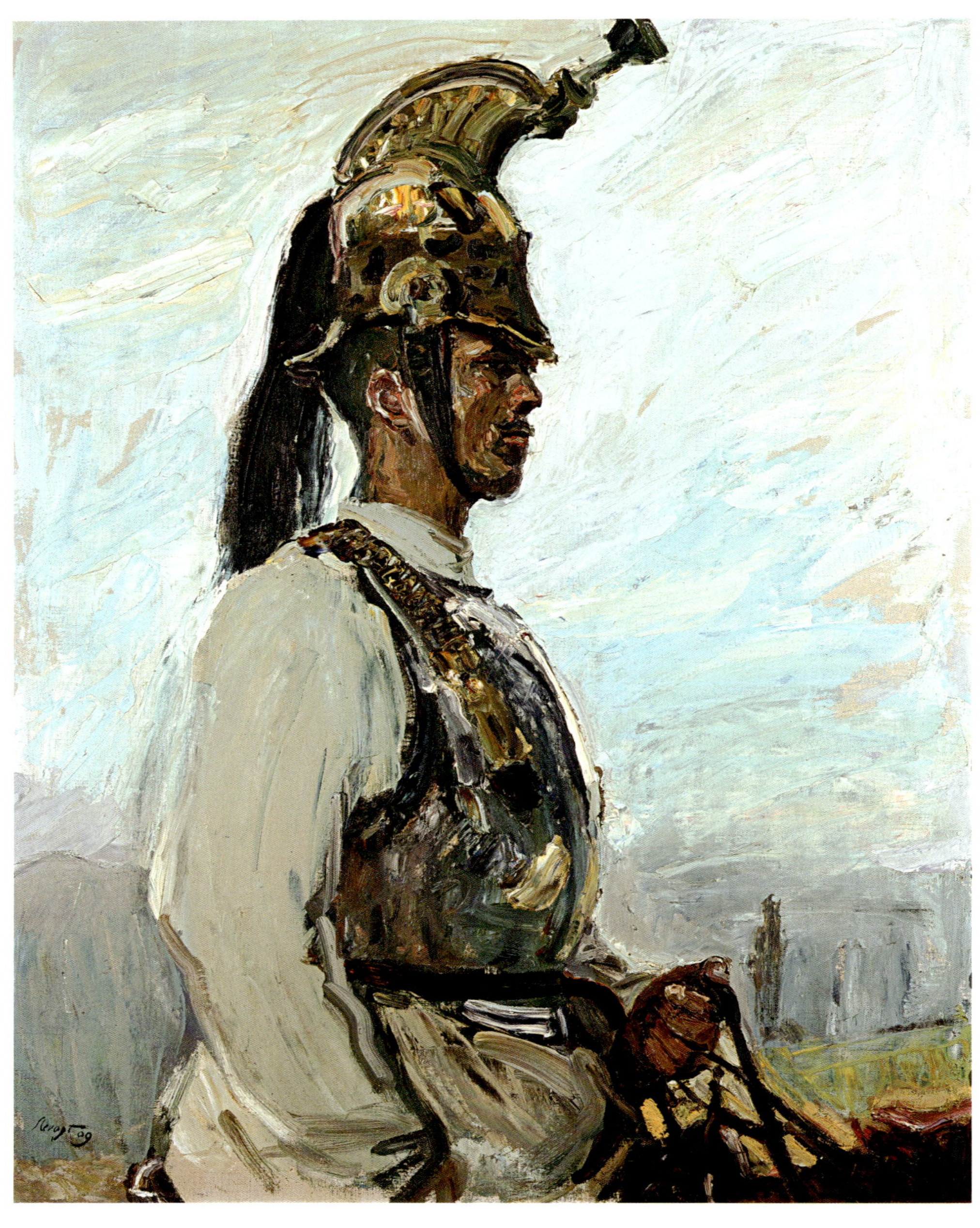

Max Slevogt
French Cuirassier on Horseback
Französischer Kürassier zu Pferd, 1909

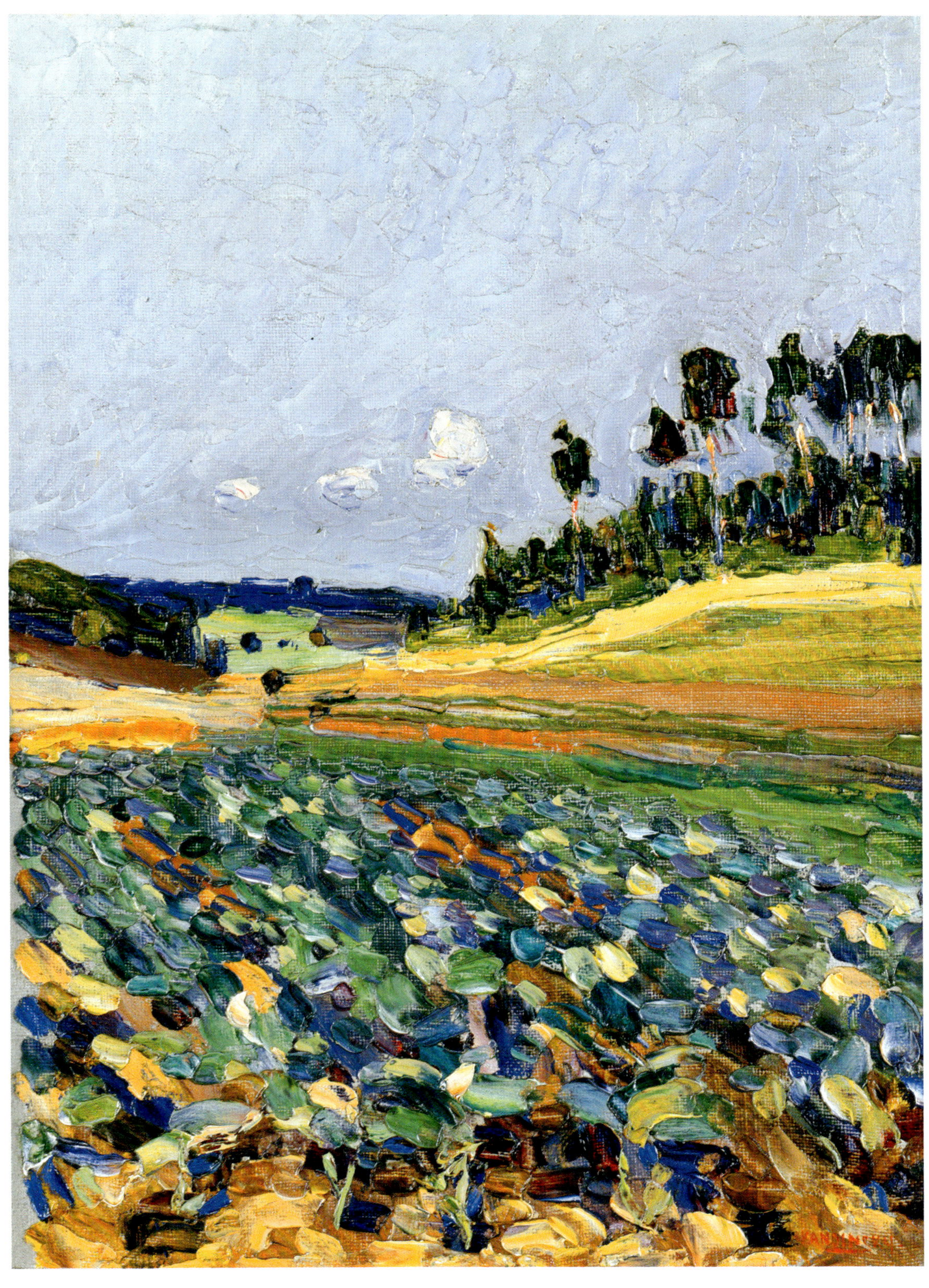

Wassily Kandinsky
Landscape at Regensburg
Landschaft bei Regensburg, 1903

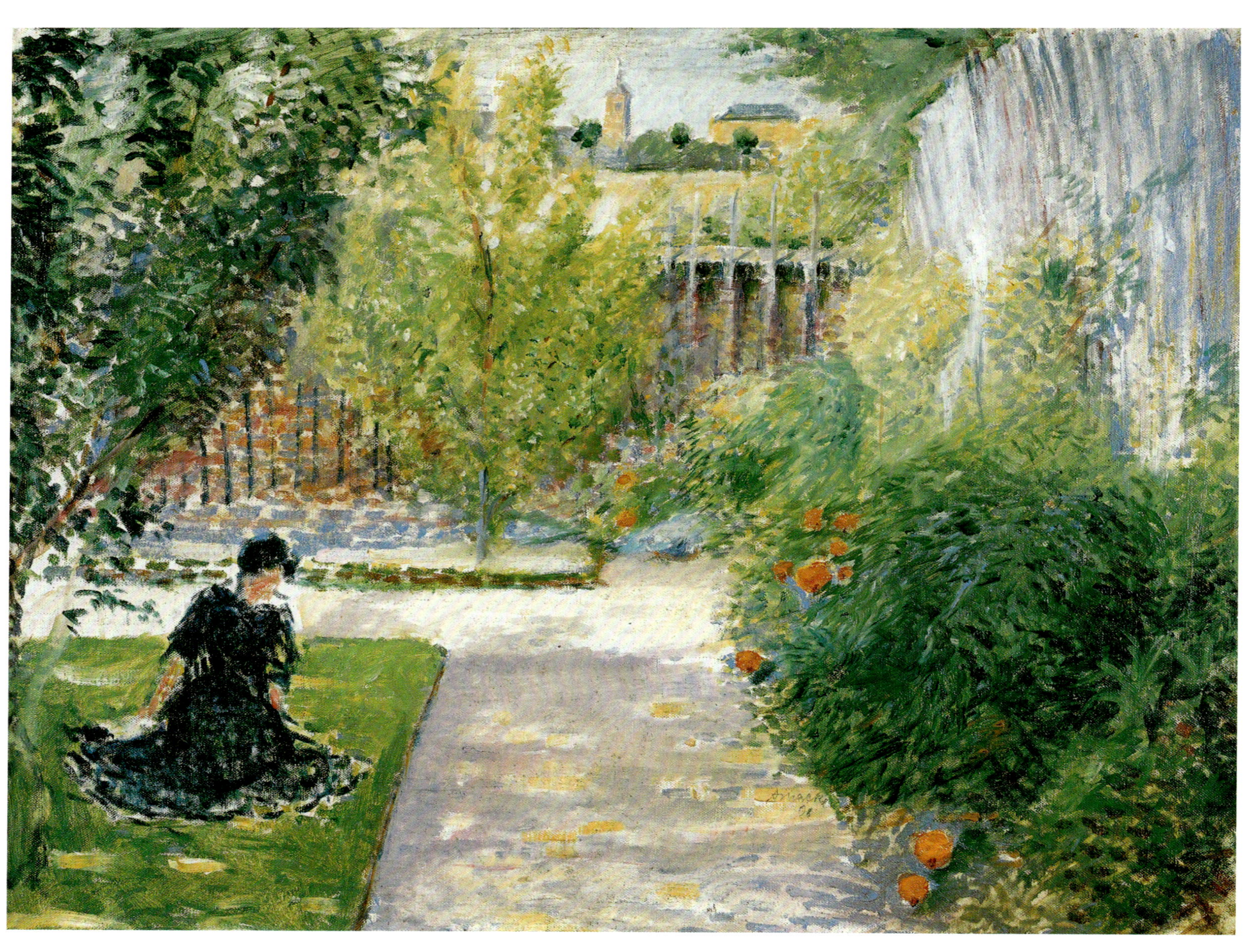

August Macke
Sunny Garden
Sonniger Garten, 1908

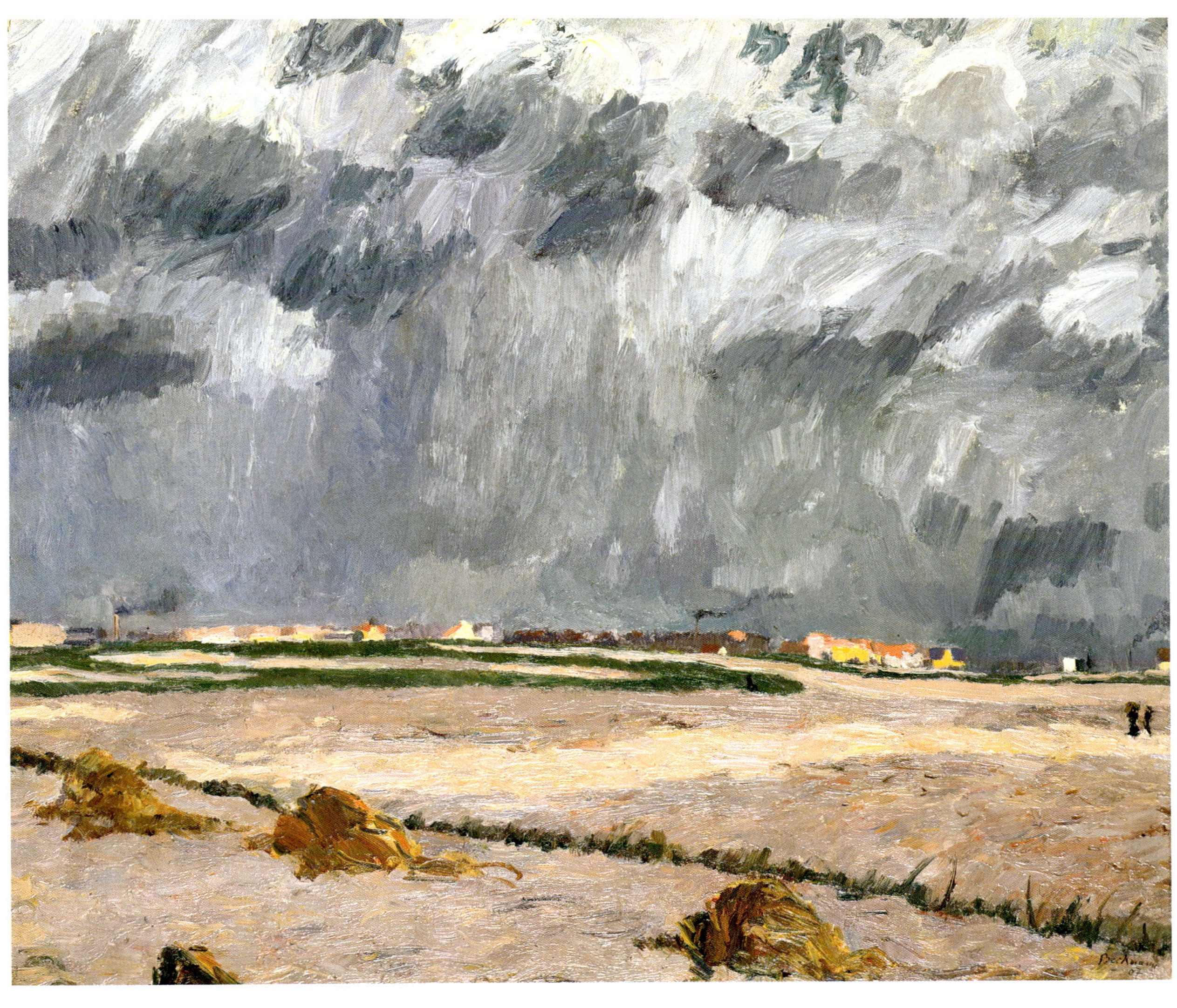

Max Beckmann
View of Lankwitz and Marienfelde
Blick auf Lankwitz und Marienfelde, 1907

CATALOGUE OF PAINTINGS

Unless indicated otherwise, the works are in the possession of the Wallraf-Richartz-Museum & Fondation Corboud of the City of Cologne or are the property of the Fondation Surpierre associated with the Wallraf.

KATALOG DER GEMÄLDE

Soweit nicht anders angegeben, befinden sich die Werke im Besitz des Wallraf-Richartz-Museums & Fondation Corboud der Stadt Köln oder sind Eigentum der mit dem Wallraf assoziierten Fondation Surpierre.

Charles Angrand

Haus unter Ölbäumen oder *Hütte in einem Obstgarten*, 1903
House under Olive Trees or *Hut in an Orchard*
La Maison dans les oliviers *ou* Chaumière dans un verger
Öl auf Leinwand Oil on canvas, 50.3 x 65.3 cm
Bezeichnet unten links Inscribed lower left:
CHARLES ANGRAND – 03
Inv.-Nr. Inv. no.: WRM Dep. FC 730

An der Schwelle oder *Der Milchtopf*, 1908
On the Threshold or *The Milk Pot*
Sur le seuil *ou* La Jatte de lait
Öl auf Leinwand Oil on canvas, 81 x 99.8 cm
Bezeichnet unten rechts Inscribed lower right:
CHARLES ANGRAND / 08
Inv.-Nr. Inv. no.: WRM Dep. 731

Paul Baum

Sommer in Flandern, 1892
Summer in Flanders
Öl auf Leinwand Oil on canvas, 61 x 78.5 cm
Bezeichnet unten rechts Inscribed lower right:
BAUM 92
Inv.-Nr. Inv. no.: WRM Dep. FC 582

Platz in St. Anna, Holland, ca. 1905
Square in St. Anna, Holland
Öl auf Leinwand Oil on canvas, 58.5 x 71 cm
Bezeichnet unten links und rechts
Inscribed lower left and right: P. Baum
Inv.-Nr. Inv. no.: WRM Dep. FC 577

Schweizer Alpenlandschaft, 1917
Swiss Alpine Landscape
Öl auf Leinwand Oil on canvas, 91.2 x 111 cm
Bezeichnet unten rechts Inscribed lower right:
P. BAUM / 1917
Inv.-Nr. Inv. no.: WRM Dep. FC 608

Jean-Frederic Bazille

Junge Frau zwischen Weinstöcken, 1869
Young Woman in a Vineyard
Jeune femme dans les vignes
Öl auf Karton Oil on cardboard, 26 x 34 cm
Bezeichnet unten rechts Inscribed lower right:
F. Bazille. / Montpellier 1869
Inv.-Nr. Inv. no.: WRM Dep. 811

Max Beckmann

Blick auf Lankwitz und Marienfelde, 1907
View of Lankwitz and Marienfelde
Öl auf Leinwand Oil on canvas,
70.5 x 81.3 cm
Bezeichnet unten rechts Inscribed lower right:
Beckmann 07
Inv.-Nr. Inv. no.: WRM Dep. FC 844

Emile Bernard

Ansicht von Pont-Aven (Landschaft von Pont-Aven oder *Ansicht des Bois d'Amour)*, 1888
View of Pont-Aven (Landscape at Pont-Aven or *View of the Bois d'Amour)*
Vue de Pont-Aven (Paysage de Pont-Aven *ou* Vue du Bois d'Amour)
Öl auf Leinwand Oil on canvas,
90.4 x 63.2 cm
Bezeichnet unten rechts Inscribed lower right:
E. Bernard
Inv.-Nr. Inv. no.: WRM Dep. FC 695

Häuser in Pont-Aven, 1890
Houses in Pont-Aven
Maisons à Pont-Aven
Öl auf Leinwand Oil on canvas,
72.4 x 92.1 cm
Bezeichnet unten rechts Inscribed lower right:
Emile Bernard 90
Inv.-Nr. Inv. no.: WRM Dep. FC 812

Liebespaar, 1891
Lovers
Le Couple d'amoureux
Öl auf Leinwand Oil on canvas,
108.5 x 83.5 cm
Bezeichnet unten rechts Inscribed lower right:
Emile Bernard 1891
Inv.-Nr. Inv. no.: WRM Dep. FC 863

Albert Besnard

Eine Wiese im Park von Calais, 1890
A Meadow in the Park in Calais
Une Prairie dans le parc de Calais
Öl auf Leinwand Oil on canvas,
100.5 x 81.5 cm
Bezeichnet unten links Inscribed lower left:
ABesnard. (A und B ligiert A and B ligated)
Inv.-Nr. Inv. no.: WRM Dep. FC 732

Pierre Bonnard

Modell mit großem Hut, 1907
Model with a Large Hat
Modèle au grand chapeau
Öl auf Leinwand Oil on canvas, 58 x 64 cm
Bezeichnet unten rechts Inscribed lower right:
Bonnard
Inv.-Nr. Inv. no.: WRM Dep. 861

Frauenakt im Spiegel, 1910
Female Nude in the Mirror
»Frou-frou«
Öl auf Leinwand Oil on canvas, 123 x 46 cm
Bezeichnet unten links Inscribed lower left:
Bonnard
Inv.-Nr. Inv. no.: WRM Dep. 446
Dauerleihgabe des On Permanent loan from the Kuratorium und Förderergesellschaft des Wallraf-Richartz-Museums / Museums Ludwig e. V.

Im Kahn (Bei Vernon), 1912
In a Rowboat (Vernon)
En Canot (Vernon)
Öl auf Leinwand Oil on canvas, 81.5 x 116 cm
Bezeichnet unten rechts Inscribed lower right:
Bonnard
Inv.-Nr. Inv. no.: WRM 3238

Weideland am Ufer der Seine, ca. 1913
Pasture on the Banks of the Seine
Le Pâturage, bord de Seine
Öl auf Leinwand Oil on canvas, 40 x 59 cm
Bezeichnet unten links Inscribed lower left:
Bonnard
Inv.-Nr. Inv. no.: WRM Dep. FC 733

Blick durch ein Fenster in eine Landschaft, ca. 1918
View of a Landscape through a Window
Paysage à travers une fenêtre
Öl auf Leinwand Oil on canvas, 61 x 33.3 cm
Bezeichnet unten rechts Inscribed lower right:
Bonnard
Inv.-Nr. Inv. no.: WRM Dep. FC 696

Die Seine bei Vernon, ca. 1922
The Seine at Vernon
La Seine à Vernon
Öl auf Leinwand Oil on canvas, 38 x 60.5 cm
Bezeichnet unten links Inscribed lower left:
Bonnard
Inv.-Nr. Inv. no.: WRM Dep. 734

François Bonvin

Stillleben mit Weintrauben, Pfirsichen und Kirschen, o. J.
Still Life with Grapes, Peaches, and Cherries, n.d.
Öl auf Leinwand Oil on canvas, 24 x 41 cm
Bezeichnet unten links Inscribed lower left:
François Bonvin
Inv.-Nr. Inv. no.: WRM 3569

Eugene Boudin

Kerhor, Fischerinnen, 1870
Kerhor, Fisherwomen
Kerhor, les pêcheuses
Öl auf Leinwand Oil on canvas,
85.5 x 121.5 cm
Bezeichnet unten links Inscribed lower left:
E. Boudin – 70
Inv.-Nr. Inv. no.: WRM Dep. FC 657

Trouville, Strandszene, 1881
Trouville, Beach Scene
Trouville, scène de plage
Öl auf Holz Oil on wood, 14 x 26 cm
Bezeichnet unten rechts Inscribed lower right:
E. Boudin; bezeichnet unten links
inscribed lower left: Trouville 81
Inv.-Nr. Inv. no.: WRM Dep. FC 735

Die Küste von Trouville, 1894
The Coast at Trouville
Le Rivage de Trouville
Öl auf Leinwand Oil on canvas,
50.5 x 74.3 cm
Bezeichnet unten rechts Inscribed lower right:
E. Boudin · 94
Inv.-Nr. Inv. no.: WRM Dep. FC 619

Rouen – Côte Sainte-Catherine im Morgennebel, 1895
Rouen – Côte Sainte-Catherine in the Morning Mist
Rouen – La Côte Sainte-Catherine, brume du matin
Öl auf Leinwand Oil on canvas,
40.5 x 55.5 cm
Bezeichnet unten links Inscribed lower left:
E. Boudin 95
Inv.-Nr. Inv. no.: WRM Dep. FC 736

Gustave Caillebotte

Garten in Trouville, ca. 1882
Garden in Trouville
Jardin à Trouville
Öl auf Leinwand Oil on canvas,
27.5 x 35.5 cm
Bezeichnet unten links Inscribed lower left:
G. Caillebotte.
Inv.-Nr. Inv. no.: WRM Dep. FC 602

Schuppen im Garten von Petit-Gennevilliers, 1882
Shed in the Garden in Petit-Gennevilliers
Hangar dans le jardin du Petit-Gennevilliers
Öl auf Leinwand Oil on canvas,
54.5 x 65.7 cm
Bezeichnet unten rechts Inscribed lower right:
G. Caillebotte
Inv.-Nr. Inv. no.: WRM Dep. 828

Die Ebene von Gennevilliers, gelbe Felder, 1884
The Yellow Fields at Gennevilliers
La Plaine de Gennevilliers, champs jaunes
Öl auf Leinwand Oil on canvas, 54 x 64.7 cm
Bezeichnet unten rechts Inscribed lower right:
G Caillebotte / 1884
Inv.-Nr. Inv. no.: WRM Dep. FC 561

Hügel bei Colombes, 1884
Hill at Colombes
Le Coteau de Colombes
Öl auf Leinwand Oil on canvas,
60.2 x 73.3 cm
Bezeichnet unten rechts Inscribed lower right:
G. Caillebotte
Inv.-Nr. Inv. no.: WRM Dep. FC 727

Nebenarm der Seine, Herbststimmung, 1890
Branch of the Seine in Autumn
Le petit bras de la Seine, effet d'automne
Öl auf Leinwand Oil on canvas, 65.2 x 54 cm
Bezeichnet unten rechts Inscribed lower right:
G. Caillebotte
Inv.-Nr. Inv. no.: WRM Dep. 689

Boote und Schuppen am Ufer der Seine, 1891
Boats and Shed on the Banks of the Seine
Barques et cabane, bord de Seine
Öl auf Leinwand Oil on canvas, 45.7 x 55 cm
Bezeichnet unten links Inscribed lower left:
G. Caillebotte
Inv.-Nr. Inv. no.: WRM Dep. FC 603

Ufer der Seine, 1891
Banks of the Seine
Bords de Seine
Öl auf Leinwand Oil on canvas, 46 x 61 cm
Inv.-Nr. Inv. no.: WRM Dep. FC 706

Trocknende Wäsche am Ufer der Seine, ca. 1892
Laundry Drying on the Banks of the Seine
Ligne séchant au bord de la Seine, Petit Gennevilliers
Öl auf Leinwand Oil on canvas, 106 x 150 cm
Bezeichnet unten links Inscribed lower left:
G. Caillebotte
Inv.-Nr. Inv. no.: WRM Dep. 447
Dauerleihgabe des On Permanent loan from the Kuratorium und Fördergesellschaft des Wallraf-Richartz-Museums / Museums Ludwig e. V.

Segelboot auf der Seine bei Argenteuil, 1893
Sailboat on the Seine at Argenteuil
Voilier sur la Seine à Argenteuil
Öl auf Leinwand Oil on canvas, 65 x 54 cm
Bezeichnet unten links Inscribed lower left:
G. Caillebotte
Inv.-Nr. Inv. no.: WRM Dep. 622
Dauerleihgabe des On Permanent loan from the Kuratorium und Fördergesellschaft des Wallraf-Richartz-Museums / Museums Ludwig e. V.

Mary Cassatt

Sara mit einem dunklen Häubchen, 1901
Sara in a Dark Bonnet with Right Hand on Arm of Chair
Öl auf Leinwand Oil on canvas, 67 x 55 cm
Inv.-Nr. Inv. no.: WRM Dep. FC 697

Paul Cezanne

Landschaft bei Aix-en-Provence, ca. 1879
Landscape at Aix-en-Provence
Paysage à Aix-en-Provence
Öl auf Leinwand Oil on canvas, 46 x 55.3 cm
Inv.-Nr. Inv. no.: WRM Dep. FC 658

Stillleben mit Birnen, ca. 1885
Still Life with Pears
Nature morte aux poires
Öl auf Leinwand Oil on canvas, 38 x 46 cm
Inv.-Nr. Inv. no.: WRM 3189

Landschaft im Westen von Aix-en-Provence, 1885/88
Landscape in the West of Aix-en-Provence
Dans la plaine de Bellevue
Öl auf Leinwand Oil on canvas, 65 x 81 cm
Inv.-Nr. Inv. no.: WRM 3188

Lovis Corinth

Kreuzabnahme, 1895
Descent from the Cross
Öl auf Leinwand Oil on canvas,
99.5 x 124.5 cm
Bezeichnet unten, rechts von der Mitte
Inscribed bottom, right from center:
LOVIS CORINTH
Inv.-Nr. Inv. no.: WRM Dep. 355
Leihgabe aus Privatbesitz On loan from a private collection

Kaisertag in Hamburg, 1911
Emperor's Day in Hamburg
Öl auf Leinwand Oil on canvas,
70.5 x 90.5 cm
Bezeichnet unten links Inscribed lower left:
LOVIS CORINTH 27 Aug 1911
Inv.-Nr. Inv. no.: WRM 2585

Großes Stillleben mit Figur (Geburtstagsbild), 1911
Large Still Life with Figure (Birthday Painting)
Öl auf Leinwand Oil on canvas,
150.5 x 200 cm
Bezeichnet oben links Inscribed upper left:
Lovis Corinth / pinxit 1911 / für s-l Petermann
Inv.-Nr. Inv. no.: WRM 2861

Selbstbildnis im weißen Kittel, 1918
Self-Portrait in a White Smock
Öl auf Leinwand Oil on canvas, 105 x 81 cm
Bezeichnet oben links Inscribed upper left:
Lovis Corinth. / 1918. / LX.
Inv.-Nr. Inv. no.: WRM 2368

Rosa Rosen, 1918
Pink Roses
Öl auf Karton Oil on cardboard, 74 x 59 cm
Bezeichnet oben links Inscribed upper left:
Lovis Corinth / 1918
Inv.-Nr. Inv. no.: WRM 3138

Rote Rosen in einem Glaskrug, 1919
Red Roses in a Glass Jug
Öl auf Lindenholz Oil on limewood, 54.5 x 36 cm
Bezeichnet unten links Inscribed lower left: Lovis Corinth. 1919.
Inv.-Nr. Inv. no.: WRM 2785

Frühlingsblumen im Kelchglas, 1924
Spring Flowers in a Goblet
Öl auf Leinwand Oil on canvas, 61 x 41.5 cm
Bezeichnet oben links Inscribed upper left: Lovis Corinth. / 1924.
Inv.-Nr. Inv. no.: WRM 1185

Walchensee-Panorama (Walchensee, Blick von der Kanzel), 1924
Lake Walchen Panorama
Öl auf Leinwand Oil on canvas, 101 x 200 cm
Bezeichnet unten, links von der Mitte Inscribed bottom, left from center: Lovis Corinth. / 1924.
Inv.-Nr. Inv. no.: WRM 2886

Jean-Baptiste-Camille Corot

Bei Avray, ca. 1860/70
Ville d'Avray
Ville d'Avray
Öl auf Leinwand Oil on canvas, 50 x 65 cm
Inv.-Nr. Inv. no.: WRM 2482

Die Dichtkunst, ca. 1865/70
Poetry
La Poésie
Öl auf Leinwand Oil on canvas, 55 x 45.5 cm
Bezeichnet unten rechts und rückseitig auf der Mittelstrebe des Keilrahmens Inscribed lower right and on reverse on center strut of stretcher: Vente / Corot
Inv.-Nr. Inv. no.: WRM 2651

Die alte Ziegelsteinbrücke bei Arleux-Palluel, 1871
The Old Brick Bridge at Arleux-Palluel
Öl auf Leinwand Oil on canvas, 51 x 90 cm
Bezeichnet unten links Inscribed lower left: Corot
Inv.-Nr. Inv. no.: WRM 3194

Gustave Courbet

Das Jagdfrühstück, 1858
The Hunters' Breakfast
Le Repas de chasse *ou* L'Hallali du chevreul
Öl auf Leinwand Oil on canvas, 207 x 325 cm
Bezeichnet unten rechts Inscribed lower right: G. Courbet.
Inv.-Nr. Inv. no.: WRM 1171

Dame auf der Terrasse, 1858
Lady on the Terrace (Lady of Frankfurt)
La Dame de Francfort
Öl auf Leinwand Oil on canvas, 104 x 140 cm
Bezeichnet unten links Inscribed lower left: G. Courbet.
Inv.-Nr. Inv. no.: WRM 2635

Meeresstrand, 1865
Seascape
Marine
Öl auf Leinwand Oil on canvas, 53.5 x 64 cm
Bezeichnet unten links Inscribed lower left: G. Courbet.
Inv.-Nr. Inv. no.: WRM 2905

Château de Chillon, 1873
Öl auf Leinwand Oil on canvas, 54.1 x 65.3 cm
Bezeichnet unten links Inscribed lower left: G. Courbet.
Inv.-Nr. Inv. no.: WRM Dep. FC 698

Ansicht des Parc des Crêtes, oberhalb von Clarens, 1874
View of the Parc des Crêtes above Clarens
Vue du Parc des Crêtes au-dessus de Clarens
Öl auf Leinwand Oil on canvas, 50 x 75 cm
Bezeichnet unten links Inscribed lower left: 74 / G. Courbet.
Inv.-Nr. Inv. no.: WRM Dep. FC 690

Lucie Cousturier

Blumenstrauß, 1910
Bouquet of Flowers
Bouquet de fleurs
Öl auf Leinwand Oil on canvas, 61 x 50 cm
Bezeichnet unten links Inscribed lower left: Lucie Cousturier
Inv.-Nr. Inv. no.: WRM Dep. FC 737

Henri Edmond Cross

Sonnenuntergang über dem Meer, 1896
Sunset over the Sea
Coucher de soleil sur la mer
Öl auf Leinwand Oil on canvas, 54.3 x 61.5 cm
Bezeichnet unten links Inscribed lower left: henri Edmond Cross 96
Inv.-Nr. Inv. no.: WRM Dep. FC 708

Landschaft der Provence, 1898
Landscape in Provence
Paysage provençal
Öl auf Leinwand Oil on canvas, 60.2 x 81.5 cm
Bezeichnet unten links Inscribed lower left: henri Edmond Cross 98
Inv.-Nr. Inv. no.: WRM Dep. FC 659

Akt in einem Baum oder *Frau im Baum*, ca. 1906
Nude in a Tree or *Woman in a Tree*
Nu dans un arbre *ou* Femme dans l'arbre
Öl auf Papier Oil on paper, 35.1 x 27 cm
Bezeichnet unten rechts Inscribed lower right: HE Cross
Inv.-Nr. Inv. no.: WRM Dep. FC 854

Die Lichtung, 1906–07
The Clearing
La Clairière
Öl auf Leinwand Oil on canvas, 162 x 131 cm
Bezeichnet unten rechts Inscribed lower right: henri Edmond Cross
Inv.-Nr. Inv. no.: WRM Dep. FC 660

Charles-François Daubigny

Der Weiher von Gylieu bei Optevoz, 1856
Gylieu Pond at Optevoz
Öl auf Lindenholz Oil on limewood, 32 x 57 cm
Bezeichnet unten rechts Inscribed lower right: C. Daubigny
Inv.-Nr. Inv. no.: WRM 3118

Feldweg, Villerville, ca. 1865
Track across the Fields, Villerville
Chemin de la ferme, Villerville
Öl auf Holz Oil on wood, 19 x 37 cm
Bezeichnet unten rechts Inscribed lower right:
Daubigny.
Inv.-Nr. Inv. no.: WRM Dep. FC 738

Mondschein am Flussufer oder
Die Ufer der Oise, ca. 1869
Moonlight on the Riverbank or
The Banks of the Oise
Clair de lune au bord de la rivière *ou*
Bords de l'Oise
Öl auf Holz Oil on wood, 26.3 x 54 cm
Bezeichnet unten links Inscribed lower left:
Daubigny
Inv.-Nr. Inv. no.: WRM Dep. FC 739

Wiese mit blühenden Obstbäumen, ca. 1870
Meadow with Blossoming Fruit Trees
Öl auf Leinwand Oil on canvas, 45 x 82 cm
Bezeichnet unten links Inscribed lower left:
Daubigny
Inv.-Nr. Inv. no.: WRM 1119

Edgar Degas

Tänzerinnen, ca. 1905
Dancers
Öl und Pastell auf Papier, auf Leinwand aufgezogen Oil and pastel on paper mounted on canvas, 46 x 94 cm
Bezeichnet unten rechts Inscribed lower right:
Degas
Inv.-Nr. Inv. no.: WRM 3122

William Degouve de Nuncques

Schneelandschaft, ca. 1910/20
Snowy Landscape
Öl auf Leinwand Oil on canvas, 66 x 57 cm
Bezeichnet unten rechts Inscribed lower right:
WD / De / N
Inv.-Nr. Inv. no.: WRM 3617

Henri Delavallee

Herbst, Dorf im Tal, ca. 1887
Autumn, Village in the Valley
Automne, village dans la vallée
Öl auf Leinwand Oil on canvas, 32.5 x 55.5 cm
Bezeichnet unten rechts Inscribed lower right:
H Delavallée
Inv.-Nr. Inv. no.: WRM Dep. FC 740

Maurice Denis

Weinlaube in Saint-Germain, ca. 1903/05
Vine Bower in Saint-Germain
La Treille à Saint-Germain
Öl auf Karton Oil on cardboard, 35 x 53 cm
Bezeichnet unten links Inscribed lower left:
M / A / U / D (ligiert ligated)
Inv.-Nr. Inv. no.: WRM Dep. FC 741

Die roséfarbene Kirche – Tilloloy, 1921
The Pink Church – Tilloloy
L'Eglise rose – Tilloloy
Öl auf Leinwand Oil on canvas, 43.2 x 76.5 cm
Bezeichnet unten links Inscribed lower left:
MAUD 21
Inv.-Nr. Inv. no.: WRM Dep. FC 742

August Deusser

Pauker und Trompeter, 1907
Drummer and Trumpeters
Öl auf Leinwand Oil on canvas, 50 x 61.5 cm
Bezeichnet unten links Inscribed lower left:
A. Deusser.
Inv.-Nr. Inv. no.: WRM 1191

Virgilio Narcisso Diaz de la Pena

Blumenstillleben, o. J.
Still Life with Flowers, n.d.
Öl auf Leinwand Oil on canvas, 93 x 72 cm
Bezeichnet unten links Inscribed lower left:
N. Diaz.
Inv.-Nr. Inv. no.: WRM 3535

Blumenstrauß in Tonvase, o. J.
Bouquet of Flowers in a Clay Vase, n.d.
Öl auf Leinwand Oil on canvas, 33.3 x 24.5 cm
Bezeichnet unten links Inscribed lower left:
N. Diaz
Inv.-Nr. Inv. no.: WRM 3575

Herbst im Wald von Fontainebleau, o. J.
Autumn in the Forest of Fontainebleau, n.d.
Öl auf Holz Oil on wood, 27.5 x 40.7 cm
Bezeichnet unten links Inscribed lower left:
N. Diaz
Inv.-Nr. Inv. no.: WRM 3541

Waldweg, o. J.
Forest Path, n.d.
Öl auf Holz Oil on wood, 26 x 19.8 cm
Bezeichnet unten links Inscribed lower left:
N. Diaz
Inv.-Nr. Inv. no.: WRM 3582

Kees van Dongen

Haus in Fleury, 1905
House in Fleury
La Maison à Fleury
Öl auf Leinwand Oil on canvas, 55.9 x 45.7 cm
Bezeichnet unten links Inscribed lower left:
van Dongen; rückseitig signiert und datiert auf dem Keilrahmen signed and dated on reverse on stretcher frame
Inv.-Nr. Inv. no.: WRM Dep. FC 661

Albert Dubois-Pillet

Quai de Lesseps – Rouen, ca. 1887
Öl auf Leinwand Oil on canvas, 31.8 x 45.7 cm
Bezeichnet unten rechts Inscribed lower right:
à Pissarro hommage / duBois Pillet; rückseitige Aufschrift auf dem Keilrahmen inscription on reverse on stretcher frame: à M. Pissarro
Inv.-Nr. Inv. no.: WRM Dep. FC 743

Felder in der Ile-de-France, ca. 1889/90
Fields, Ile-de-France
Champs en Ile-de-France
Öl auf Leinwand Oil on canvas, 31 x 41 cm
Bezeichnet unten rechts Inscribed lower right:
dUBois PillEt

Landschaft, o. J.
Landscape, n.d.
Paysage
Öl auf Leinwand Oil on canvas, 36.1 x 54.4 cm
Inv.-Nr. Inv. no.: WRM Dep. FC 609

Raoul Dufy

Boulevard Saint-Martin, 1903
Öl auf Leinwand Oil on canvas, 53 x 64 cm
Bezeichnet unten rechts Inscribed lower right:
R. Dufy
Inv.-Nr. Inv. no.: WRM Dep. FC 662

Gittertor, 1930
Paled Gate
La Grille
Öl auf Leinwand Oil on canvas,
130.2 x 162.2 cm
Bezeichnet unten rechts Inscribed lower right:
Raoul Dufy

James Ensor

Mädchen mit Puppe, 1884
Young Girl with a Doll
Öl auf Leinwand Oil on canvas, 149 x 91 cm
Bezeichnet unten rechts Inscribed lower right:
Ensor 84
Inv.-Nr. Inv. no.: WRM 2742

Skelett, Chinoiserien betrachtend, 1885
Skeleton Gazing at Chinoiseries
Squelette regardant des chinoiseries
Öl auf Leinwand Oil on canvas, 99.5 x 64.5 cm
Bezeichnet unten links Inscribed lower left:
Ensor 85
Inv.-Nr. Inv. no.: WRM 2741

Georges d'Espagnat

Garten in Verneuil, 1892/95
Garden in Verneuil
Jardin à Verneuil
Öl auf Leinwand Oil on canvas, 65 x 81 cm
Bezeichnet unten links Inscribed lower left:
gdE
Inv.-Nr. Inv. no.: WRM Dep. FC 613

Die Anglerinnen, o.J.
The Anglers, n.d.
Les Pêcheuses
Öl auf Leinwand Oil on canvas, 97 x 130.4 cm
Bezeichnet unten rechts Inscribed lower right:
gdE
Inv.-Nr. Inv. no.: WRM Dep. 860

Henri Fantin-Latour

Blühender Rhododendronzweig, 1874
Rhododendron Branch in Bloom
Öl auf Leinwand Oil on canvas, 55 x 58 cm
Bezeichnet oben links Inscribed upper left:
Fantin 74.
Inv.-Nr. Inv. no.: WRM 3146

Alfred William (genannt known as Willy) Finch

Dorf nahe der Nordseeküste, ca. 1889
Village near the North Sea Coast
Village près des côtes de la Mer du Nord
Öl auf Leinwand Oil on canvas, 57.8 x 71.3 cm
Bezeichnet unten links Inscribed lower left:
A.W.F.
Inv.-Nr. Inv. no.: WRM Dep. FC 711

Paul Gauguin

Die Seine beim Pont de Grenelle, 1875
The Seine at the Pont de Grenelle
La Seine au Pont de Grenelle
Öl auf Holz Oil on wood, 30.6 x 45.7 cm
Bezeichnet unten rechts Inscribed lower right:
P Gauguin 75
Inv.-Nr. Inv. no.: WRM Dep. FC 744

Landschaft bei Rouen, 1884
Rouen Landscape
Paysage à Rouen
Öl auf Leinwand Oil on canvas, 74 x 60 cm
Bezeichnet unten links Inscribed lower left:
P Gauguin 84
Inv.-Nr. Inv. no.: WRM Dep. FC 699

Das Ausbringen des Mists, 1884
Manuring
La Fumure des terres
Öl auf Leinwand Oil on canvas, 59.5 x 73.5 cm
Bezeichnet unten rechts Inscribed lower right:
P Gauguin / 84
Inv.-Nr. Inv. no.: WRM Dep. FC 663

Ein bretonischer Junge, 1889
Nude Breton Boy
Petit Breton nu
Öl auf Leinwand Oil on canvas, 93 x 73.5 cm
Bezeichnet unten rechts Inscribed lower right:
89 P Gauguin
Inv.-Nr. Inv. no.: WRM 3114

Leo Gausson

Die Rue des Etuves in Lagny-sur-Marne (Ansicht von Lagny-sur-Marne) oder *Frau auf der Straße*, ca. 1885
The Rue des Etuves in Lagny-sur-Marne (View of Lagny-sur-Marne) or *Woman on the Street*
La Rue des Etuves à Lagny-sur-Marne (Vue de Lagny-sur-Marne) *ou* Femme dans la rue
Öl auf Pappelholz Oil on poplar, 28.5 x 20.5 cm
Inv.-Nr. Inv. no.: WRM Dep. FC 745

Landschaft in der Umgebung von Lagny, ca. 1887/89
Landscape near Lagny
Paysage aux environs de Lagny
Öl auf Leinwand Oil on canvas, 23.2 x 29.3 cm
Bezeichnet unten rechts Inscribed lower right:
Leo Gausson
Inv.-Nr. Inv. no.: WRM Dep. FC 664

Norbert Goeneutte

Porträt einer Frau (Berthe Morisot?), ca. 1875
Portrait of a Woman (Berthe Morisot?)
Portrait de femme (Berthe Morisot?)
Öl auf Leinwand Oil on canvas, 56 x 45.8 cm
Bezeichnet oben links Inscribed upper left:
Norbert Goeneutte
Inv.-Nr. Inv. no.: WRM Dep. FC 746

Elegante Dame am Strand, o. J.
Elegant Lady on the Beach, n.d.
Elégante sur la plage
Öl auf Holz Oil on wood, 8.5 x 15.5 cm
Bezeichnet unten links Inscribed lower left:
N Goeneutte / Treport
Inv.-Nr. Inv. no.: WRM Dep. FC 747

Vincent van Gogh

Bauernkate in Nuenen, 1885
Farmhouse in Nuenen
Boerenhuis, Nuenen
Öl auf Leinwand über Holz Oil on canvas mounted on wood, 35 x 47.2 cm
Inv.-Nr. Inv. no.: WRM Dep. FC 665

Brücke von Clichy, 1887
Bridge at Clichy
Pont de Clichy
Öl auf Leinwand Oil on canvas, 54.8 x 46.1 cm
Inv.-Nr. Inv. no.: WRM Dep. 813

Die Zugbrücke, 1888
The Drawbridge
Le Pont de Langlois
Öl auf Leinwand Oil on canvas, 49.5 x 64 cm
Inv.-Nr. Inv. no.: WRM 1197

Fernand Marie Eugene le Gout-Gerard

Strickerinnen, ca. 1906
Women Knitting
Les Tricoteuses
Öl auf Papier Oil on paper, 47 x 60 cm
Bezeichnet unten rechts Inscribed lower right:
F Le Gout Gerard
Inv.-Nr. Inv. no.: WRM Dep. FC 807

Armand Guillaumin

Landschaft von Louveciennes, ca. 1872
Landscape, Louveciennes
Paysage de Louveciennes
Öl auf Leinwand Oil on canvas, 56 x 46 cm
Bezeichnet unten rechts Inscribed lower right:
Guillaumin
Inv.-Nr. Inv. no.: WRM Dep. FC 604

Bäume und Blumen, Landschaft bei Damiette, ca. 1885
Trees and Flowers, Landscape at Damiette
Arbres et fleurs, paysage à Damiette
Öl auf Leinwand Oil on canvas, 60 x 73 cm
Bezeichnet unten links Inscribed lower left:
Guillaumin; rückseitige Aufschrift auf dem Keilrahmen inscription on reverse on stretcher frame: Paysage à Damiette 7bre temps gris
Inv.-Nr. Inv. no.: WRM Dep. FC 748

Am Kanal, 1888/89
On the Canal
Au bord du canal
Öl auf Leinwand Oil on canvas, 65 x 80.7 cm
Bezeichnet unten links Inscribed lower left:
Guillaumin
Inv.-Nr. Inv. no.: WRM Dep. FC 606

Meer bei Saint-Palais, 1892
The Sea at Saint-Palais
La Mer à Saint-Palais
Öl auf Leinwand Oil on canvas, 60.4 x 93.4 cm
Bezeichnet unten links Inscribed lower left:
Guillaumin; rückseitige Aufschrift auf dem Keilrahmen inscription on reverse on stretcher frame: 4 AOUT (18)92
Inv.-Nr. Inv. no.: WRM Dep. FC 749

Felsklippe an der Landzunge von La Baumette, 1893
Rocks at the Spit of La Baumette
Rocher à la pointe de la Baumette
Öl auf Leinwand Oil on canvas, 33.2 x 46 cm
Bezeichnet unten links Inscribed lower left:
Guillaumin; rückseitige Aufschrift auf dem Keilrahmen inscription on reverse on stretcher frame: Rocher à la pointe de la Baumette / Janvier (18)93, 4h Nr. 4375
Inv.-Nr. Inv. no.: WRM Dep. FC 559

Die Ile Besse bei Agay, am Morgen, 1901
The Ile Besse at Agay, Morning Scene
L'Ile Besse à Agay, le matin
Öl auf Leinwand Oil on canvas, 65 x 70.8 cm
Bezeichnet unten links Inscribed lower left:
Guillaumin; rückseitige Aufschrift auf dem Keilrahmen inscription on reverse on stretcher frame: Agay Mai 1901 de Besse (le matin)
Inv.-Nr. Inv. no.: WRM Dep. FC 750

Der Berg Bariou, Crozant, 1918
Mount Bariou, Crozant
Le Puy Bariou, Crozant
Öl auf Leinwand Oil on canvas, 65 x 81 cm
Bezeichnet unten rechts Inscribed lower right:
Guillaumin
Inv.-Nr. Inv. no.: WRM Dep. FC 751

Karl Hagemeister

Waldbach im Vorfrühling, ca. 1900
Forest Stream in Early Spring
Öl auf Leinwand Oil on canvas,
73.5 x 118.5 cm
Bezeichnet unten rechts Inscribed lower right:
K. Hagemeister
Inv.-Nr. Inv. no.: WRM 3141

Ferdinand Hart-Nibbrig

Geuldal, Provinz Limburg, ca. 1904/05
Geuldal, Province of Limburg
Het Geuldal in Limburg
Öl auf Leinwand Oil on canvas, 46 x 60.5 cm
Bezeichnet unten rechts Inscribed lower right:
HART · NIBBRIG
Inv.-Nr. Inv. no.: WRM Dep. FC 700

Louis Hayet

Am Flussufer, 1888
Riverside
Au bord de la rivière
Öl auf Leinwand Oil on canvas, 51.5 x 71.5 cm
Bezeichnet unten rechts Inscribed lower right:
L. Hayet 88
Inv.-Nr. Inv. no.: WRM Dep. FC 752

Paris, der Eiffelturm, ca. 1889/90
Paris, the Eiffel Tower
Paris, la tour Eiffel
Öl auf Karton Oil on cardboard, 18.1 x 30.4 cm
Bezeichnet unten rechts Inscribed lower right:
L. hayet.
Inv.-Nr. Inv. no.: WRM Dep. FC 610

Junge Frau beim Zeichnen vor ihrer Staffelei, ca. 1892/94
Young Woman Drawing at her Easel
Jeune femme dessinant à son chevalet
Öl auf Papier Oil on paper, 27 x 19 cm
Bezeichnet unten rechts Inscribed lower right:
L.H.
Inv.-Nr. Inv. no.: WRM Dep. FC 806

Auguste Herbin

Die Hügel von Haute-Isle, Val-d'Oise, 1906
The Hills of Haute-Isle, Val-d'Oise
Les Coteaux à Haute-Isle, Commune du Val-d'Oise
Öl auf Leinwand Oil on canvas, 59.5 x 73 cm
Bezeichnet unten rechts Inscribed lower right:
Herbin
Inv.-Nr. Inv. no.: WRM Dep. 838

Ferdinand Hodler

Kopfstudie einer Italienerin (Giulia Leonardi), 1910
Study of the Head of an Italian Woman (Giulia Leonardi)
Öl auf Leinwand Oil on canvas, 34.5 x 40 cm
Bezeichnet unten rechts Inscribed lower right:
1910 F. Hodler
Inv.-Nr. Inv. no.: WRM 1210

Ludwig von Hofmann

Brandung, 1905
Surf
Öl auf Leinwand Oil on canvas, 82.5 x 118 cm
Bezeichnet unten links Inscribed lower left:
L v Hofmann 1905
Inv.-Nr. Inv. no.: WRM 1250

Blanche Hoschede-Monet

Weiher in Giverny oder *Der Garten,* o. J.
Pond in Giverny or *The Garden,* n.d.
L'Etang à Giverny *ou* Le Jardin
Öl auf Leinwand Oil on canvas, 58 x 71 cm
Bezeichnet unten rechts Inscribed lower right:
Blanche Monet
Inv.-Nr. Inv. no.: WRM Dep. FC 753

Eugene Isabey

Rückkehr vom Fischfang, o. J.
Return from Fishing, n.d.
Öl auf Karton Oil on cardboard, 23 x 31 cm
Inv.-Nr. Inv. no.: WRM 3398

Alexej von Jawlensky

Straße in Oberbayern, 1904
Road in Upper Bavaria
Öl auf Karton Oil on cardboard, 35.2 x 50.2 cm
Inv.-Nr. Inv. no.: WRM Dep. FC 754

Johan Barthold Jongkind

Normannische Landschaft, 1859/61
Landscape in Normandy
Öl auf Leinwand Oil on canvas, 42.3 x 56.5 cm
Bezeichnet unten rechts Inscribed lower right:
Jongkind 1859
Inv.-Nr. Inv. no.: WRM 3605

In der Umgebung von Nevers oder *Bauernhof in Saint-Parize-le-Chatel,* 1861
In the Environs of Nevers or *Farm in Saint-Parize-le-Chatel*
Aux environs de Nevers *ou*
Ferme à Saint-Parize-le-Chatel
Öl auf Leinwand Oil on canvas, 24.7 x 32.8 cm
Bezeichnet unten rechts Inscribed lower right:
Jongkind 1861
Inv.-Nr. Inv. no.: WRM Dep. FC 666

Wassily Kandinsky

Landschaft bei Regensburg, 1903
Landscape at Regensburg
Öl auf Leinwand über Karton Oil on canvas mounted on cardboard, 32.4 x 23.5 cm
Bezeichnet unten rechts Inscribed lower right:
KANDINSKY.
Inv.-Nr. Inv. no.: WRM Dep. 819

Alexander Kanoldt

Blick auf einen Park in Karlsruhe, ca. 1907
View of a Park in Karlsruhe
Öl auf Leinwand über Karton Oil on canvas mounted on cardboard, 30.7 x 48 cm
Bezeichnet unten links Inscribed lower left:
AK
Inv.-Nr. Inv. no.: WRM Dep. FC 667

Gotthardt Kuehl

Lachendes Mädchen, 1903
Young Girl Laughing
Öl auf Karton Oil on cardboard, 53.5 x 38 cm
Bezeichnet unten rechts auf der Truhe
Inscribed lower right, on the trunk:
Gotthardt Kuehl / 03
Inv.-Nr. Inv. no.: WRM 1483

Georges Lacombe

Felsen bei Vignage, Wald von Ecouves, ca. 1904/08
Rocks at Vignage, Forest of Ecouves
Rochers au Vignage, forêt d'Ecouves
Öl auf Leinwand Oil on canvas, 89 x 117 cm
Bezeichnet unten rechts Inscribed lower right:
G Lacombe
Inv.-Nr. Inv. no.: WRM Dep. FC 756

Felsen bei Vignage, Wald von Ecouves oder *Sonnenlicht auf den Buchen,* ca. 1905/08
Rocks at Vignage. Forest of Ecouves or *Sunshine on the Beeches*
Rochers au Vignage, forêt d'Ecouves *ou*
Coup de soleil sur les hêtres
Öl auf Leinwand Oil on canvas, 105 x 82.5 cm
Bezeichnet unten rechts Inscribed lower right:
GL (ligiert ligated)
Inv.-Nr. Inv. no.: WRM Dep. FC 607

Blühende Apfelbäume oder *Zwei blühende Bäume in einem Waldstück bei Vignage,* ca. 1910/14
Apple Trees in Bloom or *Two Blossoming Apple Trees in a Grove near Vignage*
Pommiers en fleurs *ou* Deux arbres en fleurs dans un sous-bois au Vignage
Öl auf Leinwand Oil on canvas, 65.2 x 81.5 cm
Bezeichnet unten rechts Inscribed lower right:
Lacombe
Inv.-Nr. Inv. no.: WRM Dep. FC 755

Achille Lauge

Promenade am Flussufer, 1888
Promenade on the Riverside
La Promenade au bord de la rivière
Öl auf Leinwand Oil on canvas, 34.5 x 44 cm
Inv.-Nr. Inv. no.: WRM Dep. FC 757

Landschaft mit blühenden Bäumen, 1898
Landscape with Trees in Bloom
Paysage aux arbres fleurissants
Öl auf Leinwand Oil on canvas, 54 x 75 cm
Bezeichnet unten rechts Inscribed lower right:
A. Laugé
Inv.-Nr. Inv. no.: WRM Dep. FC 758

Weg mit Ginster, ca. 1900
Path with Gorse
La Route aux genêts
Öl auf Leinwand Oil on canvas, 54 x 72 cm
Bezeichnet unten rechts Inscribed lower right:
A. Laugé
Inv.-Nr. Inv. no.: WRM Dep. FC 759

Vase mit Rosen, 1909
Vase with Roses
Vase avec des roses
Öl auf Leinwand Oil on canvas, 55 x 45.8 cm
Bezeichnet unten rechts Inscribed lower right:
A. Laugé / 09
Inv.-Nr. Inv. no.: WRM Dep. FC 760

Rosen, 1910
Roses
Roses
Öl auf Leinwand Oil on canvas, 54 x 38 cm
Bezeichnet unten rechts Inscribed lower right:
A Laugé / 10
Inv.-Nr. Inv. no.: WRM Dep. FC 761

Henri Lebasque

Das Dorf Champigné, Maine-et-Loire, 1893
The Village of Champigné, Maine-et-Loire
Le Village de Champigné, Maine-et-Loire
Öl auf Leinwand Oil on canvas, 41.3 x 33.2 cm
Bezeichnet unten rechts Inscribed lower right:
H. Lebasque 93
Inv.-Nr. Inv. no.: WRM Dep. FC 669

Zwei bretonische Frauen am Meer, 1897
Two Breton Women on the Seashore
Deux bretonnes au bord de la mer
Öl auf Leinwand Oil on canvas, 46.2 x 55.8 cm
Bezeichnet unten rechts Inscribed lower right:
H Lebasque 97
Inv.-Nr. Inv. no.: WRM Dep. FC 670

Ein Nachmittag im Park, ca. 1898
An Afternoon in the Park
Un Après-midi dans le parc
Öl auf Leinwand Oil on canvas, 50.5 x 61.5 cm
Bezeichnet unten links Inscribed lower left:
H. Lebasque
Inv.-Nr. Inv. no.: WRM Dep. FC 572

Schnitter in der Umgebung von Lagny, ca. 1899/1900
Reapers near Lagny
Moissonneurs aux environs de Lagny
Öl auf Leinwand Oil on canvas, 92 x 150 cm
Bezeichnet unten rechts Inscribed lower right:
H. Lebasque
Inv.-Nr. Inv. no.: WRM Dep. 857

Albert Charles Lebourg

Hondouville-sur-Iton im Nebel, ca. 1890/92
Hondouville-sur-Iton in the Fog
Hondouville-sur-Iton, effet de brume
Öl auf Leinwand Oil on canvas, 50.8 x 73 cm
Bezeichnet unten links Inscribed lower left:
AC Lebourg (A und C ligiert A and C ligated) / Hondouville sur Iton.
Inv.-Nr. Inv. no.: WRM Dep. FC 762

Weiher, ca. 1900
Pond
L'Etang
Öl auf Holz Oil on wood, 14.5 x 23.5 cm
Bezeichnet unten links Inscribed lower left:
Lebourg
Inv.-Nr. Inv. no.: WRM Dep. FC 763

Ansicht von Bouille, ca. 1900
View of Bouille
Vue de la Bouille
Öl auf Leinwand Oil on canvas, 46 x 76.5 cm
Bezeichnet unten rechts Inscribed lower right:
AC Lebourg (A und C ligiert A and C ligated); rückseitige Aufschrift inscription on reverse: Vue de la Bouille
Inv.-Nr. Inv. no.: WRM Dep. FC 583

Umgebung von Clermont-Ferrand, ca. 1900
Environs of Clermont-Ferrand
Environs de Clermont-Ferrand
Öl auf Leinwand Oil on canvas, 40.6 x 73.7 cm
Bezeichnet unten rechts Inscribed lower right:
AC Lebourg (A und C ligiert A and C ligated)
Inv.-Nr. Inv. no.: WRM Dep. FC 764

Georges Lemmen

Auf dem Deich – Der Strand von Ostende, 1890–92
On the Dyke – The Beach at Ostend
Sur la digue – La Plage à Ostende
Öl auf Leinwand Oil on canvas, 46.6 x 61.1 cm
Bezeichnet unten rechts *Inscribed lower right:*
GL (ligiert ligated)
Inv.-Nr. Inv. no.: WRM Dep. FC 765

Die Küste von Heyst, 1891
The Coast at Heyst
La Côte à Heyst
Öl auf Pappelholz Oil on poplar, 12.5 x 21.8 cm
Bezeichnet unten rechts Inscribed lower right:
GL (ligiert ligated); rückseitige Aufschrift inscription on reverse: Heyst 21 juillet 91 8 le soir
Inv.-Nr. Inv. no.: WRM Dep. FC 715

Die Küste von Heyst bei fallendem Wasser, 1891
The Coast at Heyst, Low Tide
La Côte à Heyst, marée descendante
Öl auf Pappelholz Oil on poplar, 12.3 x 21.5 cm
Bezeichnet oben links Inscribed upper left: GL (ligiert ligated); rückseitige Aufschrift inscription on reverse: Heyst mercredi 19 août 1891 / 3 heures marée descendante
Inv.-Nr. Inv. no.: WRM Dep. FC 716

Blick auf eine grüne Küste, 1891/92
View of a Green Coast
Vue de la côte, près verte
Öl auf Leinwand Oil on canvas, 16.3 x 22.3 cm
Bezeichnet unten rechts Inscribed lower right:
GL (ligiert ligated)
Inv.-Nr. Inv. no.: WRM Dep. FC 767

Die Klippen von Dover, 1892
The Cliffs of Dover
Les Falaises de Douvres
Öl auf Leinwand Oil on canvas, 16 x 23.8 cm
Bezeichnet unten rechts Inscribed lower right:
GL (ligiert ligated)
Inv.-Nr. Inv. no.: WRM Dep. FC 766

Stanislas Lepine

Der Kanal Saint-Denis im Mondschein, vom Hafen von Metz aus gesehen, ca. 1876/79
The Saint-Denis Canal in the Moonlight, Viewed from the Harbor at Metz
Le Canal Saint-Denis vu de la darse de Metz, effet de lune
Öl auf Leinwand Oil on canvas, 114.5 x 146 cm
Bezeichnet unten links Inscribed lower left:
S. Lepine
Inv.-Nr. Inv. no.: WRM Dep. FC 814

Die Insel Grande Jatte, ca. 1877/82
The Island of Grande Jatte
L'Ile de la Grande Jatte
Öl auf Leinwand Oil on canvas, 46.5 x 55.5 cm
Bezeichnet unten rechts Inscribed lower right:
S. Lepine
Inv.-Nr. Inv. no.: WRM Dep. FC 691

Andre Leveille

Springbrunnen, ca. 1903
Fountain
Le Jet d'eau
Öl auf Leinwand Oil on canvas, 146.5 x 115 cm
Bezeichnet unten rechts Inscribed lower right:
A Leveille

Max Liebermann

Marktszene, 1874
Market Scene
Öl auf Leinwand Oil on canvas, 84 x 59 cm
Bezeichnet unten rechts Inscribed lower right:
M. Liebermann 74.
Inv.-Nr. Inv. no.: WRM 2341

Die Rasenbleiche, 1882
The Bleaching Ground
Öl auf Leinwand Oil on canvas, 109 x 173 cm
Bezeichnet unten rechts Inscribed lower right:
M Liebermann 82
Inv.-Nr. Inv. no.: WRM 2939

Zwei holländische Bäuerinnen, 1898
Two Dutch Peasant Women
Öl auf Leinwand Oil on canvas, 56 x 73 cm
Bezeichnet unten rechts Inscribed lower right:
M Liebermann
Inv.-Nr. Inv. no.: WRM 2887

Reiter und Reiterin am Strand, 1903
Riders on the Beach
Öl auf Leinwand Oil on canvas, 72.5 x 101 cm
Bezeichnet unten rechts Inscribed lower right:
M. Liebermann
Inv.-Nr. Inv. no.: WRM 2819

Judengasse in Amsterdam, 1905
Jewish Quarter in Amsterdam
Öl auf Leinwand Oil on canvas, 59 x 73 cm
Bezeichnet unten links Inscribed lower left:
M. Liebermann 1905.
Inv.-Nr. Inv. no.: WRM 1189

Selbstbildnis, 1908
Self-Portrait
Öl auf Leinwand Oil on canvas, 87.5 x 71 cm
Bezeichnet oben rechts Inscribed upper right:
M. Liebermann
Inv.-Nr. Inv. no.: WRM 1186

Der barmherzige Samariter, 1911
The Good Samaritan
Öl auf Leinwand Oil on canvas, 93 x 112 cm
Bezeichnet unten rechts Inscribed lower right:
M Liebermann 1911
Inv.-Nr. Inv. no.: WRM 1187

Reitknecht mit Pferd, 1912
Groom with Horse
Öl auf Karton Oil on cardboard, 81 x 64.5 cm
Bezeichnet unten rechts Inscribed lower right:
M. Liebermann 1912.
Inv.-Nr. Inv. no.: WRM 1190

Käthe, die Tochter des Malers, zu Pferd, 1913
Käthe, the Painter's Daughter, on Horseback
Öl auf Leinwand Oil on canvas, 80 x 100 cm
Bezeichnet unten rechts Inscribed lower right:
M Liebermann 13
Inv.-Nr. Inv. no.: WRM 1183

Gustave Loiseau

Die Ufer des Flusses Sausseron, bei Nesles, ca. 1897
Banks of the River Sausseron at Nesles
Les Bords du Sausseron à Nesles
Öl auf Leinwand Oil on canvas, 81.5 x 65.5 cm
Bezeichnet unten rechts Inscribed lower right:
G LOISEAU
Inv.-Nr. Inv. no.: WRM Dep. FC 770

Landschaft im Schnee, Dorfeingang in der Bretagne, ca. 1897/1900
Landscape in the Snow, Entrance to a Village in Brittany
Paysage sous la neige, entrée de village en Bretagne
Öl auf Leinwand Oil on canvas, 74 x 93 cm
Bezeichnet unten rechts Inscribed lower right:
G LOISEAU
Inv.-Nr. Inv. no.: WRM Dep. FC 771

Der Pont Perronet in Mantes, ca. 1898
Pont Perronet in Mantes
Pont Perronet à Mantes
Öl auf Leinwand Oil on canvas, 50.5 x 61.8 cm
Bezeichnet unten links Inscribed lower left:
G LOISEAU
Inv.-Nr. Inv. no.: WRM Dep. FC 612

Dorf im Frühling, das Tal der Seine bei Les Damps, ca. 1898
Village in Spring, the Seine Valley at Les Damps
Le Village au printemps, vallée de la Seine aux Damps
Öl auf Leinwand Oil on canvas, 60 x 81 cm
Bezeichnet unten rechts Inscribed lower right:
G LOISEAU
Inv.-Nr. Inv. no.: WRM Dep. FC 772

Maximilien Luce

Saint-Tropez, 1892
Öl auf Karton Oil on cardboard, 26 x 39.8 cm
Bezeichnet unten links Inscribed lower left:
92 L S Tropez
Inv.-Nr. Inv. no.: WRM Dep. FC 773

Regenstimmung über der Seine, 1894
The Seine in the Rain
La Seine aux grésillons
Öl auf Leinwand Oil on canvas, 38 x 46 cm
Bezeichnet unten rechts Inscribed lower right:
Luce 94
Inv.-Nr. Inv. no.: WRM Dep. 846

Straßenszene in Gisors, 1895
Street Scene in Gisors
Gisors, scène de rue
Öl auf Karton Oil on cardboard, 35.8 x 49 cm
Bezeichnet unten links Inscribed lower left:
à l'ami Grave / Luce 95
Inv.-Nr. Inv. no.: WRM Dep. FC 574

Die Ebene von Les Grésillons, Poissy, 1899
The Plain of Les Grésillons, Poissy
La Plaine des Grésillons sur Poissy
Öl auf Leinwand Oil on canvas, 73 x 92.1 cm
Bezeichnet unten rechts Inscribed lower right: Luce; rückseitige Aufschrift auf dem Keilrahmen inscription on reverse on stretcher frame: Luce 1899 / La plaine des Grésillons sur Poissy
Inv.-Nr. Inv. no.: WRM Dep. FC 774

Der Fluss Eure bei Garennes, ca. 1901
The River Eure near Garennes
L'Eure à Garennes
Öl auf Karton Oil on cardboard, 28 x 41.2 cm
Bezeichnet unten rechts Inscribed lower right: Luce
Inv.-Nr. Inv. no.: WRM Dep. FC 775

Am Flussufer, 1903
On the Banks of the River
Au bord de la rivière
Öl auf Karton Oil on cardboard, 24 x 32 cm
Bezeichnet unten links Inscribed lower left: Luce 1903
Inv.-Nr. Inv. no.: WRM Dep. FC 776

Notre-Dame, Ansicht vom Quai Saint-Michel aus, 1901–04
Notre-Dame, Viewed from the Quai Saint-Michel
Notre-Dame, vue du Quai Saint-Michel
Öl auf Leinwand Oil on canvas, 101 x 118.8 cm
Bezeichnet unten links Inscribed lower left: Luce 1901 – 04
Inv.-Nr. Inv. no.: WRM Dep. FC 692

August Macke

Sonniger Garten, 1908
Sunny Garden
Öl auf Leinwand Oil on canvas, 51 x 66.3 cm
Bezeichnet rechts der Mitte (auf dem Weg) Inscribed right of center (on the path): A Macke / 08; rückseitige Aufschrift inscription on reverse: Aug. Macke 1908 (und Nachlass-Stempel and estate stamp)
Inv.-Nr. Inv. no.: WRM Dep. 815

Edouard Manet

Schwarzes Boot bei Berck, 1873
Fishing Boat on the Beach at Berck
Le Bateau noir à Berck
Öl auf Karton Oil on cardboard, 20.4 x 33.3 cm
Bezeichnet unten links Inscribed lower left: Manet
Inv.-Nr. Inv. no.: WRM Dep. 777

Spargel-Stillleben, 1880
A Bunch of Asparagus
L'Asperge
Öl auf Leinwand Oil on canvas, 46 x 55 cm
Bezeichnet unten links Inscribed lower left: Manet
Inv.-Nr. Inv. no.: WRM Dep. 318
Dauerleihgabe des On Permanent loan from the Kuratorium und Förderergesellschaft des Wallraf-Richartz-Museums / Museums Ludwig e. V.

Albert Marquet

Vorort von Paris, 1899
Suburb of Paris
Banlieue de Paris
Öl auf Karton Oil on cardboard, 23.5 x 31.5 cm
Bezeichnet unten links Inscribed lower left: marquet
Inv.-Nr. Inv. no.: WRM Dep. FC 671

Waschfrauen, Triel-sur-Seine, 1931
Washerwomen, Triel-sur-Seine
Les Lavandières, Triel-sur-Seine
Öl auf Holz Oil on wood, 33 x 41 cm
Bezeichnet unten rechts Inscribed lower right: marquet
Inv.-Nr. Inv. no.: WRM Dep. FC 778

Henri Martin

Muse mit Lyra, ca. 1890
Muse with Lyre
Muse à la lyre
Öl auf Leinwand Oil on canvas, 98 x 104 cm
Inv.-Nr. Inv. no.: WRM Dep. 858

Ins Dorf heimkehrender Bauer, ca. 1898
Peasant Returning to the Village
Paysan rentrant au village
Öl auf Leinwand Oil on canvas, 83.5 x 115 cm
Inv.-Nr. Inv. no.: WRM Dep. FC 779

La Bastide-du-Vert, ca. 1905
Öl auf Leinwand Oil on canvas, 78 x 101.5 cm

Landschaft – Haus auf dem Lande, ca. 1910
Landscape – House in the Country
Paysage – Maison à la campagne
Öl auf Leinwand Oil on canvas, 60.3 x 81.3 cm
Bezeichnet unten rechts Inscribed lower right: Henri Martin
Inv.-Nr. Inv. no.: WRM Dep. FC 672

Kind in den Armen einer Frau mit Hut oder *Mutter und Kind*, ca. 1920
Child in the Arms of a Woman Wearing a Hat or *Mother and Child*
Enfant dans les bras d'une femme au chapeau *ou* Mère et enfant
Öl auf Leinwand Oil on canvas, 45.8 x 38.3 cm
Bezeichnet unten links Inscribed lower left: Henri Martin
Inv.-Nr. Inv. no.: WRM Dep. 849

Henri Matisse

Korsika, die alte Mühle (Hof der Mühle in Ajaccio I), 1898
Corsica, the Old Mill (Mill Courtyard in Ajaccio I)
Corse, le vieux moulin
Öl auf Leinwand Oil on canvas, 38.2 x 46 cm
Bezeichnet unten rechts Inscribed lower right: Henri Matisse
Inv.-Nr. Inv. no.: WRM Dep. FC 780

Maxime Maufra

Winterlandschaft, 1890
Winter Landscape
Paysage, effet de neige
Öl auf Leinwand Oil on canvas, 55.2 x 100.4 cm
Bezeichnet unten rechts Inscribed lower right: Maxime Maufra 1890.
Inv.-Nr. Inv. no.: WRM Dep. FC 781

Segelboote in einer Bucht der Seine, 1899
Sailboats in a Bay of the Seine
Voiliers en baie de Seine
Öl auf Leinwand Oil on canvas, 60.5 x 73.7 cm
Bezeichnet unten links Inscribed lower left: Maufra 99
Inv.-Nr. Inv. no.: WRM Dep. FC 611

Regenbogen, 1901
Rainbow
L'Arc-en-ciel
Öl auf Leinwand Oil on canvas, 76 x 99 cm
Bezeichnet unten links Inscribed lower right:
MauFra 1901.
Inv.-Nr. Inv. no.: WRM Dep. FC 584

Kerhostin, nach after 1903
Öl auf Leinwand Oil on canvas, 38 x 46 cm
Bezeichnet unten rechts Inscribed lower right:
MauFra
Inv.-Nr. Inv. no.: WRM Dep. FC 783

Die Kapelle von Sainte-Avoye, Morbihan, 1908
The Chapel of Sainte-Avoye, Morbihan
La Chapelle de Sainte-Avoye, Morbihan
Öl auf Leinwand Oil on canvas, 81 x 65 cm
Bezeichnet unten links Inscribed lower left:
Maufra 1908.
Inv.-Nr. Inv. no.: WRM Dep. FC 782

Fluss bei Auray, 1909
River near Auray
La Rivière d'Auray
Öl auf Leinwand Oil on canvas, 65 x 81 cm
Bezeichnet unten rechts Inscribed lower right:
MauFra 1909.

Jean Metzinger

Bauernhof, vor 1906
Farm, before 1906
Cour de ferme
Öl auf Leinwand Oil on canvas, 56.9 x 73 cm
Bezeichnet unten links Inscribed lower left:
J. Metzinger
Inv.-Nr. Inv. no.: WRM Dep. FC 701

Landschaft mit Baum, ca. 1906
Landscape with Tree
Paysage à l'arbre rond
Öl auf Karton über Holz Oil on cardboard mounted on wood, 22 x 27.5 cm
Bezeichnet unten rechts Inscribed lower right:
Metzinger
Inv.-Nr. Inv. no.: WRM Dep. 847

Jean François Millet ?

Liegender Frauenakt, o. J.
Reclining Nude, n.d.
Öl auf Leinwand Oil on canvas, 54 x 65 cm
Bezeichnet unten rechts Inscribed lower right:
J F. Millet
Inv.-Nr. Inv. no.: WRM 3532

Claude Monet

Die Seine bei Asnières, 1873
The Seine at Asnières
La Seine à Asnières
Öl auf Leinwand Oil on canvas, 54.2 x 72.5 cm
Bezeichnet unten rechts Inscribed lower right:
Claude Monet
Inv.-Nr. Inv. no.: WRM Dep. FC 784

Fischerboote am Strand von Etretat, 1883/84
Fishing Boats at the Beach at Etretat
Bateaux de pêche et Porte d'Aval
Öl auf Leinwand Oil on canvas, 74 x 101 cm
Bezeichnet unten rechts Inscribed lower right:
Claude Monet / 1884
Inv.-Nr. Inv. no.: WRM 3120

Häuser in Falaise im Nebel, 1885
Houses in Falaise in the Fog
Maisons à Falaise, brouillard
Öl auf Leinwand Oil on canvas, 73.5 x 92.5 cm
Bezeichnet unten rechts Inscribed lower right:
Claude Monet
Inv.-Nr. Inv. no.: WRM Dep. FC 673

Seerosen, ca. 1915/17
Water Lilies
Nymphéas
Öl auf Leinwand Oil on canvas, 180 x 205 cm
Bezeichnet unten links Inscribed lower left:
Claude Monet (Atelierstempel Studio stamp)
Inv.-Nr. Inv. no.: WRM 3266

Georges Daniel de Monfreid

Landschaft in der Umgebung von Banyuls, 1891
Landscape near Banyuls
Paysage aux environs de Banyuls
Öl auf Leinwand Oil on canvas, 73 x 100 cm
Bezeichnet unten links Inscribed lower left:
Daniel / Les Escaldes Juillet 91; bezeichnet unten rechts inscribed lower right: à Paul Gauguin / à mon ami et maître genial, / Témoignage d'amitié / et de pure admiration. / Daniel
Inv.-Nr. Inv. no.: WRM Dep. 785

Chinesische Vasen (Blumen), 1892
Chinese Vases (Flowers)
Les Vases chinois (Fleurs)
Öl auf Leintuch Oil on linen, 65.5 x 45.5 cm
Bezeichnet unten rechts Inscribed lower right:
Daniel / Avril 92
Inv.-Nr. Inv. no.: WRM Dep. FC 674

Adolphe Monticelli

Landschaft bei Ganagobie, 1872
Landscape at Ganagobie
Paysage à Ganagobie
Öl auf Karton Oil on cardboard, 48 x 95 cm
Bezeichnet unten links Inscribed lower left:
Monticelli
Inv.-Nr. Inv. no.: WRM Dep. FC 709

Henry Moret

Die Zollstation, Finistère, 1899
The Customs House, Finistère
La Cabane des douaniers, Finistère
Öl auf Leinwand Oil on canvas, 60.5 x 74 cm
Bezeichnet unten rechts Inscribed lower right:
Henry Moret 99
Inv.-Nr. Inv. no.: WRM Dep. FC 786

Heidelandschaft von Saint-Guinolé bei Pont-Aven, 1900
Heathland in Saint-Guinolé near Pont-Aven
Lande de Saint-Guinolé près de Pont-Aven
Öl auf Leinwand Oil on canvas, 70 x 90 cm
Bezeichnet unten links Inscribed lower left:
Henry Moret / 1900
Inv.-Nr. Inv. no.: WRM Dep. FC 787

Küste bei Belon, Finistère, ca. 1900
Coast at Belon, Finistère
Côte de Belon, Finistère
Öl auf Leinwand Oil on canvas, 42.5 x 81.5 cm
Bezeichnet unten links Inscribed lower left:
Henry Moret; rückseitige Aufschrift auf dem Keilrahmen inscription on reverse on stretcher frame: Côte de Belon – Finistère
Inv.-Nr. Inv. no.: WRM Dep. FC 788

Nacht in Douelan, 1909
Douelan at Night
La Nuit à Douelan
Öl auf Leinwand Oil on canvas, 33.5 x 46.5 cm
Bezeichnet unten links Inscribed lower left:
Henry Moret / 09
Inv.-Nr. Inv. no.: WRM Dep. FC 573

Berthe Morisot

Boote auf der Seine, ca. 1879/80
Boats on the Seine
Bateaux sur la Seine
Öl auf Leinwand Oil on canvas, 25.5 x 50 cm
Bezeichnet unten rechts Inscribed lower right:
Berthe Morisot
Inv.-Nr. Inv. no.: WRM Dep. FC 615

Kind zwischen Stockrosen, 1881
Child in the Hollyhocks
Enfant dans les roses trémières
Öl auf Leinwand Oil on canvas, 50.5 x 42.5 cm
Bezeichnet unten rechts Inscribed lower right:
Berthe Morisot
Inv.-Nr. Inv. no.: WRM Dep. FC 614

Der Hafen von Nizza, 1881/82
The Harbor of Nice
Le Port de Nice
Öl auf Leinwand Oil on canvas, 41 x 55 cm
Bezeichnet unten rechts Inscribed lower right:
Berthe Morisot
Inv.-Nr. Inv. no.: WRM Dep. FC 710

Gabriele Münter

Villa in Sèvres, ca. 1906
Öl auf Leinwand Oil on canvas, 17.5 x 25.5 cm
Bezeichnet unten rechts Inscribed lower right: M
Inv.-Nr. Inv. no.: WRM Dep. FC 717

Edvard Munch

Åsgårdstrand, 1888/90
Öl auf Fichtenholz Oil on spruce, 24.7 x 35.2 cm
Bezeichnet unten links Inscribed lower left:
E Munch
Inv.-Nr. Inv. no.: WRM Dep. FC 718

Vier Mädchen auf der Brücke, 1905
Four Girls on the Bridge
Öl auf Leinwand Oil on canvas, 126 x 126 cm
Bezeichnet unten rechts Inscribed lower right:
E Munch; darüber above that: E Munch
(E und M ligiert E and M ligated) 1905
Inv.-Nr. Inv. no.: WRM 2816

Hippolyte Petitjean

Die Brücke, ca. 1890
The Bridge
Le Pont
Öl auf Leinwand Oil on canvas, 65.7 x 100.5 cm
Bezeichnet unten rechts Inscribed lower right:
hipp. Petitjean
Inv.-Nr. Inv. no.: WRM Dep. 816

Ländliche Szene, ca. 1898
Rural Scene
Scène champêtre
Öl auf Holz Oil on wood, 19 x 25.5 cm
Bezeichnet unten rechts Inscribed lower right:
Atelier / Hipp Petitjean
Inv.-Nr. Inv. no.: WRM Dep. FC 675

Die drei Grazien, 1917
The Three Graces
Les trois grâces
Öl auf Karton Oil on cardboard, 37.5 x 30.5 cm
Bezeichnet unten rechts Inscribed lower right:
Hipp. Petitjean.
Inv.-Nr. Inv. no.: WRM Dep. FC 676

Francis Picabia

Morgensonne im Herbst, ca. 1898
Morning Sun in Autumn
Effet d'automne, soleil du matin
Öl auf Leinwand Oil on canvas, 73.6 x 91.5 cm
Bezeichnet unten links Inscribed lower left:
Picabia.
Inv.-Nr. Inv. no.: WRM Dep. FC 677

Moret-sur-Loing im Winter, 1907
Moret-sur-Loing in Winter
Moret-sur-Loing, en hiver
Öl auf Leinwand Oil on canvas, 55 x 65 cm
Bezeichnet unten rechts Inscribed lower right:
Picabia
Inv.-Nr. Inv. no.: WRM Dep. FC 728

Der Hafen von Saint-Tropez im Sonnenlicht, 1909
The Harbor of Saint-Tropez in the Sunlight
Le Port de Saint-Tropez, effet de soleil
Öl auf Leinwand Oil on canvas, 89.8 x 117.2 cm
Bezeichnet oben links Inscribed upper left:
Picabia 1909
Inv.-Nr. Inv. no.: WRM Dep. FC 728

Camille Pissarro

L'Hermitage bei Pontoise, 1867
The Hermitage at Pontoise
L'Hermitage à Pontoise
Öl auf Leinwand Oil on canvas, 91 x 150.5 cm
Bezeichnet unten rechts Inscribed lower right:
C. Pissarro. 1867
Inv.-Nr. Inv. no.: WRM 3119

Obstgarten in Pontoise bei Sonnenuntergang, 1878
Orchard in Pontoise at Sunset
Verger à Pontoise, soleil couchant
Öl auf Leinwand Oil on canvas, 46.7 x 55.2 cm
Bezeichnet unten rechts Inscribed lower right:
Pissarro 1878
Inv.-Nr. Inv. no.: WRM Dep. FC 712

Bauernhof in Bazincourt, 1884
Farm in Bazincourt
Ferme à Bazincourt
Öl auf Leinwand Oil on canvas, 54 x 65 cm
Bezeichnet unten links Inscribed lower left:
C.P.
Inv.-Nr. Inv. no.: WRM Dep. FC 693

Obstgarten in Varengeville, 1899
Orchard in Varengeville
Un Clos à Varengeville
Öl auf Leinwand Oil on canvas, 47 x 56 cm
Bezeichnet unten links Inscribed lower left:
C. Pissarro. 99
Inv.-Nr. Inv. no.: WRM Dep. 850

Lucien Pissarro

Bauernhäuser in der Bretagne, Riec, 1910
Brittany Cottages, Riec
Öl auf Leinwand Oil on canvas, 46 x 55 cm
Atelierstempel und Datierung unten rechts
Studio stamp and date lower right
Inv.-Nr. Inv. no.: WRM Dep. FC 702

Leon Pourtau

Tal im Frühling, 1893
Valley in Spring
Vallée au printemps
Öl auf Leinwand Oil on canvas, 73.7 x 92.4 cm
Bezeichnet unten rechts Inscribed lower right:
LP 93
Inv.-Nr. Inv. no.: WRM Dep. FC 679

Die Kapelle von Sainte-Adresse, ca. 1897
The Chapel of Sainte-Adresse
La Chapelle de Sainte-Adresse
Öl auf Leinwand Oil on canvas, 33 x 41 cm
Bezeichnet unten rechts Inscribed lower right:
L. POURTAU
Inv.-Nr. Inv. no.: WRM Dep. FC 678

Fernand Loyen du Puigaudeau

Sonnenuntergang bei Croisic, bretonische Landschaft, 1895
Sunset at Croisic, Breton Landscape
Coucher du soleil au Croisic, paysage de Bretagne
Öl auf Leinwand Oil on canvas, 65 x 81 cm
Bezeichnet unten rechts Inscribed lower right:
F. du Puigaudeau
Inv.-Nr. Inv. no.: WRM Dep. FC 616

Blühende Apfelbäume, ca. 1900
Apple Trees in Bloom
Les Pommiers en fleurs
Öl auf Leinwand Oil on canvas, 60 x 73 cm
Bezeichnet unten rechts Inscribed lower right:
F. du Puigaudeau
Inv.-Nr. Inv. no.: WRM Dep. FC 789

Beim Pflücken der Stockrosen, ca. 1904
Picking Hollyhocks
La Cueillette des roses trémières
Öl auf Leinwand Oil on canvas, 66 x 92 cm
Bezeichnet unten rechts Inscribed lower right:
F. du Puigaudeau

Der Markusplatz in Venedig bei Nacht, o. J.
Piazza San Marco in Venice at Night, n.d.
La Place Saint-Marc à Venise, la nuit
Öl auf Leinwand Oil on canvas, 63.8 x 79.4 cm
Bezeichnet unten links Inscribed lower left:
F. du Puigaudeau
Inv.-Nr. Inv. no.: WRM Dep. FC 713

Jean-François Raffaelli

Notre-Dame, Paris, ca. 1890
Notre-Dame de Paris
Notre-Dame de Paris, vue de la Seine
Öl auf Leinwand Oil on canvas, 65 x 81 cm
Bezeichnet unten links Inscribed lower left:
J F RAFFAËLLI

Odilon Redon

Der Kampf mit dem Drachen, ca. 1907
Saint George and the Dragon
Saint Georges et le dragon
Öl auf Pappelholz Oil on poplar, 29.5 x 27 cm
Bezeichnet unten rechts Inscribed lower right:
Odilon Redon
Inv.-Nr. Inv. no.: WRM 2812

Die Gefangene, 1910
The Prisoner
La Captive
Öl auf Leinwand Oil on canvas, 50.5 x 65.5 cm
Bezeichnet unten links Inscribed lower left:
Odilon Redon
Inv.-Nr. Inv. no.: WRM 2957

Schmetterlinge, 1910
Butterflies
Papillons
Öl auf Karton Oil on cardboard, 35 x 26.6 cm
Bezeichnet unten rechts Inscribed lower right:
Odilon Redon
Inv.-Nr. Inv. no.: WRM Dep. 856

Auguste Renoir

Ein Paar im Grünen, ca. 1868
The Fiancés
Les Fiancés
Öl auf Leinwand Oil on canvas, 105 x 75 cm
Bezeichnet unten links Inscribed lower left:
Renoir
Inv.-Nr. Inv. no.: WRM 1199

Die Ufer der Seine bei Rueil, 1879
On the Banks of the Seine at Rueil
Paysage au bord de la Seine à Rueil
Öl auf Holz Oil on wood, 38 x 66 cm
Bezeichnet unten links Inscribed lower left:
Renoir 79
Inv.-Nr. Inv. no.: WRM Dep. FC 790

Ruhender Akt, 1890/95
Resting Nude
Öl auf Leinwand Oil on canvas, 46 x 63 cm
Bezeichnet oben rechts Inscribed upper right:
Renoir
Inv.-Nr. Inv. no.: WRM 3177

Jean Renoir nähend, 1900
Jean Renoir Sewing
Jean Renoir, cousant
Öl auf Leinwand Oil on canvas, 55 x 46 cm
Bezeichnet unten links Inscribed lower left:
Renoir.
Inv.-Nr. Inv. no.: WRM Dep. FC 680

Villeneuve-les-Avignon, 1901
Öl auf Leinwand Oil on canvas, 33 x 53.5 cm
Bezeichnet unten rechts Inscribed lower right:
Renoir
Inv.-Nr. Inv. no.: WRM Dep. FC 791

Landschaftsstudie, o. J.
Landscape Study, n.d.
Öl auf Leinwand Oil on canvas, 13.2 x 15 cm
Inv.-Nr. Inv. no.: WRM 3550

Antoine de la Rochefoucauld

Neoimpressionistische Landschaft, 1898
Neo-Impressionist Landscape
Paysage néo-impressionniste
Öl auf Leinwand Oil on canvas, 50.5 x 35.5 cm
Bezeichnet unten rechts Inscribed lower right:
A. de la Rochefoucauld. – Janvier 1898
Inv.-Nr. Inv. no.: WRM Dep. FC 668

Christian Rohlfs

Waldweg im Winter (Chaussee nach Tiefurt im Webicht bei Weimar), 1889
Forest Path in Winter (Road to Tiefurt in Webicht near Weimar)
Öl auf Leinwand Oil on canvas, 59.5 x 74.5 cm
Bezeichnet unten rechts Inscribed lower right:
C R 89
Inv.-Nr. Inv. no.: WRM 2460

Obstbäume im Schnee (Am Sandweg vor Weimar-Ehringsdorf), ca. 1898
Fruit Trees in the Snow
Öl auf Leinwand Oil on canvas, 60 x 77 cm
Inv.-Nr. Inv. no.: WRM 2523

Landschaft, 1903
Landscape
Öl auf Leinwand Oil on canvas, 62.3 x 77.4 cm
Bezeichnet unten rechts Inscribed lower right:
C Rohlfs 03
Inv.-Nr. Inv. no.: WRM Dep. FC 792

Türme von Soest, 1906
Steeples in Soest
Rückseite On reverse:
Weiblicher Akt *Female Nude*
Öl auf Karton Oil on cardboard, 67.5 x 97.5 cm
Inv.-Nr. Inv. no.: WRM 2765

Theo van Rysselberghe

Saint-Tropez, 1895
Öl auf Holz Oil on wood, 19 x 27 cm
Bezeichnet unten links Inscribed lower left:
VR (ligiert ligated); rückseitige Aufschrift inscription on reverse: van Rysselberghe – Saint-Tropez – 1895
Inv.-Nr. Inv. no.: WRM Dep. FC 793

Das Kap Gris-Nez oder *Sommernebel*, 1900
Cape Gris-Nez or *Summer Mist*
Le Cap Gris-Nez *ou* Brumes d'été
Öl auf Leinwand Oil on canvas, 65.5 x 81.6 cm
Bezeichnet unten links Inscribed lower left:
19 TVR (ligiert ligated) 00
Inv.-Nr. Inv. no.: WRM Dep. FC 714

Le Lavandou, Var, 1908
Öl auf Karton Oil on cardboard, 38 x 55.2 cm
Bezeichnet unten links Inscribed lower left:
VR (ligiert ligated) / 08; rückseitige Aufschrift inscription on reverse: Le Lavandou, dépt. du Var
Inv.-Nr. Inv. no.: WRM Dep. FC 617

Pinien in Monaco, 1917
Pines in Monaco
Pins à Monaco
Öl auf Karton Oil on cardboard, 32.8 x 40.8 cm
Bezeichnet unten rechts Inscribed lower right:
TVR (ligiert ligated) / 1917
Inv.-Nr. Inv. no.: WRM Dep. FC 703

Claude-Emile Schuffenecker

Träumendes Kind am Meer, bei Sonnenuntergang, 1884
Child Dreaming on the Seashore at Sunset
Enfant rêvant devant la mer, au coucher de soleil
Öl auf Leinwand Oil on canvas, 54.1 x 65 cm
Bezeichnet unten rechts Inscribed lower right:
E. Schuffenecker / 1884
Inv.-Nr. Inv. no.: WRM Dep. FC 694

Figur in bretonischer Heidelandschaft (Weg über einen blühenden Hügel oder *Der ansteigende Weg)*, 1886
Figure in a Breton Heathland (Path over a Hill in Bloom or *The Ascending Path)*
Personnage dans la lande bretonne (Le chemin traversant la colline en fleurs *ou* Le chemin montant)
Öl auf Leinwand Oil on canvas, 46.2 x 55.7 cm
Bezeichnet mit Atelierstempel unten links
Inscribed with studio stamp, lower left:
E (Lotusblüte lotus blossom) S
Inv.-Nr. Inv. no.: WRM Dep. FC 681

Seetang-Sammlerinnen (Am Fuße der Klippen oder *Zwei bretonische Frauen am Strand bei Ebbe)*, 1888
Kelp Gatherers (At the Foot of the Cliffs or *Two Breton Women on the Beach at Low Tide)*
Les Ramasseuses de varech (Au pied des falaises *ou* Deux bretonnes sur la plage, marée basse)
Öl auf Leinwand Oil on canvas, 53.8 x 73 cm
Bezeichnet unten rechts Inscribed lower right:
E. Schuffenecker / 1888
Inv.-Nr. Inv. no.: WRM Dep. FC 795

Notre-Dame von Paris (Notre-Dame im Schnee), 1889
Notre-Dame de Paris (Notre-Dame in the Snow)
Notre-Dame de Paris (Notre-Dame par la neige *ou* Notre-Dame sous la neige)
Öl auf Leinwand Oil on canvas, 73.6 x 54.2 cm
Bezeichnet unten links Inscribed lower left:
E. Schuffenecker / 89
Inv.-Nr. Inv. no.: WRM Dep. FC 796

Paul Serusier

Stillleben mit Birnen, 1923
Still Life with Pears
Nature morte aux poires
Öl auf Leinwand Oil on canvas, 35.5 x 53.5 cm
Bezeichnet unten links Inscribed lower left:
P Sérusier / 23
Inv.-Nr. Inv. no.: WRM Dep. FC 797

Georges Seurat

Gestalt in einer Landschaft bei Barbizon, ca. 1882
Figure in a Landscape at Barbizon
Figure massive dans un paysage à Barbizon
Öl auf Pappelholz Oil on poplar, 15.5 x 24.8 cm
Rückseitige Aufschrift Inscription on reverse:
G. Seurat. Barbizon. RC 024
Inv.-Nr. Inv. no.: WRM Dep. FC 705

Straßenszene, ca. 1883
Street Scene
Dans la rue
Öl auf Holz Oil on wood, 16.5 x 24.7 cm
Inv.-Nr. Inv. no.: WRM Dep. 822

Henri le Sidaner

Brunnen in den Tuilerien, ca. 1900
Fountain in the Tuileries
La Fontaine aux Tuileries
Bleistift und Öl auf Papier, aufgezogen auf Leinwand Pencil and oil on paper mounted on canvas, 21.3 x 18.1 cm
Bezeichnet unten links Inscribed lower left:
Le SiDANER
Inv.-Nr. Inv. no.: WRM Dep. FC 768

Pavillon mit Rosen – Gerberoy, nach 1902
Pavilion with Roses – Gerberoy, after 1902
Le Pavillon aux roses, Gerberoy
Öl auf Leinwand Oil on canvas, 73 x 60 cm
Bezeichnet unten rechts Inscribed lower right:
Le SiDANER.

Der »Weiße Garten« von Gerberoy in der Dämmerung, ca. 1907
The "White Garden" of Gerberoy at Dusk
Le Jardin blanc au crépuscule à Gerberoy
Öl auf Papier über Holz Oil on paper mounted on wood, 34 x 41.5 cm
Bezeichnet unten rechts Inscribed lower right:
Le SIDANER
Inv.-Nr. Inv. no.: WRM Dep. FC 587

Haus mit Rosen in Versailles, 1918
House with Roses in Versailles
La Maison aux roses, Versailles
Öl auf Leinwand Oil on canvas, 108.8 x 91 cm
Bezeichnet unten links Inscribed lower left:
Le SIDANER
Inv.-Nr. Inv. no.: WRM Dep. FC 704

Verschneiter kleiner Platz in Chartres, 1919
Small Square in Chartres in the Snow
Petite place à la neige, Chartres
Öl auf Leinwand Oil on canvas, 60.5 x 73.5 cm
Bezeichnet unten rechts Inscribed lower right:
Le SIDANER
Inv.-Nr. Inv. no.: WRM Dep. FC 769

Paul Signac

Die Seine bei Courbevoie (Flusslandschaft), 1883
The Seine at Courbevoie (Riverscape)
La Seine à Courbevoie (Paysage de rivière)
Öl auf Leinwand Oil on canvas, 45.2 x 81.7 cm
Bezeichnet unten links Inscribed lower left:
P. Signac / 83 / Neuilly
Inv.-Nr. Inv. no.: WRM Dep. FC 798

Saint-Tropez, Windstille, 1895
Saint-Tropez, Calm
Saint-Tropez, calme
Öl auf Holz Oil on wood, 18.5 x 27.2 cm
Bezeichnet unten rechts Inscribed lower right:
P. Signac
Inv.-Nr. Inv. no.: WRM Dep. FC 683

Capo di Noli, 1898
Öl auf Leinwand Oil on canvas, 93.5 x 75 cm
Bezeichnet unten links Inscribed lower left:
98 P. Signac
Inv.-Nr. Inv. no.: WRM Dep. FC 682

Samois, Studie Nr. 8 (Die Seine bei Samois), 1899
Samois, Study No. 8 (The Seine at Samois)
Samois, Etude n° 8 (La Seine à Samois)
Öl auf Leinwand über Karton Oil on canvas mounted on cardboard, 27.1 x 34.7 cm
Inv.-Nr. Inv. no.: WRM Dep. FC 684

Der Hafen von Concarneau, 1933
The Harbor at Concarneau
Concarneau, le port
Öl auf Leinwand Oil on canvas, 53 x 73.5 cm
Bezeichnet unten rechts Inscribed lower right:
P. Signac
Inv.-Nr. Inv. no.: WRM Dep. FC 656

Alfred Sisley

Brücke bei Hampton Court, 1874
Bridge at Hampton Court
Le Pont de Hampton Court
Öl auf Leinwand Oil on canvas, 45.5 x 61 cm
Bezeichnet unten links Inscribed lower left:
Sisley. 74
Inv.-Nr. Inv. no.: WRM 2929

Umgebung von Louveciennes, 1876
The Environs of Louveciennes
Environs de Louveciennes
Öl auf Leinwand Oil on canvas, 61 x 46 cm
Bezeichnet unten rechts Inscribed lower right:
Sisley · 76
Inv.-Nr. Inv. no.: WRM Dep. FC 707

Am Waldrand – Les Sablons, ca. 1884/85
At the Edge of the Forest – Les Sablons
A la lisière de la forêt – Les Sablons
Öl auf Leinwand Oil on canvas, 54.5 x 65.5 cm
Bezeichnet unten rechts Inscribed lower right:
Sisley
Inv.-Nr. Inv. no.: WRM Dep. 851

Die Bucht von Langland, 1897
Langland Bay
La Baie de Langland
Öl auf Leinwand Oil on canvas, 54 x 65 cm
Bezeichnet unten rechts Inscribed lower right:
Sisley – 97
Inv.-Nr. Inv. no.: WRM Dep. FC 618

Max Slevogt

Französischer Kürassier zu Pferd, 1909
French Cuirassier on Horseback
Öl auf Leinwand Oil on canvas, 99.5 x 80.5 cm
Bezeichnet unten links Inscribed lower left:
Slevogt 09
Inv.-Nr. Inv. no.: WRM 1188

Weinlaube auf Neukastel, 1917
Vine Bower in Neukastel
Öl auf Lindenholz Oil on limewood, 61 x 49.5 cm
Bezeichnet unten rechts Inscribed lower right:
21. Sept. 17.
Inv.-Nr. Inv. no.: WRM 2596

Kirschenernte, Blick von Neukastel nach Süden, 1926
Cherry Harvest, View from Neukastel to the South
Öl auf Leinwand Oil on canvas, 90.5 x 116 cm
Bezeichnet unten rechts Inscribed lower right:
Slevogt / 1926
Inv.-Nr. Inv. no.: WRM 2361

Nicolas Tarkhoff

Boulevard St. Denis, 1901
Öl auf Leinwand Oil on canvas, 57 x 80 cm
Bezeichnet unten links Inscribed lower left:
N. Tarkhoff
Inv.-Nr. Inv. no.: WRM Dep. FC 799

Ein Morgen im Frühling (Der Maler in seinem Garten), ca. 1911
A Morning in Spring (The Painter in his Garden)
Le Matin au printemps (Le Peintre dans son jardin)
Öl auf Leinwand Oil on canvas, 80.3 x 65 cm
Bezeichnet unten links Inscribed lower left:
N. Tarkhoff
Inv.-Nr. Inv. no.: WRM Dep. FC 800

Henri de Toulouse-Lautrec

Fischerboot, 1880
Fishing Boat
Barque de pêche
Öl auf Holz Oil on wood, 14 x 23.5 cm
Inv.-Nr. Inv. no.: WRM Dep. FC 719

Nizza – Auf der »Promenade des Anglais«, 1880
Nice – On the "Promenade des Anglais"
Nice – Sur la Promenade des Anglais
Öl auf Karton Oil on cardboard, 32 x 39.5 cm
Bezeichnet unten links Inscribed lower left:
TL Nice 1880
Inv.-Nr. Inv. no.: WRM Dep. 848

Heinrich Wilhelm Trübner

Auf Frauenchiemsee, ca. 1891
On Frauenchiemsee
Öl auf Leinwand Oil on canvas, 62 x 76 cm
Bezeichnet unten rechts Inscribed lower right:
W. Trübner.
Inv.-Nr. Inv. no.: WRM 2375

Fritz von Uhde

Die drei Töchter des Malers im Garten, ca. 1885
The Painter's Three Daughters in the Garden
Öl auf Leinwand Oil on canvas, 55 x 67 cm
Bezeichnet unten links Inscribed lower left:
F v Uhde
Inv.-Nr. Inv. no.: WRM 1184

Maurice Utrillo

Der Zirkus oder *Fest von Vaugirard*, 1927
The Circus or *The Festival of Vaugirard*
Le Cirque *ou* La Fête de Vaugirard
Öl auf Leinwand Oil on canvas, 60.2 x 81.2 cm
Bezeichnet unten links Inscribed lower left:
Maurice. Utrillo. V. 1927.
Inv.-Nr. Inv. no.: WRM Dep. FC 801

Felix Vallotton

Umgebung von Bex, das Tal von St. Maurice, 1909
The Environs of Bex, the Valley of St. Maurice
Environs de Bex, défilé de St. Maurice
Öl auf Leinwand Oil on canvas, 37.5 x 52 cm
Bezeichnet unten rechts Inscribed lower right:
F. VALLOTTON. 09

Louis Valtat

Unterholz, ca. 1898
Undergrowth
Sous-bois
Öl auf Leinwand Oil on canvas, 65.5 x 54.5 cm
Bezeichnet unten links Inscribed lower left:
L. Valtat
Inv.-Nr. Inv. no.: WRM Dep. 802

Der Fährmann, ca. 1905
The Ferryman
Le Passeur
Öl auf Leinwand Oil on canvas, 65.4 x 81.2 cm
Bezeichnet unten rechts Inscribed lower right:
L.V.
Inv.-Nr. Inv. no.: WRM Dep. FC 803

Maurice de Vlaminck

Die Brücke von Chatou, 1908
The Bridge at Chatou
Le Pont de Chatou
Öl auf Leinwand Oil on canvas, 46.4 x 55.3 cm
Bezeichnet unten rechts Inscribed lower right:
Vlaminck
Inv.-Nr. Inv. no.: WRM Dep. FC 729

Edouard Vuillard

Mädchen am Wäscheschrank, ca. 1894/95
Girl at the Linen Cupboard
Öl auf Karton auf Holz aufgeklebt Oil on cardboard mounted on wood, 37 x 33.5 cm
Bezeichnet unten rechts Inscribed lower right:
EV
Inv.-Nr. Inv. no.: WRM 3049

Heuhaufen im »Jardin des Etincelles« in Criqueboeuf, 1902
Haystacks in the "Jardin des Etincelles" in Criqueboeuf
Les Meules au jardin des Etincelles à Criqueboeuf
Öl auf Karton über Holz Oil on cardboard mounted on wood, 37.6 x 54 cm
Bezeichnet unten rechts Inscribed lower right:
E Vuillard
Inv.-Nr. Inv. no.: WRM Dep. FC 817

Bildnis der Schauspielerin Lucie Belin (Frau im Atelier), 1914/15
Portrait of the Actress Lucie Belin (Woman in the Studio)
Öl auf Papier, auf Leinwand aufgezogen
Oil on paper mounted on canvas, 85.5 x 94 cm
Bezeichnet unten links Inscribed lower left:
E. Vuillard
Inv.-Nr. Inv. no.: WRM 3145

Heinrich von Zügel

Rindvieh, 1900
Cattle
Öl auf Leinwand Oil on canvas, 40 x 55 cm
Bezeichnet unten rechts Inscribed lower right:
JH (ligiert ligated) Zügel 1900
Inv.-Nr. Inv. no.: WRM 2439

ARTISTS' BIOGRAPHIES

KÜNSTLER-BIOGRAFIEN

Charles Angrand
(Criquetot-sur-Ouville 1854 – 1926 Rouen)

Ab 1870 besuchte der ausgebildete Lehrer Angrand die Kunstakademie von Rouen, und seine Malerei war zunächst von einer durchaus konventionell zu nennenden Bildauffassung geprägt. Sein Schaffen war deutlich vom künstlerischen Vorbild Edouard Manets beeinflusst, und seine Maltechnik stand jener der Impressionisten nahe.
Erst als Angrand 1882 nach Paris zog und in Kontakt mit den Neoimpressionisten Seurat und Signac trat, vollzog sich ein Wandel in seinem Kunstschaffen, indem er sich der pointillistischen Malweise in konsequent gesetzten Farbtupfen zuwandte. 1884 zählte er zu den Gründungsmitgliedern der Société des artistes indépendants, an deren Pariser Ausstellungen er 1887 und 1901 teilnahm.
Ab 1891 malte Angrand allerdings nicht mehr ausschließlich im neoimpressionistischen Stil, und in den folgenden zehn Jahren widmete er sich überwiegend der Kohle- und Kreidezeichnung. Er ließ sich in dieser Zeit in der Normandie nieder, wo er 1901 auch wieder die Ölmalerei aufnahm. Fortan malte er Bilder sowohl in impressionistischer als auch in neoimpressionistischer Manier.
Angrand war gezwungen, lebenslang neben seiner Malerei seinen erlernten Beruf des Mathematiklehrers auszuüben, um seinen Lebensunterhalt zu sichern.

Educated as a teacher, Angrand enrolled at the art academy in Rouen in 1870, and his early painting reflects a thoroughly conventional approach to the visual image. His art was clearly influenced by the work of Edouard Manet, and his painting technique had much in common with that of the Impressionists.
It was not until Angrand moved to Paris in 1882 and established contact with the Neo-Impressionists Seurat and Signac that a change became evident in his art, as he adopted a Pointillist style that relied on the rigorous application of small daubs of paint. He became a founding member of the Société des Artistes Indépendants in 1883 and participated in the society's Paris exhibitions in 1887 and 1901.
Beginning in 1891, Angrand's technique was no longer exclusively Neo-Impressionist, and over the following ten years, he devoted himself primarily to charcoal and chalk drawing. He moved to Normandy during this period, where he once again turned his attention to oil painting in 1901. From that point on, his oeuvre included paintings executed in both an Impressionist and Neo-Impressionist style.
Aside from his painting, his entire life, Angrand was compelled to earn his living as a teacher of mathematics.

Paul Baum
(Meißen 1859 – 1932 San Gimignano)

Paul Baum absolvierte ab 1877 ein Kunststudium in Weimar und Dresden. In seinem Frühwerk zeigt sich deutlich das Vorbild der Pleinairmalerei der Schule von Barbizon, ab 1890 wird der Einfluss des Impressionismus sichtbar. Der persönliche Kontakt zu Pissarro und van Rysselberghe ab 1894 führte Baum um 1900 zu einer individuellen neoimpressionistischen Stilform. Diese Phase dauerte bis etwa 1909, später wandte sich der Maler allmählich von der konsequent pointillistischen Technik ab.
1902 wurde er Mitglied der Berliner Sezession. Nach Professuren an den Kunstakademien in Dresden und Kassel zwischen 1914 und 1921 zog Paul Baum 1924 in den Süden und ließ sich in seiner neuen Wahlheimat Italien in San Gimignano nieder, wo er 1932 starb.

Paul Baum gilt – neben Curt Herrmann – bis heute als der bedeutendste Vertreter der neoimpressionistischen Kunstrichtung in Deutschland.

Baum studied art in Weimar and Dresden beginning in 1877. While his early work clearly exhibits the influence of the plein-air painters of the Barbizon School, a shift toward Impressionism becomes evident in 1890. His personal contact with Pissarro and van Rysselberghe, whom he met in 1894, led Baum to adopt an individual form of Neo-Impressionism around 1900. This phase lasted until roughly 1909, after which time the painter gradually abandoned the rigorous Pointillist technique.
He joined the Berlin Secession in 1902. Following tenures as a professor at the art academies in Dresden and Kassel between 1914 and 1921, Paul Baum moved to southern Europe in 1924 and settled in his newly adopted home of San Gimignano in Italy, where he died in 1932.
Besides Curt Herrmann, Paul Baum is regarded as the most significant representative of Neo-Impressionist art in Germany.

Jean-Frederic Bazille

(Montpellier 1841 – 1870 Beaune-la-Rolande)

Bazille kam 1862 nach Paris, wo er im Atelier von Charles Gleyre die Malerkollegen Renoir, Sisley und Monet kennenlernte. Schnell bildeten die vier eine Gruppe, die sich von den anderen Schülern absonderte, weil sie dem akademischen Geist nicht gerecht zu werden schienen, der im gleyreschen Atelier vorherrschte. Gefühlsmäßig empfanden sie gewisse Widersprüche mit den Lehren Gleyres und suchten sich mit der Zeit immer mehr von diesen akademischen Prinzipien zu befreien. 1864 arbeiteten die vier Künstler erstmals gemeinsam vor der Natur, in Chailly, einer Ortschaft am Rande des Waldes von Fontainebleau, in der Nähe von Barbizon gelegen. Sie trafen hier auch auf einige der älteren Meister von Barbizon, von denen sie weitere Anregungen empfingen. Nach diesen Erfahrungen verließ Bazille in den folgenden Jahren immer wieder sein Studio und malte zeitweise in der freien Natur; allerdings ist er eher für seine Porträts und seine Figurenmalerei bekannt denn für seine Landschaften. Bazille fiel 1870, nur 29-jährig, als Freiwilliger im Deutsch-Französischen Krieg.

Bazille came to Paris in 1862, where he became acquainted with fellow painters Renoir, Sisley, and Monet at Charles Gleyre's studio. The four soon formed a group that stood apart from the other students, as they appeared unwilling to accept the academic spirit that prevailed there. They felt a certain emotional resistance to Gleyre's teachings, and as time passed, they strove increasingly to liberate themselves from his academic principles. The four artists first worked together in a natural setting in 1864 in Chailly, a town at the edge of the Forest of Fontainebleau near Barbizon. There they also met some of the older masters of Barbizon, from whom they drew further inspiration for their work. Encouraged by those experiences, Bazille often left his studio to paint outdoors during the years that followed, although he is better known for his portraits and figures than for his landscapes. Bazille volunteered for military service during the Franco-Prussian war and was killed in battle at the young age of twenty-nine.

Max Beckmann

(Leipzig 1884 – 1950 New York)

Beckmanns Anfänge als Maler waren noch deutlich geprägt von der malerischen Auseinandersetzung mit Naturerscheinungen. Vorübergehend ließ er sich dabei auf moderne postimpressionistische Techniken ein; auch den malerischen Stil des deutschen Impressionismus eignete er sich teilweise an, wobei Pastosität der Farbe, skizzenhafte Anlage oder flüssige Primamalerei, wie man sie bei den Impressionisten finden kann, in seinen Bildern fehlen.
Zwischen 1900 und 1903 durch seinen Lehrer an der Kunstschule in Weimar, Carl Frithjof Smith, in die Landschaftsmalerei eingeführt, eröffnete eine anschließende Reise nach Paris dem jungen Beckmann auch die Malerei der französischen Impressionisten. Vorübergehend malte er mit impressionistischem Pinselschwung, der aber schon bald wieder einem festeren, in geschlossenen Formen gesetzten Duktus weichen sollte. Damit einhergehend verminderte sich das impressionistische Interesse an den Wirkungen des Lichts.
Zu der expressionistischen Bewegung innerhalb der jungen, aufstrebenden Künstlergeneration auf Distanz gehend, wurde Beckmann in seinem Stil gleichwohl vom Expressionismus beeinflusst, und wie die Expressionisten neigte er in seiner Formensprache zu einfachen, unverbildeten Formen, die die künstlerischen Äußerungen besonders unmittelbar und unverstellt zum Ausdruck kommen lassen sollten. Zu der expressionistischen Gestaltungsweise fand Beckmann, der stets ein künstlerischer Einzelgänger bleiben sollte, erst nach dem Ersten Weltkrieg, dessen Erlebnisse den Maler zutiefst erschütterten. Fortan schuf er jene rätselhaft-hintergründigen Bilder des menschlichen Daseins, für die er berühmt wurde.

Beckmann's early years as a painter were still clearly characterized by his interest in painting natural phenomena. For a time, he experimented with modern, Post-Impressionist techniques, adopting aspects of the painting style of the German Impressionists, although evidence of the use of impasto, sketchy composition schemes, and a spontaneous *alla prima* technique is lacking in his paintings.
Introduced to landscape painting by Carl Frithjof Smith, his teacher at the art school in Weimar between 1900 and 1903, the young Beckmann was also exposed to the work of the French Impressionists during a subsequent trip to Paris. He painted for a while with the energetic brush of the Impressionists but soon returned to a more compact style with clearly delineated forms. His Impressionist-inspired interest in the effects of light also waned accordingly.
Although he distanced himself from the Expressionist movement that emerged within a new generation of ambitious young artists, Beckmann's style nonetheless exhibited aspects of Expressionism, and like the Expressionists, he tended to favor a visual language comprised of simple, non-depictive forms that would express his artistic statements with greater immediacy and authenticity. Under the influence of his profoundly disturbing experiences during the war years, Beckmann, who remained a lone wolf in the art scene throughout his life, did not adopt an Expressionist style until after World War One. In the years that followed, he created the enigmatic, probing images of human existence for which he would become famous.

Emile Bernard

(Lille 1868 – 1941 Paris)

Nachdem er 1886 aufgrund des Vorwurfs undisziplinierten Verhaltens des Ateliers des Pariser Malers Fernand Cormon verwiesen wurde, ging der junge Bernard nach Pont-Aven, wo er die Bekanntschaft Paul Gauguins machte. Bernards Bewunderung für das reiche Erbe mittelalterlicher Kultur in der Bretagne wie auch seine beginnende Freundschaft mit Gauguin sollten die Richtung seines weiteren künstlerischen Schaffens deutlich bestimmen.

Nach einer kurzen pointillistischen Periode entwickelte er 1887/88 eine Malerei, die mit nur geringfügig modellierten, klar umrissenen Farbflächen den dekorativen Charakter eines Motivs betonte. Dieser Stil, der auf die Glasmalerei der Gotik zurückging und darüber hinaus deutlich beeinflusst war vom japanischen Holzschnitt, erhielt die Bezeichnung Style cloisonné. Als Gauguin 1888 nach Pont-Aven zurückkehrte und hier den endgültigen Bruch mit dem Impressionismus vollzog, führte Bernard den Freund in die künstlerischen Ideen des Cloisonismus ein. Gemeinsam arbeiteten beide an einer weiteren Ausformung dieses Stils, und auf der Grundlage des Style cloisonné entstand die Kunstform des Synthetismus. Die enge Zusammenarbeit Bernards und Gauguins endete 1891 in einem heftigen Streit, weil Bernard seinen künstlerischen Beitrag zur Entwicklung des Synthetismus als missachtet ansah; Gauguin beanspruchte uneingeschränkt die Stellung als alleiniger Begründer des Synthetismus für sich und wurde zur künstlerischen Leitfigur innerhalb der Gruppe von Pont-Aven.

Nach der Abkehr vom Künstlerkreis um Gauguin bemühte sich Bernard intensiv um die Reputation der Kunst seines gerade verstorbenen Freundes Vincent van Gogh. Neben der Malerei widmete er sich auch dem Holzschnitt, dem kunstgewerblichen Zeichnen und der Buchkunst, zudem verfasste er Novellen und Theaterstücke.

Having been accused of a lack of discipline and expelled from the studio of Paris painter Fernand Cormon in 1886, the young Bernard went to Pont-Aven, where he met Gauguin. His admiration for the rich heritage of medieval culture in Brittany and his budding friendship with Gauguin had a considerable formative impact on his art during the following years.

After a brief Pointillist period, he developed a style of painting in 1887/88 in which he emphasized the decorative character of his motifs with clearly outlined fields of color that exhibit little modeling. This style, which traced its roots to Gothic glass painting and was also markedly influenced by Japanese woodcut art, was referred to as *style cloisonné*.

When Gauguin returned to Pont-Aven in 1888 and made his final break with Impressionism, Bernard introduced his friend to the artistic principles of Cloisonnism. The two worked together in refining the technique, and *style cloisonné* became the foundation for the new current known as Synthetism. The period of close collaboration between Bernard and Gauguin ended in a heated dispute in 1891. Bernard felt that his artistic contribution to Synthetism had been ignored. Gauguin claimed recognition as the sole founder of Synthetism and became the leading figure in the artists' group in Pont-Aven.

After abandoning the circle of artists associated with Gauguin, Bernard committed himself to promoting the reputation of his recently deceased friend Vincent van Gogh. Aside from painting, he also devoted himself to woodcutting, industrial design drawing, and book art in addition to authoring several novellas and plays.

Albert Besnard
(Paris 1849 – 1934 Paris)

Ausgebildet an der Ecole des Beaux-Arts als Schüler von Alexandre Cabanel, schuf Besnard zu Beginn seiner künstlerischen Laufbahn vorwiegend großformatige Historienbilder im Stile der französischen Kunst jener Zeit. Ab 1883 – nach der Rückkehr von einem dreijährigen Aufenthalt in London – wurde Besnards Schaffen mehr und mehr vom Impressionismus beeinflusst, einer Kunstrichtung, von der sich der Maler bis dahin deutlich distanziert hatte. Immer intensiver erprobte er die Möglichkeiten der Pleinairmalerei und gewann eine zunehmende Freiheit in der Anwendung der Farbe, während er sich von seinen Ursprüngen, der Kunst des offiziellen Salons, abwandte. Fortan hatte Besnards Schaffen – in Bildnissen, Freilichtbildern und dekorativen Kompositionen – als Quelle der Inspiration wie auch als vorherrschendes Thema die Stimmung des Lichts.

Das Gros der Werke Besnards wurde noch zu seinen Lebzeiten in Paris ausgestellt. Im Juni 1905 zeigte beispielsweise die dort ansässige Galerie Georges Petit eine umfassende Werkschau des Künstlers. Ab 1917 hatte Besnard die Position des Direktors der Académie de France in der Villa Medici in Rom inne.

Trained at the Ecole des Beaux-Arts under Alexandre Cabanel, Besnard produced primarily large-scale history paintings in the French style of the period. From 1883 onward—following his return from a three-year stay in London—the influence of Impressionism, a current in art from which the painter had previously clearly distanced himself, became increasingly evident in Besnard's art. With growing intensity, he explored the possibilities of plein-air painting and a more liberal use of color, as he gradually abandoned his own roots in the art of the official Salon. From that point on, the atmosphere of light served as the source of inspiration and the predominant theme in Besnard's portraits, outdoor scenes, and decorative compositions.

Most of Besnard's paintings were exhibited in Paris during his lifetime. The Galerie Georges Petit in Paris showed an extensive selection of the artist's works in June 1905. Besnard was appointed director of the Académie de France at the Villa Medici in Rome in 1917.

Pierre Bonnard
(Fontenay-aux-Roses/Seine 1867 – 1947 Le Cannet)

Bonnard widmete sich in seinem Werk hauptsächlich dem Interieur und der Landschaft. Seine anfänglich impressionistische, die Form auflösende Malweise änderte sich, bald nachdem er die Arbeiten von Gauguin und der Gruppe von Pont-Aven kennengelernt hatte. Gleichwohl sollte er sich nie gänzlich von den Prinzipien des Impressionismus lossagen. Überhaupt entzog sich Bonnards Kunst stets einer Einordnung in die vielen Stilrichtungen seiner Zeit. Er war kein Symbolist – selbst dann nicht, als er der Künstlergruppe der Nabis angehörte –, und er war erst recht kein Expressionist. Ebenso wenig stand er den Fauves nahe, und auch abstrakte Tendenzen lagen ihm fern. Früh schon waren Sammler auf ihn aufmerksam geworden, und so konnte er von seiner Kunst gut leben.

Einen Maler des bürgerlichen Glücks hat man den späten Bonnard genannt, denn seine Kunst war weder politisch, noch bewegte sie sich nach 1900 in den Bahnen des zeitgenössischen Kunstdiskurses. Doch tatsächlich führten sein stetes Bemühen um das eigentlich Malerische, um Faktur und Komposition und schließlich seine Beschäftigung mit Farbproblemen dazu, den Bildgegenstand im Bildgefüge nurmehr zum Anlass zu nehmen für die reine Darstellung von Licht und Farbe – eine Form einschleichender Abstraktion also, die in ihrer absichtsvollen Konsequenz ernsthaftere als nur dekorative Ziele verfolgte.

Schon vor dem Ersten Weltkrieg verlagerte Bonnard seinen Lebensmittelpunkt aus Paris in die Provinz und verzog schließlich 1925 nach Le Cannet an der Côte d'Azur, wo er 1947 starb.

Bonnard's oeuvre is composed primarily of interiors and landscapes. His early form-dissolving, Impressionist style changed soon after his first encounter with the works of Gauguin and the Pont-Aven group. Yet he never completely abandoned the principles of Impressionism. Bonnard's art consistently defied classification with reference to the various stylistic currents of his time. He was not a Symbolist—not even during the years of

his membership in the Nabi Group—and he was certainly not an Expressionist. He had little in common with the Fauvists and showed no interest in abstract tendencies. Collectors had discovered him in his early years, and thus he was able to live quite well from his art.
Late in his career, Bonnard earned a reputation as a painter of bourgeois contentment, for his art was neither political nor did it respond to contemporary currents of discourse on art after 1900. Yet his constant focus on the essential aspects of painting, on technique and composition, coupled with his concern with the problems of color, led him to regard the subject of his paintings as no more than the occasion for the pure depiction of light and color—in a gradually emerging form of abstraction whose deliberate consistency was devoted to more serious goals than that of mere decoration.
Bonnard moved from Paris to the countryside before the outbreak of World War One, eventually settling in Le Cannet on the Côte d'Azur in 1925, where he died in 1947.

François Bonvin
(Vaugirard 1817 – 1887 Saint-Germain-en-Laye)

Bonvin widmete sich hauptsächlich der Genremalerei und dem Stillleben. Zu seinen Schülern gehörte unter anderen der spätere Neoimpressionist Henri Edmond Cross. Bonvin vertrat eine Kunstauffassung, nach der der Bildgegenstand möglichst naturnah wiedergegeben werden sollte, schlicht aufgefasste Bildthemen charakterisieren sein Werk. Das Dargestellte lässt die genaue Beobachtung erkennen, der Bonvin das Bildsujet unterzog, wiewohl bei allem Realismus auch stets besonderes Augenmerk auf die Wirkung der Lichtstimmung gelegt ist.

Bonvin devoted himself primarily to genre and still-life painting. His students included the later Neo-Impressionist Henri Edmond Cross. Bonvin embraced a concept of art that called for the true-to-life depiction of the subject of a painting, and a straightforward rendering of pictorial themes is characteristic of his art. The painted image reflects Bonvin's precise observation of his subject, and he consistently emphasized the effects of specific atmospheres of light.

Eugene Boudin
(Honfleur 1824 – 1898 Deauville)

Wie die Maler von Barbizon so kann auch Eugène Boudin in seinen fortwährenden Bemühungen, die atmosphärischen und farblichen Veränderungen der Natur im Bild wiederzugeben, als ein Wegbereiter der Impressionisten angesehen werden.
Als Sohn eines Seemanns wuchs Boudin in Le Havre auf, und die Welt des Meeres prägte ihn für sein ganzes Leben. Dank einer finanziellen Unterstützung von Seiten der Stadt Le Havre kam der talentierte, aber mittellose Boudin nach Paris an die Kunstakademie, wo er Bildnis- und Landschaftsmalerei studierte. Drei Jahren später kehrte er nach Le Havre zurück.
Die Motive der nordfranzösischen Küste bildeten von nun an den Mittelpunkt seiner Malerei, und seine zahlreichen Marine- und Hafenbilder machten ihn berühmt. Die Wogen des Meeres und die verschiedenartigen Wolkenbildungen über der Küste stellten für ihn die bevorzugten Sujets dar, wobei er seine Malerei vor allem der Darstellung des Lichtspiels widmete. Boudin besaß einen besonderen Farbsinn, und die Frische der Farben und eine lebhafte Pinselführung zeugen von seiner Gewohnheit, in freier Natur zu malen und zu beobachten, welche Tonwerte die Dinge im Licht annehmen.
Bereits zu Lebzeiten war Boudin ein gefragter Künstler, seine Arbeit war stets von Erfolg und Anerkennung begleitet.

Like the painters of Barbizon, Boudin, who was consistently concerned with depicting shifts of atmosphere and color in nature, may be regarded as a forerunner of the Impressionist movement.
Born the son of a seaman, Boudin grew up in Le Havre, and he remained intensely interested in the world of the sea throughout his life. Thanks to financial support provided by the city of Le Havre, the talented but penniless Boudin was able to enroll at the art academy in Paris, where he studied portraiture and landscape painting. He returned to Le Havre three years later.
From that point on, the motifs of the northern coast of France were the focal point of his painting, and his many seascapes and harbor scenes made him famous. His favorite subjects included ocean waves and diverse cloud formations in the coastal sky, though his painting focused above all on the play of light. Boudin possessed a unique sense of color, and the freshness of his colors as well as his energetic brushwork bear witness to his habit of painting outdoors and observing the effects of changing light on the colors of things.
Boudin achieved considerable popularity during his lifetime, and his work consistently earned him success and recognition.

Gustave Caillebotte
(Paris 1848 – 1894 Gennevilliers)

Caillebotte nahm ab 1872 Privatstunden bei dem gefeierten Salonmaler Léon Bonnat, 1873 bestand er die Aufnahmeprüfung an der Ecole des Beaux-Arts. 1874 erwies sich seine Bekanntschaft mit Degas als wegweisend für die Entwicklung des jungen Malers, da Degas ihn mit der Gruppe der Maler zusammenbrachte, die als Impressionisten bekannt wurden.
Auf der zweiten Ausstellung der Impressionisten 1876 stellte er aus, und seit dieser Zeit unterstützte der vermögende Caillebotte seine Freunde auch als Sammler. Er war für einige Jahre ihr Mäzen und Organisator, Beteiligter und Förderer zugleich. Als sich 1880 erste Zerwürfnisse innerhalb der Gruppe abzeichneten, versuchte Caillebotte, die Gruppe zusammenzuhalten, doch blieben seine Bemühungen letztlich ohne Erfolg.
Schließlich zog er sich aus Paris zurück und wählte Petit-Gennevilliers zu seinem bevorzugten Aufenthaltsort. Abseits der lärmenden Großstadt näherte sich sein Schaffen hier immer mehr dem Werk Monets an. Neigte also sein Pariser Stil noch dem Realismus zu und war insgesamt mehr Degas verpflichtet, so waren seine Gemälde nun Interpretationen von Licht und Atmosphäre.
Weiterhin hielt er Kontakt zu Renoir und Monet, nahm aber auch zu den jüngeren Malern, den Neoimpressionisten wie Seurat und Signac, Verbindung auf. Seine bedeutenden Beiträge zur Entwicklung der impressionistischen Malerei sind lange Zeit nicht so gewürdigt worden wie sein Testament, mit dem er 1883 dem französischen Staat seine hochkarätige Sammlung von Werken seiner Künstlerfreunde vermachte.

Caillebotte took private lessons from the celebrated Salon painter Léon Bonnat beginning in 1872 and passed the entrance examination at the Ecole des Beaux-Arts in 1873. His friendship with Degas was instrumental in shaping the young painter's career, as Degas introduced him to the group of painters known as the Impressionists in 1874.
The wealthy painter exhibited at the second Impressionist exhibition in 1876 and also supported his friends as a collector in the years that followed. For several years, he not only served as their patron, organizer, and promoter, he also exhibited his own work alongside theirs. When the first

signs of dissent appeared within the group in 1880, Caillebotte tried to hold it together, but his efforts were ultimately in vain.
He finally left Paris and moved to Petit-Gennevilliers. Far from the hustle and bustle of the big city, his painting developed an increasing affinity to the work of Monet. While the style of his Paris years had been more realistic and indicative of the influence of Degas, his paintings now became interpretations of light and atmosphere.
While he stayed in touch with Renoir and Monet, he also forged ties with younger painters, including the Neo-Impressionists Seurat and Signac. For many years, his important contributions to the development of Impressionist painting were overshadowed by his will, in which he bequeathed his outstanding collection featuring works by his fellow artists to the French government in 1883.

Mary Cassatt

(Allegheny City/Pittsburgh 1844 – 1926 Mesnil-Théribus/Oise)

Mary Cassatt besuchte von 1860 bis 1862 die Pennsylvania Academy of Fine Arts in Philadelphia und ging 1865 nach Paris – von dort 1868 nach Villiers-le-Bel, um bei Manets Lehrer Thomas Couture zu arbeiten. Als der Deutsch-Französische Krieg ausbrach, ging Cassatt zurück nach Amerika, wo der große Brand in Chicago 1871 viele ihrer frühen Werke zerstörte. Bereits im Dezember desselben Jahres war sie zurück in Europa und stellte regelmäßig im Pariser Salon aus (1872–74).
Nachdem Degas sie bereits 1877 zur Teilnahme an den regelmäßigen Ausstellungen der Société des artistes indépendants aufgefordert hatte, folgte die Künstlerin 1879 erstmals dieser Einladung. In den Jahren bis 1886 folgten weitere Ausstellungsbeteiligungen bei den Indépendants; 1881 war Durand-Ruel ihr Händler geworden. 1898 unternahm Cassatt erstmals wieder eine Reise in die USA, wo sie in den folgenden zwanzig Jahren regelmäßig ausstellte.
Seit etwa 1895 entstanden Cassatts zahlreiche Mutter-Kind-Darstellungen, die Achille Segard in dem Buch *Mary Cassatt: Eine Malerin von Kindern und Müttern* behandelte, für das er ab 1912/13 Interviews mit der Künstlerin führte. In ihren intimen und gefühlvollen Darstellungen von Müttern und Kindern fand Cassatts große künstlerische Begabung besonderen Ausdruck, wobei ihr Interesse deutlich mehr auf dem Charakter der Modelle lag als auf dekorativen Details.
Als ihr Bruder Alexander 1906 starb, verbrannte die Künstlerin zahlreiche ihrer Werke. Sie starb 1926 hochbetagt auf ihrem Schloss Château Beaufresne in Mesnil-Théribus, nördlich von Paris.

Mary Cassatt attended the Pennsylvania Academy of Fine Arts in Philadelphia from 1860 until 1862, departing for Paris in 1865. From there, she traveled to Villiers-le-Bel in 1868 to work with Manet's teacher, Thomas Couture. Following the outbreak of the Franco-Prussian war, Cassatt returned to America, only to witness the destruction of many of her early works in the great Chicago Fire of 1871. In December of that same year, she went back to Europe and exhibited regularly at the Paris Salon from 1872 to 1874.
As early as in 1877, Degas encouraged her to participate in the regular exhibitions of the Société des Artistes Indépendants, and she accepted the invitation for the first time in 1879. She continued to exhibit with the Indépendants until 1886. Durand-Ruel had become her agent in 1881. In 1898, Cassatt traveled to the United States for the first time after her long absence, exhibiting there often during the following years.
The first of the mother-and-child paintings discussed in Achille Segard's book *Mary Cassatt: A Painter of Children and Mothers* (for which he interviewed the artist beginning in 1912/13) was completed in circa 1895. Cassatt's impressive talent found eloquent expression in these intimate, sensitive portraits of mothers and their children, in which she focused primarily on the characters of her models, giving less emphasis to decorative details. Following the death of her brother Alexander in 1906, the artist burned many of her works. She died after a long life at Château Beaufresne, her home in Mesnil-Théribus, north of Paris, in 1926.

Paul Cezanne

(Aix-en-Provence 1839 – 1906 Aix-en-Provence)

Nach einem Jura-Studium an der Fakultät von Aix ging der junge Cézanne 1861 nach Paris an die Académie Suisse. Eine Bewerbung um Aufnahme an der Ecole des Beaux-Arts scheiterte, und seine Bilder wurden regelmäßig vom Salon zurückgewiesen. Bereits zu diesem Zeitpunkt war sein Werk vielgestaltig, und seine dynamische Malweise in satten, kräftigen Farben sollte er später »Facture couillarde« nennen.
Die Zeit des Deutsch-Französischen Krieges verbrachte Cézanne in L'Estaque, wo er im Freien zu malen begann, und gegen Ende des Jahres 1871 ließ er sich in Auvers-sur-Oise nieder. Zu dieser Zeit brachte ihm Pissarro die künstlerischen Bestrebungen der Impressionisten nahe, und Cézanne folgte in seiner Bewunderung für Pissarro der Kunstauffassung des Älteren. Sein Bild *Das Haus des Gehängten* (1873) markiert den Wendepunkt hin zu einer neuen Stilform, jedoch entwickelte sich sein Stil mehr noch als in den Landschaften in einer Reihe von Stillleben weiter.
Auf der Impressionisten-Ausstellung des Jahres 1874 hatte Cézanne zum ersten Mal Gelegenheit, mit seiner Kunst an die Öffentlichkeit zu treten, allerdings verwehrte ihm das Publikum seine Gunst. Auch eine Einzelausstellung (1895) in Ambroise Vollards Pariser Galerie wurde vom Publikum wenig beachtet, fand aber große Bewunderung unter den Künstlerkollegen und der jüngeren Malergeneration, die erkannte, welch bedeutende Vorreiterrolle Cézanne zukam.
Cézanne war nie tatsächlich ein Vertreter der Technik und der Ideale des Impressionismus. Ihn beschäftigten vielmehr die Probleme von Form und Struktur in seinen Bildern, und er nutze die Farbe mehr zu deren Betonung denn zur Beschreibung von Licht und Atmosphäre.
Paul Cézanne starb 1906 in Aix an einer Lungenentzündung, die er sich beim Malen »sur le motif« zugezogen hatte.

After completing studies in law at the university in Aix, the young Cézanne enrolled at the Académie Suisse in Paris in 1861. His application for admission to the Ecole des Beaux-Arts was not accepted, and his paintings were regularly rejected by the Salon. His art had already become quite diverse by this time. He would later refer to his dynamic style of painting in vivid, saturated colors as "facture couillarde."
Cézanne spent the years of the Franco-Prussian war in L'Estaque, where he began painting outdoors. He settled in Auvers-sur-Oise toward the end of 1871. It was at about this time that Pissarro introduced him to the artistic ambitions of the Impressionists, and Cézanne, who admired Pissarro greatly, followed the lead of the elder painter in matters of art. His *House of the Hanged Man* (1873) marks the turning point toward a new style, which evolved more in a series of still lifes than in his landscapes, however.
Cézanne's first opportunity to present his art to a broader public came at the Impressionist exhibition in 1874, but his paintings found no favor with viewers. A solo exhibition at Ambroise Vollard's gallery in Paris (1895) was also largely ignored by the public, although it earned him the admiration of fellow artists and a younger generation of painters, who recognized Cézanne's pioneering role.

Cézanne never actually espoused the technique or the ideals of the Impressionists. He was concerned instead with problems of form and structure in his paintings, and he employed color more as a means of emphasizing these aspects than of describing light and atmosphere.
In 1906 Paul Cézanne died of pneumonia contracted while painting *sur le motif*.

Lovis Corinth
(Tapiau 1858 – 1925 Zandvoort)

Corinth wurde in Tapiau in Ostpreußen geboren und erhielt seine erste künstlerische Ausbildung an der Akademie von Königsberg. 1880 ging er an die Kunstakademie nach München, wo die künstlerische Szene um diese Zeit – neben Paris – als besonders fortschrittlich galt. Corinth schloss sich dort dem Naturalismus an, der sich zu diesem Zeitpunkt gegen die klassische Historienmalerei zu behaupten begann. In der ersten Hälfte der 1890er-Jahre kam der Maler in Berührung mit dem modernen Pleinairismus, stand in Kontakt mit den »Revolutionären« der Münchner Kunstszene und gehörte 1892 zu den Gründungsmitgliedern der Münchner Sezession.
Lovis Corinth ist vor allem durch seine späten, vehement gemalten Walchensee-Landschaften ein Begriff, aber auch durch seine lebendigen Bildnisse, unter denen die Reihe der Selbstbildnisse den sicher stärksten Eindruck hinterlässt.
Besonders in seiner Frühzeit, die noch sehr im Zeichen des akademischen Studiums stand, behandelte er auch religiöse Themen, wobei ihm speziell die Leidensgeschichte Christi die Möglichkeit zu extremen Gefühlsäußerungen, aber auch zu einer fantasievollen Handhabung des Kostüms wie zur Darstellung des nackten Körpers bot.
Corinth wird heute – neben Liebermann und Slevogt – zu den bedeutendsten Vertretern des deutschen Impressionismus gezählt, wobei in seinen späten Werken auch Anklänge des Expressionismus zu erkennen sind. Dabei wurde ihm Expressionismus nicht zum Programm, sondern war das Ergebnis eines immanenten Prozesses der Selbstfindung.

Corinth was born in Tapiau in East Prussia and received his early training in art at the academy in Königsberg. In 1880 he enrolled at the art academy in Munich, where the art scene was regarded as unusually progressive—along with that of Paris—at the time. In Munich, Corinth joined the ranks of the Naturalists, who had begun to offer an alternative to traditional history painting in those years. During the first half of the 1890s, the painter became acquainted with the modern form of plein-air painting. He was in touch with the "revolutionary figures" of the Munich art scene and joined the Munich Secession as a founding member in 1892.
Lovis Corinth is best known for his late, vehemently executed landscapes from the Lake Walchen region but also for his lifelike portraits, among which the series of self-portraits surely evokes the most vivid impressions.
He also dealt with religious themes, particularly in his early years under the influence of his academic studies, and most notably with the Passion of Christ, which offered him not only a vehicle for the expression of extreme emotions, but also an opportunity for an imaginative approach to costume and the depiction of the nude body.
Along with Liebermann und Slevogt, Corinth is today regarded as one of the most significant exponents of German Impressionism, although elements of Expressionism are also recognizable in his late works. The artist did not unyieldingly pursue the Expressionist style; rather, it was the result of an immanent process of self-discovery.

Jean-Baptiste-Camille Corot
(Paris 1796 – 1875 Paris)

Corot genoss eine kurze künstlerische Ausbildung, die ganz dem klassizistischen Stil verpflichtet war, und widmete sich dann schon früh Studien vor der Natur, unter anderem im Wald von Fontainebleau.
Von 1825 bis 1828 führte ihn eine erste Reise nach Italien, und die besonderen Lichtverhältnisse und die Farben des Südens, Natur, Architektur sowie die Relikte der Antike wirkten fortan in seiner Kunst nach. Insbesondere die Erfahrungen hinsichtlich der Pleinairmalerei, der im Italien der damaligen Zeit ein hoher Stellenwert zukam, sollten für sein weiteres Schaffen von entscheidender Bedeutung sein.
Nach seiner Rückkehr nach Frankreich behielt Corot die Pleinairmalerei bei, entwickelte sie weiter und beeinflusste damit nachhaltig die Maler der Schule von Barbizon. Wiewohl er uns in erster Linie als Landschaftsmaler vor Augen steht und als solcher einer der wichtigsten Wegbereiter auch des Impressionismus wurde, spielt die Darstellung der menschlichen Gestalt in Corots Werk ebenfalls eine wichtige, wenn auch klar begrenzte Rolle. Entscheidender ist jedoch sein künstlerischer Beitrag zur Erneuerung der französischen Landschaftsmalerei, wobei eine besondere Leistung in der gleichzeitigen Auseinandersetzung mit Naturstudie und Atelierproduktion zu sehen ist. Daneben malte Corot auch ideale Landschaften mit Szenen mythologischen Inhalts.

Corot completed a brief period of training in art dedicated entirely to the Neoclassical style before turning to studies in natural settings, among them the Forest of Fontainebleau, early in his career.
He traveled through Italy for the first time from 1825 to 1828. The unique light and colors of southern Europe, its nature and architecture, as well as the relics of antiquity had a lasting impact on his art. His experience with plein-air painting, which played an important role in Italy during those years, was of crucial importance to his later work.
After returning to France, Corot continued to paint outdoors, refining the technique and thereby exerting a lasting influence on the painters of the Barbizon School. Although regarded above all as a landscape painter—and as such one of the most significant forerunners of Impressionism—the image of the human body also plays an important, albeit clearly limited role in Corot's art. Of greater importance, however, is his contribution to the revival of French landscape painting. One of his most noteworthy achievements in this context was his unique combination of nature studies and studio production. Corot also painted idealized landscapes featuring scenes with mythological content.

Gustave Courbet
(Ornans 1819 – 1877 La-Tour-de-Peilz)

Gustave Courbet studierte ab 1839 in Paris in den Ateliers verschiedener Künstler und malte zunächst durchaus konventionelle, romantisierende Bilder. Erst als er in freundschaftlichen Kontakt mit Künstlern, Dichtern und Philosophen der Avantgarde, wie Charles Baudelaire und Pierre-Joseph Proud'hon, trat, bildete er in diesem geistigen Umfeld seinen Realismus aus. 1848/49 entstanden seine ersten realistischen Bilder. Sein Realismus widmete sich der Schilderung der Wirklichkeit – ungeschönt und kompromisslos – und brachte dem Künstler den Vorwurf ein, seine Bilder seien hässlich, sodass sein Schaffen in der Öffentlichkeit wachsende Ablehnung erfuhr.
Entsprechend wurden seine Werke 1855 von der Jury der Pariser Weltausstellung nicht angenommen. Courbets Kunstauffassung, der zufolge die

Malerei allein die Wirklichkeit, das Greifbare und Sichtbare, zum Thema haben dürfe und die eine rigide Absage an die traditionelle Kunstauffassung – wie sie von den Akademien vertreten wurde – darstellte, nach der alle Kunst die idealen Vorstellungen von Schönheit wiederzugeben hatte, entsprach nicht der Kunsterwartung des großen Publikums. Auch Courbets sozialistische Haltung erregte Kritik: Die Kunst war für Courbet kein Luxus oder private Erbauung für die Reichen, sondern ein öffentliches Medium für alle. Aus Protest errichtete der Künstler einen eigenen Holzschuppen in der Nähe der Weltausstellung, über dessen Eingang programmatisch der Titel »Le Réalisme – G. Courbet« prangte.
Politisch stand Courbet den Revolutionären von 1848 und der Kommune von 1871 nahe, in der er sich aktiv engagierte. 1873 konnte er einen Haftbefehl nicht abwenden, sodass er ins Exil in die Schweiz gehen musste, wo er 1877 starb.

Courbet studied in the studios of several different artists beginning in 1839 and painted entirely conventional, Romantic scenes during this period. It was not until he became acquainted with avant-garde artists, writers, and philosophers, such as Charles Baudelaire and Pierre-Joseph Proud'hon, that he began to develop his own form of Realism in this intellectual environment. His first Realist paintings were completed in 1848/49. His Realism focused on the unembellished, uncompromising depiction of reality. He was accused of producing ugly paintings, and his art was rejected by an increasingly large segment of the public.
Accordingly, his works were not accepted for exhibition by the jury for the Paris Exposition Universelle in 1855. His concept of art, according to which the only legitimate subject of painting was the real, palpable, visible world, conflicted with the expectations of the general public as it represented a strict rejection of the traditional view of art—as propagated by the academies—which demanded that all art reflect the ideal concepts of beauty. Courbet's socialist views also drew criticism. He regarded art not as a luxury or an object of personal pleasure and enlightenment for the rich but as a public medium meant for everyone. In a gesture of protest, the artist built a wooden shed in the vicinity of the Exposition Universelle and placed a sign over its entrance bearing the salient title "Le Réalisme—G. Courbet."
Politically, Courbet was closely associated with the revolutionaries of 1848 and the Paris Commune of 1871, in which he was actively involved. Unable to evade an arrest warrant in 1873, he fled into exile in Switzerland, where he died in 1877.

Lucie Cousturier
(Paris 1876 – 1925 Paris)

Die neoimpressionistische Malerin wurde wesentlich durch die Kunst Paul Signacs geprägt. Sie schuf Stillleben, Landschaften, Seestücke, Porträts und Figurenbilder. 1906 fanden erstmals Ausstellungen zu ihrem Werk in der Galerie Druet in Paris statt, späterhin in der Galerie Bernheim. Cousturier stellte zudem im Salon der Indépendants aus und ebenso bei der Berliner Sezession. 1907 war sie im Kunstverein München vertreten, 1908 in Brüssel im Salon der Gruppe La libre esthétique.

The Neo-Impressionist painter Cousturier was largely influenced by the art of Signac. She painted still lifes, landscapes, seascapes, portraits, and works featuring human figures. Her work was first exhibited at the Galerie Druet in Paris in 1906 and later at the Galerie Bernheim. Cousturier also exhibited at the Salon des Artistes Indépendants and with the Berlin Secession. Her paintings were shown at the Kunstverein Munich in 1907 and at the Salon of the La Libre Esthétique group in Brussels in 1908.

Henri Edmond Cross
(Douai 1856 – 1910 Saint-Clair)

Cross, 1856 als Henri Edmond Delacroix geboren, studierte von 1874 bis 1876 Jura in Lille, wo er sich gleichzeitig an der Kunstakademie einschrieb. 1876 ging er nach Paris und arbeitete dort zunächst im Atelier von Carolus Duran und François Bonvin. Um Verwechslungen mit dem berühmten Delacroix auszuschließen, malte er fortan unter dem Pseudonym Cross.
Befreundet mit den Neoimpressionisten Seurat und Signac, näherte er sich unter deren Einfluss immer mehr dem systematischen pointillistischen Malstil an, dessen Technik Seurat und Signac mit geradezu wissenschaftlicher Präzision entwickelt hatten. Gemeinsam mit ihnen gehörte er 1884 zu den Gründungsmitgliedern der Gruppe der »Unabhängigen«, deren öffentliches Forum fortan der Salon des artistes indépendants war. Bis zum Ende der 1880er-Jahre stellte er regelmäßig dort aus, ehe er sich – des Stadtlebens überdrüssig – 1891 in den Süden Frankreichs zurückzog, um dort zu arbeiten.
Die für die Malerei des Pointillismus bezeichnende Verwandlung der stofflich-charakterisierenden Oberflächenschilderung der Dingwelt in reine Malerei der Lichttöne ist in den Bildern Cross' deutlich erkennbar. Dabei kommt dem Umriss wieder eine neue lineare Qualität zu, die den Gegenstand definiert. Letztlich aber sind die unendlich differenzierten Abstufungen des Lichts Hauptthema seiner Bilder. Cross' meisterhaft angewandte Technik der optischen Mischung erreicht – bei aller Transparenz der Lichtqualität – in den Gegenstandsformen eine ganz neue, geradezu statisch wirkende Klassizität.

Born Henri Edmond Delacroix in 1856, Cross studied law in Lille from 1874 to 1876, where he also enrolled at the local art academy. He moved to Paris in 1876, initially working at the studio of Carolus Duran and François Bonvin. From that point on, he painted under the pseudonym of Cross in order to avoid confusion with the famous Delacroix.
Having become friends with the Neo-Impressionists Seurat and Signac, he gradually adopted a systematic Pointillist style under their influence, a technique Seurat and Signac had developed with almost scientific precision. He joined them in 1884 as founding members of the group of "Independents," whose public forum was the Salon des Artistes Indépendants. He exhibited regularly there until the late 1880s. Weary of city life, in 1891 he retreated to the south of France to work in a more tranquil environment.
The transformation of the superficial depiction of the material characteristics of the world of objects into pure painting composed of shades of light that is so typical of Pointillism is clearly evident in Cross's paintings. In these works, outlines take on a new linear quality that defines the object. Ultimately, however, the infinitely differentiated graduations of light are the dominant theme of his paintings. Despite the remarkable transparency of his light, Cross's masterfully applied technique of optical mixture achieves a new, almost static-looking classicistic character in the forms of objects.

Charles-François Daubigny
(Paris 1817 – 1878 Paris)

Daubigny begann seine künstlerische Ausbildung im Atelier von Pierre Asthasie Théodore Sentiès in Paris. 1838 entstanden erste Radierungen, und im selben Jahr beteiligte er sich auch erstmals am Pariser Salon, wo er in den 1840er-Jahren regelmäßig ausstellte; seine Kunst war zunächst ganz der Romantik verpflichtet.

1843 begann Daubigny im Wald von Fontainebleau zu malen und schloss sich bald darauf den Malern von Barbizon an. Seine Bilder wurden zunehmend stimmungsvoller, und ab dem Ende der 1840er-Jahre schuf er seine sogenannten »Paysages intimes«. Er folgte damit Corot und Henri Rousseau, die diese Form der empfindsamen Landschaftsmalerei entwickelt hatten.
Daubigny sollte der wohl fortschrittlichste Maler der Barbizon-Schule werden. Die stimmungsvollen Erscheinungen der Natur aufspürend, baute er seine Bilder aus leuchtend frischen Farben auf. Er entfernte sich dabei immer mehr vom Naturvorbild, doch gelangten ihm nun seine eindrucksvollsten Werke: Landschaften, oftmals dunstig verhangen, erfüllt von ruhiger Stimmung und feiner Atmosphäre.
1860 ging Daubigny nach Auvers-sur-Oise, wo er bis zu seinem Tode lebte und arbeitete.

Daubigny began his training in art in Pierre Asthasie Théodore Sentiès' studio in Paris. His earliest etchings were completed in 1838, the year of his first showing at the Paris Salon, where he exhibited regularly in the 1840s. The paintings executed in his early years were thoroughly Romantic in character.
Daubigny began painting in the Forest of Fontainebleau in 1843, joining the Barbizon painters soon thereafter. His paintings became increasingly atmospheric, and toward the end of the 1840s, he created his first *Paysages intimes*, works in which he followed the lead of Corot and Henri Rousseau, who had developed this particular form of emotional landscape painting.
Daubigny eventually became the most progressive of the Barbizon painters. In search of the atmospheric manifestations of nature, he composed his paintings in fresh, radiant colors. Evident in these paintings is a shift in which he moved progressively farther away from his natural sources, yet his most impressive works date from this period: landscapes, often shrouded in mist, dominated by a mood of tranquility and delicate atmosphere.
Daubigny moved to Auvers-sur-Oise in 1860 to live and work there until his death in 1878.

Edgar Degas
(Paris 1834 – 1917 Paris)

Degas, geboren als Hillaire Germain de Gas, Spross eines Adelsgeschlechts, besuchte 1855/56 die Ecole des Beaux-Arts in Paris. Beeinflusst wurde Degas zunächst von der Kunst Jean Auguste Dominique Ingres' – dessen persönliche Bekanntschaft der junge Mann machte –, ehe er sich mehr und mehr dem Licht als Stilmittel seiner Malerei zuwandte. 1874 war er an der ersten Ausstellung der Impressionisten beteiligt.
Ab 1877 tauchten neue Motive in seinen Bildern auf, er malte nun verstärkt Szenen aus Oper, Ballett oder Cafés sowie Darstellungen von Pferderennen und vom Alltagsleben der Großstadt Paris. Charakteristisch für seine Werke aus dieser Zeit sind vom Bildrand angeschnittene Hauptpersonen, aus dem Bildmittelpunkt heraus- und bisweilen nahe an den Betrachter herangerückt. Viele dieser Darstellungen vermitteln den Eindruck einer Momentaufnahme.
Degas' Kunst ist gekennzeichnet von einer dynamisch und spontan aufgefassten Darstellungsweise und beschäftigt sich intensiv mit der Wirkung des Lichts. Seine Bilder drücken eine große Vitalität aus und besitzen ein starkes atmosphärisches Kolorit. Dem Maler war nicht daran gelegen, dem Betrachter die Wirklichkeit ungeschönt vor Augen zu halten.

Born Hillaire Germain de Gas, the son of a noble family, Degas attended the Ecole des Beaux-Arts in Paris in 1855/56. He was initially influenced by the art of Jean Auguste Dominique Ingres—with whom he became personally acquainted as a young man—before turning his attention to light as a stylistic resource in his painting. He took part in the first Impressionist exhibition in 1874.
New motifs began to appear in his paintings in 1877. He now concentrated increasingly on opera, ballet, and café scenes as well as images from horse races and everyday life in the metropolis of Paris. Characteristic features of his paintings from this period are figures of protagonists cut off at the edge of the pictures, drawn forward from the center, and often brought very close to the viewer. Many of these scenes evoke the impression of a snapshot.
Degas' art is characterized by a dynamic, spontaneous painting style and is intensely concerned with the effects of light. His paintings express great vitality underscored by strong atmospheric coloration. The painter was not at all interested in confronting the viewer with unembellished reality.

William Degouve de Nuncques
(Monthermée 1867 – 1935 Stavelot)

Degouve de Nuncques teilte sich 1883 ein Atelier mit seinem Künstlerkollegen Jan Toorop, der ihm die symbolistische Kunstauffassung nahebrachte. Um die Mitte der 1880er-Jahre kam er in Paris in Kontakt mit Auguste Rodin, Maurice Denis und auch Pierre Puvis de Chavannes, mit dem ihn bald eine enge Freundschaft verband. Seine Darstellungen mystischen Inhalts stellte Degouve de Nuncques sowohl mit seinen Künstlerfreunden der Avantgarde, der Gruppe Les XX, als auch in den Ausstellungen der Gruppe La libre esthétique aus. Auf Reisen nach Italien, Österreich und Frankreich entstanden zahlreiche Landschaftsdarstellungen, vielfach Nachtbilder. Degouve de Nuncques ist in seinem Schaffen durchweg dem Symbolismus verhaftet, und seine Bilder offenbaren seine Visionen, die sichtbare Welt wie auch die Gedankenwelt zu verändern.

Degouve de Nuncques shared a studio with his fellow artist Jan Toorop, who introduced him to the art of Symbolism, in 1883. In Paris in the mid-1880s, he met Auguste Rodin, Maurice Denis, and Pierre Puvis de Chavannes, soon forging a close friendship with the latter. Degouve exhibited his paintings of mystical scenes with avant-garde friends, the members of the group Les XX, and at the exhibitions organized by the group known as La Libre Esthétique. While traveling in Italy, Austria, and France, he painted numerous landscapes, including a number of nocturnal scenes. The art of Degouve de Nuncques exhibits the strong influence of Symbolism, and his paintings reveal his visions of change in both the visible world and the realm of ideas.

Henri Delavallee
(Reims 1862 – 1943 Pont-Aven)

Die Bewunderung des jungen Delavallée, ab 1881 Schüler an der Ecole des Beaux-Arts in Paris, galt in den frühen Jahren vor allem der Kunst Corots, Millets und Courbets.
1881 bereiste der junge Künstler erstmals die Bretagne, und wie viele Landschaftsmaler seiner Zeit unternahm er fortan regelmäßige Reisen dorthin. Dabei lernte er 1886 in Pont-Aven auch die dortige Künstlergruppe um Gauguin kennen. Unter dem Einfluss Pissarros – und nach der Bekanntschaft mit Signac – begann er in der Technik des Divisionismus zu malen. Aus den Jahren von 1887 bis 1890 sind einige wenige pointillistische Werke

bekannt. Nach kurzer Zeit kehrte er allerdings zu einer eher lockeren, ungebundeneren – stärker von Gauguin beeinflussten – Malweise zurück. Zwischen 1888 und 1893 widmete sich Delavallée vornehmlich der Technik des Radierens, und es entstanden in diesen Jahren annähernd siebzig Kupferstiche.

1896 verließ Delavallée Frankreich und lebte bis 1901 mit seiner Frau, der Malerin Gabrielle Moreau, in der Türkei, wo er Hofmaler des Großwesirs wurde. Als einer der letzten aus dem Kreise um die Maler von Pont-Aven verstarb Henri Delavallée 1943 in Pont-Aven. Seine Werke sind heute auf der ganzen Welt verstreut, und bisweilen werden seine Bilder auch fälschlicherweise seiner Frau zugeschrieben.

The young Delavallée, who enrolled at the Ecole des Beaux-Arts in Paris in 1881, was a great admirer of the art of Corot, Millet, and Courbet during the early years of his career.

The artist first traveled to Brittany in 1881, and like many landscape painters of his time, he continued to visit the region regularly for many years. In 1886, he became acquainted with the artists associated with Gauguin in Pont-Aven. Under the influence of Pissarro—and after having met Signac—he began painting in the style of the Divisionists. Although a few Pointillist works have survived from the years between 1887 and 1890, he soon returned to a freer, less constrained painting style that reflected the influence of Gauguin.

Delavallée worked primarily in the medium of the etching between 1888 and 1893. He completed nearly seventy copper engravings during this period. Delavallée left France in 1896 and lived with his wife, the painter Gabrielle Moreau, in Turkey, where he was appointed court painter by the Grand Visir, until 1901. When he died in Pont-Aven in 1943, Henri Delavallée was one of the last surviving members of the circle, who gathered around the Pont-Aven painters. His works, some of which have been falsely attributed to his wife, are now distributed throughout the world.

Maurice Denis
(Granville 1870 – 1943 Paris)

Ab 1888 besuchte der junge Denis die Ecole des Beaux-Arts in Paris, wo er auch im Louvre die Werke der alten Meister studierte und durch häufige Besuche in den Galerien von Paul Durand-Ruel, Léon Boussod und anderen in Berührung mit der zeitgenössischen Kunst kam. Anfänglich bewunderte er vor allem die Kunst Jean Auguste Dominique Ingres', Gustave Moreaus und Pierre Puvis de Chavannes', was in seinem Frühwerk deutlich zu erkennen ist. Von großer Bedeutung für seine weitere künstlerische Entwicklung war dann aber die Tatsache, dass ihm durch Sérusier, der in Pont-Aven zusammen mit Gauguin gemalt hatte, die Kunstauffassung des Synthetismus vermittelt wurde.

Denis gehörte – neben Bonnard, Ker-Xavier Roussel, Vuillard und anderen – zu den Gründungsmitgliedern der Nabis (aus dem Hebräischen: »Propheten«), die den Illusionismus der Impressionisten ablehnten und eine in Inhalt und Form bedeutungsvolle Malerei forderten. Denis wurde einer der wichtigsten Theoretiker dieser antinaturalistischen Kunst. In der Zeitschrift *Art et Critique* veröffentlichte er das »Manifest« der Nabis, seine »Définition du Néo-traditionnisme«, wonach die Malerei mehr sein sollte als eine reine Wiedergabe der Natur.

Das Gesamtwerk Denis' ist so umfangreich wie vielgestaltig. Seine poetische Bildsprache fand Ausdruck in Gemälden, Wandbildern und Dekorationen, Entwürfen für Fenster, Mosaike und Gobelins. Daneben existiert gleichbedeutend sein druckgrafisches Schaffen – Lithografien und Buchillustrationen.

In 1888, the young Denis enrolled at the Ecole des Beaux-Arts in Paris, where he also studied the works of the old masters in the Louvre and came in contact with contemporary art through frequent visits to the galleries of Paul Durand-Ruel, Léon Boussod, and others. His early paintings clearly reflect his admiration for the art of Jean Auguste Dominique Ingres, Gustave Moreau, and Pierre Puvis de Chavannes. He was later introduced to the concepts of Synthetism by Sérusier, who had painted with Gauguin in Pont-Aven, and that experience had an appreciable impact on his subsequent development as an artist.

Denis joined Bonnard, Ker-Xavier Roussel, Vuillard, and others as a founding member of the Nabi group (from Hebrew "prophet"), who rejected the illusionism of the Impressionists and appealed for a style of painting that was meaningful in both content and form. Denis became one of the leading theorists of this anti-Naturalist art. In the Nabi "manifesto," his "Définition du Néo-traditionnisme" published in the journal *Art et Critique*, he argued that painting should be more than a pure depiction of nature.

Denis' oeuvre is both extensive and diverse. His poetic visual language is expressed in paintings, frescoes, and decorations; designs for windows; mosaics; and Gobelin tapestries. His graphic works, comprising lithographs and book illustrations, are regarded as an equally important part of his oeuvre.

August Deusser
(Köln Cologne 1870 – 1942 München Munich)

Nach seiner Zeit als Meisterschüler an der Kunstakademie Düsseldorf prägte Deusser das kulturelle Klima Düsseldorfs mit neuen Impulsen und engagierte sich an der Akademie, im Kunstverein sowie im »Malkasten«, dem intellektuellen Künstlertreffpunkt. Er organisierte zahlreiche Ausstellungen, in denen auch Künstler der französischen Avantgarde präsentiert wurden. Vom früh etablierten Historienmaler entwickelte sich Deusser zu einem Verfechter der Moderne. Er propagierte die Abkehr vom Akademismus und wandte sich entschieden den neuen Ideen der Pleinairmalerei im Sinne Liebermanns zu.

Sein energisches kulturpolitisches Engagement führte 1909 zur Gründung des Sonderbundes. Mit den Sonderbund-Ausstellungen – besonders der großen Schau in Köln von 1912 – gelang der Moderne auch im Rheinland der Durchbruch. In die Sonderbund-Jahre fällt die bedeutendste Schaffensphase Deussers. Ohne sich vom Gegenstand zu lösen, entwickelte er in Anlehnung an die Neoimpressionisten, die Fauves und Cézanne eine eigenständige freie und aufgelockerte Malweise.

After his years as a master student at the Kunstakademie Düsseldorf, Deusser helped shape the cultural climate of the city on the Rhine River by contributing a number of new impulses, and he was actively involved at the art academy, the art society, and the Malkasten, a meeting place for artists and intellectuals. He organized numerous exhibitions in which artists of the French avant-garde were also featured. Having established a reputation as a history painter early on, Deusser eventually became an advocate of Modernism. He appealed for the rejection of academic art and embraced the new concepts of plein-air painting propagated by Liebermann.

His commitment to cultural reform culminated in the founding of the Sonderbund in 1909. The Sonderbund exhibitions—most notably the major show in Cologne in 1912—played a pivotal role in helping modern art achieve its breakthrough in the Rhineland. The Sonderbund era was Deusser's most important creative period. Without abandoning the object completely, he developed a freer, less constrained, self-reliant painting style influenced by the Neo-Impressionists, the Fauvists, and Cézanne.

Virgilio Narcisso Diaz de la Pena
(Bordeaux 1808 – 1876 Mentone)

Nach autodidaktischen Anfängen als Maler, war Díaz de la Peña zunächst gezwungen, sich seinen Lebensunterhalt als Porzellanmaler zu verdienen. Als er mit der Kunst Eugène Delacroix' in Berührung kam, schloss sich Díaz der romantischen Bewegung an. Daneben begeisterten ihn vor allem die Werke Correggios. Bereits seine ersten im Salon ausgestellten Bilder waren Freilichtstudien nach Motiven aus der Umgebung von Paris und dem Wald von Fontainebleau. Solche Landschaften, von einer poetischen Lichtstimmung durchdrungen, sollten lebenslang sein Schaffen kennzeichnen. Häufig durchsetzte er diese Landschaften mit kleinen Staffagefiguren. Mit diesen sinnlich reizvollen Bildern konnte der Maler, der zum Künstlerkreis der Schule von Barbizon gezählt wird, bis zu seinem Tode großen materiellen Erfolg verzeichnen.

Following his early years as a self-taught painter, Díaz de la Peña was compelled at first to earn his living as a porcelain painter. After being introduced to the art of Eugène Delacroix, Díaz joined the Romantic movement. He was also a great admirer of the works of Correggio. His first paintings exhibited at the Salon were plein-air studies of motifs from the environs of Paris and the Forest of Fontainebleau. Landscapes of this kind, saturated with a poetic atmosphere of light, would remain typical of his art throughout his lifetime. He often incorporated small incidental figures into these landscapes. The painter, who is associated with the artists of the Barbizon School, achieved considerable financial success with these paintings with strong sensual appeal.

Cornelis Theodorus Marie (genannt known as Kees) van Dongen
(Delfshaven/Rotterdam 1877 – 1968 Monte Carlo)

Von 1894 bis 1896 besuchte van Dongen die Académie royale des Beaux-Arts in Rotterdam. Er interessierte sich besonders für die Kunst Rembrandts und Frans Hals' und schuf zunächst Porträts und Landschaften in der Art der holländischen Schule, in kühler, schwerer Farbigkeit. 1899 übersiedelte er nach Paris. Kunsthändler wie Ambroise Vollard, Eugène Druet und Berthe Weill begannen sich für sein Schaffen zu interessieren und organisierten erste Ausstellungen mit seinen Werken, die dem Künstler die erste öffentliche Anerkennung einbrachten. Sein Schaffen in diesen Jahren war deutlich von der Malerei der Impressionisten beeinflusst.
1905 stellte er im Salon d'automne aus, jenem berühmten Salon, bei dessen Besuch sich der Kunstkritiker Louis Vauxcelles zu dem berühmten Ausspruch vom »Cage aux fauves« (Käfig der wilden Tiere) veranlasst sah, der den Fauvisten ihren Namen geben sollte.
1913 lernte van Dongen die Comtesse Casati und Jasmy Jacob kennen – zwei Damen aus der mondänen Gesellschaft von Paris, die ihn in die Pariser Boheme einführten, deren gefeierter Porträtist er nach dem Ende des Ersten Weltkrieges werden sollte. Bis zum Anfang der 1930er-Jahre agierte er als Chronist der »folle époque«.
Vom Ende des Zweiten Weltkriegs bis zu seinem Tod wurden zahlreiche Ausstellungen mit den Werken van Dongens organisiert. 1968 starb der Künstler 90-jährig in Monaco.

Van Dongen attended the Académie Royale des Beaux-Arts in Rotterdam from 1894 to 1896. He was especially fascinated with the art of Rembrandt and Frans Hals, and his earliest works were portraits and landscapes in the style of the Dutch school composed in cool, weighty colors. He moved to Paris in 1899. A number of art dealers, including Ambroise Vollard, Eugène Druet, and Berthe Weill, showed an interest in his art and organized the first exhibitions of his works, through which the artist achieved early public recognition. His art during these years was clearly influenced by Impressionist paintings.
He exhibited at the Salon d'Automne in 1905, the famous salon that prompted the art critic Louis Vauxcelles to coin the famous phrase *"cage aux fauves"* (a cage of wild animals)—from which the Fauvists derived their name—during a visit.
In 1913, van Dongen made the acquaintance of Countess Casati and Jasmy Jacob—two ladies of Parisian high society who introduced him to the Paris *bohème*. He would later become its most celebrated portraitist after the end of the World War One. He served as the chronicler of the *folle époque* until the 1930s.
Numerous exhibitions of van Dongen's works were organized between the end of World War Two and the artist's death. He died in 1968 in Monaco at the age of ninety.

Albert Dubois-Pillet
(Paris 1846 – 1890 Le Puy-en-Velay)

Louis-Auguste Albert Dubois-Pillet (den Mädchennamen seiner Mutter pflegte er seinem Geburtsnamen erst ab etwa 1884 beizufügen), der eine Militärlaufbahn eingeschlagen hatte, widmete sich ab der Mitte der 1870er-Jahre auch autodidaktisch der Malerei. Als sich im Juni 1884 – aus Protest gegen die Auswahlkriterien der Jury des Salon – die abgewiesenen Künstler zur Société des artistes indépendants zusammenschlossen, zählte Dubois-Pillet zu den Initiatoren der Künstlervereinigung. Bis zu seinem Tode nahm er regelmäßig an ihren jährlichen, juryfreien Gruppenausstellungen teil. Er verfasste die Statuten der Vereinigung und avancierte zum Organisator der Gruppe.
Waren Dubois-Pillets Bilder aus den ersten Pariser Jahren noch deutlich vom Impressionismus geprägt, so sollte sein Schaffen ab 1885 immer mehr vom Neoimpressionismus beeinflusst werden. Hierzu trug vor allem auch seine enge Freundschaft mit Signac, Angrand und Seurat, dem Begründer der divisionistischen Malweise, bei. Ab 1886 malte Dubois-Pillet seine Landschaften, Stadtansichten, Genrebilder und Stillleben ganz in der pointillistischen Manier.
Der Maler starb 1890 in Le Puy, und nach seinem und Seurats Tode (1891) zog sich das Gros der französischen und belgischen Anhänger von der Société des artistes indépendants zurück. In Frankreich sollte sich erst um 1897/98 ein neues öffentliches Interesse am Neoimpressionismus herausbilden.

Louis-Auguste Albert Dubois-Pillet (he first added his mother's maiden name to his in about 1884), who originally embarked upon a career in the military, also developed an interest in painting—as an autodidact—in the mid-1870s. In June 1884, when the artists rejected by the Salon jury formed the Société des Artistes Indépendants—in protest of the jury's selection criteria—Dubois-Pillet was among the founding members of the society. He participated regularly in the group's annual, non-adjudicated exhibitions until his death. He authored the society's statutes and became one of the group's leading organizers.
While Dubois-Pillet's paintings from his early years in Paris bore the unmistakable imprint of Impressionism, his art from 1885 onward was increasingly influenced by Neo-Impressionist model. His close friendship with Signac, Angrand, and Seurat, the founder of the Divisionist style, played an important role in this process. Dubois-Pillet began painting land-

scapes, urban scenes, genre pictures, and still lifes in a decidedly Pointillist style in 1886.
The painter died in Le Puy in 1890, and after his and Seurat's death (1891), most of the French and Belgian followers left the Société des Artistes Indépendants. Renewed public interest in Neo-Impressionist art would not emerge again in France until about 1897/98.

Raoul Dufy
(Le Havre 1877 – 1953 Forcalquier)

Als Ältester aus der Gruppe der drei Fauves, die aus Le Havre stammten, ging Raoul Dufy 1900 – zur gleichen Zeit wie Georges Braque – nach Paris. Die beiden Freunde trafen dort Othon Friesz wieder, der zwei Jahre zuvor an die Ecole des Beaux-Arts gegangen war. Gemeinsam besuchten die drei Jugendfreunde das Atelier Léon Bonnats, wobei keiner der drei lange dort blieb.
Unter dem Eindruck der avantgardistischen Malerei, die er in den Galerien in der Rue Laffitte sah, erweiterte Dufy schon bald nach seiner Ankunft in Paris seine Palette und begann – gerade nach der Begegnung mit Matisses Werk im Salon der Indépendants des Jahres 1905 –, in seinen Bildern die Vereinfachung der Form voranzutreiben. 1906 stellte er im Herbstsalon seine ersten fauvistischen Gemälde aus. 1908 wandte sich Dufy, angeregt durch eine Reise mit Braque nach L'Estaque, vermehrt Kompositionen zu, die deutlich den Bildwerken Cézannes verpflichtet waren.

Raoul Dufy, the oldest member of the group of three Fauvists from Le Havre, moved to Paris in 1900—at about the same time as Georges Braque. There, the two friends were reunited with Othon Friesz, who had enrolled at the Ecole des Beaux-Arts two years earlier. The three comrades took lessons together at Léon Bonnat's studio, but none of them stayed with Bonnat very long.
Under the influence of the avant-garde paintings he viewed at galleries on the Rue Laffitte, Dufy expanded his palette soon after his arrival in Paris and embarked—shortly after his encounter with the art of Matisse at the Salon des Artistes Indépendants in 1905—on a process devoted to the simplification of form in his paintings. In 1906, he exhibited his first Fauvist works at the Salon d'Automne. Inspired by a trip to L'Estaque with Braque, Dufy focused increasingly on compositions in which the influence of Cézanne's paintings became more and more evident.

James Ensor
(Ostende Ostend 1860 – 1949 Ostende Ostend)

Der belgische Maler, Zeichner und Graveur Ensor hatte 1877 bis 1879 eine Ausbildung an der Akademie der Schönen Künste in Brüssel erhalten. Später zählte er zu den Mitbegründern der avantgardistischen Künstlergruppe Les XX.
Der Maler hatte seinen besonderen Spaß daran, den Betrachter mit skurrilen Darstellungen zu irritieren. Im sarkastischen Zusammenspiel von scheinbar freundlichem und vertrautem Ambiente mit Bildmotiven, die uns das Gruseln lehren, schaffte der Belgier Verwirrung: Ob es nicht doch eine unbekannte Welt gibt, die neben den realen Dingen existiert? Entsprechend stellte er auch die dunkle Seite der menschlichen Natur in den Mittelpunkt seines Œuvres. Mit übersteigerten Farben und Formen schuf er eine Fantasiewelt, die den belgischen Surrealismus ankündigte.
Ensors Kunst wird gemeinhin dem Symbolismus zugerechnet, wiewohl sein Schaffen auch expressionistische Züge trägt.

The Belgian painter, draftsman, and engraver Ensor was trained at the Academy of Fine Arts in Brussels from 1877 to 1879. He was later one of the cofounders of the avant-garde artists' group known as Les XX.
Ensor appeared to take great pleasure in irritating viewers with scurrilous scenes. He generated a sense of confusion with the sarcastic interplay of seemingly pleasant, familiar ambiences and motifs that engender feelings of horror. Is there in fact an unknown world that exists alongside that of real things? Accordingly, Ensor placed the dark side of human nature in the foreground of his oeuvre. Using exaggerated colors and forms, he created a fantasy world that heralded the advent of Belgian Surrealism.
Ensor's art is commonly categorized as a form of Symbolism, although his work exhibits Expressionist features as well.

Georges d'Espagnat
(Melun 1870 – 1950 Paris)

Georges d'Espagnat verspürte bereits früh die Neigung, sich der Kunst zu widmen, und ging 1888 nach Paris. Menschenscheu und freiheitsliebend, schulte sich d'Espagnat durch Louvre-Besuche und durch die Arbeit nach Modellen im Rahmen eines Unterrichts in einem kleinen Übungsraum am Boulevard du Montparnasse. Seine erste Einzelausstellung hatte der Maler 1895 in der Galerie Le Barc de Boutteville in Paris, gefolgt von einer bedeutenden Präsentation in der Galerie Durand-Ruel 1897.
Albert André und Louis Valtat zählten zu seinen Malerfreunden. Letzterer machte ihn um die Jahrhundertwende mit Renoir bekannt, und auch Bonnard, Vuillard und Denis gehörten bald zu seinem Freundeskreis.
1905 stellte d'Espagnat im Salon d'automne aus – gemeinsam mit jenen, die bald Fauves genannt werden sollten.
In den Jahren zwischen 1905 und 1910 unternahm der Künstler zahlreiche Reisen. Vor allem in den 1930er-Jahren erhielt er viele öffentliche Aufträge zur dekorativen Ausgestaltung von Bauwerken. 1936 nahm d'Espagnat eine Professur an der Pariser Ecole des Beaux-Arts an.

Georges d'Espagnat felt the urge to devote himself to art at an early age and went to Paris in 1888. Shy and devoted to the principles of liberty, he educated himself by visiting the Louvre and working from models during lessons at a small studio on the Boulevard du Montparnasse. The painter's first solo exhibition was presented at the Galerie Le Barc de Boutteville in Paris in 1895, followed by an important showing at the Galerie Durand-Ruel in 1897.
His friends and fellow artists included Albert André and Louis Valtat. The latter introduced him to Renoir around the turn of the twentieth century. Bonnard, Vuillard, and Denis soon joined his circle of friends as well.
In 1905, d'Espagnat exhibited at the Salon d'Automne—along with the artists who later came to be known as the Fauvists.
The artist traveled extensively during the years between 1905 and 1910. He received many public commissions for decorative building designs during the 1930s. D'Espagnat accepted a professorship at the Ecole des Beaux-Arts in Paris in 1936.

Henri Fantin-Latour
(Grenoble 1836 – 1904 Buré)

Fantin-Latour studierte ab 1854 an der Pariser Ecole des Beaux-Arts, ehe er 1859 Courbet begegnete, in dessen Atelier er zwei Jahre später arbeitete. 1863 zählte Fantin-Latour zu jenen Malern, die sowohl im Pariser Salon als auch im gleichzeitigen Salon des refusés ausstellten.

Obwohl ein Zeitgenosse der Impressionisten, war Fantin-Latours Kunst stärker dem Realismus verpflichtet. Bekannt wurde er vor allem durch seine Blumenstillleben, daneben schuf er aber auch zahlreiche Gruppenporträts, in denen er häufig die zeitgenössischen Pariser Maler und Schriftsteller wiedergab, die er zu seinem großen Freundeskreis zählte. Durch seine weitreichenden Kontakte sollte sein Einfluss auch bei den späteren Symbolisten zur Geltung kommen.

Henri Fantin-Latour studied at the Ecole des Beaux-Arts in Paris beginning in 1854 before meeting Courbet in 1859. He worked at Courbet's studio two years later. By 1863, Fantin-Latour had joined the ranks of painters who exhibited at both the Paris Salon and the concurrent Salon des Refusés.
Although he was a contemporary of the Impressionists, Fantin-Latour's art exhibits closer affinities to Realism. He is best known for his floral still lifes, but he also did numerous group portraits, many of which featured contemporary Parisian painters and writers from his own circle of friends. Through his extensive contacts, he also exerted considerable influence on the later Symbolist painters.

Alfred William (genannt known as Willy) Finch

(Saint-Josse-ten-Noode bei Brüssel near Brussels 1854 – 1930 Helsinki)

Willy Finch, der bei Brüssel geborene Sohn englischer Eltern, war Gründungsmitglied der XX, jener Gruppe von zwanzig Künstlern der belgischen Avantgarde, die zwischen 1884 und 1895 jährliche Ausstellungen organisierten.
Anfänglich malte Finch impressionistisch, übernahm jedoch 1887, nachdem Seurat und Pissarro bei den XX ausgestellt hatten, deren divisionistische Maltechnik und reihte sich somit als einer der ersten Belgier bei den Neoimpressionisten ein.
Zwischen 1887 und 1892 schuf er etwa fünfzehn Bilder im Stil des Divisionismus und – wiewohl direkt und offensichtlich von Seurat beeinflusst – fand in dieser Technik zu einem sehr persönlichen, individuellen Stil. In Anlehnung an sein Vorbild Seurat wählte Finch bisweilen auch Umrahmungen, die er in die Darstellung mit einbezog und in der pointillistischen Technik mit Farbtupfen besetzte.
1897 reiste Finch nach Finnland, wo er bis zu seinem Tode lebte. In Helsinki malte und lehrte er fast dreißig Jahre lang und machte den Impressionismus und den Pointillismus in Finnland erst bekannt.

Born near Brussels as the son of English parents, Willy Finch was a founding member of Les XX, the group of twenty artists of the Belgian avant-garde who organized annual exhibitions from 1884 to 1895.
Finch initially painted in the style of the Impressionists, but in 1887, following the exhibition of the work of Seurat and Pissarro at the Les XX shows, he adopted their Divisionist technique and thus joined the ranks of the first Belgian Neo-Impressionists.
He completed circa fifteen paintings in the Divisionist style between 1887 and 1892, and—directly and quite obviously influenced by Seurat—developed his own personal, highly individualistic style in this technique. Inspired by Georges Seurat, Willy Finch often integrated frames into his paintings, covering them with daubs of paint using the Pointillist technique.
Finch traveled to Finland in 1897 and remained there until his death in 1930. He painted and taught in Helsinki for nearly thirty years and is credited with introducing Impressionism and Pointillism to Finland.

Paul Gauguin

(Paris 1848 – 1903 Atuona Hiva-Oa/La Dominique, Marquesas-Inseln Marquesas Islands)

Nach beruflichen Anfängen als Matrose und Börsenmakler verschrieb sich Gauguin erst um 1883 gänzlich der Malerei. Nachdem er durch Pissarro in den Kreis der Impressionisten Einlass gefunden hatte, nahm er ab 1879 an deren Gruppenausstellungen teil.
1886 besuchte Gauguin zum ersten Mal die Bretagne. Durch die Begegnung mit der bretonischen Landschaft und ihrer Bevölkerung erschloss sich ihm eine Empfindung von Ursprünglichkeit, Vergeistigung und Mystik, die von entscheidender Bedeutung für seine gesamte weitere künstlerische Entwicklung war.
Nach einem Besuch in Panama und auf Martinique kehrte Gauguin 1888 in die Bretagne zurück. Hier vollzog er nun einen Bruch mit dem Impressionismus und entwickelte – auf der Grundlage des Cloisonismus Emile Bernards – die Kunstform des Synthetismus. Mit ungemischten Farben, großen Farbflächen und dekorativer Linienführung schuf er eine stark emotionale, symbolische Ausdrucksform, die das Motiv auf eine zeitlose, metaphysische Ebene hob. Seinen vereinfachten, formalisierten, dekorativen Stil wandte er auch im Bereich der Skulptur und des Holzschnitts an. In der Bretagne wie in Paris scharten sich die Künstler um Gauguin als den anerkannten Anführer der symbolistischen Kunst Frankreichs.
Seine fortwährende Suche nach exotischen, unverdorbenen Landstrichen führte Gauguin 1891 nach Tahiti. 1893 kehrte er nach Paris zurück, doch blieben seine Erwartungen hinsichtlich einer großen öffentlichen Anerkennung unerfüllt. Enttäuscht zog sich Gauguin 1895 auf die Marquesas-Inseln zurück, wo er 1903 starb.

Gauguin worked for a number of years as a seaman and a stockbroker, and he did not begin painting full-time until 1883. Having been introduced to the Impressionist circle by Pissarro, he began participating in their exhibitions in 1879.
Gauguin visited Brittany for the first time in 1886. The encounter with the local landscape engendered in him a sense of primal originality, spirituality, and mysticism that would play a decisive role in his development as an artist in the years to come.
After a journey to Panama and Martinique, Gauguin returned to Brittany in 1888. It was there that he abandoned Impressionism and began to develop the Synthetist style (on the basis of Emile Bernard's Cloisonnism). Working with pure colors, large fields of color, and decorative line configurations, he created a highly emotional, symbolic mode of expression that elevated the motif to a timeless, metaphysical sphere. He also applied his simplified, formalized, decorative style to sculptures and woodcuts. In Brittany as in Paris, artists were attracted to Gauguin, whom they regarded as the leading exponent of Symbolist art in France.
Gauguin's perpetual quest for exotic, unspoiled landscapes led him to Tahiti in 1891. Although he returned to Paris in 1893, the broad public recognition he anticipated was not forthcoming. Disappointed, Gauguin departed France for the Marquesas Islands, where he died in 1903.

Leo Gausson

(Lagny-sur-Marne 1860 – 1944 Lagny-sur-Marne)

In der Nähe von Paris geboren, begann Gausson seine Künstlerkarriere im Atelier des Holzschnitzers Eugène Froment, eines Freundes der Familie. Dort kam er in Kontakt mit Maximilien Luce, der ihn in die Technik des Divisionismus einführte, bei der die reinen Farben in kleinen Farbtupfen

oder -strichen auf die Leinwand oder die Holztafel aufgetragen werden und gemäß deren Theorien sich die Farben erst im Auge des Betrachters vermischen sollen. Begeistert schloss sich Gausson den Neoimpressionisten an. Die systematische Anwendung der pointillistischen Maltechnik gelangte bei Gausson zu ganz eigenen Formfindungen. Der in seinen Bildern häufig wahrnehmbare ornamentale, flächige Linienfluss sollte wenige Jahre später ein wichtiges Stilmerkmal der neuartigen Kunstform des Jugendstils sein. 1896 veranstaltete Gausson eine Sonderausstellung zu seinem Werk in der Rue Laffitte und 1899 im Théâtre Antoine. Später trat er in den Kolonialdienst ein und gab die Malerei weitgehend auf.

Born near Paris, Gausson began his career as an artist in the studio of Eugène Froment, a woodcarver and close friend of the family. He was introduced there to Luce, who taught him the technique of Divisionist painting in which pure colors are applied to the canvas or wooden panel in small daubs or strokes and—according to Divisionist theories—were mixed in the eye of the viewer. Gausson joined the ranks of the Neo-Impressionists with great enthusiasm. In Gausson's art, the systematic application of the Pointillist technique led to highly individual formal inventions. The ornamental, expansive, flowing lines frequently found in his paintings would become a characteristic feature of a new style several years later—that of Art Nouveau.

Gausson organized special exhibitions of his work in the Rue Laffitte in 1896 and at the Théâtre Antoine in 1899. He later joined the colonial service and gave up painting almost completely.

Norbert Goeneutte
(Paris 1854 – 1894 Auvers-sur-Oise)

Norbert Goeneutte brauchte den Aspekt der Verkäuflichkeit seiner Werke nie zu berücksichtigen, denn durch die finanzielle Unterstützung seines Bruders Charles war es ihm möglich, sich in völliger Unabhängigkeit der Kunst zu widmen.

Er verkehrte häufig im Café Nouvelle Athènes, in den Künstlerkreisen von Paris war er bekannt und äußerst beliebt. Im Nouvelle Athènes machte er auch die Bekanntschaft Manets und Renoirs.

Ab 1876 stellte er im Pariser Salon aus, vor allem humoristische Darstellungen von Szenen des Pariser Alltagslebens, Veduten aus Venedig, sowie Landschaften und auch Bildnisdarstellungen von sogenannten Originalen aus den einfachen Gesellschaftsschichten von Paris.

Wiewohl er nie aus dem Schatten seiner berühmteren Künstlerkollegen herausgetreten ist, sind Goeneuttes impressionistische Bilder qualitätvoll und von ansprechender Stimmungshaftigkeit.

Norbert Goeneutte was never compelled to consider the question of whether his works were saleable, as the financial support provided by his brother Charles enabled him to pursue his art in complete independence.

He was a frequent visitor to the Café Nouvelle Athènes and was well known and very popular within the artists' circles of Paris. He made the acquaintance of Manet and Renoir at the Nouvelle Athènes.

He first exhibited at the Paris Salon in 1876, showing primarily humoristic renditions of scenes from everyday life in Paris, Venice cityscapes, landscapes, and portraits of so-called originals from the lower classes of Parisian society.

Although he never emerged from the shadow of his more famous fellow artists, Goeneutte's Impressionist paintings exhibit striking quality and an appealing atmosphere.

Vincent van Gogh
(Groot-Zundert/Breda 1853 – 1890 Auvers-sur-Oise)

Van Gogh wurde sich 1880 – nach missglückten Versuchen als Kunsthändler, Lehrer und Missionar – seiner künstlerischen Berufung bewusst. Zeitlebens war er dabei auf die finanzielle Unterstützung seines Bruders Théo, eines Angestellten im Kunsthandel, angewiesen.

In seiner frühen Periode, die auch van Goghs »dunkle Periode« genannt wird, handelten seine Darstellungen vor allem von der Armut der unteren Bevölkerungsschichten. 1886 ging er nach Paris, wo er in Kontakt mit den Impressionisten kam. In dieser impressionistischen Phase gab er seine dunkeltonige Malerei zugunsten einer impressionistischen Malweise in hellen Farbtönen auf. 1888 ließ sich van Gogh in Arles nieder, wo er zeitweise eng mit Gauguin zusammenarbeitete – eine Künstlerfreundschaft, die in einem heftigen Streit endete. In Arles gelangte van Gogh mehr und mehr zu einer ganz eigenen Kunstauffassung und einem sehr persönlichen Stil. Die Bilder aus dieser Zeit sind von gesteigerter Farbigkeit und in Bildaufbau und Formgebung oft deutlich vom japanischen Farbholzschnitt beispielsweise eines Hokusai beeinflusst.

Van Gogh litt unter Anfällen und begab sich 1889 für ein Jahr in eine Nervenheilanstalt nach Saint-Rémy. Die dort entstandenen Bilder offenbaren eine wachsende Obsession für Darstellungen des Sonnenlichts, die er in einer fast expressionistisch zu nennenden Malweise ausführte. Ende Juli 1890 nahm sich Vincent van Gogh in Auvers-sur-Oise das Leben.

Van Gogh, ein Hauptmeister des Postimpressionismus, ließ niemals akademische Regeln für seine Kunst gelten, und als erster Künstler wandte er die Deformation der Form als künstlerisches Gestaltungsmittel zur Steigerung der Ausdruckskraft an. Durch sein Kunstschaffen kann er als einer der Begründer der modernen Kunst angesehen werden, war er doch für Fauvisten wie Expressionisten das wichtigste künstlerische Vorbild.

Following failed attempts to earn a living as an art dealer, a teacher, and a missionary, van Gogh realized his true calling as an artist in 1880. He was compelled to rely on his brother Théo, an art dealer, for financial support his entire life.

During his early years, which are also known as van Gogh's "dark period," his paintings focused primarily on the poverty of the lower classes. In 1886, he went to Paris, where he became acquainted with the Impressionists. During this Impressionist phase, he abandoned the dark colors of his early paintings in favor of an Impressionist style that relied on bright tones. Van Gogh moved to Arles in 1888, where he worked closely with Gauguin for a brief period. Their friendship ended in a violent dispute, however. In Arles, van Gogh gradually developed his own unique concept of art and a highly personal style. The paintings from this period are characterized by intense coloration. In terms of composition and form, they clearly suggest the strong influence of certain types of Japanese woodcuts, such as those of Hokusai.

Van Gogh suffered from bouts with mental illness and was admitted to the mental hospital in Saint-Rémy for a year in 1889. The paintings completed there reveal a growing obsession with images of sunlight, which he executed in a style that might almost be regarded as Expressionistic. He committed suicide in Auvers-sur-Oise in late July 1890.

One of the great masters of Post-Impressionism, van Gogh never accepted academic rules in his art, and he was the first artist to employ the distortion of form as a means of heightening the expressive power of his paintings. His oeuvre qualifies him as one of the founders of modern art, as he was the most important source of inspiration for both the Fauvists and the Expressionists.

Fernand Marie Eugene le Gout-Gerard
(Saint-Lô/Manche 1854 – 1924 Paris)

Fernand le Goût-Gerard war als Maler Autodidakt. Er schuf vor allem stimmungsvolle Küstenlandschaften und Ansichten von Häfen. Häufig versetzte er seine Darstellungen mit Figurenstaffage. Le Goût-Gerard unternahm Studienreisen nach Italien, wo in Venedig ein Bilderzyklus mit Ansichten der Lagune entstand, und nach Tunis. 1926, zwei Jahre nach seinem Tode, fand im Salon de la société nationale eine Gedächtnisausstellung zu seinem Werk statt. Bilder des Künstlers befinden sich heute unter anderem in den Museen von Montreal, Dijon, Rouen, Narbonne und Prag.

Fernand Le Goût-Gerard was a self-taught painter. The majority of his works are atmospheric coastal landscapes and harbor scenes. He incorporated incidental figures into many of his paintings. Le Goût-Gerard traveled to Italy, where he completed a series of views of the lagoon, and to Tunis. In 1926, two years after his death, a commemorative exhibition was organized in his honor at the Salon de la Société Nationale. Paintings by the artist are on exhibit at museums in Montreal, Dijon, Rouen, Narbonne, Prague, and other cities.

Armand Guillaumin
(Paris 1841 – 1927 Paris)

Armand Guillaumin nahm 1860 ein Zeichenstudium an der Académie Suisse auf. In dieser Zeit nahm auch seine enge Freundschaft mit Pissarro und Cézanne ihren Anfang.
Als sich nach dem Deutsch-Französischen Krieg die Beziehung zwischen jenen Künstlern, die den Spottnamen Impressionisten tragen sollten, zu festigen begann, fand sich Guillaumin in ihren Reihen. Am 27. Dezember 1873 wurde die Gründungsurkunde der Société anonyme des artistes, peintres, sculpteurs, graveurs etc. unterzeichnet, und Guillaumin zählte neben Monet, Renoir, Sisley, Degas, Morisot, Pissarro und Edmond-Joseph Béliard zu ihren Gründungsmitgliedern.
Nachdem sich die Impressionisten anfangs nur mit den Wirkungen des Lichts befasst hatten, drangen sie bald immer tiefer zum Phänomen der Farbe vor. In dem Versuch, das Farbenspiel der Natur so wiederzugeben, wie sie es wahrnahmen, lösten sie das Geschehen auf der Leinwand zunehmend in einzelne Details auf. Das vielleicht bezeichnendste Merkmal dieser Periode ist die Entwicklung einer Mikrostruktur des Bildes, indem die breiten Farbflächen zu unzähligen einzelnen farbigen Pinselstrichen verfeinert werden. Zudem erkennen wir eine deutliche Entwicklung zur Strukturierung der Form mithilfe der Pinselführung, um den Eindruck von Plastizität zu erzeugen.
Als der Letzte aus dem engeren Kreis der Impressionisten verstarb Armand Guillaumin 1927 im Alter von 86 Jahren.

Armand Guillaumin enrolled as a student of drawing at the Académie Suisse in 1860. He became friends with Pissarro and Cézanne during that period.
When the bonds that joined the artists who would later be referred to scornfully as the Impressionists grew stronger following the Franco-Prussian War, Guillaumin was among them. The founding charter of the Société Anonyme des Artistes, Peintres, Sculpteurs, Graveurs, etc., was signed on December 27, 1873, and Guillaumin joined Monet, Renoir, Sisley, Degas, Morisot, Pissarro, and Edmond-Joseph Béliard as a founding member.
After focusing initially only on the effects of light, the Impressionists soon began to delve more deeply into the phenomenon of color. In their attempts to depict the interplay of colors in nature as they perceived it, they progressively broke down the images on their canvases into individual details. Perhaps the most revealing characteristic of this period is the development of a microstructure within the painting, in which large fields of color are rendered in countless individual strokes of color. We also recognize a marked trend in favor of a more structured form achieved with brushstrokes, which evokes the impression of plasticity.
The last surviving member of the inner cercle of Impressionists, Guillaumin died in 1927 at the age of eighty-six.

Karl Hagemeister
(Werder an der Havel 1848 – 1933 Werder an der Havel)

Hagemeister begann seine künstlerische Ausbildung in Weimar bei dem Klassizisten Friedrich Preller d. Ä. In seinen frühen Wanderjahren lernte er die Malerkollegen Carl Schuch und Trübner kennen, bereiste mit ihnen unter anderem Österreich, Holland, Belgien und Italien. Stillleben und Jagdstücke kennzeichnen Hagemeisters frühes Werk, anfangs noch versetzt mit Figurenstaffage.
In seiner künstlerischen Entwicklung setzte sich Hagemeister auch mit dem Realismus Wilhelm Leibls auseinander, zählte aber nicht zum sogenannten Leibl-Kreis. Während dieser Jahre war Hagemeisters Berührung mit der aktuellen europäischen Kunst weitaus größer als die vieler anderer deutscher Maler. 1884 führte die Begegnung mit der Kunst der Impressionisten während eines Paris-Aufenthaltes zur deutlichen Aufhellung seiner Palette, und er traf während dieser Reise auch Maler der Schule von Barbizon.
1892 gehörte er mit Liebermann zu den Begründern der Berliner Sezession und zählte in Deutschland zu den bekanntesten Malern seiner Zeit.
Um 1907 erweiterte er seinen Motivkreis um Seestücke, bewegte Darstellungen der Wellen und des Meeres.

Hagemeister began his training in art in Weimar with the Classicist Friedrich Preller the Elder. During his "wandering years," he became acquainted with fellow artists Carl Schuch and Trübner and traveled with them to Austria, Holland, Belgium, Italy, and other European countries. Still lifes and hunting scenes, often featuring incidental human figures at first, appear frequently in his early oeuvre.
As his career as an artist progressed, Hagemeister developed an interest in the Realism of Wilhelm Leibl, although he did not join the so-called Leibl group. During those years, Hagemeister was exposed to a considerably broader spectrum of contemporary European art than many other German painters. His introduction to the art of the Impressionists in 1884 during a stay in Paris culminated in a significant lightening of his palette, and he also met painters of the Barbizon School during that visit.
He and Liebermann were among the founders of the Berlin Secession in 1892, and both were among the best-known painters of the period.
In around 1907, Hagemeister added seascapes—animated depictions of waves and the sea—to his repertoire of subjects.

Ferdinand Hart-Nibbrig
(Amsterdam 1866 – 1915 Laren)

Der holländische Maler und Grafiker Hart-Nibbrig absolvierte von 1883 bis 1888 ein Kunststudium an der Amsterdamer Rijksakademie van beeldende kunsten. 1888 wechselte er an die dortige Quellinus-Schule. Wenig später ging er nach Paris, wo er die Académie Julian besuchte. Dort kam er bei Fernand Cormon in Berührung mit der Kunst Seurats und Signacs, was

ihn künstlerisch nachhaltig beeinflusste. So legte er seine impressionistische Malweise um 1899 zugunsten der neuen pointillistischen Technik ab. Nach seiner Rückkehr nach Holland gab er aber auch den divisionistischen Stil letzlich wieder auf und arbeitete in der Art des Realismus mit breitem, kräftigem Pinselstrich. Hart-Nibbrigs gesamtes Werk ist von Licht und Farbe durchdrungen. Wiewohl seine Bilder auf zahlreichen bedeutenden Ausstellungen gezeigt wurden, fand der Künstler lebenslang nur bescheidene Anerkennung.

The Dutch painter and graphic artist Hart-Nibbrig studied art at the Rijksakademie van beeldende kunsten in Amsterdam from 1883 to 1888 and transferred to the Quellinus School in 1888. Soon afterwards, he went to Paris, where he attended the Académie Julian. He studied there with Fernand Cormon and was introduced to the art of Seurat and Signac, an experience that had a lasting influence on his art. He abandoned his Impressionist style in about 1899 in favor of the new Pointillist technique. But after returning to Holland, he gave up the Divisionist style and adopted a more realistic approach which relied on broad, vigorous brushstrokes. Hart-Nibbrig's entire oeuvre is full of light and color. Although his paintings have been shown at numerous major exhibitions, the artist enjoyed only modest praise during his lifetime.

Louis Hayet

(Pontoise 1864 – 1940 Cormeilles-en-Parisis)

Anfänglich verdiente sich der autodidaktisch geschulte Künstler – und Schriftsteller – Hayet seinen Lebensunterhalt als Dekorationsmaler. 1881 machte er in Pontoise die Bekanntschaft Pissarros und dessen Sohnes Lucien, durch die er 1885 Signac, ein Jahr später Seurat, kennenlernte.
Seit 1887 in Paris ansässig, beschäftigte er sich intensiv mit Michel-Eugène Chevreuls Theorie der simultanen Farbkontraste und begann in der divisionistischen Technik der Neoimpressionisten zu malen. Allerdings stellte er nur einmal, 1889, mit dieser Künstlergruppe im Salon der Indépendants aus. Ein Jahr später war er in Brüssel im Salon der XX vertreten. Nach seinem Rückzug vom neoimpressionistischen Künstlerkreis verdiente sich Hart-Nibbrig seinen Lebensunterhalt bis zu seinem Tode wieder mit dekorativer Malerei. So war er unter anderem als Bühnenbildner für das Théâtre de l'Œuvre in Paris tätig.

A self-taught artist—and writer—Hayet earned his living as a decorative painter in his early years. In 1881, he met Pissarro and his son Lucien in Pontoise and was introduced by them to Signac in 1885 and to Seurat a year later.
Having settled in Paris in 1887, he devoted himself intensely to a study of Michel-Eugène Chevreul's theory of simultaneous color contrasts and began painting in the Divisionist style of the Neo-Impressionists. He exhibited with that group of artists at the Salon des Artistes Indépendants only once (in 1889), however. He was represented at the Salon des XX in Brussels a year later. After leaving the circle of Neo-Impressionist artists, Hayet worked as a decorative painter until his death. Among other jobs, he was employed as a stage designer at the Théâtre de l'Œuvre in Paris.

Auguste Herbin

(Quievy/Cambrai 1882 – 1960 Paris)

Ab 1900 besuchte Herbin die Ecole des Beaux-Arts in Lille, ehe er sich in Paris niederließ, wo er sich zunächst den Impressionisten, dann den Fauves anschloss; ab 1913 entstanden erste vom Kubismus inspirierte Bilder. Ab 1917 folgte eine ungegenständliche, geometrische Phase, die im Konstruktivismus mündete.
1931 war Herbin Mitbegründer der Künstlervereinigung Abstraction-Création. Nach 1938 gelangte Herbin zu einer kronkreten Malerei mit strengem Flächenprinzip und einfach aufgefasstem geometrischen Formenkanon. Bereits vor dem Zweiten Weltkrieg fand sein Werk international breite Anerkennung, was sich auch nach dem Krieg fortsetzte.

Herbin enrolled at the Ecole des Beaux-Arts in Lille in 1900 before moving to Paris, where he affiliated himself first with the Impressionists and later with the Fauvists. His first Cubist-inspired paintings were completed in 1913. His abstract, geometric period began in 1917 and culminated in his embrace of Constructivist art.
Herbin was co-founder of the Abstraction-Création group in 1931. After 1938, he adopted a style of concrete painting based on a strict principle of two-dimensionality and a simple canon of geometric forms. His work gained broad international recognition before World War Two and remained popular during the post-war years.

Ferdinand Hodler

(Gürzelen/Kanton Bern Canton of Berne 1853 – 1918 Genf Geneva)

Realistische Genrebilder markieren den Beginn von Hodlers Schaffen. In seinen frühen Landschaftsbildern zeigte der Maler eine Neigung zum Impressionismus, drängte aber zunehmend zur großen Szenerie, zum Figurenbild, dessen Pathos er durch stilisierende Konturen zu unterstreichen wusste. Hodlers monumentale Historienbilder und Lebensgleichnisse der Folgejahre tragen deutliche Züge des Jugendstils und des Impressionismus. Er war zu einem der führenden Maler in Europa geworden.
Seine späten, expressionistisch anmutenden Landschaftsgemälde machten Hodler auch zu einem der bedeutendsten Maler der Alpenlandschaft.

Realistic genre paintings characterize Hodler's early oeuvre. His first landscapes reveal a tendency toward an Impressionist style, but he soon moved on to more expansive scenes, to figurative paintings whose pathos he emphasized through the use of stylized contours. Hodler's monumental history paintings and metaphorical images of the following years exhibit unmistakable characteristics of Art Nouveau and Impressionism. He had become one of the leading painters in Europe.
With his late, Expressionist-style landscapes, Hodler also earned recognition as the most important painter of the Alpine region.

Ludwig von Hofmann

(Darmstadt 1861 – 1945 Pillnitz/Sachsen Saxony)

Nach einem Studium an der Kunstakademie in Dresden (1883 bis 1886) war Hofmann von 1886 bis 1888 Meisterschüler bei Ferdinand Keller in Karlsruhe. 1889 besuchte er die Académie Julian in Paris. In den Jahren zwischen 1890 und 1903 lebte Hofmann in Berlin, wo er der Berliner Sezession angehörte. Innerhalb der Sezession vertrat Hofmann die Richtung des Jugendstils. 1903 erfolgte seine Berufung an die Großherzogliche Kunstschule nach Weimar.
Hofmanns gesamtes Schaffen ist gekennzeichnet durch zwei Pole: ekstatische Tanz- und Aktionsstudien als Ausdruck eines Höchstmaßes an Bewegung auf der einen sowie symbolisch aufgefasste friedlich-idyllische, unbewegte Ideallandschaften auf der anderen Seite, die eine harmonische Welt

suggerieren. Die Wertevorstellungen dieser schönen, unbeschwerten Welten kamen denjenigen der Jugend- und Wandervogelbewegungen nahe. Literarische Parallelen findet Hofmanns Kunstauffassung bei Hugo von Hofmannsthal.

After studying at the Kunstakademie in Dresden (1883–86), Hofmann was a master student with Ferdinand Keller in Karlsruhe from 1886 to 1888. He attended the Académie Julian in Paris in 1889. During the years between 1890 and 1903, Hofmann lived in Berlin, where he joined the Berlin Secession. Within the context of the Secession, he was a representative of Art Nouveau. He was appointed to the faculty of the Grossherzogliche Kunstschule in Weimar in 1903.
Hofmann's entire oeuvre is characterized by two opposing poles: ecstatic dance and action studies as an expression of extreme motion, on the one hand, and symbolist tranquil, idyllic, motionless landscapes suggestive of a harmonious world, on the other. The values associated with these beautiful worlds of contentment were similar to those of the "Wandervogel" movement. Literary parallels to Hofmann's concept of art are found in the writings of Hugo von Hofmannsthal.

Blanche Hoschede-Monet
(Paris 1865 – 1947 Paris)

Blanche Hoschedé-Monet war die Tochter Monets, von dem sie auch ihre ersten künstlerischen Unterweisungen empfing. Ihre Werke – überwiegend Landschaftsbilder – zeigen deutlich den Einfluss der Kunst ihres Vaters. Mit ihren reizvollen atmosphärischen Darstellungen fand Hoschedé-Monet regelmäßig Aufnahme im jährlichen Pariser Salon.

Blanche Hoschedé-Monet was the daughter of Monet, from whom she also received her early training in art. Her works—primarily landscapes—clearly reveal the influence of her father. Hoschedé-Monet's delightful, atmospheric paintings were regularly exhibited at the annual Paris Salon.

Eugene Isabey
(Paris 1803 – 1886 Lagny/Paris)

Die frühen prägenden Jahre verbrachte der Sohn eines Malers mit dem Sudium der bewunderten alten Meister im Louvre. Seine ersten Werke – überwiegend Landschaften – malte er in Aquarell. Auf Reisen in den 1820er-Jahren in die Normandie und nach England wurde seine Technik freier. Er wurde bekannt für seine romantisierenden Landschaftsdarstellungen und Seestücke, die er ebenso dramatisch wie gefällig anzulegen verstand.
In der Eigenschaft eines königlichen Marinemalers begleitete Isabey 1830 den französischen Afrika-Feldzug nach Algier und schuf zahlreiche Darstellungen des Kriegsschauplatzes. Nach seiner Rückkehr widmete er sich mehr und mehr einer historisierenden Genremalerei. Diese elegant-anekdotische Malerei machte ihn berühmt, und Louis-Philippe machte ihn zu einem seiner Hofmaler. In Isabeys späterem Werk finden sich auch starkfarbige Darstellungen von Schlachten und Überfällen.

Isabey, the son of a painter, spent his early formative years studying admired old masters in the Louvre. His first works—mostly landscapes—were watercolors. During his travels to Normandy and England in the 1820s, he developed a freer painting technique. He earned acclaim for his Romantic landscapes and seascapes, which he conceived in an equally dramatic and appealing style.
In his position as a Royal Navy painter, Isabey accompanied French troops to Algiers during the Africa campaign in 1830 and painted numerous war scenes there. After his return to France, he devoted himself increasingly to historical genre painting. His elegant, anecdotal style gained him considerable fame as well as an appointment as painter at the court of Louis-Philippe. Isabey's late oeuvre also includes a number of battle and assault scenes.

Alexej von Jawlensky
(Torschok bei Twer/Russland Russia 1864 – 1941 Wiesbaden)

Jawlensky besuchte ab 1889 die Kunstakademie in Sankt Petersburg, wo er Marianne von Werefkin kennenlernte. 1896 gingen beide gemeinsam nach München, wo sie in engen Kontakt mit der künstlerischen Avantgarde traten. Besonders mit Kandinsky verband Jawlensky eine enge Freundschaft. Das erklärte künstlerische Ziel der beiden Malerfreunde wurde die Überwindung der Akademietraditionen und eine Neubewertung des Naturbegriffs zur Schaffung einer neuen Kunstauffassung. Zu ihren Vorbildern zählten Gauguin und van Gogh, was sich bei Jawlensky früh im expressiven Gebrauch einer kräftigen, leuchtenden Farbpalette widerspiegelt. 1909 gründeten Kandinsky und Jawlensky die Neue Künstlervereinigung München, die zum Zentrum des Expressionismus im Süden Deutschlands werden sollte.
Nach einem anfänglichen »Vulkanausbruch« der Farbe, die er zunächst in einzeln gesetzten Strichen auf die Leinwand brachte, schuf Jawlensky bald »beruhigtere« Bildflächen, in ihrer Farbigkeit stärker zu Farbfeldern gegliedert, die zunehmend von festen Konturen umrissen waren. Wenngleich es ihm dabei mehr um die äußere Wiedergabe eines inneren Zustands als um Formwerte ging, gelangte seine Malerei nie – wie beispielsweise die Kandinskys – zur Gegenstandslosigkeit. Im Schweizer Exil (1914–17) widmete sich Jawlensky fast ausschließlich dem Landschaftsbild. Ab 1918 malte er wieder Porträts, wobei er die Bildnisse immer weiter reduzierte bis zu einer »Urform« des menschlichen Kopfes. Diese Darstellungen, auch bezeichnet als »neuzeitliche Ikonen«, wurden gleichsam zu Meditationsobjekten.

Jawlensky enrolled at the art academy in Saint Petersburg in 1889, where he met Marianne von Werefkin. In 1896, the two traveled to Munich, where they forged strong ties to the avant-garde art scene. Jawlensky enjoyed a particularly close friendship with Kandinsky. The two artists openly declared their intention to abandon academic traditions and reassess the interpretation of nature in order to develop a new concept of art. They were inspired by such artists as Gauguin and van Gogh, as is evident in Jawlensky's case in his expressive use of a vivid, radiant palette. Kandinsky and Jawlensky founded the Neue Künstlervereinigung München (New Munich Artists' Association) in 1909, an institution that would become a center of Expressionist art in southern Germany.
After his early "volcanic eruption" of colors, which he initially applied to the canvas in individual brushstrokes, Jawlensky soon moved on to create "calmer" paintings that are more clearly divided into distinct fields of color bordered by increasingly solid contours. Although he was more concerned with the external depiction of internal phenomena than with formal values, his painting—in contrast to that of Kandinsky—never reached the point of abstraction. During his exile in Switzerland (1914–17), Jawlensky devoted himself almost exclusively to landscape painting. He began painting portraits again in 1918, progressively reducing likenesses to "primal forms" of the human head. In a certain sense, these paintings, which are also referred to as "modern icons," became objects of meditation.

Johan Barthold Jongkind
(Lattrop 1819 – 1891 La Côte-Saint-André)

Jongkind zählte lange zu den weniger beachteten Malern der zweiten Hälfte des 19. Jahrhunderts, obwohl er in der Literatur neben Boudin immer wieder als Vorläufer und Wegbereiter des Impressionismus genannt wurde. Tatsächlich deutet die Tatsache, dass Jongkinds Bildsprache schon zum Ende der 1850er-Jahre die überkommenen Sehgewohnheiten vermissen lässt, an, wie er bereits vor den jüngeren französischen Malerkollegen die vibrierende Atmosphäre des Impressionismus zu gestalten in der Lage war. Trotz des malerisch spontanen Eindrucks bleibt die Farbe dabei stets der Ausgewogenheit der Bildkomposition verpflichtet.
Als Maler kein Revolutionär, folgte Jongkind zunächst den Traditionen der niederländischen Landschaftsmalerei des 17. Jahrhunderts. Er hellte dieser gegenüber jedoch seine Palette auf, vereinfachte sie und setzte die Farbe in kurzen, abrupten Strichen.
Eine Frankreich-Reise um 1845/46 – wohl zu Studienzwecken – löste den entscheidenden Wechsel in seinem Stil aus. Bis 1856 war Jongkind in Paris tätig, doch zeichnete sich in diesen Jahren bereits ab, was später weitgehend sein Leben ruinieren sollte, das ständige Schwanken zwischen einem ausschweifenden Leben, Alkoholismus und intensivster Arbeit.
Als der Maler 1860 aus Holland wieder nach Paris zurückkehrte, folgten Jahre harter Arbeit, aber auch wachsenden Erfolges. Zuletzt lebte Jongkind von 1878 an in Côte-Saint-André, im Hause seiner Mäzenin, Madame Fesser.

Jongkind remained one of the lesser-known painters of the later half of the nineteenth century for many years, although he is often cited in the literature along with Boudin as a pioneer and precursor of the Impressionist movement. The fact is, however, that the absence of outdated visual habits in Jongkind's pictorial language as early as in the late 1850s clearly shows that he was capable of creating the vibrant atmosphere of Impressionist painting long before the younger French painters that followed him. Despite the spontaneous quality of his painting, his colors are consistently in keeping with the balance and harmony of his pictorial compositions.
By no means a revolutionary painter, Jongkind initially followed in the footsteps of the Dutch landscape painters of the seventeenth century. In contrast to his predecessors, however, he used lighter colors, simplifying his palette and applying paint in short, abrupt strokes.
A journey to France in about 1845/46—presumably to study—triggered the crucial shift in his style. Jongkind worked in Paris until 1856, but the problems that would later bring him to the brink of ruin were evident even during those years—the constant fluctuation between a life of excess and alcoholism and periods of intense work.
The painter worked very hard after returning to Paris from Holland in 1860 but enjoyed increasing success as well. Jongkind moved to Côte-Saint-André in 1878, where he lived until his death at the home of his patroness, Madame Fesser.

Wassily Kandinsky
(Moskau Moscow 1866 – 1944 Neuilly-sur-Seine)

Kandinsky war 1896 aus Moskau nach München gekommen, wo er an der Kunstakademie bei dem Malerfürsten Franz von Stuck studierte. 1901 gründete er die private Phalanx-Kunstschule, wo er seine zukünftige Lebensgefährtin Münter kennenlernte.
Schon Kandinskys frühe Bilder wiesen mit ihrem Farbenreichtum in eine expressive Richtung, formal orientierte er sich jedoch zunächst an den französischen Neoimpressionisten. Auf Reisen nach Paris empfing er vor deren Bildern die Eindrücke bloßer Farbwirkung. In kurze, bewegte Pinselstriche zerlegte Farbwerte rhythmisieren in diesen Jahren seine Kompositionen.
1909 gründete Kandinsky zusammen mit Münter, Jawlensky, Adolf Erbslöh, Werefkin, Kanoldt, Wladimir von Bechtejeff, Karl Hofer und Alfred Kubin die Neue Künstlervereinigung München.
Nach der Begegnung mit der Kunst der Fauvisten ließ er immer mehr die Farbe zum entscheidenden formalen Element in seinen Bildern werden. Immer stärker löste er die Komposition vom Gegenstand, Farben und Formen entfalteten sich immer freier. Seine *Komposition V* war fast vollständig abstrakt. Als sie bei Ausstellungsvorbereitungen innerhalb der Neuen Künstlervereinigung auf Ablehnung stieß, rief Kandinsky mit Franz Marc eine neue Vereinigung ins Leben, den Blauen Reiter. In den 1930er-Jahren kam Kandinsky als Lehrer am Bauhaus in Kontakt mit dem russischen Konstruktivismus, woraufhin sich endgültig die geometrischen Strukturen in seinen Bildern durchsetzten.

Kandinsky came to Munich from Moscow in 1896 and enrolled as a student with the famous painter Franz von Stuck at the Kunstakademie. In 1901, he founded the private Phalanx-Kunstschule, where he met his future companion, Gabriele Münter.
The rich coloration of Kandinsky's early paintings may be seen as an early sign of a developing Expressionist orientation, yet he initially adopted the formal principles of the French Neo-Impressionists. Viewing their paintings during visits to Paris, he came away with impressions of the pure effect of color. Colors applied in short, energetic brushstrokes imbue the compositions of those years with rhythm.
Kandinsky, Münter, Jawlensky, Adolf Erbslöh, Werefkin, Kanoldt, Wladimir von Bechtejeff, Karl Hofer, and Alfred Kubin founded the Neue Künstlervereinigung München (New Munich Artists' Association) in 1909.
After becoming acquainted with the art of the Fauvists, Kandinsky used color as the crucial formal element in his paintings to an increasing extent. He progressively liberated the composition from the subject; colors and forms became freer over the course of time. His *Composition V* was almost completely abstract. When this painting was rejected by members of the Neue Künstlervereinigung, Kandinsky and Franz Marc established a new association, Der Blaue Reiter. As a teacher at the Bauhaus, Kandinsky came in contact with Russian Constructivism during the 1930s, and geometric structures dominated his paintings from that point on.

Alexander Kanoldt
(Karlsruhe 1881 – 1939 Berlin)

Ab 1899 besuchte Kanoldt zunächst die Großherzoglich-Badische Kunstgewerbeschule seiner Heimatstadt Karlsruhe und wechselte zwei Jahre später an die dortige Akademie der bildenden Künste. Mit dem Kommilitonen Adolf Erbslöh sollte ihn eine lebenslange Freundschaft verbinden. Als er anlässlich einer Ausstellung im Badischen Kunstverein im Dezember 1906 erstmals Werken der französischen Neo- und Postimpressionisten begegnete, brach eine pointillistische Phase im Schaffen Kanoldts an.
1908 kam er in München in Kontakt mit dem Künstlerkreis um Kandinsky und Jawlensky, und von 1909 bis 1912 war Alexander Kanoldt Mitglied der Neuen Künstlervereinigung München, mit der er in diesen Jahren auch regelmäßig ausstellte. 1910 war er auf der berühmten Ausstellung *Sonderbund Westdeutscher Künstler* vertreten. 1913 gehörte er neben Jawlensky, Paul Klee und anderen zu den Mitbegründern der Münchner Neuen Sezession, aus der er 1920 – aus Protest gegen Kandinskys Programm absoluter Gegenstandslosigkeit – austrat. 1925 wurde Kanoldt als Professor an die

Breslauer Akademie für Kunst und Kunstgewerbe berufen, 1927 gründete er zusammen mit anderen die Badische Sezession, die 1936 zwangsweise aufgelöst wurde.
Kanoldts Frühwerke zeigen genrehaften Naturalismus. Nach der pointillistischen Phase folgte die Auseinandersetzung mit dem Expressionismus und Kubismus. Schließlich fand er in der Neuen Sachlichkeit die ihm gemäße Kunstform.
Zur Zeit des Nationalsozialismus galten Kanoldts Werke als »entartete Kunst«.

Kanoldt enrolled at the Grossherzoglich-Badische Kunstgewerbeschule in his native city of Karlsruhe in 1899 and later transferred to the local Akademie der bildenden Künste. He forged a lifetime friendship with his fellow student Adolf Erbslöh. His first encounter with works by the French Neo-Impressionists and Post-Impressionists at an exhibition at the Badischer Kunstverein in December 1906 marked the beginning of Kanoldt's Pointillist phase.
Kanoldt came in contact with the artists associated with Kandinsky and Jawlensky in Munich in 1908. He was a member of the Neue Künstlervereinigung München (New Munich Artists' Association) from 1909 to 1912 and exhibited regularly at the association's exhibitions during those years. He took part in the famous *Sonderbund Westdeutscher Künstler* show in 1910. He joined Jawlensky, Paul Klee, and others to found the Münchner Neue Sezession (New Munich Secession) in 1913 but resigned from the organization in protest against Kandinsky's program of absolute abstract art in 1920. Kanoldt was appointed to a professorship at the Akademie für Kunst und Kunstgewerbe in Breslau in 1925. He founded the Baden Secession with several fellow artists in 1927. The organization was forced to disband in 1936.
Kanoldt's early works exhibit features of genre-style Naturalism. Following the Pointillist phase, he experimented with Expressionist and Cubist technique before discovering the style that suited him best in New Objectivity.
Kanoldt's paintings were dismissed as "degenerate art" during the Nazi era.

Gotthardt Kuehl
(Lübeck 1850 – 1915 Dresden)

Kuehl nahm 1867 ein Studium an der Königlich Sächsischen Akademie der Bildenden Künste in Dresden auf, wechselte aber bereits nach zwei Jahren an die Kunstakademie nach München, wo er Schüler in der Klasse von Wilhelm Diez wurde. Die Diez-Schule war Wegbereiter der impressionistischen Malerei im Münchner Biedermeier und stand in den 1870er-Jahren auch in enger Verbindung zum Künstlerkreis um Wilhelm Leibl. Kuehls Kunstauffassung wurde durch die Einflüsse der Diez-Schule und ihre Verbindungen entscheidend geprägt.
Er unternahm häufige Studienreisen, so auch nach Paris, wo er 1879 ansässig wurde und bald die Führung unter den deutschen Künstlern übernahm. Ab 1880 war er dort regelmäßig im Salon vertreten und verschrieb sich ab 1883 der Pleinairmalerei, deren Errungenschaften er gleichermaßen auch in seine Interieurmalerei einzubeziehen vermochte. Er griff zudem die Milieuthemen Liebermanns in seinem Werk auf und wurde – speziell nach seiner Rückkehr nach Deutschland 1889 – zum bedeutenden Vermittler französischer Entwicklungen. 1892 gehörte Kuehl zu den Mitbegründern der Münchner Sezession. 1895 zog er nach Dresden, wo er einen Lehrauftrag an der Kunstakademie annahm und weiterhin eine impressionistische Malweise pflegte, die charakterisiert war durch einen zusammenfassenden Malgestus und eine besondere koloristische Ausgewogenheit.

Kuehl enrolled in a course of study at the Königlich Sächsische Akademie der Bildenden Künste in 1867 but transferred after only two years to the Kunstakademie in Munich, where he studied with Wilhelm Diez. The Diez School paved the way for Impressionist painting during the Biedermeier period in Munich and was also closely associated with the group of artists affiliated with Wilhelm Leibl during the 1870s. Kuehl's art exhibits the significant influence of the Diez School and related approaches.
He undertook frequent study journeys, including trips to Paris, where he settled in 1879 and soon advanced to a position of leadership among the German artists in the city. Kuehl exhibited regularly at the Salon beginning in 1880. He devoted himself to plein-air painting after 1883 and sought to incorporate aspects of this technique in his interiors as well. He also took up Liebermann's milieu-related themes in his work and—especially after his return to Germany in 1889—became a leading exponent of French currents. Kuehl was one of the original founders of the Munich Secession in 1892. He moved to Dresden in 1895 and accepted a teaching position at the local art academy. He continued to paint in an Impressionist style characterized by a tendency to summarize and an extraordinary balance of color.

Georges Lacombe
(Versailles 1868 – 1916 Alençon)

Lacombe besuchte zunächst die Académie Julian in Paris und schloss sich dann – durch Vermittlung Sérusiers – der Gruppe der Nabis an. Schon bald änderte Lacombe seinen Stil und wandte sich der neoimpressionistischen Malweise zu. Von 1888 bis 1897 verbrachte er die Sommer im Departement Finistère. Hier entstanden in jenen Jahren neben Ölgemälden auch zahlreiche Skulpturen und Reliefs. Lacombe stellte regelmäßig im Herbstsalon und mit der Société des artistes indépendants aus. Nach Kriegsausbruch 1914 gab er den Künstlerberuf auf und wurde Krankenpfleger. Er starb während des Ersten Weltkrieges an den Folgen einer Infektionskrankheit.
In vielen Bildern Lacombes wird ersichtlich, welche verschiedenen Malstile um die Jahrhundertwende gleichzeitig möglich waren und sich durchdringen konnten: Während teilweise die impressionistische Malweise noch ausgeprägt gegenwärtig ist, sind auch Elemente des Symbolismus und des Jugendstils bei Lacombe erkennbar.

Lacombe attended the Académie Julian in Paris and later—having been introduced by Sérusier—joined the Nabi group. He soon altered his style and adopted the Neo-Impressionist mode of painting. From 1888 to 1897, he spent his summers in the Departement Finistère. He completed a number of paintings as well as numerous sculptures and reliefs during these stays. Lacombe exhibited regularly at the Salon d'Automne and the shows organized by the Société des Artistes Indépendants. After the outbreak of World War One in 1914, he abandoned his career in art to work as a male nurse. He died of complications following an infection during the war.
Many of Lacombe's paintings offer a good indication of the wide range of painting styles that were employed and often used in combination around the turn of the twentieth century. Although the Impressionist style is clearly evident in some works, elements of Symbolism and Art Nouveau are also discernible in Lacombe's art.

Achille Lauge
(Arzens/Carcassonne 1861 – 1944 Cailhau)

Ab 1881 studierte Laugé an der Pariser Ecole des Beaux-Arts. Ab 1889 hatte er ein Atelier in Carcassonne und unterhielt viele Freundschaften zu dort

lebenden Künstlern. Zugleich blieb er mit der Pariser Kunstwelt durch Freundschaften, regelmäßige Besuche und Ausstellungen in Kontakt und stellte gemeinsam mit den Indépendants und den Nabis aus.
Seit dem Ende seiner Pariser Zeit setzte er sich intensiv mit den Theorien des Neoimpressionismus auseinander und übernahm dessen divisionistischen Pinselstrich. Mit der Zeit wandte er sich dabei von den kleinen, systematisch gesetzten Strichen ab und fand zu einer eigenen, dem Pointillismus gleichwohl noch nahestehenden Malweise – einem leichteren Stil mit breiten und pastosen Tupfen, den er bis zum Ende seiner Schaffenszeit beibehielt. Trotz aller theoretischen Überlegungen war Laugé an der präzisen Erfassung des Gegenstandes weniger interessiert als vielmehr an den farblichen, durch Licht hervorgerufenen optischen Strukturen. Die Farbe wurde mehr und mehr zum Hauptthema in Laugés Malerei. Um die Eindrücke der Natur unmittelbar einfangen zu können, ließ sich der Künstler 1905 einen glasüberdachten Wagen bauen – ein »Atelier roulant« –, in dem er bei jedem Wetter arbeiten konnte.

Laugé enrolled at the Ecole des Beaux-Arts in Paris in 1881. He set up a studio in Carcassonne in 1889 and became friends with many of the artists who were living there at the time. Yet he maintained close contact with the Paris art world through friendships, frequent visits, and exhibitions, and he took part in exhibitions with the Indépendants and the Nabis.
After leaving Paris, he devoted himself to an intense study of Neo-Impressionist theories and adopted a Divisionist approach to brushwork. Over the course of time, he turned away from small, systematically applied brushstrokes and developed a painting technique of his own—even very close to Pointillism—a lighter style using broad, thick daubs of paint, which he retained for the remainder of his creative life. Despite his concern with theoretical considerations, Laugé was less interested in a precise rendering of his subject than with the chromatic visual structures generated by light. To an increasing extent, color became the dominant theme of his painting. In order to capture impressions of nature directly, the artist had a glass-roofed wagon built—a "studio on wheels"—in which he could work in every kind of weather.

Henri Lebasque
(Champigné/Maine-et-Loire 1865 – 1937 Le Cannet)

An der Ecole des Beaux-Arts in Paris war Lebasque Schüler von Léon Bonnat. Er pflegte enge Kontakte zu den Mitgliedern der Künstlergruppe der Nabis, die sich 1890 formierte, und 1893 beteiligte er sich am Salon der Indépendants, wo er die Bekanntschaft von Signac und Luce machte. Ab 1894 bis zu dessen Tod 1903 stand Lebasque zudem in Kontakt mit Pissarro, und seine Malerei wurde deutlich von der Kunst des Älteren beeinflusst.
Nach Ausbruch des Ersten Weltkrieges hielt Lebasque in Paris die Schrecken des Krieges in einer Folge von Lithografien fest, und noch 1917 verfolgte er – gemeinsam mit Vallotton – als Armeemaler das Kriegsgeschehen an der Front. 1918, im Jahr des Waffenstillstands, nahm ihn die Galerie Georges Petit unter Vertrag. Es folgten für den Maler zahlreiche Auftragsarbeiten zur Ausgestaltung von Bauwerken. Die erste Hälfte der 1920er-Jahre verbrachte Lebasque überwiegend auf Reisen. 1924 ließ er sich mit seiner Familie in Le Cannet nieder, wo er 1937 starb.

Lebasque studied with Léon Bonnat at the Ecole des Beaux-Arts in Paris. He maintained close ties with the members of the Nabi group, which had formed in 1890, and exhibited at the Salon des Artistes Indépendants in 1893, where he met Signac and Luce. Between 1894 and Pissarro's death in 1903, he was also in frequent contact with the elder artist, whose work clearly influenced Lebasque's painting. When World War One broke out in 1914, Lebasque returned to Paris, where he recorded the horrors of the war in a series of lithographs. Along with Vallotton, he followed the progress of the war on the front in 1917. In 1918, the year of the armistice, he signed a contract with the Galerie Georges Petit. The painter received numerous commissions for decorative art in architectural settings. Lebasque spent the first half of the 1920s traveling. In 1924, he moved with his family to Le Cannet, where he died in 1937.

Albert Charles Lebourg
(Montfort-sur-Risle/Eure 1849 – 1928 Rouen)

Nach einer Ausbildung als Architekt ging Lebourg auf Einladung eines Kunstsammlers nach Algier, wo er zwischen 1872 und 1877 an der Ecole des Beaux-Arts unterrichtete. Um das strahlende Licht Nordafrikas entsprechend wiederzugeben, fand Lebourg in Algier – ohne das Wissen um die revolutionären Theorien der Impressionisten, die die avantgardistischen Pariser Zirkel bewegten – zu einer ähnlichen Lösung. Wie die Impressionisten verspürte auch er das Bedürfnis, seine Farben aufzuhellen und mit großzügigen Pinselstrichen zu arbeiten, was den akademischen Lehren der damaligen Zeit gänzlich entgegenstand.
Nach seiner Rückkehr nach Frankreich lernte Lebourg 1878 Degas, Pissarro und Monet kennen und pflegte freundschaftliche Beziehungen zu ihnen. Er stellte auf zwei Impressionisten-Ausstellungen aus (1879 und 1880) und war von 1883 bis 1895 im Pariser Salon vertreten.
In seinen Landschaftsdarstellungen der Auvergne, der Normandie und der Ufer der Seine findet Lebourg trotz aller Nähe zu den Impressionisten zu einem durchaus eigenständigen Stil. Mit Interesse verfolgte er auch die neoimpressionistische Bewegung und setzte sich intensiv mit deren Theorien auseinander.

After completing his education as an architect, Lebourg was invited by an art collector to travel to Algiers, where he remained to teach at the Ecole des Beaux-Art from 1872 to 1877. In search of a way to represent the radiant light of North Africa, Lebourg—who knew nothing of the revolutionary Impressionist theories that were moving the avant-garde art scene in Paris—developed a very similar approach. Like the Impressionists, he felt the need to lighten his colors and to work with broad brushstrokes, which ran contrary to the academic principles of the period.
Following his return to France, in 1878 Lebourg became acquainted with Degas, Pissarro, and Monet and maintained ties of friendship with all three. He exhibited at two Impressionist exhibitions (in 1879 and 1880) and was a regular participant in the Paris Salon from 1883 to 1895.
Despite his affinities with the Impressionists, Lebourg developed a uniquely personal style in his landscapes from the Auvergne, Normandy, and the banks of the Seine. He also followed the progress of the Neo-Impressionist movement with interest and assiduously studied their theories.

Georges Lemmen
(Schaerbeek 1865 – 1916 Uccle)

Nach einem kurzen Besuch einer Zeichenschule begann Lemmen autodidaktisch zu malen – immer befreiter von Akademietraditionen. 1889 wurde er in die Künstlergruppe Les XX aufgenommen, die vehement für eine lebenswahre Kunst und gegen den Akademismus des offziellen Salons kämpfte. Auch der nach demselben Geiste ausgerichteten Gruppe La libre esthétique gehörte Lemmen seit 1894 als Gründungsmitglied an.

Wenn seine frühen Werke auch akademischen Traditionen verhaftet waren, so entstanden schon 1890 die ersten divisionistischen Werke. Die pointillistische Malweise wandte Lemmen fortan konsequent an, und von 1889 bis 1893 stellte er auch im Kreis der Neoimpressionisten bei den Indépendants aus.
Wie Henry van de Velde widmete sich auch Lemmen der angewandten Kunst und gehörte entsprechend 1894 zu den Mitbegründern der Vereinigung L'Art, die als eine interdisziplinäre Mittlerin zwischen Künstlern, Fabrikanten und Käufern von kunsthandwerklichen Objekten agierte.
Seit 1895 tauchten immer neue, freiere stilistische Elemente in Lemmens vom Neoimpressionismus bestimmten Schaffen auf. Nach 1900 sollte auch die enge Freundschaft mit Vuillard in seiner Malerei ihren Ausdruck finden.
1911 unternahm der Künstler eine Reise nach Saint-Jean-Cap-Ferrat, wo er die Pleinairmalerei intensivierte und das Licht des Südens für seine Malerei entdeckte.
Im Gegensatz zu vielen seiner Künstlerkollegen ließ Lemmen sich nicht dauerhaft im Midi nieder. Er starb 1916 in einem Vorort von Brüssel.

After attending a drawing school for a brief period of time, Lemmen began painting without further formal training—and moving progressively farther from academic traditions. In 1889, he was admitted to membership in Les XX, a group of artists committed to a true-to-life style of art and vehemently opposed to the academic principles of the official Salon. Lemmen was also a founding member of the group known as La Libre Esthétique, which embraced similar views, in 1894.
While his early works paid allegiance to academic traditions, he completed his first Divisionist paintings in 1890. From that point on, Lemmen consistently employed the Pointillist technique, and from 1889 to 1893 he also exhibited alongside the Neo-Impressionists at the shows organized by the Indépendants.
Like Henry van de Velde, Lemmen also practiced applied art and was one of the co-founders of L'Art association, which served as an interdisciplinary mediator between artists, manufacturers, and buyers of handcrafted objects.
A series of new, freer stylistic elements began to appear in Lemmen's Neo-Impressionist-oriented art in 1895. His closer friendship with Vuillard was also reflected in his painting after 1900.
In 1911, the artist traveled to Saint-Jean-Cap-Ferrat, where he pursued plein-air painting with greater intensity and discovered the light of the south for his painting.
Unlike many of his fellow artists, Lemmen did not settle permanently in the Midi. He died in a suburb of Brussels in 1916.

Stanislas Lepine
(Caen/Calvados 1835 – 1892 Paris)

Stanislas Lépine kam 1855 nach Paris und begann 1860 seine Ausbildung im Atelier von Corot. Lépine malte im Geiste seines Lehrers, denn auch ihn erfüllte eine tiefe Bewunderung und starke Passion für die Wunder der Natur.
Durch die Aufhellung seiner Palette und sein Gefallen an wechselnden atmosphärischen Stimmungen, was in seinen Stadtansichten und Landschaftsdarstellungen deutlich zum Ausdruck kommt, lassen Lépines Werke die Kunst der Impressionisten – mit denen er 1874 gemeinsam ausstellte – bereits erahnen. Seine Palette ist so licht wie jene der Schule von Barbizon, und so wird er – wie Boudin – zu den Wegbereitern des Impressionismus gezählt.
Lépines Landschaften sind nur selten mit Figuren besetzt, oder diese sind auf den Status eines Piktogramms reduziert. Hinsichtlich der Bedeutung, die Lépine hingegen dem Wasser und der Himmelszone in seinen Bildern beimaß, steht seine Kunst in der Tradition des Goldenen Zeitalters der niederländischen Malerei und offenbart daneben auch den jüngeren Einfluss der Kunst Jongkinds.
Lépine führte ein ruhiges und zurückgezogenes Leben und arbeitete stets allein. Seine Bilder konnte er nur schwer verkaufen, wenngleich sein Freund und Förderer, Graf Doria, ihm große Unterstützung zukommen ließ.

Lépine arrived in Paris in 1855 and began a course of training at Corot's studio in 1860. He painted in the spirit of his teacher, for Lépine, too, was a passionate admirer of the wonders of nature.
The lightened colors of his palette and Lépine's love of changing atmospheric moods, which is clearly evident in his urban scenes and landscapes, anticipate the art of the Impressionists—with whom he exhibited in 1874. His palette is as light and bright as that of the Barbizon painters, and thus he—like Boudin—is regarded as a forerunner of the Impressionist movement.
Lépine's landscapes seldom contain figures, and the few that appear are reduced to the status of pictograms. He attached great importance to water and the sky in his paintings, and to that extent, his art reflects the tradition of the Golden Age of Dutch painting as well as the more recent influence of Jongkind's art.
Lépine led a quiet life in relative isolation and always worked alone. He had difficulty selling his works, although his friend and patron, Count Doria, provided him with considerable support.

Andre Leveille
(Lille 1880 – 1962 Paris)

Léveillé verdiente sich seinen Lebensunterhalt zunächst mit Textilentwürfen und bildete sich in seiner Freizeit autodidaktisch als Maler. Während seine große Bewunderung der Kunst der alten Meister galt, zeigte sich Léveillé in seinem Schaffen anfangs vor allem durch die Impressionisten beeinflusst. 1911 debütierte er mit einigen Landschaftsdarstellungen in der Ausstellung der Indépendants. In den folgenden Jahren machte sich dann mehr und mehr das Vorbild Derains und Picassos in seiner Kunst bemerkbar. Nach dieser kubistischen Periode wandte sich Léveillé wieder einer naturalistischeren Darstellungsweise zu, in der allerdings stets kubistische Elemente erkennbar blieben. 1937 gab Léveillé die Malerei auf und wurde Direktor des Palais de la découverte in Paris.

Léveillé earned his living in the early years of his career with textile designs while teaching himself to paint in his spare time. A great admirer of the old masters, Léveillé's own painting was initially influenced primarily by the art of the Impressionists. He debuted at the Salon des Indépendants with several landscapes in 1911. The influence of Derain and Picasso became increasingly evident in his art in the following years. After this Cubist period, Léveillé returned to a more Naturalist style, although Cubist elements are still recognizable in these works. The artist stopped painting in 1937 and became director of the Palais de la Découverte in Paris.

Max Liebermann
(Berlin 1847 – 1935 Berlin)

Einfachheit und Größe der Natur waren Liebermann in den Bildern der französischen Realisten begegnet, welche er bei seinem ersten Paris-Auf-

enthalt 1872 kennenlernte. Courbet, Daubigny und Corot zogen ihn an, vor allem war er 1874 aber Millets wegen für einige Monate nach Barbizon gekommen. Millets Einfluss ist es auch zuzuschreiben, dass Liebermann nach Vollendung seiner Ausbildung ebenfalls an der Gestaltung von Bildern der Arbeitswelt interessiert war. In der Folgezeit traten allerdings spezifisch holländische Motive in den Vordergrund seines Interesses. Sie zeigen Liebermanns Bemühen um die schlichte Darstellung der Realität, um eine neue Sicht des Alltäglichen – eine Auffassung, die erst um 1900 zugunsten modischerer Themen aufgegeben wurde. Liebermann näherte sich zu dieser Zeit den Bestrebungen des deutschen Impressionismus an und malte nun in helleren Farben. Der Pinselduktus wurde schwungvoller, die Pinselstriche breiter und lockerer gesetzt, und um einen bewegten Eindruck des Dargestellten zu vermitteln, suchte Liebermann die Möglichkeiten des Impressionismus vollständig auszuschöpfen.

Liebermann discovered simplicity and the splendor of nature in the paintings of the French Realists he saw during his first stay in Paris in 1872. He was attracted to Courbet, Daubigny, and Corot, but it was Millet who prompted him to come to Barbizon for several months in 1874. The fact that Liebermann developed an interest in scenes from the world of labor after completing his training is also attributable to Millet's influence. In the following years, however, specifically Dutch motifs were the focus of his interest. They bear witness to Liebermann's concern with the straightforward depiction of reality and with a new perspective on the ordinary—an approach he did not abandon in favor of more fashionable subjects until about 1900. At that time, Liebermann adopted aspects of the style of the German Impressionists and began to paint in lighter colors. His brushwork became more energetic, the individual brushstrokes broader and more loosely spaced. In an effort to convey the impression of animation in the subject, Liebermann sought to exploit the potential of Impressionism to the fullest.

Gustave Loiseau

(Paris 1865 – 1935 Paris)

Loiseau lernte zunächst bei einem Dekorateur, ehe ihm eine kleine Erbschaft die Möglichkeit gab, sich ganz der Malerei zu widmen. Jedoch besuchte er auch später keine Kunstschule, sondern arbeitete als Autodidakt. 1890/91 malte er zusammen mit Gauguin, Maufra und Bernard in Pont-Aven, was nicht ohne Einfluss auf sein Schaffen blieb, und was sich vor allem an dem zeichnerischen Charakter in manchen seiner Bilder ablesen lässt.

Er entwickelte seinen Stil jedoch nicht nach dem Vorbild anderer Maler, sondern allein nach der Natur, die er – zeitlebens häufig auf Reisen – stets neu für sich entdeckte. Sein Ziel war es, die Landschaft so naturnah wie möglich wiederzugeben, und es lag ihm fern, einen anderen Künstler zu imitieren oder gar einer Theorie wie dem Divisionismus Seurats oder dem Synthetismus Gauguins zu folgen.

Seine Vorliebe galt vor allem Flusslandschaften, die er in zarten Farben auf die Leinwand zu bringen wusste. Eine sanfte Lichtstimmung, die mit ihrem goldenen Licht die Dinge zum Leuchten bringt, ist typisch für die poetische Darstellungsweise Loiseaus.

1897 nahm ihn der Galerist Durand-Ruel unter Vertrag, sodass Loiseau von da an finanziell abgesichert war.

Loiseau trained initially with a decorator before a small inheritance enabled him to devote himself exclusively to painting. He never attended an art school, however, but worked as a self-taught artist for the remainder of his life. He painted with Gauguin, Maufra, and Bernard in Pont-Aven in 1890/91, an experience that was not without influence on his art and which is evident in the graphic character of some of his paintings.

Yet he did not develop his style by imitating other painters. Instead, he worked solely from nature, which he constantly rediscovered in the course of his many travels. His goal was to render the landscape as authentically as possible, and he had no interest in imitating other painters or subscribing to such theories as Seurat's Divisionism or Gauguin's Synthetism.

His favorite scenes were river landscapes painted in delicate colors. A soft, light atmosphere whose golden light causes objects to glow is typical of Loiseau's poetic style.

Having signed a contract with gallerist Durand-Ruel in 1897, Loiseau enjoyed a measure of financial security from that point on.

Maximilien Luce

(Paris 1858 – 1941 Paris)

Nach einer Ausbildung an der Ecole des arts décoratifs in Paris verdiente sich Luce seinen Lebensunterhalt zunächst als Holzschnitzer und Lithograf. Seine ersten Gemälde waren vom Impressionismus geprägt.

Ab 1877 wurde er in seiner Malweise stark beeinflusst von Pissarro, Seurat und Signac, und begeistert von ihren neoimpressionistischen Theorien setzte er diese fortan in seiner Malerei um. Als Mitglied der Société des artistes indépendants stellte er seit 1887 auch gemeinsam mit seinen Malerfreunden aus und wurde von der zeitgenössischen Kritik sofort als einer der führenden Maler des Neoimpressionismus gefeiert.

Häufig lässt bei Luce die pointillistische Farbtechnik des Tupfens die dargestellten Dinge gleichsam entmaterialisiert erscheinen, wie hinter einem Lichtschleier. Wenige stärker hervortretende kompakte Formen gewähren den Kompositionen optischen Halt. Hauptgegenstand seiner Bilder ist das Phänomen Licht. Der leuchtende Eindruck seiner Bilder wird durch sehr locker und groß, dann wieder dicht und farbmäßig komplementär hingesetzte Farbtupfen hervorgerufen. Auch machen seine Werke deutlich, wie die konsequente Anwendung pointillistischer Farbtupftechnik letztlich zu einer neuen Qualität linearer Flächenformen führen musste: den neuen und formenden Charakter der Linie, der auf den künftigen Jugendstil vorausweist.

Den konsequent neoimpressionistischen Stil gab Luce allerdings um 1900 zugunsten einer mehr impressionistischen Malweise wieder auf.

After completing his studies at the Ecole des Arts Décoratifs in Paris, Luce earned his living initially as a woodcarver and lithographer. His earliest paintings were done in the style of the Impressionists.

The influence of Pissarro, Seurat, and Signac became increasingly evident after 1877. Fascinated by their Neo-Impressionist theories, he applied them to his own painting from that point on. After becoming a member of the Société des Artistes Indépendants in 1887, he first exhibited alongside his artist friends that same year and was immediately hailed by contemporary critics as one of the leading painters of the Neo-Impressionist movement.

Luce's Pointillist technique of applying spots of color gives the depicted objects a dematerialized look, as if they were covered by a veil. Less compact forms give the compositions certain stability. The primary subject of his paintings is the phenomenon of light. The impression of radiance evoked by his pictures is created by fields of loosely spaced, large spots of color juxtaposed with dense areas of complementary color points. His works also clearly show that the consistent application of the color-spot technique necessarily culminated in a new quality of flat linear forms, in a new and formal character of the line anticipating the Art Nouveau of later years.

Luce abandoned his rigorous Neo-Impressionist style around 1900 in favor of an approach that had more in common with Impressionism.

August Macke
(Meschede 1887 – 1914 bei near Verdun)

August Macke besuchte zwischen 1904 und 1906 die Akademie und die Kunstgewerbeschule in Düsseldorf. Zu Beginn seiner künstlerischen Laufbahn war er vor allem beeinflusst durch die Kunst des Schweizer Malers Arnold Böcklin, und seine Gemälde aus dieser Zeit sind in dunklen Tönen gehalten.

Zwischen 1907 und 1909 unternahm der junge Maler drei Reisen nach Paris, wo er sich intensiv mit der Kunst der Impressionisten und den Farbexperimenten der jüngeren Avantgarde, der Fauves, auseinander setzte. Diese Erfahrungen sollten sein weiteres Werk entscheidend prägen und letztlich der Farbexplosion in seinen Bildern den Weg bahnen. 1911 gehörte Macke neben Franz Marc, Kandinsky und Alfred Kubin zur Künstlergemeinschaft Der Blaue Reiter.

Sein verhältnismäßig kurzes Schaffen wird dem Expressionismus zugerechnet. Macke ließ 1914 mit nur 27 Jahren im Ersten Weltkrieg bei Verdun sein Leben.

Macke attended the academy and the Kunstgewerbeschule in Düsseldorf from 1904 to 1906. In the early years of his career, he was influenced above all by the art of the Swiss painter Arnold Böcklin, and his paintings from this period are composed of dark shades of color.

The young painter took three trips to Paris between 1907 and 1909, during which he undertook the intense study of the art of the Impressionists and the color experiments of the young avant-garde. The insight gained in the process would have a lasting and significant influence on his later work and ultimately pave the way for the explosion of color that came to characterize his paintings in the following years. In 1911, Macke joined Franz Marc, Kandinsky, and Alfred Kubin to form the artists' group Der Blaue Reiter.

The oeuvre he created during his relatively short career is assigned to the category of Expressionism. Macke lost his life near Verdun in 1914, the first year of World War One, at the age of twenty-seven.

Edouard Manet
(Paris 1832 – 1883 Paris)

Nicht alle Künstler, die man heute mit der Kunstauffassung des Impressionismus in Verbindung bringt, haben an den Ausstellungen der Impressionisten auch teilgenommen. Das prominenteste Beispiel hierfür ist zweifellos Edouard Manet, dessen Bilder auf keiner der acht Ausstellungen der Gruppe zu sehen waren. Trotzdem gilt er – wenngleich nicht mit seinem Gesamtwerk und vielleicht nicht einmal in seinen Hauptwerken – als wesentlicher Protagonist dieser Malerei. Allerdings wird Manets Kunst über seine Figurenbilder definiert, und gerade hier dominieren die Atelierkompositionen.

Seine frühen, von der Malerei Spaniens und besonders Diego Velázquez' beeinflussten Entwürfe sind dunkle, konturbetont durchgearbeitete Bilder, bei denen allenfalls die Delikatesse der Stoffbehandlung, changierend und durch das sich in der Kleidung fangende Licht modelliert, impressionistisch wirkt. Manchen seiner Kompositionen schließlich, in denen die Prinzipien des Pleinairismus in der Faktur greifbar werden, steht die historische Thematik entgegen. Doch sind natürlich auch unter den besonders ab den 1870er-Jahren entstandenen figuralen Kompositionen Manets Bilder, die zum Besten gehören, was der Impressionismus zu leisten imstande war. Mehr noch als in der Figurenmalerei aber tritt die Bedeutung des Gegenstandes in Manets Stillleben zugunsten der reinen Farbwirkung und der Lichtwertigkeiten zurück, bemüht sich der Maler um Schlichtheit des Gegenständlichen bei gleichzeitiger reicher Entfaltung seines malerischen Vermögens in Farbe und Faktur.

Not all of the artists we associate with the Impressionist movement actually took part in the Impressionist exhibitions. The most prominent example of an artist who did not is surely Edouard Manet, whose paintings were not shown at any of the eight exhibitions organized by the group. Yet Manet is regarded as a significant protagonist of Impressionist painting—an assessment that is not based on his entire oeuvre and perhaps not even on his most important works. Manet's art is defined primarily by his figurative paintings, among which studio compositions predominate.

Influenced by Spanish painting, in particular that of Diego Velázquez, his early works are dark, thoroughly composed pictures with prominent contours in which, at best, the only traces of an Impressionist style are found in the delicate rendering of the shimmering fabrics, which are modeled by the light shining on the clothing. With regard to some of his compositions, the principles of plein-air painting that are evident in the structure stand in opposition to the historical themes. Yet among Manet's figure compositions, especially those executed in the 1870s and later, are some of the very best paintings Impressionism was capable of producing. But to an even greater extent than in his figure paintings, the subjects of his still lifes are secondary to the pure effects of color and light. In these works, the painter sought to achieve simplicity of representation while developing his abundant gifts as a painter at the level of color and form.

Albert Marquet
(Bordeaux 1875 – 1947 Paris)

Um die Mitte der 1890er-Jahre studierte Marquet bei Gustave Moreau und Fernand Cormon an der Ecole des Beaux-Arts in Paris, wo er Matisse traf und dessen enger Freund wurde. Zu dieser Zeit war Marquet beeinflusst durch die Impressionisten, Cézanne und die Nabis.

Um 1898 begannen die gemeinsamen Bemühungen Matisses und Marquets um eine Malerei in reinen Farben und den Aufbau der Bildfläche allein durch Farbflächen – Bestrebungen, die in der Kunstform des Fauvismus aufgehen sollten. Mit der Gruppe der Fauves war Marquet im legendären Herbstsalon des Jahres 1905 vertreten.

Nach 1905 entfernte er sich allerdings mehr und mehr von der Kunst der Fauves. Während seine frühen Bilder noch einen pastosen, kräftigen, »stakkativen« Farbauftrag aufweisen und die traditionelle Perspektive nach Art der Fauves veränderten, sind seine späteren Werke gekennzeichnet durch einen wesentlich flüssigeren Malstil. Seine frühen Bilder besitzen einen Reichtum der Farbe, der später einer matten, gedeckten Tonigkeit wich, und seine Palette erreichte eine höchste Nuanciertheit der Töne.

Als der Erste Weltkrieg ausbrach, stand Marquet bereits bei der Galerie Druet unter Vertrag. Von materiellen Sorgen befreit, begann für Marquet nach 1920 eine Zeit ausgedehnter Reisen. Erst kurz vor seinem Tode ließ er sich wieder fest in Paris nieder.

Marquet studied with Gustave Moreau and Fernand Cormon during the mid-1890s at the Ecole des Beaux-Arts in Paris, where he met and became close friends with Matisse. At the time, Marquet's art was influenced above all by the Impressionists, Cézanne, and the Nabis.

In 1898 or thereabouts, Matisse and Marquet worked together in an effort to develop a style of painting in pure colors that relied solely on fields of color as a structuring principle—an effort that would culminate in the art of the Fauvists. Marquet exhibited with the Fauvists at the legendary Salon d'Automne in 1905.
He distanced himself progressively from the Fauvists after 1905, however. Whereas his early paintings are characterized by a vigorous, impasto, "staccato-style" application of paint and the altered perspective typical of the Fauvists, his later works exhibit a much more smoothly flowing technique. The rich, vivid colors of his early paintings gave way in his later works to duller, more subdued coloration, and his palette was composed of highly nuanced shades.
Marquet was already under contract to the Galerie Druet when World War One broke out. Free of financial worries, Marquet began traveling extensively after 1920. He did not return permanently to Paris until shortly before his death in 1947.

Henri Martin
(Toulouse 1860 – 1943 La Bastide-du-Vert)

Henri Martin besuchte zunächst die Ecole des Beaux-Arts in Toulouse, nahm aber ab 1879 seinen Wohnsitz in Paris. Ein Stipendium ermöglichte es ihm, im Atelier von Jean-Paul Laurens zu arbeiten. 1883 bekam er einen Preis für ein im Pariser Salon ausgestelltes Werk, und 1885 erhielt er ein Stipendium für eine Studienreise nach Italien, wo ihn besonders die Meisterwerke von Giotto und Masaccio beeindruckten. Nach seiner Rückkehr nach Paris wurde Martin vor allem durch die neoimpressionistische Malweise beeinflusst, und auch Anklänge der Kunst der Fauves finden sich in seinem Werk.

Henri Martin attended the Ecole des Beaux-Arts in Toulouse before moving to Paris in 1879. A grant enabled him to study with Jean-Paul Laurens. In 1883, he was awarded a prize for a work exhibited at the Paris Salon, and in 1885, he received a grant for a study journey in Italy, where he was impressed above all by the masterpieces of Giotto and Masaccio. After his return to Paris, Martin was influenced primarily by the Neo-Impressionist painters, and affinities with the art of the Fauvists are also evident in his works.

Henri Matisse
(Le Cateau-Cambrésis 1869 – 1954 Nizza Nice)

Nach Anfängen an der Académie Julian in Paris, ging Matisse an die Ecole des Beaux-Arts und arbeitete dort in den Ateliers von Gustave Moreau und Eugène Carrière.
Matisses erste Arbeiten waren deutlich vom Impressionismus geprägt, aber um 1898 – während eines Aufenthalts auf Korsika – begann er sich mehr und mehr für den neuartigen Gebrauch der Farbe zu interessieren, wie ihn die Neoimpressionisten praktizierten. Fortan malte er in einem verhaltenen Pointillismus.
Ab etwa 1900 entdeckte er die Farbe und die ornamentale Form für seine Kunst. Zum Durchbruch gelangte Matisses Malerei allerdings erst im ersten Dezennium des 20. Jahrhunderts, als er mit den Künstlerfreunden aus den Reihen der Fauves in Paris Werke von revolutionärer Farbgebung ausstellte. Ab 1905, als er den Divisionismus aufgab, arbeitete Matisse daran, seinen Farben eine größere Leuchtkraft zu verleihen, die den Effekt von Licht erzeugen sollte, ohne es nachzuahmen. Daneben suchte er zu einer stärkeren Strukturierung der Bildfläche zu gelangen – ein künstlerisches Ziel, das er dem Vorbild Cézannes schuldete. Nach dem Abklingen des Fauvismus wurde Matisses weiteres Schaffen noch ornamentaler und zeichnete sich durch eine immer stärkere Flächenhaftigkeit aus.
Matisse hatte an der Entstehung des Fauvismus maßgeblichen Anteil, und dessen Errungenschaften sollte er in einem umfangreichen Gesamtwerk weiterentwickeln, das eine bestimmende Größe in der Kunst des 20. und beginnenden 21. Jahrhunderts darstellt.

After early studies at the Académie Julian in Paris, Matisse enrolled at the Ecole des Beaux-Arts and worked in the Paris studios of Gustave Moreau and Eugène Carrière.
Matisse's first paintings were clearly influenced by Impressionist art, but in about 1898—during a stay on the island of Corsica—he began to develop a growing interest in the innovative use of color as practiced by the Neo-Impressionists. From that point on, he painted in a restrained Pointillist technique.
Beginning in about 1900, he discovered color and ornamental form as crucial elements of his art. He did not achieve his breakthrough as a painter until the first decade of the twentieth century, however, when he exhibited works characterized by revolutionary color along with fellow artists from the ranks of the Fauvists. Having abandoned Divisionism in 1905, Matisse focused on imbuing his colors with greater luminosity, generating the effect of light without imitating it. He also strove to achieve a more structured painting surface—a goal to which he was inspired by Cézanne. As Fauvism waned, Matisse's paintings became increasingly ornamental and oriented toward the flat surface.
Matisse played an instrumental role in the emergence of Fauvism, and he elaborated on the achievements of the Fauvists in an extensive oeuvre that contributed significantly to shaping the character of art in the twentieth and early twenty-first centuries.

Maxime Maufra
(Nantes 1861 – 1918 Poncé-sur-le-Loir)

Maufras erste Arbeiten vor der Natur entstanden 1884; deren Motive fand er vor allem an den Küsten der Bretagne. 1886 sah er erstmals impressionistische und neoimpressionistische Bilder von Pissarro, Monet, Renoir, Sisley, Gauguin, Seurat und Signac. Fortan malte er überwiegend Landschaften, die deutlich vom Impressionismus beeinflusst waren.
1890 kam Maufra nach Pont-Aven und fühlte sich dort von dem Kreis um Gauguin und dessen künstlerischen Idealen angezogen. Er schuf nun einfache und dekorative Kompositionen, im Geist und im Stil des Synthetismus. Die Betonung der linearen Formen sowie der ineinander fließende Farbauftrag und die langen Pinselstriche zeigen die genaue Kenntnis der Malerei Gauguins. Der Farbauftrag ist pastos und die Farbgebung bisweilen geradezu abstrakt. Von 1890 bis 1892 beteiligte sich Maufra auch an den Ausstellungen der Indépendants. Ab etwa 1898 war seine Malerei wieder stärker vom Impressionismus beeinflusst und wurde immer konventioneller.
Während des Ersten Weltkriegs reiste Maufra an die Front, um Lithografien vorzubereiten, die im Juni des Jahres 1917 unter dem Titel *Paysages de guerre* veröffentlicht wurden.

Maufra's first paintings from nature, featuring primarily motifs from the coast of Brittany, date from 1884. He initially encountered the Impressionist and Neo-Impressionist paintings of Pissarro, Monet, Renoir, Sisley, Gauguin, Seurat, and Signac in 1886. From that point on, he painted mostly landscapes exhibiting the marked influence of Impressionism.

Maufra traveled to Pont-Aven in 1890, strongly attracted by the artists associated with Gauguin and his ideals of art. He then began painting simple, decorative compositions in the spirit and style of Synthetism. His emphasis on linear forms, his intermingling colors, and his extended brushstrokes reveal a close familiarity with Gauguin's painting. His paint is applied in impasto; his coloration often approaches abstraction. Maufra also took part in the exhibitions of the Indépendants from 1890 to 1892. His painting was increasingly influenced by Impressionism and became progressively more conventional after 1898.
During World War One, Maufra traveled to the front to do preparatory studies for the lithographs he published under the title *Paysages de guerre* in June of 1917.

Jean Metzinger

(Nantes 1883 – 1956 Paris)

Metzinger ging 1903 nach Paris, dem damaligen Zentrum aller Kunstströmungen, und unterhielt Kontakte unter anderen zu Guillaume Apollinaire und Albert Gleizes, war befreundet mit Juan Gris und machte auch die Bekanntschaft Georges Braques und Pablo Picassos. In Picassos Art der Bildgestaltung erkannte Metzinger bereits den Beginn einer neuen Stilrichtung, deren Form der Bildauffassung erst später mit der Bezeichnung Kubismus umrissen werden sollte.
Im Salon der Indépendants des Frühjahrs 1910 war Metzinger mit einem Bild vertreten, das bereits die langsame Hinwendung des Künstlers zum analytischen Kubismus bezeugt. Auf dem Herbstsalon desselben Jahres präsentierte sich mit dem gemeinsamen Auftreten jener Künstler, die in der Folgezeit als Kubisten bezeichnet werden sollten, die Bewegung erstmals als Gruppe. Selbst die stärksten Verunglimpfungen durch ihre Widersacher konnten das Gros der kubistischen Künstler nicht von ihrem Wege abbringen, und der Kubismus überzeugte durch immer vielfältigere Ausdrucksformen der Einzelnen.
Metzinger hat seine künstlerische Entwicklung, ausgehend vom Postimpressionismus, über Divisionismus und Fauvismus zum Kubismus geführt. In den 1920er-Jahren gab er allerdings die kubistische Malweise – wie auch Picasso und Braque – auf. Erlebte die Bewegung damit auch ihr vorläufiges Ende, so blieben ihre Errungenschaften für die gestalterische Freiheit in der Malerei gleichwohl wirksam.

Metzinger moved to Paris in 1903, attracted by the center of all major currents of art at the time, where he maintained contact with such figures as Guillaume Apollinaire and Albert Gleizes, became friends with Juan Gris, and met Georges Braque and Pablo Picasso. Metzinger saw the beginning of a new stylistic movement in the way Picasso organized his paintings. It was not until later that its form of pictorial conception was to be termed Cubism. The artist exhibited a painting at the Salon des Artistes Indépendants in the spring of 1910, a work that bears witness to the artist's gradual embrace of analytical Cubism. The movement presented itself as a group at the Salon d'Automne that same year, where the artists who would later be referred to as Cubists appeared together for the first time. Even the most brutal attacks by their opponents did not cause the majority of Cubist artists to stray from their chosen path, and Cubism grew popular through the increasingly diverse forms of expression developed by individual artists.
Having begun as a Post-Impressionist, Metzinger proceeded through Divisionist and Fauvist phases before taking up the Cubist style. He abandoned Cubism in the 1920s—as did Picasso and Braque as well. Although that marked the end of the movement for the time being, its achievements on behalf of creative freedom in painting had a lasting impact.

Jean François Millet

(Gruchy 1814 – 1875 Barbizon)

Millet gehörte zum Kreis jener Landschaftsmaler, die als Schule von Barbizon bekannt geworden sind. Seine Themen sind immer wieder das bäuerliche Leben und die dörfliche Landschaft. Diese rustikalen Szenen sind in eigener Weise realistisch und zugleich von einer fast mystischen Poesie der Naturnähe und Erdverbundenheit geprägt, und auch starke Hell-Dunkel-Kontraste sind häufig in Millets Werken zu finden.

Millet belonged to the group of landscape painters known as the Barbizon School. Peasant life and the rural village landscape are recurring themes in his paintings. These rustic scenes are strikingly realistic, yet characterized at the same time by an almost mystical poetry of communion with nature and bonds to the earth. Strong light-and-dark contrasts are also frequently found in Millet's paintings.

Claude Monet

(Paris 1840 – 1926 Giverny)

Monet wuchs in Le Havre auf, wo ihn Boudin ermutigte, sich der Malerei zu widmen und nach Paris zu gehen. Dort schloss sich Monet den jungen Malern der Académie Suisse an, unter ihnen Pissarro, und er kam in Kontakt mit den Künstlern Bazille, Renoir und Sisley. Bald malte er gemeinsam mit ihnen im Wald von Fontainebleau. 1874 war er auf der ersten Impressionisten-Ausstellung vertreten, und sein Gemälde mit dem Titel *Impression, Soleil levant* verlieh der Gruppe der jungen Künstler überhaupt erst ihren Namen.
Nach 1880 zog sich Monet allmählich vom Kreis der Impressionisten zurück und übersiedelte nach Giverny. Hier legte er im Laufe der Jahre einen fantastischen Garten an, in dem seine zahlreichen Blumen- und Seerosenbilder entstanden.
In den späten 1880er-Jahren begann er mit einer neuen Art von Malerei, nachdem sein Bemühen schon von Beginn an der Fixierung atmosphärischer Wirkungen gegolten hatte. Nicht nur die Lokalfarbe der Dinge wollte er erfassen, sondern die durch Luft und Dunst veränderten Farbwerte. Der Bildgegenstand an sich wurde damit nurmehr zu einem Hilfsmittel, war nur noch Träger und Oberfläche für die Darstellung von Farbwandlungen. Der Maler versuchte, sich dem Unmöglichen soweit als möglich zu nähern: dem momentanen, in ständigem Wandel begriffenen Farbeindruck durch die Malerei dauernden Ausdruck zu verleihen. Seine letzten, in den frühen 1920er-Jahren entstandenen Gemälde nehmen daher immer weniger Notiz von den vorgegebenen Formen, sind gleichsam davon abstrahiert und wirken hauptsächlich als Farbräume. Mit Monet begann die Hinwendung zur Abstraktion, die in die Kunst der Moderne führte.

Monet grew up in Le Havre, where he was encouraged by Boudin to devote himself to painting and move to Paris. There, he joined the young painters of the Académie Suisse, among them Pissarro, and came in contact with Bazille, Renoir, and Sisley. He soon began painting with them in the Forest of Fontainebleau. Monet took part in the first Impressionist exhibition in 1874, and his painting entitled *Impression, Soleil levant* was the source of the name given to this group of young artists.
Monet gradually retreated from the circle of Impressionist artists after 1880 and moved to Giverny. It was there that he created the fantastic garden in which his many flower and water-lily paintings were done.
Having focused from the outset of his career on rendering the effects of atmosphere, he began in the late 1880s to develop a new style of painting.

He was not interested in capturing the local color of objects but rather the character of colors altered by air and mist. The pictorial subject per se became merely a tool, the medium and surface for the depiction of color transformations. The painter sought to come as close as possible to the impossible: to give permanent expression to the momentary, constantly changing color impression through painting. Thus his later paintings, completed during the early 1920s, pay increasingly little attention to existing forms. They appear as if abstracted from them, and their primary effect is that of color spaces. The turn toward abstraction that eventually led to modern art began with Monet.

Georges Daniel de Monfreid
(Paris 1856 – 1929 Corneilla-de-Conflent/Pyrénées-Orientales)

Seitdem er 1889 durch Schuffenecker in den Künstlerkreis von Pont-Aven eingeführt wurde, verband den jungen Monfreid eine enge Freundschaft mit Gauguin, der das künstlerische Tun des Jüngeren zu unterstützen suchte, indem er ihn beispielsweise noch im Jahr ihres Kennenlernens zur Beteiligung an einer Ausstellung im Café Volpini einlud – gemeinsam mit Bernard, Schuffenecker und anderen. 1906 sollte es dann auch Monfreid sein, der im Herbstalon die retrospektive Ausstellung von Werken seines Freundes Gauguin organisierte.
Allerdings führte die enge Verbindung zu Gauguin auch dazu, das Schaffen Monfreids gänzlich in den Schatten des großen Künstlerfreundes treten zu lassen. Dabei ging Monfreid in seinen Werken bisweilen so weit, traditionelle Perspektive und gängigen Bildaufbau zu vernachlässigen, was auf den Einfluss der Kunst Cézannes verweist, und seine Bilder bezeugen darüber hinaus Monfreids großes Interesse am Exotischen und an der Kultur des Orients. Tatsächlich sind aber auch viele von Monfreids Werken deutlich dem Synthetismus Gauguins verpflichtet.

After his introduction into the artists' group at Pont-Aven by Schuffenecker in 1889, the young Monfreid became close friends with Gauguin, who strove to promote the younger man's career in art where he could—by inviting him, for example, to take part that same year in an exhibition at the Café Volpini alongside Bernard, Schuffenecker, and others. It was then Monfreid who organized the retrospective exhibition of the works of his friend Gauguin at the Salon d'Automne in 1906.
It should be noted, however, that Monfreid's close friendship with Gauguin was the reason why his art was completely overshadowed by that of his great friend and fellow artist. This, despite that fact that Monfreid went so far as to neglect traditional perspective and conventional principles of composition in some of his works, an approach that is attributable to the influence of Cézanne. Monfreid's paintings also reflect his intense interest in the exotic and the culture of the Orient. Many of his works actually do exhibit the powerful influence of Gauguin's Synthetism, however.

Adolphe Monticelli
(Marseille 1824 – 1886 Marseille)

Monticelli wuchs bei einer Ziehmutter in Ganagobie auf, und so sollte er später die Besonderheit der provenzalischen Landschaft in seinen Bildern oft und gerne zur Anschauung bringen. Nach künstlerischen Anfängen in Marseille übersiedelte Monticelli 1846 nach Paris, wo er in das Atelier von Paul Delaroche eintrat. Seine ersten eigenständigen Bilder standen noch deutlich unter dem Einfluss Delaroches, waren aber auch der Kunst Richard Boningtons, Isabeys und Thomas Coutures verpflichtet.
Ab 1855 stand Monticelli in engem Kontakt mit Díaz de la Peña, mit dem er häufig gemeinsam im Atelier oder in Fontainebleau vor der Natur malte und dessen Kunst ihn deutlich beeinflusste. Langsam vollzog sich ein Wandel in Monticellis Schaffen, und es bildete sich mehr und mehr ein besonderes Interesse für das Licht heraus. Seine »Fêtes galantes« sind von einem zarten, die Umrisse des Dargestellten zerfließen lassenden Licht erfüllt. Neben genrehaften Figurenbildern schuf Monticelli auch Landschaftsbilder und Stillleben.

Monticelli was raised by a foster mother in Ganagobie, and many of his later works express the unique quality of the landscape of the Provence region. After early studies in Marseilles, Monticelli moved to Paris in 1846, where he joined the studio of Paul Delaroche. While his first original paintings reveal the unmistakable influence of Delaroche, they also reflect his admiration for the art of Richard Bonington, Isabey, and Thomas Couture. Beginning in 1855, Monticelli was in close contact with Díaz de la Peña, with whom he frequently painted in the studio or in natural settings in Fontainebleau and who exerted a significant influence on his art. Monticelli's painting style changed gradually, as he became increasingly interested in light. His *fêtes galantes* are bathed in a delicate light that sets the contours of his subjects in flux. In addition to genre-style figure paintings, Monticelli also did a number of landscapes and still lifes.

Henry Moret
(Cherbourg 1856 – 1913 Paris)

Moret entdeckte während seines Militärdienstes seine Vorliebe für die Landschaft der Bretagne, die er nicht wieder verlassen sollte – ausgenommen die Jahre seiner Ausbildung, als er bei Jean-Léon Gérôme und Jean-Paul Laurens in Paris studierte. Fünfundzwanzig Jahre lang erkundete er dann die rauhe Küste des Atlantiks und hielt sie in seinen Bildern fest.
1880 hatte Moret einen ersten Erfolg im Salon, gab aber bald seine akademische Malerei zugunsten des Impressionismus auf. 1888 ließ er sich in Pont-Aven nieder und traf dort zum erstenmal Gauguin. Diese Begegnung, die bald zu einer engen Zusammenarbeit zwischen den beiden Malern führte, sollte Morets Stil nachhaltig beeinflussen. Motivwahl, Bildaufbau und Pinselduktus in den Gemälden Morets aus dieser Zeit weisen unverkennbar den Einfluss Gauguins, aber auch van Goghs auf. Mit den Künstlern von Pont-Aven stellte Moret im Salon der Indépendants aus. Nach wie vor im impressionistischen Duktus arbeitend, übertrug Moret die neuen Theorien des Synthetismus in seine Malerei, und suggestive Farbkontraste verhelfen seinen Bildern zu einem besonderen emotionalen Gehalt. Auch nach Gauguins Abreise in die Südsee sollte Moret weiterhin in diesem modifizierten Synthetismus malen.

During his military service, Moret discovered his fascination for the landscape of Brittany, and he would never leave the region again—except for his years of study with Jean-Léon Gérôme and Jean-Paul Laurens in Paris. Then, for twenty-five years, he explored the rugged Atlantic coast and captured its features in his paintings.
After enjoying initial success at the Salon in 1880, Moret soon abandoned his academic painting style in favor of the Impressionist technique. He moved to Pont-Aven in 1888 and met Gauguin for the first time. This encounter, which was soon followed by a period of close collaboration between the two painters, was to have a lasting impact on Moret's style. The choice of subjects, the composition, and the brushwork in Moret's paintings from those years point unmistakably to the influence of Gauguin as well as of van Gogh. Moret exhibited with the artists of Pont-Aven at the

Salon des Indépendants. Still working in the Impressionist mode, Moret incorporated the new theories of Synthetism into his painting, while suggestive color contrasts imbue his paintings with a unique emotional quality. Moret continued to paint in this modified Synthetist style even after Gauguin's departure for the South Sea.

Berthe Morisot

(Bourges 1841 – 1895 Paris)

Schon früh galt Morisots besondere Bewunderung den Künstlern von Barbizon, insbesondere der Malerei Corots, dessen Schülerin sie 1860 wurde. Der Landschaftsmaler führte die junge Frau in seine Kunst ein und machte sie mit seiner Behandlung des Lichts und der Form vertraut, was für ihre weitere künstlerische Entwicklung entscheidend werden sollte.

In den Jahren von 1864 bis 1873 fanden Morisots Bilder – vornehmlich Landschaftsbilder, in denen sie bereits Licht und Farbe zum eigentlichen Gegenstand der Darstellung erhob – regelmäßig Aufnahme im Pariser Salon. 1868 lernte sie durch Fantin-Latour Edouard Manet kennen und traf auch dessen Bruder Eugène, der später ihr Mann wurde. Fortan arbeiteten Berthe und Edouard zusammen und beeinflussten sich in ihrem Schaffen gegenseitig: Unter ihrem Einfluss begann Manet, im Freien zu malen, und seine Palette hellte sich auf. In Morisots Schaffen erkennen wir eine deutliche Hinwendung zur Schilderung des modernen Alltagslebens und eine immer freiere Pinselführung. Manet schuf auch zahlreiche Porträts von Berthe Morisot; 1868 saß sie beispielsweise Modell für sein berühmtes Bild *Le Balcon.*

Gegen den Protest des Schwagers beteiligte sich Morisot 1874 an der ersten Impressionisten-Ausstellung. Fortan stellte sie nie mehr im Salon officiel aus. Wiewohl die Künstlerin – mit Ausnahme des Jahres 1879 – auch auf allen übrigen Impressionisten-Ausstellungen vertreten war, ist sie lange Zeit die wohl am wenigsten beachtete Künstlerin aus dem engeren Zirkel der Impressionisten geblieben, und vielfach wurde ihr Schaffen lediglich im Kontext der Kunst ihres Mentors Manet wahrgenommen.

Morisot was a great admirer of the artists of Barbizon School at an early age. She was particularly intrigued with the work of Corot, who became her teacher in 1860. The landscape painter introduced the young woman to his style of art and familiarized her with his approach to light and form. The experience would have a decisive impact on her development as an artist.

Morisot's paintings—for the most part landscapes in which she had already made light and color the real subjects of her works—were accepted regularly for exhibition at the Paris Salon between 1864 and 1873. She was introduced to Edouard Manet by Fantin-Latour in 1868 and also met his brother Eugène Manet, whom she later married. From that point on, Berthe and Edouard painted together and influenced each other's work. Under her influence, Manet began painting outdoors, and his palette grew progressively lighter. We recognize in Morisot's oeuvre a strong interest in the depiction of modern everyday life as well as an increasingly liberal brushwork style. Manet also created numerous portraits of Berthe Morisot. In 1868, for example, she sat for his famous painting *Le Balcon.*

Despite the protests of her brother-in-law, Morisot took part in the first Impressionist exhibition in 1874. She would never again exhibit at the Salon. Although the artist also showed works at all of the other Impressionist exhibitions—with the exception of the show in 1879—for many years she was the least recognized artist from the inner circle of Impressionists, and her art was often mentioned only within the context of the achievements of her mentor, Manet.

Gabriele Münter

(Berlin 1877 – 1962 Murnau)

Münter nahm 1902 in München das Studium der Malerei an der von Kandinsky neu ins Leben gerufenen Phalanx-Kunstschule auf und verlobte sich ein Jahr später mit ihrem Lehrer. 1906/07 entstanden zahlreiche, zumeist kleinformatige Ölbilder in impressionistischem und postimpressionistischem Stil. 1908 war Münter erstmals in Murnau, wo sie im folgenden Jahr ein Haus erwarb, in dem sie und Kandinsky gemeinsam arbeiteten.

1911 trat Münter aus Solidarität mit Franz Marc und Kandinsky aus der Neuen Künstlervereinigung München aus, die sie zu Beginn des Jahres 1909 mitbegründet hatte. An der darauf folgenden Gründung der Künstlergruppe Der Blaue Reiter war Münter ebenfalls beteiligt.

Bei Kriegsausbruch 1914 gingen Kandinsky und Münter in die Schweiz. 1916 kam es zur endgültigen Trennung des Paares, was Münter verzweifeln ließ und sie für mehrere Jahre am Arbeiten hinderte. Ab dem Ende der 1920er-Jahre lebte Gabriele Münter gemeinsam mit ihrem neuen Lebensgefährten Johannes Eichner, einem Kunsthistoriker und Philosophen, wieder in ihrem Haus in Murnau. Erst lange Zeit nach ihrer Rückkehr nach Murnau begann die Künstlerin, wieder zu malen. Seit Beginn der 1930er-Jahre entstanden in Murnau Gemälde, die an Münters Expressionismus der Vorkriegszeit erinnern. 1937 wurden sowohl ihre Werke als auch die ihres ehemaligen Lebensgefährten Kandinsky von den Nationalsozialisten als »entartete Kunst« diffamiert.

In 1902, Münter enrolled as student of painting at the new Phalanx-Kunstschule founded by Kandinsky. She became engaged to her teacher a year later. In 1906/07, she completed a number of oils, most of them in small formats, in the Impressionist and Post-Impressionist styles. Münter first visited Murnau in 1908 and bought a house there in 1909, where she and Kandinsky worked together.

As a gesture of solidarity with Franz Marc and Kandinsky, in 1911, Münter left the Neue Künstlervereinigung München (New Munich Artists' Association), which she had helped to found in 1909. She was also a co-founder of Der Blaue Reiter, which was established shortly thereafter.

Kandinsky and Münter moved to Switzerland when war broke out in 1914. After the couple separated permanently in 1916, she suffered bouts of depression and found it difficult to work for several years. In the late 1920s, Münter returned to her home in Murnau, where she lived with her new partner, Johannes Eichner, an art historian and philosopher. She did not begin painting again until long after her return to Murnau. The paintings completed in the early 1930s and the following years in Murnau are reminiscent of Münter's Expressionist works from the pre-war period. In 1937, her paintings and those of her former companion Kandinsky were declared "degenerate art" by the National Socialists.

Edvard Munch

(Løten 1863 – 1944 Ekely/Skøyen)

Zu Beginn der 1880er-Jahre von Christian Krohg und Frits Thaulow in der naturalistischen Pleinairmalerei unterrichtet, war Munch jedoch ab 1884 mehr und mehr vom Kreis um Hans Jaeger beeinflusst, der in seiner Kunst großes Gewicht auf Subjektivität und Selbstbeobachtung legte. Dies hatte zur Folge, dass Munch begann, den Inhalt seiner Bilder verstärkt auf seine persönlichen Ängste hinsichtlich Krankheit und Tod auszurichten, die ihn seit seiner Kindheit verfolgten. Außerdem malte er häufig Motive mit deutlich sexuellem Unterton, womit er seine problematische Beziehung zum anderen Geschlecht thematisierte. Um die in seinen Bildern zum Aus-

druck kommenden Emotionen zu unterstreichen, begann Munch, Licht und Farbe – innerhalb seiner naturalistischen Malerei – einen stärkeren symbolischen Gehalt zu geben.
Von 1889 bis 1892 hielt sich Munch in Paris auf und hatte ausgiebig Gelegenheit, die Impulse der zeitgenössischen französischen Kunst in sich aufzunehmen. Inspiriert durch Künstler wie Gauguin, Toulouse-Lautrec oder van Gogh, wie auch durch die symbolistische Dichtkunst, entwickelte Munch seinen symbolistisch-expressiven Stil weiter, wobei er Linie, Form und Farbe vereinfachte, um Werke voller visueller Atmosphäre zu schaffen. Nach einem Zusammenbruch im Herbst 1908 und einer anschließenden Behandlung in einer Nervenklinik in Kopenhagen kehrte Munch nach Norwegen zurück. Fortan lebte er dort die meiste Zeit sehr zurückgezogen auf seinem Besitz in Ekely außerhalb Oslos.

After receiving instruction in Naturalist plein-air painting from Christian Krohg and Frits Thaulow in the early 1880s, Munch was influenced to an increasing extent after 1884 by the artists associated with Hans Jaeger, who placed strong emphasis on subjectivity and self-exploration in his art. Consequently, Munch began to focus in his paintings on the personal fears of illness and death that had plagued him since childhood. He also painted motifs with unmistakable sexual undertones, thereby giving expression to his problematic relationship to the opposite sex. Searching for a suitable means of underscoring the emotions expressed in his paintings, Munch began to give greater symbolic weight to light and color within the context of his Naturalist painting style.
Munch lived in Paris from 1889 to 1892 and had ample opportunity to absorb the impulses of contemporary French art. Inspired by such artists as Gauguin, Toulouse-Lautrec, and van Gogh and by the poetry of the Symbolists, Munch continued to refine his Symbolist-Expressionist style, simplifying line, form, and color in order to produce works with powerful visual atmosphere.
Following a nervous breakdown in the fall of 1908 and treatment in a mental hospital in Copenhagen, Munch returned to Norway, where he lived in relative isolation at his estate in Ekely, near Oslo, for the remainder of his life.

Hippolyte Petitjean

(Mâcon/Saône-et-Loire 1854 – 1929 Paris)

Petitjean zählte ab 1885 zur Gruppe der Neoimpressionisten in Paris und war eng mit Seurat befreundet, dessen Kunstauffassung sein Schaffen nachhaltig beeinflusste. 1891 fanden Werke Petitjeans Aufnahme im Salon der Indépendants in Paris, 1893 in Brüssel. Auch in Berlin (1898) sowie Weimar (1903) und Wiesbaden (1921) wurden seine Werke gezeigt. Sein vielfach symbolistisch aufgefasstes Œuvre ist nicht umfangreich; seine zeichnerischen Fähigkeiten bei der Figurendarstellung sind vor allem durch die Auseinandersetzung mit Jean Auguste Dominique Ingres und Pierre Puvis de Chavannes geprägt.

Petitjean joined the circle of Paris Neo-Impressionists in 1885 and was a close friend of Seurat, whose views on art had a lasting impact on his own work. Paintings by Petitjean were accepted for exhibition at the Salon des Artistes Indépendants in Paris in 1891 and in Brussels in 1893. His paintings were also shown in Germany in Berlin (1898), Weimar (1903), and Wiesbaden (1921). His oeuvre, a considerable share of which exhibits marked Symbolist qualities, is not extensive. His figure drawing exhibits the unmistakable influence of Jean Auguste Dominique Ingres and Pierre Puvis de Chavannes.

Francis Picabia

(Paris 1879 – 1953 Paris)

Picabia (eigentlich Francis Martinez de Picabia) war französisch-kubanisch-spanischer Abstammung. Er begann zunächst impressionistisch zu malen, folgte dann eine zeitlang den Theorien der Neoimpressionisten und wandte sich in der Folge dem Kubismus zu. 1903 stellte er im Salon der Indépendants aus, 1911 in der Section d'or mit den Kubisten. Von 1914 bis 1916 hielt sich Picabia in New York auf und arbeitete eng mit Marcel Duchamp zusammen. Nach einer dadaistischen Phase von 1914 bis 1920 wechselte er zum Surrealismus. 1925 suchte er Anschluss an die gegenständliche Kunst und widmete sich nach 1945 der informellen Malerei. Das Werk Picabias, der auch als Dichter und Schriftsteller tätig war, zählt zu den vielgestaltigsten innerhalb der Kunst des 20. Jahrhunderts.

Picabia (whose full name was Francis Martinez de Picabia) was of French-Cuban-Spanish descent. He initially painted in an Impressionist style, then adopted the theories of the Neo-Impressionists for some time, eventually turning to Cubism. He exhibited at the Salon des Indépendants in 1903 and with the Cubists at the Section d'Or in 1911. Picabia spent the years from 1914 to 1916 in New York, where he worked in close collaboration with Marcel Duchamp. Following a Dadaist phase from 1914 to 1920, he shifted to Surrealism. In 1925, he moved toward a more representational form of art, devoting himself to Informal Painting after 1945. Picabia, who also wrote poetry and prose, produced what is regarded as one of the most diverse oeuvres of the twentieth century.

Camille Pissarro

(St. Thomas/Kleine Antillen Lesser Antilles 1830 – 1903 Paris)

Seinen ersten Zeichenunterricht erhielt Pissarro durch den dänischen Maler Fritz Melby, mit dem er von 1852 bis 1854 Venezuela bereiste und dann in Caracas ein Studio unterhielt. 1855 ließ sich Pissarro in Paris nieder und malte zunächst unter dem Einfluss von Corot überwiegend Landschaften. Ab 1859 verband ihn eine enge Freundschaft mit Monet. Pissarro zählt zu den bedeutendsten Malern des Impressionismus, und so war er 1874 auch an der ersten Impressionisten-Ausstellung beteiligt. Sowohl Cézanne als auch Gauguin erhielten durch Pissarro bedeutende künstlerische Impulse. Angeregt durch Seurat und Signac malte der Ältere ab 1885 pointillistisch, kehrte jedoch nach fünf Jahren wieder zur impressionistischen Malweise in hellen Farbtönen zurück. Sein Schaffen umfasst Landschaften, einige Stillleben, Porträts und ab 1890 ebenso Großstadtszenen. Er hinterließ auch ein umfangreiches grafisches Œuvre von Radierungen, Lithografien und Zeichnungen.

Pissarro received his first lessons in drawing from the Danish painter Fritz Melby, with whom he traveled in Venezuela from 1852 until 1854 and then shared a studio in Caracas. He moved to Paris in 1855, where he primarily painted landscapes clearly influenced by Corot. His close friendship with Monet dates from 1859. Pissarro is regarded as one of the most significant Impressionist painters, and he also took part in the first Impressionist exhibition in 1874. Both Cézanne and Gauguin were influenced in significant ways by Pissarro. Inspired by Seurat and Signac, the elder painter adopted a Pointillist technique in 1885, but returned to the Impressionist mode and began painting in bright colors five years later. His oeuvre comprises landscapes, a few still lifes, portraits, and scenes of big-city life (the latter dating from the 1890s). He also left behind an extensive body of graphic art, including etchings, lithographs, and drawings.

Lucien Pissarro

(Paris 1863 – 1944 Hewood/Dorset)

Luciens Vater Camille war sein erster und wichtigster Lehrer, und verschiedene seiner Frühwerke weisen auch neoimpressionistische Stilmerkmale auf. Lucien stellte im Salon der Indépendants in Paris ebenso aus wie bei Les XX in Brüssel. 1890 ließ er sich in England nieder, unternahm aber von dort regelmäßig Reisen in sein Heimatland Frankreich.

Luciens Kunst lässt einen präzisen Zeichenstil und eine subtile Farbgebung erkennen. Seine umfangreiche Kenntnis des Impressionismus und des Neoimpressionismus wirkte sich einflussbildend auf die Malerei in England aus. Lucien war auch als Designer und Illustrator für englische und französische Zeitschriften tätig und wurde seinerseits wiederum durch die Werke der englischen Präraffaeliten beeinflusst. 1894 gründete der Maler einen Buchverlag in der künstlerischen Tradition von William Morris.

Lucien's father, Camille, was his first and most influential teacher, and many of his early works exhibit characteristic features of Neo-Impressionist painting. Lucien exhibited at the Salon des Indépendants in Paris and at the shows organized by Les XX in Brussels. He moved to England in 1890, frequently traveling from there to his native France.

Lucien's art reveals a precise drawing style and a subtle handling of color. His close familiarity with Impressionist and Neo-Impressionist art influenced painting in England. Lucien worked as a designer and illustrator for English and French magazines and was also influenced by the art of the English Pre-Raphaelites. In 1894, the painter founded a publishing house in the artistic tradition of William Morris.

Leon Pourtau

(Bordeaux 1868 – 1898 bei einem Schiffsuntergang im Atlantik
in a ship wreck during an Atlantic crossing)

Über das kurze Leben des Künstlers gibt es nur spärliche Hinweise. Pourtau ging nach Paris, um autodidaktisch zu malen, traf dort mit Seurat zusammen und malte fortan in der pointillistischen Technik. Von seiner Hand existieren mehrere Landschaften aus der Umgebung von Lyon. Pourtau hatte dann die Idee, Chansons zu illustrieren, und so lernte er in einem Pariser Konzert-Café die Musiker der Garde républicaine – Les Concerts lamoureux kennen. Er begleitete das Ensemble auf einer Konzertreise durch Frankreich und ging dann aufs Konservatorium in Paris, wo er gleichzeitig Kurse an der Ecole des Beaux-Arts belegte. Nach Abschluss seines Musikstudiums wurde er Solist im Orchester des Grand Théâtre in Lyon. Um seinen Traum, sich nur der Malerei widmen zu können, zu verwirklichen, nahm er Konzertangebote in den USA an, und so sollte er Frankreich nie wiedersehen: Das Schiff, auf dem er die Rückreise antrat, erlitt Schiffbruch im Atlantik.

Little is known about the brief life of Pourtau. He went to Paris to paint as a self-taught artist, met Seurat there, and painted using the Pointillist technique from that time on. Several of his landscapes from the environs of Lyon have survived. Intrigued by the idea of illustrating chansons, Pourtau became acquainted with the musicians of the Garde Républicaine—Les Concerts Lamoreux at a Parisian concert café. He accompanied the ensemble on a concert tour through France and then enrolled at the conservatory in Paris, where he also took courses at the Ecole des Beaux-Arts. After completing his studies in music, he was hired as a soloist in the orchestra of the Grand Théâtre in Lyon. In hopes of realizing his dream of devoting himself exclusively to painting, he accepted offers to perform in concerts in the United States and was thus never seen in France again: The ship on which he embarked on his return journey sank while crossing the Atlantic.

Fernand Loyen du Puigaudeau

(Nantes 1864 – 1930 Croisic/Bretagne Brittany)

Puigaudeau war als Maler Autodidakt und malte zunächst im impressionistischen Stil. Nach einer Italien-Reise arbeitete er 1880 in Pont-Aven, wo er mit Gauguin zusammentraf, überdies war er gut mit Degas, Monet und Renoir bekannt. Es folgten weitere Reisen nach Afrika, Deutschland und in die Schweiz. Nach einem anschließenden Aufenthalt in Schweden kehrte der Maler in die Bretagne zurück. Hier verlieren sich seine Spuren.

Puigaudeau was a self-taught painter who began his career as an Impressionist. After returning from travels in Italy, he worked in Pont-Aven in 1880, where he met Gauguin. He was also well acquainted with Degas, Monet, and Renoir. Puigaudeau later journeyed to Africa, Germany, and Switzerland. Following a stay in Sweden, he returned to Brittany. Nothing is known of his life and work during the following years until his death.

Jean-François Raffaelli

(Paris 1850 – 1924 Paris)

Raffaëlli arbeitete als Schauspieler am Pariser Theater, ehe er sich der Malerei verschrieb. Er fand Aufnahme im Studio von Jean-Léon Gérôme und stellte 1870 erstmals im Pariser Salon aus. Bei seinen frühen Werken handelt es sich überwiegend um Genrebilder.

Ab 1879 arbeitete Raffaëlli auch im Freien und schuf zahlreiche Ansichten von Paris und der näheren Umgebung, mit denen er sehr erfolgreich war, vermochte er doch die naturnahe Wiedergabe trefflich mit lebendiger Schilderung und Atmosphäre zu verbinden.

Bei den Zusammenkünften der Künstler der Avantgarde im Café Guerbois machte Raffaëlli die Bekanntschaft von Degas, der den Maler – gegen den Willen der übrigen Impressionisten – einlud, sich an deren Gruppenausstellungen von 1880 und 1881 zu beteiligen. Raffaëllis dunkeltonige Palette stand dabei eindeutig im Widerspruch zur lichten Malerei der Impressionisten. Erst später sollte der Maler seine Palette deutlich aufhellen. Eine Einzelausstellung im Jahre 1884, auf der er Porträts und wiederum Genredarstellungen präsentierte, verhalf Raffaëlli zum endgültigen Durchbruch. Raffaëlli war auch als Kupferstecher und Lithograf tätig.

Raffaëlli performed as an actor at the theater in Paris before turning to painting. He was admitted to the studio of Jean-Léon Gérôme and exhibited for the first time at the Paris Salon in 1870. Most of his early works are genre paintings.

He began working outdoors in 1879 and completed numerous views of Paris and environs. Raffaëlli achieved considerable success with these works, in which he aptly combined true-to-life depictions with animated description and atmosphere.

Raffaëlli became acquainted with Degas at gatherings of avant-garde artists at the Café Guerbois. Despite the protests of the other Impressionists, Degas invited the painter to take part in their group exhibitions in 1880 and 1881. Raffaëlli's somber palette stood in stark contrast to the light-colored painting of the Impressionists. He did not lighten his palette significantly until later. A solo exhibition in 1884, at which he presented both portraits and genre paintings, helped him achieve his ultimate breakthrough. Raffaëlli also worked as a copper engraver and lithographer.

Odilon Redon
(Bordeaux 1840 – 1916 Paris)

Von romantischen Bildfindungen ausgehend, wandte sich Redon 1862 der Stilrichtung des Symbolismus zu und konzentrierte sich dabei zunächst ganz auf das Zeichnen; erst um 1890 entdeckte er Ölmalerei und Pastell für sich.
Obwohl ein Zeitgenosse der Impressionisten und im selben Jahr geboren wie Monet, schlug Redon einen anderen künstlerischen Weg ein. Für ihn war die Arbeit nicht getan, wenn die äußerlichen Eindrücke festgehalten waren, sondern erst, wenn das von diesen Eindrücken in seinem Innersten Ausgelöste dargestellt war. Er verstand es, Unsichtbarem Ausdruck zu verleihen, hielt Angstträume vor dem Unbekannten und den Schattenseiten des Daseins im Bilde fest. Urformen menschlichen Bewusstseins verlieh er Furcht einflößende Gestalt, malte mythische und mythologische Suggestionen.
Entsprechend ist Redons Kunstauffassung zu sehr von seiner Persönlichkeit geprägt gewesen, als dass es direkte Parallelen in der zeitgenössischen Kunst gegeben hätte. Ebenso weit entfernt von akademischer Malerei, die er bei Jean-Léon Gérôme kennengelernt hatte, wie von den Kunsttheorien der Realisten beziehungsweise Impressionisten, half Redon 1884 bei der Gründung des Salon der Indépendants. Er fand Anschluss an den symbolistisch arbeitenden Kreis der Nabis und nahm an den Ausstellungen der revolutionären Künstlergruppe Les XX in Brüssel teil. Erst im 20. Jahrhundert ist er in seiner Bedeutung als Wegbereiter einer surrealistischen Kunstauffassung anerkannt worden.

Having begun with Romantic scenes, Redon adopted a Symbolist style in 1862, initially focusing entirely on drawing. He did not take up oil painting and working with pastels until 1890.
Although he was a contemporary of the Impressionists, born in the same year as Monet, Redon pursued an entirely different course in his art. He did not regard his work as complete once external impressions had been captured, but rather only when the inner responses triggered by those impressions were made visible on the canvas. He succeeded in giving expression to the invisible, in rendering dream images reflecting fear of the unknown and the dark sides of life in his paintings. He depicted primal modes of human consciousness in frightening figures in paintings fraught with suggestive mythical and mythological references.
The influence of Redon's personality on his views on art was so strong that it is difficult to find direct parallels to the major currents in the art of his time. Equally distant from academic painting, to which he had been introduced by Jean-Léon Gérôme, and Realist or Impressionist theories of art, Redon was involved in the founding of the Salon des Indépendants in 1884. He came into contact with the Symbolist artists of the Nabi group and participated in the exhibitions of the revolutionary Les XX group in Brussels. He did not gain public recognition as an important forerunner of Surrealist art until the twentieth century.

Auguste Renoir
(Limoges 1841 – 1919 Cagnes)

Nach Unterricht im Atelier des Malers Charles Gleyre besuchte Renoir ab 1862 die Pariser Ecole des Beaux-Arts. Hier freundete er sich mit Monet, Bazille und Sisley an, und in den kommenden Jahren arbeiteten die vier Künstler häufig gemeinsam vor der Natur. 1864 und 1865 stellte Renoir im Pariser Salon aus. Zu dieser Zeit malte er noch überwiegend in den dunklen, gedeckten Farben der Romantiker und Courbets.
1868 entstanden dann unter dem Einfluss Monets die ersten impressionistischen Werke Renoirs. Als diese Bilder vom Salon zurückgewiesen wurden, animierte der Maler als Reaktion hierauf viele seiner Künstlerkollegen zur Teilnahme am Salon des refusés von 1873.
Das Problem der Farbe führte Renoir um diese Zeit zur Auseinandersetzung mit der Kunst Eugène Delacroix'. Daneben verarbeitete er in seinem Schaffen die Errungenschaften von Monet, der Licht und Farbe im Freien studierte, und von Manet, dessen Darstellungen zeitgenössischen Lebens ihn interessierten. In dieser Zeit malte Renoir nun schon ganz mit der Leichtigkeit der impressionistischen Palette. Als im folgenden Jahr die erste Impressionisten-Ausstellung abgehalten wurde, war Renoir mit drei Werken vertreten. Auch an den beiden nächsten Ausstellungen der Gruppe beteiligte er sich, war dann aber erst wieder auf der siebten Ausstellung im Jahre 1882 vertreten. Renoirs künstlerische Entwicklung ging zu diesem Zeitpunkt bereits dahin, die Formen zu vergrößern, und er baute seine Figurenbilder mehr und mehr aus kräftigen Formen auf, die durch eine geschlossene Kontur umschrieben wurden. Zu dieser Zeit feierte Renoir erste größere Erfolge mit seinen Bildern.

After taking lessons at the studio of Charles Gleyre, Renoir enrolled at the Ecole des Beaux-Arts in Paris in 1862. There he met and became friends with Monet, Bazille, and Sisley, and the four artists often painted together in natural settings over the course of the following years. Renoir exhibited at the Paris Salon in 1864 and 1865. In those years, he was still painting primarily in the dark, subdued colors of the Romanticists and Courbet.
Renoir's first Impressionist paintings were executed in 1868 under the influence of Monet. When these works were rejected by the Salon jury, the painter responded by encouraging many of his fellow artists to exhibit at the Salon des Refusés in 1873.
His concern with the problem of color prompted Renoir to focus his attention on the art of Eugène Delacroix at about this time. He also drew from the achievements of Monet, who had studied the effects of light and color in outdoor settings, and Manet, whose scenes of contemporary life he found very interesting. During those years, Renoir painted consistently with the light colors of the Impressionist palette. He was represented with three paintings at the first Impressionist exhibition the following year. He also took part in the next two exhibitions organized by the group, but not again until the seventh show in 1882. At that point, Renoir had already begun to enlarge his forms, developing his figures to an increasing extent with powerful forms with solid outlines. It was at this time that the artist first gained wide success with his paintings.

Antoine de la Rochefoucauld (Comte)
(Paris 1862 – 1959 Menilles)

Rochefoucauld, Spross einer wohlhabenden französischen Aristokratenfamilie, war sowohl Maler als auch Dichter, und auch sein Bruder Hubert war ein talentierter Maler. Bisweilen arbeiteten wohl beide gemeinsam an der Vollendung eines Werkes.
Antoine verkehrte in den späten 1880er-Jahren in den symbolistischen Zirkeln in Paris und gehörte zum Kreis um Signac. Seine finanziellen Möglichkeiten erlaubten es ihm, Malerkollegen wie Bernard und Sérusier zu unterstützen, und er gehörte zu den ersten Sammlern von Werken van Goghs und Redons.
Zwischen 1893 und 1914 stellte Rochefoucauld mehrmals im Salon der Indépendants aus und organisierte 1892 den ersten Salon de la Rose & Croix in Paris, an dem er auch selbst teilnahm und für deren Lehr- und Regel-

buch er mehrere Aufsätze verfasste. Daneben verlegte Rochefoucauld die esoterische Zeitschrift *Le Cœur*, von der – zwischen April 1893 und Juni 1894 – zehn Ausgaben erschienen.
Von Rochefoucauld sind, neben seinen pointillistischen Bildern, auch einige Landschaften im Stil der Schule von Pont-Aven bekannt.

Rochefoucauld, the son of a wealthy French aristocratic family, was both a painter and a poet. His brother Hubert was a talented painter in his own right. The brothers presumably worked together on some of their works.
Antoine frequented Symbolist circles in Paris during the late 1880s and was a member of the group associated with Signac. His financial standing enabled him to support several of his fellow artists, including Bernard and Sérusier, and he was one of the first collectors of paintings by van Gogh and Redon.
Rochefoucauld exhibited at the Salon des Indépendants between 1893 and 1914 and organized the first Salon de la Rose & Croix in Paris in 1892, a show in which he took part and for whose organizers he also wrote several articles. The artist also published the esoteric journal *Le Cœur*, of which ten issues appeared between April 1893 and June 1894.
In addition to his Pointillist paintings, Rochefoucauld also executed several landscapes in the style of the painters of Pont-Aven.

Christian Rohlfs

(Niendorf bei near Segeberg/Holstein 1849 – 1938 Hagen/Westfalen Westphalia)

Rohlfs absolvierte 1870 ein Studium der Malerei an der Kunstschule in Weimar und schuf anfangs hauptsächlich Aktdarstellungen in der Tradition des akademischen Realismus, ehe er nach 1883 zunehmend Landschaften malte, die durch eine besondere Betonung von Atmosphäre und Licht gekennzeichnet waren.
Dies mag auf eine Reise nach Paris zurückzuführen sein, auf der er die Kunst der Schule von Barbizon kennengelernt und in deren Folge er sich intensiv mit der Pleinairmalerei auseinandergesetzt hatte. Ende der 1880er-Jahre bildete Rohlfs einen ganz persönlichen Stil aus, unabhängig von der zeitgleichen Malerei des Impressionismus.
Erst nachdem er 1897 in Weimar Werke Monets kennengelernt hatte, zeigte dies Auswirkungen auf seine künstlerischen Bestrebungen. Durch Henry van de Velde wurde er 1900 mit Karl Ernst Osthaus bekannt, der ihn ein Jahr später an das Museum in Hagen (jetzt Karl Ernst Osthaus-Museum) einlud, wo er Rohlfs ein Studio einrichtete.
Erst 1902, als er Akademieprofessor in Weimar wurde, erwachte Rohlfs' Interesse am Neoimpressionismus. 1905 lernte er die Kunst van Goghs kennen sowie die Malerei der Brücke-Künstler, was seine Kunst dem Expressionismus öffnete. 1937 wurden 412 seiner Werke von den Nazis als »entartete Kunst« diffamiert.

Rohlfs completed studies in painting at the art academy in Weimar in 1870. In the early years of his career, he did primarily nudes in the tradition of academic Realism before turning his attention after 1883 to landscapes with a strong emphasis on light and atmosphere.
This change may have been prompted by a trip to Paris during which he became acquainted with the art of the Barbizon School. After returning home, he completed a significant number of plein-air paintings. In the late 1880s, Rohlfs developed a very personal style that had little in common with the art of his Impressionist contemporaries.
It was not until after Rohlfs viewed Monet's paintings in Weimar in 1897 that the influence of Impressionism became evident in his own work. In 1900, he was introduced by Henry van de Velde to Karl Ernst Osthaus, who invited him to come to the museum in Hagen (now the Karl Ernst Osthaus-Museum), where he set up a studio for Rohlfs a year later.
Rohlfs developed an interest in Neo-Impressionism about the time of his appointment as an academy professor in Weimar in 1902. He became acquainted with the art of van Gogh and the paintings of the Brücke artists in 1905, both experiences that made him more receptive to Expressionist art. In 1937, 412 of his works were declared to be as "degenerate art" by the Nazis.

Theo van Rysselberghe

(Gent 1862 – 1926 Saint-Clair/Var)

Zu Beginn der 1880er-Jahre schuf van Rysselberghe Werke in jener tachistischen Manier, die von den modernen belgischen Künstlern aus dem Realismus der 1860er-Jahre im Gegensatz zum französischen Impressionismus entwickelt worden war.
1883 gehörte van Rysselberghe zu den Gründungsmitgliedern der Künstlergruppe Les XX – neben Finch, Henry van de Velde, Felicien Rops, Jan Toorop, Lemmen, Isidore Verheyden und anderen. Gemeinsam mit ihnen stellte er auf den jährlichen Ausstellungen der Gruppe aus. Hier kam er wenige Jahre später in Berührung mit dem französischen Impressionismus wie auch mit dem Neoimpressionismus, stellten doch 1886 Monet und Renoir bei den XX aus, und 1887 war Seurat dort vertreten.
Die Bekanntschaft mit diesen Künstlern sollte von besonderer Bedeutung für van Rysselberghes weitere künstlerische Entwicklung werden: Zunächst erfolgte eine allmähliche Hinwendung des Malers zum Impressionismus, wenig später zum Neoimpressionismus. Von da an stellte der Belgier auch regelmäßig mit seinen neuen Freunden im Pariser Salon der Indépendants aus.
Stets stand er aber auch in engem Kontakt mit seinen Künstlerkollegen in Brüssel – auch noch nach 1897, als er sich in Paris niederließ. Nach 1910 siedelte van Rysselberghe nach Südfrankreich über, wo er sehr zurückgezogen lebte. In dieser Zeit erkennt man wiederum einen Wandel in seinem Schaffen: Die neoimpressionistische Malweise wich wieder mehr und mehr einem gemäßigten Impressionismus.

In the early 1880s, van Rysselberghe created works in the Tachist style which was developed by modern Belgian Realist artists of the 1860s as a countercurrent to French Impressionism.
Van Rysselberghe joined Finch, Henry van de Velde, Felicien Rops, Jan Toorop, Lemmen, Isidore Verheyden, and others as a founding member of Les XX in 1883. He put his work on display with the group at its annual exhibitions. It was there that he came in contact with French Impressionism and Neo-Impressionism several years later. Both Monet and Renoir exhibited with Les XX in 1886, Seurat a year later in 1887.
Van Rysselberghe's ties to these artists had a significant impact on his own artistic development: after gradually adopting an Impressionist style, the Belgian painter shifted toward Neo-Impressionism somewhat later. From that point on, he exhibited alongside his new friends at the Paris Salon des Artistes Indépendants.
Nonetheless, he remained in close contact with his fellow artists in Brussels—even after settling in Paris in 1897. Van Rysselberghe moved to southern France after 1910 and lived the remainder of his life in relative isolation there. Those years also witnessed a change in his art, as his Neo-Impressionist style again progressively gave way to a moderate form of Impressionism.

Claude-Emile Schuffenecker
(Fresne-Saint-Mamès 1851 – 1934 Paris)

Schuffenecker, der als Autodidakt zu malen begonnen hatte, sammelte ab 1880 Werke seiner Künstlerkollegen. Zudem kündigte er seine Stellung als Buchhalter, um sich fortan ausschließlich der Kunst zu widmen.
1884 gehörte er zu den Gründungsmitgliedern der Indépendants. Von Seurats *Une baignade, Asnières*, das dieser im selben Jahr auf der ersten Ausstellung der Gruppe zeigte, war Schuffenecker zutiefst beeindruckt. Um diese Zeit nahm er eine Stellung als Zeichenlehrer an – eine Tätigkeit, die er mehr als zwanzig Jahre lang ausüben sollte, um seinen Lebensunterhalt zu sichern.
Schuffenecker kam in Kontakt mit dem Künstlerkreis von Pont-Aven und setzte sich intensiv mit der Kunstauffassung Gauguins und dessen Theorien des Synthetismus auseinander.
1894 ersuchte Schuffenecker in einem Schreiben an Johanna Bonger, die Schwägerin Vincent van Goghs, um die Möglichkeit, Bilder des 1890 Verstorbenen erwerben zu können. Johanna, die um die große Bewunderung Claude-Emiles für van Gogh wusste, willigte ein, ihm einige Gemälde zu überlassen. Allerdings wurde Schuffeneckers finanzielle Situation in den folgenden Jahren so prekär, dass er sich 1904 gezwungen sah, seine gesamte Sammlung von rund 120 Gemälden (seine eigenen Werke eingeschlossen) zu verkaufen.

Schuffenecker, who began his career as a self-taught painter, began collecting works by his fellow artists in 1880. He also left his job as an accountant in order to devote himself entirely to art.
He was a founding member of the Indépendants in 1884. Schuffenecker was profoundly impressed with Seurat's *Une baignade, Asnières*, a painting shown at the group's exhibition that same year. At about the same time, he accepted a position as a drawing instructor, an occupation he would pursue for more than twenty years as a means of earning a living.
Schuffenecker became acquainted with the artists of Pont-Aven and undertook an intensive study of Gauguin's concept of art and his theories of Synthetism.
In 1894, the artist inquired in a letter to Johanna Bonger, Vincent van Gogh's sister-in-law, about the possibility of purchasing paintings by the artist, who had died in 1890. Johanna, who was aware that Claude-Emile was a great admirer of van Gogh, agreed to sell him several paintings. Schuffenecker's financial situation became so precarious in the following years, however, that he was compelled to sell his entire collection of some 120 paintings (including his own works) in 1904.

Paul Serusier
(Paris 1863 – 1927 Morlaix/Finistère)

Nach einem Studium der Philosophie und dem anschließenden Besuch der Académie Julian in Paris machte Sérusier 1888, während eines Urlaubs in der Bretagne, die Bekanntschaft Gauguins und jenes Künstlerkreises, der sich in Pont-Aven um ihn scharte. Unter Gauguins Anleitung malte Sérusier während dieses Aufenthaltes auf dem Deckel einer Zigarrenkiste ein kleines Bild, *Landschaft im Bois d'Amour*, besser bekannt als *Der Talisman*. Diese fast abstrakte Landschaft sollte den Status einer Ikone erlangen, denn anhand ihrer erläuterte Sérusier nach seiner Rückkehr nach Paris seinen Mitstudenten Gauguins künstlerische Innovationen. Noch Jahrzehnte später trat Sérusier für die Errungenschaften des Synthetismus ein, veröffentlichte er 1921 mit seiner Schrift *ABC de la Peinture* doch gleichsam dessen Manifest.
1888 gehörte Sérusier – neben Denis, Vuillard, Bonnard, Vallotton und Ker-Xavier Roussel – zu den Gründungsmitgliedern der Künstlergruppe der Nabis. Diese Gruppe stand zunächst noch deutlich unter dem Einfluss von Gauguins Synthetismus, lehnte den Illusionismus der Impressionisten ab und forderte eine nach Inhalt und Form bedeutungsvolle Malerei. Entsprechend standen die Nabis auch in Verbindung mit den Zirkeln der symbolistischen Dichter in Paris, an deren Versammlungen und Gesprächskreisen sie häufig teilnahmen. Bereits um die Mitte der 1890er-Jahre ließ der Zusammenhalt der Gruppe allerdings nach, und der Kreis der Nabis brach auseinander. Sérusier verstarb 1927 unbeachtet von der Öffentlichkeit im Finistère.

After completing studies in philosophy and attending the Académie Julian in Paris, Sérusier became acquainted with Gauguin and the artists associated with him in Pont-Aven during holidays in Brittany in 1888. Under Gauguin's guidance, Sérusier painted a small picture on the cover of a cigar box during his visit: *Landscape in the Bois d'Amour*, better known as *The Talisman*. This almost abstract landscape would later attain the status of an icon, as Sérusier used it after returning to Paris to explain Gauguin's artistic innovations to his fellow students. Decades later, Sérusier defended the achievements of Synthetism in his publication entitled *ABC de la Peinture* (1921), a late manifesto of the movement.
Sérusier joined Denis, Vuillard, Bonnard, Vallotton, and Ker-Xavier Roussel to found the artists' group known as the Nabis in 1888. At first, the group was clearly influenced by Gauguin's Synthetism. Its members rejected the illusionism of the Impressionists and appealed for a style of painting that was meaningful in both form and content. Accordingly, the Nabis also established ties with groups associated with the Symbolist poets in Paris and frequently took part in their meetings and discussions. In the mid-1890s, solidarity within the group began to wane, and the Nabis eventually disbanded. Sérusier's death in 1927 attracted virtually no public notice.

Georges Seurat
(Paris 1859 – 1891 Paris)

Schon während seiner Zeit an der Ecole des Beaux-Arts setzte sich Seurat eingehend mit wissenschaftlichen Schriften über Geometrie, Physik und über die Gesetze der Optik auseinander – vor allem mit den Abhandlungen der Wissenschaftler Michel-Eugène Chevreul, Charles Henry, Charles Blanc, Humbert de Superville und David Sutter. Darüber hinaus studierte Seurat die Arbeiten von James Clerk Maxwell und N. O. Rood.
Basierend auf diesen theoretischen Schriften und ausgehend von einer Kunstauffassung, die die Malerei des Impressionismus – die den flüchtigen Augenblick festzuhalten suchte – weiterzuführen gedachte, entwickelte Seurat eine Kunst, die aus der Summe flüchtiger Momente (dem Vergänglichen) das Unvergängliche – sozusagen die allgemeingültige Summe, die Synthese aller Augenblicke – filtern und im Bild festhalten sollte.
Auf der Basis seiner Experimente mit Farbwerten gelangte Seurat zu einer »synthetischen« Malerei. Er setzte die Farbe, in ihre einzelnen Töne zerlegt, in Punkten und Tupfen auf den Bildträger, wobei er Bildeinheit und -aufbau wiederherstellte, indem er erneut strikt jene formalen Kompositionsgesetze berücksichtigte, die die Impressionisten bewusst außer Acht gelassen hatten. Farben wurden nebeneinandergesetzt und erzeugen Farbflächen, die sich allein ob der Verschiedenheit ihrer Tonwerte voneinander absetzen. Eine lineare Zeichnung als Trennlinie zwischen den Farbfeldern war mithin kaum mehr vonnöten. Diese neuartige Malerei, die auf den Gesetzen der Farbzerlegung gründete, wurde Divisionismus genannt.

As a student at the Ecole des Beaux-Arts, Seurat devoted himself to a rigorous study of scientific publications in the fields of geometry, physics, and the laws of optics—most notably with the writings of Michel-Eugène Chevreul, Charles Henry, Charles Blanc, Humbert de Superville, and David Sutter. Seurat also studied the work of James Clerk Maxwell and N. O. Rood.
On the basis of these theoretical writings and a concept of art devoted to pursuing the Impressionist philosophy—which aimed at capturing the fleeting moment—to a higher level, Seurat developed a mode of painting that sought to filter out the permanent—the universal core, the synthesis of all moments, so to speak—from the sum total of all such moments (the transitory) and render it in the painted image.
Through his experiments with color values, Seurat arrived at a form of "synthetic" painting. He placed color, broken down into its component shades, in points and spots on the canvas, restoring the unity and structure of the whole by adhering strictly to the very laws of composition the Impressionists had ignored. Colors were juxtaposed to generate color fields that stood apart from each other by virtue of their tonal values alone. A linear marking as a dividing line between color fields was hardly necessary. This new style of painting based on the laws of the fragmentation of color synthesis was called Divisionism.

Henri le Sidaner
(Port-Louis/Mauritius 1862 – 1939 Versailles)

Von 1880 bis 1885 studierte Sidaner an der Ecole des Beaux-Arts in Paris unter Alexandre Cabanel und stellte ab 1887 regelmäßig im Salon officiel aus. 1889 nahm ihn der Pariser Galerist Georges Petit unter Vertrag und ermöglichte ihm Ausstellungen in Paris, London und New York.
Von 1896 bis 1900 ist eine symbolistische Phase im Schaffen Sidaners zu erkennen, wobei seine Themenwahl durch literarische Vorlagen angeregt wurde. 1900 besuchte Sidaner den kleinen Ort Gerberoy nordwestlich von Beauvais und erwarb dort 1902 ein Haus, das mit seinem Garten eine Quelle der Inspiration für viele seiner Gemälde war. Von Gerberoy aus unternahm er zahlreiche Reisen, unter anderem nach Holland, Venedig und London. Bis zu seinem Lebensende erhielt Sidaner zahlreiche Auszeichnungen und Ehrungen und war ab 1937 Präsident der Académie des Beaux-Arts in Paris.
In Sidaners Werk vermischen sich Impressionismus und Neoimpressionismus in einer äußerst differenzierten und harmonischen Valeurstechnik. Seine Landschaften, Interieurs und Blumenbilder sind oft charakterisiert durch eine Malweise, die den dargestellten Gegenstand in einen Dunstschleier hüllt. Zahlreich sind auch seine Darstellungen von Landschaften bei Morgen- oder Abenddämmerung.

Sidaner studied at the Ecole des Beaux-Arts in Paris with Alexandre Cabanel from 1880 to 1885 and exhibited regularly at the Salon beginning in 1887. He signed a contract with gallerist Georges Petit in 1889, and the agent arranged for him to show his work at exhibitions in Paris, London, and New York.
A Symbolist phase becomes discernible in Sidaner's art between 1896 and 1900. His choice of subjects was stimulated by literary sources. In 1900, Sidaner visited Gerberoy, a small village northwest of Beauvais, where he bought a house in 1902. His home and garden would serve as an important source of inspiration for many of his paintings. He traveled extensively from Gerberoy, visiting Holland, Venice, and London, among other places. Sidaner received numerous awards and honors during his lifetime and was elected President of the Académie des Beaux-Arts in Paris in 1937.
Sidaner's oeuvre contains a mixture of Impressionist and Neo-Impressionist works rendered in an extremely distinctive, harmonious color value technique. Many of his landscapes, interiors, and floral paintings are characterized by a painting style that envelops objects in a veil of mist. He also painted numerous landscape scenes with dawn and twilight atmospheres.

Paul Signac
(Paris 1863 – 1935 Paris)

Der Besuch einer Monet-Retrospektive bewog Signac 1880, eine Laufbahn als Maler anzustreben, und seine frühen Werke – vom Impressionismus geprägte Landschaften und Stillleben – verweisen denn auch deutlich auf die Vorbildhaftigkeit Monets wie auch Sisleys.
1884 lernte er Seurat kennen, und noch im selben Jahr zählten die beiden zu den Gründungsmitgliedern der Société des artistes indépendants. Seurat machte Signac mit der von ihm entwickelten Kunstform des Divisionismus vertraut, und schon bald verschrieb sich Signac gänzlich dieser Technik.
Auf Einladung von Pissarro, der zu dieser Zeit ebenfalls dem Divisionismus zuneigte, nahmen Signac und einige seiner Künstlerfreunde 1886 an der letzten Impressionisten-Ausstellung teil, die so letztlich zur Manifestierung des Divisionismus beitragen sollte.
Signac begann um 1890, fast ausschließlich in seinem Atelier nach Skizzen und Aquarellen zu malen, die er vor der Natur fertigte. Ab 1895 veränderte sich seine divisionistische Pinselführung von Farbpunkten hin zu größeren, immer leuchtenderen Farbtupfen.
Signac kann neben Seurat als der wohl bedeutendste Vertreter des Neoimpressionismus angesehen werden. Zeit seines Lebens war er an jeder Ausstellung der Société des artistes indépendants beteiligt. Signacs anziehendes Wesen und seine Begeisterungsfähigkeit ließen ihn – bald nach Seurats Tode – zum Oberhaupt der neoimpressionistischen Gruppe avancieren. Indem er sowohl den Fauves als auch den Kubisten die Beteiligung am Salon der Indépendants ermöglichte, konnte Signac den engen Zusammenschluss der Indépendants mit den Künstlern der neuen Avantgarde herbeiführen und dadurch sicherstellen, dass der Neoimpressionismus noch geraume Zeit an den Entwicklungen der modernen Kunst teilhatte.

Signac viewed a Monet retrospective in 1880, and the experience inspired him to take up painting. His early works—landscapes and still lifes in the Impressionist style—also point clearly to the influence of Monet and Sisley.
He met Seurat in 1884, and the two joined other painters to found the Société des Artistes Indépendants that same year. Seurat introduced him to Divisionism, a style he had developed himself, and Signac soon devoted himself exclusively to the technique.
In response to an invitation from Pissarro, who was also painting in a Divisionist style at the time, Signac and several of his fellow artists took part in the last Impressionist exhibition in 1886, a show that ultimately contributed to the manifestation of Divisionism.
Around 1890, Signac began painting almost exclusively in his studio from sketches and watercolors executed in natural settings. Beginning in 1895, his Divisionist technique began to change, as points of color gave way to large, increasingly radiant daubs.
Signac and Seurat may safely be regarded as the most important representatives of Neo-Impressionism. Signac participated in every exhibition organized by the Société des Artistes Indépendants during his lifetime. By virtue of his personal appeal and enthusiasm, he advanced—soon after Seurat's death—to the status of the leader of the Neo-Impressionist group. Having enabled the Fauvists and the Cubists to participate in the Salon of

the Indépendants, Signac paved the way for the close alliance between the Indépendants and the artists of the new avant-garde, thereby ensuring that Neo-Impressionism would play a role in developments in modern art for some time to come.

Alfred Sisley
(Paris 1839 – 1899 Moret-sur-Loing)

Im Atelier seines Lehrers Charles Gleyre machte Sisley die Bekanntschaft Monets, Renoirs und Bazilles, und 1863 arbeiteten die vier Künstler erstmals gemeinsam im Wald von Fontainebleau in der freien Natur. Allerdings begann er erst um 1870, freier und in helleren Farben zu malen, übernahm die Chromatik der impressionistischen Palette und setzte Pinselstriche lichter Farben gesondert nebeneinander.

Seine frühen Landschaften – auch jene, die er im offiziellen Salon der Jahre 1866 und 1870 präsentieren konnte – sind hingegen in einer dunklen Palette von gedecktem Braun gemalt, denn wiewohl er die reaktionären Akademietraditionen ablehnte, erachtete er die Kunst Corots und Courbets für vorbildlich. Bereits in diesen frühen Werken wird sein besonderes Gefühl für den Bildraum, den Bildaufbau und den Kontrast zwischen Licht und Schatten und ein untrügliches Gespür für die Wirkung der Farbtöne erkennbar.

Als 1874 die erste gemeinsame Ausstellung der Gruppe der Impressionisten stattfand, war Alfred Sisley dort mit fünf Landschaften vertreten. Insgesamt sollte er sich an vier der acht Impressionisten-Ausstellungen beteiligen.

Ab 1883 stellte sich für Sisley durch Verkäufe seiner Bilder langsam eine gewisse finanzielle Sicherheit ein, gleichwohl straften ihn die Kritiker weiterhin mit Missachtung. Von seinen Malerkollegen hingegen wurde Sisley bereits zu Lebzeiten große Bewunderung entgegengebracht. Diese Wertschätzung sollte seinem Werk bald nach seinem Tode auch von der öffentlichen Meinung, von Sammlern und Kunstkritikern zuerkannt werden. Heute gilt Sisley als einer der bedeutendsten Vertreter der Malerei des Impressionismus.

Sisley became acquainted with Monet, Renoir, and Bazille at the studio of his teacher Charles Gleyre, and the four artists first worked together, painting from nature in the Forest of Fontainebleau, in 1863. Sisley did not begin painting in a freer style and with lighter colors until 1870, however, when he adopted the chromatic scheme of the Impressionist palette and placed distinct strokes of light colors next to one another.

In contrast, his early landscapes—including those he presented at the official Salon in 1866 and 1870—were painted with a dark palette of subdued browns, for although he rejected the reactionary traditions of academic art, he regarded the art of Corot and Courbet as exemplary models. His unique sense of pictorial space, composition, and contrasts of light and shadow, and his unerring grasp of the effects of specific colors are evident even in these early paintings.

Sisley presented five landscapes at the first exhibition organized by the Impressionists in 1874. He took part in four of the eight Impressionist exhibitions in all.

After his paintings began to sell in 1883, Sisley gradually achieved a measure of financial security. Yet critics continued to dismiss his work for some time.

Sisley's fellow painters expressed great admiration for his art even during his lifetime, however, and his oeuvre gained both public recognition and the respect of collectors and critics soon after his death. He is regarded today as one of the most important exponents of Impressionist painting.

Max Slevogt
(Landshut 1868 – 1932 Neukastel)

Slevogt studierte von 1884 bis 1890 an der Münchner Akademie bei Wilhelm Diez. 1889/90 bereiste er Italien, Holland und Ägypten. Entscheidende Prägung erfuhr sein Schaffen vor allem durch Wilhelm Leibl.

Slevogts frühe Werke vom Ende der 1890er-Jahre riefen aufgrund ihres Realismus in München vehemente Ablehnung hervor. Der Maler ging daraufhin von München fort und ließ sich in Berlin nieder. Dieser Wechsel der Umgebung ging mit einer Weiterentwicklung seines persönlichen Stils einher. Die dunkle Tonalität seiner Akademiejahre überwindend, gelangte Slevogt um 1907 zu einer aufgehellteren Palette. Ein Stil, der impressionistisch zu nennen ist, nahm zu dieser Zeit seinen Anfang. In späteren Jahren sollte Slevogts Malerei die Bildgegenstände in ihren Formen immer stärker in Farbe und Licht auflösen. Dabei vermittelt ein pastoser Farbauftrag einen Einblick in den schnellen Schaffensprozess und verstärkt den Eindruck, dass Slevogts Kompositionen ganz von der momentanen Impression bestimmt waren.

Slevogt studied at the academy in Munich with Wilhelm Diez from 1884 to 1890. He traveled in Italy, Holland, and Egypt in 1889/90. His art was influenced above all by Wilhelm Leibl.

Due to their Realist style, Slevogt's early works from the late 1890s were received with considerable hostility in Munich. The painter left Munich and moved to Berlin. This change of surroundings went hand in hand with a progressive shift in his personal style. Abandoning the dark coloration of his years at the academy, Slevogt developed a lighter palette around 1907. And it was at this point that he began to paint in an Impressionist style. In his later years, the forms of the subjects of his paintings progressively dissolved into fields of light and color. Slevogt's use of impasto conveys the sense of the speed with which he worked and underscores the importance of momentary impressions in his compositions.

Nicolas Tarkhoff
(Moskau Moscow 1871 – 1930 Orsay)

Auf einer Reise lernte Tarkhoff 1897 K. A. Korowin kennen, den wohl bedeutendsten Impressionisten Russlands, der ihn für den Impressionismus begeistern konnte. 1899 übersiedelte Tarkhoff nach Paris, wo er für kurze Zeit an der Ecole des Beaux-Arts die Klassen von Jean-Paul Laurens und Luc Olivier Merson besuchte. Nach seinem Umzug nach Paris setzte schon bald künstlerischer Erfolg ein: Bedeutende Sammler interessierten sich für die Werke des Malers, und auch der französische Staat kaufte Werke des Künstlers an. Er stellte regelmäßig im Salon der Indépendants wie auch im Salon d'automne aus. 1913 war Tarkhoff an der *Armory Show* in New York, Boston und Chicago beteiligt.

Zu den bekanntesten Werken Tarkhoffs zählen seine impressionistischen Stadtbilder, die mit ihrem stark überhöhten Betrachterstandpunkt deutlich dem Vorbild Pissarros verpflichtet sind. Mehr und mehr gewannen diese Darstellungen an Dynamik, indem er die verschwommenen Bewegungen der Menschen mit immer raffinierteren Lichtnuancen durchsetzte. Von Tarkhoffs Straßenszenen wurde nicht nur der Fauvist van Dongen beeinflusst. Ab 1904 schuf Tarkhoff zunehmend farbintensivere Werke, in denen der Künstler der Auffassung des fauvistischen Kreises um Matisse nahesteht.

While traveling in 1897, Tarkhoff met Konstantin A. Korovin, the leading Russian Impressionist, who inspired his enthusiasm for Impressionist paint-

ing. In 1899, Tarkhoff moved to Paris, where he briefly attended the Ecole des Beaux-Arts as a student of Jean-Paul Laurens and Luc Olivier Merson. He achieved early success as an artist soon after settling in Paris. Important collectors showed an interest in the painter's works, and the French government also purchased several of his paintings. He exhibited regularly at the Salon des Indépendants and the Salon d'Automne. Tarkhoff took part in the *Armory Show* in New York, Boston, and Chicago in 1913.
Among Tarkhoff's best-known works are his Impressionist cityscapes, works whose extremely elevated perspective clearly reveals the influence of Pissarro. These scenes grew increasingly dynamic as he incorporated progressively sophisticated nuances of light into the blurred movements of the human figures. Tarkhoff's street scenes influenced a number of artists, including the Fauvist van Dongen. Beginning in 1904, Tarkhoff painted an ever more number of works with more vivid coloration that display affinities with the Fauvists associated with Matisse.

Henri de Toulouse-Lautrec
(Albi 1864 – 1901 Malromé)

Toulouse-Lautrec erhielt ab 1882 eine akademische Malausbildung, und selbst die Tatsache, dass durch zwei Unfälle beide Beine verkrüppelt waren, konnte ihn von der Berufung zur Malerei nicht abbringen. Toulouse-Lautrec machte die Bekanntschaft van Goghs und Bernards, aber vor allem waren es die Begegnungen mit dem Impressionismus und mit der Kunst des japanischen Farbholzschnitts, die letztlich eine Änderung seiner akademisch geprägten Malerei bewirkten.
Ab 1886 war Toulouse-Lautrec ein oft gesehener Gast in den Cabarets, Cafés und Theatern – später auch Bordellen – am Montmartre, und die dortigen Personen und Szenen wurden ihm Inspirationsquelle und bevorzugtes Bildthema. Sein Atelier nahm er bald am Montmartre und zog tags wie nachts durch die Straßen auf der Suche nach Motiven.
Oft bis ins Karikaturistische verzerrt gab Toulouse-Lautrec die Menschen in seinen Porträts wieder. Die Bildausschnitte wählte er unkonventionell und verlieh seinen Darstellungen dadurch etwas Dynamisches und zugleich Beunruhigendes.
Der internationale Erfolg setzte 1888 nach einer Beteiligung an der Ausstellung der belgischen Künstlergruppe Les XX ein. Ab den 1890er-Jahren fertigte er Plakatentwürfe, womit er in Frankreich wie im Ausland bekannt wurde. Daneben war er auch als Illustrator und als Bühnenbildner tätig.
Toulouse-Lautrecs Schaffen hat zweifelsohne der Kunst des Jugendstils den Weg bereitet, und die starke Farbigkeit der Flächen und die geschwungene, deutlich akzentuierte Linienführung, die wir in seinen Bildern finden, sollten dort wieder zur Anwendung kommen.

Toulouse-Lautrec began his academic training as a painter in 1882, and even the fact that both of his legs were crippled as the result of two accidents was not enough to prevent him from pursuing his calling as an artist. Toulouse-Lautrec was acquainted with van Gogh and Bernard, but it was above all his encounters with Impressionism and the art of Japanese colored woodcuts that ultimately brought about a change in his academic painting style.
The artist was a frequent guest at cabarets, cafés, and theaters—and later at brothels—around Montmartre in the years after 1886, and the local people and scenes became a source of inspiration and a favorite subject for his paintings. He soon moved into a studio at Montmartre and could be seen strolling through the streets day and night in search of motifs.
The human figures in his portraits are often distorted to the point of caricature. His choice of unconventional details gives his scenes a certain dynamic, yet disturbing, character.
He earned international acclaim with his presentation at the exhibition organized by the Belgian group Les XX in 1888. Toulouse-Lautrec began designing posters in the 1890s, works with which he attracted attention both in France and abroad. He also worked as an illustrator and stage designer.
Toulouse-Lautrec's work undoubtedly paved the way for Art Nouveau, and the vivid fields of color and clearly accentuated lines we find in his paintings would be used again by the artists of that current.

Heinrich Wilhelm Trübner
(Heidelberg 1851 – 1917 Karlsruhe)

Trübner studierte 1867/68 an der Kunstschule in Karlsruhe, wo er die Historienmalerei des Schlachtenmalers Wilhelm Diez kennenlernte. Später ging er an die Kunstakademie nach München, wo er auf der *Ersten Internationalen Kunstausstellung* die Werke Courbets sah. Hier kam er auch in Kontakt mit der Kunst Wilhelm Leibls, der prägend für den Jüngeren wurde, nachdem dieser ihn nach 1870 persönlich kennenlernte und daraufhin dessen Kreis angehörte.
Trübners zwischen Realismus und Pleinairmalerei stehende Arbeiten zeichnen sich durch einen fleckenhaften Auftrag bei feinster Farbabstufung und eine tonige Zusammenfassung gedämpfter Farben aus, die ab den späten 1880er-Jahren deutlich aufhellten. In theoretischen Schriften formulierte er die Forderung, der Farbe die wichtigste Rolle in der Malerei zuzuweisen.
In seinem Schaffen folgte er stilistisch dem Realismus, dem Naturalismus und in seinem Spätwerk dem Impressionismus.

Trübner studied at the academy in Karlsruhe in 1867/68 and became acquainted there with the history paintings of battle painter Wilhelm Diez. He then transferred to the Kunstakademie in Munich, where he saw works by Courbet at the *Erste Internationale Kunstausstellung* (First International Art Exhibition). In Munich, he also encountered the art of Wilhelm Leibl, who exerted a strong influence on the younger artist after the two met and Trübner was introduced to Leibl's circle of friends after 1870.
Trübner's works, which occupy a position between Realism and plein-air painting, are characterized by a patchy application of fine color gradations and tonal concentration of subdued colors, which became markedly lighter in the late 1880s. In his theoretical writings, he appealed for the recognition of color as the most important aspect of painting.
The style of his art reflects the influences of Realism, Naturalism, and, in his later years, Impressionism.

Fritz von Uhde
(Wolkenburg/Sachsen Saxony 1848 – 1911 München Munich)

In einer Zeit miteinander konkurrierender Kunstströmungen, als Realismus gegen Naturalismus antrat, beide sich gegen den Impressionismus abgrenzten, Pointillismus und Symbolismus Avantgarde waren und allerorten Sezessionen vom Konflikt zwischen Konservativen und Modernen kündeten, spielte Uhde eine führende Rolle nicht nur im Münchner Kunstgeschehen. Sein Gesamtwerk war vielschichtig, angesiedelt im Spannungsfeld zwischen Realismus, Symbolismus und Impressionismus.
Uhde war vergleichsweise spät zur Malerei gekommen. Erst 1877 quittierte er den Militärdienst, um sich als Künstler zu versuchen. Er fand zu einer ästhetischen Erfolgsformel, malte aktualisierte, »moderne« Andachtsbilder und traf damit den Geschmack der bürgerlichen Käuferschichten.

Finanzielle Unabhängigkeit sowie anhaltende, wenn auch kontroverse Popularität waren Uhde von nun an sicher.
Daneben fand Uhde – vornehmlich in Darstellungen seiner drei Töchter – zu einer Modernität des Ausdrucks, der ihn in die vorderste Reihe der deutschen Impressionisten rückt.
In Uhdes Spätwerk sollten die verschiedenen Stränge seines Œuvres zusammenlaufen – in den fast klassisch anmutenden Engelbildern, für die wiederum seine Töchter Modell standen.
Mit diesen Arbeiten wie auch mit seinen früheren Bildern eines »Arme-Leute-Jesus«, mit denen er die Geschichte des Neuen Testaments in enge Beziehung zu seiner Gegenwart setzte und damit neue, tief empfundene Darstellungen schuf, wurde Uhde zum Vorläufer der modernen Kirchenkunst des 20. Jahrhunderts.

During a period of competition among rival currents of art in which Realism vied to displace Naturalism and both movements sought to set themselves apart from Impressionism, Pointillism and Symbolism, and while secession movements in many cities bore witness to the conflict between Conservatives and Modernists, von Uhde played an important role in and beyond the pale of the Munich art scene. His oeuvre is a complex body of work that reflects the tensions between Realism, Symbolism, and Impressionism.
Von Uhde turned to painting relatively late in life. It was not until 1877 that he left military service to embark upon a career as an artist. He developed an aesthetic formula for success and painted "modernized" devotional images that catered to the tastes of a bourgeois clientele. From that point on, von Uhde enjoyed financial security and sustained, though often controversial, popularity.
At the same time, von Uhde developed a modern form of expression—primarily in portraits of his three daughters—that placed him at the forefront of the German Impressionist movement.
The various strands of the artist's oeuvre came together in his late work—in the almost classical depictions of angels for which his daughters once again posed as models.
With these works as well as his early paintings of a "Jesus of the poor," with which he forged a link between the story of the New Testament and his own times and created images of a new, profoundly emotional character, von Uhde became a forerunner of modern church art of the twentieth century.

Maurice Utrillo
(Paris 1883 – 1955 Dax)

Utrillo, der Sohn Suzanne Valadons, Malerin und Ateliermodell, malte zwischen 1903 und 1906 in der Umgebung von Paris Bilder in sehr dunklen Farbtönen und mit dichtem Pinselduktus. Ab 1907 hellte er seine Palette auf und begann ab etwa 1910 verstärkt mit verschiedenen Weißtönen zu arbeiten, weshalb diese Periode auch als seine »Weiße Periode« bezeichnet wird. Ab 1909 beteiligte sich Utrillo regelmäßig am Salon der Indépendants sowie am Salon d'automne.
Von 1914 an veränderte sich sein Malstil unter dem Einfluss seiner Mutter zusehends, wurde zeichenhafter, farbintensiver und eher cloisonistisch. Für diese Entwicklung, die Utrillos Schaffen nahm, ist der Gegensatz zwischen hellen, klaren und den sie gleichsam »umfassenden«, dunklen Farben charakteristisch. Andererseits besteht eine Besonderheit seines Schaffens in der Gestaltung des Bildraumes: Mit der Darstellung von Straßenfluchten und den massigen Volumina der Häuser schuf Utrillo – zeitgleich zum Werk der Kubisten – eine Kunst, die die Gesetze der Komposition und des Bildaufbaus streng beachtete.
Die Genauigkeit der Zeichnung und die Art der Wiedergabe der Figuren macht klar, warum man versucht hat, seine Malerei in die Nähe der naiven Malerei zu rücken.
Wiewohl er noch zu seinen Lebzeiten internationale Berühmtheit genoss, nahm Utrillos künstlerisches Vermögen in seiner späten Schaffenszeit immer stärker ab, und immer häufiger erschöpften sich seine Sujets in Wiederholungen.

Utrillo, the son of painter and studio model Suzanne Valadon, painted scenes in very dark colors and brushstrokes applied in dense patterns in the environs of Paris between 1903 and 1906. He began working with lighter colors in 1907, and focused increasingly on various shades of white beginning in about 1910, which is why those years are often referred to as his White Period. Utrillo made the first of many presentations at the Salon des Indépendants and the Salon d'Automne in 1909.
His painting style began to change appreciably under the influence of his mother in 1914, growing increasingly graphic as his colors grew more vivid and he moved closer to the Cloisonnist technique. A characteristic feature of this trend in his art is the opposition between light, clear colors and dark, "surrounding" tones. Another unique characteristic of his art is his approach to pictorial space. With his depictions of streets narrowing toward the background and massive buildings, Utrillo created—concurrent with developments in Cubist art—a style that relied strictly on the laws of composition and pictorial structure.
The precision of his drawing and the manner in which he depicted human figures explain the attempts to associate his art with Naïve painting.
Although Utrillo achieved international fame during his lifetime, his later work suggests that his artistic talents were waning, as his subjects became increasingly exhausted in repetition.

Felix Vallotton
(Lausanne 1865 – 1925 Paris)

Der Schweizer Vallotton übersiedelte als 17-Jähriger aus seiner Heimatstadt nach Paris. Dort schloss er sich 1892 dem Kreis der Nabis an und stellte bis 1903 gemeinsam mit ihnen aus. Mit formal wie psychologisch scharfen Holzschnitten in kühnem Schwarz-Weiß wurde er alsbald berühmt. Daneben war er in den Jahren von 1890 bis 1897 auch als Kunstkritiker tätig.
Nach einer Übergangsperiode begab sich Vallotton zu Beginn des 20. Jahrhunderts auf eigene künstlerische Wege, am Rande der Avantgarde. Interieur- und Genreszenen sowie Schwarz-Weiß-Radierungen gab er auf, um sich ab 1907 fast ausschließlich der Bildnismalerei zu widmen.
Der menschliche Körper, die Aktmalerei, sowie Landschaften und Stillleben faszinierten ihn. Vallotton war ein exakter, wahrheitsfanatischer Beobachter und zugleich ein großartiger Stilist, dem die Ornamentik nie Nebensache wurde, sowie ein Meister der fantasievollen Koloristik. Selten malte einer seiner Zeitgenossen Aktbilder in solcher Intensität, als »nackte Wahrheit«, oder verwandelte wirkliche Landschaften in derart traumverwunschene poetische Fantasielandschaften, wie Vallotton es tat.

A native of Switzerland, Vallotton moved from the city of his birth to Paris at the age of seventeen. There, he joined the Nabi group in 1892 and exhibited with them until 1903. He soon gained acclaim with formally and psychologically penetrating woodcuts in bold black and white. He also worked as an art critic from 1890 to 1897.
Following a period of transition, Vallotton embarked upon new paths of his own along the fringes of the avant-garde in the early years of the twentieth

century. He abandoned interior and genre scenes and black-and-white etchings to devote himself almost entirely to portrait painting from 1907 onward.
Vallotton was fascinated by the human body and with painting nudes as well as landscapes and still lifes. He was both a precise observer, obsessed with authenticity, and an outstanding stylist for whom the ornamental was never of secondary importance. He was also a master of imaginative coloration. Only very few of his contemporaries painted nudes with such intensity as "the naked truth" or transformed real landscapes into such enchanted dream landscapes as Vallotton.

Louis Valtat
(Dieppe 1869 – 1952 Paris)

Valtat ging 1887 nach Paris an die Ecole des Beaux-Arts, besuchte dort das Atelier Gustave Moreaus und wurde 1891 an der Académie Julian Schüler von Jules Dupré. Hier lernte er Bonnard und Vuillard kennen, die sein frühes Schaffen beeinflussen sollten. Bereits 1893 stellte Valtat im Salon der Indépendants aus und nahm fortan regelmäßig an den Ausstellungen der Gruppe teil.
Er verkehrte weiterhin mit Bonnard und Vuillard und auch mit den anderen Künstlern der Nabis-Gruppe, die regelmäßig im Café Volpini zusammenkamen. Unter dem Einfluss dieses Künstlerzirkels gab er bald die pointillistische Technik auf, in der er anfänglich gemalt hatte, und sein Pinselstrich wurde zunehmend länger und gleichmäßiger. In den Jahren ab 1905 sollte er neben Matisse und Marquet zu einem der führenden Vertreter des Fauvismus werden.
In den Anfängen schuf Valtat vor allem Ansichten der Stadt Paris, Zeugnisse des lebhaften Treibens der Großstadt, sowie Porträts, doch erst nach und nach gelang sein künstlerisches Temperament zum Durchbruch. In kraftvollem Kolorit schuf er Werke, für die er Anregungen auf seinen zahlreichen Reisen empfing.

Valtat moved to Paris in 1887 to enroll at the Ecole des Beaux-Arts and work in the studio of Gustave Moreau. In 1891 he became a student of Jules Dupré at the Académie Julian, where he met Bonnard and Vuillard, both of whom would exert a noticeable influence on his early work. Valtat exhibited at the Salon des Indépendants in 1893 and participated regularly in the group's exhibitions in the following years.
Valtat remained in close contact with Bonnard, Vuillard, and other members of the Nabi group, who met regularly at the Café Volpini. Under the influence of these artists, he soon abandoned the Pointillist technique of his early years, and his brushstrokes grew longer and more uniform. He joined Matisse and Marquet as one of the leading representatives of Fauvism after 1905.
In his early years, Valtat painted predominantly Parisian city scenes, documents of the hustle and bustle of the big city, and portraits, but his artistic temperament gradually approached a breakthrough. Working with vivid colors, he created a number of works inspired by experiences gathered during his extensive travels.

Maurice de Vlaminck
(Paris 1876 – 1958 Rueil-la-Gadelière)

In der ersten Hälfte der 1890er-Jahre kam Vlaminck bei dem Maler Henri Rigal, Vertreter einer naiven Kunst, in Berührung mit den Grundlagen der Malerei. Seiner Berufung zur Kunst wurde er sich allerdings erst bewusst, als er die Bekanntschaft André Derains machte, und fortan widmete er sich ganz der Malerei. Gemeinsam mieteten Derain und Vlaminck ein Atelier in Chatou. Aufgewühlt durch den Anblick der Werke van Goghs, die er auf einer 1901 von der Galerie Bernheim-Jeune ausgerichteten Ausstellung gesehen hatte, entwickelte Vlaminck seine Malerei weiter. Die Grundlagen zur späteren Teilhabe an den Errungenschaften der Fauves wurden zu diesem Zeitpunkt gelegt.
Auf Veranlassung von Matisse beteiligte sich Vlaminck 1905 erstmals am Salon der Indépendants und sechs Monate später am denkwürdigen Salon d'automne. Dort präsentierte er Werke, die sich durch eine fast brutale Chromatik auszeichneten. Neben Matisse, Derain und van Dongen gehört Vlaminck zu den bedeutendsten Vertretern des Fauvismus.
Ab 1907 erkennen wir bei ihm eine weniger ungestüme Farbigkeit und eine Hinwendung zu einer stärkeren Festigung der Bildanlage nach dem Vorbild Cézannes.

Vlaminck was introduced to the fundamental principles of painting by the artist Henri Rigal, a representative of Naïve art, in the first half of the 1890s. Yet he first became aware of his true calling as an artist upon meeting André Derain, after which he devoted himself completely to painting. Derain and Vlaminck rented a studio in Chatou. Profoundly moved by the paintings of van Gogh he had encountered at an exhibition organized by the Galerie Bernheim-Jeune in 1901, Vlaminck began to develop his own style of painting. It was during this period that he laid the foundation for his later contribution to the achievements of the Fauvists.
At the instigation of Matisse, Vlaminck took part in the Salon des Indépendants for the first time in 1905. Six months later, he presented works at the distinguished Salon d'Automne. These paintings were characterized by an almost brutal use of color. Along with Matisse, Derain, and van Dongen, Vlaminck is regarded as one of the most important representatives of Fauvism.
Beginning in 1907, we recognize a trend toward less vigorous coloration and greater stability of composition in keeping with the example set by Cézanne.

Edouard Vuillard
(Cuiseaux 1868 – 1940 La Baule)

Zunächst arbeitete Vuillard noch ganz im Stil einer ornamentalen Malerei, die gegen die realistische und impressionistische Spiegelung der Wirklichkeit gerichtet war und der angewandten Kunst starke Impulse vermittelte. Entscheidend für seine Entwicklung wurde die Freundschaft mit Denis, Ker-Xavier Roussel, Bonnard und Sérusier, mit denen er seit 1888 die Académie Julian besuchte. Dort schlossen sich die Freunde bald unter dem Einfluss von Gauguin zu einer Gruppe zusammen, die sich den Namen Nabis gab, das hebräische Wort für Propheten. Gemäß ihren Theorien sahen die Nabis die vornehmlichste Aufgabe des Künstlers darin, die Natur zu stilisieren, indem sie nur die Hauptformen und -farben des Naturdetails im Bild umsetzten und so eine hinter der Naturform stehende Idee deutlich machten. Die Natur wurde von der Gruppe nur zum Vorwand genommen, um ein unabhängiges, nach künstlerischen Gesetzen komponiertes, ornamental gesehenes Werk zu schaffen.
Vuillard beschäftigte sich allerdings nur bis etwa 1900 mit dieser symbolhaft-ornamentalen Malerei und machte sich deren letztliche Hinwendung zu christlich-mystischen Bildinhalten nicht zu eigen. Seine überwiegend dem intimen Interieur gewidmete Thematik führte ihn vielmehr zu einer Malerei, in der die Stilisierung an Bedeutung verlor, die Bilder räumlicher wurden und sich den einst bekämpften Prinzipien einer der Impression verpflichteten Malerei annäherten.

Vuillard initially painted in a largely ornamental style in opposition to Realist and Impressionist approaches to the depiction of reality. These works provided important impulses for applied art.
Crucial to his development as an artist were his relationships with Denis, Ker-Xavier Roussel, Bonnard, and Sérusier, with whom he studied at the Académie Julian beginning in 1888. Under the influence of Gauguin, the friends soon formed the group known as the Nabis—the Hebrew word for prophet. According to their theories, the Nabis regarded the stylized depiction of nature as the foremost goal of the artist. This was to be achieved by rendering only the primary forms and colors of the natural detail in the painting and, in this way, to give expression to the idea underlying the natural form. The group used nature as a pretense for the creation of an ornamental work composed in accordance with the laws of art.
Vuillard's interest in this symbolic, ornamental style of painting lasted only until about 1900, however, and he rejected its ultimate devotion to Christian and mystical subjects. Mostly concerned with the intimate interior, his thematic interest led him instead to a style of painting in which stylization became less important as his paintings grew more space-oriented and returned in part to the once disputed principles of a kind of painting concerned with spontaneous impressions.

Heinrich von Zügel
(Murrhardt/Württemberg 1850 – 1941 München Munich)

Nach Anfängen an der Münchner Akademie beschloss der junge Zügel unter dem Einfluss der Diez-Schule, selbstständig zu arbeiten. Sein Tun war erfolgreich: 1883 erhielt er auf der Weltausstellung in Wien die Große Goldene Medaille, und im Verlauf der 1880er-Jahre tätigten verschiedene Museen in Deutschland Ankäufe seiner Werke. In den 1890er-Jahren widmete sich der Maler vor allem der Landschaftsmalerei. Es folgten Berufungen an die Akademie nach Karlsruhe (1894/95) und eine Professur in München (1895–1922).
Unterbrochen nur von den Wirren des Ersten Weltkrieges, entstand bis in die 1930er-Jahre ein vielgestaltiges, umfangreiches Œuvre. Allerdings blieb Zügel in seinem zeichnerischen und malerischen Werk im Wesentlichen der Tier- und Landschaftsdarstellung treu.

After his early years at the Munich academy, the young Zügel, under the influence of the Diez School, resolved to become an independent artist. His work led to success. In 1883, he was awarded the Grand Gold Medal at the World's Fair in Vienna, and various museums in Germany purchased his works during the 1880s. During the following decade, the painter devoted himself largely to landscape painting. He was later appointed to a position at the academy in Karlsruhe (1894–95) and a professorship in Munich (1895–1922).
Interrupted only by the vicissitudes of World War One, Zügel had developed a diverse and extensive oeuvre by the 1930s. In his drawings and paintings, however, he focused primarily on the depiction of animals and landscape scenes.

SELECTED BIBLIO-GRAPHY

AUSWAHL-BIBLIO-GRAFIE

Gert von der Osten & Horst Keller (Hrsg. eds.), *Katalog der Gemälde des 19. Jahrhunderts im Wallraf-Richartz-Museum (Kataloge des Wallraf-Richartz-Museums,* Bd. vol. 1), bearb. v. comp. by Rolf Andree, Köln Cologne 1964

Wallraf-Richartz-Museum Köln. Vollständiges Verzeichnis der Gemäldesammlung, bearb. v. comp. by Christian Heße & Martina Schlagenhaufer, Köln & Mailand Cologne & Milan 1986

Wallraf-Richartz-Museum Köln. Von Stefan Lochner bis Paul Cézanne. 120 Meisterwerke der Gemäldesammlung, Köln & Mailand Cologne & Milan 1986

Les lumières de l'impressionnisme. Musée du Petit Palais, Genève – La Collection Corboud, Ausst.-Kat. exh. cat. Daimaru Museum, Tokyo; Art Gallery in Kushiro City Hall; The Museum of Art, Kintetsu; Fukuoka Art Museum, Tokyo 1993

Bildwelten des Impressionismus. Meisterwerke aus der Sammlung des Petit Palais in Genf, Ausst.-Kat. exh. cat. Wallraf-Richartz-Museum, Köln Cologne, Leipzig 1994

Rainer Budde (Hrsg. ed.), *Vom Spiel der Farbe. Armand Guillaumin (1841–1927) – Ein vergessener Impressionist,* Ausst.-Kat. exh. cat. Wallraf-Richartz-Museum, Köln Cologne, Gent Ghent 1996

Rainer Budde (Hrsg. ed.), *Pointillismus – Auf den Spuren von Georges Seurat / Pointillisme – Sur les traces de Seurat,* Ausst.-Kat. exh. cat. Wallraf-Richartz-Museum, Köln Cologne; Fondation de l'Hermitage, Lausanne, München Munich & New York 1997

Monet, Renoir et les Impressionnistes, Ausst.-Kat. exh. cat. Tobu Museum of Art, Tokyo; Hokkaido Obihiro Museum of Art; The Okayama Prefectural Museum of Art; Nara Prefectural Museum of Art, Tokyo 1998

Rainer Budde & Barbara Schaefer (Hrsg. eds.), *Miracle de la couleur,* Ausst.-Kat. exh. cat. Wallraf-Richartz-Museum – Fondation Corboud, Köln Cologne 2001

Impressionism. Wallraf-Richartz-Museum – Foundation Corboud, Ausst.-Kat. exh. cat. Hokkaido Asahikawa Museum of Art; Shizuoka Prefectural Museum of Art; Sogo Museum of Art, Yokohama; Onomichi City Museum of Art; Koriyama City Museum of Art, Tokyo 2002/03

Miracle de la couleur – impressionisme en post-impressionisme, Ausst.-Kat. exh. cat. Kunsthalle Rotterdam, Zwolle 2003

Wallraf-Richartz-Museum – Fondation Corboud, Köln. Museumsführer, hrsg. vom ed. by Wallraf-Richartz-Museum – Fondation Corboud & Museumsdienst Köln, 2. Aufl. 2nd. ed., Köln Cologne 2004

Ingrid Mössinger & Beate Ritter (Hrsg. eds.), *Couleur et lumière – französische Malerei von 1870 bis 1918. Werke aus dem Wallraf-Richartz-Museum – Fondation Corboud (Köln),* Ausst.-Kat. exh. cat. Kunstsammlungen Chemnitz, Bielefeld 2004

Götz Czymmek, *Französische Malerei des 19. Jahrhunderts 1 – mit Ausnahme der Bilder der Fondation Corboud (Wallraf-Richartz-Museum – Fondation Corboud, Köln. Bildhefte zur Sammlung,* Bd. vol. 12), Köln Cologne 2005

Impresionismo. Obras maestras del Museo Wallraf-Richartz – Fundación Corboud, Ausst.-Kat. exh. cat. Fundación Pedro Barrié de la Maza, La Coruña; Fundación Pedro Barrié de la Maza, Vigo, 2005/06

Barbara Schaefer, *Französische Malerei des 19. Jahrhunderts II – Die Impressionisten und ihre Nachfolger – Die Bilder der Fondation Corboud. Mit einem Beitrag von Götz Czymmek (Wallraf-Richartz-Museum & Fondation Corboud, Köln. Bildhefte zur Sammlung,* Bd. vol. 13), Köln Cologne 2006

Iris Schaefer, Caroline von Saint-George & Katja Lewerentz, *Impressionismus – Wie das Licht auf die Leinwand kam* *Painting Light—The Hidden Techniques of the Impressionists,* Ausst.-Kat. exh. cat. Wallraf-Richartz-Museum & Fondation Corboud, Köln Cologne; Palazzo Strozzi, Florenz Florence, Genf Geneva & Mailand Milan 2008

Herausgeber Editor
Andreas Blühm

Organisation und Redaktion
Organization and Editing
Barbara Schaefer

Verlagslektorat Copyediting
Regina Dorneich (Deutsch German),
Rebecca van Dyck (Englisch English)

Übersetzungen (Deutsch – Englisch)
Translations (German – English)
John Southard

Grafische Gestaltung Graphic design
Andreas Platzgummer

Satz Typesetting
Weyhing digital, Ostfildern

Schrift Typeface
Trump Mediaeval (von by Georg Trump)

Reproduktionen und Gesamtherstellung
Reproductions and printing
Dr. Cantz'sche Druckerei, Ostfildern

Papier Paper
BVS matt, 150 g/m²

Buchbinderei Binding
Thomas Müntzer, Bad Langensalza

Erschienen im Published by
Hatje Cantz Verlag
Zeppelinstraße 32
73760 Ostfildern
Deutschland Germany
Tel. +49 711 4405-200
Fax +49 711 4405-220
www.hatjecantz.com

Hatje Cantz books are available internationally at selected bookstores. For more information about our distribution partners please visit our homepage at www.hatjecantz.com.

ISBN 978-3-7757-2092-2

Printed in Germany

Umschlagabbildung Cover illustration
Auguste Renoir, *Ein Paar im Grünen*
The Fiancés, ca. 1868

Fotonachweis Photo credits
Archiv des Museums Museum archives:
S. pp. 11, 14, 17, 18, 91, 92 unten rechts lower right, 113, 137 unten links lower left, 142, 179, 210 oben links upper left, 213 unten rechts lower right, 216, 222 unten rechts lower right, 225, 228 unten rechts lower right, 229
Alle übrigen Fotografien All other photographs:
Rheinisches Bildarchiv, Köln Cologne